Galitz's

Human Machine Interaction

Galitz's

Human Machine Interaction

Adapted by:

Dr. Dhananjay R. Kalbande
Professor & HOD
Computer Engineering Department
Sardar Patel Institute of Technology
Mumbai

Prashant Kanade
Assistant Professor
Computer Engineering Department
Vivekanand Education Society's Institute of Technology
Mumbai

Sridari Iyer
Assistant Professor
Computer Engineering Department
St. Francis Institute of Technology
Mumbai

WILEY

Human Machine Interaction

[Adaptation of An Essential Guide to User Interface Design by Wilbert O. Galitz, 2nd edition (ISBN: 9780471084648)]

Other Wiley Editorial Offices:

John Wiley & Sons, Inc. 111 River Street, Hoboken, NJ 07030, USA

Wiley-VCH Verlag GmbH, Pappellaee 3, D-69469 Weinheim, Germany

John Wiley & Sons Australia Ltd, 42 McDougall Street, Milton, Queensland 4064, Australia

John Wiley & Sons (Asia) Pte Ltd, 1 Fusionopolis Walk #07-01 Solaris, South Tower, Singapore 138628

John Wiley & Sons Canada Ltd, 22 Worcester Road, Etobicoke, Ontario, Canada, M9W 1L1

Reprint: 2017

ISBN: 978-81-265-5868-1

www.wileyindia.com

Printed at: Gopaljee Enterprises Delhi

Contents

Preface

Human Machine Interaction is a field of research that demands equal knowledge about human psychology and technology. Norman can be considered as the father of this field, as he was the first person to find this relation between humans and interface designs. The original book *Essential Guide to User Interface Design*, 2nd edition, provides details on what can be accepted as a good design.

In this adaptation of the book, which we have named *Human Machine Interaction*, we have specified a systematic approach for designing clear, easy-to-understand-and-use interfaces and screens for graphical and Web systems. This adaptation is to give insight on human psychology. What exactly happens to us, and why do we do things in a particular way. By understanding the human characteristics, you can develop better human-centric designs that have a greater chance of success in the market.

We have been teaching Human Computer Interaction to our students from the aesthetical view point. A gap was always felt to relate these concepts to human psychology. *For example, it is commonly advised to reduce the use of the color red. So the user interface designing books suggest various design guidelines for effective use of red in minimal quantity.* Since the reason to avoid red is unknown, it becomes an abstract concept to the reader or the designer. Through this book, we give an insight on how colors are perceived by the human eye, and how each color has a different effect on our brain. When a designer is exposed to many such concepts, he/she may get confused, and may not know how to prioritize the guidelines. This can again lead to poor designs.

With this understanding and the design guidelines, the reader will know the importance of each guideline and its significance on humans. Guidelines alone, without this explanation, are like the superstitions told by our ancestors – "Don't stitch after sunset". Your immediate reaction would be "Why not?" This book attempts to bridge the gap between the humans and technology.

This is the first ever book that describes Human Machine Interaction designing. The system development methodology has changed in the last few years. Initially, the customer or ultimate end user was not involved in system development and designing of the software systems. This evolution is discussed in the book while discussing Goal Directed Design. Design methodology evolved and expanded as interface technology changed and research knowledge expanded.

This adaptation focuses exclusively on user's perspective for digital systems. The major part is already described in The Essential Guide to User Interface Design. This is a small contribution to focus mainly on the overall user-oriented interface for computer-based systems.

New to the Adaptation

This book contains three new chapters to focus on bridging the gap between humans and technology, and nine chapters from the original book that focus on the design guidelines. By reading this book, you will not only know the guidelines to create the best designs, but also the reason behind the existence of those guidelines. We are sure this knowledge will help you make better design decisions, and all your products will be successful among your users.

This book blends the results of screen design research, knowledge concerning people, knowledge about the hardware and software capabilities of the interface, and few practical experiences (which are much lesser than the span of 40 years in display-based systems of Hon'ble Wilbert O. Galitz).

Organization of the Book

This book comprises 14 chapters which are divided into five parts.

1. Chapter 1 provides an insight into the history of UI design; hardware, software and operating environments; psychopathology of everyday things and psychology of everyday actions.
2. Chapter 2, Goal Directed Design, explains the mistakes performed while designing a computer system; the design and design software evolution process; how to recognize the goals; goal directed design process; implementation model and mental model; etc.
3. Chapter 3 reviews the two dominant user interfaces today, the graphical user interface (GUI) and the World Wide Web (WWW or Web). GUI interfaces are looked at in terms of their components, characteristics, and advantages over the older text-based systems. Web interfaces are compared to both GUI interfaces and conventional printed documents. The differing characteristics of three distinct Web environments, the Internet, intranet, and extranet are also summarized. This chapter concludes with a statement of the basic underlying principles for interface design.
4. Chapter 4 discusses design guidelines; their perception; Gestalt principles; visual structure; color; vision; memory; six behavioral patterns; recognition and recall; learning and actors affecting learning.

5. Chapter 5 helps us to choose the right kind of menu. It involves understanding how menus are used and selecting the proper kinds for specific tasks. The principles of menu design are described, and the purpose and proper usage of various menu types are detailed. In this chapter, Web site navigation schemes are also discussed.
6. Chapter 6 helps us to choose the right kind of window. It involves understanding how windows are used and selecting the proper kinds for the tasks. The elements of windows are described, and the purpose and proper usage of various types of windows are detailed.
7. Chapter 7 helps us to choose the right kind of device-based controls. It involves identifying the characteristics and capabilities of these various control mechanisms and providing the proper ones for users and their tasks. In addition to the keyboard, a system or Web site might offer the user a mouse, trackball, joystick, graphic tablet, touch screen, light pen, or some other similar device.
8. Chapter 8 helps us to choose the right kind of screen-based controls. It involves identifying the characteristics and capabilities of these various screen-based controls and guidelines for providing the proper ones for users and their tasks. The designer is presented an array of screen-based controls to choose from. Selecting the right one for the user and the task is often difficult. But, as with device-based controls, making the right choice is critical to system success. A proper fit between user and control will lead to fast, accurate performance. A poor fit will result in lower productivity, more errors, and often user dissatisfaction.
9. Creating text and messages in a form the user wants and understands is absolutely necessary for system acceptance and success. Rules for writing text and messages for systems and Web sites are presented in Chapter 9.
10. Chapter 10 presents the guidelines for presenting to the user feedback concerning the system and its processing status. It also describes the system response times necessary to meet user needs. It also describes the kinds of guidance and assistance that should be included in a system, and presents important design guidelines for the various kinds.
11. Graphics, including icons and images, are an integral part of design. Design guidelines for various types of graphics are presented in Chapter 11. Icons are also described, including a discussion of what kinds of icons exist, what influences their usability, and how they should be designed so they are meaningful and recognizable.
12. Color, if used properly, can emphasize the logical organization of a screen, facilitate the discrimination of screen components, accentuate differences, and make displays more interesting. If used improperly, color can be distracting and cause visual fatigue, impairing a system's usability. Chapter 12 involves understanding color and how to use it effectively on textual and statistical graphics screens, and in Web sites.

Scattered throughout the book are many illustrations of design, both good and bad. These illustrations have been made as generic as possible, without intending to reflect any one graphical product or system. In view of the ever-changing interface landscape, this seems the most practical approach. Some of the examples are self-imagination of authors and some are adopted from few literatures; there may be illustrative bias in this direction.

Also provided in Part V of the book are Practical and Case Studies.

Who Should Read This Book

This book, while essentially an introduction to Human Machine Interaction, will be useful for any

GUI system, Web page and application developers. For the developer with limited experience, a reading of its entire contents is appropriate. For the more experienced developer, a perusal of its extensive contents will undoubtedly identify topics of further interest. The experienced developer will also find suitable guidelines useful in identifying topics to be read more thoroughly. We have included various case studies that all readers will also find very helpful to carry out further research in the futuristic digital designs. This book can be handy reference guide in their development efforts.

Readers who are teachers in design-oriented courses as well as technological courses like Computer Engineering, Information Technology and Computer Applications can use this book as a useful reference in interface designing.

Thank you for your interest in Human Machine Interaction. The readers are welcome to contact the authors/publishers with feedback or comment.

AUTHORS

Acknowledgments

Our gratitude to Wiley India Pvt. Ltd. for providing us an opportunity and motivation to present the adaptation of the book written by Wilbert O. Galitz. We would also like to thank Amey Patankar and Meenakshi Sehrawat for editorial guidance and support.

Our gratitude is also extended to the multitude of user interface researchers and designers – without their work this book would not have been possible. We would also like to acknowledge and thank, for their contributions, several people who have been instrumental in the shaping up of our career in teaching.

Finally, we would like to thank our families and other important people without whose support this book would not have been possible.

AUTHORS

About the Authors

Dr Dhananjay Kalbande is currently a Professor and Head in Department of Computer Engineering, Sardar Patel Institute of Technology, Andheri (West), Mumbai, India. He has completed B.E. in Computer Technology, Master of Engineering in Information Technology and obtained Ph.D. from University of Mumbai, Mumbai in 2011. He has over 16+ years of experience in teaching and research. He is recognized as Ph.D. guide in Mumbai and Nagpur University, currently guiding 6 research scholars in the area of Soft Computing, Mobile Cloud Computing and Imaging Analysis. His area of interest is Soft Computing, Human Computing Interaction, Mobile Device Applications, Decision making, etc. He has authored two books, namely, GUI and MIS. He has delivered and conducted the workshop plus seminar talk on Neural Network & Fuzzy Logic, dot Net. Outcome based accreditation process for Engineering Institutes. He has more than 42 papers published in International conference and journals.

Prashant Kanade is Assistant Professor, Computer Engineering Department, Vivekanand Education Society's Institute of Technology, Mumbai. He holds more than 12 years of experience in teaching. Other than teaching, he is associated with other major academic responsibilities at his Institute.

He is involved in technological as well as management related activities in various social organizations. He holds 8 national and international publications to his credit. He is also a creative writer for street plays and theatre shows.

Ms Sridari Iyer is a computer engineer, working as an Assistant Professor in St. Francis Institute of Technology, affiliated to Mumbai University. She has about 10 years of work experience, of which 7 years is in teaching. She is a very dynamic and creative person with a strong inclination towards research.

She holds one international conference paper to her credit, and is awaiting more.

She has a passion for writing, and is pursuing a Masters in English out of her own interest.

Unit One

Human

CHAPTER

1

Human

Introduction

We are moving towards a world of automation with a goal to reach *The Era of Machines*. Each day our machines are remodeled with more features that can ease our task further. For example, washing clothes was a household chore. People found it cumbersome, so a machine was invented. These semi-automatic washing machines required human intervention, so fully automatic machines came into existence. Further these machines are enhanced each day to provide more features, like temperature, soak, dry, etc. Now we are trying to add intelligence to these machines, so that they can automatically set the wash time, decide on the amount of soap required, and so on. We are in a competitive world, and adding new functionalities is the only approach for a business to stay successful. In Figure 1.1 we depict the evolution of washing machines.

Figure 1.1 Evolution of washing clothes.

Imagine you have purchased a washing machine that is just launched. The promoting advertisements say that this machine can decide the amount of soap required, set its own temperature and timer. The advertisement even says there is no need of any kind of installation. You just need to connect the water pipes and you are good to wash. You make an online purchase, and this product has arrived at your door step. You open the wrapper, and find this machine really huge, as compared to your previous machine. The color given to its body is bright fuchsia with shiny gold rims. Your jaw drops a little. Even if pink were to be your favorite color, you may not prefer it on a home appliance. Now you place it in the destined location and want to connect the inlet and outlet pipes. The designer has concealed these valves so that the machine looks elegant. You will land up searching these valves for a while, reach out for the manual, and then discover them. The same thing happens with the power adaptor. Let us say, that you have managed to make these connections now.

Similarly the door has a concealed handle, to maintain the elegance. Again you read the manual and learn to open the door. Now you put a few clothes in it, and want to try the first wash. You are wondering how to start it There is no display unit in the front of the machine, where it is supposed to be. You start searching for it, and again reach out for the manual. The designer has placed a power button on the side to avoid the accidental presses. You find this idea interesting, and now press on the start button, but nothing happens. Then you realize you have not added soap. From the manual you discover that the soap tray is placed on the side, next to the power button. Now, you drag the machine from its location, because the side wall does not allow you to open the soap tray. You add some soap and press the power again. The machine does nothing. You are anxious and wonder if the machine is defective. You read the manual over and over again, search the machine for more buttons, but nothing is visible anywhere. So you decide to call the customer care. After waiting on their line for more than twenty minutes, you get to speak to an executive. He says that the machine is fully automatic and you do not need to do anything more than that. You read the manual again, word by word. You check all your connections, the power source. You search for a display panel everywhere on the machine. You press the power button a few more times, and wait for a few hours. Nothing happens.

What has gone wrong here? Is the machine really faulty? How could you decide that? Now everything about the machine will disturb you. The bright fuchsia body and shiny gold handles, the number of times you had read the manual, you had to move the machine just to add soap, the 20minutes wait on the customer care line, your search for the valves and soap tray, the invisible display unit, everything annoys you. Finally, you log into the online portal and book for a refund. This will leave the company with one unhappy customer, and lose thousands of potential customers who would read your reviews.

The millions of rupees spent on the research and innovation of all the features have become useless. Is the machine really faulty, or is the customer so dumb? Of course the machine works fine, but it did not have a good way of interacting with the user. The designer wanted to make the system simple to use, by eliminating all interactions. The machine is designed to start at the press of the button and the rest of the process is made automatic. It first calculates the temperature of water required, decides the amount of time and soap, and then goes into soak mode. But this was not known to you, so you pressed the button again. That shut down the system. Again you press the power button and wait to see no change, and press the button again, that stopped it.

An interface is the way in which the machine is presented to the human.

Each person has a different level of intelligence and experience. Human Machine Interaction is the field of research that concentrates on how to present the functionality of a system to the user. A huge amount of study on human psychology is required to build a good interface. Every single aspect about the target users' needs to be considered, such as their interests, behaviors, needs, likes, dislikes, experience, challenges, etc.

Technology may change rapidly, but people change slowly. Hence a research on human psychology will yield results that remain true forever. This book aims at bridging the gap between human psychology and the upcoming technologies, so that we design more human-centric models. As the saying "only a good listener can be a good speaker", in HMI we can say "only a good observer can be a good designer".

History of User Interface Designing

We begin our computer engineering and information technology courses with generations of computers. Similar to that user interfaces also have generations.

A machine can be defined as anything that can reduce manual effort.

First Generation: Machines that Reduce Physical Labor

The earliest machine that can be thought of is the hand-axe, a machine to transform lateral force into a transverse split. The handle is the interface to access this tool. A long wooden piece that is rounded smoothly is used to ensure a good grip. The shape, size, weight and texture of the wedge and the handle decide the outcome. The crude handmade axes of Stone-age gradually improved in aesthetics as well as purpose. Look at the axes in Figure 1.2(a). You can easily identify the woodcutting axe from a battle axe, just by their appearance. Slowly more machines were invented, such as boomerangs,

(a) (b)

Figure 1.2 Machines to reduce manual labor.

slingshots, wheel and axle, pulley, levers, etc. For each of these machines, their physical appearance such as their shape, size, material used, weight, etc., decided their utility. Figure 1.2(b) shows a few machines that are used to reduce physical labor.

Second Generation: Machines that Displayed Output

These machines calculate the speed of wind, temperature, time, etc. They showed humans some kind of readings. The presentation of data to the user can be called as its interface. The units of measurements, the shape and size of pointers, color, scale, etc., made a difference to the ease of use of the machine.

The earliest known machine of this genre is a sundial. In the beginning, only a gnomon (a vertical pillar) was used. The length of its shadow indicated time. Slowly a dial was built onto which the gnomon was installed. The precision required to space the numbers on the dial determined the accuracy of time read. Gradually the dial included various data such as directions, zodiac constellations etc. Figure 1.3 shows a few machines that provide us with some readings of the environment.

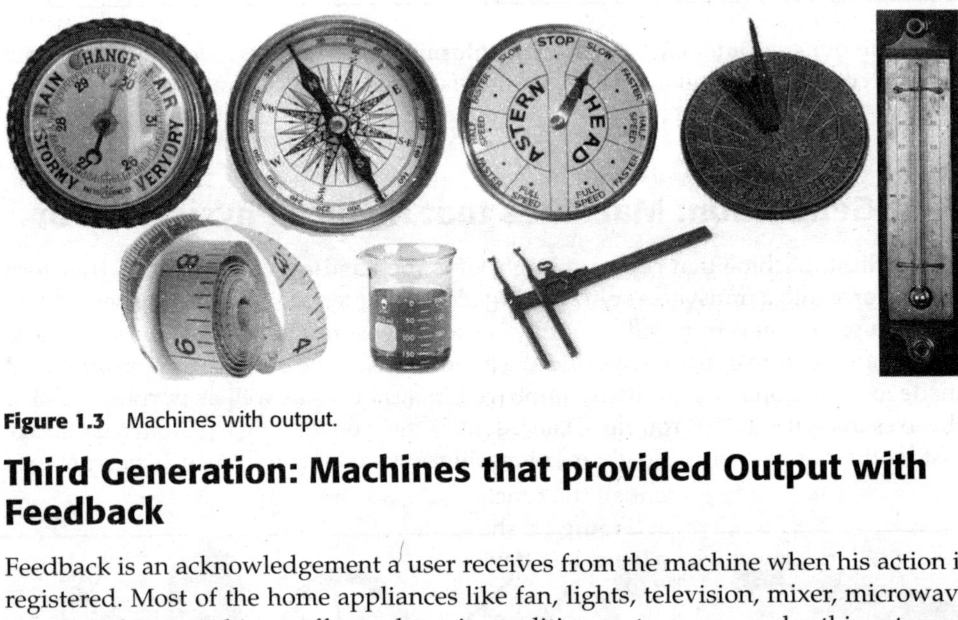

Figure 1.3 Machines with output.

Third Generation: Machines that provided Output with Feedback

Feedback is an acknowledgement a user receives from the machine when his action is registered. Most of the home appliances like fan, lights, television, mixer, microwave oven, washing machine, coffee maker, air-conditioner etc., come under this category. For example, if user presses on the channel change button of a television remote, the user can see the channel change on the screen. User can immediately see the effect of his action.

Here the interface is the part through which the user is able to make the system perform some action such as switches, knobs, remote controls etc. The design of this interface is totally the deciding factor of the entire product's usability. We can see in our houses how each of our appliances has evolved over time, and also their usability. Electrical switches have become safer and softer to handle, mixer knobs are easier to operate now, TV remotes got standardized, etc. Most of us are familiar with most of such machines. We have operated an older version when we were children, and now we have modern ones. With a keen eye, you can observe how the interfaces of each of these devices have evolved over time. Figure 1.4 shows a few machines that provide feedback to users' actions.

Figure 1.4 Machines with feedback.

Fourth Generation: Machines with Computing Power

The innovation of computers has motivated research in various fields. Earlier providing functionality itself was a challenge, and was a field of research. Today we have options, and we are free to discard the ones we are not comfortable with. For example, earlier people learnt DOS commands to work with a computer. Today no one puts so much effort to learn to use a system. They just shift to a system which is easier to use. Human Computer Interaction is a field of research that emerged due to this competition. Here the focus is on easing the communication between the user and a computer.

Earlier only text-based screens were available. With the introduction of graphics, the scope of creativity in user interfaces has magnified. Technology is changing rapidly, and we have new computing devices every day. From the huge main frame computers we have shrunk to smart- watches, which have the same capabilities! Today's biggest challenge is to present all the functionalities in that limited display space and in the most user friendly way. Figure 1.5 shows the various computing devices we use. We can see the way in which their sizes have shrunk over time, but their functionalities have increased.

Figure 1.5 Computing machines.

Fifth Generation: Intelligent Machines

With artificial intelligence in boom, traditional input methods are proving to insufficient. We are making machines that can adapt to the humans by continuous learning. These systems require the freedom to learn from the environment. Here the user need not learn how to use the system. Instead these systems learn how the user is going to operate the system. These systems are capable of acquiring inputs independently, as well as learn by analyzing them. Most of the prediction systems, business intelligent systems, tracking systems, sensors, etc., are intelligent. With traditional input methods, these systems cannot provide the desired outcomes. Figure 1.6(a) shows automobiles with obstacle sensors. Input is taken directly from the environment, and is not typed into or pointed by any particular human.

Consider an automatic air conditioner. It scans the room to get number of people, fetches the outside temperature, and then automatically adjusts its temperature to the optimal value. For such systems keyboard, mouse or even a touchscreen restrict the learning of the machine. Natural language processing is an upcoming field that allows humans to freely talk to the computer in their own language, and the computer will interpret it correctly as depicted in Figure 1.6(b).

These systems also learn about humans from their actions. The restriction to hold a device in his hand and provide inputs in a specific way will not help the machine learn. With voice inputs, body gestures or brain signals, all such restrictions are removed, and there is a wider scope of machine learning. In voice UIs, the user communicates with the computer completely with his voice. Gesture UIs on the other hand take input from users' bodily movements. While the brain-computer UIs, can operate the systems with just the brain signals. Users need not give any external output in anyway.

(a) Obstacle sensors in automobiles

(b) Natural language processing

Figure 1.6 Intelligent machines.

Future: Augmented Reality

This concept is the opposite of virtual reality. You may have come across many games that involve building a new city, a farm or a house and family. This is virtual reality, where the real world is replaced by a virtual world. In augmented reality, the virtual world is brought into a user's reality. We watch many sci-fi movies where a human is able to enter into a video game, or one of the game characters come into our real world. We see video conferences with 3D holograms, sunglasses that able to pull out database records about the things in your line of sight, and reprogrammed humans. Such is the scope of augmented reality. Here not only the input methods should have freedom, even the output has to be unrestricted. You cannot travel into a user's reality by making him hold a 4 × 6 inch screen in his hand. The future of UIs is to make the line between reality and virtual world so blurred, that we can miss it easily. Figure 1.7 gives an idea of what kind of output is perceived by augmented reality.

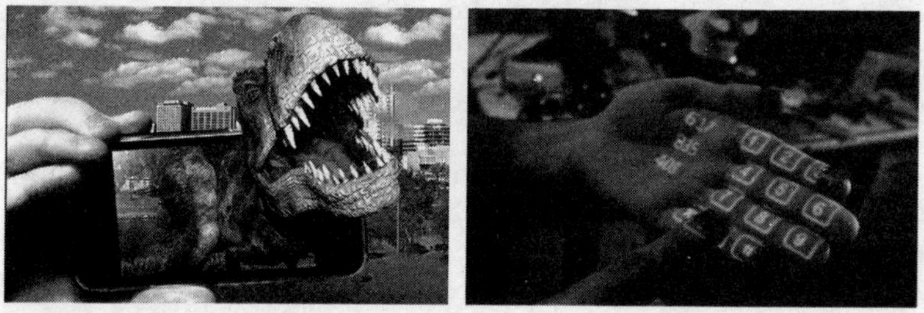

Figure 1.7 Augmented reality.

Hardware, Software and Operating Environments

Hardware

Hardware was the most important utility in earlier generations of computing. They were sole game players, as hardware use to drive the software. But in the current scenario, it is quite the opposite. Today we can choose the hardware as per the requirement of the user, and can top it up with any software application. The hardware options available are plenty, and one need not compromise like earlier times.

Software

Software is the tool with which we can create an effective user interface. Again we have a very large range of software that can be chosen. Based on the requirement of the task, and the underlying hardware, we need to decide on the software. It can be lower level languages, such as Assembly Level Languages, or high level languages, like C, C++, Java, and so on. There are many front-end developer tools, with which we can create an audio/visual experience for the user, such as Visual Basic, HTML5, PHP, animators, etc.

Operating Environment

Though there is huge turnover in the software and hardware, the major focus is on the end user and based on that the designs are decided. Our design decision should fulfill the user-level acceptance test and the modification should be provided immediately after any suggestion. The operation environment should follow a process within that certain level of pitfalls should be avoided.

Following are the some key points that define the golden rules of user interface design:

- Friends, family members, colleagues are not representatives of target users.
- User requirements should be understood by a team and not by an individual.
- Goal should be to minimize user difficulties.
- The hardware (device) and software balance should be maintained.

User Interface

User interface is not necessarily a computer or mobile screen. It is the medium through which a user sees the machine. It may be in the form of hard copies, computer screen operation environments, remote controls, or just the appearance of machine itself. A good UI will ensure that the target audience will be able to understand the functionality of the system by just seeing it. User requirements should be identified well in advance before designing the interface. In this chapter we focus mainly on the major factors about humans that need to be considered before the actual design process.

The Psychopathology of Everyday Things

The topic name is very intriguing for one. By breaking it down, word-by-word, it will be easier to understand the idea behind this topic. First, we will break the word *psychopathology* as:

psycho = mind; *pathos* = suffering/disease; *logy* = study.

Psychopathology: The study of mental illness

Psychopathology of everyday things: How the design of our everyday things can make us crazy.

Have you ever walked into a closed door? It is very frustrating to bang your head on the glass, and then realize that the door was meant to be pulled, and not pushed. This is a common experience, but it is not the fault of the user. Had the handles been designed in such a manner that it leaves enough clues for the human mind to recognize, this error would not occur. These are called Norman doors – A common term used to say that these doors are not comprehensible to the human mind. The door in Figure 1.8 is a PULL door. You can realize that by closely observing the hinges. But the absence of handles makes it seem like this is a PUSH door.

Figure 1.8 Norman Doors.

Complexity of Modern Devices

Every product is launched with something different. A business believes in thinking out of the box. Sometimes they are with enhanced features, or sometimes with just a new appearance. They make a namesake interface to make sure all their features are accessible to the user. The designers rarely make an effort to analyze the utility of their new design.

Sometimes, the designer just wants to make a difference, and creates existing products with a new appearance, such as the Norman pots or the coffee cup shown in Figure 1.9. The coffee cup sure has an interesting appearance, but the designer again has not considered the difficulty of the user to drink from it.

Technology is advancing at a great pace and the designs are not that competent. Focus of the developer is to equip the machines with more features, and exquisite appearances, but very less on the utility. A designer has to ensure that these features are presented in a simple and comprehensible way to the user, yet ensure perfect usability. Instead, they leave the user confused and make him feel incompetent to use such a high end product.

Most of us face trouble using simple day-to-day devices. To figure out the buttons on our TV or AC remote, we feel the need of an engineering degree. A new TV may be upgraded with many new features, but a user sees all these features through the remote that is in the user's hand. If the remote control confuses the user, then all the

Figure 1.9 Confusing designs.

features provided become useless. Look at all the remote controls shown in Figure 1.10. Not all are easy to simple or easy to use by a novice user.

Figure 1.10 Remote controls.

Be it any appliance or software, technologies keep upgrading. Be it in microwaves ovens, air conditioners, washing machines, mixers, coffee makers, gas stoves, computers, mobile phones, wrist watches or treadmills, computing power is added. As the features increase, the complexity of the interface too grows. It is the responsibility of the designers to make these features available to the user in the most usable way.

Human-Centered Design

Human-centered designing is to consider all the aspects of the destined user, such as his interests, behaviors, needs, likes, dislikes, skill set, experience, challenges, etc., and build products that users will be able to easily adapt to. Analyzing the human characteristics is the requirement of the product design, and user satisfaction is the designer's goal.

Each person has some kind of experience of the real world, and their intelligence will use this experience to learn new features. It is the creativity of the designer to find this knowledge of the user, and exploit it to their advantage. For example, when you look at a suitcase, you know that it can be opened and you can place things inside it. Using the image of a suitcase on the computer screen will tell the user that it can be opened, and they will be able to find something inside it.

Conceptual model is the mental image a human has built. To be able to find things inside a suitcase is the mental image. Similarly, when you have to make a note of a few points, you look for a pen and paper. This is again the mental image formed for writing. As a good designer you should be able to use these mental models of the user, as well as be able to create mental models for the user. For example, Microsoft Word has become the mental model of a text editor unanimously.

Conceptual models define a good design as the communication between the designer and the user. The designer must be able to explain the entire product to the user by just the appearance of it. These models are very critical for a good user experience. If the end product does not map to the mental images of the user, the product is not a success.

Norman talks of four aspects through which these conceptual models can be used and/or constructed.

1. **Feedback:** The effect of every action. A feedback in any form is very critical to the user. In the earlier washing machine example, the user did not get any kind of feedback from the system. That made the user assume the system is faulty. Every single user action has to be acknowledged immediately.
2. **Constraints:** Prevent the user from making mistakes. Instead of having an option for the user to make a mistake and then forgiving them, make sure your user can never make a mistake. For example, you want your user to enter a date. Show a pick-n-click calendar, instead of a textbox. This will eliminate all possibilities of syntax mismatches (see Figure 1.11).

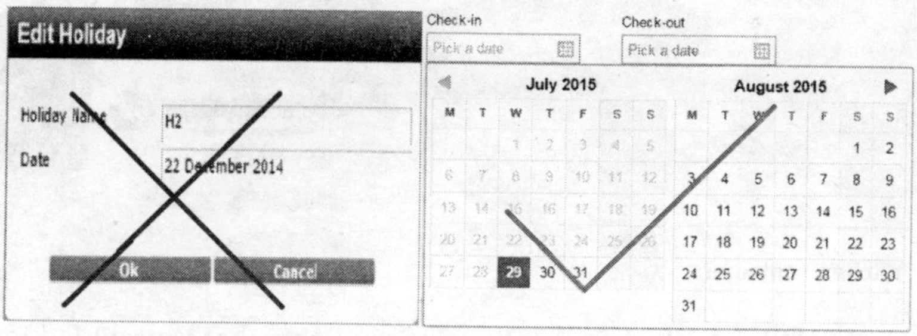

Figure 1.11 Constraints for date entry.

To leave messages everywhere, such as "Click here", "Insert this way", etc., are the qualities of a poor design.

3. **Affordances:** Convey the rules by leaving visual clues. To make sure that the appropriate actions are perceivable, and non-accessible ones are not invisible. By just the appearance of any object, its functionality must be clear to the user. Example, by looking at the handles, we should know how the door opens.
4. **Power of observation:** Learn from the struggle of others. As a normal person, we do not have a keen eye to observe. In fact when someone is making a mistake or struggling with a system, we tend to make fun of them or judge them to be incapable. As a HMI student, you need to observe them. Their struggle could be genuine and their mistakes could be innocent. As designers, we need to consider every such aspect of the user, and ensure that he/she gets a good experience.

Norman's Fundamental Principles of Interaction

Affordances

These are the little aspects that tell the human what needs to be done. This concept was introduced by psychologist J. J. Gibson. He defines affordances as "*the qualities of the physical world that suggest the possibility of interaction relative to the ability of an actor (person or animal) to interact*". He stated three fundamental qualities of an affordance:

- An affordance exists relative to the action capabilities of a particular actor.
- The existence of an affordance is independent of the actor's ability to perceive it (emphasis added).
- An affordance does not change as the needs and goals of the actor change.

You may notice many containers in your kitchen. Each opens in its own way. Not many have any instructions printed on them. They may open with a screw movement or by a pull/ press technique, while some have a locking feature. How are you able to identify one from the other? From the containers in Figure 1.12, are you able to guess the way each can be opened? Is it the shape or size of the body? Or is it the shape of the lid? Or do both participate? Those features of the physical appearance than contribute in explaining to the user the mechanism with which it operates can be called as its affordances. Here the shape of the lid and body are the affordances of the container.

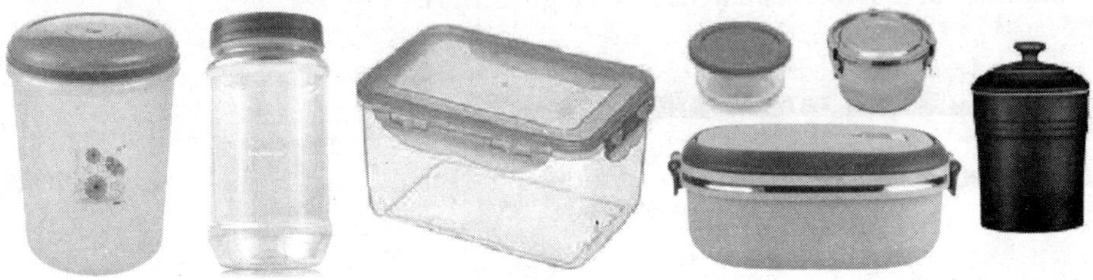

Figure 1.12 Kitchen containers.

For example, when you see the handle of a cup, you know that is provided to lift the cup. Similarly, when you see a 3D button on the screen, you tend to click on it. The blinking vertical line tells you that you can type here (Figure 1.13). Similarly, a round red button in a remote control tells the user that it can be pressed to power on or off the system. *Affordances are the visual clues that lead the user to understand the functionality of the object.* It is the most critical aspect of a design. As a designer, you should first realize the users' level of experience and intelligence. Only then you can make a design that would be predictable to the user.

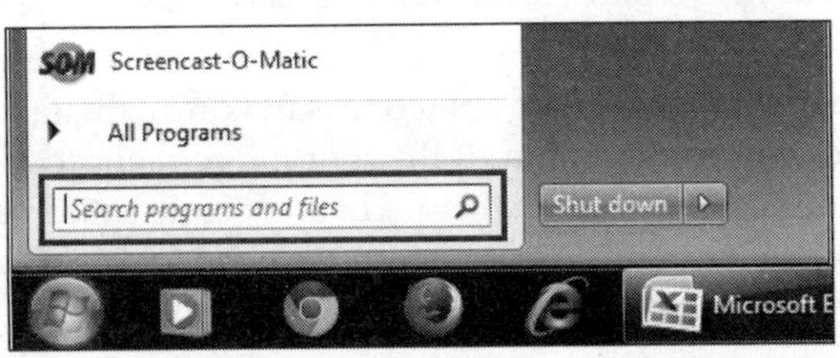

Figure 1.13 Textbox with blinking cursor.

Signifiers

This is a physical form of showing the functionality to the user, such as a sound, a printed word, or an image. For example, writing the word "PUSH" on a door is a clear way to tell the user that the door will open when pushed. Sometimes, affordances are not clear enough to tell the user the functionality of the object. A signifier removes all such ambiguity. In an ATM machine the card insert slot can be confusing at times. You may wonder whether you need to swipe the card and remove it, or let the machine absorb the card. In such cases, you may add a signifier INSERT or SWIPE (Figure 1.14).

Figure 1.14 Signifiers.

Affordances, Perceived Affordances and Signifiers

Perceived affordance is what the user understands by looking at the object. It may not be the same as what the designer intended it to be. This concept was introduced by Norman. Sometimes we look at an object and assume its purpose. In Figure 1.15(a) the panel of a lift is shown. Here it is easy for the user to assume that the glowing arrows are pushable. Only after pushing it the user will realize that it is just a label, and it cannot be pushed. After that realization starts the next confusion. To go down, should you press the square beside the down arrow, or the one beneath it?

Another example, many novice users look at the two *Enter* keys on a keyboard as shown in Figure 1.15(b), and assume they have different functionalities. The intention of the designer was to increase the usability. Since most of the keyboards have these two *Enter* keys in different shapes, many novice users easily form this assumption. Sometimes you may even hear them say "Press this ENTER key, not that one!"

(a) Lift panel (b) Keyboard with two Enter keys

Figure 1.15 Perceived affordances.

Mapping

To present the relationship between two objects is mapping. Here we shall map actions to consequences. Every user action has to be acknowledged in some way. In the beginning of the chapter we saw how a poor feedback system can frustrate the user, to the extent of returning his brand new washing machine. Had his actions been acknowledged in some way, his anxiety will reduce and will have a happy customer.

It is also important to have a good mapping between the action and consequence. The user must be able to predict the consequence of his action beforehand. If the user moves his mouse to the right, the pointer on the screen also moves to the right. It is easy for the user to learn this mapping and remember it too, because the movement of the hand directly affects the movement of the pointer. They work synchronously. Such mapping can be termed as natural.

Steering a car wheel in the clockwise direction, turns the car to the right. Most of us are trained to view the clockwise rotation is a rightward movement, hence this too becomes a natural mapping. Similarly to increase the volume of a device, we turn the knob clockwise. It is imbibed in most humans to assume an increase as we go rightwards. Could be because of the mathematics teacher in our schools who taught us the greater than symbol "<".

Sometimes the fan regulators get fixed the opposite way (Figure 1.16). It may be due to the negligence of a careless electrician. Even after months or years of its usage, you will still try to rotate it the opposite way, and curse the electrician for his poor job.

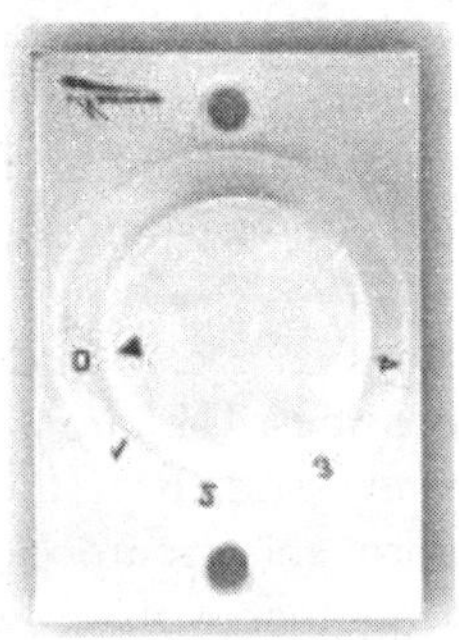

Figure 1.16 Fan regulator.

Switches provide immediate feedback to the user about his action. You push a switch, a light glows. Imagine you are sitting in a room of switches, all of whose light bulbs are in other rooms. How long will it take for you to learn the mapping of the switches to their correct bulbs? You take time because you are not able to see the consequence of your action. You need to train your brain systematically with repeated usage to remember this mapping. It is not a natural process. Only when a user can see the consequence of his action, he will learn and remember its functionality.

Exploit the physical analogies and traditions of your user to create the best products. It is easier for us to operate a machine with the knowledge we already possess than to learn and remember something new. Use natural mapping as much as possible.

Feedback

Feedback is the best and the fastest way of learning. We humans always work on a trial-and-error method. We want to try to use the product first and learn it during the course. You do not want to theoretically study and earn a degree on how to use your mobile phone before purchasing it. You go to the store and pick the latest model that is affordable for you. You believe you will be able to learn its working as you start using it. Unlike old phones, these days mobile phones come with a lot of features on a small display screen. Not all icons provided are comprehensible of their exact use. It takes time for one to learn all these functionalities.

Feedback should not only be prompt, but also predictable to the user. A correct mapping of the actions and consequences creates a good feedback system.

Conceptual Models

The affordances induce a thought of action. Signifiers affirm that thought. Mapping his action to a consequence provides a feedback. Good feedback encourages learning. Repeated learning creates a mental model in the user about the system.

"I think the system does this" is different from what the system actually does. A conceptual model is developed gradually in the user's mind after repeated interactions with a system. A design model is the conceptual model of the designer, and not the user. They can be very different from each other if the system is not well designed.

A driver's mental model says that the press of the accelerator pedal of a car makes the car go faster. The design model is to provide more fuel to the engine when the accelerator is pressed. Here the mental pictures may be different, but the consequence is the same. Hence there is no problem.

Here is a customer care center joke that was commonly shared a few years back.

Executive: How may I help you?
Customer: The coffee cup holder of my PC broke this morning, and I'm still in warranty.
Executive: I'm sorry I do not understand. Was this cup holder given to you as a compliment with our computer?
Customer: No. It is inside your computer. I press this button, and it pops out.
Executive: But we do not have any computers that come with cup holders. Is there anything written on this button?
Customer: Yes. HD DVD

You may laugh at this joke. But there were many who really used the CD ROM tray as their coffee cup holders. A novice user does not know anything about computers or discs, but is familiar with the concept of placing coffee cups in round slots. He finds a tray with a slot that easily fits his cup, and in the ideal height to place his coffee while working on the computer (Figure 1.17). He in fact compliments the designers for their thoughtfulness. Can you really laugh at these users? Here the mental model of the user is a coffee cup holder, whereas the design was to insert discs.

Figure 1.17 Cup Holder Tray.

It is the responsibility of the designer to first understand the mental model of users, and try to make a product that will agree to it. To make a user learn a new concept, and develop a mental model about the product will be difficult, as well as time consuming. Creativity for a designer is essential, but not at the cost of making the users feel incompetent.

Conceptual models is a vast concept that is covered in detail later in this book. This section should give you a basic idea of its significance.

Psychology of Everyday Actions

How do People do Things

Humans' first response to a poor design is self-blame. We feel incompetent to use the product. We first try the trial-and-error method. When that fails, we ask people around us to help us. When they too give up, we reach out to the user manual. Even after this if the product is incomprehensible, we call the customer care. We make every effort to learn about the product, because humans have the tendency to believe that the new product is beyond their level of expertise and they have to make an effort to understand it.

Also, humans also have a tendency to compare themselves. If the product has a good market value, but they are not able to figure it out, then the human feels incompetent to use the product. Only after we have tried everything under the sun, and the market reviews are bad, we tend to blame the product.

As a designer we can exploit this nature of humans. We can build high-end systems with complex designs and ask our end users to adapt themselves to it, and we can be sure that they will make every effort to do it as well. The disadvantage of this approach is that, humans can get exhausted trying to adapt to new technologies. At one point, they will settle down for something known and easy to use, over a complex system that they need to learn all over again.

Our aim should not be to make humans adapt to our product.
Instead to build products that can adapt to the humans.

When we look at a product, we should know how to use it without any external help. Only then we can say that the product is good. We may be able to use it out of our experience or our intelligence. Either way, we can call that design successful.

Seven Stages of Action and Three Levels of Processing

Seven Stages of Action

Norman states that human actions have two aspects, execution and evaluation. We perform an action (execution) and then analyze our action if that is what we wanted (evaluation). Every action is performed in seven stages as given below:

1. Forming the goal

Execution

2. Forming the intention (plan)

3. Specifying an action (specify)
4. Executing the action (perform)

Evaluation

5. Perceiving the state of the world (perceive)
6. Interpreting the state of the world (reflect)
7. Evaluating the outcome (compare)

To understand this concept, let us take a macro example. You are alone at home and bored, so you go and watch a movie. Though this looks simple, our human brain executed it in the following way:

1. I want to kill my boredom (goal)
2. Movie seems to be a good idea (plan)
3. Check for the nearest cinema and show time (specify)
4. Purchase a ticket and go sit in the movie hall. (perform)
5. You watch the audio visual effects of the movie (perceive)
6. You interpret the effects to your understanding (reflect)
7. After the movie, you say to yourself "that was a good time pass" (compare)

Similar stages take place even in our micro activities. Let us take the example of a single action. You are driving a nail into a piece of furniture.

1. This nail has to hold these two blocks together (goal)
2. This location seems perfect (plan)
3. Hold the nail at that point (specify)
4. Start hammering it (perform)
5. I can see the hammer striking the nail, and hear the sound (perceive)
6. This nail seems to be going in straight (reflect)
7. At the end, I move the blocks to check if the nail has fastened them together (compare)

Though the action may look simple, most of the time we go through all these stages to perform it. There is always a gap between what we wanted to do, and what we have done. Norman calls this as *The Gulfs of Execution and Evaluation*. In the first case, what you wanted was to kill boredom, and what had done was watched a movie. In the second case, you wanted to fasten two wooden blocks together, and hammered a nail into it. Most of the time, what we do does not satisfy our goal. We can use this human feature in interface designing too. Since we know how exactly the user is going to perform every action, we can decide the flow for him.

- **Gulf of Execution:** The distance between the options available and the user's goal is the gulf of execution. You need to find if the system provides actions that correspond to the intentions of the person.
- **Gulf of Evaluation:** The amount of effort a person has to put to interpret the options available on the system and determine if they will match his intentions.

These seven stages of action are very much effective in deciding the user's perspective of the interface. If end user expectations are not properly analyzed while performing some actions users will

(a) Fail at few points out of which they may try to represent some different action
(b) User interface will not be user friendly
(c) User actions may be scattered
(d) User may end up with non-satisfactory results.

Three Levels of Processing

- **Visceral level:** The most immediate level of processing. Here the human reacts to audio, visual and other aspects of a product before experiencing it. The look and feel of the product dominates the user in this level. An immediate decision is made about what is good, bad, safe or dangerous. Bright colors, sweet taste, melody, good aroma, smooth surface, etc., are appreciated in this level. Our brain is trained to like or dislike based on our cultural beliefs and social upbringing. Girls like pink; boys like blue; Indians like spicy food; Brazilians like Samba; English like tea; etc. A taste needs to be developed to like bitter gourd or beer. As the saying, "beauty is in the eyes of the beholder", each person finds something more attractive than the other.

  Visceral design often corresponds to creating an aesthetically pleasing appearance. The creative skills of a visual and graphic designer alone creates an impact on the user. Only after this level approves of the product, we proceed towards working with it. If at this level, we react with a negative feeling, the other levels will need tremendous effort to accept the product over long periods of time.

  The designer of a product with high end features may find it absurd to choose a good color for the product. But for the user, this becomes one of the most critical deciding factors.

- **Behavioral level:** The middle level of processing. The emotional brain takes control of the decision making. We react to the products at a deeper level than that of visceral. We get annoyed or frustrated with complex systems. We enjoy working on familiar and simple environments. This level manages our simple, everyday actions. Here functionality of the product takes prime importance.

  In behavioral design, semantics, and usability practices are primarily addressed. It tells the user how to "behave" or "respond" to a communication or feedback given by the product. For example, a dialog box with an error or warning message tells the user what needs to be done next. Or a simple ON and OFF mark on an electrical switch tells us how to operate the switch.

- **Reflective level:** The last level of processing. A careful analysis and reflection of all the incidents or experiences is made. The meaning of an experience is stored in our brain.

  Through reflection, we try to share our experiences by designing models and convert them into prototype. Reflective design is nothing but the effort to develop long-term relationships with the customers. Thus, reflective design can tell us about the customer's inclination towards various ranges of products.

Knowing the three levels at which we process information (Figure 1.18), the seven stages of our actions can be understood better. Each stage of action works on a particular level. Through Figure 1.19, Norman gives an overview of this mapping.

At the reflective level a need is identified which becomes our goal. Analyzing our past experiences or future requirements, we make a plan to achieve this goal. Then based on our mood, likes and dislikes we choose a method to execute that plan. The behavioral level is responsible for this action. Most of the time our decisions are affected by our emotions. This level has the strongest influence over a human being. At the visceral level we actually perform the specified method. All the physical aspects of performing the task are considered. Our senses of vision, hearing, smell, touch and taste are used to perceive the action being performed. These perceptions are then interpreted and given a meaning by the behavioral level again. Finally the reflective level analyses our experience and compares it with the initial goal. It stores this experience as positive or negative for future reference.

Let us consider the same example of watching a movie because we were bored. The stages of action that were followed to execute it were seen in the earlier section.

1. **Goal:** I want to kill my boredom. The reflective level has analyzed your situation as boredom, and realizes from past experience that it should be avoided.
2. **Plan:** Movie seems to be a good idea. Again the reflective layer gathers from past experiences that a movie is a good distraction.

LOOK & FEEL	➔ ➔	Visceral level	➔ ➔	MOTOR SKILLS
	➔ ➔	Behavioral level	➔ ➔	
	➔ ➔	Reflective design	➔ ➔	

Figure 1.18 Three levels of processing.

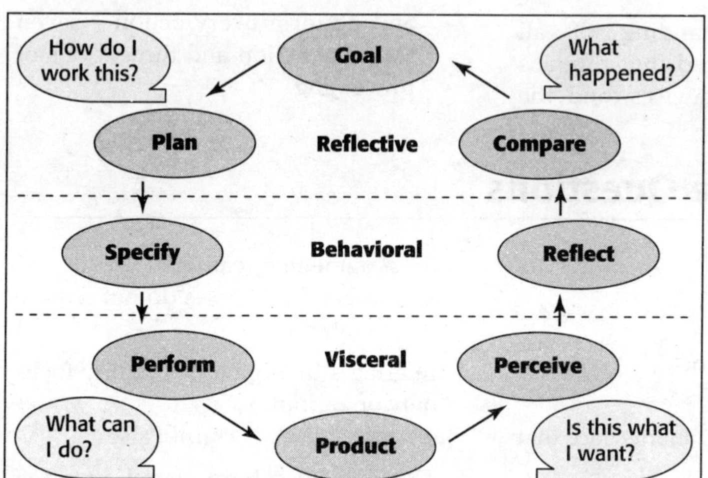

Figure 1.19 Seven stages of action and three levels of processing.

3. **Specify:** Check for the nearest cinema and show time. Now the behavioral layer has its likes and dislikes. It takes the responsibility of choosing the perfect movie for the moment.
4. **Perform:** Purchase a ticket and go sit in the movie hall. The visceral layer takes care of the physical activities, like choosing the seat, making payment, reaching the movie hall and watching the movie.
5. **Perceive:** You watch the audio visual effects of the movie. The visceral level appreciates the various audio and visual effects of the movie. The actions presented, the sound effects, the direction, etc., creates an impression about the movie.
6. **Reflect:** You interpret the effects to your understanding. Now the behavioral level reacts to these perceptions with an emotion. We relate ourselves with one of the actors emotionally. We cry, laugh and get angry while watching the movie. This level appreciates the story line of the movie.
7. **Compare:** After the movie, you say to yourself "that was a good time pass". Now the reflective level gives a meaning to the entire experience, by comparing it with the goal. It sure killed the boredom. So it was a good idea. The next time you feel bored you will consider watching another movie.

Summary

Through this chapter we introduce

- The aim of this field. The, aim to not make humans adapt to a product. Instead to build products that can adapt to the humans.
- Evolution of user interfaces by classifying machines into five generations.
- A basic understanding of all the problems faced by humans with day-to-day devices, and the need for a designer to look into these issues.
- Norman's principles of interactions – Affordances, Signifiers, Perceived Signifiers, Mapping, Feedback & Conceptual Model.
- A realization on human psychology that reveals how people think and perform every action – seven stages of action and three levels of processing.

Multiple Choice Questions

1. Interface is
   (a) GUI
   (b) Interaction method
   (c) Physical appearance
   (d) All of these
2. Data mining requires an interface that is of
   (a) Fourth generation machines
   (b) Fifth generation machines
   (c) Augmented reality
   (d) Backend processes do not require an interface.
3. Interfaces in augmented reality focus only on output.
   (a) True (b) False
4. The image of a horn placed on top of the button in a car is a

(a) Affordance
(b) Signifier
(c) Perceived signifier
(d) Feedback

5. We are able to differentiate between a battle axe and a woodcutter's axe because of their
   (a) Affordances
   (b) Signifiers
   (c) Decoration
   (d) Place of display
6. Revamping the appearance of an existing device makes it
   (a) More user friendly
   (b) Business competent
   (c) Complex to use
   (d) Annoying to the user
7. Natural mapping is relationship between
   (a) Mental model and design model
   (b) Cognitive skills and consequences
   (c) User and machine
   (d) Nature and culture
8. Norman doors are
   (a) Doors without handles
   (b) Revolving doors, as in a mall
   (c) Confusing doors
   (d) Invisible glass doors
9. Affordances work on
   (a) Visceral level
   (b) Behavioral level
   (c) Reflective level
   (d) All of these.
10. Match the following:

(a) Visceral level	(i) Emotional
(b) Behavioral level	(ii) Experience
(c) Reflective level	(iii) Reactive
(d) Conceptual model	(iv) Analytical

Review Questions

1. Explain the history of user interfaces.
2. How does the complexity of modern devices add to the psychopathology of these things?
3. What is a human-centric design?
4. Give Norman's fundamental principles of interaction.
5. Compare affordances and perceived affordances.
6. What is the difference between mapping and feedback?
7. How does feedback help in developing mental models?
8. Why do humans blame themselves for a poorly designed product?
9. Explain the seven stages of action and three levels of processing with suitable examples.
10. Explain the gulf of execution and evaluation with an example.
11. Sit next to an elderly person working with a computer. Observe the mistakes they are making. Note down their reactions. Try to find out their mental image of the system in use. Identify at what level of processing they are facing the problems.
12. Pick an appliance in your house that is used the most. Observe all the options given on it, and try to create the design model of this product.
13. A light bulb is faulty in your house and you need to replace it with a new one. Describe the seven stages of action that you will follow to change this bulb, along with the level of processing in each.

CHAPTER 2

Goal Directed Design

In the last chapter we have discussed about the human behavior and some key concepts of interaction in the real-world scenario before actually beginning with the system design. In this chapter, we will discuss the design issues related to the specific tasks that need to be carried out as per the user's requirement. Nowadays user interface is essential for almost all categories of the systems, namely, hardware, software, and other supporting equipment. We can call it as a digital system. A mobile phone, tablet PC (Tab), hand-held ticketing machine and even a standalone computer software and web interface can be called as a digital system.

If all the above-mentioned systems are not well equipped with a better interface design, then their use, usage, and usability will definitely be challenging.

The nine basic questions are as follows:

1. Who are the users of the system?
2. What are the users' tasks and goals?
3. What are the users' expectation levels with the document, and documents like it?
4. What functions do the users need from the interface?
5. What information might the users need, and in what form do they need it?
6. How do users think the system should work?
7. What are the extreme environments?
8. Is the user multitasking?
9. Does the interface utilize different inputs modes such as touching, spoken, gestures, or orientation?

Mistakes Performed While Designing a Computer System

Most of the computer system designers think that operations such as mouse click, drag and drop, writing an email, or any system related operation performed by them with ease is possible for everyone. It is assumed that the person or end user is a skilled computer operator and expected that he will understand all necessary actions that are required to be carried out while using the system. Developers think exactly what is being built. Challenges are not solved while using the system and that may cause the failure in use, usage, and usability of the system. In addition to the mistakes normally carried out by the designers, the other general observations are as follows:

- Developers expect people to think like Computers.
- Developers asks user to perform difficult operations (that may not be difficult for developers).
- The resultant Software design will have poor behavior.
- Users are ignored.

If all the system operations are considered related to end user's expectations and his skills, these ill effects of the poor design can be avoided.

Design

As we are discussing human machine interface, we should make a conscious effort to consider humanity. Here the major focus is designing the digital or computer system.

"Computer System Design is the process that consists of a user-oriented approach where all meaningful activities are systematically framed together and utmost importance is given to the person who is going to use that system."

Following are the activities involved in design process:

- Understanding user requirements.
- Understanding purpose of the user.
- Understanding the work environments.

For understanding user requirement, we should consider the desire, need, and enhance the user ability to perform the task. Purpose of understanding user's requirement is to provide feasibility to use the system. Finally, the work environment is the place where the system is being used, whether it is a stand-alone computer terminal, an information kiosk at the public place, an automated cash deposit machine, or self-billing section in the departmental store or a mall.

Software Evolution Process

Figure 2.1 shows various phases of evolution of software development process. The first phase is when developers develop systems without considering the user and

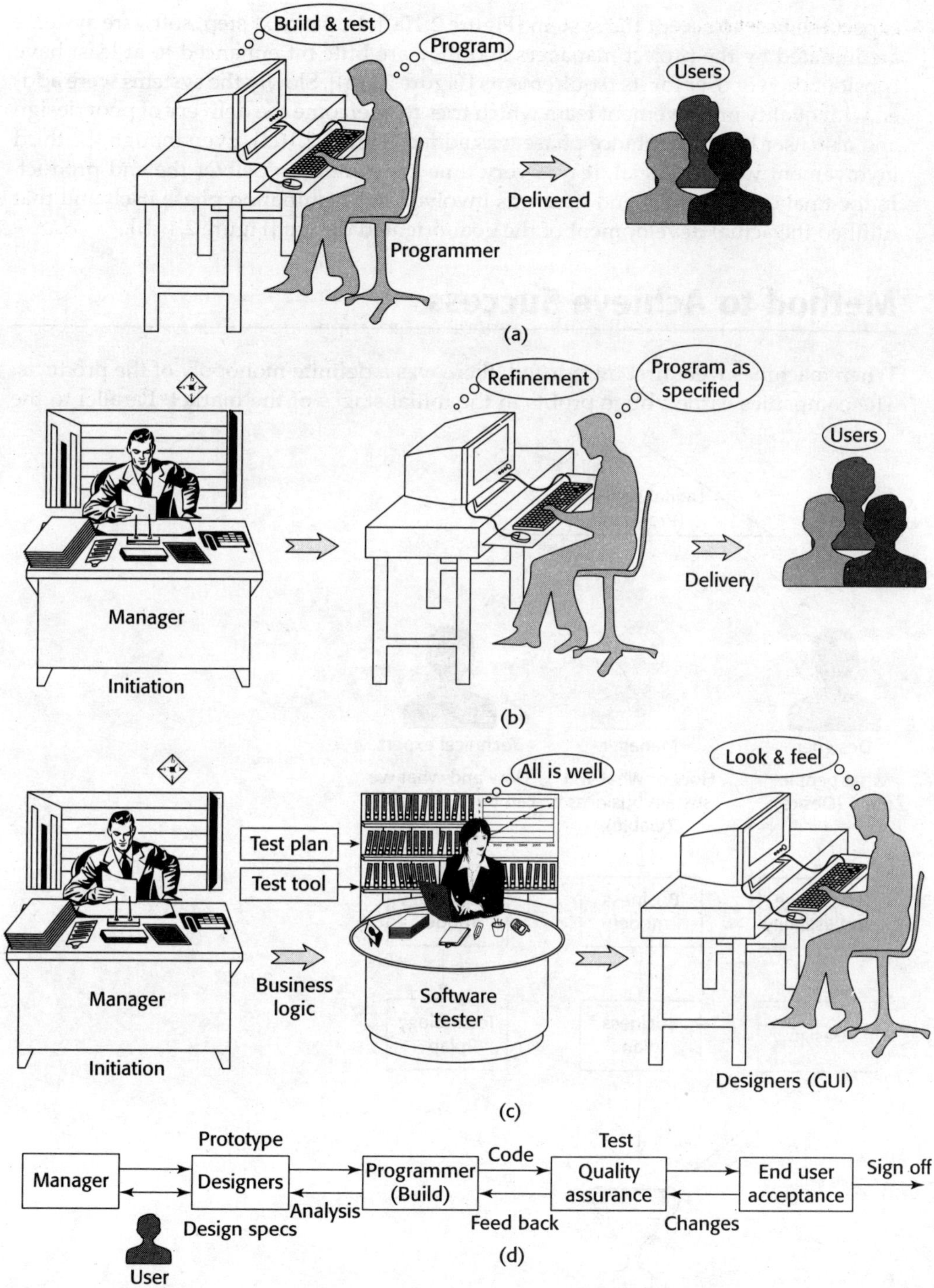

Figure 2.1 Showcasing different stages: (a) when systems were delivered; (b) when software Engineering was adopted; (c) when software testing was introduced; (d) stakeholder's involvement in the current design approach.

expect the user to accept the system [Figure 2.1(a)]. In the next step, software systems are initiated by the project managers and they are little bit enhanced to at least have consideration of user for its requirements [Figure 2.1(b)]. Slowly the systems were added with quality improvement team which tries to overcome the delivery of poor design and also user level acceptance phase was added [Figure 2.1(c)]. Even though the third involvement was beneficial, it was very time consuming to deliver the end product. In the final evolution the end user was involved in the initiation phase itself and that fulfilled the actual development of the goal-oriented design [Figure 2.1(d)].

Method to Achieve Success

When machines were first introduced, there was a definite monopoly of the products. The companies earned huge profits in the initial stages of the market. Parallel to the

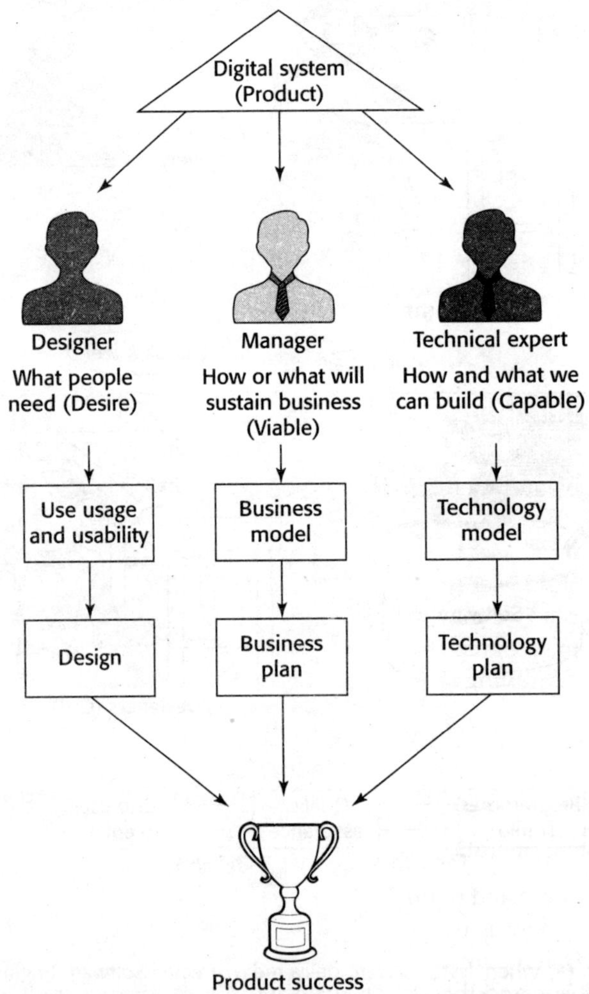

Figure 2.2 Desirability, viability and capability to achieve success in Digital products or software system delivery.

supply of the existing products, the companies were looking for new business opportunities and there was also a tough competition in the market. Companies strived to provide new range of products with considerable feasibility to the user. This was possible when design phase was introduced in manufacturing industry. Slowly, computers were also involved and that was having a limitless behavior. Designs very much decide the success of the product. To achieve success, we should have our computer interface with desirability, viability, and capability (see Figure 2.1).

- **Desirability:** What does the end user needs?
- **Viability:** How can we sustain the business? (How to ensure use, usage, and usability?)
- **Capability:** What can we deliver by using latest available technology?

Recognize the Goals

Some questions worth pondering about are:

- What are the goals?
- How do we identify them?
- How can we confirm the sure goals?
- Are goals common to all?
- Can they be different each time?

To understand the goal directed design, we should better understand the user goals and how they can help to design relevant interactive behavior.

User goals are often quite different from what we actually think; for example, let us consider that purchase in-charge of the organization may require the information of the equipment purchased by all other departments in specific format, as a developer we may think that he wants a list of equipment as name of the equipment, the date of purchase the cost, and status of the equipment. Purchase in-charge may be asking the same list of equipment along with the cost of the equipment as on date by calculating its depreciation from the date of purchase. He may also want to gather information about utilization of the equipment. End user will definitely help to recognize goals that he may think are essential; in this case we may miss to identify the other user's goals. It should be a collective approach to recognize goals of all stakeholders at clients end.

The prototype presented after identifying the exact goals must ensure that

- It is user-friendly.
- It provides feasibility for the user.
- User is able to effectively operate the system.
- User is able to enjoy the system operation.

The user interface should be communicated to the end user for acceptance well before the coding begins. Change management is easier w.r.t. user interface if it is required to be updated. Interface design will have minimum changes if there is a focus on the users, the tasks users need to perform, and their goals.

Project management approach for user interface design also plays an important role. In project management, there is an approach to map our goals with the tasks and activities to be carried out by the user. It is always recommended that this mapping can be involved. The goals and tasks are two different entities. They help to meet the ultimate requirements. Donald Norman has also recommended the Activity Centric Design (ACD). ACD influence to propose a design that effectively helps to understand *how people interact with the world*. Most of the times, traditional efforts generate inadequate results. ACD also makes some important steps to highlight the users perspective in design. It helps in dividing the task according to the concepts discussed in Chapter 1 and basic questions discussed in the beginning phase of this chapter. Recognizing the goals enhances the quality of design to understand the expectations of end user and activities relation to that. To summarize we can say that goals are human centric they change very slowly whereas activities may be ask to change each new time.

Following are few real-life scenarios that help to understand goals and activities. It is recommended that teacher using this book should motivate students to discuss about the goals and activities for the following systems:

1. Automated customer care interface using the telephone.
2. Information kiosk for the bank customers and its ease of use for first time users.
3. Self-check-out counter for Departmental Store or Mall.
4. Online Purchase. (Kindly have a case study of few popular online shopping portals.)
5. Mobile app for performing shopping or finance transactions.

Goal Directed Design Process

To create the interface pertaining to user and specific to goal, it is necessary to bridge the gap between user and developer. This is possible only by having the proper nature of research. The research approach will help to identify:

- How users use the system?
- What all technological systems can be incorporated?
- Can any information resources be utilized?
- Is there any way of integration?

Designers can play the role of researchers and by the year 2000 software companies did appointed few engineers as market researchers. The traditional market survey was carried out by almost all companies to identify need of the market and technically sound people were involved in the market survey. Instead of promoting the products they were asked to identify the systems used at various organizations and their next requirements. Figure 2.3 shows the process of conducting market research.

Goal directed design is nothing but various phases along with the market research that provides the solution which meet the requirements and goals of the end users. Figure 2.4 is the goal directed design process.

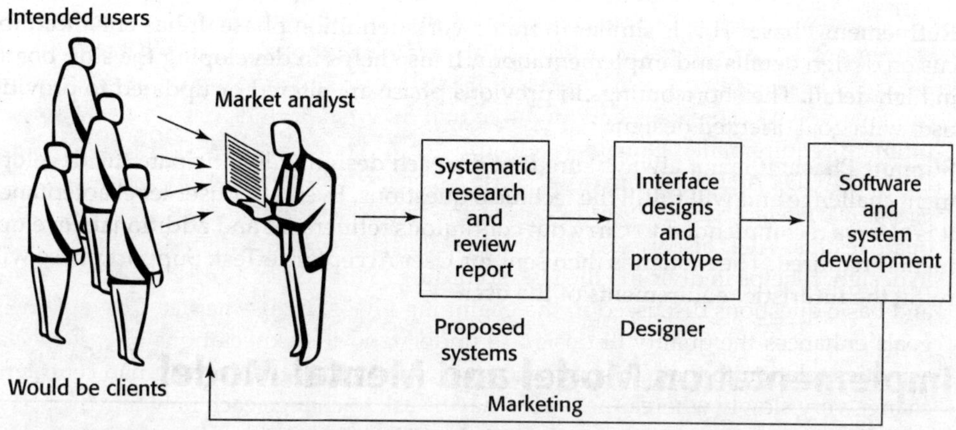

Figure 2.3 Process of conducting market research to decide the target areas for system.

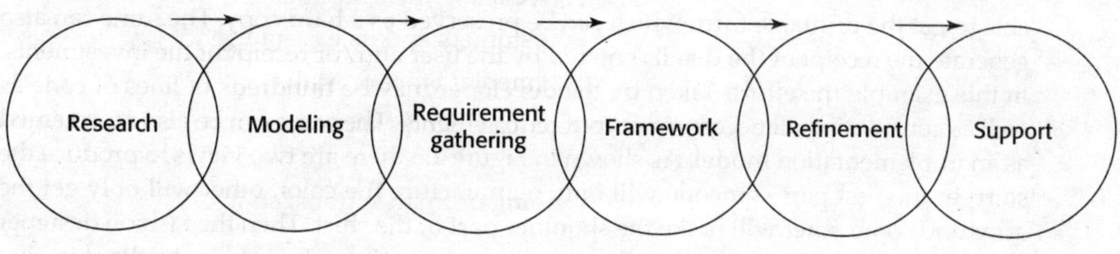

Figure 2.4 Goal directed design process.

Research Phase: This is nothing but the initial phase to bridge the gap between the user and developer. It consists of field survey by conducting contextual interviews and observations. The research generates the information about potential or actual users. Interview report of the stakeholders consists of information of people who are involved in research, some competitive products, what exactly is expected and general responses received. The research helps to identify behavior patterns and personas in the modeling phase as well as constraints that must be satisfied.

Modeling Phase: The outcome of research phase is synthesized into domain and user models. Domain model includes information flow and work flow. We can identify the detailed persona, composite user arch types that represent distinct behavior attitude, aptitude, and goals and motivations identified in research phase.

Requirements Definition Phase: This phase provides the much needed connectivity between the user and other models and design framework. It also focuses on most important tasks.

Framework Phase: In this phase a basic framework for the system behavior, visual design as well as physical form of the design is proposed. In this phase interaction team may specify the interaction framework. At the concluding state of interaction design we can evolve visual framework to discuss the color schemes and visual style. Detailed discussion on interaction design can be carried out differently.

Refinement Phase: This is similar to framework definition phase. It has enhanced focus on design details and implementations. It also helps in developing the storyboard in high detail. The shortcomings in previous phase are altered or updated to provide user with goal oriented design.

Support Phase: It is not always sure that the each design will anticipate the development challenge and will fulfill the technical questions. Even after user level acceptance it is always recommended to carry out continuous refinement and additional development if required. The system is then sent for User Acceptance Test. Support phase will fulfill the futuristic requirements of the user.

Implementation Model and Mental Model

If user is working with a website to provide his/her details for an investments in mutual fund; he/she will get an input form developed in HTML or any script language. The input details will be inserted into some database and when user confirms his/her details, the system will recall the user details and frame them in a simple html page and will enable to get the printable form which can be preserved as a hard copy. The same can also generate the receipt of the details entered by the user and/or receipt of the investments. In this example the efforts taken by the developer may be hundreds of lines of code as well as considering all necessary output requirements. The same can be also represented as an implementation model. As shown in Figure 2.5 there are two views to produce the shirt: In the first part someone will only manufacture the color, other will only get the arms and some other will make the shoulder part of the shirt. Then the fashion designer will decide how to integrate the all parts and make various styles to make the shirt that suits the fashion statement. In other parts, whole shirt will be as per the person's choice and that will be actual mental model. First part is implementation model.

The person or the customer who is getting the result will have some level of satisfaction after receipt of the details he/she has entered and he/she is able to recall the system record linked with his/her login credentials. He/she will not strive to know the program or operating environment used to generate the records. This behavior is called as a mental model or conceptual model. People may not be interested to know

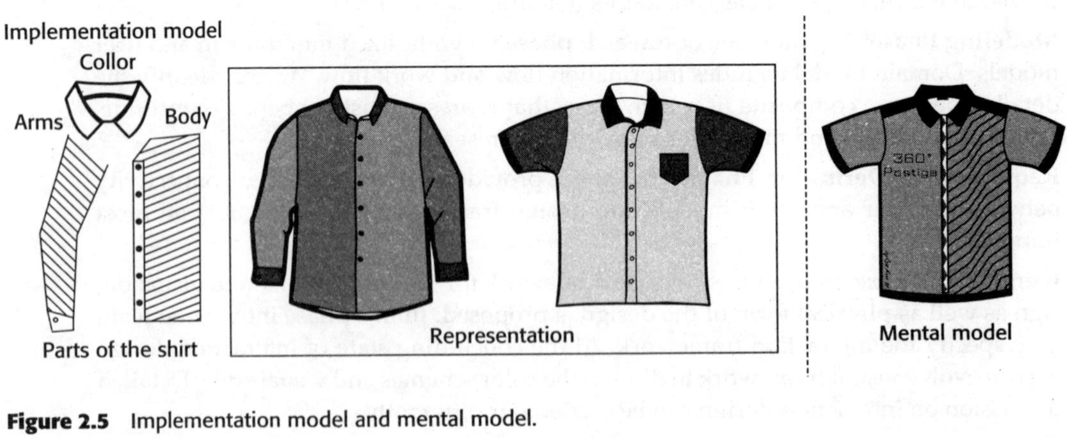

Figure 2.5 Implementation model and mental model.

all the details how complex is the mechanism that actually is used to build the system. Implementation and mental models are totally distinct from each other.

Case Study: Identify the current generation Software development tools and try to identify its implementation model. For example, Microsoft dot net, PHP MySQL, Oracle, Java, Java scripts, HTML 5, IOS, Android App Development.

Beginners, Experts and Intermediates

Developers need to verify the effect of their design decisions on the end users for any computer system and user interface. Websites, applications, or other user interfaces or services designed should have feasible impact on users. We already have discussed that it is necessary to identify the potential users of the system. Apart from the need to understand the business case and idea, identification of user is the most important thing. Prior to starting any design work there should be clear cut idea of the business, potential users who will experience the system, and how we can provide added value for the system.

User Experience Design: Perspective of Beginners, Intermediates, or Experts

It is a biggest challenge to address the needs and requirements of all those users? If we make a comment to build the system for everyone then we are designing for no one. However, in today's market environment where users are coming from all walks of life and with different experiences, we need to achieve the right balance between designing for beginners or experts is an increasingly complex and important task.

Most Users are Neither Beginners Nor Experts

When we design user interfaces we try to understand who our end users are: Are they beginners with no prior computing experience (or, at least, without experience using the system you are designing) or, perhaps, they may be excellent users (experts) who can find their way around easily? In the majority of situations, our users do not belong to similar group or they are from different categories – rather, they may be mixed bunch of people. They are members of the user community with different levels of experience and familiarity with the interfaces you are designing.

Skill spectrum can be divided into three parts. The first part consists of beginners, the middle is where so-called intermediates belong, and the third part is for experts. The categories can be decided from the age, IQ level, skillset, and distribution of population distributions. According to research done by experts in the field of Human Machine Interface the experience level of people performing a specific UI activity tends to follow the Gauss classic statistical bell curve. See Figure 2.6.

If you position the beginners at the left-hand side and experts to right-hand side, the largest, central part is where the majority of users fit. Their skill level can be characterized as intermediate and therefore the term "intermediates" is often used for them.

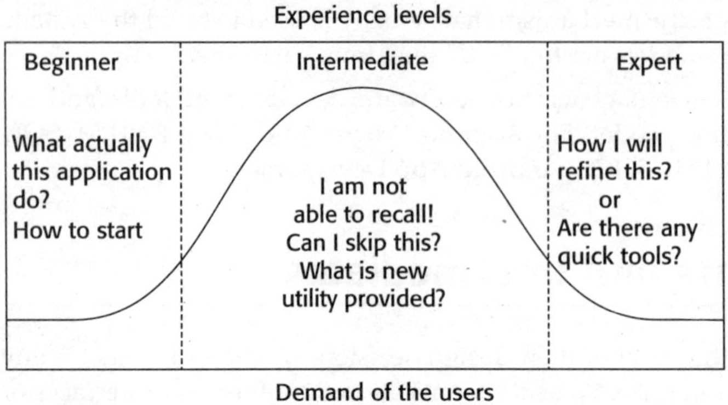

Figure 2.6 User experience levels in demand curve (Bell Curve).

It is obvious from the picture that most of the users are neither beginners nor experts—they are intermediates.

Skill Spectrum Dynamics

Let us recall your first phase of programming of higher level programming: When you start typing a code at the beginning, you may have referred the programming guidelines by a tutor or reference books. When you earned an experience of few lines of code you learnt some shortcuts and grasped a number of available concepts and features that enabled you to be more productive. In other words, you were graduated from the beginners to the intermediates part of the skill spectrum. See Figure 2.7 which shows the practice set for typewriter to enhance the typing skills. Professional typewriters use specific fingers to type in specific keys. They are trained for the same accordingly. The practice session enhances the level of typewriting from basic typewriter to 20 WPM (words per minute), 30 WPM, 40 WPM, etc.

If we perform various practice sessions to use the system, then we can achieve some expert level of experience. Try to recall how typewriters earn their skills or how musicians graduate from amateur to maestros. We will also take another example that most of us have experienced.

Remember when you started to learn how to ride a bicycle: You were beginner for the very first moments, after that you learnt some skills and moved into joining the intermediates. Just some people have developed into experts riding bicycles as pros. Under heavy pressure and competition—sooner or later—they will again fall into the category of intermediates.

The bottom line is—all users do gravitate towards the central part of the skill spectrum. We all do spend some time as beginners, but we learn how to use a specific tool or technology and soon we are intermediates.

As UI designers and consultants, our premier concern is to deliver high quality, enjoyable, and valuable experiences for our users, clients, businesses. Our goal, when we look at the user interface design discipline, is to create user interfaces that will look appealing and useful for all users—but that will be able to adapt and support the fact that users are migrating from beginners to intermediates. Also, we need to be smart

Figure 2.7 Lesson given for typewriters to earn skills. LHS gives the lesson for initial typewriting course and RHS shows the keys and figure position.

and reasonable enough to allow intermediate users to move towards becoming experts so that they can extend their abilities and increase their productivity and satisfaction.

It is probably easiest to summarize it all by saying that we need to be very pragmatic—accommodate the beginners and experts but optimize our UIs to the largest segment of the users—intermediates.

Accommodating Beginners

This is the only phase we are all definitely going to get a taste of. For how long we will stay beginners is almost completely up to User Interface and interaction designers. Bear in mind that users usually will go from beginners to intermediates, but they might, as well, just turn away and quit using the product if they do not find it easy enough and understandable for them to use. To make sure that users will start using the UI and move to becoming intermediates later, as designers we must ensure that the things they see, use, and feel in the UI resonate well with their mental models and their perception of the UI.

If you have ever conducted or watched serious usability study where users were complete beginners, you would have noticed that at least two major focus areas within the UI for them: menus and messages in dialog boxes. They tend to browse through the menus and their hierarchical architectures, reading all the labels and basically trying to get an overview and understanding of where specific options and features are positioned. And as for dialogs and notifications – they tend to read them slower, trying to understand them thoroughly even though in many cases they do not feel very confident about executing or cancelling specific actions.

It is wrong, however, to assume that beginners will rely heavily on help and support systems. The main purpose of those systems is to serve as reminders, reference points —not always as starting points. However, adding walkthroughs that appear for beginners and guiding them through the user interface, explaining the main ideas, concepts, and scope of the particular software is good idea. Just make sure that users who do not need those instructions anymore can easily turn them off.

Figure 2.8 shows the installation wizard (Open Office) which is necessary when you ask the user to install any software application.

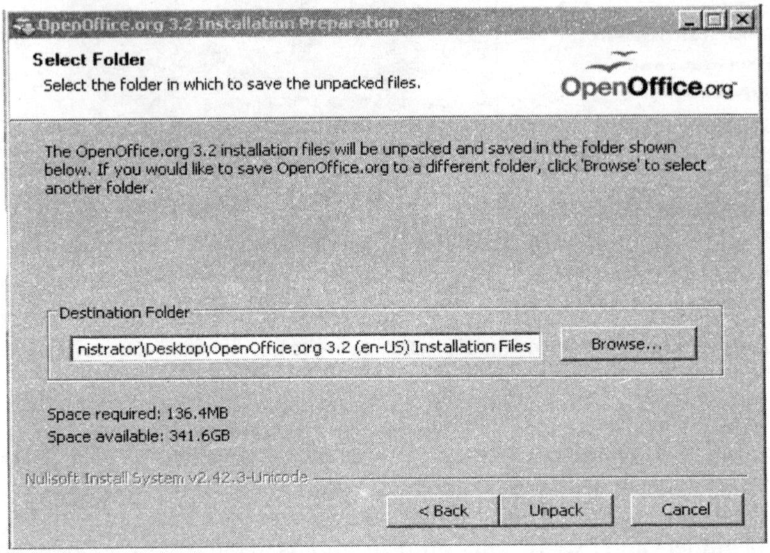

Figure 2.8 The guideline or wizard for user to install Open Office software on computer system.

The important—probably fundamental—thing is the fact that nobody wants to remain a beginner for the entire period of using any application. Our measure goal is to make sure that users should be effectively able to use the software or user application and make them expert in using it. Just try to recall the typical office assistant provided by Microsoft Office as shown in Figure 2.9.

Figure 2.9 Office assistant introduced by Microsoft to help users who were new to Microsoft office.

Intermediates

While beginners were looking for answers to questions like "What does this program do?", "Where do I start?", and "How do I use this?", intermediates are looking for access to desired features. The answers to the questions asked a few lines above are at the beginning. Now they will have some different requirements. The basic skills are grasped. Since they are familiar with the basics—they will now go and look for reference manuals—in these cases having good help and support systems can be extremely useful.

Another UI pattern really helping a lot is the usage of ToolTips. Though beginners will find so-called "rich tooltips" useful as well, intermediates (and even experts to some extent) will use ToolTips as helpful notes showing the functions and features in the simplest way. See Figure 2.10 that shows the magnified ToolTip provided in Libero office.

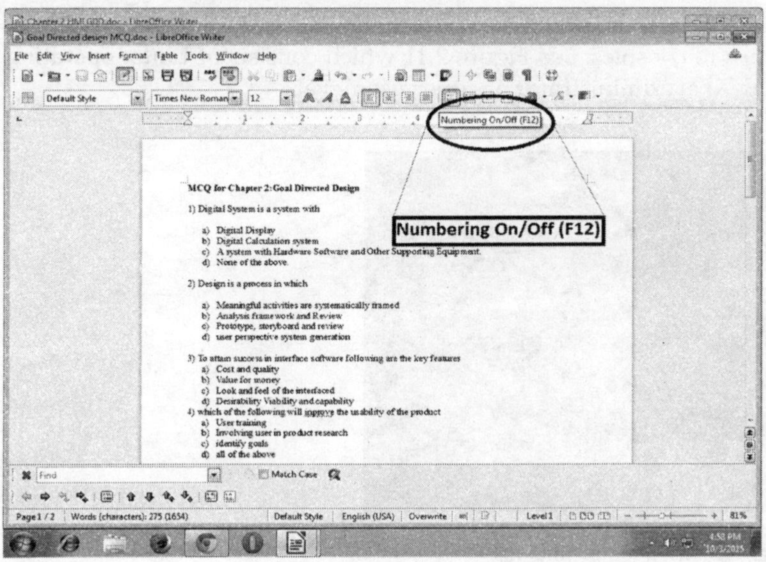

Figure 2.10 Shortcuts provided on Libero office software in its word processor.

Majority of the users are intermediates. We should optimize user experiences and, as a first touch point, user interfaces, for intermediates. The technical obstacles and policies do not interfere with your design thinking. After all, most resources should be applied to accommodate the majority of users.

Accommodating Experts

Though their number is much smaller than intermediates and it is probably even smaller than the number of beginners, experts are an extremely important group of users. Their number might be small figures but their impact and influence is extremely high and important. After all, we all tend to trust experts and ask them for advice and help. Large companies like Adobe, Microsoft, IBM, Google, and others have recognized the importance of experts and pretty much all of them have some expert communities.

Experts require some more functionalities and abilities. Also, if an expert says that some application or website is not very good, those words do carry some significance and beginners and the general public might judge your designs only by what some experts have said about it.

Your user interfaces should enable experts to use them and become more productive with them. Of course, you have optimized your UI for intermediates, you have helped beginners to get the idea and develop a good feeling about your application—now you need to make sure that even experts will have a good time and be productive and satisfied while using your UI.

Experts might be into some rarely used features needed for really complex scenarios. They will definitely require some shortcuts and abilities to manipulate the UI without the mouse (think about keyboard shortcuts). They will be looking into possibilities for significant customizations, automation, and maybe even for some level of extensibility.

They will even find that some graphical user interfaces are, in fact, slowing them down and might turn to consoles. See Figure 2.11 which consists of Linux operating system commands used at administrator or super-user level.

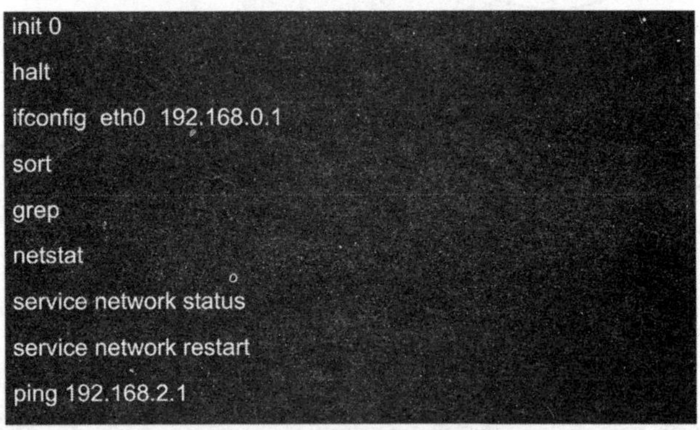

Figure 2.11 Linux OS administration commands.

It is clear that all those functionalities are rarely or never used by intermediates, not to mention beginners. However, experts do need them for their very specific tasks and you should organize and architecture your UI to enable them to find them and use them. Luckily, it is generally accepted that experts will not usually be distracted by features and approaches put in place for intermediates.

Understanding Users

The success of any product or digital design is totally dependent on how it meets the requirements of stakeholders and the product itself. The designer should always understand the user. It is not the case that the designer should understand who the user is but the experience level of the user should be totally accommodated.

The deep knowledge of the user can not only be achieved by analyzing the numbers obtained in quantitative study during market research but also the deep knowledge about the user will be obtained in various qualitative research techniques.

Qualitative versus Quantitative Research

QUANTITATIVE RESEARCH	QUALITATIVE RESEARCH
It is a statistics of the human activities that answers questions like "how much" or "how many".	The detailed information that provides the knowledge about behavior, attitude, and aptitude of the user.
Quantitative research helps to forecast the use, usage, and usability of the interface.	It helps to identify any existing same or similar products are available.
Quantitative research will only try to resolve the quantity of the copies of the product to be delivered to certain group of users.	Qualitative research also helps in environmental contexts of the product being designed.
Quantitative research will help in earlier dialog between the developers and end users. It will also tend to make a decision that how many end users need to be asked detailed questions related to qualitative research.	Qualitative research provides the creditability and authority to design team, as the design decisions are traced from the quantitative research.

Value of Qualitative Research

Qualitative research is a more superior technique than quantitative research. It helps to understand the domain of the context and constraints of the digital system being developed. As it provides the behavior, attitude, and aptitude of the users, it helps to identify design patterns to be adopted in development of the interface. It provides vision to the management to make more informative and communication oriented product.

If there is a decision to make ticket vending machines for state transport bus service and which need to be installed at various bus depots, the qualitative research will play an effective role as quantitative research will confirm the number of passengers. It will also tell the number of passengers who collect the tickets just before they board the bus on their intended route, how many collect their tickets from the bus conductors, etc. In other way, if we conduct the qualitative research we will come to know the following:

- How many passengers will actually be able to get the tickets from such systems?
- How many people use digital products such as mobile phones, smart cards, or credit cards?
- What kind of system is to be designed?
- Automatic ticket vending that accepts bank notes or the machine that is specific to smart cards?

In qualitative research we have to adopt various types of techniques that will enhance our interface design decisions.

- Stakeholder Interview.

- Subject Matter Expert (SME) Interview.
- User and Customer Interview.
- User Observation or Ethnographic Study.
- Literature Review.
- Product or Design Audits.

Stakeholder Interview

We know that stakeholder is anyone who is directly or indirectly associated with the product, that is, the user, owner, and developer. In the recent trends of the business, the involvement of the stakeholder plays an important role; we already have mentioned this in Figure 2.1(d) in evolution phase of the design. The type of information that must be gathered from stakeholder interview involves:

- **Primary vision of the product:** Who's who in the process and how it will be benefit the day to day needs.
- **Budget and the schedule:** This is directly related to project management approach as need to satisfy the scope of the product being developed.
- **Technical and non-technical issues:** This tells that the business logic needs to be provided as per the user's requirement.
- **Business drivers:** It is always necessary to identify what exactly is product or business trying to achieve. The need hierarchy of all stakeholders should be satisfied.
- **Stakeholder's perception:** The maximum efforts should be taken to provide dedicated help to the end user so that the end user acceptance level will be elevated.

SME Interviews

These are the experts who will be major role players in using as well as evaluating the system. They can use the product effectively as well as they train others to use it effectively. They may be the actual end users or may be appointed by client to test or evaluate their use. One point is very often observed that the SMEs are experts but they are not the designers; hence sometimes they may give a scattered evaluation for the system under consideration. Following are few additional points that should be perfectly described about SMEs:

- **SMEs are often expert users:** They have domain knowledge and they will perfectly provide the design requirements. They are not current users but they know how system interface should have action flow.
- **SMEs are Experts but they are not Designers:** SMEs have exact knowledge to improve the overall usage of the product. They can give the rough draft or required layout of the proposed system design. SMEs are not design experts but their analysis is valuable support for designers.
- **SME help in regulating the standards:** Industrial, Pharmaceutical, financial, or food product industries have certain regulations and they need to be reflected in the final desired output of the ultimate module of the system. These few stan-

dards need to be reflected in the business logic or user interface where SMEs will give general guidelines. Let us say in an example of a final print file for bill generated from user interface the necessary tax references should be made available. The government certificate number that clears the authority to collect necessary charges should be clearly printed on the bill see Figure 2.12.

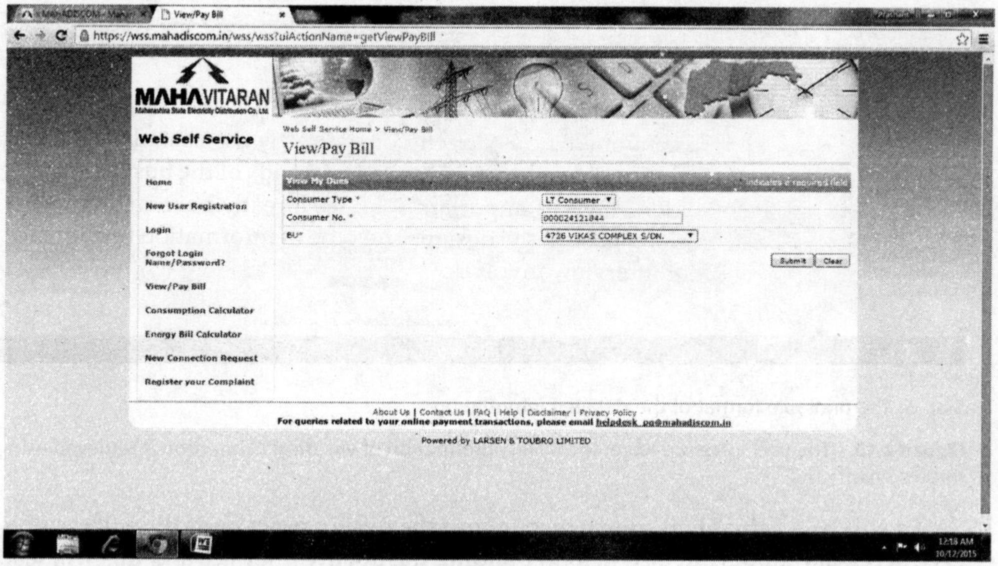

Step 1: The Graphical User Interface to accept the key information for which information is to be retrieved

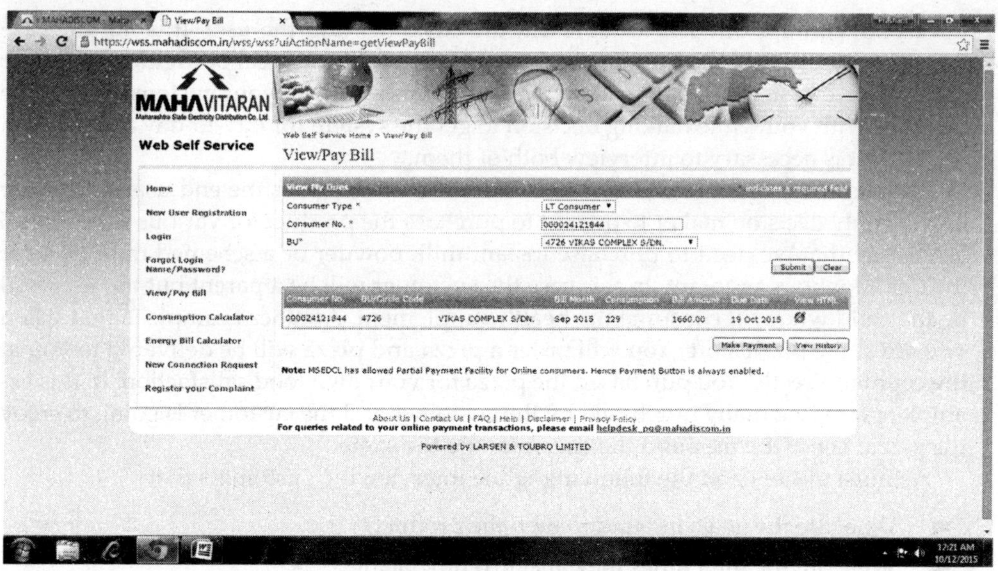

Step 2: The initial response from the system related to key information

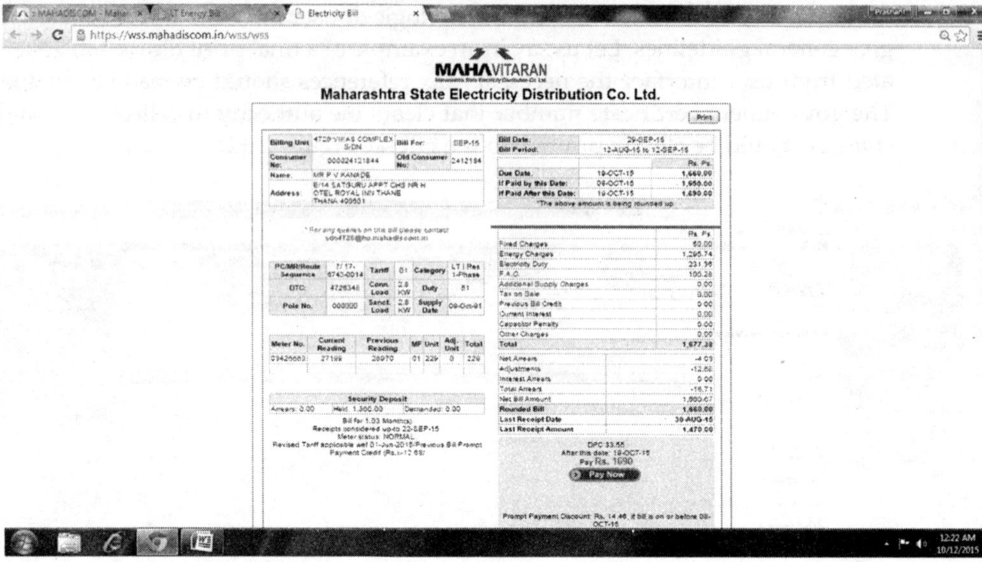

Step 3: The printable format of the detailed information

Figure 2.12 The user interface to get the billing information of electrical connection is retrieved using three steps.

SMEs will be a valuable resource throughout the design process: SMEs will not only give necessary inputs but also help in building the quality interface and this will lead to effective expected outcome.

Customer Interviews

Let us not confuse our self to represent the customer and the user. It is not the case that customer will be the ultimate end user if it is a technological or digital product or any software system. It may be the case that the user will be your customer if he/she interacts with you while making decision to get the system for day-to-day activities. In that case it is necessary to interview both of them.

It is necessary to understand who is the owner and who is the end user. Customer may be only decision maker to own or to purchase the product for various set of users. Let us say that we need to purchase instant milk powder or a schemed milk powder for a child who is an infant. In this case the customer will be a parent but the user will be the child who will consume the health supplement. Another example is that when you are at the pizza store: You will order a pizza and pizza will be delivered to you at the counter directly. You purchased the pizza for your own food satisfaction. In this example, pizza is actually purchased by the customer and the customer is going to enjoy the pizza; hence the user and the customer are the same.

We must understand the following while interviewing customers that:

- What are the goals in mind to own the product?
- What are the difficulties they are currently facing?
- Who makes the decision and what is the proper channel for decision making?

- Who's who in the decision making process?
- What is the business logic applied (Domain Knowledge)?

Just like subject matter experts, customer may also help to improve the quality of the product being delivered. Suggestions from customer also make a valid sense to improve the product outcome. As already mentioned it is necessary to interview both customers and ultimate users. It may be designing a new product or updating or enhancing the existing product. It is always recommended to interview the potential users of the system.

Following are the major outcomes in our qualitative research:

- How the product is involved in the day-to-day activities.
- Domain knowledge of the system that is used and one that will be used after delivery.
- Goals and motivations.
- Mental model (a forecast of the system or user interface).
- Problems faced in performing day-to-day activities.

User Observation and Ethnographic Interviews

We can simply make conclusions by carefully observing the users. The user should not be asked every minute thing in the form of question but his behavior can be observed and some conclusions can be made. The combination of immersive observation and directed interview is called as ethnographic interview. This is also called as contextual inquiry. This sometimes helps to achieve qualitative research. Following are the four major principles for having contextual inquiry:

- **Context:** Interview should be in the free environment and should not be in a special room. We can gather information while user is allowed to freely discuss on the work he carries out.
- **Partnership:** Ask few set of questions while user is actually performing some activities and parallel to it observe the user behavior. As user is not asked to fully concentrate on interview and more focused on the day to day actions it will give broader idea about the user behavior about the system under usage.
- **Interpretation:** Interviewer must gather the actual information and make interpretation based on the actual data captured and should have a pure interpretation of the responses made by the person and not his own experiences.
- **Focus:** Major focus should be on the relevant information that needs to be captured and not on the questions that may have non-functional data.

We also should have improved contextual inquiry and for the same we need to have shortened interview process so that users will not provide the irrelevant information due to much more long discussions. There may be possibility to create scattered use cases if we involve lot many people in design process. To avoid such problem we should keep smaller design teams. Proper planning wins the game; hence we should be prepared enough with exacts goals already defined much ahead of time. As already observed in software engineering, we should not have tunnel view for any design; we should also look beyond the business context.

There are various phases of ethnographic interviews and they are as follows:

- **Early-stage interview:** Early stage consists of interviews related to gathering domain knowledge; in this stage broad and open-ended questions are asked.
- **Middle-stage interview:** In the middle phase, some detailed clarifications are made.
- **Later-stage interview:** In the later stage, close-ended questions are asked to get further adjustments, so that modifications can be done if required.

Let us now have a quick look on the major focus on success of ethnographic interviews:

- Interviews should be conducted at workplace where actual activities are carried out.
- Change questions each time.
- Focus on goals and not task environment.
- Do not ask user to design anything.
- Forget about the implementation platform or technology.
- Create a storyboard or promote storytelling.
- Ask for templates or samples (if any).
- Do not try to get answers as per your assumptions. (You like blue color do not you?)

Case Study: Try to identify other type of research techniques adopted such as focus groups, market demography, card sorting, and identification of use, usage, and usability.

Modeling Users: Persona and Goals

As all users do not hold the same characteristics. We need to have summary of various observations of the users and create some model to represent the usefulness or test the same. Using our research to create descriptive model of interaction design, we add some flavors to it that is referred as personas.

Personas help us to provide the precise way of thinking and representing how users behave, how users think, what exactly they are willing to accomplish, and why they want to do so. Personas are composite architypes based on behavioral data gathered from many actual users from which we capture some percent of information. We have already discussed how we can gather the information.

Personas help us to **determine, communicate, build consequences, measure, and contribute** the design quality of the product. It also helps to fit the product as per the experience level of the user. Personas also help us to resolve three design issues – elastic user, self-referential design, and edge cases. Personas are represented as individual people, group of users that may be architypes and stereotypes. Personas may also explore ranges of behavior and they must have motivations for the users.

Goals: As we know that personas provide contextual information for behaviors; **goals** are basic drivers for such behaviors. Persona without goal can provide an effective tool

Table 2.1 Experience Goals, End Goals, and Life Goals

EXPERIENCE	END GOALS	LIFE GOALS
Look and feel	Awareness of problems	Live good life
Enjoyment	Stay concerned	Success achievement
Relaxation	Time management	Become popular for good work
Alert or remain focused	Effectiveness	Make investments
Get the things done	Best results	Make others happy

but it will not be a utility. Goal serves as a magnifier through which designer considers the functionality of the product. Goals motivate the usage pattern and tell how personas desire to use the product as well as get the fruitful results after using the product.

Goals also motivate to design the product by focusing on three levels of cognitive processing. The three levels of cognitive processing are already discussed in Chapter 1. There are three types of goals and they are described in small context in Table 2.1.

Steps in Constructing Personas

Personas can be created by adopting various techniques and they are specified below. The detailed description of each methodology is beyond the scope of this book.

1. Identify behavioral variables.
2. Map interview subjects to behavioral variables.
3. Identify behavioral patterns.
4. Synthesize characteristics and relevant goals.
5. Check for redundancy and completeness.
6. Expand description of attributes and behaviors.
7. Designate persona types.

Multiple Choice Questions

1. Digital system is a system with
   (a) Digital display
   (b) Digital calculation system
   (c) Hardware, software and other supporting equipment
   (d) None of the above

2. Design is a process in which there is/are
   (a) Meaningful activities are systematically framed
   (b) Analysis framework and review
   (c) Prototype, storyboard and review
   (d) User perspective system generation

3. To attain success in interface software, following are the key features
   (a) Cost and quality
   (b) Value for money
   (c) Look and feel of the interfaced
   (d) Desirability, viability and capability

4. Which of the following will improve the usability of the product?
   (a) User training
   (b) Involving user in product research
   (c) Identifying goals
   (d) All of the above

5. Goal directed design must ensure
   (a) User friendliness, feasibility and effective environments
   (b) Visually pleasing composition
   (c) End user acceptance
   (d) All of the above
6. ACD stands for
   (a) Accumulated connection device
   (b) Alternate computational development
   (c) Activity centric design
   (d) Advance computer Display
7. SME is nothing but
   (a) Small manufacturing enterprise
   (b) Small machine equipment
   (c) System manageable execution
   (d) Subject matter expert
8. Which statement is true from the following?
   (i) Users have fixed experience level
   (ii) Expert will remain experts once use the product
   (iii) Users are neither beginners nor experts
   (a) Only (i)
   (b) Only (ii)
   (c) Only (iii)
   (d) Both (i) and (ii)
9. Overall consideration to generate the accurate and desired output is
   (a) Analytical model
   (b) Implementation model
   (c) Research model
   (d) All of the above
10. Overall consideration of visually pleasing composition is
   (a) Implementation model
   (b) Mental model
   (c) Prototype
   (d) Design phase

Review Questions

1. Explain the goal directed design process in brief.
2. What do you mean by implementation model and mental model?
3. What are various experience levels of the users? How can we attain the intermediate level of user experience?
4. Specify the design requirement for various levels of users.
5. Explain the persona and model in brief.
6. What are the various types of ethnographic interviews? How the success of such interviews can be achieved.
7. Explain SME based refinement with suitable example.
8. You are required to provide a computer based interactive program for purchase section of organization. The system consists of proposing the goods to be purchased and its full list of equipment. The sanctioning authority will approve the list. The final approval will be from chief officer and then purchase officer will generate the purchase order. Provide the first phase of research questions and try to identify stakeholders of the system.
9. We are expected to build a mobile application for mathematics tutor. How will the personas be represented for the required mobile based application?
10. There is need to specify requirements at SME (Subject Matter Expert) Level. As an SME provide the proper sequence for online matrimony web portal.
11. Discuss few real-life scenarios where design of graphical user interface will enhance the end users' performance in use of the computer-based application.

Unit

Two

Designing

CHAPTER

3

Graphical User Interface

The graphical user interface differed significantly from its text-based forefather. The Web interface differs from a GUI interface in significant ways also, not all differences, however, can be considered interface advancements. In this chapter, the characteristics of a GUI interface will be reviewed, including the concept it introduced: direct manipulation. Then, Web characteristics will be reviewed, including the differences between GUI and Web interface design, and the differences between printed page and Web design.

The Graphical User Interface

In brief, a graphical user interface can be defined as follows. A *user interface,* as recently described, is a collection of techniques and mechanisms to interact with something. In a *graphical* interface, the primary interaction mechanism is a pointing device of some kind. This device is the electronic equivalent to the human hand. What the user interacts with is a collection of elements referred to as *objects.* They can be seen, heard, touched, or otherwise perceived. Objects are always visible to the user and are used to perform tasks. They are interacted with as entities independent of all other objects. People perform operations, called *actions,* on objects. The operations include accessing and modifying objects by pointing, selecting, and manipulating. All objects have standard resulting behaviors.

The Popularity of Graphics

Graphics revolutionized design and the user interface. A graphical screen bore scant resemblance to its earlier text-based colleagues. Whereas the older text-based screen possessed a one-dimensional, text-oriented, form-like quality, graphic screens assumed a three-dimensional look. Information floated in windows, small rectangular boxes seemed to rise above the background plane. Windows could also float above other windows. Controls appeared to rise above the screen and move when activated. Lines appeared to be etched into the screen. Information could appear, and disappear, as needed, and in some cases text could be replaced by graphical images called icons. These icons could represent objects or actions.

Screen navigation and commands are executed through menu bars and pull-downs. Menus "pop up" on the screen. In the screen body, selection fields such as radio buttons, check boxes, list boxes, and palettes coexisted with the reliable old text entry field. More sophisticated text entry fields with attached or drop-down menus of alternatives also became available. Screen objects and actions were selected through use of pointing mechanisms, such as the mouse or joystick, instead of the traditional keyboard.

Increased computer power and the vast improvement in the display enable the user's actions to be reacted to quickly, dynamically, and meaningfully. This new interface is characterized as representing one's "desktop" with scattered notes, papers, and objects such as files, trays, and trashcans arrayed around the screen. It is sometimes referred to as the WIMP interface: windows, icons, menus, and pointers.

Graphic presentation of information utilizes a person's information-processing capabilities much more effectively than other presentation methods. Properly used, it reduces the requirement for perceptual and mental information recoding and reorganization, and also reduces the memory loads. It permits faster information transfer between computers and people by permitting more visual comparisons of amounts, trends, or relationships; more compact representation of information; and simplification of the perception of structure. Graphics also can add appeal or charm to the interface and permit greater customization to create a unique corporate or organization style.

The Concept of Direct Manipulation

The term used to describe this style of interaction for graphical systems was first used by Shneiderman (1982). He called them "direct manipulation" systems, suggesting that they possess the following characteristics:

The system is portrayed as an extension of the real world. It is assumed that a person is already familiar with the objects and actions in his or her environment of interest. The system simply replicates them and portrays them on a different medium, the screen. A person has the power to access and modify these objects, among which are windows. A person is allowed to work in a familiar environment and in a familiar way, focusing on the data, not the application and tools. The physical organization of the system, which most often is unfamiliar, is hidden from view and is not a distraction.

Continuous visibility of objects and actions. Like one's desktop, objects are continuously visible. Reminders of actions to be performed are also obvious, labeled buttons replacing complex syntax and command names. Cursor action and motion occurs in physically obvious and intuitively natural ways. Nelson (1980) described this concept as "virtual reality," a representation of reality that can be manipulated. Hatfield (1981) is credited with calling it "WYSIWYG" (what you see is what you get). Rutkowski (1982) described it as "transparency," where one's intellect is applied to the task, not the tool. Hutchins, Hollan, and Norman (1986) considered it direct involvement with the world of objects rather than communicating with an intermediary.

One problem in direct manipulation, however, is that there is no direct analogy on the desk for all necessary windowing operations. A piece of paper on one's desk maintains a constant size, never shrinking or growing. Windows can do both. Solving this problem required embedding a control panel, a familiar concept to most people, in a window's border. This control panel is manipulated, not the window itself.

Actions are rapid and incremental with visible display of results. Since tactile feedback is not yet possible (as would occur with one's hand when one touches something), the results of actions are immediately displayed visually on the screen in their new and current form. Auditory feedback may also be provided. The impact of a previous action is quickly seen, and the evolution of tasks is continuous and effortless.

Incremental actions are easily reversible. Finally, actions, if discovered to be incorrect or not desired, can be easily undone.

Earlier Direct Manipulation Systems

Using the above definition, the concept of direct manipulation actually preceded the first graphical system. The earliest full-screen text editors possessed similar characteristics. Screens of text resembling a piece of paper on one's desk could be created (extension of real world) and then reviewed in their entirety (continuous visibility). Editing or restructuring could be easily accomplished (through rapid incremental actions) and the results immediately seen. Actions could be reversed when necessary. It took the advent of graphical systems to crystallize the direct manipulation concept, however.

Indirect Manipulation

In practice, direct manipulation of *all* screen objects and actions may not be feasible because of the following:

- The operation may be difficult to conceptualize in the graphical system.
- The graphics capability of the system may be limited.
- The amount of space available for placing manipulation controls in the window border may be limited.

- It may be difficult for people to learn and remember all the necessary operations and actions.

When this occurs, *indirect manipulation* is provided. Indirect manipulation substitutes words and text, such as pull-down or pop-up menus, for symbols, and substitutes typing for pointing. Most window systems are a combination of both direct and indirect manipulation. A menu may be accessed by pointing at a menu icon and then selecting it (direct manipulation). The menu itself, however, is a textual list of operations (indirect manipulation). When an operation is selected from the list, by pointing or typing, the system executes it as a command.

Which style of interaction—direct manipulation, indirect manipulation, or a combination of both—is best, under what conditions and for whom, remains a question whose answer still eludes us.

Graphical Systems: Advantages and Disadvantages

Graphical systems burst upon the office with great promise. The simplified interface they presented was thought to reduce the memory requirements imposed on the user, make more effective use of one's information-processing capabilities, and dramatically reduce system learning requirements. Experience indicates that for many people they have done all these things.

Advantages

The success of graphical systems has been attributed to a host of factors. The following have been commonly referenced in literature and endorsed by their advocates as advantages of these systems.

Symbols recognized faster than text. Research has found that symbols can be recognized faster and more accurately than text, and that the graphical attributes of icons, such as shape and color, are very useful for quickly classifying objects, elements, or text by some common property. An example of a good classification scheme that speeds up recognition are the icons developed for indicating the kind of message being presented to the user of the system. The text of an informational message is preceded by an "i" in a circle, a warning message by an exclamation point, and a critical message by another unique symbol. These icons allow speedy recognition of the type of message being presented.

Faster learning. Research has also found that a graphical, pictorial representation aids learning, and symbols can also be easily learned.

Faster use and problem solving. Visual or spatial representation of information has been found to be easier to retain and manipulate and leads to faster and more successful problem solving. Symbols have also been found to be effective in conveying simple instructions.

Easier remembering. Because of greater simplicity, it is easier for casual users to retain operational concepts.

More natural. Graphic representations of objects are thought to be more natural and closer to innate human capabilities. In human beings, actions and visual skills emerged before languages. It has also been suggested that symbolic displays are more natural and advantageous because the human mind has a powerful image memory.

Exploits visual/spatial cues. Spatial relationships are usually found to be understood more quickly than verbal representations. Visually thinking is believed to be better than logical thinking.

Fosters more concrete thinking. Displayed objects are directly in the high-level task domain, or directly usable in their presented form. There is no need mentally to decompose tasks into multiple commands with complex syntactic form. The need for abstract thinking is therefore minimized.

Provides context. Displayed objects are visible, providing a picture of the current context.

Fewer errors. More concrete thinking affords fewer opportunities for errors. Reversibility of actions reduces error rates because it is always possible to undo the last step. Error messages are less frequently needed.

Increased feeling of control. The user initiates actions and feels in control. This increases user confidence and hastens system mastery.

Immediate feedback. The results of actions furthering user goals can be seen immediately. Learning is quickened. If the response is not in the desired direction, the direction can be changed quickly.

Predictable system responses. Predictable system responses also speed learning.

Easily reversible actions. The user has more control. This ability to reverse unwanted actions also increases user confidence and hastens system mastery.

Less anxiety concerning use. Hesitant or new users feel less anxiety when using the system because it is so easily comprehended, is easy to control, and has predictable responses and reversible actions.

More attractive. Direct-manipulation systems are more entertaining, cleverer, and more appealing. This is especially important for the cautious or skeptical user.

May consume less space. Icons may take up less space than the equivalent in words. More information can often be packed in a given area of the screen. This, however, is not always the case.

Replaces national languages. Language-based systems are seldom universally applicable. Language translations frequently cause problems in a text-based system. Icons possess much more universality than text and are much more easily comprehended worldwide.

Easily augmented with text displays. Where graphical design limitations exist, direct-manipulation systems can easily be augmented with text displays. The reverse is not true.

Low typing requirements. Pointing and selection controls, such as the mouse or trackball, eliminate the need for typing skills.

Smooth transition from command language system. Moving from a command language to a direct-manipulation system has been found to be easy. The reverse is not true.

Disadvantages

The body of positive research, hypotheses, and comment concerning graphical systems is being challenged by some studies, findings, and opinions that indicate that graphical representation and interaction may not necessarily always be better. Indeed, in some cases, it may be poorer than pure textual or alphanumeric displays. Trying to force all system components into a graphical format may be doing a disservice to the user. Some also feel that, as graphical systems are becoming increasingly sophisticated and continue to expand, interfaces have become increasingly more complex, sometimes arcane, and even bizarre. Among the disadvantages put forth are these:

Greater design complexity. The elements and techniques available to the graphical screen designer far outnumber those that were at the disposal of the text-based screen designer. Controls and basic alternatives must be chosen from a pile of choices numbering in excess of 50. (Conversely, alternatives available to the text-based screen designer numbered about 15.) This design potential may not necessarily result in better design, unless the choices are thoughtfully selected and consistently and simply applied. Proper window types must also be chosen and colors selected from a seemingly unending rainbow of alternatives. With graphics, the skill of the designer is increasingly challenged. Poor design can undermine acceptance.

Learning still necessary. The first time one encounters many graphical systems, what to do is not immediately obvious. The meanings of many words and icons may not be known. It is not often possible to guess their meanings, especially the more arbitrary symbols. How to use a pointing device may also have to be learned. A severe learning and remembering requirement is imposed on many users, and it takes a while to get up to speed. A text-based system could easily be structured to incorporate a set of clear instructions: (1) Do this, (2) now do this, and so on.

System providers estimate that becoming accustomed to a graphical interface should require about eight hours of training. Other experts say the learning time is closer to 20 or 30 hours.

Lack of experimentally-derived design guidelines. The graphical interface is still burdened today by a lack of widely available experimentally-derived design guidelines. Early on, more developer interest existed in solving technical rather than usability issues, so few studies to aid in making design decisions were performed. Today, studies being performed in usability laboratories are rarely published. This occurs because of a number of factors. First, builders of platforms and packages will not publish their study results because they want to maintain a competitive advantage. If a better way is found to do something, or present something, why tell the competition? Let them make the same mistake, or find the answer themselves.

Second, the studies are often specific to a particular function or task. They may not be generally applicable. Third, it takes time and effort to publish something. The developer in today's office seldom has the time. Finally, it is also difficult to develop studies evaluating design alternatives because of increased GUI complexity. Too many variables that must be controlled make meaningful cause-and-effect relationships very difficult to uncover.

Consequently, there is too little understanding of how most design aspects relate to productivity and satisfaction.

Inconsistencies in technique and terminology. Many differences in technique, terminology, and look and feel exist among various graphical system providers, and even among successive versions of the same system. These inconsistencies occur because of copyright and legal implications, product differentiation considerations, and our expanding knowledge about the interface. The result is that learning, and relearning, for both designers and users is much more difficult than it should be.

Working domain is the present. While direct-manipulation systems provide context, they also require the user to work in the "present." Hulteen (1988), in a parody of "WYSIWYG," suggests "What you see is all you get." Walker (1989) argued that language takes you out of the here and now and the visually present. Language, she continues, makes it easier to find things.

Not always familiar. Symbolic representations may not be as familiar as words or numbers. We have been exposed to words and numbers for a long time. Research has found that numeric symbols elicit faster responses than graphic symbols in a visual search task. One developer had to modify a new system during testing by replacing iconic representations with a textual outline format. The users, lawyers, were unfamiliar with icons and demanded a more familiar format.

Human comprehension limitations. Human limitations may also exist in terms of one's ability to deal with the increased complexity of the graphical interface. The variety of visual displays can still challenge all but the most sophisticated users. The number of different icons that can be introduced is also restricted because of limitations in human comprehension. Studies continually find that the number of different symbols a person can differentiate and deal with is much more limited than text. Some researchers note that claims for the easy understanding of pictograms are exaggerated, and that recognizing icons requires much perceptual learning, abstracting ability, and intelligence.

The motor skills required may also challenge all but the most sophisticated users. Correctly double-clicking a mouse, for example, is difficult for some people.

Window manipulation requirements. Window handling and manipulation times are still excessive and repetitive. This wastes time and interrupts the decision-making needed to perform tasks and jobs.

Production limitations. The number of symbols that can be clearly produced using today's technology is still limited. A body of recognizable symbols must be produced that are equally legible and equally recognizable using differing technologies. This is extremely difficult today.

Few tested icons exist. Icons, like typefaces, must appear in different sizes, weights, and styles. As with text, an entire font of clearly recognizable symbols must be developed. It is not simply a question of developing an icon and simply enlarging or reducing it. Changing an icon's size can differentially affect symbol line widths, open areas, and so forth, dramatically affecting its recognizability. Typeface design is literally the product of 300 years of experimentation and study. Icons must be researched, designed, tested, and then introduced into the marketplace. The consequences of poor or improper design will be confusion and lower productivity for users.

Inefficient for touch typists. For an experienced touch typist, the keyboard is a very fast and powerful device. Moving a mouse or some other pointing mechanism may be slower.

Inefficient for expert users. Inefficiencies develop when there are more objects and actions than can fit on the screen. Concatenation for a command language is impossible.

Not always the preferred style of interaction. Not all users prefer a pure iconic interface. A study comparing commands illustrated by icons, icons with text, or text-only, found that users preferred alternatives with textual captions.

Not always fastest style of interaction. Another study has found that graphic instructions on an automated bank teller machine were inferior to textual instructions.

Increased chances of clutter and confusion. A graphical system does not guarantee elimination of clutter on a screen. Instead, the chance for clutter is increased, thereby increasing the possibility of confusion. How much screen clutter one can deal with is open to speculation. The possibility that clutter may exist is evidenced by the fact that many people, when working with a window, expand it to fill the entire display screen. This may be done to reduce visual screen clutter. Mori and Hayashi (1993) found that visible windows, not the focus of attention, degraded performance in the window being worked on.

The futz and fiddle factor. With the proliferation of computer games, computer usage can be wasteful of time. Stromoski (1993) estimates that five hours a week in the office are spent playing and tinkering. Experts have said that the most used program in Microsoft Windows is Solitaire! Tinkering includes activities such as creating garish documents reflecting almost every object property (font size, style, color, and so on.) available.

Futzing and fiddling does have some benefits, however. It is a tool for learning how to use a mouse, for example, and it is a vehicle for exploring the system and becoming familiar with its capabilities. It is of value when done in moderation.

May consume more screen space. Not all applications will consume less screen space. A listing of names and telephone numbers in a textual format will be more efficient to scan than a card file.

Hardware limitations. Good design also requires hardware of adequate power, processing speed, screen resolution, and graphic capability. Insufficiencies in these areas can prevent a graphic system's full potential from being realized.

Some Studies and a Conclusion

The many benefits of one interaction style versus another are anecdotal. This has often made the debate between advocates of graphical and other styles of interaction more emotional than scientific. This is certainly true for many of the arguments. Over the past couple of decades a variety of studies have been performed comparing graphical systems with other interaction styles. In some usability studies graphical systems were found superior, in other studies other interaction techniques were found superior, and in some cases no differences were found. Perhaps the best conclusion was drawn by Whiteside, Jones, Levy, and Wixon (1985) who compared the usability characteristics of seven systems, including the direct-manipulation, menu, and command language styles of interaction. They found that user performance did not depend on the type of system. There were large differences in learnability and usability among all. How well the system was *designed* was the best indicator of success, not the style of interaction.

Research and experience have shown that different interface styles also have different strengths and weaknesses. Some concepts and tasks are very hard to convey symbolically and do not seem to be suited for a pure graphical presentation. Other concepts and tasks, however, may be well suited to such an approach. Which tasks are best suited for which styles still needs continuing study. Finally, all users may not like all aspects of a graphical system. The design should reflect this. In summary, the following is clear:

- The design of an interface, and not its interaction style, is the best determinant of ease of use.
- User preferences must be considered in choosing an interaction style.
- In the overwhelming majority of cases, words are more meaningful to users than icons.
- The content of a graphic screen is critical to its usefulness. The wrong presentation or a cluttered presentation may actually lead to greater confusion, not less.
- The success of a graphical system depends on the skills of its designers in following established principles of usability.

Characteristics of the Graphical User Interface

A graphical system possesses a set of defining concepts. Included are sophisticated visual presentation, pick-and-click interaction, a restricted set of interface options, visualization, object orientation, extensive use of a person's recognition memory, and concurrent performance of functions.

Sophisticated Visual Presentation

Visual presentation is the visual aspect of the interface. It is what people see on the screen. The sophistication of a graphical system permits displaying lines, including drawings and icons. It also permits the displaying of a variety of character fonts, including different sizes and styles. The display of 16 million or more colors is possible on some screens. Graphics also permit animation and the presentation of photographs and motion video.

The meaningful interface elements visually presented to the user in a graphical system include windows (primary, secondary, or dialog boxes), menus (menu bar, pull-down, pop-up, cascading), icons to represent objects such as programs or files, assorted screen-based controls (text boxes, list boxes, combination boxes, settings, scroll bars, and buttons), and a mouse pointer and cursor. The objective is to reflect visually on the screen the real world of the user as realistically, meaningfully, simply, and clearly as possible.

Pick-and-Click Interaction

Elements of a graphical screen upon which some action is to be performed must first be identified. The motor activity required of a person to identify this element for a proposed action is commonly referred to as *pick*, the signal to perform an action as *click*. The primary mechanism for performing this pick-and-click is most often the mouse and its buttons. The user moves the mouse pointer to the relevant element (pick) and the action is signaled (click). Pointing allows rapid selection and feedback. The eye, hand, and mind seem to work smoothly and efficiently together.

The secondary mechanism for performing these selection actions is the keyboard. Most systems permit pick-and-click to be performed using the keyboard as well.

Restricted Set of Interface Options

The array of alternatives available to the user is what is presented on the screen or what may be retrieved through what is presented on the screen, nothing less, nothing more. This concept fostered the acronym WYSIWYG.

Visualization

Visualization is a cognitive process that allows people to understand information that is difficult to perceive, because it is either too voluminous or too abstract. It involves changing an entity's representation to reveal gradually the structure and/or function of the underlying system or process. Presenting specialized graphic portrayals facilitates visualization. The best visualization method for an activity depends on what people are trying to learn from the data. The goal is not necessarily to reproduce a realistic graphical image, but to produce one that conveys the most relevant information. Effective visualizations can facilitate mental insights, increase productivity, and foster faster and more accurate use of data.

Object Orientation

A graphical system consists of objects and actions. *Objects* are what people see on the screen. They are manipulated as a single unit. A well-designed system keeps users focused on objects, not on how to carry out actions. Objects can be composed of *subobjects.*

For example, an object may be a document. The document's subobjects may be a paragraph, sentence, word, and letter.

IBM's System Application Architecture Common User Access Advanced Interface Design Reference (SAA CUA) (IBM, 1991) breaks objects into three meaningful classes: data, container, and device. *Data objects* present information. This information, either text or graphics, normally appears in the body of the screen. It is, essentially, the screen-based controls for information collection or presentation organized on the screen.

Container objects are objects to hold other objects. They are used to group two or more related objects for easy access and retrieval. There are three kinds of container objects: the workplace, folders, and workareas. The *workplace* is the desktop, the storage area for all objects. *Folders* are general-purpose containers for long-term storage of objects. *Workareas* are temporary storage folders used for storing multiple objects currently being worked on.

Device objects represent physical objects in the real world, such as printers or trash baskets. These objects may contain others for acting upon. A file, for example, may be placed in a printer for printing of its contents.

Microsoft Windows specifies the characteristics of objects depending upon the relationships that exist between them. Objects can exist within the context of other objects, and one object may affect the way another object appears or behaves. These relationships are called collections, constraints, composites, and containers.

A *collection* is the simplest relationship—the objects sharing a common aspect. A collection might be the result of a query or a multiple selection of objects. Operations can be applied to a collection of objects.

A *constraint* is a stronger object relationship. Changing an object in a set affects some other object in the set. A document being organized into pages is an example of a constraint.

A *composite* exists when the relationship between objects becomes so significant that the aggregation itself can be identified as an object. Examples include a range of cells organized into a spreadsheet, or a collection of words organized into a paragraph.

A *container* is an object in which other objects exist. Examples include text in a document or documents in a folder. A container often influences the behavior of its content. It may add or suppress certain properties or operations of objects placed within it, control access to its content, or control access to kinds of objects it will accept.

These relationships help define an object's *type*. Similar traits and behaviors exist in objects of the same object type.

Another important object characteristic is *persistence*. Persistence is the maintenance of a state once it is established. An object's state (for example, window size, cursor location, scroll position, and so on) should always be automatically preserved when the user changes it.

Properties or Attributes of Objects

Objects also have properties or attributes. Properties are the unique characteristics of an object. Properties help to describe an object and can be changed by users. Examples of properties are text styles (such as normal or italics), font sizes (such as 10 or 12 points), or window background colors (such as black or blue).

Actions

In addition to objects are actions. People take actions on objects. They manipulate objects in specific ways (commands) or modify the properties of objects (property or attribute specification).

Commands are actions that manipulate objects. They may be performed in a variety of ways, including by direct manipulation or through a command button. They are executed immediately when selected. Once executed, they cease to be relevant. Examples of commands are opening a document, printing a document, closing a window, and quitting an application.

Property/attribute specification actions establish or modify the attributes or properties of objects. When selected, they remain in effect until deselected. Examples include selecting cascaded windows to be displayed, a particular font style, or a particular color.

The following is a typical *property/attribute specification sequence:*

1. The user selects an object—for example, several words of text.
2. The user then selects an action to apply to that object, such as the action BOLD.
3. The selected words are made bold and will remain bold until selected and changed again.

A series of actions may be performed on a selected object. Performing a series of actions on an object also permits and encourages system learning through exploration.

Application versus Object or Data Orientation

Earlier graphical systems were usually application-oriented, a continuation of the philosophy that enveloped text-based systems. When a text-based system was developed, it was called an application. As graphical systems evolved, developers usually thought in terms of applications as well. When a real picture of the user began to emerge, it finally became evident that people thought in terms of tasks, not applications. They choose objects and then act upon them.

An application-oriented approach takes an action:object approach, like this:

Action> 1. An application is opened (for example, word processing).
Object> 2. A file or other object selected (for example, a memo).

An object-oriented object:action approach does this:

Object> 1. An object is chosen (a memo).
Action> 2. An application is selected (word processing).

The object-action approach permits people to more easily focus on their task and minimizes the visibility of the operating system and separate applications. Many experienced users may have difficulty in switching from one approach to another since an old interaction behavior must be unlearned and a new one learned. New users should not experience these problems, since it more accurately reflects a person's thinking. In any one interface, it is critical that a consistent orientation be maintained, either an object:action or an action:object approach.

Views

Views are ways of looking at an object's information. IBM's SAA CUA describes four kinds of views: composed, contents, settings, and help.

Composed views present information and the objects contained within an object. They are typically associated with data objects and are specific to tasks and products being worked with. *Contents* views list the components of objects. *Settings* views permit seeing and changing object properties. *Help* views provide all the help functions.

Use of Recognition Memory

Continuous visibility of objects and actions encourages use of a person's more powerful recognition memory. The "out of sight, out of mind" problem is eliminated.

Concurrent Performance of Functions

Graphic systems may do two or more things at one time. Multiple programs may run simultaneously. When a system is not busy on a primary task, it may process background tasks (cooperative multitasking). When applications are running as truly separate tasks, the system may divide the processing power into time slices and allocate portions to each application (preemptive multitasking). Data may also be transferred between programs. It may be temporarily stored on a "clipboard" for later transfer or be automatically swapped between programs.

The Web User Interface

The expansion of the World Wide Web since the early 1990s has been truly amazing. Once simply a communication medium for scientists and researchers, its many and pervasive tentacles have spread deeply into businesses, organizations, and homes around the world. Unlike earlier text-based and GUI systems that were developed and nurtured in an organization's Data Processing and Information Systems groups, the Web's roots were sown in a market-driven society thirsting for convenience and information.

Web interface design is essentially the design of navigation and the presentation of information. It is about content, not data. Proper interface design is largely a matter of properly balancing the structure and relationships of menus, content, and other linked documents or graphics. The design goal is to build a hierarchy of menus and pages that feels natural, is well structured, is easy to use, and is truthful. The Web is a navigation environment where people move between pages of information, not an application environment. It is also a graphically rich environment.

Web interface design is difficult for a number of reasons. First, its underlying design language, HTML, was never intended for creating screens to be used by the general population. Its scope of users was expected to be technical. HTML was limited in objects and interaction styles and did not provide a means for presenting information in the most effective way for people. Next, browser navigation retreated to the pre-GUI era. This era was characterized by a "command" field whose contents had to be learned, and a navigational organization and structure that lay hidden beneath a mostly dark and blank screen. GUIs eliminated the absolute necessity for a command field, providing menus related to the task and the current contextual situation. Browser navigation is mostly confined to a "Back" and "Forward" concept, but "back-to-where" and "forward-to-where" is often unremembered or unknown. Ill-timed use of the Back button can destroy many minutes worth of work. Remaining navigation was willed to Web pages themselves, where the situation only worsened. Numerous links were provided to destinations unknown, invisible navigation buttons lay unrecognizable on the screen, and linked jumps two paragraphs down the page were indistinguishable from those that went to the Ukraine. Also, form completion and submission was essentially a form of batch processing. Forms were completed, transmitted, and then edited instead of the editing being interactive, occurring as the entry process was accomplished. Web interface design is now struggling to recover from these giant steps backward.

Web interface design is also more difficult because the main issues concern information architecture and task flow, neither of which is easy to standardize. It is more difficult because of the availability of the various types of multimedia, and the desire of many designers to use something simply because it is available. It is more difficult because users are ill defined, and the user's tools so variable in nature.

Today, then, the Web interface is a victim of its poor foundation. It is also a victim of its explosive and haphazard growth. Looking forward, interface design tools will mature, research-based design guidelines will become increasingly available (and will be applied), and knowledge of users and their needs will expand. Then, the ultimate goal of a Web that feels natural, is well structured, and is easy to use will reach fruition.

The Popularity of the Web

While the introduction of the graphical user interface revolutionized the user interface, the Web has revolutionized computing. It allows millions of people scattered across the globe to communicate, access information, publish, and be heard. It allows people to control much of the display and the rendering of Web pages. Aspects such as typography and colors can be changed, graphics turned off, and decisions made whether or not to transmit certain data over nonsecure channels or whether to accept or refuse cookies. Nowhere in the history of computing has the user been given so much control.

Web usage has reflected this popularity. The number of Internet hosts has risen dramatically. In 1984, hosts online exceeded 1,000; in 1987, 10,000; in 1989, 100,000, in 1990, 300,000; in 1992 hosts exceeded one million. Commercialization of the Internet saw even greater expansion of the growth rate. In 1993, Internet traffic was expanding at a 341,634 percent annual growth rate. In 1996, there were nearly 10 million hosts online and 40 million connected people (PBS Timeline).

User control has had some decided disadvantages for some Web site owners as well. Users have become much more discerning about good design. Slow download times, confusing navigation, confusing page organization, disturbing animation, or other undesirable site features often results in user abandonment of the site for others with a more agreeable interface. People are quick to vote with their mouse, and these warnings should not go unheeded.

Characteristics of a Web Interface

A Web interface possesses a number of characteristics, some similar to a GUI interface, and, as has already been shown, some different. In the following paragraphs many of these specific commonalities and differences will be examined. Also, the differing characteristics of printed page design and Web page design will be compared.

GUI versus Web Page Design

GUI and Web interface design do have similarities. Both are software designs, they are used by people, they are interactive, they are heavily visual experiences presented through screens, and they are composed of many similar components. Significant differences do exist, however. The following paragraphs highlight the other most significant differences. Table 3.1 provides a summary listing. Parts of this discussion are based upon Berry (2000) and Nielsen (1997a).

Devices. In *GUI* design, the characteristics of interface devices such as monitors and modems are well defined, and design variations tend to be restricted. Monitor display capabilities, such as installed fonts and screen size, are established and easily considered in the design process. In *Web* design, no assumptions about the user's interface devices can be made. User devices may range from handheld mechanisms to high-end workstations. (In GUI design, the difference in screen area between a laptop and a high-end workstation is a factor of six, in Web page design this difference may be as high as 100.) Connection speed bandwidths may also vary by a factor of 1,000. Consequently, WYSIWYG no longer exists in page design. In GUI design, the layout of a screen will look exactly as specified, Web page look will be greatly influenced by both the hardware and software. With the Web, the designer has to relinquish full control and share responsibility for the interface with users and their hardware and software.

User focus. *GUI* systems are about well-defined applications and data, about transactions and processes. Thorough attention must usually be addressed to tasks in need of completion. The *Web* is about information and navigation, an environment where people move back and forth in an unstructured way among many pages of information. Web use is most often characterized browsing and visual scanning of information to find what information is needed.

Data/information. *GUI* data is typically created and used by known and trusted sources, people in the user's organization or reputable and reliable companies and organizations. The properties of the system's data are generally known, and the information is typically organized in an understandable and meaningful fashion. A notion of shared data exists, as does a notion of data privacy. The *Web* is full of unknown content typically placed there by others unknown to the user. Typical users don't put information on the Web (except for publishing their own pages). The reliability and truthfulness of found information cannot always be ascertained and trusted. Web content is usually highly variable in organization, and the privacy of the information is often suspect.

User tasks. *GUI* system users install, configure, personalize, start, use, and upgrade programs. They open, use, and close data files. Fairly long times are spent within

Table 3.1 GUI versus Web Design

	GUI	WEB
Devices	User hardware variations limited. User hardware characteristics well defined. Screens appear exactly as specified.	User hardware variations enormous. Screen appearance influenced by hardware being used.
User Focus	Data and applications.	Information and navigation.
Data/ Information	Typically created and used by known and trusted sources. Properties generally known. Typically placed into system by users or known people and organizations. Typically organized in a meaningful fashion. A notion of private and shared data exists.	Full of unknown content. Source not always trusted. Often not placed onto the Web by users or known people and organizations. Highly variable organization. Privacy often suspect.
User Tasks	Install, configure, personalize, start, use, and upgrade programs. Open, use, and close data files. Fairly long times spent within an application. Familiarity with applications often achieved.	Link to a site, browse or read pages, fill out forms, register for services, participate in transactions, download and save things. Movement between pages and sites very rapid. Familiarity with many sites not established.
User's Conceptual Space	Controlled and constrained by program.	Infinite and generally unorganized.
Presentation Elements	Windows, menus, controls, data, toolbars, messages, and so on. Many transient, dynamically appearing and disappearing. Presented as specified by designer. Generally standardized by toolkits and style guides.	Two components, browser and page. Within page, any combination of text, images, audio, video, and animation. May not be presented as specified by the designer—dependent on browser, monitor, and user specifications. Little standardization.

Navigation	Through menus, lists, trees, dialogs, and wizards. Not a strong and visible concept. Constrained by design. Generally standardized by toolkits and style guides.	Through links, bookmarks, and typed URLs. Significant and highly visible concept. Few constraints, frequently causing a lost "sense of place." Few standards. Typically part of page design, fostering a lack of consistency.
Context	Enables maintenance of a better sense of context. Restricted navigation paths. Multiple viewable windows.	Poorer maintenance of a sense of context. Single-page entities. Unlimited navigation paths. Contextual clues become limited or are difficult to find.
Interaction	Interactions such as clicking menu choices, pressing buttons, selecting list choices, and cut/copy/paste occur within context of active program.	Basic interaction is a single click. This can cause extreme changes in context, which may not be noticed.
Response Time	Nearly instantaneous.	Quite variable, depending on transmission speeds, page content, and so on. Long times can upset the user.
Visual Style	Typically prescribed and constrained by toolkit. Visual creativity allowed but difficult. Little significant personalization.	Fosters a more artistic, individual, and unrestricted presentation style. Complicated by differing browser and display capabilities, and bandwidth limitations. Limited personalization available.
System Capability	Unlimited capability proportional to sophistication of hardware and software.	Limited by constraints imposed by the hardware, browser, software, client support, and user willingness to allow features because of response time, security, and privacy concerns.
Task Efficiency	Targeted to a specific audience with specific tasks. Only limited by the amount of programming undertaken to support it.	Limited by browser and network capabilities. Actual user audience usually not well understood. Often intended for anyone and everyone.

(*continues*)

Table 3.1 *(Continued)*

	GUI	WEB
Consistency	Major objective exists within and across applications. Aided by platform toolkit and design guidelines. Universal consistency in GUI products generally created through toolkits and design guidelines.	Sites tend to establish their own identity. Frequently standards set within a site. Frequent ignoring of GUI guidelines for identical components, especially controls.
User Assistance	Integral part of most systems and applications. Accessed through standard mechanisms. Documentation, both online and offline, usually provided. Personal support desk also usually provided.	No similar help systems. The little available help is built into the page. Customer service support, if provided, oriented to product or service offered.
Integration	Seamless integration of all applications into the platform environment a major objective. Toolkits and components are key elements in accomplishing this objective.	Apparent for some basic functions within most Web sites (navigation, printing, and so on.) Sites tend to achieve individual distinction rather than integration.
Security	Tightly controlled, proportional to degree of willingness to invest resources and effort. Not an issue for most home PC users.	Renowned for security exposures. Browser-provided security options typically not understood by average users. When employed, may have function-limiting side effects.
Reliability	Tightly controlled in business systems, proportional to degree of willingness to invest resources and effort.	Susceptible to disruptions caused by user, telephone line and cable providers, Internet service providers, hosting servers, and remotely accessed sites.

an individual application, and people become familiar with many of its features and its design. *Web* users do things like linking to sites, browsing or reading pages, filling out forms, registering for services, participating in transactions, and downloading and saving things. Movement between pages and sites is often a very rapid activity, with people not gaining familiarity with many sites. The typical Web user has no notion of programs and tends to be much less aware of computer mechanics. Most GUI and Web users to not want to spend the effort required to set up or install anything.

User's conceptual space. In a *GUI* environment the user's conceptual space is controlled by the program and application. A user's access to data is constrained, and space is made available where their data can be stored and managed. A *Web* user's space is infinite and generally unorganized. Little opportunity for meaningful organization of personal information exists.

Presentation elements. The main presentation elements for *GUIs* are various kinds of windows, menus, controls, toolbars, messages, and data. Many elements are transient, dynamically appearing and disappearing based upon the current context of the interaction. They are also generally standardized as a result of the toolkits and style guides used. Elements are presented on screens exactly as specified by the designer. *Web* systems possess two components: the browser and page. Many browsers are substantially GUI applications with traditional GUI presentation elements. Within a page itself, however, any combination of text, images, audio, video, and animation may exist. Complex, cluttered, and visually distracting pages are easy to generate and often exist. This occurs because many designers have focused on implementing that which is new, pretty, or attention getting, with little thought given to usability. The availability of interface style guides and guidelines to aid the design process is not known (or they are ignored). Common toolkits and industry conventions, however, are now being proposed and will be slowly adopted. Also contributing to page design problems is the fact that a page may not be presented exactly as specified by the designer. The exact look of a page is dependent on browser and monitor used. Extreme variations in screen sizes for presenting pages can and do exist. Finally, the user can change the look of a page by modifying its properties.

Navigation. *GUI* users navigate through structured menus, lists, trees, dialogs, and wizards. Paths are constrained by design (grayed out menu choices, for example), and the navigation mechanisms standardized by toolkits and style guides. Navigation is a weakly established concept, a supplement to more important task functions and actions. Some aspects of a GUI do provide a strong sense of navigation, the ellipsis on "to another window" intent indicators such as "Open...," command buttons such as "OK" and "Cancel" that direct the user's focus to another window, and wizards. Others aspects of GUI design do not provide a strong sense of navigation—button pressing, for example, that does not result in something visible happening (for example, pressing an Apply button).

Web users control their own navigation through links, bookmarks, and typed URLs. Navigation is a significant and highly visible concept with few constraints. The immense size of the Web, and the user's ability to easily wander just about anywhere, frequently causes a lost "sense of place," or "Where am I right now?"

feeling. Web navigation has few standards beyond the browser's Back button and underlined links. Typically most navigation is part of page design that fosters a lack of consistency, and often confuses users. Establishing a continual sense of place for the user is a critical aspect of Web page design.

Context. *GUI* systems enable the user to maintain a better sense of context. Paths are restricted, and multiple overlapping windows may be presented and be visible, enabling users to remember how what they are doing fits into the overall task picture. *Web* pages are single entities with almost unlimited navigation paths. They do not bring up separate dialog boxes to ask questions, provide or request supplemental information, or present messages. Contextual clues become limited or are hard to find.

Interaction. *GUI* interactions consist of such activities as clicking menu choices, pressing buttons, selecting choices from list, keying data, and cutting, copying, or pasting within context established by an open window and an active program. The basic *Web* interaction is a single click. This click can cause extreme changes in context such as moving to another site or changing the displayed information within a site. The user may not notice subtle changes when they occur. Additionally, the browser provides parallel mechanisms like the Back button that may function differently depending on context. The distinction between an action and a navigation link is not always obvious.

Response time. Compared to the Web, response times with a *GUI* system are fairly stable, if not nearly instantaneous. *Web* response times can be quite variable, and often aggravatingly slow. Line transmission speeds, system loads, and page content can have a dramatic impact. Long response times can upset and frustrate users.

Visual style. In *GUI* systems, the visual style is typically prescribed and constrained by toolkit. (Exceptions are entertainment and multimedia applications.) Visual creativity in screen design is allowed but it is difficult to do. While some user options and style choices do exist, little opportunity exists for screen personalization. In *Web* page design, a more artistic, individual, and unrestricted presentation style is allowed and encouraged. Much design freedom exists, but differing browser and display capabilities, multiple screen sizes, and bandwidth limitations, often complicate and restrict this freedom. Limited personalization of the system is available, at a browser or site level, for users.

System capability. *GUI* system capabilities are only limited in proportion to the capability of the hardware in terms of speed, memory, and configuration, and the sophistication of the software. The *Web* is more constrained, being limited by constraints imposed by the hardware, browser, and software. It is also limited by the willingness of the page owner to provide certain functions and elements, and the willingness of the user to allow features because of response time, security, and privacy issues and concerns.

Task efficiency. *GUI* systems are targeted to a specific audience performing specific tasks. Generally, the efficiency of performing a task is only limited by the amount of programming undertaken to support it. Browser and network capabilities limit *Web* task efficiency. The actual user audience is usually not well understood, since many Web sites are intended for anyone and everyone.

Consistency. Consistency in *GUI* system design is a major objective in most development efforts. While they are far from perfect, an attempt is made to be consistent both within applications and across applications. Many organizations possess interface and screen design standards and toolkits to aid in the standardization process. Toolkits and guidelines also allow a certain degree of universal consistency in GUI products. In *Web* page design, the heavy emphasis on graphics, a lack of design standards, and the desire of Web sites to establish their own identities results in very little consistency across sites. Web sites often establish standards within a site, but in too many instances developers ignore guidelines existing for GUI components used in Web pages. These problems are especially found in the presentation of screen controls on pages.

User assistance. User assistance is an integral part of most *GUI* systems applications. This assistance is accessed through standard mechanisms such as the F1 key and Help menus. Message and status areas are also provided on the screen. Documentation, both online and offline, is normally provided, as is a support desk to answer user questions and provide guidance and assistance. *Web* pages do not yet provide similar help systems. What little help that is available is built into the page. Customer service support, if provided, is generally oriented to the product or service offered. GUI browsers may provide GUI-type assistance, so the user sees two different assistance approaches. Deficiencies in Web page help then become more obvious.

Integration. A primary goal of most *GUI* applications is the seamless integration of all pieces. Common functions are supported across applications and import/export capabilities exist. Again, toolkits and their components are key elements in accomplishing this objective. In *Web* design, some integration is apparent within a site for basic functions such as navigation and printing. But because sites strive for individual distinction, interoperability between sites is almost nonexistent.

Security. In a *GUI* environment, security and data access can be tightly controlled, in proportion to the degree of willingness of an organization to invest resources and effort. For home applications, security is not an issue for most PC users. The *Web* is renowned for security exposures. This is a major inhibitor of Web use for both businesses and consumers. Browser-provided security options have typically not been well understood by average Web users. When employed, these security options often have function-limiting side effects. (Disabled cookies, for example.) Attempts to create a more trustworthy appearance are being made through the use of security levels and passwords to assure users that the Web is a secure environment.

Reliability. Like security, reliability in *GUI* systems is established and controlled in proportion to the degree of willingness of an organization to invest resources and effort. The computer being used influences reliability as does, if applicable, the local area network. Both are in the control of the using organization. *Web* reliability is susceptible to disruptions from many directions. Telephone line and cable providers, Internet service providers, hosting servers, and remotely accessed sites all can contribute to the problem. Accessed applications and user mistakes may also cause reliability problems. A lack of reliability can be a great inhibitor of Web use.

In conclusion, from a design implication perspective, GUI and Web differences can be extensive. Today, these differences must be considered in any Web page design, although many GUI interface design techniques and guidelines are applicable in page design. Tomorrow, many of these GUI-Web differences will diminish or disappear as the discrepancies are addressed by technology.

In developing a Web system, always evaluate each GUI guideline for direct applicability in any development effort. Also, do not simply transport a GUI application or design "en toto" to the Web without evaluating it in terms of the implications described above. Some applications or designs may require significant changes, others a simple "fine-tuning." One so far unmentioned aspect that both GUI and Web systems *do* have in common, is "know your user." Involving them throughout the redesign process will ensure the best transition to the Web.

Printed Pages versus Web Pages

While Internet history spans but a few years, that of the printed page measures more than five and one-half centuries. Research and experience with printed pages through these centuries has created a fundamental and accepted set of guidelines for editorial style, element presentation, and text organization. Many of the basic guidelines, clear, comprehensive, and consistent, can and are being applied to Web page design. Web page design, however, is different in many aspects from the design of books, documents, newspapers, and other similar materials. These differences require a rethinking, researching, and reformulating of a number of these guidelines for use in Web page design. Many of these differences have already been identified. Others will surface as Web experience grows and research is conducted. In the following paragraphs, the major differences between print and Web page design are briefly described. Implications for Web page design are also summarized.

Page size. Printed pages are generally larger than their Web counterparts. They are also fixed in size, not variable like Web pages. A printed page can be designed as one entity, the designer being assured that the completed final product will possess an integrated and complete look. Web pages, while usually designed as a complete entity, are presented in pieces, pieces whose dimensions differ depending on the user's technology (browser, monitor, and so on). The visual impact of the printed page is maintained in hard-copy form, while on the Web all that usually exists are snapshots of page areas. The visual impact of a Web page is substantially degraded, and the user may never see some parts of the page because their existence is not known or require scrolling to bring into view. The design implications: the top of a Web page is its most important element, and signals to the user must always be provided that parts of a page lie below the surface.

Page rendering. Printed pages are immensely superior to Web pages in rendering. Printed pages are presented as complete entities, and their entire contents are available for reading or review immediately upon appearance. Web pages elements are often rendered slowly, depending upon things like line transmission speeds and page content. Dozens of seconds may be consumed waiting for a page to completely appear. Impatient users may not wait, moving on to somewhere else. Design implications: Provide page content that downloads fast, and give people elements to read immediately so the sense of passing time is diminished. (The ultimate goal: a bandwidth fast enough to download a Web page as fast as one can turn a paper page.)

Page layout. With the printed page, layout is precise with much attention given to it. With Web pages layout is more of an approximation, being negatively influenced by deficiencies in design toolkits and the characteristics of the user's browser and hardware, particularly screen sizes. Design implication: Understand the restrictions and design for the most common user tools.

Page resolution. Today, the resolution of displayed print characters still exceeds that of screen characters, and screen reading is still slower than reading from a document. Design implication: Provide an easy way to print long Web documents. (The ultimate goal: a screen resolution sharp enough to render type crisply enough so that screen reading speed reaches that of newspaper reading.)

User focus. Printed pages present people with entire sets of information. Estimations of effort needed to deal with the document are fairly easily made, size and the nature of the material being strong contributors. Some printed pages may be read sequentially (a novel) and others (a newspaper) partially and somewhat sequentially (the sports section first, perhaps?). Others forms of printed material may simply be skimmed (a sales brochure), but this skimming is usually systematic in some way. Web pages present people with individual snapshots of information, often with few clues as to structure and sequence, and rarely with a few cues as to length and depth. People also have a sense that the body of Web information potentially available is almost unlimited, and that information paths can lead everywhere and anywhere. With few content size cues available and a huge information base, a common resulting behavior of Web users is to skim the information presented, looking for what is most relevant to their task or need. This is done for personal efficiency and so as not to tax one's patience. Design implications: Create easy to scan pages and limit the word count of textual content. Also, provide overviews of information organization schemes, clear descriptions of where links lead, and estimations of sizes of linked pages and materials.

Page navigation. Navigating printed materials is as simple as page turning. It is a motor skilled learned early in life and never thought of as navigation or a design element. Substantial interaction between pages is rare, since the process is essentially sequential. Navigating the Web requires innumerable decisions concerning which of many possible links should be followed. It requires asking oneself questions such as these: What is at the end of this link? Where is it? Will it address my need or solve my problem? Design implications are similar to the above—provide overviews of information organization schemes and clear descriptions of where links lead.

Sense of place. With paper documents you derive a sense of where you are through a mixture of graphic and editorial organization, and size cues supplied by the design of the document. The document is an object with physical characteristics. Paging through printed material is an orderly process, sequential and understandable. Electronic documents provide none of these physical cues. All that is visible is a small collection of text, graphics, and links hinting that much else lies *somewhere* underneath. Moving through the Web links can cause radical shifts in location and context. Paging using the browser's Back button steps one back through links visited and may involve passing through different documents. Fixed locations that provide cues to support one's memory concerning the location of things are nonexistent. All these factors cause a person to easily lose a sense of place and lead to confusion. Design implication: Build cues into Web pages to aid the user in maintaining a sense of place.

Interactivity. Printed page design involves letting the eyes traverse static information, selectively looking at information and using spatial combinations to make page elements enhance and explain each other. Web design involves letting the hands move the information (scrolling, pointing, expanding, clicking, and so on) in conjunction with the eyes. Information relationships, static or dynamic, are expressed chronologically as part of the interaction and user movements. Doing is more memorable and makes a stronger impact than simply seeing. No print precedents exist for this style of interaction. A better understanding of this process (as well as better hardware and software) is needed to enhance interactivity.

Page independence. Because moving between Web pages is so easy, and almost any page in a site can be accessed from anywhere else, pages must be made freestanding. Every page is independent, and its topic and contents must be explained without assumptions about any previous page seen by the user. Printed pages, being sequential, fairly standardized in organization, and providing a clear sense of place, are not considered independent. Specific types of content (table of contents, author, index, and so on) are easily found in well-established document locations. Design implication: Provide informative headers and footers on each Web page.

In conclusion, many of the basic print guidelines can be applied to Web page design. As shown above, however, printed material design differs from Web page design in many aspects. New guidelines must continue to be developed, implemented, and modified as necessary as technology advances and our understanding of Web interaction increases. For the moment, apply existing guidelines where relevant, and new guidelines as necessary.

The Merging of Graphical Business Systems and the Web

Another strength of the Web lies in its ability to link databases and processing occurring on a variety of machines within a company or organization. Within a closed system, queries against databases can be made, internal communication performed, and information useful for employees can be made available. Current systems can also be implemented with more traditional GUI interfaces. The graphical business system and the Web will merge into a common entity. These Web systems are called intranets.

Characteristics of an Intranet versus the Internet

An intranet has many of the same characteristics as the Internet. They differ, however, in some important ways. The following discussion is partly based upon Nielsen (1997b).

Users. The users of intranets, being organization employees, know a lot about the organization, its structure, its products, its jargon, and its culture. Internet sites are used by customers and others who know much less about the organization, and often care less about it. The intranet user's characteristics and needs can be much more specifically defined then can those of the general Internet user.

Tasks. An intranet is used for an organization's everyday activities, including complex transactions, queries, and communications. The Internet is mainly used to find information, with a supplementary use being simple transactions.

Type of information. An intranet will contain detailed information needed for organizational functioning. Information will often be added or modified. The Internet will usually present more stable information: marketing and customer or client information, reports, and so forth.

Amount of information. Typically, an intranet site will be much larger than an organization's Internet site. Massive amounts of information and processes seem to be needed to make an organization function. It has been estimated that an intranet site can be ten to one hundred times larger than its corresponding public site.

Hardware and software. Since intranets exist in a controlled environment, the kinds of computers, monitors, browsers, and other software can be restricted or standardized. The need for cross-platform compatibility is minimized or eliminated, permitting more predictable design. Upgraded communications also permit intranets to run from a hundred to a thousand times faster than typical Internet access can. This allows the use of rich graphics and multimedia, screen elements that contribute to very slow download times for most Internet users.

Design philosophy. Implementation on the intranet of current text-based and GUI applications will present a user model similar to those that have existed in other domains. This will cause a swing back to more traditional GUI designs—designs that will also incorporate the visual appeal of the Web, but eliminate many of its useless, promotional, and distracting features. The resulting GUI hybrids will be richer and much more effective.

Extranets

An extranet is a special set of intranet Web pages that can be accessed from outside an organization or company. Typical examples include those for letting customers check on an order's status or letting suppliers view requests for proposals. An extranet is a blend of the public Internet and the intranet, and its design should reflect this.

Principles of User Interface Design

An interface must really be just an extension of a person. This means that the system and its software must reflect a person's capabilities and respond to his or her specific needs. It should be useful, accomplishing some business objectives faster and more efficiently than the previously used method or tool did. It must also be easy to learn, for people want to do, not learn to do. Finally, the system must be easy and fun to use, evoking a sense of pleasure and accomplishment not tedium and frustration.

The interface itself should serve as both a connector and a separator: a connector in that it ties the user to the power of the computer, and a separator in that it minimizes the possibility of the participants damaging one another. While the damage the user inflicts on the computer tends to be physical (a frustrated pounding of the keyboard), the damage caused by the computer is more psychological (a threat to one's self-esteem).

Throughout the history of the human-computer interface, various researchers and writers have attempted to define a set of general principles of interface design. What follows is a compilation of these principles. They reflect not only what we know today, but also what we think we know today. Many are based on research, others on the collective thinking of behaviorists working with user interfaces. These principles will continue to evolve, expand, and be refined as our experience with GUIs and the Web increases. We will begin with the first set of published principles, those for the Xerox STAR.

Principles for the Xerox STAR

The design of the Xerox STAR was guided by a set of principles that evolved over its lengthy development process (Smith, Harslem, Irby, Kimball, and Verplank, 1982; Verplank, 1988). These principles established the foundation for graphical interfaces.

The illusion of manipulable objects. Displayed objects that are selectable and manipulable must be created. A design challenge is to invent a set of displayable objects that are represented meaningfully and appropriately for the intended application. It must be clear that these objects can be selected, and how to select them must be self-evident. When they are selected should also be obvious, because it should be clear that the selected object will be the focus of the next action. Verplank calls this "graphics with handles on it." Standalone icons easily fulfilled this requirement. The handles for windows were placed in the borders (window-specific commands, pop-up menus, scroll bars, and so on).

Visual order and viewer focus. Attention must be drawn, at the proper time, to the important and relevant elements of the display. Effective visual contrast between various components of the screen is used to achieve this goal (STAR was monochromatic so color was not used). Animation is also used to draw attention, as is sound. Feedback must also be provided to the user. Since the pointer is usually the focus of viewer attention, it is a useful mechanism for providing this feedback (by changing shapes).

Revealed structure. The distance between one's intention and the effect must be minimized. Most often, the distance between intention and effect is lengthened as system power increases. The relationship between intention and effect must be tightened and made as apparent as possible to the user. The underlying structure is often revealed during the selection process.

Consistency. Consistency aids learning. Consistency is provided in such areas as element location, grammar, font shapes, styles, and sizes, selection indicators, and contrast and emphasis techniques.

Appropriate effect or emotional impact. The interface must provide the appropriate emotional effect for the product and its market. Is it a corporate, professional, and secure business system? Should it reflect the fantasy, wizardry, and bad puns of computer games?

A match with the medium. The interface must also reflect the capabilities of the device on which it will be displayed. Quality of screen images will be greatly affected by a device's resolution and color-generation capabilities.

General Principles

The design goals in creating a user interface are described below. They are fundamental to the design and implementation of all effective interfaces, including GUI and Web ones. These principles are general characteristics of the interface, and they apply to all aspects. The compilation is presented alphabetically, and the ordering is not intended to imply degree of importance. They are derived from the various principles described in Galitz (1992), IBM (1991, 2001), Mayhew (1992), Microsoft (1992, 1995, 2001), Open Software Foundation (1993), and Verplank (1988).

Aesthetically Pleasing

- Provide visual appeal by following these presentation and graphic design principles:
  — Provide meaningful contrast between screen elements.
  — Create groupings.
  — Align screen elements and groups.
  — Provide three-dimensional representation.
  — Use color and graphics effectively and simply.

A design aesthetic, or visually pleasing composition, is attractive to the eye. It draws attention subliminally, conveying a message clearly and quickly. Visual appeal makes a computer system accessible and inviting. A lack of visually pleasing composition is disorienting, obscures the intent and meaning, and slows down and confuses the user. Visual appeal is terribly important today because most human-computer communication occurs in the visual realm.

Visual appeal is provided by following the presentation and graphic design principles to be discussed, including providing meaningful contrast between screen elements, creating spatial groupings, aligning screen elements, providing three-dimensional representation, and using color and graphics effectively. Good design combines power, functionality, and simplicity with a pleasing appearance.

Clarity

- The interface should be visually, conceptually, and linguistically clear, including:
  - — Visual elements
  - — Functions
  - — Metaphors
  - — Words and text

The interface must be clear in visual appearance, concept, and wording. Visual elements should be understandable, relating to the user's real-world concepts and functions. Metaphors, or analogies, should be realistic and simple. Interface words and text should be simple, unambiguous, and free of computer jargon.

Compatibility

- Provide compatibility with the following:
  - — The user
  - — The task and job
  - — The product
- Adopt the user's perspective.

User compatibility. Design must be appropriate and compatible with the needs of the user or client. Effective design starts with understanding the user's needs and adopting the user's point of view. One very common error among designers is to assume that users are all alike. A glance around the office should quickly put this assumption to rest. Another common error is to assume that all users think, feel, and behave exactly like the developer. Studies have proven otherwise. Users have quite different needs, aspirations, and attitudes than developers. A system reflecting only the knowledge and attitudes of its designers cannot be successful.

"Know the user" is *the* fundamental principle in interface design. User compatibility can only happen if understanding truly occurs.

Task and job compatibility. The organization of a system should match the tasks a person must do to perform the job. The structure and flow of functions should permit easy transition between tasks. The user must never be forced to navigate between applications or many screens to complete routine daily tasks.

Product compatibility. The intended user of a new system is often the user of other systems or earlier versions of the new system. Habits, expectations, and a level of knowledge have been established and will be brought to bear when learning the new system. If these habits, expectations, and knowledge cannot be applied to the new system, confusion results and learning requirements are greatly increased. While compatibility across products must always be considered in relation to improving interfaces, making new systems compatible with existing systems will take advantage of what users already know and reduce the necessity for new learning.

Comprehensibility

- A system should be easily learned and understood. A user should know the following:
  - — What to look at
  - — What to do
  - — When to do it
  - — Where to do it
  - — Why to do it
  - — How to do it
- The flow of actions, responses, visual presentations, and information should be in a sensible order that is easy to recollect and place in context.

A system should be understandable, flowing in a comprehensible and meaningful order. Strong clues to the operation of objects should be presented. The steps to complete a task should be obvious. Reading and digesting long explanations should never be necessary.

Configurability

- Permit easy personalization, configuration, and reconfiguration of settings.
  - — Enhances a sense of control.
  - — Encourages an active role in understanding.

Easy personalization and customization through configuration and reconfiguration of a system enhances a sense of control, encourages an active role in understanding, and allows for personal preferences and differences in experience levels. It also leads to higher user satisfaction.

Some people will prefer to personalize a system to better meet their preferences. Other people will not, accepting what is given. Still others will experiment with reconfiguration and then give up, running out of patience or time. For these latter groups of users a good default configuration must be provided.

Consistency

- A system should look, act, and operate the same throughout. Similar components should:
  - — Have a similar look.
  - — Have similar uses.
  - — Operate similarly.
- The same action should always yield the same result.
- The function of elements should not change.
- The position of standard elements should not change.

Design consistency is the common thread that runs throughout these guidelines. It is the cardinal rule of all design activities. Consistency is important because it can reduce requirements for human learning by allowing skills learned in one situation to be transferred to another like it. While any new system must impose some learning requirements on its users, it should avoid encumbering productive learning with nonproductive, unnecessary activity. Consistency also aids learning of the system's mental model.

In addition to increased learning requirements, *inconsistency* in design has a number of other prerequisites and by-products, including:

- More specialization by system users.
- Greater demand for higher skills.
- More preparation time and less production time.
- More frequent changes in procedures.
- More error-tolerant systems (because errors are more likely).
- More kinds of documentation.
- More time to find information in documents.
- More unlearning and learning when systems are changed.
- More demands on supervisors and managers.
- More things to do wrong.

Inconsistencies in design are caused by differences in people. Several designers might each design the same system differently. Inconsistencies also occur when those performing design activities are pressured by time constraints. All too often the solutions in those cases are exceptions that the user must learn to handle. People, however, perceive a system as a single entity. To them, it should look, act, and feel similar throughout. Excess learning requirements become a barrier to users achieving and maintaining high performance and can ultimately influence user acceptance of the system.

Can consistency make a big difference? One study found that user thinking time nearly doubled when the position of screen elements, such as titles and field captions, was varied on a series of menu screens.

Design consistency is achieved by developing and applying design standards or guidelines. In the late 1980s the computer industry and many using organizations finally awakened to the need for them, and a flurry of graphical user interface guideline documents were developed and published. These guidelines specify the appearance and behavior of the GUI user interface. They describe the windows, menus, and various controls available, including what they look like and how they work. They also provide some guidance on when to use the various components.

Examples of industry-produced guidelines include Apple's *Macintosh Human Interface Guidelines* (1992b), Digital Equipment Corporation's *XUI Style Guide* (1988), IBM's *System Application Architecture Common User Access* (1987, 1989a, 1989b, 1991, 1992), Sun Microsystem's *OPEN LOOK Graphical User Interface Application Style Guidelines*

(1990), Open Software Foundation's *OSF/MOTIF Style Guide* (1993), and Microsoft's *The Windows Interface* (1992) and *The Windows Interface Guidelines for Software Design* (1995).

The Web has burst upon the scene with few standards and guidelines to direct design. Many GUI and printed material principles are applicable but they have been applied in a haphazard manner. New research-based guidelines are desperately needed.

Organizations working on traditional interface guidelines or standards include the International Standards Organization (ISO), the American National Standards Institute (ANSI), and the Human Factors and Ergonomics Society (Billingsley, 1996). The development of Web design guidelines has been one focus of the World Wide Web Consortium (2001).

Control

- The user must control the interaction.
  - — Actions should result from explicit user requests.
  - — Actions should be performed quickly.
  - — Actions should be capable of interruption or termination.
  - — The user should never be interrupted for errors.
- The context maintained must be from the perspective of the user.
- The means to achieve goals should be flexible and compatible with the user's skills, experiences, habits, and preferences.
- Avoid modes since they constrain the actions available to the user.
- Permit the user to customize aspects of the interface, while always providing a proper set of defaults.

Control is feeling in charge, feeling that the system is responding to your actions. Feeling that a machine is controlling you is demoralizing and frustrating. The interface should present a tool-like appearance. Control is achieved when a person, working at his or her own pace, is able to determine what to do, how to do it, and then is easily able to get it done. Simple, predictable, consistent, flexible, customizable, and passive interfaces provide control. Lack of control is signaled by unavailable systems, long delays in system responses, surprising system actions, tedious and long procedures that cannot be circumvented, difficulties in obtaining necessary information, and the inability to achieve the desired results. The feeling of control has been found to be an excellent mitigator of the work stress associated with many automated systems

In general, avoid modes since they restrict the actions available to the user at any given time. If modes must be used, they should be visually obvious (for example, a changed mouse pointer shape). Existing modes must also be easy to learn and easy to remove.

Directness

- Provide direct ways to accomplish tasks.
  - — Available alternatives should be visible.
  - — The effect of actions on objects should be visible.

Tasks should be performed directly. Available alternatives should be visible, reducing the user's mental workload. Directness is also best provided by the object-action sequence of direct-manipulation systems. Tasks are performed by directly selecting an object, then selecting an action to be performed, and then seeing the action being performed.

Efficiency

- Minimize eye and hand movements, and other control actions.
  - — Transitions between various system controls should flow easily and freely.
  - — Navigation paths should be as short as possible.
  - — Eye movement through a screen should be obvious and sequential.
- Anticipate the user's wants and needs whenever possible.

Eye and hand movements must not be wasted. One's attention must be captured by relevant elements of the screen when needed. Sequential eye movements between screen elements should be predictable, obvious, and short. Web pages must be easily scannable. All navigation paths should be as short as possible. Manual transitions between various system controls should also be as short as possible. Avoid frequent transitions between input devices such as the keyboard and mouse.

Always try to anticipate the user's wants and needs. At each step in a process, present to the user all the information and tools needed to complete the process. Do not require user to search for and gather necessary information and tools.

Familiarity

- Employ familiar concepts and use a language that is familiar to the user.
- Keep the interface natural, mimicking the user's behavior patterns.
- Use real-world metaphors.

Build on the user's existing knowledge. Build into the interface concepts, terminology, workflows, and spatial arrangements already familiar to the user. Operations should mimic one's behavior patterns; dialogs should mimic one's thought processes and vocabulary. Familiar concepts enable people to get started and become productive quickly.

Flexibility

- A system must be sensitive to the differing needs of its users, enabling a level and type of performance based upon:
  — Each user's knowledge and skills.
  — Each user's experience.
  — Each user's personal preference.
  — Each user's habits.
  — The conditions at that moment.

Flexibility is the system's ability to respond to individual differences in people. Permit people to choose the method of interaction that is most appropriate to their situation. People should be able to interact with a system in terms of their own particular needs, including knowledge, experience, and personal preference. Flexibility is accomplished by providing multiple ways to access application functions and perform tasks. It is also accomplished through permitting system customization. Another benefit of flexibility is that it contributes to increased user control. A flexible system is a versatile system.

Flexibility is not without dangers. Highly flexible systems can confuse inexperienced people, causing them to make more errors. For this reason, flexibility appears desirable only for experienced users. The novice user should not be exposed to system flexibility at the start, but only as experience is gained. The concept of "progressive disclosure," to be discussed in the simplicity guideline to follow, is also applicable here.

Another problem with flexibility is that it may not always be used, some people prefer to continue doing things in the way they first learned. A variety of factors may account for this, including an unwillingness to invest in additional learning, or, perhaps, new ways may not be obvious. The former problem may be addressed by making the new ways as easy and safe to learn as possible, the latter by including in training and reference materials not only information about how to do things, but when they are likely to be useful.

Forgiveness

- Tolerate and forgive common and unavoidable human errors.
- Prevent errors from occurring whenever possible.
- Protect against possible catastrophic errors.
- When an error does occur, provide constructive messages.

It is often said "to err is human." The corollary to that statement, at least in computer systems, might be "to forgive is good design." People will make mistakes; a system should tolerate those that are common and unavoidable. A forgiving system keeps people out of trouble.

People like to explore and learn by trial and error. A system oversensitive to erroneous inputs will discourage users from exploring and trying new things. Learning will be inhibited, and people will be overcautious, working slowly and carefully to avoid mistakes. Productivity will then suffer. A fear of making a mistake and not being able to recover from it has always been a primary contributor to fear of dealing with computers.

Prevent errors from occurring by anticipating where mistakes may occur and designing to prevent them. Permit people to review, change, and undo actions whenever necessary. Make it very difficult to perform actions that can have tragic results. When errors do occur, present clear instructions on how to correct them.

Predictability

- The user should be able to anticipate the natural progression of each task.
  - — Provide distinct and recognizable screen elements.
  - — Provide cues to the result of an action to be performed.
- All expectations should be fulfilled uniformly and completely.

Tasks, displays, and movement through a system should be anticipatable based on the user's previous knowledge or experience. All actions should lead to results the user expects. Screen elements should be distinct and recognizable. Current operations should provide clues as to what will come next. Anticipation, or predictability, reduces mistakes and enables tasks to be completed more quickly. All expectations possessed by the user should be fulfilled uniformly and completely. Predictability is greatly enhanced by design consistency.

Recovery

- A system should permit:
  - — Commands or actions to be abolished or reversed.
  - — Immediate return to a certain point if difficulties arise.
- Ensure that users never lose their work as a result of:
  - — An error on their part.
  - — Hardware, software, or communication problems.

A person should be able to retract an action by issuing an *undo* command. Knowing that an action can be reversed reduces much of the distress of new users, who often worry about doing something wrong. The return point could be the previous action, previous screen, a recent closure point, or the beginning of some predetermined period, such as back 10 screens or some number of minutes. Reversing or abolishing an action is analogous to using an eraser to eliminate a pencil mark on a piece of paper.

The goal is stability, or returning easily to the right track when a wrong track has been taken. Recovery should be obvious, automatic, and easy and natural to perform. In short, it should be hard to get into deep water or go too far astray. Easy recovery from an action greatly facilitates learning by trial and error and exploration. If an action is not reversible, and its consequences are critical, it should be made difficult to accomplish. Always ensure that users never lose their work as a result of their own errors or technical glitches.

Responsiveness

- The system must rapidly respond to the user's requests.
- Provide immediate acknowledgment for all user actions:
  - — Visual.
  - — Textual.
  - — Auditory.

A user request must be responded to quickly. Knowledge of results, or feedback, is a necessary learning ingredient. It shapes human performance and instills confidence. All requests to the system must be acknowledged in some way. Feedback may be visual, the change in the shape of the mouse pointer, or textual, taking the form of a message. It may also be auditory, consisting of a unique sound or tone.

Never leave the screen blank for more than a moment, because the user may think the system has failed. If a request requires an unusually long processing time, or one that is longer than customary, provide an interim "in-progress" message. Also provide some unique form of communication if a user action results in a problem or possible problem.

Substantial or more informative feedback is most important for the casual or new system user. Expert users are often content to receive more modest feedback.

Simplicity

- Provide as simple an interface as possible.
- Five ways to provide simplicity:
  - — Use progressive disclosure, hiding things until they are needed.
    - Present common and necessary functions first.
    - Prominently feature important functions.
    - Hide more sophisticated and less frequently used functions.
  - — Provide defaults.
  - — Minimize screen alignment points.
  - — Make common actions simple at the expense of uncommon actions being made harder.
  - — Provide uniformity and consistency.

Simplicity is the opposite of complexity. Complexity is a measure of the number of choices available at any point in the human-computer interaction. A great deal of functionality and power is usually associated with high complexity. Complexity most often overwhelms and confuses new and casual users of systems. Complex systems are often not fully used, or used ineffectively, because a person may follow known but more cumbersome methods instead of easier but undiscovered or unfamiliar methods.

A system lacking complexity may have a different set of faults. It may be tedious to use or not accomplish much. It is better, however, to provide less functionality that will get effectively used than to provide too much functionality, yielding an interface hopelessly complex and extremely difficult to use. Complexity, then, is a two-edged sword. To effectively solve problems, it must be present without being apparent. The goal, then, is to provide a complex system while masking the complexity through a simple interface. There are several ways to minimize this complexity.

Progressive disclosure. Introduce system components gradually so the full complexity of the system is not visible at first encounter. Teach fundamentals first. Then, slowly introduce advanced or more sophisticated functions. This is called the layered, or spiral, approach to learning. Such an approach was first described by Carroll and Carrithers (1984) who called it the "Training-Wheels System." They found that by disabling portions of the system that were not needed and could lead to errors and confusion, improved system learning efficiency was achieved.

Provide defaults. Providing defaults is another form of system layering. When a system is first presented, provide a set of defaults for all system-configurable items. The new user will not be burdened with these decisions and can concentrate on the fundamentals first. Defaults can later be changed, if desired, as experience increases.

Minimize screen alignment points. A larger number of alignment points of elements displayed on a screen are associated with greater screen visual complexity. Minimizing these alignment points minimizes visual complexity. This concept will be discussed more fully later.

Make common actions simple. Make common actions within a system easier to accomplish than uncommon actions. The benefit will be greater overall system efficiency.

Provide uniformity and consistency. Inconsistency is really a foolish form of complexity. It forces a person to learn that things that appear different are not different.

Transparency

- Permit the user to focus on the task or job, without concern for the mechanics of the interface.
  - — Workings and reminders of workings inside the computer should be invisible to the user.

Never force the user to think about the technical details of the system. One's thoughts must be directed to the task, not the computer communication process. Reminders of the mechanics of the interface occur through the use of technical jargon, the heavy use of codes, and the presentation of computer concepts and representations.

Trade-Offs

- Final design will be based on a series of trade-offs balancing often-conflicting design principles.
- People's requirements always take precedence over technical requirements.

Design guidelines often cover a great deal of territory and often conflict with one another or with technical requirements. In such conflicts the designer must weigh the alternatives and reach a decision based on trade-offs concerning accuracy, time, cost, and ease of use. Making these trade-offs intelligently requires a thorough understanding of the user and all design considerations. The ultimate solution will be a blend of experimental data, good judgment, and the important user needs.

This leads to a second cardinal rule of graphical system development: *Human requirements always take precedence over technical requirements.* It may be easier for the designer to write a program or build a device that neglects user ease, but final system judgment will always come down to one simple fact: How well does the system meet the needs of the user?

Multiple Choice Questions

1. HCI was earlier referred as
   (a) Computer Human Interaction
   (b) Human interaction process
   (c) Interaction design process
   (d) Interface design method
2. Interaction based on windows, icons, menus, and pointers is called the
   (a) WICP (b) WIMP
   (c) WIMD (d) WIWD
3. A GUI
   (a) Uses buttons, menus, and icons
   (b) Should be easy for a user to manipulate
   (c) Stands for Graphic Use Interaction
   (d) Both (a) and (b)
   (e) All of the above
4. Which is not a feature of a GUI that makes learning a program easy for users?
   (a) Online help
   (b) WYSIWYG formatting
   (c) Dialog boxes
   (d) Detailed key strokes and commands
   (e) Icons
5. GUI stands for
   (a) Graphics user interaction
   (b) Graphical user interface
   (c) Graphics usual interface
   (d) None of these
6. The visual language includes ________ for representing visual sentences.
   (a) Visual language
   (b) Icons
   (c) Both (a) and (b)
   (d) None of these
7. Following are the benefits of good design:
   (a) To Increase productivity.
   (b) To produce the result quickly.
   (c) For good recognition of the system.
   (d) None of above.

8. Direct manipulation system means
   (a) One in which the user is able to select an object and then specify which actions are to be taken
   (b) One in which the user is able to select an object and then does not specify which actions are to be taken
   (c) One in which the user is not able to select an object but specify which actions are to be taken
   (d) One in which the user is able to select and perform the action on object
9. The process of physically selecting the files and dragging them to the trash is an example of
   (a) Indirect manipulation system
   (b) Direct manipulation system
   (c) Both (a) and (b)
   (d) None of the above
10. Indirect manipulation results from
    (a) Operations being difficult to conceptualize in the graphical system
    (b) Graphics capability of the system is not limited
    (c) Difficulties for people to learn and remember all the necessary operations and actions
    (d) None of the above
11. What is the difference between the printed page and web page?
    (a) Printed pages are smaller than web pages
    (b) Printed pages are larger than web pages
    (c) Printed pages and web pages are equal in size
    (d) Printed pages are fixed in size but variable like web pages
12. "Use real-world metaphors" will match with the following UI design principle:
    (a) Directness (b) Efficiency
    (c) Familiarity (d) Flexibility
13. "Providing meaningful contrast between screen elements" will match with the following UI design principle:
    (a) Accessibility
    (b) Aesthetically pleasing
    (c) Availability
    (d) Clarity
14. "Systems should be designed to be usable, without modification, by as many people as possible" will match with the following UI design principle:
    (a) Accessibility
    (b) Aesthetically pleasing
    (c) Availability
    (d) Clarity
15. "Enhances a sense of control" will match with the following UI design principle:
    (a) Compatibility
    (b) Configurability
    (c) Consistency
    (d) Control
16. "Have a similar look" will match with the following UI design principle:
    (a) Compatibility
    (b) Configurability
    (c) Consistency
    (d) Control
17. "The effect of actions on objects should be visible" will match with the following UI design principle:
    (a) Compatibility
    (b) Configurability
    (c) Directness
    (d) Responsiveness
18. "Prevent errors from occurring whenever possible" will match with the following UI design principle:
    (a) Familiarity
    (b) Flexibility
    (c) Forgiveness
    (d) Responsiveness

19. "System's design can be used by everyone, regardless of a person's physical capabilities" will match with the following UI design principle:
    (a) Perceptibility
    (b) Operability
    (c) Predictability
    (d) Responsiveness

20. "Provide as simple an interface as possible" will match with the following UI design principle:
    (a) Perceptibility
    (b) Simplicity
    (c) Clarity
    (d) Availability

Review Questions

1. Define user interface. State the benefits of good UI.
2. Explain the factors by which user gets distracted from the computer system.
3. What are the characteristics of a good interface design?
4. Describe the various visual pleasing compositions with their qualities for good screen design.
5. Explain in detail the following principles of UI design:
    (a) Aesthetically Pleasing
    (b) Clarity
    (c) Compatibility
    (d) Forgiveness
    (e) Consistency
    (f) Robustness
    (g) Simplicity
6. Describe economics (or Human Factors) and how economics and HCI are related.
7. Write down the 8 golden rules that provide interface design.
8. What are the 4 interfaces that give name WIMP? Describe one of them in brief.
9. Give Norman's 7 that provide a useful summary of his user centered design philosophy.
10. Justify: 'Dialogue between user and System is influenced by the style of the interface'.
11. Distinguish between GUI and Web Page Design.
12. Distinguish between printed page and Web Page.
13. Explain the general principals of user interface design.
14. Apply HCI principles for designing the user interface for Automatic Ticket Vending Machine (ATVM) machine for ABC metro train. It should allow user to select the source and destination and to buy a ticket. Assume suitable data and screen elements and draw the interface.
15. Apply any five HCI principles to design the user interface for Academic Calendar and Event planner for college. It should allow student to see any event organized by the department in the college. Students should register, view the venue and select the event. The report should be generated at the end of the event and will be passed to all faculties with attendance and event details. Assume suitable data and draw interface.

CHAPTER

4

Design Guidelines: Designing with Mind in Mind

Introduction

User experience is the most important aspect of an interface design. If the user finds the interface easy to comprehend and is motivated to stay with your interface, we conclude that the user has had a good experience. Not every interface that we see these days is good. Earlier developers concentrated on the functionality of the system, and left out the part on how to expose this functionality to the user.

These days, developers are aware of this need to enhance the user experience. But our graphical interfaces are so high end that the developer may tend to over-do the features, which in return shall reduce the user experience. For example, the availability of 16 million colors in a normal operating system can also be a disadvantage. The developer may make the page extremely colorful, which will not be a good experience for the user. The interface design shown in Figure 1 in Appendix to Chapter 4 is a classic example of a poor interface design, due to over-use of colors.

An optimal use of all the graphical features available, and achieving maximum user experience, has become a challenge for every developer. Many companies have started to hire user experience designers, who can understand the human psychology, and come up with designs that will not only provide a good user experience, but can also enhance the business of the organization.

Our world is very competitive, with each one of us equipped with various skills. In applied sciences like physics or chemistry, researchers patent their research, but publishes it for future reference. But business strives on the "survival of the fittest" principle. Once a business has managed to design a successful interface, they will not share their secret with others. This makes the next designer as naïve as the first one. There is no re-use of the knowledge gained by the former designer, leading to waste of time and effort by the next.

Thus, Human Machine Interaction has emerged as a new field of studies that researches on the human psychology, analyzes human responses, and develops guidelines to create good interfaces that can provide the best user experience. This chapter covers some of the important aspects about human characteristics that are required for a good user interface.

Perception

What the user perceives is an important aspect to be considered. Perception is what human eye sees, but not necessarily the reality. Our brain has a great influence on what we see. The images in our vision are sent as signals to the brain, which in turn interprets them into something known.

Illusion and perception are related terms that are often confused with each other. Though both are not reality, they are not the same. Illusion is a distortion of our senses. Majority of the people will respond to the deception in a similar way, whereas perception is an interpretation of the inputs from our senses. It is subjective to an individual. For example, mirage is an excellent example of illusion. The refraction of light forces our vision to perceive water on a dry surface. Every single person at that spot will be able to visualize the mirage. It is not a game played by our brain on our vision. But an environment is created for the brain to believe this deception.

Perception, on the other hand, is the way in which our brain assumes the reality. Missing values can be filled in, gaps in images can be completed, spelling mistakes can be ignored, and relations between objects can be drawn based on their appearance. There cannot be any condition on the way an object can be perceived. It will totally depend on an individual and his/her context at that given instance of time.

For example, this snetecne taht you are redanig now, has a lot of sp3llnig msitaeks. Are you reading it as you see, or are you interpreting it into the correct words?

Perception is based on

- **Experience:** For example, imagine you are booking a seat online for a movie show. An image is shown to you of all the seats in the hall, with the screen and passage. You have logged well in advance for this show, and you see that all the seats are gray. We immediately assume that the hall is full, and will try to look for another show time. Even if the designer has mentioned in bold letters that the gray seats are the available ones, we ignore this text, and we conclude that the show is fully booked. After going through a lot of scrutinizing, some of us may gradually come to the understanding that the gray seats are the available ones. The designer may have used gray, as it may match the theme of the website, or it is the color of their business. But for a user, gray is perceived as an unavailable option. This perception is due to the past experience of the user, or his/her understanding of the world around him, which marks unavailability as "grayed out".

- **Current context:** In English there are many words whose meanings change based on the context it is being used in. The moment we hear the word *"heavy"*, we associate it with the weight of a product. Consider the following sentences

  There was a heavy downpour yesterday.
  These heavy duty nails are hard to drive.
  I heaved a sigh with a heavy heart.

  We perceive the meaning of a word, based on the context it is being used in.
- **Future goals:** Imagine you enter a crowded hall looking for your friend. After a long search, you finally meet him. You are relaxed now. This friend asks you if you happened to see another friend who was supposed to be in the same room. Would you have noticed? Your goal was to find this friend, which you did. You did scan the room looking for this friend's face. But did you take note of all the others in the room? Similarly when a user browses looking for a specific information, the rest of the data presented may get ignored.

Gestalt Principles

Gestalt is a German word, meaning *unified whole*. It is a set of theories developed by German psychologists on visual perception. This theory shows how human eye tends to see the object in front of it as an entire whole, instead of its parts and their details. German psychologist Kurt Koffka stated that "The whole is *other* than the sum of the parts". He refused to use the term *greater* instead of *other* in his statement, as this is not a mathematical concept. He explained that the parts as such may have some or no meaning, but the human eye tends to interpret it to a completely different object when viewed all at once. For example, Figure. 4.1(a) seems like an elegant pattern, a decorated square, while Figure 4.1(b) shows the shape used to bring this pattern. Figure 4.1(b) by itself does not make sense to the user, but a combination of these images seems like a pattern to the human eye. Our human mind always tries to make sense even out of chaos.

There is still a great deal of argument on what is perceived first, whether it is the image in the front, or the background, or both together as a whole. There are a few principles formed on this Gestalt's theory.

(a) (b)

Figure 4.1 (a) Unified whole perception. (b) Parts of the whole.

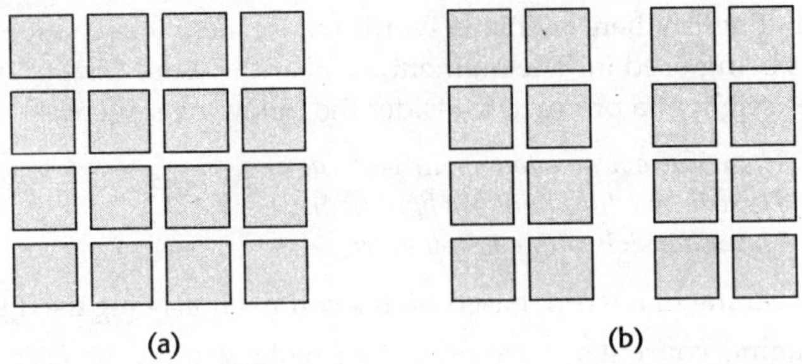

Figure 4.2 (a) One group. (b) Two groups.

1. **Proximity:** When the objects are identical in all aspects, that is, color, shape, and size, then the displacement alone of these objects will affect their purpose. Our brain tends to cluster objects that are close to each other as one group. For example, imagine you walk into a school. All children will appear the same because of their uniforms, but will not stay together. They will sit amidst their friend circles. When you see a group of children sitting together you immediately conclude that either they are all from the same class or they are a group of friends. This theory of proximity can be exploited to group objects of similar purpose together. Figure 4.2(a) will be perceived as one group of elements, while Figure 4.2(b) will be perceived as two groups.

   Moreover proximity is more powerful than color coding. In both parts of Figure 4.2 all elements are of the same color; hence you may feel they are grouped together. In Figure 4.3(a) the elements are of two different colors, and will be identified as two groups. But Figure 4.3(b) proves that proximity is more powerful than color code. Now you may assume that the black cells are highlighted elements of that group, but you will not declare them as belonging to a different group.

2. **Similarity:** Objects of similar appearance, that is, same shape, size, color, and texture, will appear to be elements of the same group. In Figure 4.4, all elements are different. There is no similarity among any of these elements. But in Figure 4.5(a), we try to find some level of similarity. We will identify all the squares as one group and the circles to be another. In Figure 4.5(b) the groups are based on the size.

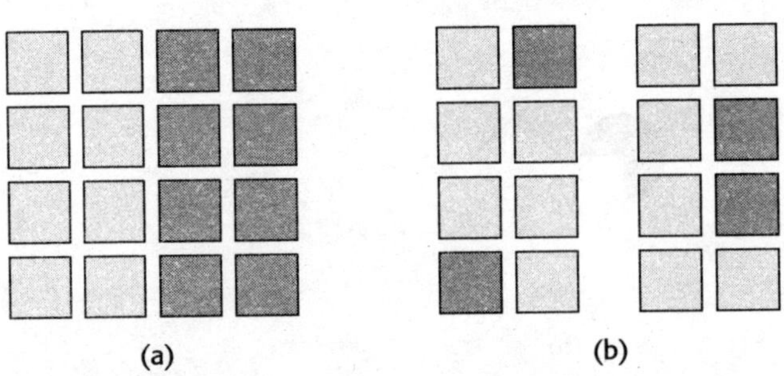

Figure 4.3 (a) Two groups. (b) Two groups only.

Figure 4.4 Different elements.

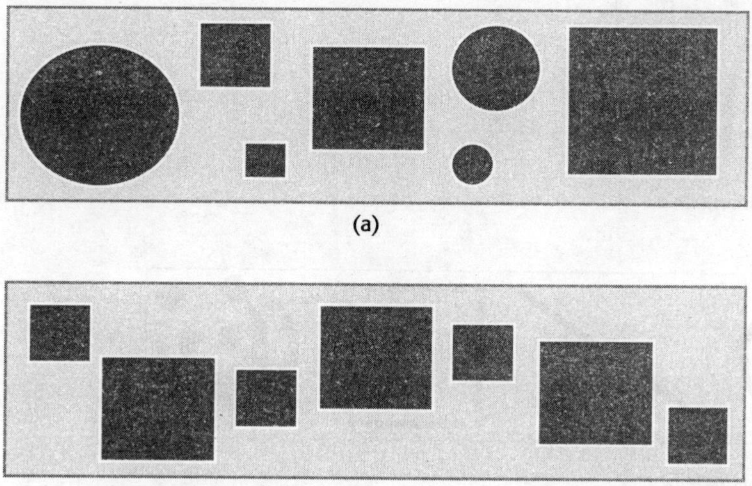

(a)

(b)

Figure 4.5 (a) Similarity based on shape. (b) Similarity based on size.

This theory can not only be used to group objects of similar purposes together, but also to show dissimilarity, as shown in Figure 4.6.

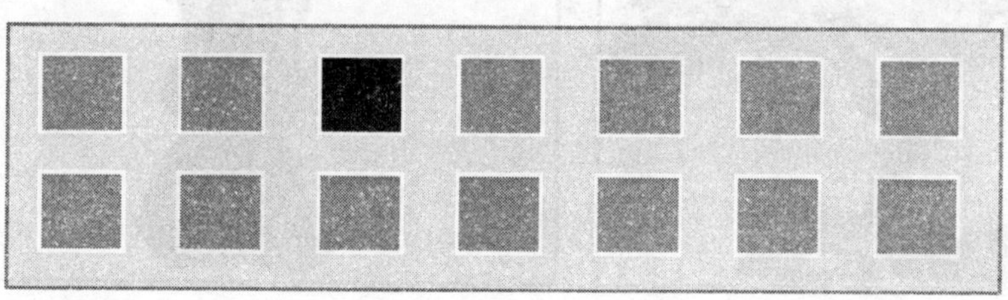

Figure 4.6 Dissimilarity.

3. **Continuity:** We do not give much importance to the gaps in an image. In Figure 4.7 though the lines are hidden behind a circle, we still assume the lines to be continuous. Similarly when you see the many railway tracks crossing each other, we are able to follow each track till the end, and do not get mixed up with the others.
4. **Closure:** Our human eye tends to complete the missing parts of an image. Circles with missing arches are seen as complete circles, or dashed lines will be seen as a solid line, as shown in Figure 4.8.

5. **Figure/Ground:** Here our mind separates the image into two parts—figure (foreground) and ground (background). Ideally the foreground has elements are of priority, while background is everything else. Figure 4.9 shows images that can seem different when viewed closely. Do you see the tree or the animals? Do you see the apple or the faces?

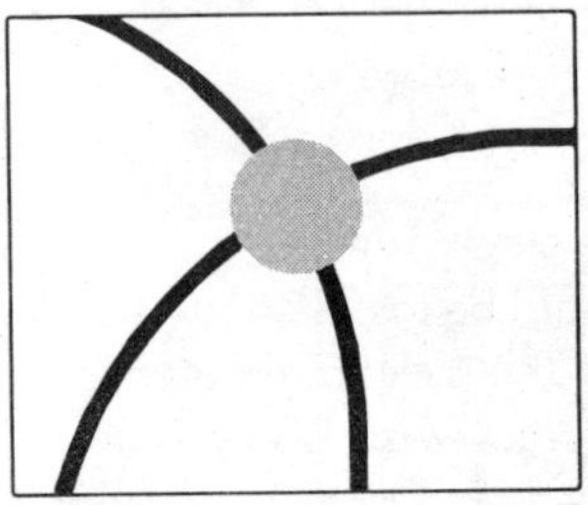

Figure 4.7 Crossing lines.

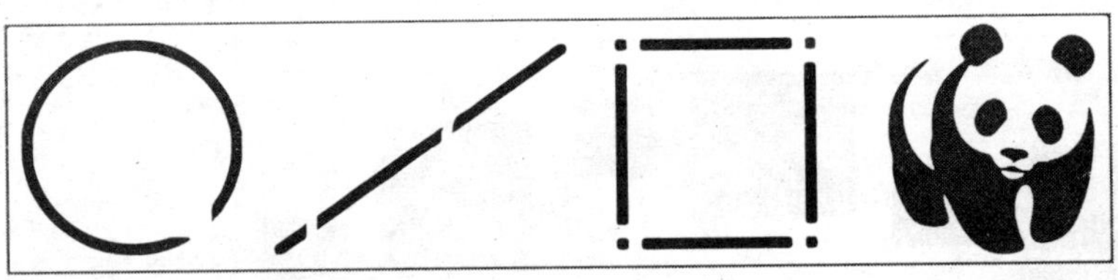

Figure 4.8 Closure.

Figure 4.9 Figure and ground.

Visual Structure

Structure Reduces Scan Time

When long numbers that are important for the user to remember have to be presented, like account numbers, customer IDs, or telephone numbers, it will be good to break

Customer ID:	**1234567890123456**

(a)

Customer ID:	**123** - **456** - **78901234** - **56** (City) (Branch) (Account no.) (Type)

(b)

Figure 4.10 (a) Single field display. (b) Multiple fields with explanation.

down the number into three-to-four digits. A better practice would be to explain to the user what each of those fields mean. This will make it easy for the user to remember the number forever. For example, you need to provide a customer with his account number of 16 digits. Figure 4.10(a) displays all the digits in a single field, while Figure 4.10(b) displays it in three fields. Which do you think will be easier for the user to remember?

Data-Specific Controls Enhance Structure

Imagine you are designing a site for resale of old furniture. As a customer who wishes to purchase second-hand furniture, one will want to locate his/her best buy by going through the least number of advertisements. His/her criteria will be price, pick-up location, and the type of furniture that he/she wants, that is, bed, sofa, wardrobe, etc. As a designer you need to ensure that the seller has mentioned all these details in his/her advertisement in such a way that the buyer is able to locate this deal.

Figure 4.11(a) presents a form for the seller to enter the details of his/her furniture. Here the seller is free to describe everything in his/her own words. All the fields such as pick-up location, type of furniture, price and contact details, are mandatory. What could be the disadvantage of this type of entry?

Your database in the backend will create a new record for each new location or furniture type. One seller will be listed under *Borivali,* while another seller will be listed under *Borivli,* even though both of them are located at the same locality. Some entries could be formed due to ignorance of spellings, and others could be typing mistakes. Some sellers will want to describe their bookshelf as a *book rack*, some as *book case* or a *bookshelf.* All these sellers intend to sell the same type of furniture, but will be stored under different categories in the database. Such errors will reduce the number of listings a buyer views on his search.

You can avoid this by limiting the seller's freedom to describe the furniture in his own words. You can create a database with common entries and that can be displayed to the seller in the form of drop down lists. Here the seller will be forced to choose one locality from the given list. This will make sure that all listings in a particular location will be displayed to the desired buyer. Figure 4.11(b) displays the same form of Figure 4.11(a) with data controls that can reduce most erroneous entries.

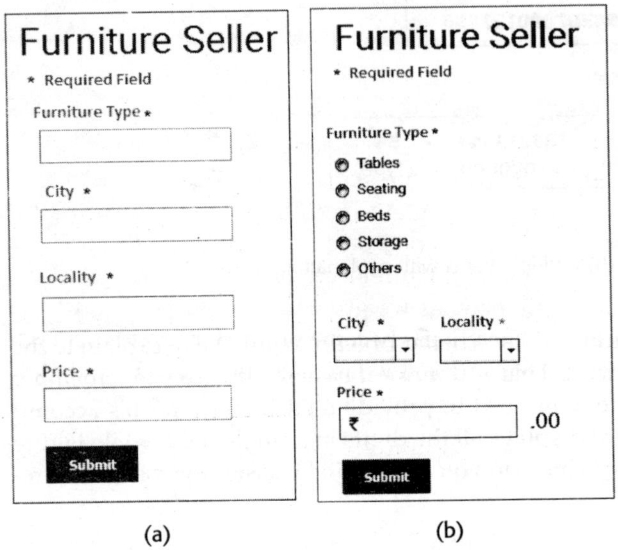

Figure 4.11 (a) Free inputs. (b) Controlled inputs.

Visual Hierarchy

When large amounts of information have to be presented to the reader, he/she will often get lost in it. The user can get confused on what he/she is looking for, or not be able to remember what he/she came here to find. When data is presented with a good structure, it is easier for him/her to locate and find what he/she wants. For example, if you want the telephone number of a particular organization, you will not like to search for it amidst the huge amounts of data about the organization. It will be easier if there is a separate tab that mentions about the contact details (Figure 4.12).

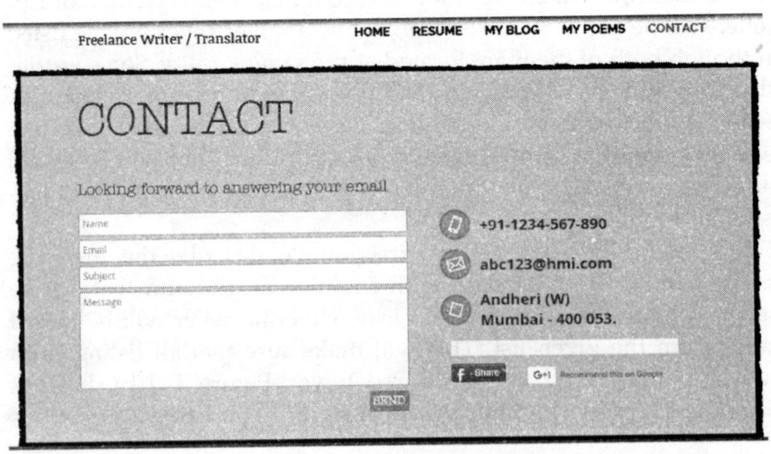

Figure 4.12 Contact tab.

Reading is Unnatural

Language versus Reading

Unlike reading and writing, the speaking and understanding of spoken language is a natural human ability because these are the skills human brain learned during the early stages of evolution for communication. As a result, normal humans are born with ability to learn the languages they are exposed to without any systematic training. The human brain develops the neural structure necessary to support the learning of a spoken language during the childhood. As we grow up, we start to learn other skills using different parts of the brain. These parts become prominent over time, decreasing our ability to learn a language. Learning a new language in adolescence is equivalent to learning a new skill. It requires a systematic training of our brain over long periods of time. Think of the way in which you learnt your mother tongue, and the way in which you learnt other languages in school. You may look around at your neighbors who have moved in from a different state for the sake of employment. While the adults still struggle to interact in the local language, their children would have gained fluency over it.

In contrast to learning a language, writing and reading do not exist in the early stages of the human brain development. Even in the process of human evolution, these skills have been acquired very late. Man, a social being, learned to communicate with each other using gestures and languages, but script is a very recent development when compared to the existence of mankind on this planet.

Human brain by itself does not show any special ability to read. Reading is an artificial skill that is learned by systematic training like playing musical instruments or balancing a bicycle, etc. Learning to read involves training the brain to recognize visual patterns. A gamut from low to high levels runs to recognize patterns that our brains learn.

Initially basic visual features are recognized by brain like shapes, lines, and contours. These do not require any special learning for their recognition. They combine to form various patterns that humans learn to identify as characters, numbers, alphabets, and other symbols. Depending on the type of script, these symbols combine and get recognized as words, and its further forms such as phrases, sentences, and paragraphs. The process of learning to read is a step-by-step and systematic training given to our brain, but not a natural process.

Feature Driven versus Context Driven

As stated earlier, reading is a trained process to recognize patterns. This can be either a bottom-up (feature-driven) process or a top-down (context-driven) process. Either shapes can be recognized as letters and words, and then interpreted to mean something. Or meaningful phrases or paragraphs can be broken down into words and characters.

In feature-driven reading, the visual system first identifies simple features like line segments in a certain orientation or curves of a certain radius on a page or display, and then combines them into more complex features, such as angles, multiple curves, shapes, and patterns. The brain recognizes certain shapes as characters or symbols representing letters, numbers, or words. In ideographic scripts, such as Chinese script *hanzi*, symbols represent entire words or concepts. In alphabetic scripts, groups of letters are perceived as morphemes and words. In all types of scripts, sequences of words are parsed into phrases, sentences, and paragraphs that have meaning. Feature-driven reading is also referred to as "bottom-up" or "context-free". Ability to identify basic features like lines or curve natural ability of brain but recognition of morphemes, words, and phrases has to be learned. Initially the identification process is non-automatic and requires conscious analysis of letters and words but after enough practice these patterns become common and the identification becomes automatic.

Context-driven or top-down reading, on the other hand, works in the opposite way. It starts with recognition of sentences or the paragraphs, and then breaking them down into words and characters. Here our brain first tries to find the meaning of the sentence or paragraph, and does not read every word in it. Try reading the below line quickly.

All that glitters is is not gold.

Invariably you would have read the above sentence as "All that glitters is not gold", and would not have noticed the repetition of "is" in the line. Here your brain first comprehends the meaning of the entire phrase, and even links it to the context in which it is used. In fact, the whole line may get interpreted into one word like *deception.* This is context-driven reading. Try reading the below lines.

Evrey night my draems, I see you, I f 1 you.**
That is how I know you go on

This is the lyrics of that famous song that was featured in the movie Titanic (1997). Most of us know the lyrics and there is no need to read. Here you would have easily overlooked the spelling mistakes and that the missing word "in", in the first line. You also know what to replace the asterisk with. You can easily read the second line even though only it is partly visible. Here the brain has pre-interpreted the meaning of the sentences before reading every word or character in it.

Now try reading the below sentence.

Sift flour before making pancakes.

Here our brain is reading every word of the sentence, putting them together and then deriving its meaning. This is feature-driven reading. Context-level reading occurs only when the phrases or concepts are familiar to the reader.

Parts of Brain Used for Reading

In recent decades, various techniques for observing the operation of functioning brains in living people have been developed. It allows researchers to observe the behavior of different areas of a brain, including the sequence in which they respond. Using these methods, researchers discovered the neural pathways involved in reading differ for novice and skilled readers. Visual cortex is first to respond for all readers and after that, the pathways diverge as explained below.

Novice: First the area of the brain above and behind Wernicke's area becomes active where alphabetic scripts such as English and Hindi, words are "sounded out" and assembled then the letters are analyzed and matched with their corresponding sounds. The word-analysis area then communicates with Broca's area and the frontal lobe, where meaning of the word is identified. For ideographic languages, where whole word is represented by symbol, and often has a graphical correspondence to their meaning, sounding out of words is not part of reading.

Advanced: For skilled readers instead of word analysis area, the area behind the ear, not far from the visual cortex (occipito-temporal), becomes active. This area recognizes words as a whole without sounding them out, and then that activates pathways toward the front of the brain that finds the word's meaning and forms a mental image.

Findings from brain scan methods do not indicate the exact processes in the brain. But the theory of use of different processes used by skilled and novice readers is widely accepted.

Poor Design Can Affect Reading

For skilled readers, bad presentation will reduce context based reading to a feature based reading. This will become a conscious effort, and decrease the efficiency of the reader. For an unskilled reader, poor presentation will lead to complete withdrawal from reading itself.

- **Uncommon or unfamiliar vocabulary:** Words that are not commonly in use should be avoided. On a car steering, you may place the symbol of a horn or write "HORN" to indicate it. If you see "TOCSIN" instead, what will you be able to make of it? On a computer interface technical jargons are used, such as "authenticate", "authorize", "default", "reboot", "processor", "malware", "ADSL", "IP", "ISP", "CPU", "RAM", "host", "pixel", "modem", "router", etc. All computer geeks may be familiar with all these terms, but for people from other domains, such as a real estate agent, furniture dealer, or a receptionist, such words become very difficult to decode and then understand the message. As a designer, it is your responsibility to make all users comfortable.

  You can use simple words and simple language to convey your information. Instead of scaring the user with "authorization failed" or "access denied", you may simply state "incorrect username or password".

  It is best to avoid abbreviations completely, unless it is a very generic one like "USA", "GMT", "AM/PM", "BC/AD" or "FM". In fact it is better to use the abbreviation in such cases, because a user may not know what "Frequency Modulation" is, but will be familiar with "FM".

- **Difficult script and typefaces:** You may be tempted to use the various fonts available and make the interface interesting. But it is important to test its readability before employing it. Our brain recognizes each symbol by its visual features.

  Is this font easy to read? It sure looks interesting, but are you not taking an extra effort to comprehend it?

  Only when the font is familiar, we move up from feature-driven reading to context-driven reading.

- **Tiny fonts:** How often do you read the "fine print" disclaimer note on an insurance form? Even though we know it is important, we still sign at the bottom of the page without reading it. Why do you think this information is presented in such small fonts? Most of the warnings and unpleasant information is part of the disclaimer. If this is presented to you in bold fonts, you will read through each line carefully and understand the implications negatively. This will scare you from buying an insurance, ever. It is an advertising tactic followed commonly by most agencies. The positive and enticing offers are in bold large fonts, while the actual risks are in extremely small fonts. The intention behind using tiny fonts should be only to ensure that your user skips this information easily.
- **Text on noisy background:** Having text written on a textured background reduces readability. Here the vision is distracted to the bright colors on the background, and the focus from the text present is lost. Compare the texts given in Figure 4.13. Which text is more readable? You may use images in the background in case of personalized greetings. Here the photographs have a greater priority over the simple "Miss you" or "Have a nice day" text messages (Figure 4.14). In all other cases, it is better to have simple, plain backgrounds.
- **Information buried in repetition:** "Two grains of rice from a bag of hay" is an old saying used when too much unnecessary information is presented. Reading the same information repeatedly, may be in different tenses, will make the reader assume there is nothing more in it. He will skip the entire section after reading a few lines. You may have presented important information later in the section, but this will be overlooked easily as a repetition.

  While writing an exam you may have experienced answering a question that you partially know. You tend to write whatever little you know repeatedly, in different voices and tenses. Why do you do this? You want to create an impression

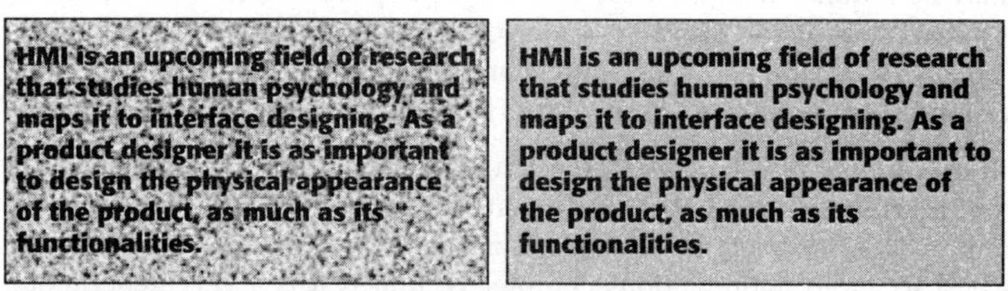

Figure 4.13 Textured and plain background.

Figure 4.14 Text on photographs.

HMI is an upcoming field of research that studies human psychology and maps it to interface designing. As a product designer it is as important to design the physical appearance of the product, as much as its functionalities.

Figure 4.15 Center aligned text.

that the rest of the answer is as valid as the little information known to you, while secretly wishing that your entire answer is not read word by word.

- **Centered text or right aligned:** Most of us are trained to read from left to right. Unconsciously our eyes jump to the exact left most point at which the previous line started. In a centered or right aligned text, each line begins at a different place. The reader has to make a conscious effort to find the beginning of each new line. Reading will not be an automatic process anymore. Try reading the text shown in Figure 4.15. Where does your eye take you at the end of each line?

  This style of presentation is encouraged in a wedding invitation or poetry, because you do not want your reader to skip even a single word of information. You want him to consciously read every word, analyze it and even remember it. Normally you want your reader to automatically read and comprehend the gist of the paragraph.

Guidelines to Support Reading

You cannot do away with only images. Comics and novels tell stories, but the effect they leave on the reader is completely different. A novel gives the freedom of imagination to the user, while a comic restricts our thinking to the image shown in front of us. Similarly a concept can be explained only using text. Can you imagine learning a new subject by just looking at a few images? You will need an interpretation of the images shown, and that will be in text.

When there is important information needs to be read by the user, it becomes the designer's responsibility to present it correctly. You want to encourage reading. Below are some guidelines to ensure you have a happy reader.

- **Avoid the poor designs discussed above:** non-standard fonts, tiny fonts, complicated backgrounds, and center or right alignments.
- **Use simple language**. You do not want your reader to refer to a dictionary at every word.
- **Use visual hierarchy**. When sections have headings and bulleted points, a reader is able to grasp the gist faster. If the same is presented in endless paragraphs, the reader will get bored and assume there is nothing important in there.

Minimize the Need for Reading

Imagine you are answering a survey questionnaire. If the questions are asked in a few words, you will be encouraged to complete the survey. If each question runs into paragraphs, will you have to patience to read each first, understand and then answer it?

As mentioned earlier, reading is not a natural process. It does need an extra level of processing as compared to images. Though you cannot omit reading completely, it is better to keep it minimal. You may use images or single words as much as possible and avoid writing sentences where ever possible.

Color

What Is Color Vision?

The retina is a surface at the back of our eye that responds to the images we see. There are two types of receptors on the retina, called *rods* and *cones*. Rods detect light levels and cones detect colors. There are about 120 million rods and six million cones and most of it is populated in the fovea region.

Rods are not much in use when we work indoors or in bright day light. In fully bright or artificially lit environments, only cones provide most of the input to the brain. We use rods only in the dark, such as on a starlit night or when we are having a candle-light dinner. Most of the time, our vision is completely dependent on our cones. You can assume that the rods can just recognize the levels of brightness of light and objects as anything that obstructs this light source. The rest of the image recognition is done by our cones.

Again cones are of three types that respond to three different wavelengths – red, green, and blue. Each cone can respond to a range of colors within a certain frequency range.

- **Low frequency cones:** Most sensitive to middle (yellow) and low (red) range of light. But this cone is sensitive to almost the entire range of light. About 64% of the cones are sensitive to this frequency and are most used by us.
- **Medium frequency cones:** Most sensitive to middle (greens and yellows) to higher range of frequencies. They are not very sensitive to the low range (reds). About 32% of the cones are sensitive to this mid-range frequency. These are less used as compared to the red cones, but are frequently in use.
- **High frequency cones:** Most sensitive to high ranges of frequencies (violets and blues), but do not respond to the middle (greens and yellows) or low (reds and orange) levels. About 2% of the cones respond to this frequency. This cone is hardly used by the retina.

This is in contrast to the working of a digital camera. Here each receptor responds to only its range of frequencies. Morgan Kauffman graphically compares how a retina and a camera respond to each frequency range. Figure 2(a) in Appendix to Chapter 4 shows how the retina responds to color, while Figure 2(b) in Appendix to Chapter 4 shows how a camera responds to color.

Since red can be sensed only by the low frequency cones, prolonged exposure to red will fatigue these cones alone, while the other cones remain unutilized. Blue, on the other hand, can be sensed by all three types of cones. This ensures equal distribution of load on the retina, and hence a relaxed vision.

Our brain has a proportional calculation applied to the inputs from the three cones to compute the color of the object in vision. The low frequency cone has the maximum participation, while the high frequency cone has the least.

Just as we have three color channels (red, green, blue), the cones also combine to produce three "color-opponent" channels, such as, red-green, yellow-blue, and black-white. These colors send a strong signal to the brain, and can be distinguished from each other faster than all other colors. The basic six colors are shown in Figure 3 in Appendix to Chapter 4.

Edge Contrast versus Brightness

We are more sensitive to difference in colors than to variations in brightness. In Figure 4 in Appendix to Chapter 4 the fonts in both blocks are of the same color, and the backgrounds are of the same level of saturation. In the first block, the font and background belong to the same hue, with a variation only in the level of saturation. While in the second block, the font and background belong to different hues. Which block is more legible?

You may even find it hard to believe that both blocks have their fonts of the same color, because the background influences your vision to think otherwise. This concept has to be retained even while designing buttons on any machine. If you want your user to take notice, then the object needs to stand out. Only contrast colors can catch the attention of the human eye. You may try to maintain the appearance of your model with monochromatic designs, but usability should be the aim.

Presentation of Colors

Our ability to identify colors totally depends on the way they are presented to us. We are easily able to overlook a caterpillar on a leaf or a chameleon. This is because the contrast between the two objects is so low that from a distance we are not able to distinguish them. Only after we make a keen observation they become visible to us. The number of colors we can identify totally depends on the way it is presented to us. There are three main factors that affect our ability to distinguish colors:

1. **Low saturation:** When two shades of very low saturation are placed next to each other, we are hardly able to distinguish between them. You may observe the walls in your house. It is a good practice to use light colors on walls, so that the rooms look bigger and more light is reflected by them. Mostly three walls are painted with a pale shade, and the fourth wall is painted in contrast. How would it be if you were to paint the fourth wall too with another pale shade? Figure 5(a) in Appendix to Chapter 4 shows two pale shades next to each other. Colors are different, blue and green. They fall in different ranges of the spectrum, but the saturation levels of both are same. Are you able to identify the difference between them in a glimpse?
2. **Patch size:** When the size of the object is very small, we will not be able to identify its exact color. In Figure 5(b) in Appendix to Chapter 4, it is not easy to

distinguish the color of the smaller circles, while it is easy to identify the shades in the bigger circles. Similarly fonts have a very small area, and it is not easy to identify the color on it.

3. **Distance:** Proximity of the objects also makes it hard for us to identify its color. In Figure 5(c) in Appendix to Chapter 4 the brown patches that are away from each other will look like they are of the same color. Only when observed together, we are able to discriminate between the shades. This is the identical twin effect. You will not be able to identify who you are interacting with if you meet only one of them. But when they are together, you will be able to notice the small differences in them.

Color Blindness

People who are color blind are not completely incapable of recognizing colors. It is a difference in the way our brain calculates the inputs from our cones. Most commonly red/green blindness is noticed. The cones of low frequency or middle frequency do not provide adequate input to the brain.

Figure 6 in Appendix to Chapter 4 gives the distribution of cone cells in the fovea of an individual with normal color vision and a color blind. Note that the center of the fovea holds very few blue-sensitive cones in either case. There is also a blue/purple blindness, black/blue blindness, and red/black blindness.

In red/green blindness, the following pairs cannot be distinguished:

- Dark red from black
- Blue from purple
- Light green from white
- Green from khaki

While designing interfaces, it is important to consider all types of users. You cannot design a pie chart with blue and purple next to each other, and make your color blind user feel incompetent. The best way to check if the colors chosen are appropriate is to convert the image to grayscale. If you are able to distinguish the colors there, then your product is good to go!

Factors that Affect Colors

- **Variations in display units:** Digital systems have various display technologies that depend on its drivers, hardware, and operating systems. The color chosen by the designer need not always be the color viewed by the user. You may have chosen beige, but your user can see it as yellow. Similar differences can happen on machines. The intended color may not be possible to create by the manufacturer of your product.
- **Grayscale displays:** Most of the displays are color today, but there are requirements to print too. Not always a color printer is available. Hence the designer should also consider a grayscale version of the display. Figure 4.16 is the

Figure 4.16 Grayscale image.

grayscale image of Figure 4 in Appendix to Chapter 4. Since the saturation is same, the two blocks look exactly identical.

- **Display angle:** Many display units give a better vision when viewed from the front, than from an angle. The colors are poorly displayed, or inversely displayed when viewed from a different angle.
- **Ambience:** Most of us have this experience of sunlight falling on our computer or television screens. The display gets blurred, and we almost immediately get up to draw the curtains. In artificially lit environments, the colors may be displayed as intended, but it will be wrong to assume all your users will always be indoors.

Vision

Fovea versus Peripheral Vision

Fovea is a very small depression on the surface of the retina that forms the focal point. It occupies about 1% of the area on the retina, but is responsible for providing more than 50% of the visual input to the brain. Unlike a digital camera where all types of receptors are spread uniformly throughout the entire surface, the fovea is completely saturated with cones, but does not have any rods. As we move away from the fovea to the rest of the retina, the number of cones keeps decreasing while the number of rods increases. The center of the fovea has only red and green cones. As we move a few millimeters away from the center, blue cones start to appear. Rods are saturated on the outer edges of the retina, and they are responsible for our peripheral vision. Our peripheral vision responds only to the changes in light levels and not to the changes in color.

Notice the reaction of our eyes when exposed to a heavy beam of light. You go blind for a few moments after that. This is because in normal lighting we use our cones for vision. When the beam hits our eye, rods take over the control. A chemical reaction takes places in the retina that shifts the controls from rods to cones and cones to rods. The changes in light levels induce this chemical reaction. Our eyes usually take a few seconds to adjust when we move between places of different light levels. We can also call this chemical reaction as a shift from our foveal vision to peripheral vision or vice versa. The control is passed on to the peripheral vision only when there is a drastic change in the level of lighting. Else we mostly use the fovea for vision.

Figure 7 in Appendix to Chapter 4 gives a pictorial idea of the distribution of the rods and cones over the retina. The central part contains only red and green cones. The next circle contains all three cones, with minimal blue cones. Rods are shown here in yellow and they saturate gradually as we move from the fovea. Everyone has a blind spot on the retina where there are absolutely no rods or cones.

As you read this page, notice that you are shifting your eye from one word to another. Or are you able to read the entire page without any eye movement? If you were to click a picture of this page using your camera, you will be able to do it in one shot, but your eye will not be able to do it. Our foveal vision is so small that it can capture only a few words at a time. While you look at one word, the rest of the page and your environment fall in your peripheral vision.

Use of Peripheral Vision

Most of the useful input is provided by the fovea. The peripheral vision has only rods which are not required most of the time. Then you might wonder about the purpose of this area of vision.

Imagine drawing a line with a pencil. You may assume the tip of your pencil as our foveal vision, and the hand dragging the pencil as our peripheral vision. With this analogy you can understand the need for the peripheral vision. It guides our fovea to the next object that needs to be viewed.

Since peripheral vision has more of rods, it will respond only to light level changes. Objects that blink or move bring a variation in the level of light from that particular region. This can catch the attention of rods. Due to the absence of cones in the peripheral region, color changes do not come into notice. Hence stationary objects in the peripheral view are as good as they not being there.

You may have noticed this while playing "hidden object" games. You may spend hours searching for a particular object which is right in front of you. The object is placed in a way that is not so easy to identify. When you decide to give up and ask for help, the object starts to blink. The motion is easily identified by our eyes, and we click on the object.

Using this concept, you can force your user to shift his attention to the next object of your choice. You need to catch his attention through some movement. This can be used to guide the user through your system. Without referring any instruction manual, the user will be able to work in the same order that you intended for him.

Making Messages Visible

The common practices followed to ensure a message is seen by your user are as follows:

- **Display it where the user is currently looking.** In a GUI, you need to predict the most probable location of the user's view and place the message there. In machine interfaces the display unit is limited to a small area. Here you may use the entire space to display critical messages. This will ensure your user sees it, and it does not get ignored.
- **Indicate error clearly.** Humans prefer to get a gist of the message before reading every word of it and understanding it. They are not academicians. Placing symbols as shown in Fig. 4.17 to indicate the type of message will convey the meaning immediately. This will help the user take corrective measures instead of losing interest in your systems.

Figure 4.17

- **Use of red.** Red always alerts the user and catches their attention easily. A blinking red object is sure to interrupt users' activities and attract them. Too much of red can scare your user to even abandon the system. So use red sparingly, but meaningfully.
- **Pop-up messages.** This is hard to overlook by anyone. It will appear in front of the screen where the user is working. Use this only for critical messages. You do not want to jerk your user out of his chair for typing a wrong password.
- **Use of sound.** Even a small beep will catch the attention faster than most visual gimmicks. User will immediately be alarmed that his/her action was wrong, and he/she will take a corrective measure. The sound sends a signal to the user's brain that his/her action was a mistake or unauthorized. Again this is a powerful method of interruption, and should be used as sparingly as possible. You do not want to embarrass your user at his/her work place by making him/her look like a technologically challenged idiot or a hacker!
- **Flash or blink.** When an object flashes or blinks, there is a change of light level in that area. This catches the attention of the peripheral vision, which will immediately draw to the fovea to that point. You can use this for important notifications that the user should not miss. Too many blinking objects can be a distraction and can make your user forget why he/she is on that page.

Memory

Short- versus Long-Term Memory

Short-term memory retains information for a few seconds, up to about a minute, while long-term memory retains information for longer periods of time, that is, hours, days, months, and years. In a computer, we can call the cache memory as short term, and other memory devices such as RAM, hard disk, DVDs, flash drives, etc., to be long term.

Earlier theories have proved these two functions of a human brain are distinct, and memory cells are located at different parts of the brain. This theory is proved by memory loss patients. They either suffer from short-term memory loss or long-term memory loss. Also, the pace at which we forget new things and the amount of experiences we are able to recollect from our past, totally contrast the retention capacities of the brain. So we may assume these two memories to be two different entities. In Figure 4.18 the relation between sensory organs and memory is depicted.

Figure 4.18 Earlier memory definition.

But modern researchers prove that both short-term and long-term memories belong to the same storage function, and are stimulated by perception. Perception is the information computed by the brain from the inputs obtained from our sensory organs. Each sensory organ dumps its information into a specific sensory modality area. Here only low-level features are detected, such as contrast edges, diagonal lines, high pitched tones, sour taste, and the color red or rightward directions. These features are sent to a downstream area where they combine to form high-level features, such as friend Amy, apple, fear, duck, etc.

Perception also Largely Depends on the Context

When you are on a dance floor and you hear loud, fast paced music, you respond to it with grace. You automatically shake a limb or two in its rhythm. But your response to the same song will be completely different if it is played in your bedroom while you are trying to read something important. On the dance floor the song is perceived with pleasure, while in your bedroom it is perceived with annoyance.

Similarly, darkness in a familiar place can induce lust or sleep but in an unfamiliar place, it will bring fear. Or a chocolate offered to you by your friend will have a totally different response as compared to that when it is offered to you by a complete stranger. The chocolates are same, and may even be of your preference, but your response will not be the same. Your friend's gesture will be perceived as care or love and will be accepted happily. But the stranger's gesture will not be welcomed so warmly.

Characteristics and Implications of Short Term Memory

Short-term memory is characterized by its low storage capacity and its high volatility.

George Miller, a psychologist, proposed in 1956 the theory of *"The Magical Number Seven, Plus or Minus Two"*. Here Miller measures the amount of information that can be stored in our short-term memory to be around five to nine *chunks*. A chunk is any piece of meaningful information, a symbol, an image, a word, a character, a name, a person, a place, a sound, an odor, or any such item. About five to nine unrelated chunks of information can be stored by an individual for about 20–30 seconds. For a person familiar with a language, a chunk can be word or even a phrase. But for a person who is not familiar with that language, each letter could also be a chunk. Try the following exercise to realize this concept.

Read the line given below and close this book. Get up from your chair and walk five steps and come back. Now write down what you had read.

silke Hersteller sind die reichsten Leute in der Stadt.

How many words were you able to recollect? The above sentence is in Deutsche. The same sentence is translated in English below. Now try the same exercise on this.

Silk manufacturers are the richest people in the city.

How difficult was it for you to recollect every word of this sentence?

A similar effect can be noticed when we are reading the map of a known and an unknown city. You will be able to remember most of the roads and localities on the map of a known city, but you will hardly be able to recollect one or two names from the map of an unfamiliar city. The same thing happens with sounds. If you listen to a set of sounds that compile into a musical tune, you will be able to reproduce this music. Here the entire tune can be considered as one chunk of information. But if you hear a few sound notes that are not connected, it will not be that easy to recollect them, as each sound will get stored as a separate chunk in our memory.

Volatility is the other critical feature of short-term memory. You may assume that as new information comes in, the old data gets wiped out. Do not relate the concept of short-term memory to a digital storage device. It is not always so that the new data shall overwrite the oldest data. Here new neurons will store the new information and start to provide input to the brain. Connections from the older neurons will be cut off from providing inputs. Most of the time, neurons with information that are unfamiliar or unconnected will be chosen to let go. Since we lose input from the older neurons, we forget the information stored in it. We lose track of our actions. Sometimes we just cannot remember why we entered a room, or why we started a certain conversation.

Design Implications of Short Term Memory Characteristics

Since we know the low storage capacities and the high volatility of human memory, we have to make interfaces that can help the user to remember his/her actions and proceed towards accomplishing his/her goal. A few factors affect the usability of a design with respect to a human's limited and volatile memory.

- **Mode:** An application can be presented to the user in more than one mode. This provides more functionality with lesser controls. For example, in the *Paint* program of Microsoft, a click-and-drag operation can select an area of the image, perform free-hand drawing or pre-defined shapes like rectangle or circles, depending upon the mode selected by the user at that point in time. Since the same control is reused, it becomes easier for the user to learn this control and use it freely. But this can also be the cause of errors, as user may forget which mode he/she is right now in. He/she may intend to select an area, but will land up drawing a line on it.

  These errors can be minimized by providing a continuously, visible feedback to the user about the mode he/she is currently in.
- **Search results:** People search for something, but often forget their own search criteria. Unless the interface displays to the user his/her search criteria, the user

will blame the system to be pulling out the wrong results. The display of his/her criteria reduces the burden on his/her brain to remember it.

- **Instructions:** It is not easy for the human mind to remember all the instructions to be followed. Imagine you are trying your hand at *Origami*, the Japanese paper folding art, for the first time. You want to make a lotus. There are about 14 steps in it. Would you prefer to read all the instructions first, close the manual, and then start folding your paper? Or would you prefer to read one instruction, do it alongside, and then read the next instruction?

If a task has a lot of steps to be performed, it is always better to take the user one step at a time, instead of loading him/her with all the information at the beginning.

Characteristics and Implications of Long-Term Memory

Long-term memory does not specify how long. There is no time bound on this storage. It can be from a few hours up to infinity. It stores information for periods longer than the short-term memory, although functionality is slightly different. Here memories are not stored in one neuron, or one in pattern, or in one location. Many related patterns overlap to form a memory. They activate each other. You can assume this as a distributed storage. But this is prone to a lot of weaknesses, such as the following:

- **Error prone:** Perceptions bias memory. The recording may not be accurate. Only a meaning or feeling will get stored forever, and not necessarily the event. In analogy to computers, you can assume long-term memories as highly compressed forms of storage.

  It need not be true that the event actually happened to you. You may have experienced that joy or grief, and recorded that feeling. Later in life you believe that was your experience. For example, I clearly remember a day of my childhood when I had fallen off the staircase and hit my head on a bucket. But my mother says it happened to my sister. One of us is wrong now.

  Similarly, you may remember that it is possible to insert slide numbers in a PowerPoint presentation. But you forgot how to actually do it. Only a part of the event is recorded in your memory.

- **Impressionist:** Each memory is stored in a different level of detail. The perception that affected you most emotionally, will get stored more in detail. You may still remember your first day at nursery school, where the pain of getting separated from your mother for the first time was unbearable. But you may have forgotten your first day at college. Storage based on emotional value will not be accurate. In fact, the emotional factors at the time of recording or retrieval can also alter the memories.

- **Free associative:** Since every memory is not stored as a single unit, we are free to associate any memory along with any other memory. You may link events of different times to be one continuous event. I clearly remember the day I got chicken pox was the same day my sister got admitted in a hospital for typhoid. Reality check: I got chicken pox in my fourth grade, and my sister got typhoid in her fourth grade. We have an age difference of three years between us.

- **Idiosyncratic:** We remember each person for a particular trait, like that nosy aunt, that funny uncle, or that shabby cousin, etc. I remember my aunt had caught me sneaking out of my house at one time. My sister says it was the neighbor who caught me, and my aunt was not even in town at that time. My notion about my aunt is "being nosy". Since only a nosy person keeps track of others, the event of me getting trailed got associated with her.
- **Retroactively alterable:** When reminiscing your childhood with your best friend about a mischief that you both had planted together, you will argue that it was your idea, while your friend will claim it to be theirs. Both of you may even gathered enough evidences to prove yourselves. Our long-term memory stores the details that fit our concept. It does not need what actually happened.

The most important characteristic is we require external aids to remember. Old school records hinted that my chicken pox and my sister's typhoid were not on the same day. We rely on calendars, diaries, ledgers etc., to recollect old events. Humans are known to be dependent on such tools right from the beginning of time. Excavations have revealed knotted ropes, cave paintings, etc., that suggests our requirement for external help to remember.

Design Implications of Long-Term Memory Characteristics

Technology has various tools that can aid one to remember, such as alarms, calendars, diaries, blogs, cameras, timers, and many more. Designers have realized this need of humans, and have provided various ways to augment our memory.

The only task with which interactive systems burden our memory is by asking us to remember passwords. We can neither write it down, nor can we share it with anyone. If we write it down, then we need to place that note in a safe place, not reachable by others and unforgettable to us.

Earlier ATM pins had a lot of restrictions on them. They would instruct the user to choose a pin that was easy to remember, had 6–10 digits, could not have started with a 0, and could not have been the user's birthdate. This burdened the user to not only remember an unfamiliar number, but also the number of digits in it. Today, all pins are 4 digits, and do not have any such restrictions. You are free to use your birthdate too, as long as you feel safe, and you can remember it.

Consistency also helps long-term memory. Since we know the idiosyncratic nature of our mind, we can exploit this by making sure certain traits never change. When you develop a new application, you do not want to introduce new keyboard short cuts for copy and paste.

Six Behavioral Patterns

- We focus on our goals and pay little attention to our tools. You reach home after a long day and you are desperate to have a cup of tea. You go to the kitchen, pick up the first utensil you see on the rack, and start preparing your tea. At that moment would you be interested in learning all the additional functionality your stove can provide? Or would you be interested in getting the water boiled?

Most of us these days have got hooked on to Whatsapp. It has become the most preferable way to socialize. Have you realised all the changes that Whatsapp has gone through since it was introduced? You sure may have noticed a few, but not necessary all. Your goal is to chat with a friend. Little do we realize all the latest updates that got incorporated in it.

Similarly, when you want to type a document, you will be interested in getting your hands on a text editor. You will not be exploring all the features of the editor at that time. The basic features will suffice your need.

- We use external aids to keep track of what we are doing. Most of us use an *expense manager* to note our expenses. Earlier, people used to write them down on books. But to remember all our expenses was never considered as efficient. We use *To-Do* lists to plan out our tasks or checklists to ensure everything is remembered. Though a human brain is very powerful, it still has limitations. The short-term memory characteristics indulge a user to seek help from external aids.

  Even simple actions like inserting a bookmark in a half-read novel, or using fingers or objects for counting, shows how little we are able to remember the status of our activities.

- We follow information "scent" toward our goal. Again, take the example of making tea. The ingredients of your interest in the kitchen will be tea leaves and sugar. The rest of the spices or grains neatly stacked and displayed on your rack will even go unnoticed. Your next interest will be on finding your tea cup and a strainer. Since your goal is to have a cup of tea, only those items that are involved in its process will catch your attention, and nothing else.

  Similarly when you are trying to book a ticket for a movie show, keywords such as "choose seats" or "make payment" will catch your attention. The rest of the advertisements and offers spread over the screen will be of little interest to you at that time.

- We prefer familiar paths. As the saying goes "all roads lead to Rome", there may be more than one route to reach your destination. But when you are in a hurry, you will always take the most familiar route, even when you know that it is not the shortest route.

  Similarly in the exams, you will solve a problem in the same way that you have practiced it. Even if your friend has taught you a shorter and easier way to solve the same problem in half the time, minutes before the exam, you still will not risk trying that method in the exam.

  Even though we know change is inevitable, we still resist it for as long as it can be managed.

  To book a travel ticket when you are in a hurry, you will always go to the site that you are most familiar with. And will follow the same process as before, that is, first pick the source and destination cities, then the dates, then airlines, then enter passenger details, and then make the payment. You do not want to skip or postpone any step, or let the system choose it automatically for you. You want to be sure that you make the right choice because most flight tickets are expensive and non-refundable.

- Our thought cycle: goal, execute, evaluate. The seven stages of action are explained in Chapter 1. We first form a goal. Then execute it by planning, specifying and performing. Then we evaluate the action by perceiving, reflecting and comparing it with the goal. If the action did not suffice the goal, repeat the process with another action. This cycle can go on until the goal is met.

  Every single action, big or small, is performed through these stages. Bigger goals are broken down into smaller goals and then executed.
- After we achieve a task's primary goal, we often forget clean-up steps. The goal-execute-evaluate cycle mostly works with the short term memory because this is the current action in hand, and our full attention is focused on it. Based on the task in hand, our focus keeps shifting from higher goals to lower goals, and then back to higher goals. Since volatility is the prime characteristic of short term memory, the moment a goal is achieved, everything related to it is wiped out.

  You may often notice people forget to
  - Take their keys off the door after opening it.
  - Switch off the lights before leaving home.
  - Return the stranger's pen after signing.
  - Log out of their inbox before leaving the cyber cafe.
  - Close quotation marks at the end of the quote.
  - Close the containers after use.

  These people call themselves absent-minded. The truth is their attention shift is faster. Their brain concludes a task to be completed as soon as the goal is ticked, and everything related to it is erased. The goal to enter the house is completed the moment the door opens, and so, the key remains on the door itself.

  This behavior of humans is quite predictable, and can be avoided with a smart design. Your interface can prompt the user to complete the task. ATM machines beep when the card is not collected back from the system within a few seconds. MS Word prompts you to save the file before closing it.

Recognition and Recall

Recognition is Easy but Recall is Hard

Has this ever happened to you when you suddenly remember an event from your past, you are not able to recollect who was along with you on that day? Instead when you meet a person from the past, you are able to recollect them along with some events of that time?

To understand why and how this happens, we need to understand what is recognition and recall.

Sensory organs send signals to the brain which cause a neural pattern to be formed giving the human a perception. Stored neural patterns are mapped with these perceptions, giving the human a feeling of recognition. When a perception is similar to the stored pattern in our memory, it becomes easier to stimulate that neural pattern.

Repeated activation of the same neural patterns makes them easier for reactivation. Thus, we can define recognition as a mapping of perceptions to long-term memory.

For example, humans living in the wild can hear a bush movement and know if it is a deer or a tiger. The sound generated by the movement in the bushes is sent as signals to the brain, creating a neural pattern. This pattern is matched with the other sound patterns that are stored in the memory. The closest match will be activated, and the human is able to recognize the sound. This retrieved sound pattern is associated with an animal, deduced out of his/her past experience. Hence the sound perceived from the bushes gets recognized as a deer.

Recall, on the other hand, is a trial to reactivate old neural patterns without any input pattern. It is like performing a search without a keyword. You randomly go through all the files of a folder. People do recall memories without any perceptual input. But this happens in random, and can rarely be caused intentionally.

Most children dislike History because they need to remember people they have never met, and times they have never been in. A conscious effort is made to create these neural patterns, store them and reactivate them as often as possible, so that it can be recalled when required. Similarly, we call certain people as witty, or with a good presence of mind. These people are able to reactivate stored neural patterns more quickly. The more often you reactivate patterns, the quicker you are able to access them. Either way, recall is not a natural activity. It is a systematically trained process of our brain.

Design Implications

Graphics can create a perception that can be recognized. We need not strain the user to recall things from his memory.

- **See and choose is better can recall and type.**
  Imagine you are looking for an old photograph that was saved in your computer years back. Which will be easier? To go through all the saved images and find it or to remember its name and search for it?

  These days, our mobile phones save people with their photographs. When you hear the name "Riya", you try your best to recall who this person was. But when the image of Riya is in front of you, you immediately know who she is. Sometimes, as we flip through our contacts we suddenly remember to make that call we had forgotten about. Many times we sit and wonder "who was I supposed to call at that time?"

  Of course GUI has replaced text based screens successfully. Now we don't have to remember commands like "dir" and "cp". We just open a folder, view its contents, and copy/paste it to where required.

- **Use pictures wherever possible to convey function.**
  Images are a natural way of recognition, as compared to reading. Though text gives freedom of imagination to the user, it is very subjective. No two people imagine the same thing.

  Imagine you are given two options "save to disk" or "save to drive". There are no supporting images. Each person will have a different explanation. Someone who is familiar with cloud computing will immediately understand this

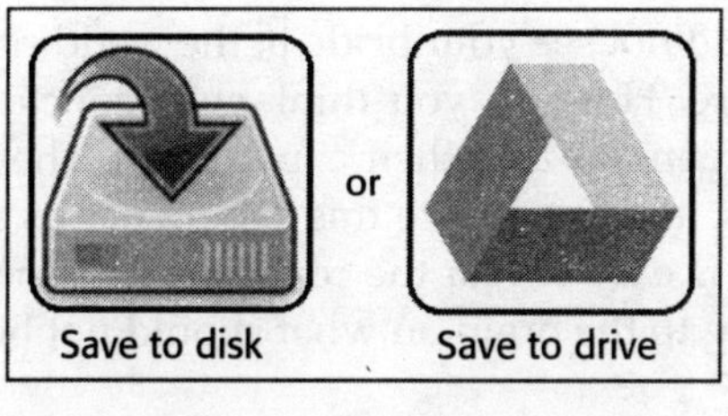

Figure 4.19 Save to disk or drive?

difference. For novice users, these two options will look the same, because both hard-drive and hard-disk refer to the same storage component. One may even assume that "save to drive" is to save on the hard-drive, while "save to disk" is to write on a CD. All such ambiguities are removed when supported with an image, as shown in Figure 4.19.

Learning

Three Brains

Brain is an organ that is found in every living organism on this planet. The variance in the level of development of brain brings the difference in the species. Human brain has three parts, and each has its own functionality and importance.

- **Old brain:** Also called the animal brain. It is reflexive in nature. It classifies everything in three classes—edible, danger or sexy. It handles the involuntary actions of our body, such as breathing, digestion, etc. This brain can be found in all living beings—from microorganisms to human beings. It is located at the part where spinal cord enters the base of the brain.
- **Mid brain:** Also called the emotional brain. It is reactive in nature. It reacts to everything with an emotion, such as joy, sadness, fear, aggression, anger, apprehension, etc. This brain is found in most birds and lower mammals. It is located in between the old brain and the new brain, that is, the cortex.
- **New brain:** Also called as intelligence. It is analytical in nature. It controls intentional, purposeful and conscious activity, including planning. This brain is found only in evolved mammals like apes, monkeys, dolphins, whales, elephants and humans. Human mind is more rational than other animals and uses this brain more than the other species. It is located in the cortex region.

For humans, the mid brain has a greater level of influence. Hence our actions and behaviors are affected by our emotions.

Learning from Experience is Easier

We have grown up listening to a lot of superstitions like "broken mirror indicates accident", or "black cat crossing your way brings bad luck", or "seven is a lucky number", or "thirteen is an unlucky number", or "you should not see your bride in the wedding gown before the wedding", and many such more. How do you think such conclusions have been drawn? Humans have a habit of generalizing their experiences. They observe their environments, analyze their actions, and generalize this experience as a fact. Since most of us react from our mid brain, it is easy to fear the consequences and not repeat the experience. This becomes a learning to the brain on what should not be done or what can be done.

But this type of learning from our experiences or others' is not perfect because:

- **Complex situations:** Most of the time our environment is unpredictable with many factors to affect it. If only one aspect is considered based on a certain experience, the situation need not yield the same results. For example, stock market prices.
- **Self-experience:** Experiences from our own lives or our close ones have greater impact, than what we hear or read about. You may have read or heard many times to avoid *thirteen*, but you will believe it completely only when something goes wrong drastically after choosing it. Similarly, you may read a lot of reviews about a university being good, but you will dare to apply to it only when a friend, who is studying there, approves of it.
- **Learning from mistakes:** "To err is human" is a fact. The mid brain makes a human react emotionally to situations. Making mistakes is not always the problem, but not learning the right lesson from it is far more damaging. Moreover, humans easily forget their actions, and tend to repeat their mistakes too.
- **Over-generalization:** Learning from experience is the way most of the organisms survive. In lower mammals these experiences are saved in their genes as instincts. A new born cat will be scared of a long, black wire. The earlier generations of cats have the experience of dealing with snakes and this has been saved in its memory. The cat is made to react to the wire by this instinct. The old brain and mid brain can store experiences, and influence our action. There is no need for a cortex to learn from experience. Humans are more evolved, and are able to rationalize their surroundings better. We do not react by our instincts, but the quality of generalizing our experiences still remain.

Performed, Learned Actions are Easy

To perform any action for the first time, we use our cortex. We analyze the situation and understand it. We are completely conscious at each step and are constantly deriving conclusions about our actions. But once this experience is gained, it gets saved in our old and mid brains. Repeated exposure to the same task, gradually reduces the usage of the new brain, and increases the usage of our old and mid brains. For example, riding a bicycle. When you are trying it for the first time, the amount of analysis your brain does and the learning it gains are tremendous. Every single movement of your body is observed, and its implications are stored. Your new brain is completely put to task. But once you gain the balance, the new brain does not have any further role to play. The old and mid brains take over, making cycling an involuntary action for you. Soon you listen to songs while you cycle your way home.

Many such day-to-day activities have become involuntary without us realizing, like brushing teeth, playing a musical instrument, riding a geared automobile, or using the computer mouse, etc.

Problem Solving and Calculation are Hard

Problem solving is the most intellectual process of a human. It requires control over most fundamental skills. Most animals, birds and other living organisms have only the old brain and the mid brain. With this they are able to perform all the involuntary actions, and also react to stimuli. Their reaction is predictable, as they learn from experience: Some of their own, and some of their ancestors, instincts. They can never handle a situation in a different or an innovative way. Problem solving, on the other hand, is trying to handle a situation in a way that was never done before. To think of a solution that was never known before. Only a new brain is capable of handling such complexity.

Imagine a dog stuck alone in an elevator that has caught fire. What would it do? Bark to call for help. Run away from the fire. Try to dig the elevator floor with its paws. Keep barking until help comes its way.

Imagine a man stuck alone in an elevator that has caught fire. What would he do? Bang on the door to call for help. Try to force open the doors. Press all the buttons repeatedly. Bang on the door some more. When all the known methods seem to fail, the realization will dawn on him that if he does not do something different soon, the fire will consume him. This is when the new brain takes over. He will try to explore the air vent even though he has never done this before.

Problem solving requires new neural patterns to be constructed. The old patterns contribute in the formation of this pattern. This process is always context based, and occurs only during a necessity. Problem solving is a whole process which includes problem-finding, problem-shaping and problem-solving. In simple terms, we can define problem solving as, reaching to a goal from our current state.

Problems are of two types

- Well defined (mathematical): Playing a chess game.
  - The current state is clear.
  - Only a finite set of operations are available, i.e., there are rules.
  - The goal is definite.
- Ill defined (personal): "I want a well settled future."
  - Current state keeps varying, with our tasks.
  - Infinite possibilities, no rules.
  - Goal keeps moving from higher to lower, and vice versa.

Factors Affecting Learning

In the previous section we saw how our brain learns. Anything done for the first time is a controlled and conscious effort by the new brain. After a long process of observation and analysis, conclusions are drawn and saved as experiences. Only after the new brain disengages itself, and the mid brain takes charge of the action, we can call it an involuntary or automatic activity. This in short can be called as learning. There are many factors that affect this process.

1. We learn faster when operation is task-focused, simple, and consistent. We know that repeated exposure to the same action makes it an automatic activity. To repeat a certain experience, it is necessary to reproduce the same environment. To learn to use a tool, we must learn to translate our desired action into the functionality provided by the tool. For example, you want to speak to your friend over the telephone. You need to translate this person into his/her phone number and dial it onto the keypad of your phone. Or if you want some cash in hand, you need to translate this requirement into the options provided by an ATM machine.

   There is always a gap between what a user wants, and what options a tool provides. This is called as "Gulf of Execution" by Norman. A person who wants to use this tool has to make an explicit, cognitive effort to learn the options provided, their consequences and map to his/her requirements. This effort usually distracts the user from actually performing the task. For example, a person has been driving a gearless vehicle for many years and is comfortable with its balance and road judgement. His/Her consciousness will be used only on choosing the best route to reach a particular place. Suddenly if he is given a geared vehicle, his consciousness will be more on the clutch and gears, and less on the roads or reaching his destination. A similar experience is shared by most of us, when we had to shift from Windows 7 to Windows 8.

   (a) Task analysis:

   - First you need to understand the goal of the user. For example, "I want some cash", or "I have to go to London", or "I need a house", can be the goals of users.
   - Next research on the ways in which your user achieves these goals currently. To buy a house, your user goes to a particular locality and tells the agent his/her requirements. The agent shows the available houses based on his/her criteria. User views these places and makes a decision to purchase it or not.
   - Rank the tasks based on their importance. First find the requirements about the house. Then find appropriate houses. Show the houses to the users. Ask for his/her decision.
   - Decide the sub-steps in each task. List the points to be considered when collecting the requirements from the user about his/her dream home; his/her locality of interest, budget, etc.
   - Find the result of each task. You will know your user's preferred locality.
   - Decide how to use these results. Filter the listed properties based on this locality.

- Decide the user of each task. Buyer lists the requirements of the house. Seller lists the available properties. Agent connects the buyers to the sellers.
- Know how these tasks are currently done. The agent writes down the details of the properties from the seller, and maps them to the buyer's requirements.
- Find out the problems in the current methods. Each agent has only a set of listings.
- Know the common terminologies used, for example, locality, budget, BHK, etc.
- Differentiate the tasks performed by each user. Buyer's requirements. Seller's property details. Agent's mapping constraints.
- Know how these users communicate with each other. Buyers and sellers contact the agent.

Once these questions have been answered, you will have a clear idea of the task. The next step will be to understand the conceptual model of these tasks. A user wants to buy a house in a locality in a specific budget with certain amenities. He/she wishes to see as many options available, before finalising on one.

Now design a tool that can map to this mental model of the user. You need to consider the user's level of expertise to use a computer and his/her current environments.

(b) Objects/actions analysis: Every conceptual model will have a set of objects and actions. Conceptual objects project the application to the user, and actions are performed on these objects. Attributes are the characteristics of the object. Here buyer, seller, and agent are objects. Buyers search. Seller lists. Agent connects. Buyer's attributes include his/her requirements.

(c) As simple as possible: Simple here means having as less concepts as possible. A buyer may dream to have a house with a swimming pool, fitness centre, modular kitchen, elevator, balcony, vitrified tiles, and close to his/her work, within a specific budget. But can you list down all his/her requirements or only the most important ones only? What would be the most important attributes? As the number of concepts increase, the complexity of the system increases.

(d) Consistency: To effectively reproduce the same environment helps the user in reliving the same experience. The more he/she is exposed to it, the faster his/her activities become automatic. If you can create an environment that he/she is already exposed to, the learning becomes faster. Since humans use the mid brain more, do not force your users to learn something new unless there is a dire necessity.

(e) The objects/actions matrix: Create a table with objects on one axis, and actions on the other. Check each valid cell. This creates a visual presentation of the complexity of your conceptual model. The more cells are checked, the better utilization of your system.

If you were to design a picture edit tool, then your object/action matrix would look like the one given in Figure 4.20.

Objects / Actions	Create	Delete	Move	Resize	Copy
Line	✔	✔	✔	✔	✔
Circle	✔	✔	✔	✔	✔
Rectangle	✔	✔	✔	✔	✔
Text box	✔	✔	✔	✔	✔
Picture box	✔	✔	✔	✔	✔

Figure 4.20 Object/Action Matrix.

A check on all the boxes implies that all objects shall behave in the same way. This will make it easy for the user to learn your tool.

(f) Keystroke consistency: Even if you do not have a degree in typing, using a keyboard is a motor activity for those who spend much time with computers. You never search for the Ctrl or Enter on the keyboard. Most of the keys are familiar to your fingers, and they do not expect your new brain to help them. If you are making a text editor you may allow the users to use Ctrl+E for centre alignment or Ctrl+C to copy, and so on.

You could also intelligently map the common keyboard shortcuts to your application. For example, if you are making a website for a bank, you may allow Ctrl+O to open an account. Since the keyword "open" forces your fingers to reach out for Ctrl and "O" keys. Similarly, you could allow Ctrl+Z to reset all fields of a form, and so on.

2. We learn faster when vocabulary is task-focused, familiar, and consistent

(a) Terminology should be task-focused. Every industry has a set of terminology used internally. It is important for the designer to find out these and use them, else the user will have to learn the new terms along with the new interface that you are going to build for them.

Imagine you are making an application for a vegetable vendor who wants to keep track of his profits. Until now he writes down his income and expenses on a note book. He calls his income as "input" and expenditure as "output". Even though the words "input" and "output" have other significances, you still need to use them here to mean "income" and "expense". You do not want to confuse your user by teaching him technology. Instead you want to build an application that he will be comfortable using.

(b) Terminology should be familiar. Familiarity reduces the time to learn. Familiar words will encourage automatic reading, while unfamiliar words will need conscious effort for reading. This effort is stored in the short term memory, as they are unfamiliar words. Our brain concludes that if something has not been known until now, then it is not something useful. It does not save such information to the long term memory.

(c) Terminology should be consistent. A poem gets boring when too many words are repeated, whereas an application gets interesting when same words are repeated. The reason is, in a poem, you want to appreciate the creativity, but you see repetition. Whereas on an application, you want to achieve your goal, and their creativity is just confusing and annoying.

Repeated exposure of the same environment to your user, increases familiarity, this in turn causes learning.

(d) Developing task-focused, familiar, consistent terminology is easier with a good conceptual model. When you interact with your users and understand their conceptual model, you also get to know their internal terminologies. You can easily map which function is termed as what by them, and incorporate the same in your design model.

3. We learn faster when risk is low: Imagine you are on a rock climbing trek for the first time. You are the base of a steep, 4500 feet tall mountain. There are safety ropes tied on to you and enough members to guide you all the way to the peak. You will bravely try to climb because you know nothing will happen even if you were to fall. Initially you may find it difficult, and may even slip a few times. But after a while, you will learn the knack of using the mountain's notches to your benefit. On the other hand, if you are provided with no safety measures, and even a single slip could get you killed, how far would you go on this trek?

   With computers the errors are not fatal. But if the application crashes or hangs during usage, your user will invariably blame himself to be the cause, and abandon your system. It is important to predict all possible errors and handle the exceptions in advance.

   An efficient system will not allow its users to make any errors in the first place. You can achieve this by:

   (a) Placing constraints on input data fields.

   (b) Notifying the user immediately of his/her errors.

   (c) Deactivating invalid options.

   (d) Ensuring all actions are easily reversible.

   (e) Providing audio/visual feedback for all his actions.

Time

This chapter has discussed about how we form perceptions, how we remember, and how we learn. By exploiting all the human characteristics discussed, we can even train our users to behave the way we want with our designs. Ever imagined how much time can be given for these?

Responsiveness

Responsiveness and performance are co-dependent, but they are not the same. Imagine you call the customer care of your mobile phone with an issue. The executive listens to your problem, lodges a complaint, gives you a token number, and informs you that you will get a call back from the technical department within 24 hours. At the end of this call, is your issue resolved? No. But are you unhappy with this executive? No. This is the difference between responsiveness and performance. The executive has responded to your problem, but not solved it. Performance can be measured by the number of actions processed within a particular time interval, whereas responsiveness is the time taken to respond an action.

It is necessary for every system to be responsive, as this will reduce the anxiety of the user. Timely feedback has to be given for all actions. It is not necessary that the actions be completed immediately, but they need to be acknowledged. When you give a delete command on a huge file, it will take time for the action to be completed. But you cannot leave your user blank for that period of time. You need to inform the user that his/her delete command is accepted by the system, and the deletion process is going on. You may even provide a visual feedback on the pace at which the deletion is taking place. Without feedback, your user may either try to repeatedly delete the same file, or assume that the system has crashed, because the user does not know what is happening inside the system.

While your Windows system is shutting down, you try to open a new application, the system does not ignore this action. It gives a message that this application cannot be opened now, as the system is shutting down. Ignoring a user's action is far worse than not being able to perform that action.

The Many Time Constants of the Human Brain

- Shortest silence detectable = 1 millisecond (0.001 second)
  If there is a gap of 1 ms between two sounds, we are able to realize it. Each word we speak is a composition of different sounds at different intervals. If the gap is less than 1 ms, we will hear it as a continuous sound. Our hearing is processed faster than our vision. Our eardrums oscillate to sound vibrations, which get converted into electrical pulses and transmitted to the brain. Since this is a mechanical process and not a neural activity, it works faster than the rods and cones.
- Shortest visual response = 5 millisecond (0.005 second)
  If an image is exposed to our eyes for less than 5 ms, you will not be aware that you are seeing it. Within 5–10 ms, the low-level processing units of our visiosn are able to register a footprint of the image. Repeated short exposures can help the brain compile the whole image gradually.

  Have you tried to read something written on a moving train? If the train is at full speed, you will not be able to read anything. But if it is comparatively slow and the banner is printed on every coach, you will be able to read it by the time all the coaches pass.

  Within 5–10 ms, you may not be able to capture any details, but if the same image is shown to you again you will approve to have seen it before.

  Subliminal perception is created by the exposure to any stimuli below the threshold for conscious perception. Here we will not consciously realize the vision, but our unconscious mind gets the message. It is a powerful technique to influence the unconscious mind and is used by psychologists in hypnotherapy. In 1950s an experiment was conducted to test this theory. In a movie hall, "DRINK COCA COLA" was flashed on the screen for less 5 ms. No one realized this, but most of the people drank Coca Cola during the interval.
- Reflex = 80 millisecond (0.08 second)
  The time taken by us to react to stimuli. It is the time taken by the involuntary motor response system to sense danger. When something approaches towards

our eyes, the speed at which we close our eyelids, or the time after which we flinch or jerk when we touch a hot plate, is about 0.08 seconds.

- Form a perception = 100 millisecond (0.1 second)
  This is the time taken by an image on the retina to reach the brain as neural patterns. A conscious perception of our vision is formed in this time. We are able to detect moving objects and track their movements at this speed.
- Detect perceptions = 140 millisecond (0.14 second)
  When two events occur one after another where the first event is the cause of the second, then our brain can deduce this relation only if the gap is less than 0.14 seconds. For example while typing, the press of a key appears on screen as a character. If the lag between the key press and symbol display is more than 0.14 seconds, our attention will be diverted. We will feel that the system has become slow. The automatic activity of typing will become a conscious activity.
- Subitize = 200 millisecond (0.2 second)
  Subtizing is a rapid judgement made by the brain on the number of items seen without counting. I shall hold two buttons on my palm, expose it to you for 0.2 seconds and then close my fist. You will be able to tell there were two buttons in my hand without counting. We are capable of subtizing a maximum of four–five items. After that we start counting. Counting takes up to 0.3 seconds per item.
- Attention blink = 500 millisecond (0.5 second)
  This is amount of time we take to shift our attention from one thought to another. For example, if two keywords are given to you and you are asked to spot them in fast conversation that has these words one after the other, majority chances are that you will not hear the second keyword. This is because when we heard the first keyword, our brain was busy making a note to have heard it during which time the second word was heard.
- Visual motor reaction = 700 millisecond (0.7 second)
- Gap in conversation = 0.5 to 2 seconds
- Unit task = 10 seconds

Engineering Approximations of Time Constants: Orders of Magnitude

It is important to respect these thresholds while creating an application to give the exact perception to the user as intended. Else the stimuli can go unnoticed, or can have other effects that were not intended. For easier calculations, all time delays are rounded off. We measure them as 1 millisecond, 1 second, 10 seconds. Following are a few approximations:

- Shortest silence detectable = 1 millisecond (Actual time is 1 millisecond)
- Shortest visual response = 10 millisecond (Actual time is 5 millisecond)
- Subitize = 0.1 second (Actual time is 0.2 second)
- Attention blink = 1 second (Actual time is 0.5 second)

Designing to Meet Real-Time Human Interaction Deadlines

You want your system to be robust, responsive, interactive etc. This can be achieved if the system is able to react to the human within a specified period of time. If it takes too long, the user will get bored and frustrated. If it is too fast, the user will feel incompetent to match its pace and give up. All animations have to be in the pace at which a human can comfortably perceive it.

Achieving Responsiveness is Important

Responsiveness cannot be attained by use of high-end or faster hardware. It is a design problem, not an implementation problem. A blank screen during the copy of files from one folder to another cannot be fixed by increasing the RAM or processor. You need a design modification. A progress bar to show continuous status of the activity, will be the solution.

It is important to respond to every action of the user within the specified period of time. That makes the system responsive. Users will patiently wait for even five minutes to get their files copied, as long as they are being informed about the activity. If the estimated time to copy and the percentage of completion is visible to the user, he will not become anxious. May be, five minutes to copy a file is a system of poor performance, but this will not annoy the user.

True or False

1. Illusion is fake, but perception is real.
2. Proximity is more powerful than similarity.
3. "Learning to read" is a similar process as "learning to skate".
4. Ideographic scripts encourage context-driven reading, while alphabetic scripts are feature-driven.
5. We can have a perfect vision of images even without any rods in the retina.
6. Foveal vision guides our peripheral vision to the next object.
7. Familiarity can increase the number of chunks stored in short term memory.
8. Only people with high IQ levels use their new brain.
9. Responsiveness of a system affects its performance.
10. Light travels faster than sound. Similarly, video reaches our brain before Audio.

Review Questions

1. Why is the understanding of human psychology required?
2. What are the factors that influence perceptions?

3. State and explain the principles of Gestalt's theory.
4. Explain the effect on data structure when appropriate data controls are not used.
5. Compare language and reading.
6. What could be the disadvantages of using context-driven reading?
7. Explain the color vision of our eye.
8. What are the factors that affect the distinguishability of colors?
9. Compare foveal and peripheral visions.
10. How will over use of red affect your application?
11. Compare "methods to make a message visible" to "the boy who cried wolf".
12. Bring out the relation between perception and memory.
13. Why are we dependent on external aids to track our own activities?
14. What are the behavioral patterns seen in humans that affect designing?
15. What makes recall hard and recognition easy?
16. Compare the generalizing habit of humans to the instincts in an animal.
17. Why is learning from our experiences not a good way?
18. What are the factors that affect learning?
19. How can you use subliminal perception effectively in your design?
20. Why is it necessary for your system to match the human time thresholds?

Appendix to Chapter 4

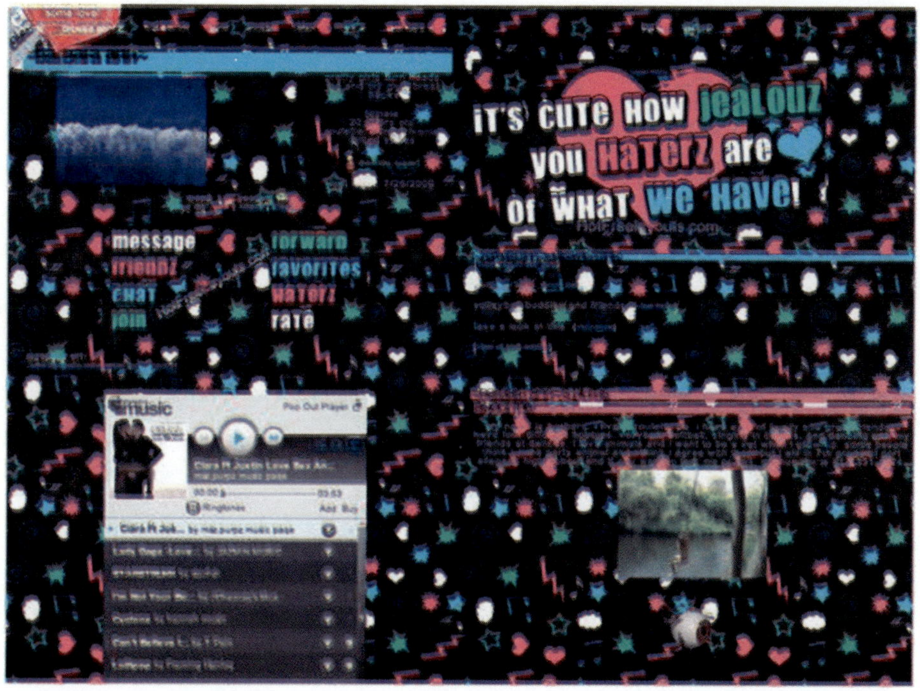

Figure 1 Overuse of color.

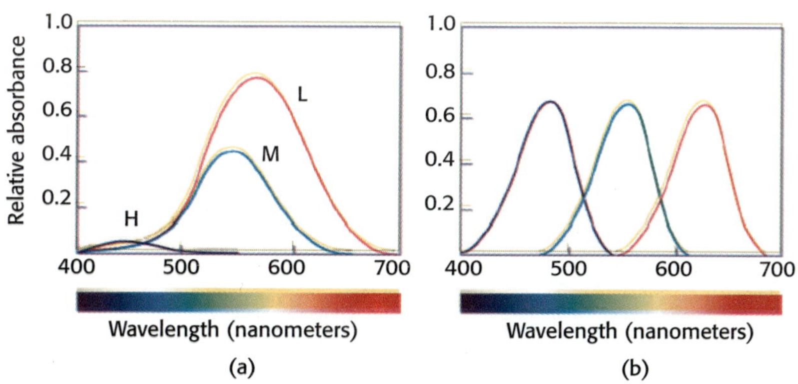

Figure 2 Response to color by (a) human eye and (b) digital camera.

Figure 3 Basic colors.

Figure 4 Brightness versus contrast.

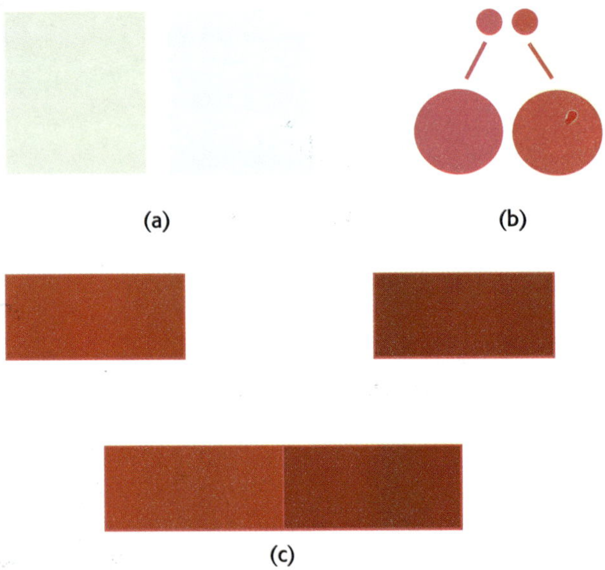

Figure 5 (a) Low saturation. (b) Patch size. (c) Distance.

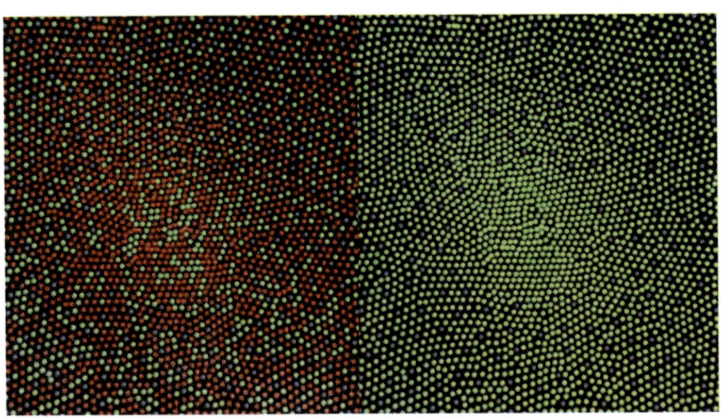

(a) Normal person (b) Color blind

Figure 6 Distribution of cone cells in fovea.

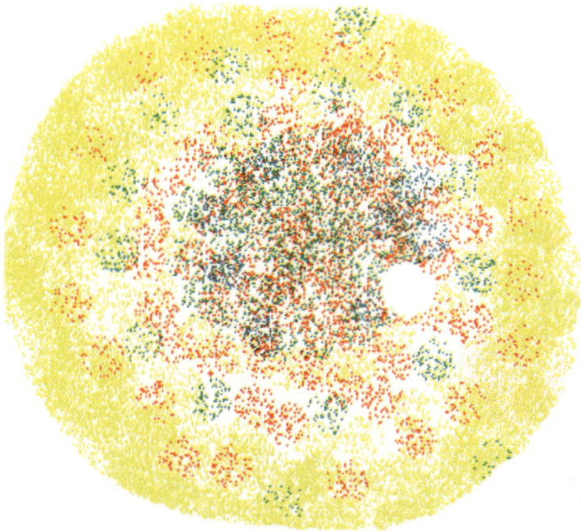

Figure 7 Rods and cones on retina.

Unit

Three

Interaction Styles

CHAPTER 5

Menus

A system contains large amounts of information and performs a variety of functions. Regardless of its purpose, the system must provide some means to tell people about the information it possesses or the things it can do. This is accomplished by displaying listings of the choices or alternatives the user has at appropriate points while using the system, or creating a string of listings that lead a person from a series of general descriptors through increasingly specific categories on following listings until the lowest level listing is reached. This lowest level listing provides the desired choices. These listings of choices are commonly called menus. Menus are a major form of navigation through a system and, if properly designed, assist the user in developing a mental model of the system. In this chapter, the following menu topics will be addressed.

- The structures of menus.
- The functions of menus.
- The content of menus.
- Formatting menus.
- Writing menus.
- Navigation using menus.
- Web site navigation and links.
- Types of graphical menus.

Menus are effective because they utilize the more powerful human capability of recognition rather than the weaker capability of recall. Working with menus reminds people of available options and information that they may not be aware of or have forgotten.

Menus are not without problems, however. New and inexperienced system users might find learning large systems difficult. Menu information must often be remembered and integrated across a series of screens. If each menu is viewed in isolation, relationships between menus may be difficult to grasp. Words and phrases with multiple meanings may also be wrongly interpreted because of the user's inability to see relationships between menus. Ambiguities, also, may not be correctly resolved if the user makes incorrect assumptions about menu structure. The frequent result is that people make mistakes and can get lost in the hierarchical structure.

Experienced system users, while finding menus helpful at first, may find them tedious as they learn the system. Continually having to step through a series of menus to achieve the desired objective can be time-consuming and frustrating. Therefore, the design of menu systems must consider the conflicting needs of both inexperienced and experienced users.

Graphical and Web systems are heavily menu-oriented. They vary in form and are applied in diverse ways. In graphical systems they are used to designate commands, properties that apply to an object, documents, and windows. When selected, a graphical menu item may lead to another menu, cause a window to be displayed, or directly cause an action to be performed. To accomplish these goals, a graphical system presents a variety of menu styles to choose from. Included are entities commonly called menu bars, and menus called pull-downs, pop-ups, cascades, tearoffs, and iconic. In Web site design, common menus include textual links to other pages, command buttons, and both graphical and textual toolbars.

In this chapter, graphical and Web system menus will be addressed. It will begin with a description of the kinds of menu structures available and their content, and then present a series of general menu design guidelines for formatting, phrasing, selecting choices, and navigating menus. Next, Web-specific navigation issues and guidelines will be discussed. Finally, specific types of graphical menus will be described, recommendations for proper usage given, and relevant specific guidelines summarized.

Structures of Menus

Menus vary in form from very simple to very complex. They may range from small dialog boxes requesting the user to choose between one of two alternatives, to hierarchical tree schemes with many branches and level of depth. A menu's structure defines the amount of control given to the user in performing a task. The most common structures are the following.

Single Menus

In this simplest form of menu, a single screen or window is presented to seek the user's input or request an action to be performed, as illustrated in Figure 5.1. In using the Internet, for example, at a point in the dialog people may be asked if they wish to "Stay Connected" or "Disconnect." In playing a game, choices presented may be "novice," "intermediate," or "expert." Single menus conceptually require choices from this sin-

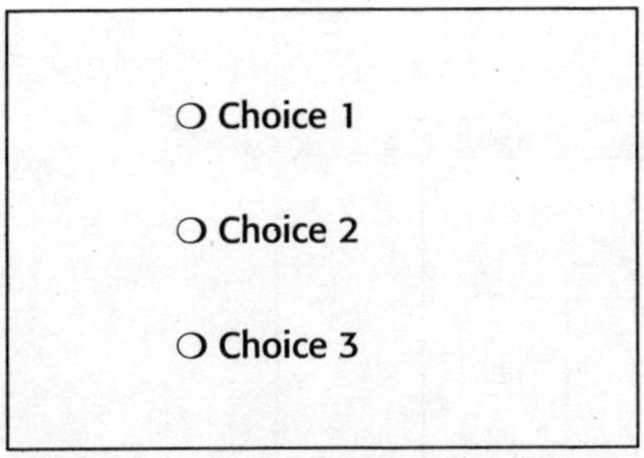

Figure 5.1 Single menu.

gle menu only, and no other menus will follow necessitating additional user choices. The user need only consider the immediate consequences of the item being chosen and need not be concerned with any other additional system menus. While other single menus may exist in the system and might be encountered later, these other menus are not perceived by the user as comprising a series of choices.

A single menu may be iterative if it requires data to be entered into it and this data input is subject to a validity check that fails. The menu will then be represented to the user with a message requesting reentry of valid data.

Sequential Linear Menus

Sequential linear menus are presented on a series of screens possessing only one path. The menu screens are presented in a preset order, and, generally, their objective is for specifying parameters or for entering data. The length of the path may be short, or long, depending upon the nature of the information being collected. All the menus are important to the process at hand and must be answered in some manner by the user. A sequential linear menu is illustrated in Figure 5.2.

Sequential path menus have several shortcomings. A long sequence may become tedious as menu after menu is presented. The user may not remember an answer to a previous question, a question important to the currently presented choices. The user may also want to return to a previous menu to change an answer or look at an answer, an awkward process that must be allowed. Finally, the user may, conceptually, want to complete the menus in a different order than which they are being presented.

Simultaneous Menus

Instead of being presented on separate screens, all menu options are available simultaneously, as illustrated in Figure 5.3. The menu may be completed in the order desired by the user, choices being skipped and returned to later. All alternatives are visible for reminding of choices, comparing choices, and changing answers. The tedium associated with a long series of sequential menus is greatly reduced.

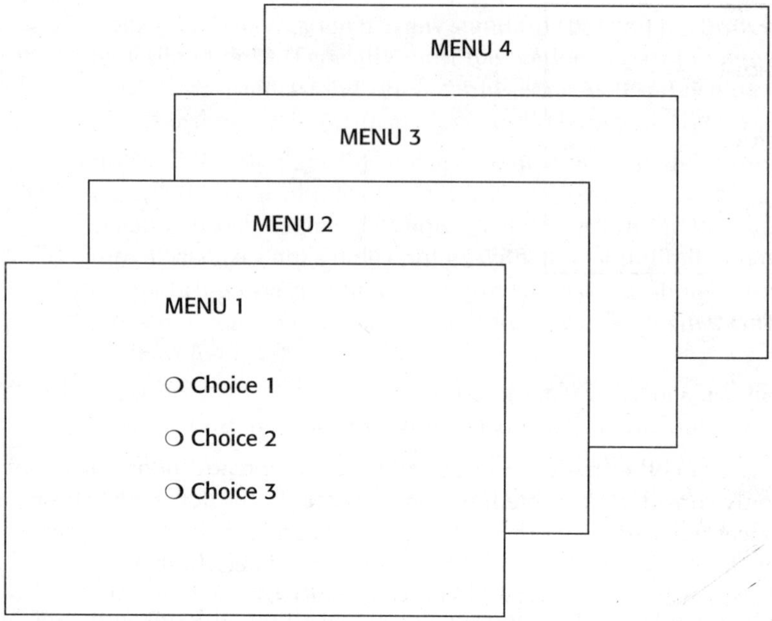

Figure 5.2 Sequential linear menus.

Problems with simultaneous menus are that for large collections of menu alternatives screen clutter can easily occur, and screen paging or scrolling may still be necessary to view all the choices. This type of menu must also clearly indicate menu choice relationships and dependencies, something better accomplished in a linear menu string, or a hierarchical menu described next. Presenting many menu dependencies and relationships on a screen, especially if poorly indicated, can also be very confusing for a novice user.

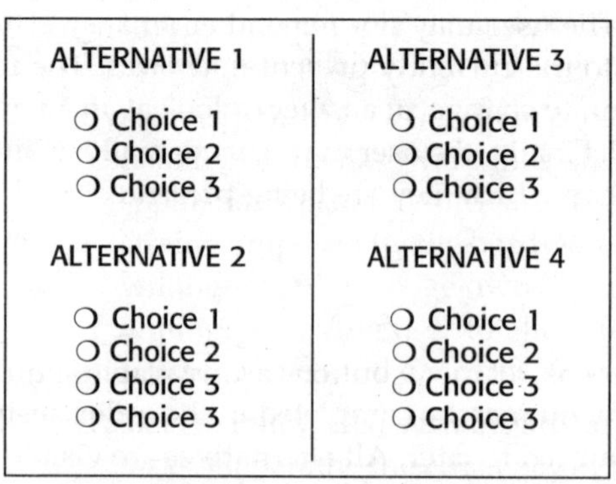

Figure 5.3 Simultaneous menus.

Hierarchical Menus

When many relationships exist between menu alternatives, and some menu options are only appropriate depending upon a previous menu selection, a hierarchical structure is the best solution. A hierarchical structure results in an increasing refinement of choice as menus are stepped through, for example, from options, to suboptions, from categories to subcategories, from pages to sections to subsections, and so on. A hierarchical structure can best be represented as an inverse tree, leading to more and more branches as one moves downward through it. Hierarchical structures are characterized by depth and breadth, depth being the number of choice levels one must traverse to reach the destination, breadth being the number of alternatives found at each level. Menu depth and breadth has been a well-researched topic and will be fully discussed in succeeding pages. Common examples of hierarchical design today are found in menu bars with their associated pull-downs, and in Web sites with their navigation links.

The order and structure of branching in a hierarchy is preset and the normal order of flow one-way, top down. A disadvantage of a hierarchical scheme is that the defined branching order may not fit the users conception of the task flow. If users are not familiar with the hierarchical menu, or are unable to predict what suboptions lie below a particular choice, they may go down wrong paths and find it necessary to go back up the tree to change a choice, or perhaps even return to the top-level menu. It is important, then, that hierarchies be consistent with user expectations, and that choice uncertainties be reduced as much as possible. It must also be easy to back upward through the tree to facilitate exploration of the tree.

A hierarchical menu is illustrated in Figure 5.4. Note that the top level of the tree is considered level 0 with subsequent levels numbered sequentially beginning with number 1. Starting at the top, level 0, two selections, or mouse clicks, are required to reach level 2.

Connected Menus

Connected menus are networks of menus all interconnected in some manner. Movement through a structure of menus is not restricted to a hierarchical tree, but is permitted between most or all menus in the network. From the user's perspective there is no top-down traversal of the menu system but an almost unhindered wandering between any two menus of interest. A connected menu system may be cyclical, with movement permitted in either direction between menus, or acyclical, with movement permitted in only one direction. These menus also vary in connectivity, the extent to which menus are linked by multiple paths. (In a hierarchical menu system, the ability to go back to a previous menu or to return to the top-level menu are also examples, although restricted, of connected menus.)

The biggest advantage of a connected menu network is that it gives the user full control over the navigation flow. Its disadvantage is its complexity, and its navigation may be daunting for an inexperienced user. An example connected menu structure is represented in Figure 5.5.

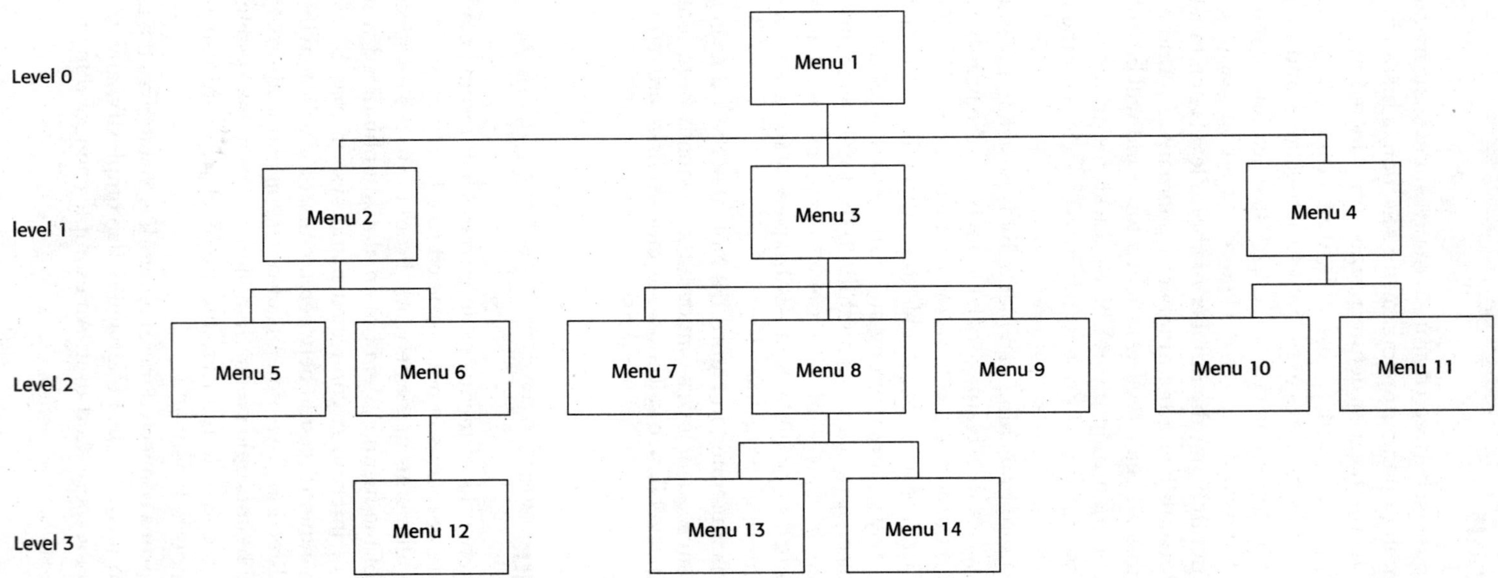

Figure 5.4 Hierarchical menus.

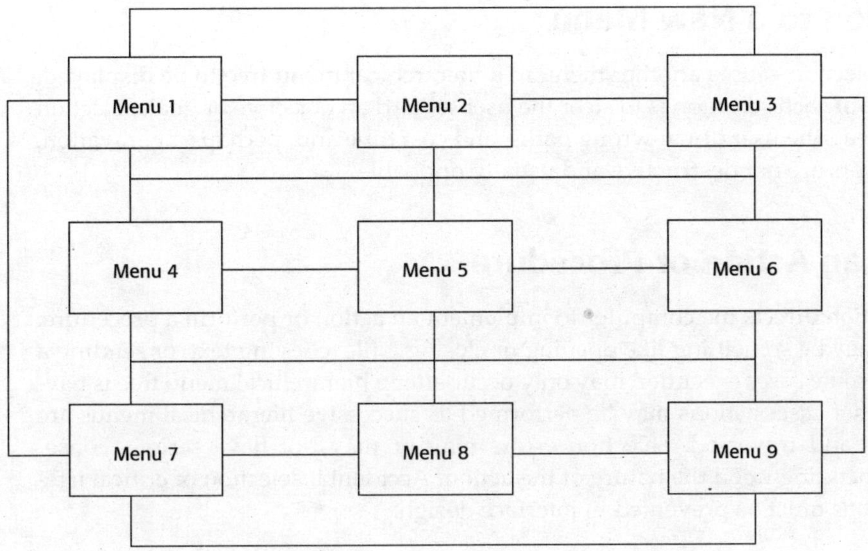

Figure 5.5 Connected menus.

Event-Trapping Menus

Event Trapping menus provide an ever-present background of control over the system's state and parameters while the user is working on a foreground task. They are, in essence, a set of simultaneous menus imposed on hierarchical menus. In a graphical system, for example, existing together are a simultaneous menu, the menu bar, and a hierarchy—the menu bar and its pull-downs. Event-trapping menus generally serve one of three functions. (1) They may immediately change some parameter in the current environment (bold a piece of text), (2) they may take the user out of the current environment to perform a function without leaving the current environment (perform a spell check), or (3) they may exit the current environment and allow the user to move to a totally new environment (Exit).

These menus can also change content based upon the system state, or an event, existing at that moment. A Paste option in a word-processing application, for example, will only function if there is something in a clipboard to paste. A Grid option on a pull-down, as another example, will toggle between a "Hide Grid" or "Show Grid" state, depending upon whether or not a grid is displayed on the screen at that moment. Event-Trapping menus such as menu bars are constantly available to aid in establishing a sense of context, or where one is, while things may be changing in the foreground.

Functions of Menus

From the user's perspective, a menu can be used to perform several functions, to *navigate* to a new menu, to *execute* an action or procedure, to *display* information, or to *input* data or parameters.

Navigation to a New Menu

Each user selection causes another menu in a hierarchical menu tree to be displayed. The purpose of each selection is to steer the user toward an objective or goal. Selection errors may lead the user down wrong paths, and cost time and, perhaps, aggravation, but these errors are nondestructive and usually undoable.

Execute an Action or Procedure

A user selection directs the computer to implement an action or perform a procedure. The action may be something like opening or closing a file, copying text, or sending a message. In some cases execution may only occur after a hierarchical menu tree is navigated. In other cases actions may be performed as successive hierarchical menus are encountered and traversed. Selection errors may or may not have serious consequences, depending upon the nature of the action. Accidental selection of critical irreversible actions must be prevented in interface design.

Displaying Information

The main purpose of selecting a menu choice may simply be to display information. The user may be searching for specific information in a database or browsing the Web. The user's focus is primarily on the information desired and less on the selection function. In many cases, information retrieval may occur only after a hierarchical menu tree is navigated. The content material and the user's interests will determine the paths followed. Users may spend considerable time and effort understanding and processing uncovered information in order to evaluate subsequently displayed menu choices. Wrong turns in the process will again cost time and perhaps aggravation, but these errors are nondestructive and usually undoable.

Data or Parameter Input

Each selection specifies a piece of input data for the system or provides a parameter value. Data or values may be input on a single menu or spread over a hierarchy of menus. The user's focus is primarily on the information being provided and, again, less on the selection function. Selection errors can easily be corrected if detected by the system.

Content of Menus

A menu consists of four elements, its *context*, its *title*, its *choice descriptions*, and its *completion instructions*. These concepts are introduced here and will be expanded in detailed guidelines to follow on succeeding pages.

Menu Context

A menu's context provides information to keep the user oriented. This kind of information is critical in complex or hierarchical menu systems, where loss of position or disorientation can easily occur. Feedback is necessary that tells users where they are in a process, what their past choices were, and possibly how much farther they still have to navigate. Human memory being what it is, where one is and how one got there all too easily slip from consciousness.

Verbal linkage, spatial linkage, or both may be used to provide navigation feedback. *Verbal linkage* involves providing, on the current menu screen, a listing of choices made on previous menus that have led to this position. It also involves assuring the user that the displayed menu is the menu desired. Its title should mirror the option selected on the previous menu, and its content should reflect its title. *Spatial linkage* can be accomplished by graphic methods. Each succeeding menu screen can be displayed overlapping the previous menu screen so a succession of choices can be seen in a single view. A sense of progress and distance can then be easily ascertained.

Menu Title

A menu's title provides the context for the current set of choices. The title must reflect the choice selected on the previously displayed menu.

Choice Descriptions

Choice descriptions are the alternatives available to the user. These descriptions can range from a mnemonic, numeric, or alphabetized listing of choices to single words or phrases to full sentences or more. The style chosen will reflect the experience of the user (novice or expert), the nature of the choices (well-learned alternatives or not), the nature of the selection mechanism (keyboard or mouse), and the nature of the system (business system application or Web page).

Completion Instructions

Completion instructions tell users how to indicate their choices. They may include the rationale for why the user is being asked to make this choice and the impact the choice will have on subsequent processes. Explicit instructions may be needed for first time or casual users of a system. Experienced users will find overly verbose instructions unnecessary. The needs of all system users, and the nature of the system, must again be considered in creating this kind of on-screen guidance.

Formatting of Menus

The human-computer interface has a rich history of experimental studies with menus, the results of which can and have been applied to graphical screen and Web page menu design and presentation. What follows is a series of guidelines for formatting menus.

Consistency

- Provide consistency with the user's expectations.
- Provide consistency in menu:
  — Formatting, including organization, presentation, and choice ordering.
  — Phrasing, including titles, choice descriptions, and instructions.
  — Choice selection methods.
  — Navigation schemes.

Like all aspects of screen design, menu design consistency is an integral component of system usability. Menu formatting, phrasing, choice selection, and navigation must be consistent throughout a graphical system or Web site.

Display

- If continual or frequent references to menu options are necessary, permanently display the menu in an area of the screen that will not obscure other screen data.
- If only occasional references to menu options are necessary, the menu may be presented on demand.
  — Critical options should be continuously displayed, however.

Whether to display a menu continually, or on demand, is determined by the menu's frequency of use. Always permanently display menus that are frequently referenced. This will provide memory support and immediate access to what is needed most. Occasionally needed menus may be presented on request via pop-ups or pull-downs. Critical options, however, should always be continuously displayed. Wright, Lickorish, and Milroy (1994) found superior performance for permanently displayed menus as opposed to menus that had to be retrieved through mouse clicks. They speculate that because retrieving a menu for display requires more actions, this may also impair people's memory for other tasks being performed.

Presentation

- Ensure that a menu and its choices are obvious to the user by presenting them with a unique and consistent structure, location, and/or display technique.
- Ensure that other system components do not possess the same visual qualities as menu choices.

A menu and its choices should be immediately recognizable by the user as being a menu of choices. This can be accomplished through giving the menu a distinctive and consistent structure and presenting it in a consistent screen or page location. Presentation techniques must, of course, be compatible with those used for other purposes on the remainder of the screen. A good way to set a menu off from the remainder of the screen is to enclose it in a box or display it using a background that contrasts with the remainder of the screen Techniques chosen should be consistent throughout the system. Web page navigation links, which may be scattered throughout a page, are displayed underlined and in a unique color to differentiate and identify them.

Ensure that other system elements do not possess qualities that allow users to confuse them with menu choices. In Web page design, for example, the underlining of any system component other than navigation links is not recommended because of the possibility that they may be confused with links.

Organization

- Provide a general or main menu.
- Display:
  - — All relevant alternatives.
  - — Only relevant alternatives.
    - • Delete or gray-out inactive choices.
- Match the menu structure to the structure of the task.
  - — Organization should reflect the most efficient sequence of steps to accomplish a person's most frequent or most likely goals.
- Minimize number of menu levels within limits of clarity.
  - — For Web sites, restrict it to two levels (requiring two mouse clicks) for fastest performance.
- Be conservative in the number of menu choices presented on a screen:
  - — Without logical groupings of elements, limit choices to 4 to 8.
  - — With logical groupings of elements, limit choices to 18 to 24.
- Provide decreasing direction menus, if sensible.
- Never require menus to be scrolled.
- Provide users with an easy way to restructure a menu according to how work is accomplished.

In organizing a menu, the goal is to simply and effectively reveal its structure, while also reducing the number of actions needed to locate the target item.

General menu. The top-level menu in a hierarchical menu scheme should be a general or main menu, consisting of basic system options. This will provide a consistent starting point for all system activities and a "home base" to which the user may always return.

Relevant alternatives. A menu should provide all relevant alternatives, and only relevant alternatives, at the point at which it is displayed. Including irrelevant choices on a menu screen increases learning requirements and has been found to interfere with performance. There are two exceptions to this rule, however. Alternatives that are conditionally inactive may be displayed along with the conditionally active choices, if the active choices can be visually highlighted in some manner (such as through bolding or reverse video), or the inactive choices can be visually subdued (perhaps as through graying them out). One study, however, found that completely eliminating inactive alternatives on a menu resulted in faster choice access time, when compared to leaving inactive alternatives on a menu but displayed in a subdued manner. This study concludes that eliminating conditionally inactive choices from a menu appears to be the best approach. Mayhew (1992) suggests that while deletion does provide an advantage to expert users of keyboard-driven menus, graying out seems to be advantageous to novices in systems using pointer-driven selection devices. She concludes that since menus are geared toward novices, graying appears to be the best overall choice. In general, today's graphical systems follow the gray-out approach for inactive menu choices. Whatever method is chosen should be consistently followed throughout a system.

Options to be implemented in the future may also be displayed if they can be visually marked in some way (through a display technique or some other annotation).

Matching menu structure to the tasks. Menus should be organized according to how people structure their tasks. They should reflect the most efficient sequence of steps to accomplish a person's most frequent or likely goals.

Minimize number of levels. The issue that must be addressed in creating a multi-level menu structure is determining how many items will be placed on one menu (its breadth) and how many levels it will consume (its depth). In general, the more choices contained on a menu (greater breadth), the less will be its depth; the fewer choices on a menu (less breadth), the greater will be its depth.

The advantages of a menu system with greater *breadth* and less depth are:

- Fewer steps and shorter time to reach one's objective.
- Fewer opportunities to wander down wrong paths.
- Easier learning by allowing the user to see relationships of menu items.

A broad menu's disadvantages are:

- A more crowded menu that may reduce the clarity of the wording of choices.
- Increased likelihood of confusing similar choices because they are seen together.

The advantages of greater *depth* are:

- Less crowding on the menu.
- Fewer choices to be scanned.
- Easier hiding of inappropriate choices.
- Less likelihood of confusing similar choices since there is less likelihood that they will be seen together.

Greater depth disadvantages are:

- More steps and longer time to reach one's objective.
- More difficulties in learning since relationships between elements cannot always be seen.
- More difficulties in predicting what lies below, resulting in increased likelihood of going down wrong paths or getting lost.
- Higher error rates.

In text-based and graphical systems, a good number of studies have looked at the breadth-depth issue in recent years. Some have concluded that breadth is preferable to depth in terms of either greater speed or fewer errors, that a low number of levels (two to three) and an intermediate number of choices (4 to 8) results in faster, more accurate performance as opposed to fewer or greater numbers of levels and choices, and that 4 to 8 choices per menu screen is best. Another study found that one level was easiest to learn, and a couple of studies have concluded that a menu could contain up to 64 items if it were organized into logical groups. The least desirable alternative in almost all cases was deep-level menus that simply presented the user with a binary choice (select one of two alternatives) on each menu.

In Web site design, two recent studies have also looked at the breadth-depth issue (Zaphiris and Mtei, 1998; Larson and Czerwinski 1998). Both found that a two-level (two mouse click) Web site was searched faster than those containing more levels.

The conclusion that one might derive from these studies is this: Fewer levels of menus aid the decision-making process, but trying to put too many choices on a single menu also has a negative impact. The final solution is a compromise: Minimize the number of levels within limits of clarity. What is clarity? The studies seem to indicate that, if the choices to be displayed cannot be segmented into logical categories, then confine the number of alternatives displayed to 4 to 8 per menu. If logical categorization is possible, and meaningful, logical category names can be established, and then a larger number of choices can be presented. The maximum number of alternatives will, however, be dependent upon the size of the words needed to describe the alternatives to the user. Wordy captions will greatly restrict the number of alternatives capable of being displayed. There is one exception to these basic principles. Large linearly ordered, well-learned listings, such as months of the year, or numbers, would be better presented in a one-level menu, rather than by breaking them into multiple levels.

Limit the number of choices. Be conservative in the number of menu choices presented on a screen. If the choices cannot be logically grouped, restrict the number to 4 to 8. If the choices can be grouped, 18 to 24 can be displayed, with no more than 10 items within a group.

Mayhew (1992) suggests that if the menu choices are complex and/or there are no groupings of items, choices presented should be restricted to *10 or fewer*. This recommendation is similar to the eight or fewer recommendations above. If the menu choices are not complex, items on the menu can be grouped, and the users are infrequent or casual, she recommends *20 or fewer* choices. If the menu choices are not complex, items on the menu can be grouped, and the users are frequent or expert, she suggests *21 or more* choices can be provided.

MAXIM **The best journey is the one with the fewest steps.**

Provide decreasing direction menus. In addition to breadth and depth, direction has been found to affect menu choice selection performance. In a multilevel menu, a *decreasing* direction structure presents successively fewer choices as each lower level is traversed. An *increasing* direction structure presents successively more choices as each lower level is traversed. Bishu and Zhan (1992) in a study of 16 and 32 item iconic menus found that decreasing direction menus were significantly faster and more accurate than increasing menus.

Scrolling. Never require menus to be scrolled. Keep all choices visible at all times.

Easy to restructure. Menus should be capable of being restructured by a user. Not everyone works the same way.

Complexity

- Provide both simple and complex menus.
- Simple: a minimal set of actions and menus.
- Complex: a complete set of actions and menus.

Providing two sets of menus will more effectively satisfy the differing needs of the novice and expert user. The novice or casual user often only requires a minimal set of actions and menus to accomplish tasks. The expert may prefer a full set of options. Make selection, and changing, between simple and complex menus easy to accomplish, preferably through a menu bar choice. IBM's SAA CUA refers to these menus as *short* and *full*

Item Arrangement

- Align alternatives or choices into single columns whenever possible.
  — Orient for top-to-bottom reading.
  — Left-justify descriptions.
- If a horizontal orientation of descriptions must be maintained:
  — Organize for left-to-right reading.

For scanning ease, menu choices should be left-justified and aligned vertically into columns. Research has found that columnar menus and listings are searched much faster than horizontally-oriented menus. Do not array a menu in multiple columns.

When menus are included on other screens, space constraints often exist, and the menu must be arrayed horizontally. If a single-row (horizontal) orientation is necessary organize for left-to-right reading. If two or more rows are available for displaying choices, organize for top-to-bottom, then left-to-right reading to facilitate visual scanning.

Ordering

- Order lists of choices by their natural order, or
- For lists associated with numbers, use numeric order.
- For textual lists with a small number of options (seven or less), order by:
  — Sequence of occurrence.
  — Frequency of occurrence.
  — Importance.
  — Semantic similarity.
- Use alphabetic order for:
  — Long lists (eight or more options).
  — Short lists with no obvious pattern or frequency.
- Separate potentially destructive actions from frequently chosen items.
- If option usage changes, do not reorder menus.
- Maintain a consistent ordering of options on all related menus.
  — For variable-length menus, maintain consistent relative positions.
  — For fixed-length menus, maintain consistent absolute positions.

Within information categories included on a menu, or in menus in which categories are not possible, options must be ordered in meaningful ways. When a menu contains multiple categories of information, the ordering of categories will follow these same principles. A meaningful ordering is necessary to:

- Facilitate search for an item.
- Provide information about the structure and relationships among items.
- Provide compatibility with the user's mental model of the item structure.
- Enhance the user's ability to anticipate a choice's location.

When items are organized along some dimension or characteristic, the user can use that information to locate items faster. An alphabetized list, for example, provides an indication of approximately where in the listing an item beginning with a particular letter will be found. Understanding structure and relationships, item similarities and dissimilarities, can also aid in focusing attention on that which is relevant. Any incompatibility with the user's mental model will disrupt searching as the user tries to make sense of something that had been well understood, but now is now being presented in a way that has not been well learned. Months of the year presented in alphabetic order, for example, would be very disrupting.

Experienced users often anticipate the location of a desired choice within a familiar menu. Hornof and Kieras (1999), in studying how items are selected from pull-down menus, found that people often make an initial eye and mouse-positioning movement toward the expected choice location before the pull-down even appeared on the screen. They also found that choices in the top three positions of the pull-down were selected faster then those in other positions. This may have been caused by users' ability to better predict a choice's location at the top, and/or the shorter mouse movement required from the menu bar to the pull-down. Observational studies also reveal that experienced users also anticipate the location of command buttons appearing within a window. While waiting for a window to appear upon which a command button will be immediately "clicked," the pointer is often positioned at the button's expected location before the window appears.

Another study, Byrne, John, Wehrle, and Crow, 1999, studied how people search unfamiliar pull-down menus. They found that the search primarily flowed from menu top to bottom, and that the initial eye fixation was usually the focused on the choice in the topmost menu position. Almost all recorded eye fixations were on one of the first three items.

Both of the studies point out the importance of presenting important menu items at the top of menu arrays, and providing consistency in menu organization schemes and menu locations. Common ordering schemes for menus, then, are the following:

Natural ordering. If items have a natural sequence, such as chapters in a book, days in a week, or months in the year, the ordering scheme should follow this natural sequence. The screen viewer will have learned these ordering schemes very well.

Numeric ordering. Use numeric ordering for choices associated with numbers, for example, type size, baud rate, or number of pixels.

Small number of options. For groupings with a small number of options (about seven or fewer), *sequence of use, frequency of use,* or *importance* are good ordering schemes. Also consider ordering by *semantic similarity*, along a semantic dimension such as impact, potency, or emphasis. Type style, for example, may be ordered by emphasis from least to most: regular, underlined, italicized, and bold.

Alphabetic order. For a large number of options, alphabetic ordering of alternatives is desirable. Alphabetic ordering is also recommended for small lists where no frequency or sequence pattern is obvious.

It has been found that alphabetically ordered menus can be searched much faster than randomly ordered menus. One study, for example, found that an 18-item alphabetic menu was visually searched four times faster than a randomly organized menu. Search time was a function of saccadic eye movements through the display. Search patterns were random, but fewer eye movements were required with the alphabetic arrangement. After 20 trials, however, only one eye movement was required for all conditions, and search time was the same. Another study has found that the longer the list, the greater the value of an alphabetic ordering scheme. As list length increased, the time to find items in longer random lists increased significantly faster than the time to find items in longer alphabetic lists.

Learning of a randomly ordered menu will eventually take place, but this learning will be greatly aided by a meaningful choice-ordering scheme.

Separate destructive choices. Destructive menu choices, such as delete or clear, should be positioned as far away from frequently chosen choices as possible to minimize the chance of accidental selection.

Do not reorder menus. Adaptivity is thought to be a desirable quality of a computer system. This may not be so for menu option ordering. A study compared static or fixed menus with dynamic menus whose options were continually reordered based upon the frequency in which they were chosen. Dynamic menus were slower to use and less preferred than static menus. The continual reordering interfered with menu order learning.

Consistency between menus. Options found on more than one menu should be consistently positioned on all menus. If menus are of variable length, maintain relative positioning of all item options (for example, always place Exit at the bottom or end of the list). If menus are of fixed length, place options in the same physical position within the list.

Groupings

- Create groupings of items that are logical, distinctive, meaningful, and mutually exclusive.
- Categorize them in such a way as to:
  — Maximize the similarity of items within a category.
  — Minimize the similarity of items across categories.
- Present no more than six or seven groupings on a screen.
- Order categorized groupings in a meaningful way.
- If meaningful categories cannot be developed and more than eight options must be displayed on a screen, create arbitrary visual groupings that:
  — Consist of about four or five but never more than seven options.
  — Are of equal size.
- Separate groupings created through either:
  — Wider spacing, or
  — A thin ruled line.
- Provide immediate access to critical or frequently chosen items.

Create groupings. Items displayed on menus should be logically grouped to aid learning and speed up the visual search process. Studies have demonstrated that logically categorized menus are easier to learn and result in faster and more accurate performance. Categorical organization may facilitate the transition from novice to expert user because information is visually represented in the way people think about it.

Categorizing. Groupings should also cover all the possibilities and contain items that are non-overlapping. While some collections of information will be easily partitioned into logical groups, others may be very difficult to partition. Some users may not understand the designer's organizational framework, and there may be differences among users based on experience. Thus, no perfect solution may exist for all, and extensive testing and refinement may be necessary to create the most natural and comprehensible solution.

Number. Limit the number of groupings on a screen to six or seven. The total number of items within all the groupings should not exceed about 18 to 24.

Ordering. Groupings of menu items may be ordered following the guidelines described in "Ordering" above. Ordering alternatives include alphabetic, sequence of use, frequency of use, importance, and semantic similarity.

Arbitrary visual groupings. Uncategorized menus should be broken in arbitrary visual groupings through the use of space or lines. Groups should be as equal in size as possible and consist of about four or five options. Groupings should never exceed more than seven options.

Separation. Perceptually separate groupings by a leaving a wider spacing between groupings, or by inscribing line separators between groupings. Guidelines for displaying line separators follow.

Critical choices. Choices that are critical or frequently chosen should be accessible as quickly and through as few steps as possible. Place them on the highest-level menu, whenever possible.

Line Separators

- Separate vertically arrayed groupings with subtle solid lines.
- Separate vertically arrayed subgroupings with subtle dotted or dashed lines.
- For subgroupings within a category:
  — Left-justify the lines under the first letter of the columnized choice descriptions.
  — Right-justify the lines under the last character of the longest choice description.
- For independent groupings:
  — Extend the line to the left and right menu borders.

Inscribing subtle solid or dashed lines between groupings can reinforce groupings and subgroupings of vertically arrayed related choices. For breaking subgroupings within one category, the line or lines should only extend from the first character of the descriptions to the end of the longest description, as shown in Figure 5.6. Many graphical platforms always extend the line from menu border to border, as illustrated in

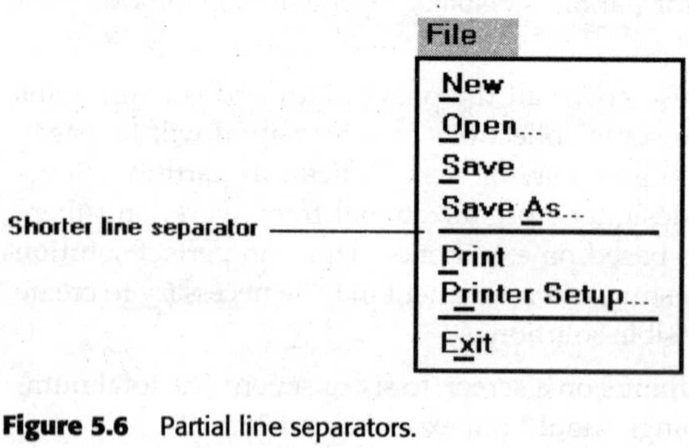

Figure 5.6 Partial line separators.

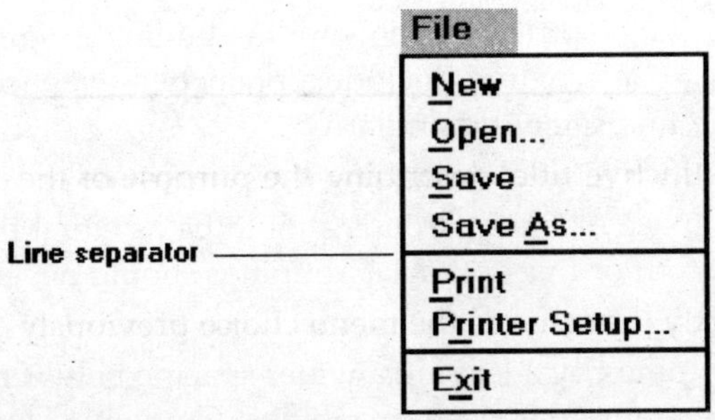

Figure 5.7 Extended line separators.

Figure 5.7. This extended line results in too strong a visual separation between what are related menu parts. Visual separation should exist, but it should not be too overpowering.

For independent groups of choices, extend the horizontal line from menu border to border. This will indicate to the user that the groupings are independent of one another. In summary, use a partial line for separating related choices; use an extended line for separating unrelated or independent choices.

Phrasing the Menu

A menu must communicate to the user information about:

- The nature and purpose of the menu itself.
- The nature and purpose of each presented choice.
- How the proper choice or choices may be selected.

Writing the content of menu components, the menu's title, the choice descriptions, and instructions, is often made difficult because of the varying experience levels of the menu users. At one extreme, there is the desire to explain, on the screen, everything in great detail. On the other hand, brevity is also important because of screen space constraints and limits on what people want to read. These conflicting goals often cause a trade-off between thoroughness and brevity. Also important in hierarchical menu systems is the role menus play in enabling a person to maintain a sense of place, or "Where am I now?" Also very important is a menu's ability to enable the user to accurately predict where a choice will lead, or what it will cause to happen, preventing user tedium and frustration. So, the menu content must be informative, but not intrusive. And it must balance the needs of all its expected users.

Following are guidelines for creating menu titles, choice descriptions, Web navigation links, and menu instructions. The standard graphical system conventions inscribed on menus, intent indicators, keyboard equivalents, and keyboard accelerators, are also described.

Menu Titles

- Main menu:
  - — Create a short, simple, clear, and distinctive title, describing the purpose of the entire series of choices.
- Submenus:
  - — Submenu titles must be worded exactly the same as the menu choice previously selected to display them.
- General:
  - — Locate the title at the top of the listing of choices.
  - — Spell out the title fully using either an:
    - Uppercase font.
    - Mixed-case font in the headline style.
  - — Superfluous titles may be omitted.

A meaningful menu title aids in defining the context of the menu and increases menu comprehension. An experimental study has demonstrated the value of titles to comprehension. Study participants were presented the detailed steps to perform a function. A descriptive title for the steps was (A) not included, (B) presented at the start of the steps, and (C) presented at the end of the steps. Participants given a title at the start of the steps (B), reported higher comprehension and recalled twice as many items as those who were not given a title (A), or who were presented the title at the end (C). The title established the context of the task, and knowing this context greatly aided comprehension.

Main menu. The menu title should immediately orient the viewer to the menu's content and purpose. It should be a short, clear, distinctive, and descriptive title, representing the entire series of choices. It's an important contextual and navigation component. A title such as MAIN MENU OPTIONS provides no information except that the user is probably at the top of a hierarchical menu tree.

Submenus. Submenu titles must be worded exactly the same way as the menu choice previously selected to display them. This will provide structural continuity and assure users that they are progressing as expected through a menu hierarchy.

General. Locate the title at the top of a listing of choices, in the title bar if one is available. Display the title in uppercase or in a mixed-case font using the headline style of presentation. When using the headline style, capitalize the first letter of each significant title word. The case style chosen should be consistently used on all menus. Superfluous titles, titles that add nothing to the understanding of menu content and context, may be omitted. A pop-up menu requested during a text-editing task, for example, is displayed within the context of the task being performed. The presented choice descriptions by themselves (Copy, Font, and so on) provide the necessary context. Message windows do not need a title either; the text of the message provides the context.

Menu Choice Descriptions

- Create meaningful choice descriptions that are familiar, fully spelled out, concise, and distinctive.
- Descriptions may be single words, compound words, or multiple words or phrases.
  — Exception: Menu bar items should be a single word (if possible).
- Place the keyword first, usually a verb.
- Use the headline style, capitalizing the first letter of each significant word in the choice description.
- Use task-oriented not data-oriented wording.
- Use parallel construction.
- A menu choice must never have the same wording as its menu title.
- Identical choices on different menus should be worded identically.
- Choices should not be numbered.
  — Exception: If the listing is numeric in nature, graphic, or a list of varying items, it may be numbered.
- If menu options will be used in conjunction with a command language, the capitalization and syntax of the choices should be consistent with the command language.
- Word choices as commands to the computer.

Meaningful. Menu item descriptions should be composed of familiar and fully spelled out words. While abbreviations may occasionally be necessary, they should be kept to a minimum. If you are using an abbreviation, only use those that are standard or well known. Descriptions should also be concise, containing as few words as possible, and distinctive, constructed of words that make each choice clearly different from all others. Repeated use of the same word or words in multiple choice descriptions hinders distinctiveness and signals the necessity for creating a grouping whose title is based upon the repeated word.

Use high-imagery keywords, words that elicit a mental image of the object or action. Avoid low-imagery words that have more general connotations. For example, when obtaining a printout of a screen, the term "print" is much more descriptive than "list."

In creating menu item descriptions, never assume that the description chosen by the designer will have the same meaning to the user. A study has found that the probability of two people choosing the same name or description for something ranged from 8 to 18 percent. Names chosen by experts were no better than those chosen by nonexperts. Therefore, iteratively test and refine the choices to achieve as much agreement in meaning by users as possible.

Size. Item descriptions may be single words, compound words, multiple words, or phrases. Menu bar items should be a single word, if possible. If a menu bar item must be a multiple word, visually tie the two words together by incorporating a hyphen between them. Web page content links will typically be phrases. Link writing guidelines will be thoroughly described in Chapter 9.

Keyword first. Arrange multi-item descriptions so that the descriptive and unique words appear at its beginning. This optimizes scanning and recognition while the user is learning the menu. Description phrasing and wording should also be consistent across all menus to aid learning further.

Capitalization. Use the headline style of presentation. Capitalize the first letter of each significant choice description word.

Task-oriented wording. Task-oriented wording is preferable to data-oriented wording. Task-oriented wording usually positions a verb first, such as *Manage Customer Information*. An example of data-oriented wording would be to simply say *Customers.* What is being done with, for, or to customers is unclear in the latter.

Parallel construction. When choices are composed of phrases, use a parallel word construction in creating descriptions for related choices. Parallel construction would be: *Print* a File, *Execute* a Program, and *Eject* a Disk. An example of non-parallel construction is: *Print*; *Execute* a Program, and Disk *Eject.*

Relationship to title. A menu choice must never have the same wording as the title of the menu on which it is presented.

Consistency across menus. Identical choices on different menus should be worded the same.

Numbering. Items should not be numbered unless the listing is numeric in nature, graphic, or a list of varying items.

Command language. If menu options will be used in conjunction with a command language, the capitalization and syntax of the captions should be consistent with those of the command language.

Word as a command to computer. Phrase all menu choices as commands to the computer whenever possible. For example, say:

Choose one:

Save and exit

Exit without saving

rather than:

Do you want to save and exit?

- Yes
- No

Wording a choice as a command to the computer more clearly describes the action of what the command accomplishes. The Yes/No alternatives shown above must be comprehended in conjunction with the question being asked. Wording a choice as a command also provides choice phrasing that is consistent with other system commands. A system, for example, often contains the standard commands *Save* and *Exit*. In addition, command wording enhances the learning of command mnemonics. Finally, this wording implies that the initiative is with the user in the dialog, not with the computer.

Menu Instructions

- For novice or inexperienced users, provide menu completion instructions.
  — Place the instructions in a position just preceding the part, or parts, of the menu to which they apply.
    - Left-justify the instruction and indent the related menu choice descriptions a minimum of three spaces to the right.
    - Leave a space line, if possible, between the instructions and the related menu choice descriptions.
  — Present instructions in a mixed-case font in sentence style.
- For expert users, make these instructions easy to ignore by:
  — Presenting them in a consistent location.
  — Displaying them in a unique type style and/or color.

People not familiar with a system and its menus may need guidance on how to complete a menu. Their needs may, however, have to be balanced against the needs of experienced users who may not want or desire such assistance. To satisfy the needs of all kinds of users at the same time necessitates that menu instructions be included on a menu, but that these instructions be easily ignored by those who do not need them.

Novice or inexperienced users. Provide explicit menu completion instructions for novice or inexperienced menu users. Place the instructions in a position just preceding the part, or parts, of the menu to which they apply. Left-justify the instruction and indent the related menu choice descriptions a minimum of three spaces to the right. Leave a space line, if possible, between the instructions and the choice descriptions. Present the instructions in a mixed-case, sentence-style font.

Expert users. When instructions are included on menus, they must be visually recognized as instructions. This will allow them to be easily ignored by the expert user when they are not needed, or no longer needed. Therefore, some visual as-pect of the instruction must indicate that it *is* an instruction. The form user then immediately recognizes them as instructions, and they can be read or ignored as is desired.

To make instructions immediately recognizable as instructions on a menu, then, present them in a unique font or color. If one of these methods is used, however, cau-tions concerning the excessive use of different font styles (and colors, as will be shown in Chapter 12 "Colors") must be heeded. Another, but less visually strong, technique is to identify the technique simply by its location. Begin the instruction to the left of the screen elements to which it applies, the left-justification identifying it as an instruction.

Try to leave a space line between the instruction and the elements to which it relates, whenever possible. Screen space constraints may not always permit a space line, however. Guidelines for writing text, including instructions, will be found in Chapter 9.

Intent Indicators

- Cascade indicator:
  - — To indicate that selection of an item will lead to a submenu, place a triangle or right-pointing solid arrow following the choice.
  - — A cascade indicator must designate every cascaded menu.
- To a window indicator:
  - — For choices that result in displaying a window to collect more information, place an ellipsis (. . .) immediately following the choice.
    - Exceptions—do not use when an action:
      - – Causes a warning window to be displayed.
      - – May or may not lead to a window.
- Direct action items:
  - — For choices that directly perform an action, no special indicator should be placed on the menu.

Providing an indication of what will happen when a menu item is selected can enhance predictability and exploration of a graphical system. If a choice leads to another lower-level menu, include a *cascade indicator*, a right-pointing arrow, following the item description. If a choice leads *to a window*, include an ellipsis following the item description. Items causing a direct action will have no indicator. These intent indicators are illustrated in Figure 5.8.

IBM's SAA CUA designates choices leading to submenus or windows as *routing* choices, and items causing direct actions as *action* choices. A Microsoft Windows *intent indicator* simply implies that additional information is needed. This additional infor-

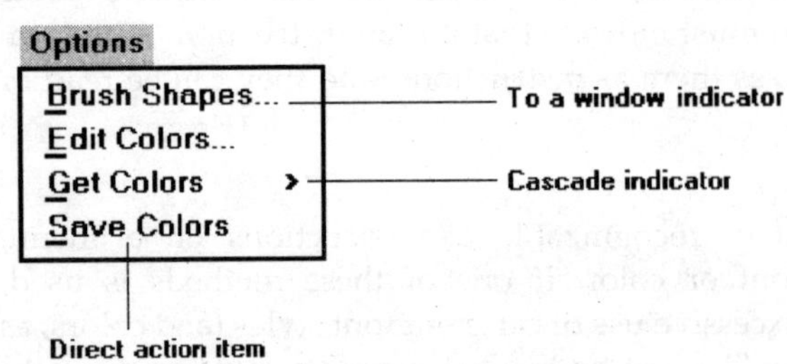

Figure 5.8 Intent indicators.

mation request is usually presented in a window, but it need not necessarily be restricted to a window.

Keyboard Equivalents

- To facilitate keyboard selection of a menu choice, each menu item should be assigned a keyboard equivalent mnemonic.
- The mnemonic should be the first character of the menu item's description.
  - — If duplication exists in first characters, use another character in the duplicated item's description.
  - — Preferably choose the first succeeding consonant.
- Designate the mnemonic character by underlining it.
- Use industry-standard keyboard access equivalents when they exist.

Keyboard selection. The ability to select a menu alternative through the keyboard should always be provided. This is accomplished by providing a keyboard *equivalent* for each menu alternative.

Mnemonics. Keyboard equivalents that have meaningful associations with their corresponding choices will be more easily learned and remembered. Studies have found that simple truncation is a good method for creating mnemonics. Therefore, the first letter of the item description is the recommended mnemonic. Unfortunately, in following this method, duplications easily occur, so an alternative principle must also be provided. A simple scheme is to use the second consonant for duplicate items. This duplication-breaking scheme need not always be faithfully followed, however. Occasionally another letter in the menu item may be more meaningful to the user. In these cases, it should be selected.

Designation. Mnemonic codes can be visually indicated in a number of ways. The recommended method is an underline beneath the proper character within the choice. Other methods—a different character color, different character intensity, or a contrasting color bar through the relevant character—are visually more complex and should be avoided. Underlined keyboard equivalents are illustrated in Figure 5.9.

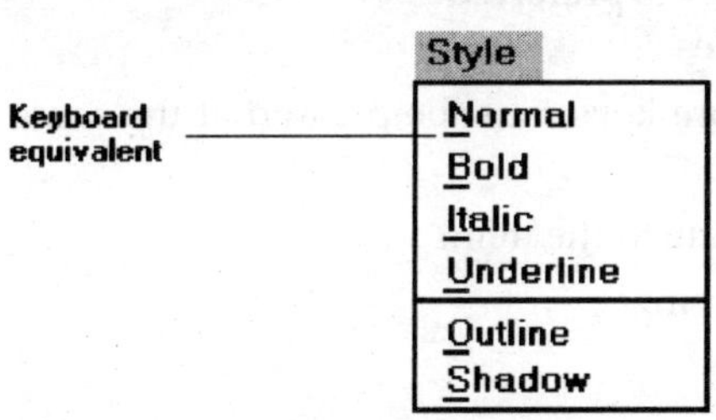

Figure 5.9 Keyboard equivalents.

Table 5.1 Standard Keyboard Equivalents

About	Help	Print	Send To
Apply	Help Topics	Print Preview	Show
Back	Insert	Properties	Size
Browse	Maximize	Redo	Split
Close	Minimize	Repeat	Stop
Copy	Move	Restore	Undo
Cut	New	Resume	View
Delete	Next	Retry	Yes
Edit	No	Rerun	
Exit	Open	Save	
File	Paste	Save As	
Find	Page Setup	Select All	

A great deal of commonality exists among these equivalents since they represent a wide variety of functions, many of which will rarely appear together on a single menu. If two actions with the same equivalents will be used within the same menu, one equivalent will have to be modified to make it unique.

Industry standards. Standard industry keyboard equivalents have been established for many common system menu choices. Where these standard equivalents have been established, they should be followed. Microsoft Windows calls keyboard equivalents *access keys.* Standard keyboard equivalents are shown in Table 5.1.

Keyboard Accelerators

- For frequently used items, provide a keyboard accelerator to facilitate keyboard selection.
- The accelerator may be one function key or a combination of keys.
  — Function key shortcuts are easier to learn than modifier plus letter shortcuts.
- Pressing no more than two keys simultaneously is preferred.
  — Do not exceed three simultaneous keystrokes.
- Use a plus (+) sign to indicate that two or more keys must be pressed at the same time.
- Accelerators should have some associative value to the item.
- Identify the keys by their actual key top engraving.
- If keyboard terminology differences exist, use:
  — The most common keyboard terminology.
  — Terminology contained on the newest PCs.

- Separate the accelerator from the item description by three spaces.
- Right-align the key descriptions.
- Do not use accelerators for:
  — Menu items that have cascaded menus.
  — Pop-up menus.
- Use industry-standard keyboard accelerators when they exist.

Accelerators are keys, or combinations of keys, that invoke an action regardless of cursor or pointer position. They are most commonly used to activate a menu item without opening the menu. They are most useful for frequent activities performed by experienced users. IBM's SAA CUA and Microsoft Windows calls these keys *shortcut* keys. They may also be called *hot keys*. Many products have, within their guidelines, standard accelerator key recommendations as well as rules for creating new accelerator keys.

For frequently used items, assign a key, or combination of keys, to accomplish an action. Function key shortcuts are usually easier to learn than modifier plus letter shortcuts. Pressing no more than two keys simultaneously is preferred; three keystrokes is the maximum. Use a plus (+) sign to indicate on the screen menu that two or more keys must be pressed at the same time.

Accelerators should have some associative value to the item and be identified by their actual key-top engraving. In situations where multiple kinds of keyboards exist, and there are keyboard terminology differences, use the term most commonly found on the keyboards or use the term contained on the newest PC, if evolution to the new PCs is expected.

Display the accelerator right-aligned and enclosed in parentheses to the right of the choice. Incorporating these key names within parentheses indicates that they are prompts (which they actually are) and that they may easily be ignored when not being used. Most graphic systems do not place them within parentheses, giving them much too strong a visual emphasis. See Figure 5.10.

Do not use accelerators for menu items that lead to cascaded menus. Also, do not use accelerators on pop-up menus, because they are mouse driven. Use standard keyboard accelerators when they exist. Standard industry accelerators are shown in Table 5.2.

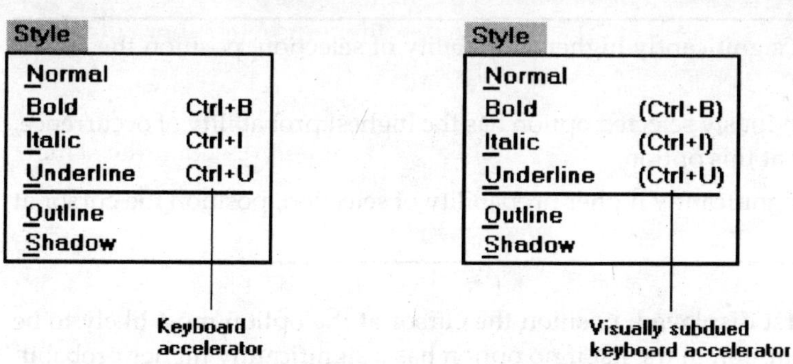

Figure 5.10 Keyboard accelerators.

Table 5.2 Standard Keyboard Accelerators

THIS ACCELERATOR:	DESIGNATES THIS ACTION:
Ctrl+C	Copy
Ctrl+N	New
Ctrl+O	Open
Ctrl+P	Print
Ctrl+S	Save
Ctrl+V	Paste
Ctrl+X	Cut
Ctrl+Z	Undo
F1	Display contextual help window
Shift+F1	Activate context-sensitive help
Shift+F10	Display pop-up menu
Spacebar	Select (single mouse click)
Esc	Cancel
Alt	Activate a menu bar

Selecting Menu Choices

Menu items can be selected by pointing at the choice with a mechanical pointer, by pointing at the choice through the keyboard, or by keying a value designating the choice.

Initial Cursor Positioning

- If one option has a significantly higher probability of selection, position the cursor at that option.
- If repeating the previously selected option has the highest probability of occurrence, position the cursor at this option.
- If no option has a significantly higher probability of selection, position the cursor at the first option.

When a menu is first displayed, position the cursor at the option most likely to be chosen, or at the first option in the list if no option has a significantly higher probability of selection. If repeating the previously selected option has the highest probability of occurrence, position the cursor at this option.

Choice Selection

- Pointers:
  - — Select the choice by directly pointing at it with a mechanical device such as a mouse or trackball pointer, or light pen, or pointing with one's finger.
  - — Visually indicate:
    - Which options can be selected.
    - When the option is directly under the pointer and can be selected.
  - — Visually distinguish single- and multiple-choice menu alternatives.
  - — If pointing with a mechanical device is the selection method used:
    - The selectable target area should be at least twice the size of the active area of the pointing device or displayed pointer. In no case should it be less than 6 millimeters square.
    - Adequate separation must be provided between adjacent target areas.
  - — If finger pointing is the selection method used:
    - The touch area must be a minimum of 20 to 30 millimeters square.
    - The touch area must encompass the entire caption plus one character around it.
- Keyboard:
  - — If moving the cursor to a menu choice:
    - The up and down arrow keys should move the cursor up or down vertically oriented menu options.
    - The left and right cursor keys should move the cursor left or right between horizontally oriented menu options.
  - — If keying a choice identifier value within an entry field:
    - Locate the entry field at the bottom of the last choice in the array of choices.
    - Uppercase, lowercase, and mixed -case typed entries should all be acceptable.
- Selection/execution:
  - — Provide separate actions for selecting and executing menu options.
  - — Indicate the selected choice through either:
    - Highlighting it with a distinctive display technique.
    - Modifying the shape of the cursor.
  - — Permit unselecting choice before execution.
    - If a menu is multiple choice, permit all options to be selected before execution.
- Combining techniques:
  - — Permit alternative selection techniques, to provide flexibility.

Pointers. Items can be selected by being pointed at using a mechanical device such as a mouse, trackball, or light pen, or through touch pointing using one's finger (for touch-sensitive screens). Pressing a key, such as Transmit or Enter, or a mouse button, signals the choice to the computer. Always visually indicate in a distinctive manner which options are selectable and when the option is under the pointer and can be selected. Visually distinguish single- and multiple-choice arrays of menu choices.

An adequate pointing target area should be provided. This area should be at least twice the size of the active area of the displayed pointer of the pointing device. In no case should it be less than 6 millimeters square. To avoid unintended activation of the wrong option, provide adequate separation between selectable areas. Highlighting of the area when selected will also provide indication of an incorrect choice.

If finger pointing is the selection method used, an even larger touch area must be provided, a minimum of 20 to 30 millimeters. Single-character positions on a screen make poor targets for most fingers. Also, keep in mind that using a finger to signify a choice can be taxing on arm muscles, so this approach should only be used in casual or infrequent use situations.

Keyboard. If the user is moving the screen cursor to a menu choice, the up and down arrow keys should move the cursor up and down a vertical column of menu options. The left and right arrow keys should move the cursor left and right across a horizontal array of options. If the user is keying a choice identifier value within an entry field, locate the entry field at the bottom of the last choice in the array of choices. If the user is keying a mnemonic value, the entry should be acceptable in any case (upper, lower, and mixed).

Selection/execution. Provide separate actions for selecting and executing menu options. For example, require typing the mnemonic to select, and then a press of the *Enter* or *Return* key to execute. Or, with a mouse, require moving the pointer to the option to select, and then clicking to execute. Always permit erroneous selections to be unselected and, in a multiple-choice menu, permit all options to be selected before execution.

The item selected should be highlighted in some way through a distinctive display technique such as bolding or changing its color. An alternative is to change the shape of the pointer itself. These methods provide direct visual feedback that the proper choice has been selected, reducing the probability of errors in choice selection.

Combining techniques. Permit alternative selection techniques to provide flexibility. If a pointing method is used, also provide a keyboard alternative to accomplish the same task. Pointing will probably be easier for the novice, but many experts prefer the keyboard alternative.

Defaults

- Provide a default whenever possible.
- Display as bold text.

Defaults aid system learning and enhance efficiency. Provide as many as possible. Indicate a default by displaying it in a bold text.

Unavailable Choices

- Unavailable choices should be dimmed or "grayed out."
- Do not add or remove items from a menu unless the user takes explicit action to add or remove them through the application.

Choices not available to the user should be made visually distinctive by dimming them or graying them out. They must not compete with active items for the user's attention. Items should not be added or removed from a menu unless the user takes explicit action to do so. Allowing the system to change menu items takes control away from the user and can also lead to user confusion.

Mark Toggles or Settings

- Purpose:
  - — Use to designate that an item or feature is active or inactive over a relatively long period of time.
  - — Use to provide a reminder that an item or feature is active or inactive.
- Guidelines:
  - — Position the indicator directly to the left of the option.
  - — For situations where several nonexclusive choices may be selected, consider including one alternative that deselects all the items and reverts the state to the "normal" condition.

Purpose. Mark toggles or settings, illustrated in Figure 5.11, are menu items that toggle between active and not active. When it is active, an indicator is displayed adjacent to the item description. For nonexclusive choices, a check mark is displayed; for mutually exclusive choices, another distinctive symbol, such as a diamond or circle, is displayed. When the item is not active, no mark or symbol will appear.

Examples of items using mark toggles are: having a specific application automatically loaded after the system is loaded, having windows automatically reduced to icons when they are made inactive, or making a setting without requiring a dialog box. The purpose of mark toggles is to activate or deactivate an attribute by setting one menu item.

Advantages/disadvantages. Mark toggles provide a visual indication of the state of an item. They are accessed quickly but may not always be visible. Mark toggles are best suited to items or features that remain active or inactive over relatively long periods of time. They provide good reminders of the state that exists.

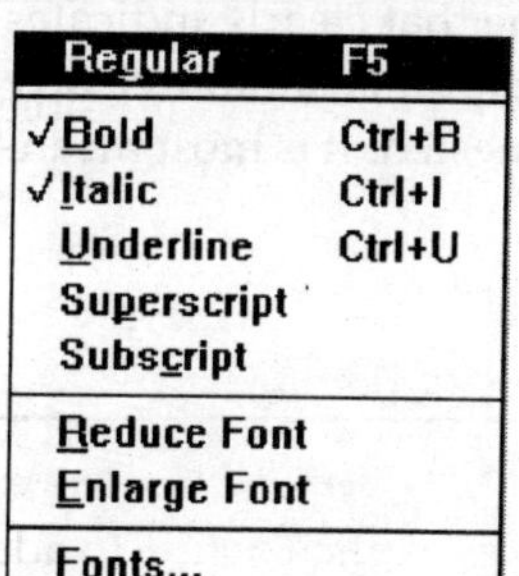

Figure 5.11 Mark toggles.

Guidelines. Position the mark toggle indicator directly to the left of the menu option. In situations where several nonexclusive choices may be selected on one menu, consider including one alternative that deselects all the items and reverts the state to the normal condition, as illustrated by "Regular" in Figure 5.11.

Toggled Menu Items

- Purpose:
  - — Use to designate two opposite commands that are accessed frequently.
  - — Use when the menu item displayed will clearly indicate that the opposite condition currently exists.
- Guidelines:
  - — Provide a meaningful, fully spelled-out description of the action.
  - — Begin with a verb that unambiguously represents the outcome of the command.
  - — Use mixed-case letters, with the first letter of each word capitalized.

Purpose. A toggled menu item is a one menu item command that toggles back and forth between the current state and its alternative state. When the menu item is first displayed, it reflects the alternative state to the condition that currently exists. For example, in Figure 5.12, if a background grid is currently being displayed, the menu item reads *Hide Grid*. When Hide Grid is selected, the grid is removed from the window, and the menu item dynamically changes to reflect the opposite action. It will now read *Show Grid*. When a grid is again requested, it will change back to Hide Grid. The purpose of toggled menu item is to use a single menu item to designate and activate the one, opposite, alternative of a two-state command setting.

Advantages/disadvantages. Toggled menu items shorten menus, decrease visual clutter, provide quicker access, and foster faster comprehension of the command action. When they are located on a pull-down menu, however, the actions themselves are not always visible. The opposite action reflecting the current state of the attribute, since it too is not visible, can cause uncertainty for novice users concerning what the state actually is. Toggled menu items are also limited in use to commands only.

Guidelines. Use toggled menu items to designate two opposite commands that are accessed frequently. The menu item displayed must be one that clearly indicates that the opposite condition currently exists. The menu captions should clearly state what would happen if the menu item action were requested. It is most meaningful to begin the command with a verb.

Figure 5.12 Toggled menu item.

Navigating Menus

Navigation, and an efficient navigational structure, is the most important element in system usability. A simple and clear navigational structure is the backbone upon which all system features are draped. In Web site design, the most successful sites have been found to be those with easy to use and understand navigational systems. No amount of graphical "sparkle" has yet been able to overcome a poor navigational design. A system's organizational structure and its navigational tools, including elements such as menus, links, toolbars, and command buttons influence the system's navigational ease of use. So, of course, does the size of the system, as well as the navigational aids available, including site maps and indexes. In Web site navigation design, the unique, often incompatible, relationship the browser has to the Web site application being presented can also strain navigation ease.

Web Site Navigation Problems

To fully understand what comprises good navigation, let's first look at some Web site navigational issues and problems, both technical and usage-related. The Web and its navigation is undoubtedly the most complex interface facing people today.

Technical issues. Unlike a graphical system application, whose screens tend to flow in an orderly and predictable manner, a Web application is composed of pages, each of which can, theoretically, be linked to any other page in the application. The graphical application user normally begins a process at a prescribed starting point and proceeds sequentially until a process or task is finished. Web users can perform tasks or satisfy needs at will, easily moving between most screens in the application "spider web" in any order desired, and even jumping to other spider webs when the urge arises. In an analogy to driving a car, the graphical system user is essentially following a freeway in Nevada. The Web user is wandering around in downtown Boston without a road map and, encountering a road link (a bridge over the Charles River), suddenly finds himself in Cambridge.

The graphical system user must deal with only one operating system whose navigational characteristics are standard and fairly consistent. The Web user must confront two navigational systems, that of the browser being used and that of the Web site being viewed. A click of the browser Back button, for example, simply redisplays the page that was previously displayed on the screen. This page may have been in another Web site, and the user is transported there. Neither Web site application is aware of this change. Nothing that might have been done on the page "moved back from" is changed. To move around within a Web site requires links within the Web site, either in the form of textual links or command buttons. The data must always be thought of as separate from the controls used to display it, not as being seamless, as occurs in graphical systems. Web users, especially novices, often do not recognize where the browser ends and the Web site application begins.

Another problem: Because of the rapidly evolving and expanding nature of the Web, Web sites also have a tendency to grow and grow. As more and more is added, what may have been initially a reasonable structure and menu scheme slowly dissolves into a confusing mass of listings and linked pages. The result is unrelated information that is presented in no particular order.

Usage problems. The two most serious user problems in Web navigation are the heavy mental loads imposed to use the Web and the feeling of spatial disorientation that often occurs. This problem may also occur in hierarchically structured graphical systems. The *cognitive or mental overhead* the user must expend in making decisions concerning which links to follow, or to abandon, can be overwhelming. Often, there are too many links presented on a page, many of whose meanings are not clear. Links frequently offer few clues to where they lead, how much information will be found at the other end, and how this information relates to the currently displayed page. For the user to reach a goal, each link's relevance to the task at hand must be determined. Another problem is that not all links on a page are always obvious. This often leads to much trial-and-error behavior; the user aimlessly clicking to see what happens.

Feelings of *disorientation* are easily experienced when one becomes "lost in Web space." Studies have shown that most people do not seem to become familiar with the layout of sites or develop useful mental models of their structure (Spool, Scanlon, Schroeder, Snyder, and DeAngelo, 1997). Many people also don't understand where they are in a Web site's information structure (Nielsen, 2000). A scrolling page can lead to loss of local context when the basic navigational elements, such as links to other local pages in the Web site disappear. There are then no familiar landmarks to then navigate by. Long chains of links to reach relevant material can be tedious and also lead to loss of context, and a "Where Am I?" reaction.

A recent research paper found that 39 percent of users of shopping sites failed in their buying attempts because the sites were too difficult to navigate. If people get buried in information, or lost on a side trip with no signposts or landmarks in sight, the most frequently implemented solution to the problem is to abandon the entire process.

Navigation Goals

A well-designed navigation system facilitates quick and easy navigation between components whose structure and relationship are easily comprehendible. For the user, answers to the following questions must be obvious at all times during an interaction:

- Where am I now?
- Where did I come from?
- Where can I go from here?
- How can I get there quickly?

Sometimes referred to as "wayfinding," a good navigational scheme, and the proper navigational tools, will minimize, if not eliminate, the problems associated with cognitive or mental overload and feelings of disorientation. General system navigation guidelines include the following.

Control

- For multilevel menus, provide one simple action to:
  — Return to the next higher-level menu.
  — Return to the main menu.
- Provide multiple pathways through a menu hierarchy whenever possible.

Navigation through menu levels should be accomplished through simple actions. It should always be very easy to return to the next higher-level menu and the main, general, or top menu. Provide multiple pathways, whenever possible, through a hierarchical menu structure.

Menu Navigation Aids

- To aid menu navigation and learning, provide an easily accessible:
  — Menu map or overview of the menu hierarchy.
  — A "look ahead" at the next level of choices, alternatives that will be presented when a currently viewed choice is selected.
  — Navigation history.

Menu maps. As has been discussed, as one wanders deeper into a multilevel menu system, it is increasingly difficult to maintain a sense of position or orientation The result is that getting lost in the menu maze is quite easy to do. The value of a menu map in reducing disorientation has been demonstrated in some studies. In these studies, providing a graphic representation of the menu structure in map form, either in hard copy or online, resulted in fewer errors or wrong choices, faster navigation, and greater user satisfaction when compared to providing no guides or simply providing indexes or narrative descriptions of the menu structure. So, menu maps or graphic representations of the menu structure are desirable and should be included on top-level menu screens. They should also be included in the system documentation where available, and through Help function.

Look-aheads. Menu navigation and learning will be assisted if a person is able to browse the next level of choices before the currently displayed choice is selected. As the cursor moves across a menu bar, for example, the pull-down menu may be automatically dropped, permitting review of the choices available if that menu bar item is selected. Such look-aheads are useful if ambiguity exists at higher-level choice points. They have been found to decrease errors and improve satisfaction. Menu search time may be longer, however.

Navigation history. It has been found that being able to view, on the screen, the path one is following improves learning and performance, and reduces feelings of disorientation. Provide a navigation history that summarizes the menu choices made leading to the currently displayed menu or screen.

Web Site Navigation

Understanding a Web site's navigational scheme is made more difficult because Web sites usually have much less *perceived* structure than typical graphical system applications. Web pages can be of any length and possess any number of links to any number of other pages. The user can wander at will or whim through multitudes of links, pages, and Web sites, and any meaningful structure a Web site design does possess can easily disappear from one's memory in the maze of directional twists and turns being made. The potential for getting lost is extremely high, unless numerous, obvious, and understandable landmarks are available as a guide.

The section focuses specifically on Web site navigation design. It will review typical Web site organizational schemes; the navigational components of a site, including the browser command buttons, links, Web site toolbars, and Web site command buttons; and the characteristics and components of a Web site that contribute to maintaining a "sense of place." In designing a Web site navigation scheme there are two things to always remember. Never assume that users know as much about a site as the site designers do (this has been said before), and, any page can be an entry point into the Web site.

Web Site Organization

- Divide content into logical fragments, units, or chunks.
- Establish a hierarchy of generality or importance.
- Structure the relationships among content fragments, units, or chunks.
  — Establish global or site-wide navigation requirements.
- Create a well-balanced hierarchical tree.
  — Restrict to two levels requiring no more than two clicks to reach deepest content, whenever possible.

It is easier to develop a clear and comprehendible navigation scheme if the Web site is organized and structured in a meaningful way. The design goal is a proper balance of menus and pages that can be easily and efficiently moved between.

Logical fragments, units, or chunks. Because of limitations in short-term human memory, smaller discrete fragments or chunks of information are often easier to navigate than long, undifferentiated units. The concept employed in Web site design, in reaction to this human memory frailty, is called *hypertext*. Hypertext is a nonlinear way of organizing information based upon the following principles:

- A large body of information exists that can be organized into fragments.
- The fragments relate to one another.
- The user needs only a small fraction of the fragments at any one time.

In organizing a Web site, information is first divided into logical fragments, units, or chunks. Coherent chunks that focus on a single topic is the desired goal.

These small chunks of related information are easier to organize into the modular groups of information that will compose the organization scheme, and form the basis for hypertext links to be described shortly.

Hierarchy of generality or importance. Having identified the information units, information is now organized in according to importance or generality, from general to specific. A hierarchical tree is the most recommended organization scheme, Sun Microsystems (1998) suggests that whenever possible:

- State conclusions and link to supporting details.
- Enumerate categories of information and link them to detailed listings.
- Summarize information and link to full-length treatments.

A document organizational tree structure, (table of contents, chapters, sections, and subsections) is a good scheme, since people are very familiar with, and have an excellent mental model of this organization. Such a structure provides information about information sequence, information quantity, and the relationships existing between components. Other organizational schemes include topics followed by subtopics, or prioritization from most to least important. The objective is to allow the user to scan the page and then select relevant and useful content for further review. Excessive fragmentation of a long, sequential story, however, should be avoided. Reading will be impeded and printing made more difficult.

Structure the relationships. Identify the relationships that exist between various elements in the hierarchical tree. In a large Web site, two levels of navigation will exist. The first is movement within the subject area. This navigation includes moving *within a branch*—up to a parent page or down to a child page. It also involves navigating across branches to sibling pages or other sections of a site. What other points on other tree branches it will be beneficial to go directly to then, must be established. The second navigation type is *global or site-wide.* What other site features, such as search a facility, site maps, and other major content areas should be mentioned on each page? Do not mention all features on all pages. Restrict the number presented to the several most useful features.

To unveil the Web site's structure, use *progressive disclosure*. Heading levels, shown in varying type sizes (as on paper), will be helpful in aiding understanding of site organization.

Hierarchical tree. Web sites pages should be organized as offshoots of a single home page. If a site has a large number of information categories, and each category contains a lot of content, create submenus to aid navigation. The design goal: a well-balanced hierarchical tree that facilitates quick access to all information and also helps people understand how the site is organized. The so-called spoke design, where every page is linked to every other page, has been found to lead to lower usability.

Hierarchical breadth has been found by many research studies to be greatly preferable to hierarchy depth. A few menus with a larger number of choices are better than a large number of menus each with a smaller amount of choices.

When menu levels go to four, five, or more, the chance of users becoming lost or disoriented is greatly increased. As studies have found (Zaphiris and Mtei, 1998; Larson and Czerwinski, 1998), restrict, whenever possible, the hierarchical tree to two levels requiring no more than two clicks to reach the deepest content. A two-level structure encompasses a home page and two additional levels below it.

Components of a Web Navigation System

To move between Web site information fragments necessitates the creation of navigation *links*. They are contained within a framework of tools or controls, including the browser's command buttons, textual phrases, Web site navigation bars, and Web site command buttons. Collectively, these are all referred to as links. Links are one of the most discussed issues in Web site design.

A link functions as a menu choice that, when selected, results in the connected information being displayed, or results in a file being opened or downloaded. A movement link may transport the user to another location within a page, to a new site page, or to another Web site. Originally, due to the nature of technology at the time hypertext was employed in computer systems, links consisted of textual or binary files. Utilization of hypertext on the Web allowed links to by created using images as well as text, so the term *hypermedia* was coined to reflect this expanded nature.

In addition to being the critical component in Web navigation, links give the user an idea of what a Web site, document, or page is all about. The wording of a textual link should enable a person to predict what lies submerged below, or what will happen if it is activated. This lets the user determine whether a link should be followed, reading the page continued, reading the page ended, or a retreat to an earlier point initiated. This is a complex cost-benefit calculation that the user makes many times in a Web interaction session.

Providing an extensive collection of link navigation tools will focus the user on the Web site itself and its content, drawing attention away from the general-purpose browser links. Making these tools consistent and predictable will help the user create an understandable mental model of the site and its organization. To begin, several general link guidelines are:

- All navigation controls must:
  — Make sense in the absence of site context.
  — Be continually available.
  — Be obvious and distinctive.
  — Be consistent in appearance, function, and ordering.
  — Possess a textual label or description.
  — Offer multiple navigation paths.

Sensible. All navigation controls, in the absence of site context, must make sense to the user. The user may have "lost" the context, or the page or Web site may have been entered from almost anywhere.

Available. All navigational controls must be easy to access. If they are not readily available, the full advantages of hypermedia may not be achieved.

Obvious and distinctive. A navigation link or control must look like a navigation control. Its appearance to the user must immediately suggest that it is an entity to be clicked or otherwise selected. This is accomplished through a tool's appearance as well as its location. Non-obvious control choices lead to aimless and tedious page clicking and ultimately confusion and frustration. Conversely, do not make any other screen element look like a navigation tool if it is not one.

The obviousness of a link is called its *affordance*. A control with high affordance will be quickly identified as a control. Bailey (2000) in a study compared the link affordances of the home pages for two large Web sites. Each page contained 29 links. The link affordance rate for one site was 97 percent (participants, on the average, identified 28.2 page links). The rate for the other site was only 76 percent (the average link identification rate being 21.9 per page). This difference was statistically significant. Because of the non-obviousness of one-quarter of the poorer sites links, its users would have spent longer times searching for links, and would probably not have even discovered some links.

Techniques to create the necessary affordance and distinctiveness differ depending upon the kind of link. Guidelines enabling the various controls to achieve distinctiveness are described in the following control-specific sections.

Consistent. Like all elements of the interface, navigation links, toolbars, and command buttons must be consistent in appearance and behavior.

Textual. All navigation must have a textual label or description. Navigation using textual descriptions is much preferable to graphical-only navigation because the purpose and function of graphic images are often unclear. They also take longer to download. Textual links are also necessary for users who do not have graphics, or who have chosen not to display graphics.

Provide multiple navigation paths. Offer multiple paths or ways to move around the Web. Provide structural components such as site maps, a table of contents, and indexes to go directly to a point of interest, provide content links to move around nonsequentially, and provide command buttons, such as *Next* and *Previous,* to move sequentially.

Browser Command Buttons

- Hide the split between the browser and the Web site application by including navigational controls within the application.

The browser being used in interacting with the Web provides its own command buttons. As discussed earlier, pressing the browser *Back* and *Forward* buttons can create confusion because they can transport a user in and out of a Web site. Novice users often do not recognize where browser control ends and application control starts, and vice versa. Rather then relying on the browser's buttons, provide navigation controls within the application for movement within the application. They can take the form of links or command buttons such as *Next* and *Previous.*

Web Site Navigation Bars

- Provide a global navigation bar at the top of each page.
- Provide a local category or topical links navigation bar on the left side of a page.
- Place minor illustrative, parenthetical, or footnote links at the end of the page.
- For long pages, provide a navigation bar repeating important global or local links at the page bottom.

A Web site navigation bar is a menu, an array of textual phrases, graphical images or icons, or command buttons, as illustrated in Figures 5.13, 5.14, and 5.15. A Web site contains at least three levels of navigation links, *global*, or site-wide, links, indicating the site's total scope or categories of available information; *local* specific navigation links within the category or topical area being displayed; and *minor* illustrative, parenthetical, or footnote links. An evolving standard in design is to locate the global links at the page top, the categorical links in a columnar array down the pages left side, and the minor links at the page bottom. This structure, illustrated in Figure 5.16, separates navigation from content, making it easy for users to find each.

Locating the global links at the page top makes sense if one considers the logical flow of information through a screen. A selection from this global area eventually results in display of a page and its content, a top-to-bottom sequential eye flow. The left-justified category navigation area would, however, have been better positioned on the right. Given the common cultural left-to-right reading sequence, upon completion of reading of a page's content the eyes will be flowing right toward the right side of the screen. Finding the navigation links next needed would be more efficient. A right positioning of these links would also place them next to a scroll bar, a common focus of the user's attention on screens being scrolled. This vertically arrayed category navigation listing, while optimizing visual scanning of alternatives, is quite wasteful of screen space, consuming about 20 percent of a screen's pixels. Its space-consuming orientation is a usability trade-off, ease of scanning being enhanced at the expense of screen efficiency. All in all, navigation consistency reduces learning and avoids user confusion, so to now change its location would probably unleash greater problems.

For long scrolling pages, repeat important global or local links at the page bottom. When finishing a page, the user, then, will not have to scroll upward to locate important navigation links.

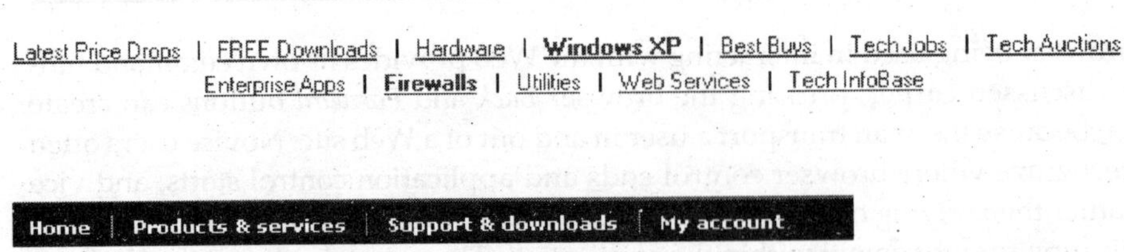

Figure 5.13 Textual explicit listing navigation bars.

Figure 5.14 Graphical or iconic navigation bars.

Figure 5.15 Command button navigation bar.

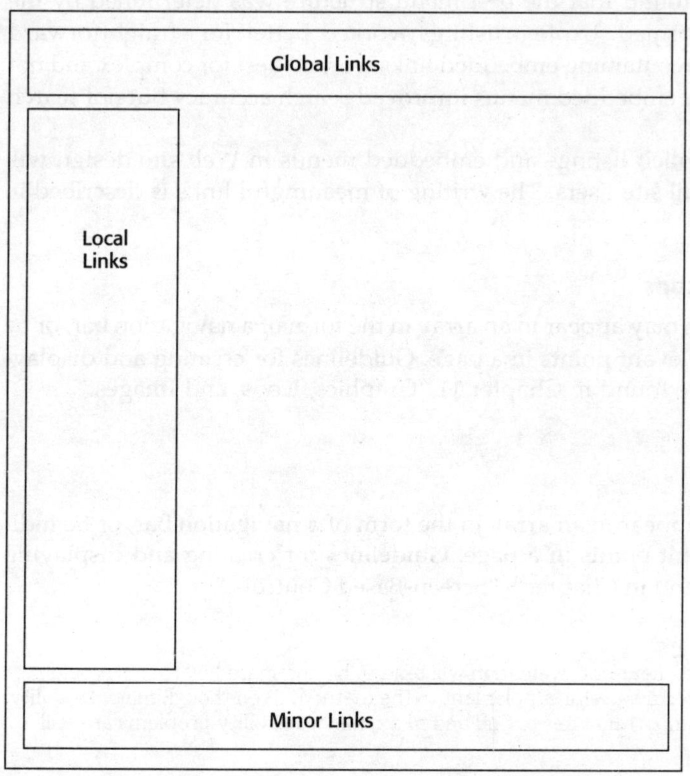

Figure 5.16 Web navigation component locations.

Textual Phrases

- Provide a mix of textual phrase links:
  - — In explicit menus.
  - — Embedded within page text.

Textual phrases are words, or short pieces of highlighted text, serving as links. Textual phrase links possess two distinct structures, explicit and embedded. An *explicit* menu is a listing of textual phrase links set apart from the main page content, often in a toolbar. These listings usually include links to various Web site topics, links to site global features such as the site map or search facility, and perhaps links to other related sites. These listings closely resemble typical screen menu arrays in their structure and presentation. A typical explicit menu is shown in Figure 5.13. An *embedded* menu is a link contained within the textual content of a page. Certain words or phrases are designated as links, highlighted, and when selected display the linked component for the user. An embedded menu is illustrated in Figure 5.17. Web sites usually contain both explicit link listings and embedded links in various mixes.

Lai and Waugh (1995) studied the effect of explicit listing hierarchical menus and embedded menus on a search task. They compared the three menu structures, menus composed solely of explicit listings, solely embedded menus, and mixed explicit and embedded menus. They found that the best menu structure was determined by the kind of search task performed. Explicit listings worked better for straightforward search tasks, while menus containing embedded links worked best for complex and not fully known searches. The embedded menus improved search accuracy but not search efficiency.

Providing a mix of explicit listings and embedded menus in Web site design will best satisfy the needs of all site users. The writing of meaningful links is described in Chapter 9.

Graphical Images or Icons

Graphical images or icons may appear in an array in the form of a navigation bar, or be individually located at relevant points in a page. Guidelines for creating and displaying graphics and icons are found in Chapter 11 "Graphics, Icons, and Images."

Command Buttons

Command buttons may appear in an array in the form of a navigation bar, or be individually located at relevant points in a page. Guidelines for creating and displaying command buttons are found in Chapter 8 "Screen-Based Controls."

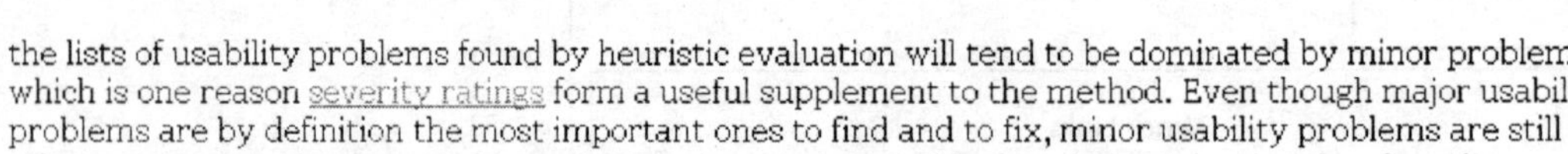
the lists of usability problems found by heuristic evaluation will tend to be dominated by minor problems, which is one reason severity ratings form a useful supplement to the method. Even though major usability problems are by definition the most important ones to find and to fix, minor usability problems are still

Figure 5.17 Embedded link menu.

Other Web Site Navigation Elements

In addition to Navigation bars, a number of other Web site elements are also important components of the Web navigation system. Among these are overviews, including executive summaries, site maps, indexes, and tables of contents. Other elements are historical trails and search engines.

Overviews

- Provide:
  - — An executive summary that provides a preview of the site and contains links to all major concepts.
  - — A site map illustrating the site's hierarchical structure and the relationships of components.
  - — Both global and local maps.
  - — An alphabetized site index.
  - — A table of contents.
- Allow accessibility from any point in the Web site.

Overviews provide a top-level view of a site's organization and content. Having an understanding of how a site is organized, the landmarks available within it, and the content it contains; assists the navigation process. In driving an automobile, referring to a road map before embarking on trip usually results in reaching one's destination faster, easier recovery from inadvertent wrong turns, a better ability to handle any unexpected detours that may be encountered, and a less stressful trip.

Overviews are most useful if provided in several forms. They may be needed during a Web interaction as well as before starting into a site. A graphical system help function, for example, may be available in tutorial form, be accessible by topics, or be organized in alphabetic form for easy scanning. It is difficult to predict the user's exact need at any moment in a session.

An *executive summary* will provide an overview of the site in narrative form and contain links to all major concepts. A *site map* will illustrate the site's hierarchical structure in either graphical or textual form. These elements provide a prospective on one's position in the spatial hierarchy. Maps may be made available at both a global or local level within the site, depending upon the site's complexity. An alphabetized site *index* will permit quick access through keywords and specific topics. A *table of contents*, structured as in a printed book, will permit review of major topics and the subtopics within. All of a Web site's overview elements should be accessible from any point within the site.

Historical Trails

- Provide:
  - — Breadcrumb Trails.
    - Locate at the top of the page below the navigation links.
  - — History Lists.

— History Trees.
— Footprints.
— Bookmarks.

Historical navigation aids try to show the user's position in an information space by showing where they have come from, or where they have been. Seeing a navigation path enables a user to better understand the context of the currently displayed page. Displayed paths also provide a means to easily return to places of interest. A *breadcrumb trail* in a hierarchical Web site structure is a sequential textual listing of pages traversed from the parent page to the page currently being displayed. A trail, illustrated in Figure 5.18, is also a series of links that permit the user to go back to any page in the sequence with one click. At this moment no standard exists for how to separate the page names in a trail. Symbols used include an arrow (->), a colon (:), a greater than sign (>), and a slash (/). Until a standard evolves, any of the above symbols remain acceptable. Do not use anything else, however. Position a breadcrumb trail at the top of the page below any existing navigation links.

A *history list* is a sequential textual listing of sites or pages visited over a specific time period, a session, a day, or some other time period. A *history tree* is an overview map of a site's structure with pages already visited marked by an indicator such as a plus sign, check mark, or asterisk. The markings serve as *footprints*, guiding the user back to pages of interest, and/or signaling which have already been seen and may no longer be of interest. A *bookmark* is similar to a history list except that it is designated by the user to mark locations of continuing interest.

Search Facility

■ Provide a search facility.

Another form of navigation support is provided by a site search facility. Provide such a facility within larger sites.

Web Site Navigation Guidelines

How many links should exist on a page? How should textual links be presented to make them obvious? What kinds of links should be included on a page? These and similar questions are addressed next.

useit.com → Papers and Essays → Heuristic Evaluation → List of Heuristics

IBM developerWorks : Web architecture : Web architecture articles

Weather > Pacific Rim > Australia > **Sydney**

Figure 5.18 Breadcrumb trails.

Scrolling

- Do not require scrolling of navigation-only pages.
- Minimize the need for scrolling to view all links on pages containing content.
- Never require horizontal scrolling.

Never require scrolling of navigation-only pages. Besides being tedious, not being able to see all links at the same time makes comparison of the alternatives for selection purposes much more difficult. For scrollable content pages, minimize the need to scroll to see all links. Also, ensure that all related links on a screen are seen together to facilitate comparison. Never require horizontal scrolling. It makes text reading difficult and users dislike it.

Number of Links

- Every page should contain at least one link.
- Be conservative in the total number of links presented on a screen:
  - — Without logical groupings of elements, limit links to 4 to 8.
  - — With logical groupings of elements, limit links to 18 to 24.
- Restrict embedded links to those most important, pertinent, and interesting.
  - — Place less relevant links in a listing.

One link. At a minimum, every page should contain at least one link. To follow a path and then reach a dead end is frustrating. Also, a dead-end page, if accessed from another Web site, provides no means for the user to navigate to other site pages.

Conservative number. How many links presented on a page is ultimately determined by the complexity of the site and its content. Menu research indicates that without choice groupings, links should be limited to 4 to 8, with groupings, limited to 18 to 24. Some experts in Web design recommend even fewer, a maximum of 8 to 12 links. In general, the more links contained on a page, the more decisions concerning which link to follow are imposed on the user. Where any link ambiguity exists, the odds of guessing correctly which link to follow diminish. A smaller number of links also increases the likelihood that those being looked for will be noticed. It is not necessary to mention all features of a site on all pages. To reduce the number of links, restrict those presented to the most important site content or useful features.

Embedded links. The trade-off that must be addressed in creating embedded links is linkability versus readability. Embedded links can be a distraction and reduce page readability, especially if used in abundance. They may also be overlooked in text scanning, especially if the scanning is not carefully done. Embedded links, however, can provide more meaningful context, adjacent phrases or sentence words being useful in understanding the link's purpose. The best trade-off is to incorporate embedded links in moderation. Reserve them for the most important, pertinent, and interesting document points. If other relevant content exists, present it in an explicit link listing.

Presenting Links

- Link text:
  - — Underline all link text, including that:
    - Embedded in page content.
    - Contained in explicit menu listings.
    - Contained in headings.
    - Used as graphical labels.
  - — Distinguish between unselected/unvisited links and selected/visited links.
    - Make unselected/unvisited links blue.
    - Make selected/visited links purple.
- Kinds of links:
  - — Distinguish links leading to different Web destinations through a differentiating symbol:
    - Precede links to content within the same page with a pound sign (#).
      - For links moving downward in the page, use: #The principles of design.
      - For links moving upward in the page use: #^ Principles introduction.
    - Precede links to external or foreign sites with another unique symbol such as an asterisk (*): * Additional information.
    - Do not precede links to other site pages with any symbol:
      - More principles of design.
  - — Also distinguish links leading to different Web destinations by presenting them in consistent locations.
- Graphical links:
  - — Distinguish graphical links from decorative graphics through:
    - Underlining graphical text labels.
- Links in toolbars:
  - — Distinguish links contained in toolbars through:
    - Presenting in consistent locations.
    - Using different colored backgrounds.

Links must be easy to find. They must not be confused with other screen graphics or textual content. Having to search for links can be a tedious and frustrating process. Whether a link has been navigated before must also be obvious. When looking for something new, continually embarking down a path already traveled can also be frustrating.

Link text. To identify a link, the well-established convention is to *underline* the link text. All link text must be underlined, including that embedded in page content, that presented in explicit listings, that contained in headings, and that taking the form of labels in graphical images.

Unselected/unvisited links must be *distinguishable* from selected/visited links. The ability to understand what links have been followed is one of the few standard navigational aids available in browsers. Stick with the default colors of *blue* for links already followed and *purple* for links not yet ventured down. While the choice of blue as a text color was poor because of its degraded reading ability it is now well learned. Its use is recommended because it is now very familiar. Using nonstandard link colors can lead to severe problems. It is difficult to remember what color means what, increasing link selection errors. It can also lead to confusion with normal underlined text in a document.

Kinds of links. Visually distinguish links leading to different Web destinations. A link that simply moves within a page, if unknown to the user, can be confusing, leading people to follow a link prematurely. A link that moves to another Web site can be aggravating if the user was not ready to move on. A link's destination should be as predictable as the content at the other end. One way to distinguish these different kinds of links is to precede the link text with a unique symbol if it does not simply lead to a new page within a Web site being viewed. To create distinctiveness, precede links to content *within the same page* with a pound sign (#). For links moving to content downward in the page, use the pound sign by itself. For links moving to content upward in the page use, the pound sign with an upward pointing arrow (#^). For links to *external or foreign* sites, precede the text with another unique symbol such as an asterisk (*). For links to *other site pages,* do not adorn the text with any symbol. A destination convention has yet to be established in Web site design. When one is established, it should be applied.

Designation of different destinations can also be accomplished by grouping links by kind, giving them a descriptive heading, and placing them in unique and consistent *locations* on a page. In the margins, for example, or at the page's top or bottom. Locating within-page links at the page's top would make most sense; locating links to other or foreign sites at the page bottom would be the most logical choice.

Graphical links. If care is not exercised, graphical links may be confused with decorative graphics. A principle of graphical or icon design is to always provide a text label. (See Chapter 11.) Distinguish graphical links by underlining the graphical text labels, as is done with plain link text.

Links in toolbars. Distinguish links contained in toolbars from page content by presenting the toolbars in consistent locations, and/or displaying them in backgrounds of a contrasting color to the page content. Global toolbars, most often in iconic or button form, are becoming consistently arrayed across the top of a page. Category or topical toolbars are now commonly arrayed down the left side of the page. Toolbars containing textual listings that contrast less with textual page content, can be emphasized and differentiated through presenting them with a background that contrasts with the content.

Some kinds of links to avoid are summarized in Table 5.3.

Other Link Guidelines

In general, many of the principles in menu design presented earlier in this chapter, and to be presented in Chapter 8, also apply to presenting and organizing links. These guidelines should be reviewed in conjunction with this brief summary that follows.

Table 5.3 Links to Avoid (or Links to Aggravate the User)

Orphan Link	A link leading to a page that does not possess any navigation options.
Boomerang Link	A links that returns to the exact same spot.
Gotcha Link	A link that leads to little or no content.
False Alarm Link	A warning to not follow a link you really should follow.
Mystery Link	A link that does not look like a link because it is not properly labeled or does not possess a raised appearance.
Link-mania	Linking every time the same keyword is mentioned in a page.
Link-drunk	A long succession of links that must be followed to reach the destination.
Stairmaster Links	No *Next* link in a series of pages, necessitating continual return to a table of contents.
Gratuitous Link	A link to other sites to return a favor.
Missed opportunities	For useful links.

- Writing:
  - — Provide links to satisfy a range of user needs.
  - — Create descriptive links clearly indicating their destination or resulting action.
- Grouping:
  - — Group links by the most relevant menu-grouping scheme.
  - — Separate visually the following types of navigation:
    - Upward to the immediate parent page.
    - Upward to the beginning of the section or category of information.
    - Across to main sections or categories of information.
    - To basic utilities.
- Ordering:
  - — Order links by the most relevant menu choice-ordering scheme.
- Heading:
  - — Where appropriate, provide a listing heading describing the organizing category, principle, or theme.
- Size:
  - — Provide graphical images and command buttons of sufficient and equal size.
- Spacing:
  - — Create equal spacing between choices graphical image and textual listing toolbars.
- Inapplicability:
  - — Disable and display dimmed links conditionally not applicable.

Writing. People with a *broad range* of needs and interests will use Web sites. Create links to satisfy disparate goals. Redundant links (different links to the same page) may be useful in satisfying these varied needs. A link should be *descriptive*, clearly indicating its destination or resulting action. The success of the link will be depen-dent on how well the user can predict where the link will lead. Descriptiveness aids prediction. Complete guidelines for writing link text will be found in Chapter 9.

Grouping. Place links of a similar purpose and function together. Develop groupings using the most relevant grouping scheme. In Web navigation, it useful to visually separate the following types of links: upward to the immediate parent page, upward to the beginning of the presented section or category of information, across to main sections or categories of information, and to basic utilities. People make better link choices when they can readily eliminate wrong links. Grouping helps this process.

Ordering. Arrange the links by the most relevant menu-choice-ordering scheme, such as importance, frequency of use, or sequence of use, as previously described.

Headings. When appropriate, provide an introductory word or phrase at top of the link list as a heading. Inform viewers about the list's organizing category, principle, or theme. Establishing list context will aid users in selecting the correct link.

Size. To achieve balance, create a visually pleasing composition, make all links readily identifiable as links, create icons and command buttons of equal size. The size of any text inscribed on icons or buttons should also be consistent in size. In addition, explicit listings of textual links should be of the same size.

Spacing. To also achieve balance, and a visually pleasing composition, all groups of links composed of icons, command buttons, listings of textual links should be equally spaced.

Inapplicability. Links that are irrelevant in a given situation should be disabled and displayed dimmed out.

Kinds of Links

- Within a page:
  - — For long pages, include links to internal page content.
- Within a Web site:
  - — On all pages include links to:
    - The Web site home page.
    - Global Web site features.
    - Other main pages, navigation points, or categories.
    - The likely Web site starting point.
    - Main pages with links to the page.
  - — On sequential pages, include links to the:
    - Next page.
    - Previous page.
  - — Also consider including links to:
    - Places of related interest.
    - Important pages.

- Background or explanatory information.
- Supplemental information.
- New or changed content.
- Web site Quit or Exit.

■ External links:

— Most appropriate for informational sites.

— Provide links to relevant information on other Web sites.

- Related content.
- Reference information.
- Background reading.

— Place external links on a separate page.

— Provide an indication when a link goes outside the current site.

Within a page. For long pages, include links to for important content within the page. Place these links at the top of the page and identify them, by a heading or symbol (see discussion above), as internal links.

Within a Web site, on all pages include the following links:

Home page. A home link will transport the user directly to the site's home page, a stable and safe anchor point to escape to in times of difficulty. Easy access is also achieved when the user is ready to start over, or ready to commence a new navigation. A home link eliminates the necessity for sequential backward movement up through a series of pages.

Global features. Provides links to a site's global features, including the highest level of information categories and utilities such as the Search facility.

Other main pages, navigation points, sections, or categories. Do not link to all sections of the site from all pages; to do so will be overwhelming. To provide easy navigation throughout a site, provide links to a site's major navigation points, sections, or categories of information. Pages linked to must possess substantive content.

MYTH **Why do users need a road map of a Web site. They'll know where to go.**

The likely Web site starting point. Provide links to the site's likely starting point, the home page, a site map, or an index.

Main pages with links to page. Provide links back to the main pages that have links to the displayed page. A return link describing the page one is going back to provides better predictability and much clearer context. It also provides escapability. While the browser's Back button will accomplish the same thing, it does not say what it is going back too, in case the user has forgotten where arrival was from. It also keeps navigation within the application itself (as opposed to the browser).

For *sequential* pages, provide easily accessible links to adjacent pages:

Next. To allow sequential movement downward through pages, place a Next link at the end of each page. Explain, whenever possible, what will happen or where one will go when the link is selected. Without this link, the user will have to continually refer to a table of contents or menu listing to continue navigation. This link will also allow users, should they choose, to leaf through the site as they would a printed book.

Previous. Also include Previous link returning the user to the prior page in the Web site structure, thereby reversing direction in screen navigation. The browser Back button will only return the user to the last page *viewed*. This will facilitate movement through a site for those entering from another Web site into the page. Leafing backward through the page hierarchy will also be easy. Locate this link at the end of the page. For long pages, also include a Previous link at the page top.

Also consider including links such as the following:

Places of related interest. Provide links to other pages with related content. Wherever the user's attention is likely to be captured, provide a direct link to related places. Also, during a search, especially when using a search facility, people rarely land directly on the desired page. Often, however, they get close. Provide links to the answers they are most likely looking for.

Important pages. Provide links to important or high-priority areas or pages you want to make sure the user sees.

Background or explanatory information. Provide links to background or explanatory information to aid users who do not have the necessary knowledge to understand or use the page. Every page must be considered independent, and its content must be understood based upon the assumption that the user has seen no other related pages.

Supplemental information. Use links to provide supplemental information like definitions of terms and abbreviations

New or changed content. Draw attention to new or changed content by making it easy to notice and go directly to. A prominently placed *What's New?* link can be used for this purpose.

Quit or Exit. The Web has no way to stop running an application without closing the browser or leaving by a link. Non-Web platforms have clearly marked exit paths, including a *Quit* or *Exit* on the File Menu. Provide this command so the users can confirm that an application is finished and any entered data should be saved. This command may be included on a special exit page showing external links and other useful information.

Provide *external* links to other relevant Web sites and information sources. There is some evidence that the inclusion of outbound links increases a site's credibility. It indicates that the site authors have done their homework, and they are not afraid to let users visit other sites.

Informational sites. Links to external or foreign sites are most appropriate for informational sites, where browsing is a primary usage purpose. In applications, where a task must be completed, focusing on the task is the most important aspect of design.

Related content. Provide links to relevant information on other Web sites, including sites with similar content to that mentioned in your Web site. Also provide links to other resources, repositories, reference information, and background reading.

Separate page. Whenever possible, locate links that go outside of the Web site on a separate page. To accomplish this, use a *See Also* link to this additional page. Placing these links on a separate page will not disrupt the flow of the displayed pages, and not tempt people to leave the site before they have adequately reviewed it.

Outside indication. Identify links leading away from the site by a heading or a unique symbol (see discussion above). Also inform users that they are leaving the displayed site for another Web site.

Link Maintenance

- Maintain correct internal links.
- Frequently check and correct external links.

As sites are modified, internal links may have to be revised. Carefully check sequential pages if *Next* and *Previous* links are used within the site. External links should also be checked and corrected frequently. Due to the volatile nature of the Web, a linked site's content may change, its location may change, or a site may cease to exist. The credibility of a site's entire content suffers if it is not properly maintained.

Maintaining a Sense of Place

As has been said several times, a sense of place—where one currently is in the labyrinth of the Web—is often difficult to maintain. A site's organizational structure is often complex, and the boundaries between sites often seem nonexistent. Navigation links can transport a person from anywhere to anywhere, as does the *Star Trek* spaceship transporter machine. (While this machine moves humanoids to a new environment, the Web moves the new environment to the humanoid.) These radical shifts in context created by jumping around information space through links can be extremely confusing. It is important that one's location be continually reinforced, because people desire stability and assurance that they are where they think they are. They also need a sense of exactly where they can go from their current location.

Paper documents create a sense of where one is located through a mixture of graphical and textual cues supplied by the design of the book, including the varying fonts and images used. Cues are also provided by the organizational scheme outlined in the table of contents, and the physical sensation of the entire book itself. Looking at where a bookmark is placed in a novel provides an excellent indication of one's location in the reading space. The answers to questions like "Can I finish before the aircraft lands and the business conference starts?" are capable of being predicted with some reliability. Electronic documents provide few of these physical cues. To provide a sense of place, plentiful and explicit cues relating to site context and organization must be provided. These cues are provided by the site's overall design characteristics and the specific orientation elements included within the Web site.

Design Characteristics That Aid in Maintaining a Sense of Place

- To assist maintaining a sense of place within a Web site:
  - — Provide a simple hierarchical tree structure.
  - — Provide ease of movement to important site features.
- To assist maintaining a sense of place across multiple Web sites:
  - — Provide consistency in all Web site design elements, including:
    - Graphical identity schemes.
    - Component presentation.
    - Component organization and location.

Within a Web site. A simple hierarchical tree structure with obvious and linked major categories is an easily understood organization scheme. Easy identification of important site features, and ease of movement to them, is also important.

Across multiple Web sites. Design consistency contributes significantly to maintaining one's sense of place when one is moving between multiple sites. Design consistency gives a site a unique look and feel that becomes obvious as links are followed within it. Moving to a new site will be clearly evident when the design scheme changes. Consistency in the graphical identity scheme, use of colors, patterns, graphics, font styles, and so forth, will be the most noticeable aspects. Consistency in component presentation, organization, and location are also very important.

Design Elements That Aid in Maintaining a Sense of Place

- Provide a home base.
- Use recurring navigation tools on all pages.
- Use recurring elements on all pages.
- Provide page numbers for sequential pages.
- Provide ongoing feedback that shows where users are in a site.
- Provide on-demand aids that illustrate the user's location within a site.
  - — Site maps.
  - — Table of contents.
- Provide clearly written link labels.

Home base. As previously mentioned, a site's home page is a stable, concrete, and safe anchor point to escape to in times of difficulty.

Recurring navigation tools. Standard navigation tools should appear on every page. In addition to creating uniformity in sight appearance, recurring tools create a more stable page environment, enhance navigation learning, and increase the user's control of the dialog.

Recurring page elements. Repeated page elements, such as titles, banners, logos, and icons, also create site uniformity. Omanson, Cline, Kilpatrick, and Dunkerton (1998) found that the page element that most significantly aided user orientation was the site logo.

Page numbers. For a long series of sequential pages provide page numbers on each page to indicate where in the page string one is located. Another useful feature is to convert page numbers into links and present them on each page. A search, for example, may return a dozen pages of matches. At the bottom of each page inscribe, in link form, page numbers, as follows:

1 2 3 4 5 6 7 8 9 10 11 12

An estimation of document length is obtained, and the pages need not be viewed in sequential order.

Ongoing feedback showing location in Web site. Provide an historical trail, such as a breadcrumb trail, that shows where the user is located within a branch of a site. In addition to providing context for the displayed page, the trail permits easy return to any page up the trail.

On-demand aids illustrating location. Navigation aids, such as a site map or table of contents, when retrieved should show exactly where the user's current location fits within the structure of the site. The current position should be highlighted within the presented information structure. Ideally, in a site map, the complete navigation path from the home page through intermediate pages to the current page should be presented.

Clearly written links. Labels that clearly indicate the function of the link, its destination, or its resulting action, reduce disorientation. Bad links are less likely to be followed and aimless wandering reduced.

Kinds of Graphical Menus

Providing the proper kinds of graphical menus to perform system tasks is also critical to system success. The best kind of menu to use in each situation depends on several factors. The following must be considered:

- The number of items to be presented in the menu.
- How often the menu is used.
- How often the menu contents may change.

Each kind of common graphical menu will be described in terms of purpose, advantages, disadvantages, and suggested proper usage. Design guidelines for each kind are also presented. A proper usage summary for the various kinds of menus will be found in Table 5.4 at the end of the menu discussion.

Menu Bar

- Proper usage:
  - — To identify and provide access to common and frequently used application actions that take place in a wide variety of different windows.
  - — A menu bar choice by itself should not initiate an action.

The highest-level graphical system menu is commonly called the menu bar. A menu bar consists of a collection of descriptions that serve as headings or titles for a series of actions on an associated pull-down menu. A menu bar choice by itself should not initiate an action.

The menu is typically arrayed in a horizontal row at the top of a window. Occasionally a menu bar is referred to as a collection of menu *titles.* In reality it is a menu in itself, and it is appropriate to simply refer to it as a *menu*. A menu bar is the starting point for many dialogs. Consistency in menu bar design and use will present to the user a stable, familiar, and comfortable starting point for all interactions. Menu bars are most effectively used for presenting common, frequent, or critical actions used on many windows in a variety of circumstances.

Menu bars often consist of a series of textual words, as represented in Figure 5.19. Macintosh, Presentation Manager, and Microsoft Windows illustrate examples of this textual approach. Some products have placed the choices within buttons, as represented in Figure 5.20. An example of this approach is Sun Microsystems' Open Look, which calls them *menu buttons*. There are also combinations of both. OSF/Motif presents a list of textual choices, but when one is selected, it resembles a button. Motif refers to these as *cascade buttons*.

Each menu bar item is the top level of a hierarchical menu. It will have a pull-down menu associated with it, detailing the specific actions that may be performed. Some products have tried to circumvent this pull-down rule and have included items in menu bars that are direct actions themselves. These direct action items have frequently been designated by an exclamation point (!) following the menu bar description. The inclusion of direct items in a menu bar should be avoided. It creates inconsistency in menu bar use and may easily cause an action to be erroneously selected. Menu bars should always possess an associated pull-down menu.

Figure 5.19 Menu bar composed of text.

Figure 5.20 Menu bar composed of buttons.

Menu bars are used to present application alternatives or choices to the screen user. Typically, each system provides a default set of menu bar commands (for example, File, Edit, View, Window, Help).

The *advantages* of menu bars are that they:

- Are always visible, reminding the user of their existence.
- Are easy to browse through.
- Are easy to locate consistently on the screen.
- Usually do not obscure the screen working area.
- Usually are not obscured by windows and dialog boxes.
- Allow for use of keyboard equivalents.

The *disadvantages* of menu bars are that:

- They consume a full row of screen space.
- They require looking away from the main working area to find.
- They require moving pointer from the main working area to select.
- The menu options are smaller than full-size buttons, slowing selection time.
- Their horizontal orientation is less efficient for scanning.
- Their horizontal orientation limits number of choices that can be displayed.

Display

- All primary windows must have a menu bar.
- All menu bars must have an associated pull-down menu containing at least two choices.
- Do not allow the user to turn off the display of the menu bar.
- If all the items in its associated pull-down menu are disabled, then disable the menu bar item.
  - Display the disabled item in a visually subdued manner.
  - However, the disabled pull-down menu must always be capable of being pulled-down so that the choices may be seen.

All primary windows must have a menu bar. Because a menu bar choice should not initiate an action, all menu bars must have an associated pull-down menu with at least two choices. If a planned menu bar choice has one or no choices, combine it within another menu bar category. Do not leave it as a separate category. Secondary windows may use their primary window bar. (Window types are described in Chapter 6.)

Never permit the menu bar to be turned off, because reminders of system actions will be eliminated and possibly forgotten by inexperienced users. If all the items in its associated pull-down menu are disabled, then disable the menu bar item but continue to display it in a visually subdued manner. The disabled pull-down menu must always be capable of being pulled down so that the choices may be seen. This will facilitate system exploration and learning.

Location

- Position choices horizontally over the entire row at the top of the screen, just below the screen title.
- A large number of choices may necessitate display over two rows.

Choices should be positioned horizontally across the top of the screen below the screen title. A typical bar is composed of no more than about seven or eight choices. Due to screen space constraints, and limitations in human information-processing capabilities, a maximum of seven or eight is reasonable. In the event that more are needed, a second line of choices may be added. Try to avoid a second line, however.

Title

- The window title will be the menu bar title.

The window title will serve as the menu bar title.

Item Descriptions

- The menu item descriptions must clearly reflect the kinds of choices available in the associated pull-down menus.
- Menu item descriptions will be the "titles" for pull-down menus associated with them.
- Use mixed-case letters to describe choices.
- Use single-word choices whenever possible.
- Do not display choices that are never available to the user.

The menu item descriptions must clearly reflect alternatives available in the associated pull-down menus. Choices should be composed of mixed-case single words. Typically, only the first letter of the choice is capitalized. Acronyms, abbreviations, or proper nouns that are normally capitalized may be capitalized. Choices should never be numbered.

If a multiple-word item must be used for clarity, consider including a hyphen between the multiple words to associate the words and differentiate them from other items. Do not display choices that are never available to the user.

Organization

- Follow standard platform ordering schemes where they exist.
  - — Place application-specific choices where they fit best.

- Order choices left-to-right with:
  — Most frequent choices to the left.
  — Related information grouped together.
- Choices found on more than one menu bar should be consistently positioned.
- Left-justify choices within the line.
- When choices can be logically grouped, provide visual logical groupings, if possible.
- Help, when included, should be located at the right side of the bar.

File   Edit   Options   Window   Help

Figure 5.21

Follow standard platform ordering schemes where they exist. Place application-specific choices where they fit best. Order all choices left-to-right, with the most frequently elected choices to the left and related information grouped together. Choices found on more than one menu bar should be consistently positioned.

Left-justify all choices within the line (as opposed to centering them when there are not enough choices to completely fill the line). However, always locate Help, when included, at the far right side. Right side positioning will always keep Help in a consistent location within the bar. Also, provide visual groupings of all related choices, if space on the bar permits.

Layout

- Indent the first choice one space from the left margin.
- Leave at least three spaces between each of the succeeding choices (except for Help which will be right-justified).
- Leave one space between the final choice and the right margin.

xFilexxxEdit   Options   Window   Helpx

Figure 5.22

The spacing recommendations above are intended to provide clear delineation of choices, leave ample room for the selection cursor, provide a legible selected choice, and provide efficiency in bar design.

Separation

- Separate the bar from the remainder of the screen by:
  — A different background, or
  — Solid lines above and below.

In addition to being identified by its location at the top, the bar should be identifiable by a contrasting display technique. The most effective way to do this is through the use of a different background, either reversed polarity (black on white for the bar, contrasted with white on black for the screen body), or a color different from the adjacent title and screen body. When a color is used, it must be chosen in conjunction with good color principles in Chapter 12. Affecting the background color choice will be the foreground or choice description color, the selection indicator to be described next, and the screen body background color. The contrast of the bar to the remainder of the screen should be moderate, neither too vivid nor too subtle.

Other Components

- Keyboard equivalent mnemonics should be included on menu bars.
- Keyboard accelerators, to a window indicators, and cascade indicators need not be included.

While keyboard mnemonics should be included on menu bars, keyboard accelerators and other intent indicators should not because a menu bar selection will always lead to a pull-down menu.

Selection Indication

- Keyboard cursor:
  - — Use a reverse video, or reverse color, selection cursor to surround the choice.
  - — Cover the entire choice, including one blank space before and after the choice word.

Figure 5.23

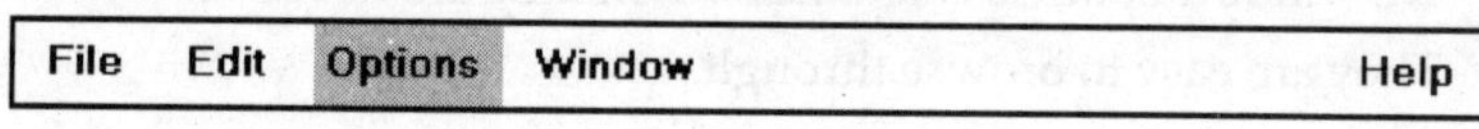

- Pointer:
  - — Use reverse video, or reverse color, to highlight the selected choice.

When using the keyboard, the selection cursor should be indicated by a contrasting reverse video or reverse color bar surrounding the choice. The cursor should extend at least one space to each side of the choice word. When using a pointer, use a reverse video or reverse color to highlight the choice when it is selected.

The recommended reverse color combination is simply to reverse the foreground and background colors of the unselected choices. Colors chosen must be those that are completely legible in either polarity. Some good combinations would include: black-white, blue-white, and black-cyan. Other contrasting color combinations may, of course, also be used. Since limitations exist in the number of colors that may be used on a screen, however, the colors chosen for menu bars must be selected in conjunction with the colors of other screen components. Since a menu bar can be identified by its location, the use of a completely different color to identify it can be redundant and unnecessary. It is more practical to reserve the use of color for other less identifiable screen components.

Pull-Down Menu

- Proper usage:
  - — To initiate frequently used application actions that take place on a wide variety of different windows.
  - — A small number of items.
  - — Items best represented textually.
  - — Items whose content rarely changes.

Selection of an alternative from the menu bar results in the display of the exact actions available to the user. These choices are displayed in a vertically arrayed listing that appears to pull down from the bar. Hence, these listings, as illustrated in Figure 5.24, are typically referred to as *pull-downs*. Other identification terms may be used, such as d*rop-downs*.

Pull-downs are first-level menus used to provide access to common and frequently used application actions that take place on a wide variety of different windows. They are most useful for a small number of rarely changing items, usually about 5 to 10. Larger numbers of choices become awkward to use, being best handled by incorporating cascade menus (see discussion that follows). Pull-downs are best suited for items represented textually, but graphical presentations, such as colors, patterns, and shades, may also be used.

The *advantages* of pull-down menus are:

- The menu bar cues a reminder of their existence.
- They may be located relatively consistently on the screen.
- No window space is consumed when they are not used.
- They are easy to browse through.
- Their vertical orientation is most efficient for scanning.
- Their vertical orientation is most efficient for grouping.
- Their vertical orientation permits more choices to be displayed.
- They allow for display of both keyboard equivalents and accelerators.

The *disadvantages* of pull-down menus are:

- They require searching and selecting from another menu before seeing options.
- They require looking away from main working area to read.

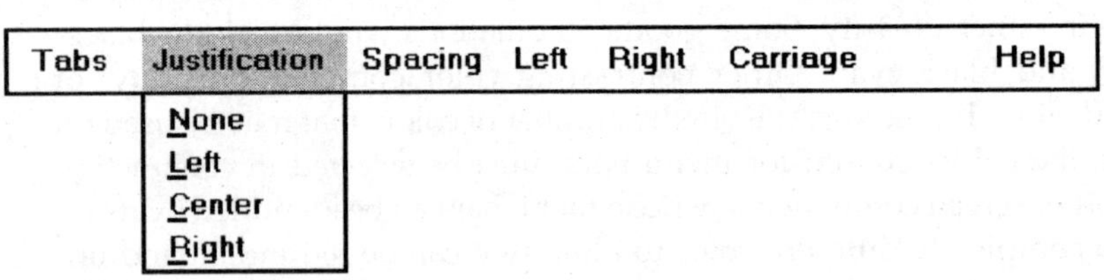

Figure 5.24 Menu bar pull-down.

- The require moving the pointer out of working area to select (unless using keyboard equivalents).
- The items are smaller than full-size buttons, slowing selection time.
- The may obscure the screen working area.

Display

- Display all possible alternatives.
- Gray-out or dim items that cannot be chosen due to the current state of an application.

Display all possible alternatives on a pull-down. Gray-out or dim items that cannot be chosen due to the current state of an application. If all items are, at any one point, not applicable, they must still be capable of being retrieved for perusal through the menu bar.

Location

- Position the pull-down directly below the selected menu bar choice.

The pull-down will be located directly below the menu bar choice by which it is selected.

Size

- Must contain a minimum of two choices.
- Restrict to no more than 5 to 10 choices, preferably 8 or less.

A typical pull-down consists of about 5 to 10 choices, although more or less are sometimes seen. A pull-down should always contain more than one choice. Because of their vertical orientation, there is space for more choices containing longer descriptions than on a menu bar, and they can easily be positioned on one screen.

Title

- Not necessary on a pull-down menu. The title will be the name of the menu bar item chosen.

The name of the item chosen on the menu bar serves as the title of a pull-down menu.

Item Descriptions

- Use mixed-case, headline-style words to describe choices.
  - — If the choices can be displayed graphically, for example, as fill-in patterns, shades, or colors, textual descriptions are not necessary.
- Do not:
  - — Identify a menu item by the same wording as its menu title.
  - — Change the meaning of menu items through use of the Shift key.
  - — Use scrolling in pull-downs.
  - — Place instructions in pull-downs.

Choices should be composed of mixed-case, headline-style words. For multiword choice descriptions, capitalize the first letter of each significant word. Acronyms, abbreviations, or proper nouns that are normally capitalized may be capitalized. If the choices can be displayed graphically, such as fill-in patterns, shades, or colors, textual descriptions are not necessary.

Never identify a pull-down menu item by the same wording as its menu bar title. The menu bar title must reflect all the items within the pull-down. Never change the meaning of items through use of the Shift key. Shift key activations are extremely error-prone, and their use should be reserved for key accelerators. Also, do not use scrolling in, or place instructions within, a pull-down.

Organization

- Follow standard platform ordering schemes when they exist.
  - — Place application-specific choices where they fit best.
- Place frequent or critical items at the top.
- Separate destructive choices from other choices.
- Align choices into columns, with:
  - — Most frequent choices toward the top.
  - — Related choices grouped together.
  - — Choices found on more than one pull-down consistently positioned.
- Left-align choice descriptions.
- Multicolumn menus are not desirable. If necessary, organize top-to-bottom, then left-to-right.

Follow standard platform ordering schemes when they exist. Place application-specific choices where they fit best. Place frequent or critical items at the top of the listing, and separate destructive choices from other choices. Align all pull-down choices into columns with their descriptions left-aligned. Locate most frequently chosen alternatives toward the top, and group related choices together. Choices found on more than one pull-down should be consistently positioned. Multicolumn menus are not desirable; if necessary, organize pull-downs from top-to-bottom, then left-to-right.

Layout

- Leave the menu bar choice leading to the pull-down highlighted in the selected manner (reverse video or reverse color).
- Physically, the pull-down menu must be wide enough to accommodate the longest menu item description and its cascade or accelerator indicator.
- Align the first character of the pull-down descriptions under the second character of the applicable menu bar choice.
- Horizontally, separate the pull-down choice descriptions from the pull-down borders by two spaces on the left side and at least two spaces on the right side.
  - — The left-side border will align with the left side of the highlighted menu bar choice.
  - — The right-side border should extend, at minimum, to the right side of its highlighted menu bar choice.

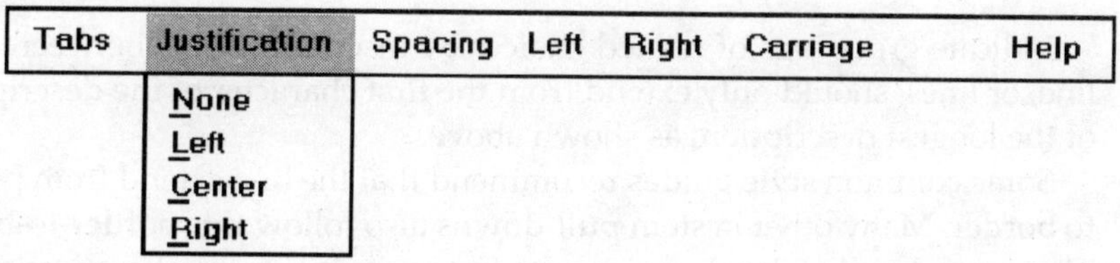

Figure 5.25

  - — Pull-downs for choices on the far right side of the menu bar, or long pull-down descriptions, may require alignment to the left of their menu bar choice to maintain visibility and clarity.

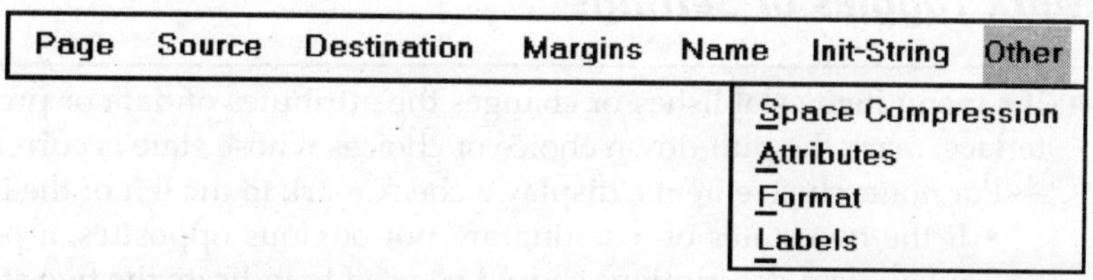

Figure 5.26

The menu bar choice leading to the pull-down should remain highlighted in the selected manner. Columnized pull-down descriptions should be aligned beginning under the second character position of the applicable bar choice. Pull-down borders should be positioned for balance and for maximum legibility and clarity of the choice descriptions. Leave two spaces to the left of the descriptions to align the left pull-down border with the left border of the selected menu bar choice. Leave a minimum of two spaces after the longest description and the right pull-down border. At the minimum, the right pull-down border should extend to the right border of the highlighted menu bar choice. Menu bar choices located at the far right, or long pull-down choice descriptions, may require alignment to the left of the applicable choice, however.

Groupings

- Provide groupings of related pull-down choices:
  — Incorporate a solid line between major groupings.
  — Incorporate a dotted or dashed line between subgroups.
  — Left-justify the lines under the first letter of the columnized choice descriptions.
  — Right-justify the lines under the last character of the longest choice description.
  — Display the solid line in the same color as the choice descriptions.

Figure 5.27

Indicate groupings of related choices by inscribing a line between each group. The line, or lines, should only extend from the first character of the descriptions to the end of the longest description, as shown above.

Some common style guides recommend that the line extend from pull-down border to border. Many other system pull-downs also follow this border-to-border approach. This extended line, however, results in too strong a visual separation between pull-down parts. The parts should be separated but not too strongly.

Mark Toggles or Settings

- If a menu item establishes or changes the attributes of data or properties of the interface, mark the pull-down choice or choices whose state is current or active "on."
  — For nonexclusive items, display a check mark to the left of the item description.
    - If the two states of a setting are not obvious opposites, a pair of alternating menu item descriptions should be used to indicate the two states.
  — For exclusive choices, precede the choice with a contrasting symbol such as a diamond or circle.

If a menu item is made permanently active or "on" when selected, this can be made clear to the user by providing a mark by the item. For nonexclusive or independent items, display a check mark to the left of the item description. For exclusive or interdependent choices, precede the choice with a different and contrasting symbol such as a diamond or circle. Microsoft Windows indicates active choices of this nature with an *option button mark.*

If a setting containing two states does not consist of clear and obvious opposites, a pair of alternating menu item descriptions should be used to indicate the two states.

Pull-Downs Leading to Another Pull-Down

- If a pull-down choice leads to another pull-down, provide a cascade indicator as follows:
  - — Place an arrow or right-pointing triangle after the choice description.
  - — Align the triangles to the right side of the pull-down.
  - — Display the triangle in the same color as the choice descriptions.

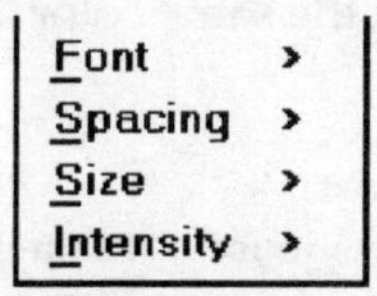

Figure 5.28

Occasionally a secondary or second level pull-down (or cascading pull-down, as it is frequently called) may be desirable if the first pull-down leads to another short series of choices. Or, it may be desirable if the first pull-down has a large number of choices that are capable of being logically grouped. The existence of this second-level, hidden pull-down should be indicated to the user on the first pull-down in a consistent manner. A simple way to do this is to include a right-pointing triangle to the right of the applicable choice description. These triangles should be aligned to the right side of the pull-down.

Pull-Downs Leading to a Window

- For pull-down choices leading to a window:
  - — Place an ellipsis (three dots) after the choice description.
  - — Do not separate the dots from the description by a space.
  - — Display the ellipsis in the same color as the choice descriptions.

Figure 5.29

When a window results from the selection of a pull-down choice, a visual indication of this fact is desirable. An ellipsis inscribed after the choice description is a good indicator that a window will appear.

Keyboard Equivalents and Accelerators

- Provide unique mnemonic codes by which choices may be selected through the typewriter keyboard.
  - — Indicate the mnemonic code by underlining the proper character.

- Provide key accelerators for choice selection.
  - — Identify the keys by their actual key-top engravings.
  - — Use a plus (+) sign to indicate that two or more keys must be pressed at the same time.
  - — Enclose the key names within parentheses ( ).
  - — Right-align the key names, beginning at least three spaces to the right of the longest choice description.
  - — Display the key alternatives in the same color as the choice descriptions.

Find...	(Ctrl+F)
Find Next	(F3)
Find Previous	(Shift+F3)
Replace...	(Ctrl+R)

Figure 5.30

Enabling the user to select pull-down choices through the keyboard provides flexibility and efficiency in the dialogue. One method of doing this is to provide single-character mnemonic codes that, when typed, will also cause the choice to be invoked. Mnemonic codes can be visually indicated in a number of ways. The recommended method is an underline beneath the proper character within the choice. Standard mnemonic codes for common commands were listed in Table 5.1.

Another method is to assign accelerators (one key, or a combination of keys) to accomplish the action. Identify these keys exactly as they are engraved on the keyboard; indicate simultaneous depression through use of a plus sign, and right-align the accelerator description and position it to the right of the choice description. Accelerators should be reserved for the most common commands. Standard accelerators are listed in Table 5.2.

Separation

- Separate the pull-down from the remainder of the screen, but visually relate it to the menu bar by:
  - — Using a background color the same as the menu bar.
  - — Displaying choice descriptions in the same color as the menu bar.
  - — Incorporating a solid-line border completely around the pull-down in the same color as the choice descriptions.
- A drop shadow (a heavier shaded line along two borders that meet) may also be included.

In addition to being identified by its position below the menu bar, the pull-down should visually relate to the menu bar and also visually contrast with the screen body. The most effective way to do this is to use the same foreground and background colors that are used on the menu bar but ensure that these colors adequately contrast with the screen body background. Because good contrasting background colors are often limited, a solid-line border of the same color as the choice descriptions will clearly delineate the pull-down border. A drop shadow, when included, will give the pull-down a three-dimensional effect.

Selection Cursor

- Use a reverse video, or reverse color, selection cursor the same color as the menu bar to surround the choice.
- Create a consistently sized cursor as wide as the pull-down menu.

Figure 5.31

The selection cursor should be a contrasting reverse video or reverse color bar of a consistent size encompassing the selected choice. The reverse color combination should be the same as the one that appears within the menu bar. Create a consistently sized cursor as wide as the pull-down menu.

Cascading Menus

- Proper usage:
  - — To reduce the number of choices presented together for selection (reduce menu breadth).
  - — When a menu specifies many alternatives and the alternatives can be grouped in meaningful related sets on a lower-level menu.
  - — When a choice leads to a short, fixed list of single-choice properties.
  - — When there are several fixed sets of related options.
  - — To simplify a menu.
  - — Avoid using for frequent, repetitive commands.

A cascading menu is a submenu derived from a higher-level menu, most typically a pull-down. Cascades may also be attached to other cascades or pop-up menus, however. Cascading menus are located to the right of the menu item on the previous menu to which they are related, as illustrated in Figure 5.32. Menu items that lead to cascading menus are typically indicated by a right-pointing triangle.

Cascading menus are developed to simplify menus by reducing the number of choices that appear together on one menu. Cascades can be used when many alternatives exist that can be grouped meaningfully. The top-level menu may contain the grouping category headings and the cascaded menu the items in each group. Any menu choices with a fixed set of related options may utilize cascades.

The *advantages* of cascading menus are that:

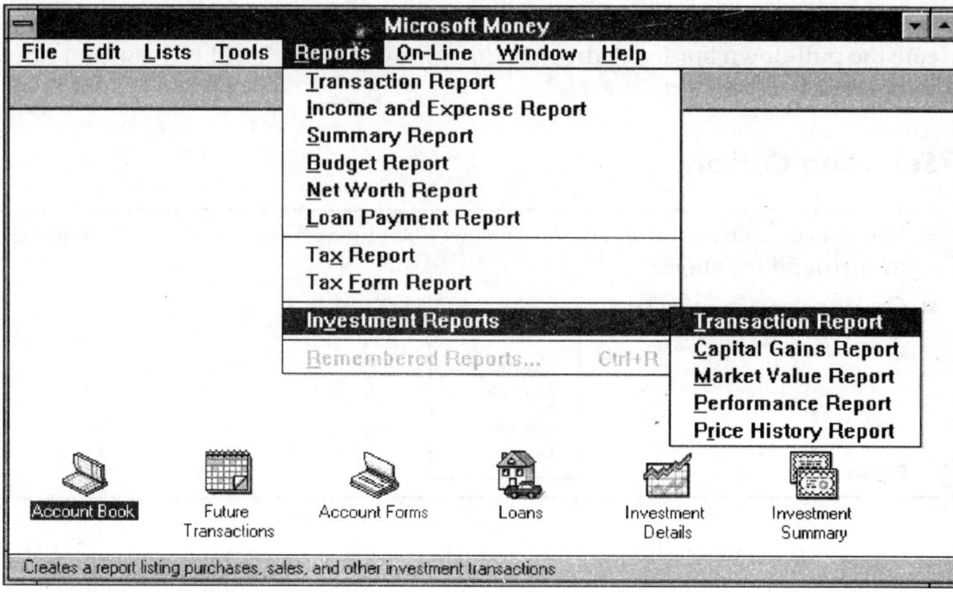

Figure 5.32 Cascading menu.

- The top-level menus are simplified because some choices are hidden.
- More first-letter mnemonics are available because menus possess fewer alternatives.
- High-level command browsing is easier because subtopics are hidden.

The *disadvantages* of cascading menus are:

- Access to submenu items requires more steps.
- Access to submenu items requires a change in pointer movement direction.
- Exhaustive browsing is more difficult; some alternatives remain hidden as pull-downs become visible.

Changing pointer movement from a vertically oriented menu such as a pull-down to an adjacent cascade is an error-prone manual movement. Sliding the mouse and its pointer horizontally is not a very precise hand movement. As the pointer moves horizontally across the menu from which the cascade is selected it has a tendency to move vertically as well, sometimes exiting the menu over an item above or below the desired choice. When this occurs in Microsoft Windows the cascade displayed is not the one desired, but the cascade for the adjacent choice over which the pointer exited. The wrong cascade is then presented to the user, and the selection process must be repeated. Apple minimizes this problem by presenting a movement "cone" for the selected choice. This cone gradually widens as it approaches the cascade, extending somewhat over the adjacent choices. If the mouse and pointer exit the menu within an adjacent choice, but still within this cone, the originally designated cascade is still presented. The Apple solution is much more understanding of human motor limitations.

Cascade Indicator

- Place an arrow or right-pointing triangle to the right of each menu choice description leading to a cascade menu.
- Separate the indicator from the choice description by one space.
- Display the indicator in the same color as the choice descriptions.

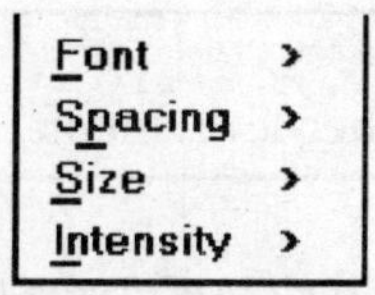

Figure 5.33

To indicate that another lower-level menu will appear when a menu item is selected, place an arrow or right-pointing triangle immediately to its right. Display the cascade indicator in the same color as the choice descriptions.

Location

- Position the first choice in the cascading menu immediately to the right of the selected choice.
- Leave the choice leading to the cascading menu highlighted.

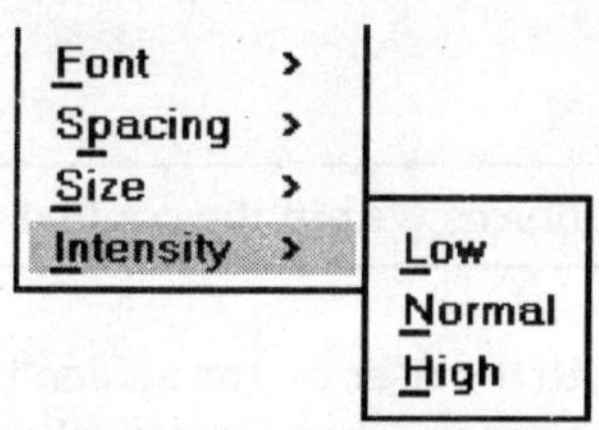

Figure 5.34

Cascading menus should be positioned so that the first choice in the cascading menu is immediately to the right of the selected choice. The choice leading to the cascade should remain highlighted in some way so that the cascade path is obvious.

Levels

- Do not exceed three menu levels (two cascades).
  — Only one cascading menu is preferred.

Each additional cascade level presented reduces ease of access and increases visual clutter. The number of cascade levels presented should represent a balance between menu simplification, ease in menu comprehension, and ease in item selection. Whenever possible, do not exceed three levels of menus (original and two cascades). Try to limit cascades to one. If too many cascade levels are derived, create additional pull-down menus, or provide a window for some alternatives. A window is useful for establishing independent settings or the setting of multiple options. A toolbar may also be used to eliminate the necessity for traversing cascades.

Title

- Not necessary on the cascading menu.
  — The title will be the name of the higher-level menu item chosen.

The title of the cascading menu will be the choice selected on the menu from which it cascades.

Other Guidelines

- Follow the organization, content, layout, separation, and selection cursor guidelines for the kind of menu from which the menu cascades.

The design of a cascade menu should follow all relevant guidelines for the family of menus to which it belongs. Included are organization, content, layout, and selection cursor.

Pop-up Menus

- Use to present alternatives or choices within the context of the task.

Choices may also be presented to the user on the screen through *pop-up* menus, vertically arrayed listings that only appear when specifically requested. Pop-up menus may be requested when the mouse pointer is positioned over a designated or *hot* area of the screen (a window border or text, for example) or over a designated icon. In look, they usually resemble pull-down menus, as shown in Figure 5.35.

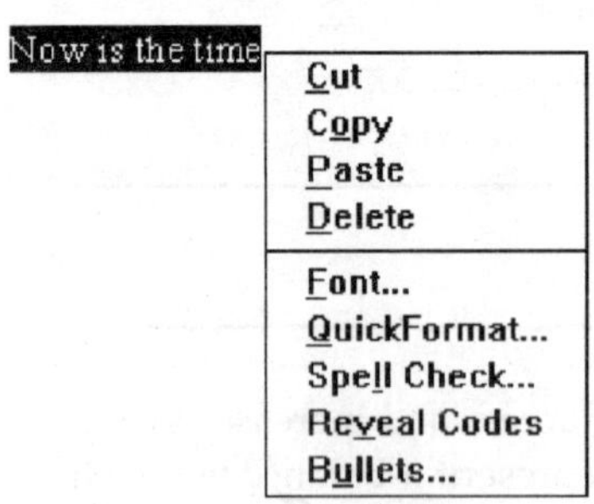

Figure 5.35 Pop-up menu.

The kinds of choices displayed in pop-up menus are context sensitive, depending on where the pointer is positioned when the request is made. They are most useful for presenting alternatives within the context of the user's immediate task. If positioned over text, for example, a pop-up might include text-specific commands.

The *advantages* of pop-up menus are:

- They appear in the working area.
- They do not use window space when not displayed.
- No pointer movement is needed if selected by button.
- Their vertical orientation is most efficient scanning.
- Their vertical orientation most efficient for grouping.
- Their vertical orientation allows more choices to be displayed.
- They may be able to remain showing ("pinned") when used frequently.
- They allow for display of both keyboard equivalents and accelerators.

The *disadvantages* of pop-up menus are:

- Their existence must be learned and remembered.
- Means for selecting them must be learned and remembered.
- They require a special action to see the menu (mouse click).
- Items are smaller than full-size buttons, slowing selection time.
- They may obscure the screen working area.
- Their display locations may not be consistent.

For experienced users, pop-up menus are an alternative to retrieve frequently used contextual choices in pull-down menus. Choices should be limited in number and stable or infrequently changing in content.

Windows contains many contextual pop-up menus. They are also referred to as *context menus* or *shortcut menus*. Examples include the *window pop-up* and an *icon pop-up*, which presents operations of the objects represented by icons.

Display

- Provide a pop-up menu for common, frequent, contextual actions.
  — If the pointer is positioned over an object possessing more than one quality (for example, both text and graphics), at minimum present actions common to all object qualities.
- Items that cannot be chosen due to the current state of an application should not be displayed.
- Continue to display a pop-up until:
  — A choice is selected.
  — An action outside the pop-up is initiated.
  — The user removes the pop-up.

Provide a pop-up menu for common, frequent, contextual actions. If the pointer is positioned over an object possessing more than one quality (for example, both text and graphics), at minimum present actions common to all object qualities. Items that cannot be chosen due to the current state of an application should not be displayed.

Continue to display a pop-up until the user selects a choice, initiates an action outside the pop-up, or requests that the pop-up be removed.

Location

- Position the pop-up:
  — Centered and to the right of the object from which it was requested.
  — Close enough to the pointer so that the pointer can be easily moved onto the menu.
  — But not so close that the pointer is positioned on an item, possibly leading to accidental selection.
- If the pointer is positioned in such a manner that the pop-up would appear off-screen or clipped, position the menu:
  — As close as possible to the object, but not covering the object.
  — So that it appears fully on the screen.

Position a pop-up menu in a consistent location relative to the object from which it is requested. The preferable location is centered to the right. Locate the pop-up close enough to the pointer so that the pointer can be easily moved onto the menu. Positioning of the pointer on the menu itself could lead to accidental selection of an action.

If the pointer is positioned in such a manner that a right-centered position would force the pop-up partially or fully off the screen, locate the pop-up fully on the screen as close as possible to the object. Do not move the pointer to make a menu fit in the most desirable location.

Size

- Restrict the pop-up to no more than 5 to 10 choices, preferably 8 or less.

Limit pop-up menus to about eight choices or fewer. If a large number of choices are needed, consider creating cascading menus. Minimize the number of levels of cascades, however, to provide ease of access and prevent visual clutter.

Title

- Not necessary on a pop-up menu.
- If included, clearly describe the menu's purpose.
- Locate in a centered position at the top.

- Display in uppercase or mixed-case letters.
- Separate it from the menu items by a line extending from the left menu border to the right border.

A title is not necessary on a pop-up menu, since it is an expert feature. Some graphical platforms include titles, others do not. Microsoft Windows does not. If a title is included, it should clearly reflect the menu's purpose. This will avoid any possible confusion that may occur if the wrong menu is accidentally selected and displayed. The title should be set off from the item descriptions by using uppercase letters or mixed-case letters in the headline style.

Other Guidelines

- Arrange logically organized and grouped choices into columns.
- If items are also contained in pull-down menus, organize pop-up menus in the same manner.
- Left-align choice descriptions.
- Use mixed-case headline-style words to describe choices.
- Separate groups with a solid line the length of the longest choice description.
- If the choice leads to a pop-up window, place an ellipsis after the choice description.
- To separate the pop-up from the screen background:
  — Use a contrasting, but complementary background.
  — Incorporate a solid line border around the pull-down.

Follow the same menu guidelines as for pull-down menus regarding organization, content, layout, separation, and selection cursor.

Tear-off Menus

- Follow all relevant guidelines for pull-down menus.

A tear-off menu is a pull-down menu that can be positioned anywhere on the screen for constant referral. As such, it possesses all the characteristics of a pull-down. It may also be called a *pushpin, detachable,* or *roll-up* menu. Its purpose is to present alternatives or choices to the screen user that are needed infrequently at some times and heavily at other times.

Advantages/disadvantages. No space is consumed on the screen when the menu is not needed. When needed, it can remain continuously displayed. It does require extra steps to retrieve, and it may obscure the screen working area.

Tear-off menus are most useful for expert users. Use these menus in situations where the items are sometimes frequently selected and other times infrequently selected. Items

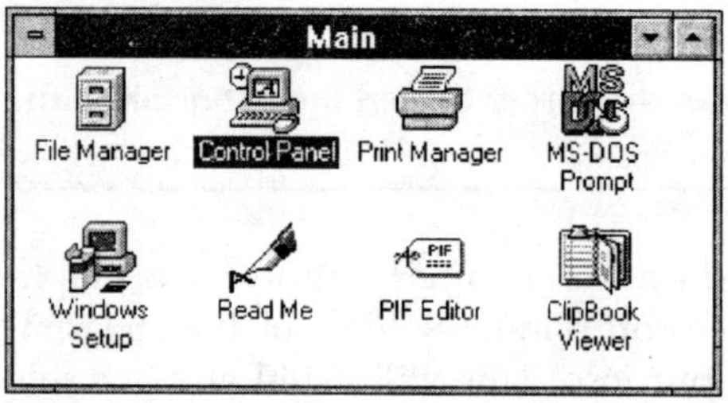

Figure 5.36 Iconic menu (from Microsoft Windows).

should be small in number and rarely change in content. A typical use would be to detach and permanently leave displayed a pull-down menu when it must be frequently used.

Since a tear-off menu is a pull-down style, all pull-down guidelines should be followed.

Iconic Menus

- Use to remind users of the functions, commands, attributes, or application choices available.
- Create icons that:
  - — Help enhance recognition and hasten option selection.
  - — Are concrete and meaningful.
  - — Clearly represent choices.

An iconic menu is the portrayal of menu items or objects in a graphic or pictorial form, as illustrated in Figure 5.36.

The purpose of an iconic menu is to remind users of the functions, commands, attributes, or application choices available.

Advantages/disadvantages. Pictures help facilitate memory of applications, and their larger size increases speed of selection. Pictures do, however, consume considerably more screen space than text, and they are difficult to organize for scanning efficiency. To create meaningful icons requires special skills and an extended amount of time. Iconic menus should be used to designate applications or special functions within an application. Icons must be meaningful and clear. They should help enhance recognition and hasten option selection. See Chapter 11 for a complete review of icon design guidelines.

Pie Menus

- Consider using for:
  - — Mouse-driven selections, with one- or two-level hierarchies, short lists, and choices conducive to the format.

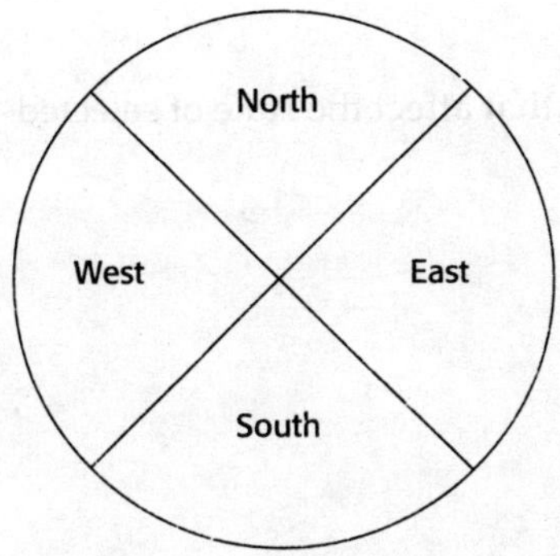

Figure 5.37 Pie menu.

A pie menu is a circular representation of menu items, as illustrated in Figure 5.37, that can be used as an alternative to a pull-down or pop-up menu. Research has found that this style of menu yields higher performance than the typical vertical array, especially when the menu tasks are unrelated. Their basic advantage is that, when presented with the mouse pointer positioned in the pie's center, average movement to any pie wedge is shorter. Mayhew (1992) concludes that pie menus might work well for mouse-driven selections with one- or two-level hierarchies, short choice listings, and data conducive to the format. Performance advantages for keyboard selection are doubtful, however.

Default Menu Items

Every system will provide a set of standard menu items. Using the default items will reduce design time and encourage interface consistency. System learning time will also be reduced. Microsoft Windows, for example, provides the following standard and optional menu bar items and pull-down actions. Always follow industry standards for naming, menu bar choices, ordering, and keyboard equivalents and accelerators.

File

A standard element, the File menu provides all the commands needed to open, create, and save files. Some standard File functions are:

- New
- Open
- Close
- Save
- Save As
- Print Preview
- Print
- Exit

Edit

A standard element, the Edit menu provides commands that affect the state of selected objects. Some standard Edit functions are:

- Undo
- Cut
- Copy
- Paste
- Select All
- Find
- Replace

View

An optional element, the View menu provides commands that affect the perspective, details, and appearance of the application. They affect the view, not the data itself. The view functions are application-specific and include the following:

- Toolbars
- Status Bar
- Magnify
- Zoom In
- Zoom Out
- Grid Points

Window

The Window menu, an optional element, provides commands to manipulate entire windows. Included are items such as:

- New Window
- Arrange All
- Hide
- Show

Help

The Help menu, a standard element, provides Help commands, including:

- Contents
- Search for Help On
- How to Use Help
- About (Application)

Table 5.4 Menu Proper Usage Summary

Menu Bar	To identify and provide access to: • Common and frequently used application actions. • Actions that take place in a wide variety of different windows.
Pull-Down Menu	For frequently used application actions that take place in a wide variety of different windows: • A small number of items (5–10). • Items rarely changing in content.
Cascading Menu	To simplify a higher-level menu. To provide easier browsing of a higher-level menu. For mutually exclusive choices. Restrict to 1–2 cascades.
Pop-Up Menu	For: • Frequent users. • Frequently used contextual commands. • A small number of items (5–10). • Items rarely changing in content. • Items that require a small amount of screen space.
Tear-Off Menu	For items: • Sometimes frequently selected. • Sometimes infrequently selected. • Small in number (5–10). • Rarely changing in content.
Iconic Menu	To designate applications available. To designate special functions within an application.

These standard menu items also have a prescribed order on the menu bar: File, Edit, View, Window, and Help. Items on their related pull-down menus also follow standard orders.

Standard menus and items should always be used when creating an application. Refer to a system's design documentation for exact details concerning what menu items are available and how they are used.

Functions Not Represented by Default Items

Having established the usability of the standard menu functions, additional system functions must be identified. Commands to accomplish these functions must be created and added to the pertinent menus. Command design guidelines include the following.

Labels

- General:
  - — Provide a label for each command.
  - — Use labels that indicate:
    - The purpose of the command, or
    - The result of what happens when the command is selected.
  - — Use familiar, short, clear, concise words.
  - — Use distinctive wording.
  - — Use mixed case, with the first letter capitalized.
  - — Begin commands with verbs or adjectives, not nouns.
  - — Preferably, use only one word.
    - If multiple words are required for clarity, capitalize the first letter of each significant word.
    - Do not use sentences as labels.
  - — Provide an ellipsis (. . .) to indicate that another window will result from selection of a command.
    - Do not use the ellipsis when the following window is a confirmation or warning.
- Dynamic labels:
  - — As contexts change, dynamically change the label wording to make its meaning clearer in the new context.
    - For example, after a cut operation, Undo may be changed to Undo Cut.

Provide a clear label for each command, indicating the purpose of the command or the result of what happens when the command is selected. Preferably, use single-word commands. If multiple words are required for clarity, capitalize the first letter of each significant word. Provide an ellipsis to indicate that another window will result from selection of a command, but do not use the ellipsis when the resulting window is a confirmation or warning. As contexts change, the label wording may be dynamically changed to make its meaning clearer in the new context. For example, after a cut operation, Undo may be changed to Undo Cut. This is called a *toggled menu item* and was previously described.

Disabled Commands

- When a command is not available, indicate its disabled status by displaying it grayed out or subdued.
- If selection of a disabled command is attempted, provide a message in the information area that the "Help" function will explain why it is disabled.

When a command is not available, indicate its disabled status by displaying it grayed out or subdued. If selection of a disabled command is attempted, provide a message in the information area that the Help function will explain why it is disabled. Help, of course, must provide the proper explanation.

Navigation and Selection

- General:
  - — Permit multiple methods for selecting commands.
- Keyboard equivalents:
  - — Assign a mnemonic for each command.
  - — A mnemonic should be as meaningful as possible. Use:
    - The first letter of the command, or if duplications exist,
    - The first letter of another word in the command, or
    - Another significant consonant in the command.
  - — For standard commands, use mnemonics provided by the tool set.
- Keyboard accelerators:
  - — Assign keyboard accelerators for frequently used commands.
  - — For standard commands, use keyboard accelerators provided by the tool set.

Permit commands to be implemented through the keyboard as well. Provide keyboard equivalents or accelerators. Finally, the menus needed must be designed following principles of effective menu design earlier in this chapter.

Graphical Menu Examples

What follows are examples of poor and proper menu design.

Example 1

An improperly presented menu bar and pull-down.

Menu 1.1

What are the problems in the way this menu bar and pull-down menu are presented? (1) Keyboard mnemonics are designated by capital letters. Note the uncommon shape of "foRmat," "cuT," and "clEar" when the mnemonic is not the first letter of the word. (2) Item groupings do not exist in the pull-down. The differences in basic functions are not obvious, and the more destructive operations (Undo, Clear, and Delete) are positioned close to standard actions, increasing the potential for accidental selection. (3) The keyboard accelerators are adjacent to the choice descriptions and not set off in any way. Therefore, these alternate, and supplemental, actions visually compete with choice descriptions for the viewer's attention.

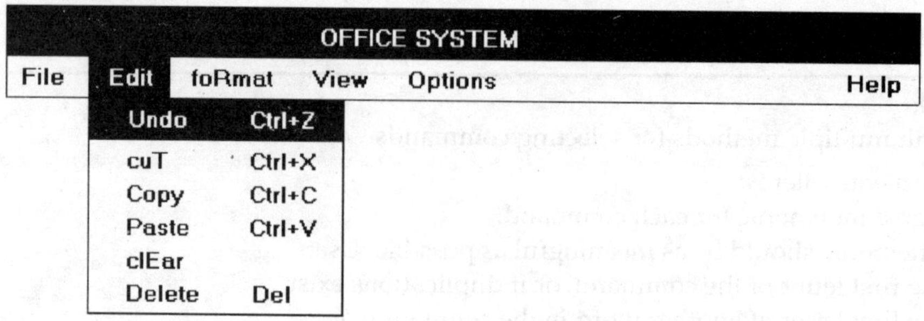

Menu 1.1

Menu 1.2

Keyboard mnemonics are designated by underlines, not capital letters. Choice descriptions now assume more common and recognizable shapes. Groupings, through use of white space, are established for choices in the pull-down. The different functions are much more obvious and separation is provided for the destructive actions. The different groupings are visually reinforced through use of separating lines. The lines are not extended to the pull-down border so as not to completely disassociate the choices. Keyboard alternatives are right-aligned to move them further from the choice descriptions. They are also enclosed in parentheses to visually deemphasize them, thereby reducing their visual competition with the choices. Choice descriptions are now more obvious.

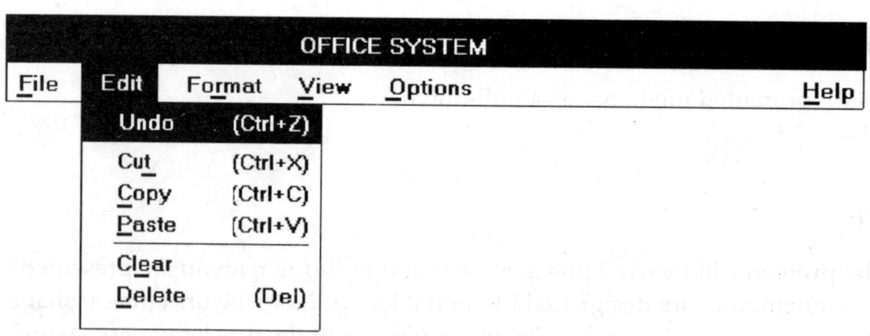

Menu 1.2

Example 2

An improperly organized menu bar and pull-down.

Menu 2.1

A very poor menu bar—all alternatives are presented creating a very crowded series of choices in a difficult-to-scan horizontal array. No groupings are provided and an alphabetic order causes intermixing of what appear to be different functions. While menu breadth is preferred to excessive menu depth, too many choices are presented here.

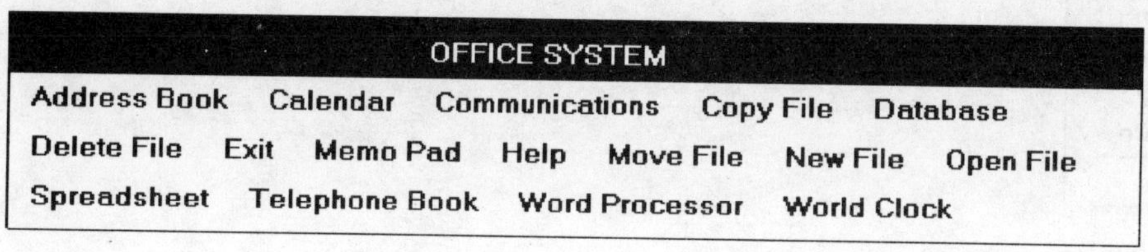

Menu 2.1

Menus 2.2 and 2.3

A better, but still poor menu bar—while File, Function, and Help are now presented separately, the cascading Function menu requires an excessive number of steps to complete selection. Note the number of levels needed to access the Address or Telephone book. Excessive levels of depth are difficult to scan and lead to one's getting lost. Some have referred to this problem as cascade confusion.

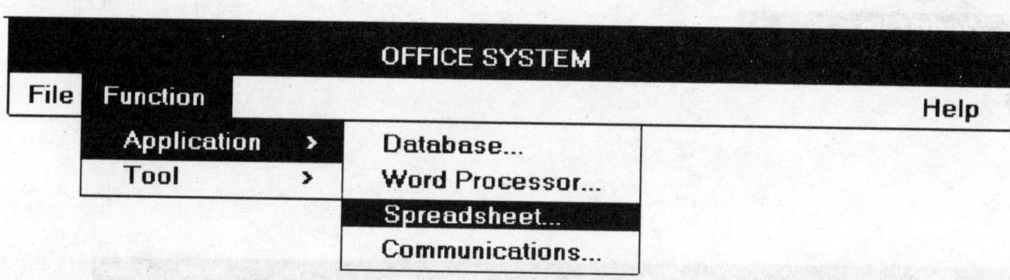

Menu 2.2

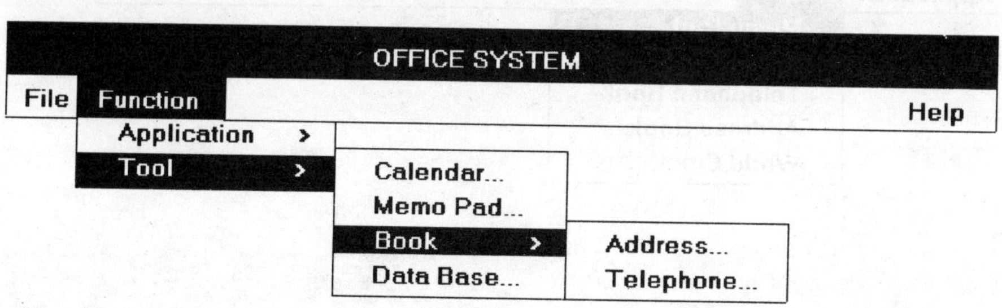

Menu 2.3

Menus 2.4, 2.5, and 2.6

A much more reasonable solution—Application and Tool menu bar items are created and all alternatives now exist on one pull-down menu. The number of steps necessary to reach any alternative is minimized and easier scanning of all items is permitted.

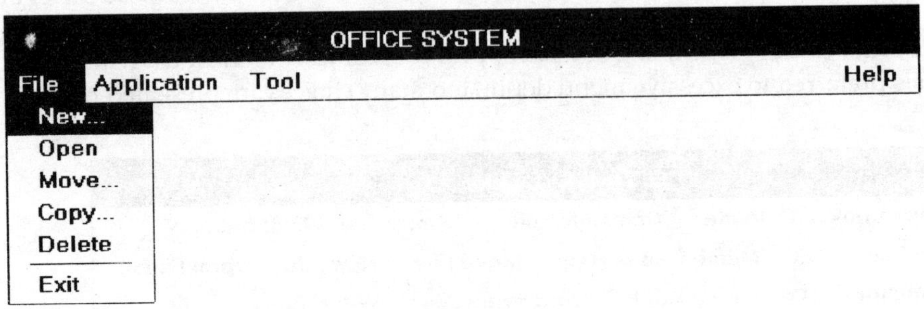

Menu 2.4

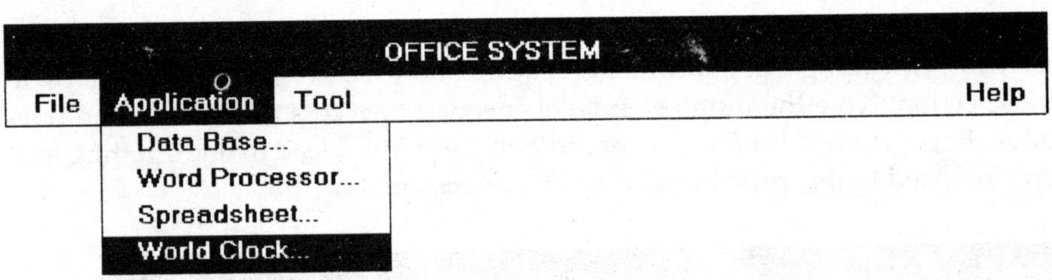

Menu 2.5

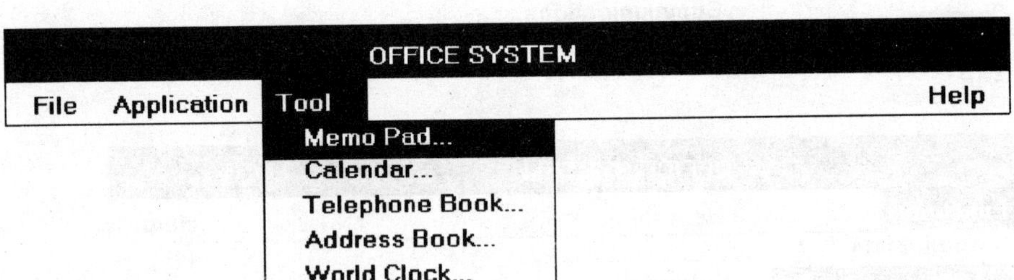

Menu 2.6

Menu 2.7A through 2.7J

Illustrated is a collection of textual Web site global navigation bars showing various presentation styles. Menu A is horizontally arrayed with good separation between alternate choices. No delimiters between the choices are included. Menu B uses the symbol >> to designate the choices. Menus C, D, E, and F use a vertical line to separate the choices, a very common technique used today in textual navigation presentation. All choices are arrayed horizontally, with Menu F comprising two lines. Menu G is composed of four columns. This menu would be scanned horizontally between columns and vertically within a column. Spacing and choice content make this obvious. Menus H and I are composed of fewer choices than Menu G and are arrayed for vertical scanning.

The vertical menu arrangements do make scanning of the choices much easier. Whenever possible, orient menus in the manner illustrated by Menus G, H, and I. If a horizontal array is used, a separation delimiter is recommended. A vertical line separator is recommended. This will give the choices a more "button-like" appearance, and this style commonly appears on Web pages.

Menu 2.7A

Menu 2.7B

Menu 2.7C

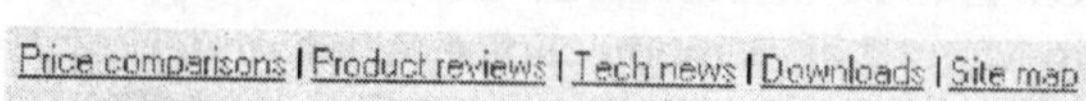

Menu 2.7D

Menu 2.7E

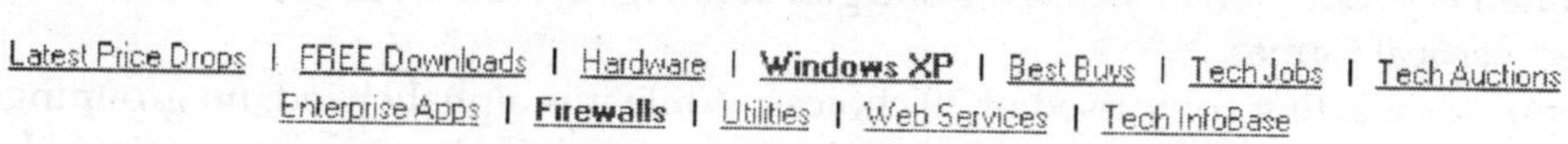

Menu 2.7F

Menu 2.7G

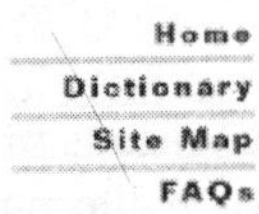

Menu 2.7H

Menu 2.7I

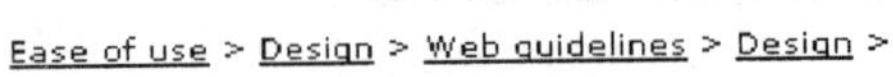

Menu 2.7J

Menus A, B, E, F, G, H, and I, use the headline style of presentation (all significant words capitalized). The remaining menus (C, D) use sentence style (only the initial word is capitalized). The recommendation in this book, for reasons previously described, is for captions and menu choices is to be displayed in the headline style. For another reason, look at the illustration in Menu 2.7J. A menu choice, when underlined, can have letters with descenders degraded, destroying the shape of the word. This is especially critical if the letter is the first word. Capitalization of a letter avoids this problem.

Menus 2.8A through 2.8E

Illustrated is a collection of local Web site global navigation bars. All are arrayed in the desired vertical format.

Menu A is a listing comprised of 20 choices. While it is alphabetized, no groupings of choices exist. It would have been much better presented with groupings related by topic. If topical grouping was not possible, visual grouping of the menu choices should have been accomplished either by leaving a space line after every five choices, or by providing a bolder or distinctively different line after every fifth choice.

Menu B, composed of nine choices, is grouped, with separation of groups by horizontal lines. Ordering appears to be by frequency of use. It is a simple and well-constructed menu.

Menu 2.8A

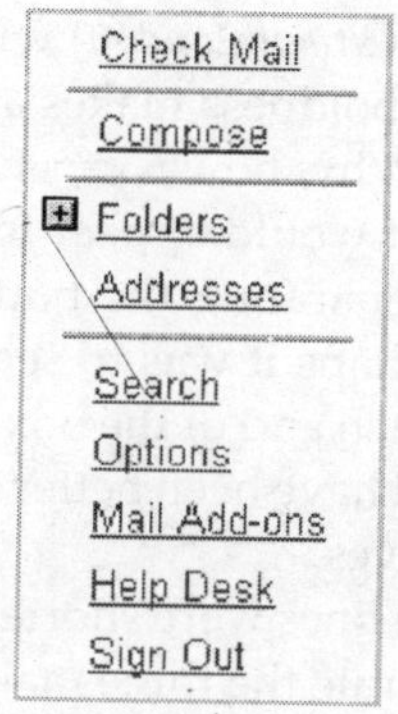

Menu 2.8B

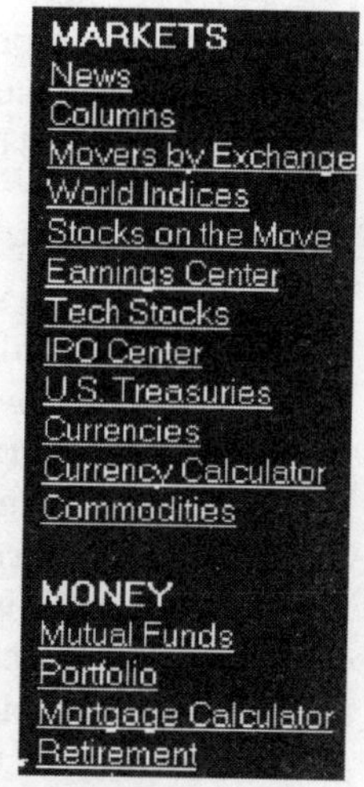

Menu 2.8C

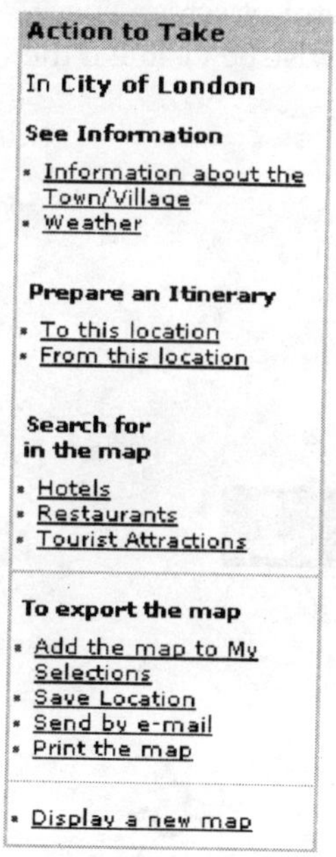

Menu 2.8D

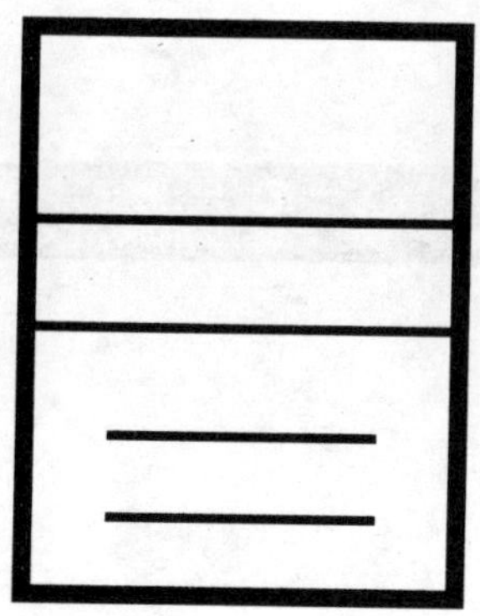

Menu 2.8E

Menu C is composed of two groups, with headings for each group. The headings, being capitalized, stand out well. The orderings schemes within groupings are not immediately obvious, however. In the *MARKETS* section, subgroupings of choices are desirable.

Menu D contains a heading (*In City of London*) with five subheadings. A larger size makes the heading stand out, and boldness makes all headings stand out. Sections are grouped and visually separated. Why, however, is the subheading "Search for in the map" positioned over two lines? It would appear to easily fit on one line. What is the purpose of the horizontal lines separating the bottom three groupings? Since these groupings all relate to "map" perhaps it was to separate the three map components. The horizontal line extending to each end of the box implies too great a separation and no relationship, however. It would have been better to inscribe a shorter line extending no wider than the choices themselves.

Also worth considering, if these lines were shortened, would be to include two lines the entire width of the box to separate the three major menu sections. This recommendation is illustrated in Menu 2.8E.

Menus 2.9A through 2.9C

Illustrated is a collection of global navigation bars containing icons.

Do these icons add to screen usability? When searching through these menu arrays do you look at the icons or words? Menu C is particularly wasteful of screen space, forcing below the screen and out of sight content that might otherwise be visible if the navigation bar were more reasonably sized.

Menu 2.9A

Menu 2.9B

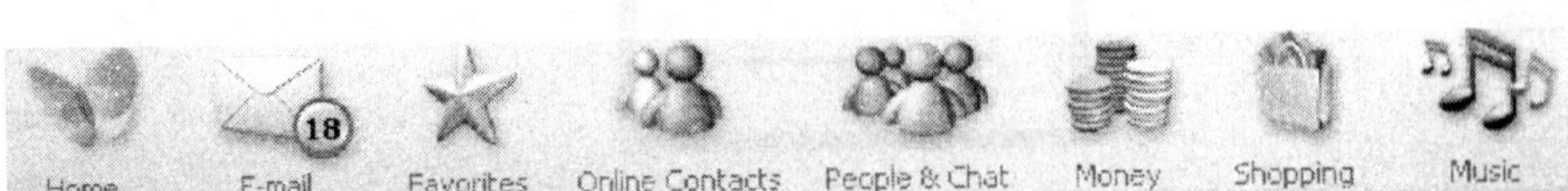

Menu 2.9C

Menu 2.10

Menu 2.10 is an interesting menu, combining a two-level menu with an historical trail. The top level, individual pages, has led to the selection of layout on the submenu. The path followed exists within the displayed menu. All lowercase letters for menu choices is not recommended, however. Headline-style presentation would have been much better.

Menu 2.10

Multiple Choice Questions

1. In sequential menus,
   (a) All menu options are available separately
   (b) All menu options are available simultaneously
   (c) Menu options are represented on a series of screens possessing only one path
   (d) A single screen is presented to seek the user's input
   (e) None of the above

2. Tear-off menus are used for
   (a) Frequent users and frequently used contextual commands
   (b) Frequently used application actions that take place in a wide variety of different windows
   (c) Items sometimes frequently or infrequently selected
   (d) Both (a) and (b)
   (e) None of the above

3. Pull down menus are used for
   (a) Frequent users and frequently used contextual commands
   (b) Frequently used application actions that take place in a wide variety of different windows
   (c) Items sometimes frequently or infrequently selected
   (d) Both (b) and (c)
   (e) None of the above

4. Pop-up menus are used for
   (a) Frequent users and frequently used contextual commands
   (b) Frequently used application actions that take place in a wide variety of different windows
   (c) Items sometimes frequently or infrequently selected
   (d) Both (a) and (c)
   (e) None of the above

5. What is the name of the control for putting menus on a form?
   (a) FormMenu
   (b) MenuForm
   (c) MenuControl
   (d) MainMenu
   (e) Menu

6. The standard prefix for a menu item is
   (a) men (b) meu
   (c) mit (d) mni
   (e) mnu

7. Which menu object property places a check mark in the display of the menu text?
(a) Check (b) Checked
(c) CheckMark (d) CheckOn
(e) RadioCheck

8. Which symbol creates an access key in the text of a menu item?
(a) @ (b) #
(c) $ (d) %
(e) &

Review Questions

1. Describe the different types of graphical menus in HCI applications.

2. List and describe the various contents of Menus.

3. Describe the guidelines for formatting the menus.

4. Explain the use of cascade indicator and window indicator with suitable examples.

5. Draw and explain with example, the use of sequential menus.

6. Draw and explain with example, the use of hierarchical menus.

7. Draw and explain with example, the use of event trapping menus.

8. Define the following terms:
(a) Keyboard equivalent
(b) Keyboard accelerators

9. A restaurant manager wants to design the food menu system for easy and quick selection of food items by customers. What will be suitable menu structure, type of menus? Draw the UI for various menus. Explain and justify.

10. Describe how ordering helps in better predicting the choices, location of items in menus.

11. While grouping menu items, how can a partial line be used for separating related choices?

12. While grouping menu items, how can an extended line be used for separating unrelated or independent choices?

13. Describe different menu instructions to be included on a menu for novice users and expert users.

14. Explain with example the use of Mark Toggles in Menus.

15. Describe various components of a Web Navigation System.

CHAPTER

6

Windows

A window is an area of the screen, usually rectangular in shape, defined by a border that contains a particular view of some area of the computer or some portion of a person's dialog with the computer. It can be moved and rendered independently on the screen. A window may be small, containing a short message or a single field, or it may be large, consuming most or all of the available display space. A display may contain one, two, or more windows within its boundaries. In this chapter the following is addressed:

- A window's characteristics.
- A window's components.
- A window's presentation styles.
- The types of windows available.
- Organizing window system functions.
- A window's operations.
- Web system frames and pop-up windows.

Window Characteristics

A window is seen to possess the following characteristics:

- A name or title, allowing it to be identified.
- A size in height and width (which can vary).

- A state, accessible or active, or not accessible. (Only active windows can have their contents altered.)
- Visibility—the portion that can be seen. (A window may be partially or fully hidden behind another window, or the information within a window may extend beyond the window's display area.)
- A location, relative to the display boundary.
- Presentation, that is, its arrangement in relation to other windows. It may be tiled, overlapping, or cascading.
- Management capabilities, methods for manipulation of the window on the screen.
- Its highlight, that is, the part that is selected.
- The function, task, or application to which it is dedicated.

The Attraction of Windows

The value of windowing is best seen in the context of a task or job. A person performs a variety of tasks, often in a fairly unstructured manner. A person is asked to monitor and manipulate data from a variety of sources, synthesize information, summarize information, and reorganize information. Things are seldom completed in a continuous time frame. Outside events such as telephone calls, supervisor or customer requests, and deadlines force shifts in emphasis and focus. Tasks start, stop, and start again. Materials used in dealing with the tasks are usually scattered about one's desk, being strategically positioned in the workspace to make handling the task as efficient as possible. This spatial mapping of tools helps people organize their work and provides reminders of uncompleted tasks. As work progresses and priorities change, materials are reorganized to reflect the changes.

Single-screen technology supports this work structure very poorly. Since only one screen of information can be viewed at one time, comparing or integrating information from different sources and on different screens often requires extensive use of one's memory. To support memory, a person is often forced to write notes or obtain printed copies of screens. Switching between tasks is difficult and disruptive, and later returning to a task requires an extensive and costly restructuring of the work environment.

The appeal of windowing is that it allows the display workspace to mirror the desk workspace much more closely. This dramatically reduces one's short-term memory load. One's ability to do mental calculations is limited by how well one keeps track of one's place, one's interim conclusions and products, and, finally, the results. Windows act as external memories that are an extension of one's internal memory. Windows also make it much easier to switch between tasks and to maintain one's context, since one does not have to reestablish one's place continually. In addition, Windows provide access to more information than would normally be available on a single display of the same size. Overwriting, or placing more important information on top of that of less importance at that moment, does this.

While all the advantages and disadvantages of windows are still not completely understood, windows do seem to be useful in the following ways.

Presentation of Different Levels of Information

Information can be examined in increasing levels of detail. A document table of contents can be presented in a window. A chapter or topic selected from this window can be simultaneously displayed in more detail in an adjoining window. Deeper levels are also possible in additional windows.

Presentation of Multiple Kinds of Information

Variable information needed to complete a task can be displayed simultaneously in adjacent windows. An order-processing system window could collect a customer account number in one window and retrieve the customer's name and shipping address in another window. A third window could collect details of the order, after which another window could present factory availability of and shipping dates for the desired items. Significant windows could remain displayed so that details may be modified as needed prior to order completion. Low inventory levels or delayed shipping dates might require changing the order.

Sequential Presentation of Levels or Kinds of Information

Steps to accomplish a task can be sequentially presented through windows. Successive windows are presented until all the required details are collected. Key windows may remain displayed, but others appear and disappear as necessary. This sequential preparation is especially useful if the information-collection process leads down various paths. An insurance application, for example, will include different types of coverage. A requested type of coverage might necessitate the collection of specific details about that type of coverage. This information can be entered into a window presented to collect the unique data. The windows disappear after data entry, and additional windows appear when needed.

Access to Different Sources of Information

Independent sources of information may have to be accessed at the same time. This information may reside in different host computers, operating systems, applications, files, or areas of the same file. It may be presented on the screen alongside the problem, greatly facilitating its solution. For instance, a writer may have to refer to several parts of a text being written at the same time. Or, a travel agent may have to compare several travel destinations for a particularly demanding client.

Combining Multiple Sources of Information

Text from several documents may have to be reviewed and combined into one. Pertinent information is selected from one window and copied into another.

Performing More Than One Task

More than one task can be performed at one time. While waiting for a long, complex procedure to finish, another can be performed. Tasks of higher priority can interrupt less important ones. The interrupted task can then be resumed without the necessity to "close down" and "restart."

Reminding

Windows can be used to remind the viewer of things likely to be of use in the near future. Examples might be menus of choices available, a history of the path followed or the command choices to that point, or the time of an important meeting.

Monitoring

Changes, both internal and external, can be monitored. Data in one window can be modified and its effect on data in another window can be studied. External events, such as changes in stock prices, out of normal range conditions, or system messages can be watched while another major activity is carried out.

Multiple Representations of the Same Task

The same thing can be looked at in several ways—for example, alternate drafts of a speech, different versions of a screen, or different graphical representations of the same data. A maintenance procedure may be presented in the form of textual steps and illustrated graphically at the same time.

Constraints in Window System Design

Windowing systems, in spite of their appeal and obvious benefits, have failed to completely live up to their expectations. In the past, a windows user interface has been described as "chaotic" because of the great amount of time users must spend doing such things as pointing at tiny boxes in window borders, resizing windows, moving windows, closing windows, and so forth. The problems with windowing systems can be attributed to three factors: historical considerations, hardware limitations, and human limitations.

Historical Considerations

Historically, system developers have been much more interested in solving hardware problems than in user considerations. Since technical issues abound, they have received the most attention. There has been very little research addressing design issues and their impact on the usability of window systems. Therefore, there are few concrete window design guidelines to aid designers.

This lack of guidelines makes it difficult to develop acceptable and agreeable window standards. While many companies have developed style guides, they are very general and limited in scope to their products. Standardization is also made more difficult by the complexity and range of alternatives available to the designer. Without user performance data, it is difficult to compare realistically the different alternatives, and design choices become a matter of preference.

Standardization of the interface is also inhibited by other factors. Some software developers, who are proud of their originality, see standards as a threat to creativity and its perceived monetary rewards. Some companies are wary of standards because they fear that other companies are promoting standards that reflect their own approach. Finally, some companies have threatened, or brought, legal action against anyone who adopts an approach similar to their own.

The result is that developers of new systems create another new variation each time they design a product, and users must cope with a new interface each time they encounter a new windowing system.

Hardware Limitations

Many of today's screens are not large enough to take full advantage of windowing capabilities. As a result, many windows are still of "Post-It" dimensions. As already mentioned, there is some evidence that many users of personal computers expand their windows to cover a full screen. Either seeing all the contents of one window is preferable to seeing small parts of many windows or the operational and visual complexity of multiple windows is not wanted.

Also, the slower processing speeds and smaller memory sizes of some computers may inhibit the use of windows. A drain on the computer's resources may limit feedback and animation capabilities, thereby reducing the system's usability. Poor screen resolution and graphics capability may also deter effective use of windows by not permitting sharp and realistic drawings and shapes.

Human Limitations

A windowing system, because it is more complex, requires the learning and using of more operations. Much practice is needed to master them. These window management operations are placed on top of other system operations, and window management can become an end in itself. This can severely detract from the task at hand. In one study comparing full screens with screens containing overlapping windows, task completion times were longer with the window screens, but the non-window screens generated more user errors. After eliminating screen arrangement time, however, task solution times were shorter with windows. The results suggest that advantages for windows do exist, but they can be negated by excessive window manipulation requirements.

It is also suggested that to be truly effective, window manipulation must occur implicitly as a result of user task actions, not as a result of explicit window management actions by the user.

Other Limitations

Other possible window problems include the necessity for window borders to consume valuable screen space, and that small windows providing access to large amounts of information can lead to excessive, bothersome scrolling.

Where To?

In spite of their problems, windows do have enormous benefits and are here to stay. So, we must cope with their constraints for now and, in the meantime, enjoy the benefits they possess.

Components of a Window

A typical window may be composed of up to a dozen or so elements. Some appear on all windows; others only on certain kinds of windows, or under certain conditions. For consistency purposes, these elements should always be located in the same position within a window. Most windowing systems provide consistent locations for elements in their own windows. Some inconsistencies do exist in element locations between different systems, however, as do some differences in what the elements are named, or what graphic images or icons are chosen to identify them. What follows is a description of typical window components and their purposes, with emphasis on the most popular windowing system, *Microsoft Windows*. Specifically reviewed will be primary windows, secondary windows, and a form of secondary window called the dialog box. An illustration of a primary window is found in Figure 6.1. Illustrations of secondary

Figure 6.1 Microsoft Windows primary window.

windows and dialog boxes are illustrated in Figures 6.8 and 6.13. How these different types of windows are used will be described in a later section in this chapter. A summary of window components for these types of windows is also found in Table 6.1.

Frame

A window will have a frame or border, usually rectangular in shape, to define its boundaries and distinguish it from other windows. While a border need not be rectangular, this shape is a preferred shape for most people. Also, textual materials, which are usually read from left to right, fit most efficiently within this structure. The border comprises a line of variable thickness and color. This variation can be used as an aid in identifying the type of window being displayed. Windows filling an entire screen may use the screen edge as the border. If a window is resizable, it may contain control points for sizing it. If the window cannot be resized, the border coincides with the edge of the window.

Title Bar

The title bar is the top edge of the window, inside its border and extending its entire width. This title bar is also referred to by some platforms as the *caption, caption bar*, or *title area*. The title bar contains a descriptive title identifying the purpose or content of the window. In Microsoft Windows, the title bar may also possess, at the extreme left and right ends, control buttons (described below) for retrieving the system menu and performing window resizing. The title bar also serves as a control point for moving the window and as an access point for commands that apply to a window. For example, as an access point, when a user clicks on the title bar using the secondary mouse button, the pop-up or shortcut menu for the window appears. Pressing the Alt-Spacebar key combination also displays the shortcut menu for the window. Title bars are included on all primary and secondary windows. Title bar text writing guidelines are described in Chapter 9 "Text Messages."

Microsoft recommends that one never place application commands or other controls in the title bar. Doing so may conflict with the special user controls Windows adds for configurations that support multiple languages.

Title Bar Icon

Located at the left corner of the title bar in a primary window, this button is used in Windows to retrieve a pull-down menu of commands that apply to the object in the window. It is 16 × 16 version of the icon of the object being viewed. When clicked with the secondary mouse button, the commands applying to the object are presented. Microsoft suggests that:

- If the window contains a tool or utility (that is, an application that does not create, load, and save its own data files), a small version of the application's icon should be placed there instead.

Table 6.1 Microsoft Windows Components

COMPONENT	WINDOWS CONTAINING COMPONENT		
	PRIMARY	SECONDARY	DIALOG BOX
Frame or Border • Boundary to define shape. • If sizable, contains control points for resizing.	X	X	X
Title Bar Text • Name of object being viewed in window. • Control point for moving window.	X	X	X
Title Bar Icon • Small version of icon for object being viewed. • Access point for commands that apply to the object.	X		
Title Bar Buttons • Shortcuts to specific commands.	X	X	X
Close	X	X	X
Minimize/Maximize/Restore	X		
What's This? – Displays context-sensitive Help about any object displayed on window.		X	X
Menu Bar • Provides basic and common application commands.	X		
Status Bar • An area used to display status information about what is displayed in window.	X		
Scroll Bar • Standard control to support scrolling.	X		
Size Grip • Control to resize window, located at right side of status bar.	X		

- If the application creates, loads, and saves documents or data files and the window represents the view of one of its files, a small version of the icon that represents its document or data file type should be placed there.
- Even if the user has not yet saved the file, display the data file icon rather than the application icon, and again display the data file icon after the user saves the file.

Window Sizing Buttons

Located at the right corner of the title bar, these buttons are used to manipulate the size of a window. The leftmost button, the *minimize* button— inscribed with a short horizontal line toward the bottom of the button—is used to reduce a window to its minimum size, usually an icon. It also hides all associated windows. The *maximize* button—typically inscribed with a large box—enlarges a window to its maximum size, usually the entire screen. When a screen is maximized, the *restore* button replaces the maximize button, since the window can no longer be increased in size. The restore button—typically inscribed with a pair overlapping boxes—returns a window to the size it had before a minimize or maximize action was performed. A *close* button—typically inscribed with an X—closes the window. Minimize, maximize, and close buttons are shown in Figure 6.1. These command buttons are graphical equivalents to the actions available through the Title Bar icon.

Sizing buttons are included on primary windows only. All buttons on a primary window's title bar must have equivalent commands on the pop-up or shortcut menu for that window.

When these buttons are displayed, use the following guidelines:

- When a window does not support a command, do not display its command button.
- The *Close* button always appears as the rightmost button. Leave a gap between it and any other buttons.
- The *Minimize* button always precedes the *Maximize* button.
- The *Restore* button always replaces the *Maximize* button or the *Minimize* button when that command is carried out.

What's This? Button

The *What's This?* Button, which appears on secondary windows and dialog boxes, is used to invoke the What's This? Windows command to provide contextual Help about objects displayed within a secondary window. When provided, it is located in the upper-right corner of the title bar, just to the left of the close button. It is inscribed with a question mark, as illustrated in Figure 6.2.

On a primary window this command is accessed from the Help drop-down menu. This command may also be included as a button on a toolbar or as a command on a pop-up menu for a specific object. This command is described more fully in Chapter 10 "Feedback and Guidance."

Figure 6.2 What's This? button.

Menu Bar

A menu bar is used to organize and provide access to actions. It is located horizontally at the top of the window, just below the title bar. A menu bar contains a list of topics or items that, when selected, are displayed on a pull-down menu beneath the choice. A system will typically provide a default set of menu actions that can be augmented by an application. In the past, some platforms have called the menu bar an *action bar*. Menu bar design guidelines were presented in Chapter 5 "Menus." The contents of the menu bar and its pull-downs are determined by the application's functionality and the context in which the user is interacting with it.

Status Bar

Information of use to the user can be displayed in a designated screen area or areas. They may be located at the top of the screen in some platforms and called a *status area*, or at the screen's bottom. Microsoft recommends the bottom location and refers to this area as the *status bar*. It is also referred to by other platforms as a *message area* or *message bar*.

Microsoft Windows suggests using the status bar to display information about the current state of what is being viewed in the window, descriptive messages about a selected menu or toolbar button, or other noninteractive information. It may also be used to explain menu and control bar items as the items are highlighted by the user.

Scroll Bars

When all display information cannot be presented in a window, the additional information must be found and made visible. This is accomplished by scrolling the display's contents through use of a scroll bar. A scroll bar is an elongated rectangular container consisting of a scroll area or shaft, a slider box or elevator, and arrows or anchors at each end. For vertical scrolling, the scroll bar is positioned at the far right side of the work area, extending its entire length. Horizontal scrolling is accomplished through a scroll bar located at the bottom of the work area. Scroll bars are more fully described in Chapter 8 "Screen-Based Controls."

Split Box

A window can be split into two or more pieces or panes by manipulating a *split box* located above a vertical scroll bar or to the left of a horizontal scroll bar. A split box is sometimes referred to as a *split bar*. A window can be split into two or more separate viewing areas that are called *panes*. Splitting a window permits multiple views of an object. A split window allows the user to:

- Examine two parts of a document at the same time.
- Display different, yet simultaneous, views of the same information.

To support the splitting of a window that is not presplit by design, include a split box. The split box should be just large enough for the user to successfully target it with the pointer; the default size of a size handle, such as the window's sizing border, is a good guideline.

Toolbar

Toolbars, illustrated in Figure 6.3, are permanently displayed panels or arrays of choices or commands that must be accessed quickly. They are sometimes called *command bars*. Toolbars are designed to provide quick access to specific commands or options. Specialized toolbars are sometimes referred to as *ribbons, toolboxes, rulers,* or *palettes*. Each toolbar band includes a single-grip handle to enable the user to resize or rearrange the toolbars. When the user moves the pointer over the grip, it changes to a two-headed arrow. When the user drags the grip, the pointer changes to a split move pointer. To resize the toolbar to its maximum or minimum size, the user clicks the grip.

Toolbars may occupy a fixed position or be movable. The design of toolbars is discussed in Chapter 8.

Command Area

In situations where it is useful for a command to be typed into a screen, a command area can be provided. The desired location of the command area is at the bottom of the window. If a horizontal scroll bar is included in the window, position the command area just below it. If a message area is included on the screen, locate the command area just above it.

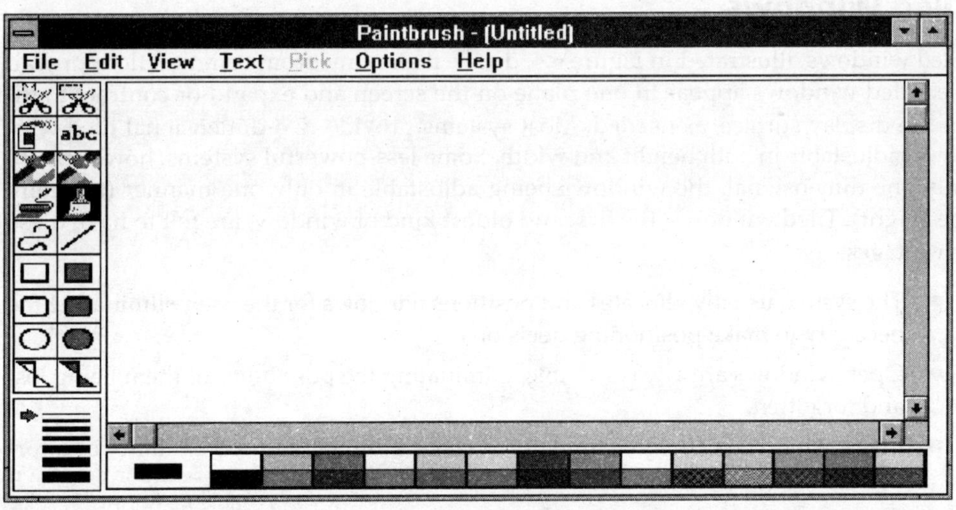

Figure 6.3 Toolbars.

Size Grip

A size grip is a Microsoft Windows special handle included in a window to permit it to be resized. When the grip is dragged the window resizes, following the same conventions as the sizing border. Three angled parallel lines in the lower-right corner of a window designate the size grip. If the window possesses a status bar, the grip is positioned at the bar's right end. Otherwise, it is located at the bottom of a vertical scroll bar, the right side of a horizontal scroll bar, or the junction point of the two bars. A size grip is shown in the lower-right corner of Figure 6.2.

Work Area

The work area is the portion of the screen where the user performs tasks. It is the open area inside the window's border and contains relevant peripheral screen components such as the menu bar, scroll bars, or message bars. The work area may consist of an open area for typing, or it may contain controls (such as text boxes and list boxes) or customized forms (such as spreadsheets). The work area may also be referred to as the *client area*.

Window Presentation Styles

The presentation style of a window refers to its spatial relationship to other windows. There are two basic styles, commonly called tiled or overlapping. In early windowing days, most systems commonly used one or the other style exclusively, seldom using both at the same time. Now, the user is usually permitted to select the style to be presented on the display.

Tiled Windows

Tiled windows, illustrated in Figure 6.4, derive their name from common floor or wall tile. Tiled windows appear in one plane on the screen and expand or contract to fill up the display surface, as needed. Most systems provide two-dimensional tiled windows, adjustable in both height and width. Some less-powerful systems, however, are only one-dimensional, the windows being adjustable in only one manner (typically the height). Tiled windows, the first and oldest kind of window, are felt to have these advantages:

- The system usually allocates and positions windows for the user, eliminating the necessity to make positioning decisions.
- Open windows are always visible, eliminating the possibility of them being lost and forgotten.
- Every window is always completely visible, eliminating the possibility of information being hidden.
- They are perceived as less complex than overlapping windows, possibly because there are fewer management operations or they seem less "magical."

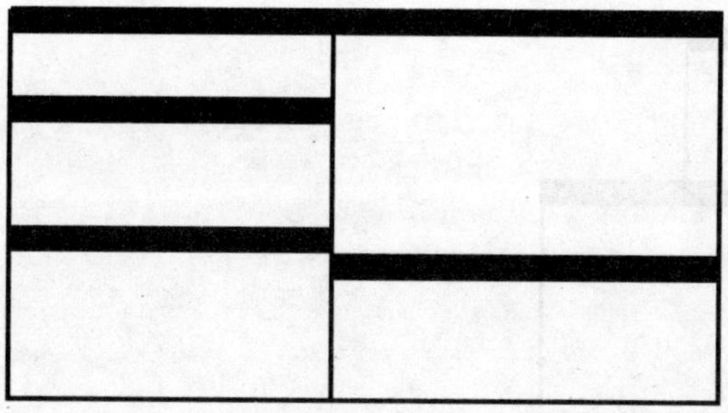

Figure 6.4 Tiled windows.

- They are easier, according to studies, for novice or inexperienced people to learn and use.
- They yield better user performance for tasks where the data requires little window manipulation to complete the task.

Perceived disadvantages include the following:

- Only a limited number can be displayed in the screen area available.
- As windows are opened or closed, existing windows change in size. This can be annoying.
- As windows change in size or position, the movement can be disconcerting.
- As the number of displayed windows increases, each window can get very tiny.
- The changes in sizes and locations made by the system are difficult to predict.
- The configuration of windows provided by the system may not meet the user's needs.
- They are perceived as crowded and more visually complex because window borders are flush against one another, and they fill up the whole screen. Crowding is accentuated if borders contain scroll bars or control icons. Viewer attention may be drawn to the border, not the data.
- They permit less user control because the system actively manages the windows.

Overlapping Windows

Overlapping windows, illustrated in Figure 6.5, may be placed on top of one another like papers on a desk. They possess a three-dimensional quality, appearing to lie on different planes. Users can control the location of these windows, as well as the plane in which they appear. The sizes of some types of windows may also be changed. Most systems today normally use this style of window. They have the following advantages:

- Visually, their look is three-dimensional, resembling the desktop that is familiar to the user.
- Greater control allows the user to organize the windows to meet his or her needs.
- Windows can maintain larger sizes.

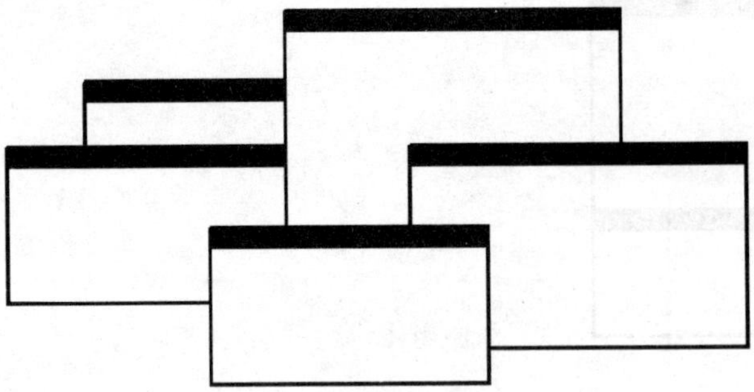

Figure 6.5 Overlapping windows.

- Windows can maintain consistent sizes.
- Windows can maintain consistent positions.
- Screen space conservation is not a problem, because windows can be placed on top of one another.
- There is less pressure to close or delete windows no longer needed.
- The possibility exists for less visual crowding and complexity. Larger borders can be maintained around window information, and the window is more clearly set off against its background. Windows can also be expanded to fill the entire display.
- They yield better user performance for tasks where the data requires much window manipulation to complete the task.

Disadvantages include the following:

- They are operationally much more complex than tiled windows. More control functions require greater user attention and manipulation.
- Information in windows can be obscured behind other windows.
- Windows themselves can be lost behind other windows and be presumed not to exist.
- That overlapping windows represent a three-dimensional space is not always realized by the user.
- Control freedom increases the possibility for greater visual complexity and crowding. Too many windows, or improper offsetting, can be visually overwhelming.

Cascading Windows

A special type of overlapping window has the windows automatically arranged in a regular progression. Each window is slightly offset from others, as illustrated in Figure 6.6. Advantages of this approach include the following:

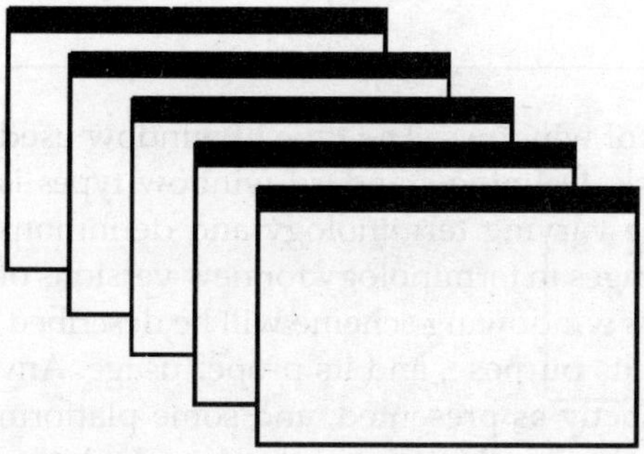

Figure 6.6 Cascading windows.

- No window is ever completely hidden.
- Bringing any window to the front is easier.
- It provides simplicity in visual presentation and cleanness.

Picking a Presentation Style

- Use tiled windows for:
  — Single-task activities.
  — Data that needs to be seen simultaneously.
  — Tasks requiring little window manipulation.
  — Novice or inexperienced users.
- Use overlapping windows for:
  — Switching between tasks.
  — Tasks necessitating a greater amount of window manipulation.
  — Expert or experienced users.
  — Unpredictable display contents.

Tiled windows. Tiled windows seem to be better for single-task activities and data that must be seen simultaneously. A study found that tasks requiring little window manipulation were carried out faster using tiled windows. They also found that novice users performed better with tiled windows, regardless of the task.

Overlapping windows. Overlapping windows seem to be better for situations that necessitate switching between tasks. A research study concluded that tasks requiring much window manipulation could be performed faster with overlapping windows but only if user window expertise existed. For novice users, tasks requiring much window manipulation were carried out faster with tiled windows. Therefore, the advantage to overlapping windows comes only after a certain level of expertise is achieved. Overlapping windows are the preferred presentation scheme.

Types of Windows

People's tasks must be structured into a series of windows. The type of window used will depend on the nature and flow of the task. Defining standard window types is again difficult across platforms because of the varying terminology and definitions used by different windowing systems, and changes in terminology for new versions of systems. For simplicity, the Microsoft Windows windowing scheme will be described. Summarized are a description of the window, its purpose, and its proper usage. Any other platform's windows may not behave exactly as presented, and some platform windows may exhibit characteristics common to more than one of the described window types.

Primary Window

- Proper usage:
  - — Should represent an independent function or application.
  - — Use to present constantly used window components and controls.
    - Menu bar items that are:
      - — Used frequently.
      - — Used by most, or all, primary or secondary windows.
    - Controls used by dependent windows.
  - — Use for presenting information that is continually updated.
    - For example, date and time.
  - — Use for providing context for dependent windows to be created.
  - — Do not:
    - Divide an independent function into two or more primary windows.
    - Present unrelated functions in one primary window.

The *primary* window is the first one that appears on a screen when an activity or action is started. It is required for every function or application, possessing a menu bar and some basic action controls, as previously described. It should present the framework for the function's commands and data, and provide top-level context for dependent windows. It has also been variously referred to as the *application* window or the *main* window. In addition, it may be referred to as the *parent* window if one or more *child* windows exist. A Microsoft Windows primary window is shown in Figure 6.7.

The primary window is the main focal point of the user's activities and should represent an independent function. Avoid dividing an independent function into two or more primary windows, and avoid presenting unrelated functions in a single primary window. This tends to confuse people.

Independent functions should begin in a primary window. A primary window should contain constantly used window components such as frequently used menu bar items and controls (for example, control bars) used by dependent windows. Also include in a primary window continually updated information such as the date and time. The components of a primary window are summarized in Table 6.2.

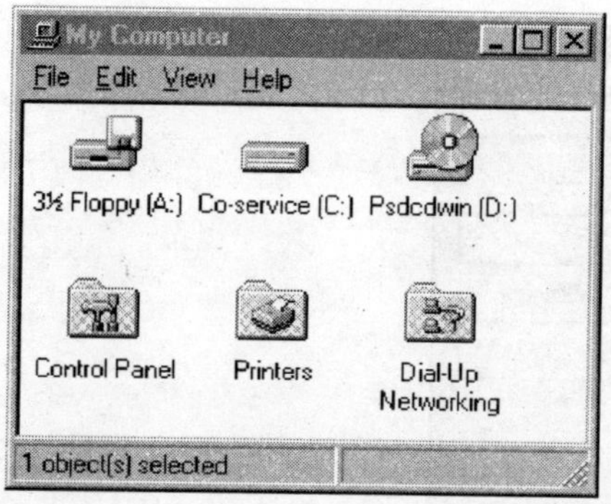

Figure 6.7 Microsoft Windows primary window.

Secondary Windows

- Proper usage:
  - — For performing subordinate, supplemental, or ancillary actions that are:
    - Extended or more complex in nature.
    - Related to objects in the primary window.
  - — For presenting frequently or occasionally used window components.
- Important guidelines:
  - — Should typically not appear as an entry on the taskbar.
  - — A secondary window should not be larger than 263 dialog units x 263 dialog units.

Secondary windows are supplemental windows. Secondary windows may be dependent upon a primary window or displayed independently of the primary window. They structurally resemble a primary window, possessing some of the same action controls (Close button) and possibly a What's This? button.

A *dependent* secondary window is one common type. It can only be displayed from a command on the interface of its primary window. It is typically associated with a single data object, and appears on top of the active window when requested. It is movable, and scrollable. If necessary, it uses the primary window's menu bar. Most systems permit the use of multiple secondary windows to complete a task. In general, dependent secondary windows are closed when the primary window closes, and hidden when their primary window is hidden or minimized.

An *independent* secondary window can be opened independently of a primary window—for example, a property sheet displayed when the user clicks the Properties command on the menu of a desktop icon. An independent secondary window can typically be closed without regard to the state of any primary window unless there is an obvious relationship to the primary window.

A Microsoft Windows secondary Window is illustrated in Figure 6.8.

Proper usage. Although secondary windows share many characteristics with primary windows, they also differ from primary windows in behavior and use. Secondary

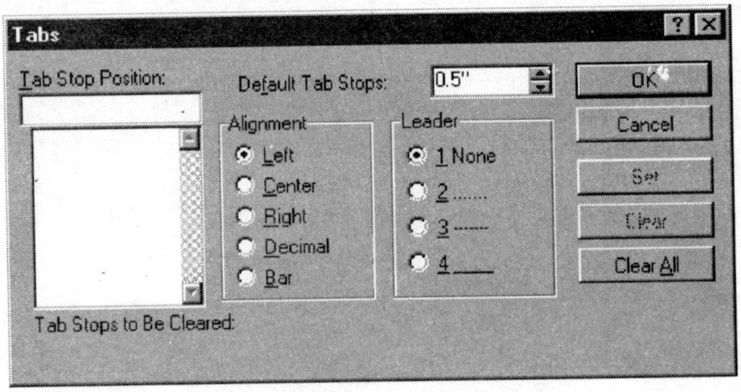

Figure 6.8 Microsoft Windows secondary window.

windows are used to perform supplemental or subordinate tasks, or tasks that are extended in nature. Frequently and occasionally used window components should also be presented in secondary windows. Microsoft Windows possesses several types of secondary windows called *dialog boxes, property sheets, property inspectors, message boxes, palette windows,* and *pop-up* windows.

Guidelines. A secondary window should typically not appear as an entry on the taskbar. Secondary windows obtain or display supplemental information that is usually related to the objects that appear in a primary window.

A secondary window is typically smaller than its associated primary window and smaller than the minimum display resolution. Microsoft recommends not displaying any secondary window larger than 263 dialog units × 263 dialog units. Microsoft defines size and location of user-interface elements not in pixels but in *dialog units* (DLUs), a device-independent unit of measure.

- One horizontal DLU is equal to one-fourth of the average character width for the current system font.
- One vertical DLU is equal to one-eighth of the average character height for the current system font.

These sizes keep the window from becoming too large to display at most resolutions. However, they still provide reasonable space to display supportive information, such as Help information, that applies.

The components of a secondary window are summarized in Table 6.2.

Modal and Modeless

- Modal:
  - — Use when interaction with any other window must not be permitted.
  - — Use for:
    - Presenting information.
      - — For example, messages (sometimes called a message box).

- Receiving user input.
  — For example, data or information (sometimes called a prompt box).
- Asking questions.
  — For example, data, information, or directions (sometimes called a question box).

— Use carefully because it constrains what the user can do.

- Modeless:
  — Use when interaction with other windows must be permitted.
  — Use when interaction with other windows must be repeated.

A secondary window can be modal or modeless.

Modal. Most secondary windows will be *modal*. Modal windows will not permit interaction with another window until the current dialog is completed. It remains displayed until the appropriate action is taken, after which it is removed from the screen. Modal dialog boxes typically request critical information or actions that must be reacted to before the dialog can continue. Since modal dialog boxes constrain what the user can do, limit their use to situations in which additional information is required to complete a command or when it is important to prevent any further interaction until satisfying a condition.

Modeless. A *modeless* dialog box permits the user to engage in parallel dialogs. Switching between the box and its associated window is permitted. Other tasks may be performed while a modeless dialog box is displayed, and it may be left on the screen after a response has been made to it. Actions leading to a modeless dialog box can be canceled, causing the box to be removed from the screen.

Use a modeless dialog box when interaction with a primary window or another secondary window must be permitted, for example, during the accessing of the Help function. Also, use a modeless dialog box when interaction with other windows must be repeated; for example, in a word search operation.

Cascading and Unfolding

- Cascading:
  — Purpose:
    - To provide advanced options at a lower level in a complex dialog.

  — Guidelines:
    - Provide a command button leading to the next dialog box with a "To a Window" indicator, an ellipsis (. . .).
    - Present the additional dialog box in cascaded form.
    - Provide no more than two cascades in a given path.
    - Do not cover previous critical information.
      — Title Bar.
      — Relevant displayed information.
    - If independent, close the secondary window from which it was opened.

- Unfolding:
  - — Purpose:
    - To provide advanced options at the same level in a complex dialog.
  - — Guidelines:
    - Provide a command button with an expanding dialog symbol (>>).
    - Expand to right or downward.

Access to additional options can be accomplished by inclusion of a command button that opens another secondary window. These multiple secondary windows needed to complete a task may be presented in two forms, cascading or expanding.

Cascading. A *cascading* window keeps the original window displayed, with the dependent window displayed on top, offset slightly to the right and below the original secondary window. A cascade, illustrated in Figures 6.9 and 6.10, is generally used when advanced options at a lower level in a complex dialog must be presented. An indication that the dialog will be cascading is signaled by an ellipsis placed in the command button used to display the additional dialog box. Because of the confusion that can develop with too many cascades, restrict the number of

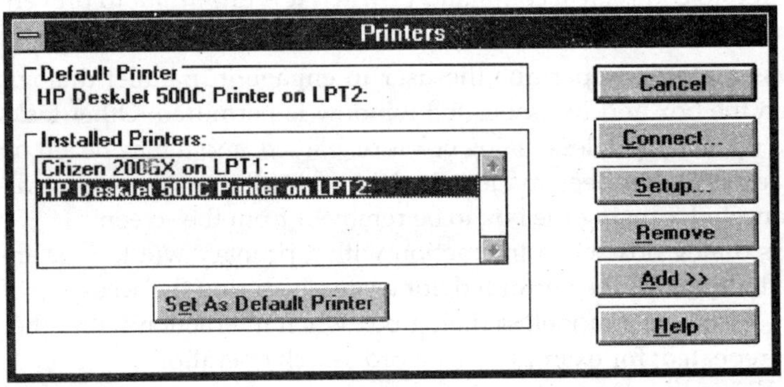

Figure 6.9 Printers secondary window with Connect... cascade button.

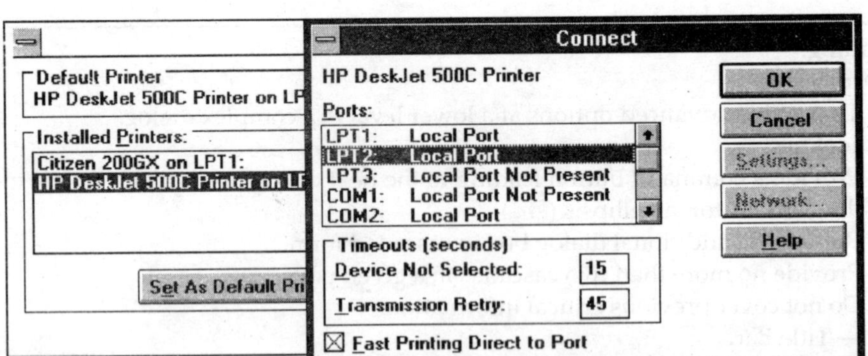

Figure 6.10 Cascading Connect secondary window.

cascades to no more than two in a given path. Do not cover information on the upper-level dialog boxes that may have to be referred to, such as box title bars and other critical or relevant information. If the cascaded window is independent in its operation, close the secondary window from which it was opened and display only the new window.

Unfolding. An *unfolding* secondary window expands to reveal additional options, a form of progressive disclosure. Unfolding windows, sometimes called *expanding* windows, are generally used to provide advanced options at the same level in a complex dialog. They are good alternatives when the interface contains a fixed set of options or controls that seldom need to be accessed. An unfolding window is illustrated in Figures 6.11 and 6.12. An indication that the dialog will be expanding is signaled by a double arrow (>>) placed in the command button used to display

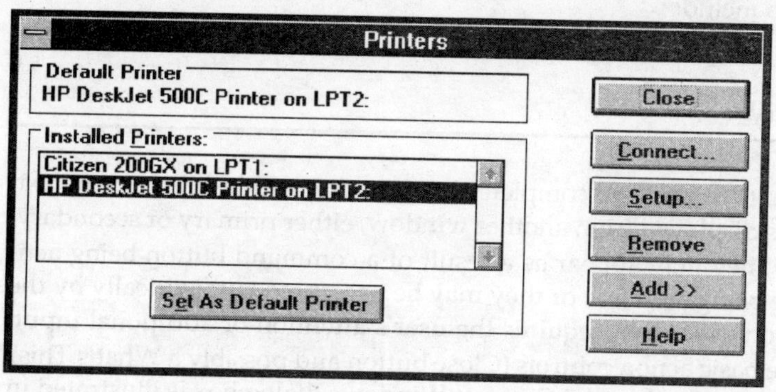

Figure 6.11 Printers secondary window with *Add* >> unfolding button.

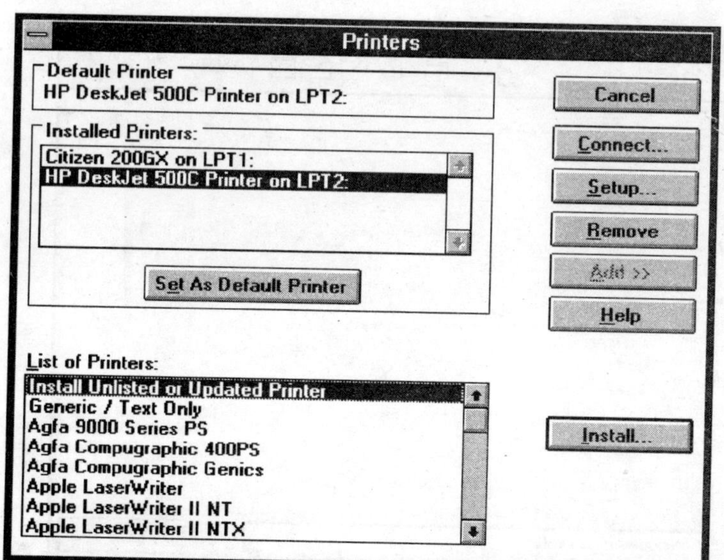

Figure 6.12 Unfolded Printers secondary window.

the additional dialog box. Expand the box to right, preferably, or downward if screen space constraints exist. As an option, the same button can be used to "refold" the additional part of the window.

Dialog Boxes

- Use for presenting brief messages.
- Use for requesting specific, transient actions.
- Use for performing actions that:
  - — Take a short time to complete.
  - — Are not frequently changed.
- Command buttons to include:
  - — OK.
  - — Cancel.
  - — Others as necessary.

Dialog boxes are used to extend and complete an interaction within a limited context. Dialog boxes are always displayed from another window, either primary or secondary, or another dialog box. They may appear as a result of a command button being activated or a menu choice being selected, or they may be presented automatically by the system when a condition exists that requires the user's attention or additional input. They may possess some basic action controls (Close button and possibly a What's This? button), but do not have a menu bar. A Microsoft Windows dialog box is illustrated in Figure 6.13.

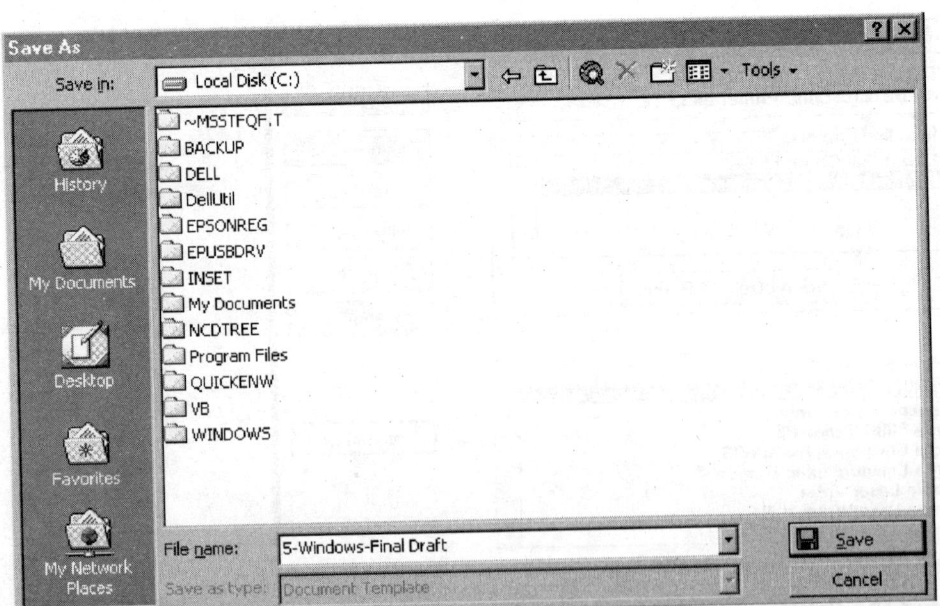

Figure 6.13 Microsoft Windows dialog box.

Most windowing systems provide standard dialog boxes for common functions, some examples being *Open, Save As*, and *Print*. Many platforms also recommend a set of standard command buttons for use in the various kinds of dialog boxes, such as OK, Cancel, and so on. Dialog boxes are of two types, modal and modeless, as recently described. They may also cascade or unfold.

Uses. Dialog boxes are used for presenting brief amounts of information or to request specific transient actions. Dialog box actions will usually be those that do not occur frequently.

Command buttons. Dialog boxes commonly include OK and Cancel command buttons. OK and Cancel buttons work best in dialog boxes that allow the user to set the parameters for a particular command. OK is typically defined as the default command button when the dialog box window opens. Other command buttons may be included in a dialog box in addition to or instead of the OK and Cancel buttons. Follow the design conventions for command buttons found in Chapter 8.

Property Sheets and Property Inspectors

The properties of an object in an interface can be displayed in a variety of ways. For example, the image and name of an icon on the desktop reflect specific properties of that object, as do other interface components such as toolbars, status bars, and even scroll bars. Secondary windows provide two other techniques for displaying properties, *property sheets* and *property inspectors.*

Property Sheets

- Use for presenting the complete set of properties for an object.
- Categorize and group within property pages, as necessary.
  - — Use tabbed property pages for grouping peer-related property sets.
  - — The recommended sizes for property sheets are:
    - 252 DLUs wide x 218 DLUs high
    - 227 DLUs wide x 215 DLUs high
    - 212 DLUs wide x 188 DLUs high
  - — Command buttons to include:
    - OK.
    - Cancel.
    - Apply.
    - Reset.
    - Others as necessary.
  - — For single property sheets, place the commands on the sheet.
  - — For tabbed property pages, place the commands outside the tabbed pages.

Use. A property sheet is the most common way to present an object's complete set of properties in a secondary window. A property sheet is a modeless secondary window that displays the user-accessible properties of an object, properties that may be viewed but not necessarily edited. A single page property sheet is illustrated in Figure 6.14.

Property pages. Because there can be many properties for an object and the object's context, the categorization and grouping of properties within sets may be necessary. A technique for supporting navigation to groups of properties in a property sheet is a tabbed *property page*, where each set of properties is presented within the window as a separate page. Each page tab is labeled with the name of the set, as shown in Figure 6.15. Use tabbed property pages for grouping peer-related property sets, tabs are described in Chapter 8.

Size. The sizes recommended for property sheets by Microsoft are shown above. These will create a window smaller than its associated window and smaller than the minimum display resolution.

Command buttons. Property sheets typically allow the values for a property to be changed, and then applied. Include the following common command buttons for handling the application of property changes. For common property sheet transaction buttons, use OK, Cancel, and Apply. A Reset command button to cancel pending changes without closing the window can also be included. Other command buttons can be included in property sheets. Avoid including a Help command button. If a Help button seems necessary, the best solution is to simplify the window.

Command buttons on *tabbed property pages* should be located outside of the tabbed page but still within the window. Buttons placed on a page imply that the action being performed applies *only* to that page. Buttons outside the pages imply

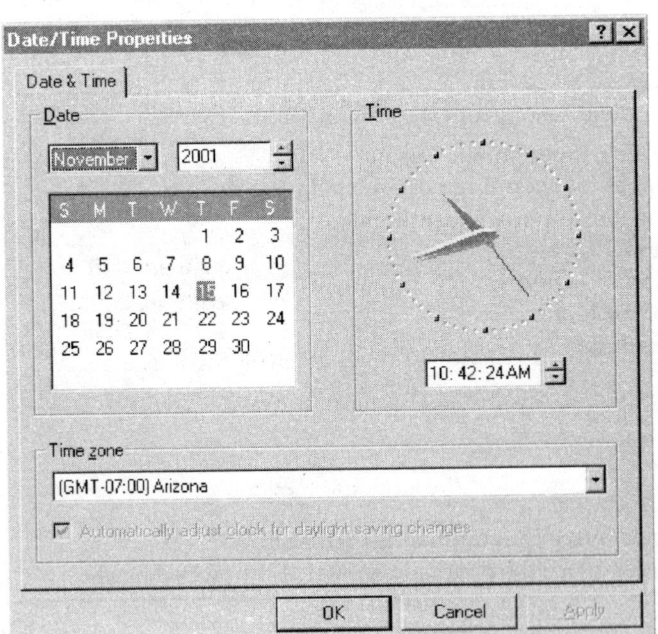

Figure 6.14 Microsoft Windows property sheet.

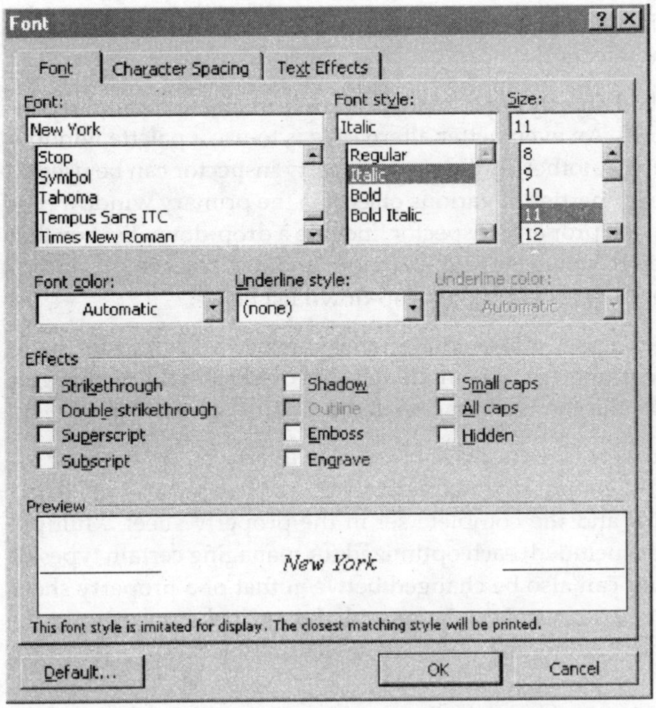

Figure 6.15 Microsoft Windows property sheet tabbed pages.

the action performed applies to *all* pages. This is the desired positioning because, most often, the tabs are considered by the user as simple grouping or navigation techniques. If the properties are to be applied on a page-by-page basis, however, then place the command and buttons on the property pages, and always in the same location on each page. When the user switches pages without selecting a command button, any property value changes for that page are applied. In these situations, it is useful to prompt the user by displaying a message box that asks whether to apply or discard any changes made.

Property Inspectors

- Use for displaying only the most common or frequently accessed object properties.
- Make changes dynamically.

Use. Display only the most common or frequently accessed properties in a property inspector. Properties of an object are displayed by using a dynamic viewer or browser that reflects the properties of the current selection. A property inspector differs from a property sheet. Even when a property sheet window is modeless, the window is typically modal with respect to the object for the properties being displayed. If the user selects another object, the property sheet continues to display the properties of the original object. A property inspector, on the other hand, always reflects the current selection.

A palette window (described shortly) or a toolbar is used to create a property inspector, as shown in Figure 6.16. An even better alternative is to use a palette window that the user can also configure. Another control in a property inspector can be used to enable the user to display the properties of various objects in the primary window. For example, as the first control in the property inspector, include a drop-down list box that displays the name of the object being viewed. To view another object's properties within the inspector, the object is selected in the drop-down list box.

Dynamic changes. Changes a user makes in a property inspector should be made dynamically. That is, the property value in the selected object should be changed as soon as the user makes the change in the related property control.

Property inspectors and property sheets are not exclusive interfaces. Both can be included in an interface. The most common or frequently accessed properties can be displayed in a property inspector and the complete set in the property sheet. Multiple property inspectors can also be included, each optimized for managing certain types of objects. An interface's behavior can also be changed between that of a property sheet and that of a property inspector. A control can be provided that "locks" its view, making it modal to the current object, rather than tracking the entire selection.

Message Boxes

- Use for displaying a message about a particular situation or condition.
- Command buttons to include:
  — OK.
  — Cancel.
  — Help.
  — Yes and No.
  — Stop.
  — Buttons to correct the action that caused the message box to be displayed.
- Enable the title bar close box only if the message includes a cancel button.
- Designate the most frequent or least destructive option as the default command button.

Use. A message box, as illustrated in Figure 6.17, is a secondary window that displays a message about a particular situation or condition.

Figure 6.16 Microsoft Windows property inspector.

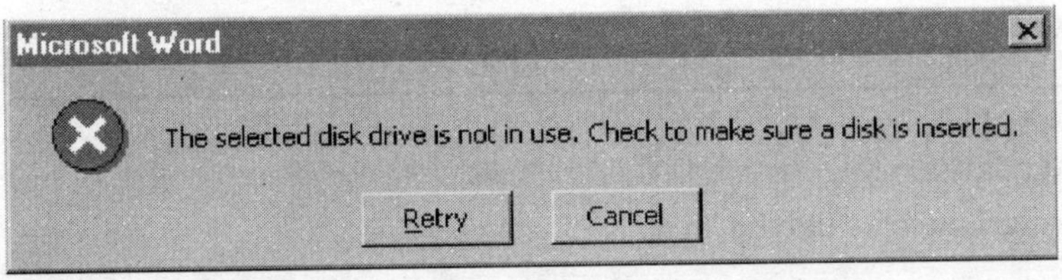

Figure 6.17 Microsoft Windows message box.

Command buttons. Typically, message boxes contain only command buttons with the appropriate responses or choices offered to the user. The command buttons used should allow the message box interaction to be simple and efficient. Microsoft suggests providing the following:

- If a message requires no choices to be made but only acknowledgment, include an OK button and, optionally, a Help button.
- If the message requires the user to make a choice, include a command button for each option.
- Include OK and Cancel buttons only when the user has the option of continuing or stopping the action.
- Use Yes and No buttons when the user must decide how to continue.
- If these choices are too ambiguous, label the command buttons with the names of specific actions, for example, *Save* and *Delete.*

Command buttons to correct the action that caused the message box to be displayed can also be included in a message box. For example, if the message box indicates that the user must switch to another application window to take corrective action, a button that opens that application window can also be included.

Stop. If Cancel is used as a command button in a message box, remember that to users, cancel implies that the state of the process or task that started the message is being restored. If you use Cancel to interrupt a process and the state cannot be restored, use *Stop* instead.

Help. A Help button can be included in a message box for messages needing more detail. This allows the message text to be more succinct.

If other command buttons are needed, consider the potential increase in complexity that their inclusion will cause.

Close box. Enable the title bar Close box only if the message includes a Cancel button. Otherwise, the meaning of the Close operation may be ambiguous.

Default. Designate the most frequent or least destructive option as the default command button.

A definition of message types, and guidelines for writing message, are found in Chapter 9.

Palette Windows

- Use to present a set of controls.
- Design as resizable.
  — Alternately, design them as fixed in size.

Use. Palette windows are modeless secondary windows that present a set of controls, as shown in Figure 6.18. Palette windows are distinguished by their visual appearance, a collection of images, colors or patterns. The title bar for a palette window is shorter and includes only a *close* button.

Sizing. A palette window can be defined as fixed in size, or, more typically, resizable by the user. Two techniques should indicate when the window is resizable, changing the pointer image to the size pointer, and placing a *size* command in the window's shortcut menu. Preserve the window's size and position so the window can be restored if it, or its associated primary window, is closed and then reopened.

Pop-up Windows

- Use pop-up windows to display:
  — Additional information when an abbreviated form of the information is the main presentation.
  — Textual labels for graphical controls.
  — Context-sensitive Help information.

Pop-up windows can be used to display additional information when an abbreviated form of the information is the main presentation technique, as illustrated in Figure 6.19. Other examples of pop-up windows used to display contextual information are *ToolTips* and *balloon tips* that provide the names for controls in graphical toolbars. Pop-up windows are also used to provide context-sensitive Help information. Pop-up windows do not contain standard secondary window components such as a title bar and close button.

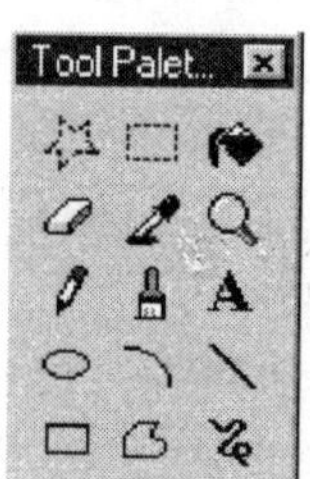

Figure 6.18 Microsoft Windows palette window.

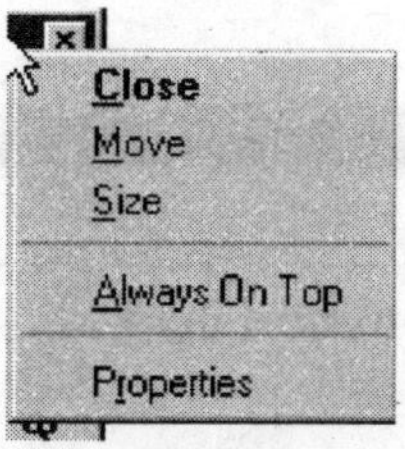

Figure 6.19 Microsoft Windows pop-up window.

Table 6.2 Microsoft Windows Window Types and Components

PRIMARY WINDOW	
Purpose:	To perform a major interaction.
Components:	Frame or border. Title bar. –Access point for commands that apply to the window, with commands displayed in a pop-up menu. Title Bar icon. –Small version of the icon of the object being viewed. –Access point for commands that apply to the object being displayed in the window, with commands displayed in a pop-up window. Title bar text. Title bar buttons to: close/minimize/maximize /restore a window. Menu bar. Status bar. Scroll bar. Size grip.
SECONDARY WINDOWS	
Purpose:	To obtain or display supplemental information related to the objects in the primary window.
Components:	Frame or border. Title bar. Title bar text. Close button. What's This? button. –Context-sensitive Help about components displayed in the window; this is optional.
Kinds:	Modal and modeless.

(continues)

Table 6.2 Continued

SECONDARY WINDOWS	
Dialog Boxes	
Purpose:	To obtain additional information needed to carry out a particular command or task.
Description:	Secondary window. Contains the following common dialog box interfaces: – Open/Replace/Find. – Save As /Print/Print Setup. – Page Setup/Font/Color.
Property Inspectors	
Purpose:	To display the most common or frequently accessed properties of a current selection, usually of a particular type of object.
Description:	A modeless secondary window. Typically modal with respect to the object for which it displays properties.
Usage:	Displayed when requested from selected object.
Property Sheets	
Purpose:	For presenting the complete set of properties for an object.
Description:	A modeless secondary window. Typically modal with respect to the object for which it displays properties.
Usage:	Displayed when requested from selected object.
Message Boxes	
Purpose:	To provide information about a particular situation or condition.
Description:	Secondary window. Types of message boxes: – Information/Warning/Critical.
Palette Windows	
Purpose:	To present a set of controls such as palettes or toolbars.
Description:	Modeless secondary window.

Table 6.2 Continued

SECONDARY WINDOWS	
Pop-Up Windows	
Purpose:	To display additional information when an abbreviated form of the information is the main presentation.
Description:	Secondary window. Does not contain standard secondary window components such as title bar and close button. Example: ToolTip.

Window Management

Microsoft Windows also provides several window management schemes, a *single-document interface, a multiple-document interface, workbooks*, and *projects*. To choose the right scheme to present an application's collection of related tasks or processes, consider a number of design factors, including: the intended users and their skill level, the application and its objects or tasks, and the most effective use of display space. These window management schemes are not exclusive design techniques. They may be combined, or others developed. These techniques, however, are the most frequently used schemes. Each is briefly described below. For greater detail, see Microsoft (2001).

Single-Document Interface

- Description:
  — A single primary window with a set of secondary windows.
- Proper usage:
  — Where object and window have a simple, one-to-one relationship.
  — Where the object's primary presentation or use is as a single unit.
  — To support alternate views with a control that allows the view to be changed.
  — To support simultaneous views by splitting the window into panes.
- Advantages:
  — Most common usage.
  — Window manipulation is easier and less confusing.
  — Data-centered approach.
- Disadvantage:
  — Information is displayed or edited in separate windows.

Often, the window interface can be established using a single primary window. A single-document window design is sufficient when the object's primary presentation or use is as a single unit, such as a folder or document, even when the object contains different types. In a single-document window design, the primary window provides the primary view or work area. Secondary windows can be used for supplemental forms of input, and to view information about objects presented in the primary window.

Multiple-Document Interface

- Description:
  - — A technique for managing a set of windows where documents are opened into windows.
  - — Contains:
    - A single primary window, called the parent.
    - A set of related document or child windows, each also essentially a primary window.
  - — Each child window is constrained to appear only within the parent window.
  - — The child windows share the parent window's operational elements.
  - — The parent window's elements can be dynamically changed to reflect the requirements of the active child window.
- Proper usage:
  - — To present multiple occurrences of an object.
  - — To compare data within two or more windows.
  - — To present multiple parts of an application.
  - — Best suited for viewing homogeneous object types.
  - — To clearly segregate the objects and their windows used in a task.
- Advantages:
  - — The child windows share the parent window's interface components (menus, toolbars, and status bars), making it a very space-efficient interface.
  - — Useful for managing a set of objects.
  - — Provides a grouping and focus for a set of activities within the larger environment of the desktop.
- Disadvantages:
  - — Reinforces an application as the primary focus.
  - — Containment for secondary windows within child windows does not exist, obscuring window relationships and possibly creating confusion.
  - — Because the parent window does not actually contain objects, context cannot always be maintained on closing and opening.
  - — The relationship between files and their windows is abstract, making an MDI application more challenging for beginning users to learn.
  - — Confining child windows to the parent window can be inconvenient or inappropriate for some tasks.
  - — The nested nature of child windows may make it difficult for the user to distinguish a child window in a parent window from a primary window that is a peer with the parent window but is positioned on top.

A multiple-document interface (MDI) may be used when multiple views of an object, or multiple documents, must be looked at simultaneously. The purpose of this scheme of windows is to provide multiple views of the same object, to permit comparisons among related objects, and to present multiple parts of an application. An MDI interface consists of multiple document windows that are easy to move between, essentially primary windows constrained to appear only within the parent windows boundary (instead of on the desktop). These windows may be referred to by a name that describes their contents, such as "Main" in Windows Program Manager. When minimized, they are displayed at the bottom of their parent window in iconic form. They are also resizable, movable, and scrollable. The primary window menu bar content may change dynamically, depending on the MDI window with the focus.

MAXIM **The information to make a decision *must be there* when the decision is needed.**

With MDI, the parent window provides a visual and operational framework for its child windows. Child windows typically share the menu bar of the parent window and can also share other parts of the parent's interface, such as a toolbar or status bar. These components can be changed to reflect the commands and attributes of the child window active at that moment. Secondary windows displayed as a result of interaction within the MDI parent or child window (dialog boxes, message boxes, or property sheets, for example), typically are not contained or clipped by the parent window. These windows should activate and display content according to the conventions for secondary windows associated with a primary window.

If an MDI document is opened, the MDI parent window opens first, and then the child window for the document opens within it. When the user closes the parent window, all of its child windows are closed. Where possible, the state of a child window, such as its size and position within the parent window, should be preserved and restored when the user reopens the file.

Workbooks

- Description:
  - — A window or task management technique that consists of a set of views organized like a tabbed notebook.
  - — It is based upon the metaphor of a book or notebook.
  - — Views of objects are presented as sections within the workbook's primary windows; child windows do not exist.
  - — Each section represents a view of data.
  - — Tabs can be included and used to navigate between sections.
  - — Otherwise, its characteristics and behavior are similar to those of the multiple-document interface with all child windows maximized.
- Proper usage:
  - — To manage a set of views of an object.
  - — To optimize quick navigation of multiple views.
  - — For content where the order of the sections is significant.

- Advantages:
  - — Provides a grouping and focus for a set of activities within the larger environment of the desktop.
  - — Conserves screen real estate.
  - — Provides the greater simplicity of the single-document window interface.
  - — Provides greater simplicity by eliminating child window management.
  - — Preserves some management capabilities of the multiple-document interface.
- Disadvantage:
  - — Cannot present simultaneous views.

A workbook is a scheme for managing a set of views that uses the metaphor of a book or notebook. Within the workbook, views of objects, in the form of sections, are presented within the workbook's primary window, rather than in individual child windows. Tabs are used as a navigational interface to move between different sections. (Tabs are described in Chapter 8.) Order the tabs to fit the content and organization of the presented information. Each tabbed section represents a view of data. One section can be used to list the workbook's table of contents.

Projects

- Description:
  - — A technique that consists of a container: a project window holding a set of objects.
  - — The objects being held within the project window can be opened in primary windows that are peers with the project window.
  - — Visual containment of the peer windows within the project window is not necessary.
  - — Each opened peer window must possess its own menu bar and other interface elements.
  - — Each opened peer window can have its own entry on the task bar.
  - — When a project window is closed, all the peer windows of objects also close.
  - — When the project window is opened, the peer windows of the contained objects are restored to their former positions.
  - — Peer windows of a project may be restored without the project window itself being restored.
- Proper usage:
  - — To manage a set of objects that do not necessarily need to be contained.
  - — When child windows are not to be constrained.
- Advantages:
  - — Provides a grouping and focus for a set of activities within the larger environment of the desktop.
  - — Preserves some management capabilities of the multiple document interface.
  - — Provides the greatest flexibility in the placement and arrangement of windows.

- Disadvantage:
  - — Increased complexity due to difficulty in differentiating peer primary windows of the project from windows of other applications.

A project is similar to a multiple-document interface (MDI), but does not visually contain the child windows. Objects represented by icons contained within it can be opened into primary windows that are peers with the parent window. Opened peer windows in the project do not share the menu bar or other areas contained with the parent window. Each opened peer window within the project must possess its own menu bar and other interface elements. (A palette window can be developed for sharing by all project windows, however.) Each peer child window can have its own entry on the taskbar.

Organizing Window Functions

Information and functions must be presented to people when and where they need them. Proper organization and support of tasks by windows will only be derived through a thorough and clear analysis of user tasks.

Window Organization

- Organize windows to support user tasks.
- Support the most common tasks in the most efficient sequence of steps.
- Use primary windows to:
  - — Begin an interaction and provide a top-level context for dependent windows.
  - — Perform a major interaction.
- Use secondary windows to:
  - — Extend the interaction.
  - — Obtain or display supplemental information related to the primary window.
- Use dialog boxes for:
  - — Infrequently used or needed information.
  - — "Nice-to-know" information.

People most often think in terms of tasks, not functions or applications. Windows must be organized to support this thinking. The design goal is to support the most common user tasks in the most efficient manner or fewest steps. Less frequently performed tasks are candidates for less efficiency or more steps.

Mayhew (1992) suggests that poor functional organization usually occurs because of one of, or a combination of, these factors:

- Emphasis on technical ease of implementation rather than proper analysis of user tasks.

- Focus on applications, features, functions, or data types instead of tasks.
- Organization of the design team into applications, with little cross-team communication.
- Blindly mimicking the manual world and carrying over manual inefficiencies to the computer system.

Emphasis on implementation ease puts the needs of the designer before the needs of the customer. Focusing on tasks conforms to the model of how people think. Application orientation imposes an unnatural boundary between functions, and lack of cross-team communication seldom yields consistent task procedures. Mimicking "what is" will never permit the capabilities of the computer system to be properly exploited.

Recommended usages for the various window types are summarized in the above guidelines. These recommendations were discussed more fully earlier in this chapter.

Number of Windows

- Minimize the number of windows needed to accomplish an objective.

A person does not work with windows simply for the joy of working with windows. Windows are a means to an end, a method of accomplishing something. Multiple windows on a display, as discussed elsewhere in this text, can be confusing, can increase the load on the human visual system, or may be too small to effectively present what needs to be contained within them.

Guidelines that appeared in early stages of window evolution concerning the maximum number of windows that a person could deal with were quite generous, a limit of seven or eight being suggested. As experience with windows has increased, these numbers have gradually fallen. One study found the mean number of windows maintained for experienced users was 3.7. Today, based on expressions of window users, a recommendation of displaying no more than two or three at one time seems most realistic. The guidelines on limitations for items like cascades (1–2) reflect today's feelings. The exact number of windows a person can effectively deal with at one time will ultimately depend on both the capabilities of the user and the characteristics of the task. Some users and situations may permit handling of more than three windows; for other users and situations, three windows may be two too many.

The general rule: Minimize the number of windows used to accomplish an objective. Use a single window whenever possible. Consider, however, the user's task. Don't clutter up a single window with rarely used information when it can be placed on a second, infrequently used, window.

Window Operations

Guidelines for windows operations are still evolving. Because of the paucity of published research data, many of the guidelines are still more anecdotal and intuitive than scientific. Guidelines will continue to develop and change as our understanding of, and experiences with, the windows interface continue to increase. Today, the following operational guidelines seem appropriate.

Active Window

- A window should be made active with as few steps as possible.
- Visually differentiate the active window from other windows.

While a system supports the display of multiple windows, the user generally works within a single window at one. This window, called the active window, may be designated either by the system or the user. Many systems make a window active when it is the object of another windowing operation. It is assumed that if users wish to change one aspect of a window's structure, they also wish to change its contents. They should also be permitted to move to and make any window active with as few steps as possible. This can be accomplished by simply allowing the user to move the selection cursor to the window's interior and then signal by pressing a key or button. For hidden windows, a menu of open windows might be presented from which the user selects a new open window.

In some situations, it may be desirable to allow multiple open windows. One research study compared a single open window with multiple open windows in performing queries and found that multiple open windows were described by people as more "natural." Performance was slower with multiple open windows, however. The study concluded that if user acceptance is important, multiple open windows might be the better alternative. If speed of task handling is critical, a single active window is more desirable.

Visually differentiate the active window from other windows. It is important that the user be able to quickly identify the active window. Methods to do this include a contrasting window title bar, border, or background color. An "active" indicator in the window border, which is turned on or off, may also be used. A combination of two or more of these visual cues may be used as well. The visual cue selected should be of moderate intensity, neither too powerful nor too subtle. Powerful cues will be distracting; subtle cues will be easily overlooked.

General Guidelines

- Design easy to use and learn windowing operations.
  — Direct manipulation seems to be a faster and more intuitive interaction style than indirect manipulation for many windowing operations.
- Minimize the number of window operations necessary to achieve a desired effect.
- Make navigating between windows particularly easy and efficient to do.
- Make the setting up of windows particularly easy to remember.
- In overlapping systems, provide powerful commands for arranging windows on the screen in user-tailorable configurations.

Easy to use. Design easy to use and learn window operations. The complexity of a windowing system should not cancel out its potential advantages. Operations must be carefully designed to achieve simplicity. As has been suggested, the ideal is that window manipulations should occur *implicitly* as a result of the user's task actions, not as a result of explicit, conscious, window management actions.

Minimize number. Minimize the number of window operations needed to achieve a desired effect. Establish the kinds of window operations that people are likely to want, and minimize the number of operations that must be performed to attain these configurations.

Easy navigation. Make navigating between windows easy and efficient. A study found that navigation between windows was the most frequent manipulation activity performed. High-frequency operations should always be easy to do.

Setting up. Make the process of setting up windows easy to remember. A study found that window arrangement (opening, resizing, moving, and so on) was a less frequent activity. Low-frequency operations should always be easy to learn.

User-tailorable configurations. In overlapping systems, provide powerful commands for arranging windows in user-tailorable configurations. When an overlapping window system is used, provide easy operations to achieve desired windowing configurations. Specific configurations should be capable of being created, named, and recalled.

Opening a Window

- Provide an iconic representation or textual list of available windows.
  - — If opening with an expansion of an icon, animate the icon expansion.
- When opening a window:
  - — Position the opening window in the most forward plane of the screen.
  - — Adapt the window to the size and shape of the monitor on which it will be presented.
  - — Designate it as the active window.
  - — Set it off against a neutral background.
  - — Ensure that its title bar is visible.
- When a primary window is opened or restored, position it on top.
  - — Restore all secondary windows to the states that existed when the primary window was closed.
- When a dependent secondary window is opened, position it on top of its associated primary window.
  - — Position a secondary window with peer windows on top of its peers.
  - — Present layered or cascaded windows with any related peer secondary windows.
- When a dependent secondary window is activated, its primary window and related peer windows should also be positioned at the top.
- If more than one object is selected and opened, display each object in a separate window. Designate the last window selected as the active window.

- Display a window in the same state as when it was last accessed.
  - If the task, however, requires a particular sequence of windows, use a fixed or consistent presentation sequence.
- With tiled windows, provide an easy way to resize and move newly opened windows.

Typically, when windows are opened, they are designated as active and positioned in the most forward plane of the screen so that they can be used immediately. When opening a window one should not assume a fixed monitor size, but reflect the size of the monitor on which the window will actually be displayed. The window's title bar must be visible. To focus attention on the newly opened window, display the screen background behind the window in a neutral or subdued manner. When opening windows from an iconic representation, gradually expand the window so that the movement is visible. This will aid association of the icon with the window in the mind of the viewer.

When a primary window is opened or restored, position it at the top. Restore all secondary windows to the states that existed when the primary window was closed. When a dependent secondary window is opened, position it on top of its associated primary window. If a secondary windows has peers, position it on top of its peers. Present layered or cascaded windows with any related peer secondary windows.

When a dependent secondary window is activated, its primary window and related peer windows should also be positioned at the top. If more than one object is selected and opened, display each object in a separate window. Designate the last window selected as the active window. Always display a window in the same state as when it was last accessed. If the task, however, requires a particular sequence of windows, use a fixed or consistent presentation sequence.

The first opened tiled window will consume the entire screen. Subsequent windows are usually positioned by defaults in the system. The system positioning of these subsequent windows may not always be consistent with the user's needs. The system should allow the user to change the default positions, or provide a way for the user to move and resize the system-provided windows easily.

Sizing Windows

- Provide large-enough windows to:
  - Present all relevant and expected information for the task.
  - Avoid hiding important information.
  - Avoid crowding or visual confusion.
  - Minimize the need for scrolling.
    - But use less than the full size of the entire screen.
- If a window is too large, determine:
  - Is all the information needed?
  - Is all the information related?
- Otherwise, make the window as small as possible.
  - Optimum window sizes:

- For text, about 12 lines.
- For alphanumeric information, about seven lines.

Larger windows seem to have these advantages:

- They permit displaying of more information.
- They facilitate learning: Data relationships and groupings are more obvious.
- Less window manipulation requirements exist.
- Breadth is preferred to depth (based on menu research).
- More efficient data validation and data correction can be performed.

Disadvantages include:

- Longer pointer movements are required.
- Windows are more crowded.
- More visual scanning is required.
- Other windows more easily obscure parts of the window.
- It is not as easy to hide inappropriate data.

Always provide large enough windows to present all the relevant and expected information for the task. Never hide important or critical information, and minimize the need for scrolling. A study has found that very small windows requiring a significant amount of scrolling appear to increase decision-making time. Scrolling is also a cumbersome operation. To avoid scrolling, consider using unfolding dialog boxes, cascading windows, or a tab control. Avoid, however, making a window's default size the full size of the display. Doing so leads to any underlying windows being completely hidden from the user's view. The option to maximize primary and secondary windows always exists.

If, through analysis and design, a window appears to be too large, determine:

- Is all the information needed?
- Is all the information related?

Important, critical, or frequently used information must be maintained on a screen, but perhaps information exists that is needed or used infrequently, for example. only 10 to 20 percent of the time. This kind of information is a good candidate for placement on another window or dialog box. Perhaps information is included on a screen that is not related to the task being performed. This kind of information should be located with the information to which it is related. As a last resort, consider shortening some window control captions or other included window text to achieve a proper fit.

At least two studies have looked at optimum window sizes. Procedural text in window sizes of 6, 12, and 24 lines were evaluated by one study. Fastest and most accurate completion occurred with the 12-line window. The retrieval of alphanumeric information was compared in 7-, 13-, and 19-line windows in another study. A seven-line window was found to be more than adequate.

Window Placement

- Considerations:
  - — In placing a window on the display, consider:
    - The use of the window.
    - The overall display dimensions.
    - The reason for the window's appearance.
- General:
  - — Position the window so it is entirely visible.
  - — If the window is being restored, place the window where it last appeared.
  - — If the window is new, and a location has not yet been established, place it:
    - At the point of the viewer's attention, usually the location of the pointer or cursor.
    - In a position convenient to navigate to.
    - So that it is not obscuring important or related underlying window information.
  - — For multiple windows, give each additional window its own unique and discernible location.
    - A cascading presentation is recommended.
  - — In a multiple-monitor configuration, display the secondary window on the same monitor as its primary window.
  - — If none of the above location considerations apply, then:
    - Horizontally center a secondary window within its primary window just below the title bar, menu bar, and any docked toolbars.
  - — If the user then moves the window, display it at this new location the next time the user opens the window.
    - Adjust it as necessary to the current display configuration.
  - — Do not let the user move a window to a position where it cannot be easily repositioned.
- Dialog boxes:
  - — If the dialog box relates to the entire system, center it on screen.
  - — Keep key information on the underlying screen visible.
  - — If one dialog box calls another, make the new one movable whenever possible.

Considerations. In placing a window on the display, consider how the window is used in relation to other windows, the overall dimensions of the display, and the reason that the window is being presented.

General. First, locate the window so it is fully visible. If the window is being restored, locate it where it last appeared. If the window is new and the location has not yet been established, place it at the point of the viewer's attention. This will usually be the location of the pointer or cursor. Also, place the window in a position where it will be convenient to navigate to, and where it will not obscure important underlying screen information. Preferred positions are essentially below and right. The suggested order of placement is below right, below, right, top right, below left, top, left, top left.

In a multiple-monitor configuration, display the secondary window on the same monitor as its primary window. If none of these situations applies, horizontally center a secondary window within the primary window, just below the title bar, menu bar, and any docked toolbars. Give each additional window its own unique location. A cascading presentation, from upper left to lower right is recommended. If the user then moves the window, display it at this new location the next time the user opens the window, adjusted as necessary for the current display configuration. Do not let the user move a window to a position where it cannot be easily repositioned.

Dialog boxes. If a dialog box relates to the entire system, center it on display, keeping key information on an underlying window visible. If one dialog box calls another, make the new one movable whenever possible.

Window Separation

- Crisply, clearly, and pleasingly demarcate a window from the background of the screen on which it appears.
  - — Provide a surrounding solid line border for the window.
  - — Provide a window background that sets the window off well against the overall screen background.
  - — Consider incorporating a drop shadow beneath the window.

Component separation is especially critical in a graphics environment because of the spatial layering that can occur. All windows must be clearly set off from the underlying screen or windows. The demarcation must be crisp and visually pleasing. A solid single-line border is recommended for this purpose. Also provide a window background that sets the window off well against the overall screen background. If color is used, exercise caution and choose compatible colors. (See Chapter 12 "Colors.") Another alternative is to use for the window a lighter shade of the color used for the screen background. Changes in the density of shades are often more visually pleasing than different colors. To emphasize the three-dimensional aspects of graphic windows, incorporate a drop shadow beneath each window.

Moving a Window

- Permit the user to change the position of all windows.
- Change the pointer shape to indicate that the move selection is successful.
- Move the entire window as the pointer moves.
  - — If it is impossible to move the entire window, move the window outline while leaving the window displayed in its original position.
- Permit the moving of a window without its being active.

An indication that the move operation has been successfully selected and that the move may begin should be indicated to the user by changing the pointer's shape. This will provide feedback indicating that it is safe to begin the move operation and will avoid false starts. Ideally, the entire window should move along with the pointer. If the entire window cannot be moved, move the window outline while leaving the full window displayed on the screen. Displaying only the window's outline during the move operation, and not the window itself, may make it harder for the user to decide when the window has been repositioned correctly. It may be necessary for a window to be moved without being active. This should be possible. The action of moving the window may implicitly activate it, however.

Resizing a Window

- Permit the user to change the size of primary windows.
  - — Unless the information displayed in the window is fixed or cannot be scaled to provide more information.
- Change the pointer shape to indicate that the resizing selection is successful.
- The simplest operation is to anchor the upper-left corner and resize from the lower-right corner.
  - — Also permit resizing from any point on the window.
- Show the changing window as the pointer moves.
  - — If it is impossible to show the entire window being resized, show the window's outline while leaving the window displayed in its original position.
- When window size changes and content remains the same:
  - — Change image size proportionally as window size changes.
- If resizing creates a window or image too small for easy use, do one of the following:
  - — Clip (truncate) information arranged in some logical structure or layout when minimum size is attained, or
  - — When no layout considerations exist, format (restructure) information as size is reduced, or
  - — Remove less useful information (if it can be determined), or
  - — When minimum size is attained, replace information with a message that indicates that the minimum size has been reached and that the window must be enlarged to continue working.
- Permit resizing a window without its being active.

Make your primary windows resizable unless the information displayed in the window is fixed or cannot be scaled to provide the user with more information. (For example, a calculator window.)

An indication that the resize operation has been successfully selected, and that the move may begin, should be indicated to the user by changing the pointer's shape. This will provide the necessary feedback that it is safe to begin the resizing and will avoid false starts. The simplest operation for the user, conceptually, is always to resize from the lower-right corner and anchor the window in the upper-left corner. Flexibility can be provided by permitting resizing to occur from any point on the border (the anchor is always opposite the pulling point), but conceptually this is more complex. Some people may have difficulty predicting which window sides or corners will be resized from specific pulling points.

Ideally, the entire window should move along with the pointer. If the entire window cannot be moved, move the window outline while leaving the full window displayed on the screen. Displaying only the window's outline during the move operation, and not the window itself, may make it harder for the user to decide when the window has been repositioned correctly.

The effect of a resizing operation on the window's contents usually depends on the application. In enlarging, more data may be displayed, a larger image may be created, or blank space may be added around the image. In reducing, less data may be displayed, the image may be made smaller, blank space may be eliminated, or the data may be reformatted. If resizing creates a window or image too small for easy use, clip or truncate information arranged in some logical structure, format, or layout. When no layout considerations exist, as is the case for text, format or restructure the displayed information. Also consider removing less useful information, if it can be determined. When the minimum size has been attained and any additional attempts to reduce window size occur, replace the information with a message that indicates that the minimum size has been reached and that the window must be enlarged to continue working.

It may be necessary for a window to be resized without being active. This should be possible. The action of moving the window may implicitly activate it, however.

Other Operations

- Permit primary windows to be maximized, minimized, and restored.

Maximizing. Maximizing a window increases the size of the window to its largest optimum size. The system default setting for the maximum size is as large as the display. This should be adjustable, as necessary.

Minimizing. Minimizing a window reduces it to its smallest size.

Restoring. Restoring returns a window to its previous size and position after the user has maximized or minimized it.

Window Shuffling

- Window shuffling must be easy to accomplish.

Window shuffling should be easy to perform in as few steps as possible. One method is to permit the toggling of the two most recently displayed windows. Another is to permit rapid window shuffling and the swapping of the front window and the second or back window.

Keyboard Control/Mouseless Operation

- Window actions should be capable of being performed through the keyboard as well as with a mouse.

- Keyboard alternatives should be designated through use of mnemonic codes as much as possible.
- Keyboard designations should be capable of being modified by the user.

All window actions should be capable of being performed using the keyboard as well as the mouse. This will provide a more efficient alternative for applications that contain tasks that are primarily keyboard-oriented, for users skilled in touch typing, and for any other situations in which frequent movement between keyboard and mouse may be required. The use of mnemonic codes to reflect window mouse actions will greatly aid user learning of the keyboard alternatives. To provide the user flexibility, all keyboard designations should be capable of being user modified.

Closing a Window

- Close a window when:
  - — The user requests that it be closed.
  - — The user performs the action required in the window.
  - — The window has no further relevance.
- If a primary window is closed, also close all of its secondary windows.
- When a window is closed, save its current state, including size and position, for use when the window is opened again.

Close a window when the user requests it to be closed, when the action required in the window is performed, or when the window has no further relevance to the task being performed. If the closed window is a primary window, also close its associated secondary windows. When a window is closed, it is important that its current state, including size and position, be saved for use when the window is again opened.

Web Systems

Web systems have limited windowing capabilities. The *frame* concept does provide window-like ability, and JavaScript does provide *pop-up* windows.

Frames

- Description:
  - — Multiple Web screen panes that permit the displaying of multiple documents on a page.
  - — These documents can be independently viewed, scrolled, and updated.
  - — The documents are presented in a tiled format.
- Proper usage:
  - — For content expected to change frequently.
  - — To allow users to change partial screen content.
  - — To permit users to compare multiple pieces of information.

- Guidelines:
  - — Use only a few frames (three or less) at a given time.
  - — Choose sizes based upon the type of information to be presented.
  - — Never force viewers to resize frames to see information.
  - — Never use more than one scrolling region on a page.

Description. The Web is, historically, essentially a single page (or, by analogy, a single window) entity. While providing significant interface benefits, it is also a reversal of the interface evolution process that led from single-screen technology to windowing. To counteract this shortcoming, *frames* were created. A frame is an independent pane of information presented in a Web page, or, again by analogy, as multiple windows. Frames, however, are presented as tiled, with no overlapping capability. The interaction richness, support, and contextual cues provided by overlapping windows are lacking. Frames, then, allow the displaying of multiple documents on a single Web page. These multiple documents can be independently viewed, scrolled, and updated.

Proper usage. Frames are useful in situations where portions of the page content are expected to change frequently. The volatile information can be separated from other page content and placed within a frame, thereby requiring only a portion of the page's content to be modified. Frames are also useful for allowing the user to change page content; navigation links can be placed in one frame and the resulting content displayed within another frame. As different links are selected, the content in the related frame changes. Finally, frames more effectively allow users to compare multiple pieces of related information displayed within the different frames.

Advantages and disadvantages. Frames, like most interface entities, have advantages and disadvantages. At this moment in their existence, the disadvantages seem to outweigh the advantages. These disadvantages, however, are being whittled away as Web technology advances.

Frames *advantages* mostly cluster around their ability to reduce the user's content comprehension mental load. These include the following:

- They decrease the user's need to jump back and forth between screens, thereby reducing navigation-related cognitive overhead.
- They increase the user's opportunity to request, view, and compare multiple sources of information.
- They allow content pages to be developed independently of navigation pages.

The *disadvantages* mostly cluster around navigational shortcomings, including:

- The difference between a single Web page and a page with frames is not always obvious to the user.
- They suffer some of the shortcomings of tiled screens:
  - — Only a limited number can be displayed in the available screen area.
  - — They are perceived as crowded and more visually complex because frame borders are flush against one another and they fill up the whole screen.

Crowding is accentuated if the borders contain scroll bars and/or control icons. Viewer attention may be drawn to the border, not the data.

- Frames-based pages behave differently from regular Web pages.
  — Page-printing difficulties and problems can exist.
  — Page interaction can be clumsy.
  — URLs cannot be e-mailed to other users.
- Frames will not work on older browsers.

Past problems, now being addressed and mostly solved, have included difficulties in bookmarking pages, difficulties in creating browser history lists, and inconsistencies in behavior of the browser's Back button. So, while no longer an interface disaster, frames do make a page clumsy to work with. One study has found that well-designed frames didn't hinder users, but they didn't help, either. A review of the top 100 Web sites (in 1999) found that one common characteristic they all shared was no use of frames.

Guidelines. Guidelines to consider in using frames are the following: Use no more than three frames at a time. Using more will shrink each frame's usable area to the point where little space will be available for presenting content. Then, users will not be able to see much and be forced to scroll. Choose frame sizes based upon the type of information you want to present. Navigational links, for example, should be presented in a small frame and the corresponding information in a larger adjacent frame. Never force people to resize frames to see information. If people feel they must resize frames, the page design is poor. Finally, do not use more than one scrolling region in frames contained on a page. This may be confusing to many users.

Technological advances in frames will continue to occur. Knowledge related to frame usability will also advance. Always be aware of the latest developments.

Pop-Up Windows

- Be extremely cautious in the use of pop-up windows.

JavaScript pop-up windows began appearing on the Web in 1996. Their use is multiplying and, in the view of almost all Web users, polluting screens. Because they are most frequently used in advertising, they have become a source of great aggravation to almost every user. Anecdotal evidence suggests that when a pop-up window begins to appear, most people close them before they are rendered. So, if a pop-up window is used, it may never be completely seen or read by the user. Use them with extreme caution.

Multiple Choice Questions

1. Tiled Windows are
   (a) Visible and eliminate the possibility of information being hidden
   (b) Invisible and eliminate the possibility of information being hidden
   (c) Visible and eliminate the possibility of them being lost or forgotten
   (d) Both (a) and (b)
   (e) Both (a) and (c)
2. Overlapping windows are best suitable for
   (a) Single-task activities
   (b) Switching between task
   (c) Data that need to be seen simultaneously
   (d) Both (a) and (b)
   (e) Both (a) and (c)
3. Tiled windows are best suitable for
   (a) Single-task activities
   (b) Switching between task
   (c) Data that need to be seen simultaneously
   (d) Both (a) and (b)
   (e) Both (a) and (c)
4. A dependent secondary window
   (a) Appears on top of the primary window's menu bar
   (b) Can be opened independently of a primary window
   (c) Gets closed when the primary window closes
   (d) Both (a) and (b)
   (e) Both (a) and (c)
5. An independent secondary window is
   (a) Appears on top of the primary window's menu bar
   (b) Can be opened independently of a primary window
   (c) Gets closed when the primary window closes
   (d) Both (a) and (b)
   (e) Both (a) and (c)
6. Modal dialog box is
   (a) Used when interaction with any other window must be permitted
   (b) Used when interaction with any other window must not be permitted
   (c) Used when interaction with any other window must not be repeated
   (d) Both (a) and (c)
   (e) None of the above
7. Modeless dialog box is
   (a) Used when interaction with any other window must be permitted
   (b) Used when interaction with any other window must not be permitted
   (c) Used when interaction with any other window must be repeated
   (d) Both (a) and (b)
   (e) Both (a) and (c)
8. A property sheet is a
   (a) a model secondary window
   (b) a modeless secondary window
   (c) Both (a) and (b)
   (d) None of the above
9. Which is not a standard dialog box?
   (a) ColorDialog (b) FontDialog
   (c) OpenDialog (d) PrintDialog
   (e) ZoomDialog
10. How are dialog boxes implemented in a program?
   (a) A dialog box is generated programmatically
   (b) A dialog control is placed in the component tray
   (c) A dialog control is placed on the form
   (d) Both (a) and (b)
   (e) All of the above

11. Which property is the same in the OpenFileDialog and the SaveFileDialog control?
    (a) FileName
    (b) Filter
    (c) InitialDirectory
    (d) Both (a) and (b)
    (e) All of the above

12. Which dialog control has a Document property?
    (a) PrintDialog
    (b) PrintPreview
    (c) PageSetupDialog
    (d) Both (a) and (b)
    (e) All of the above

Review Questions

1. Describe the various characteristics of windows.
2. Describe the types of windows used in GUI applications.
3. Define the following:
   (a) Model dialogue box/message box
   (b) Modeless
   (c) Property sheet
   (d) Property inspector
   (e) Cascade and Window indicators
4. Describe the different types of Windows Presentation Styles.
5. Describe the various components of windows.
6. Describe different types of secondary window.
7. Distinguish between secondary dependent and independent windows with example.
8. Describe briefly four different interaction styles used to accommodate the dialogue between user and computer.
9. State the different states of check-button.
10. Distinguish between SDI and MDI scheme.
11. Describe the advantages and disadvantages for various windows management schemes.
12. How can visually the active window be differentiated from other windows?
13. Give your comments on following window operations:
    (a) Maximizing a window
    (b) Minimizing a window
    (c) Closing a window
    (d) Restoring a window
14. Explain the windowing capabilities of web system with example.

CHAPTER

7

Device-Based Controls

Device-based controls, often called input devices, are the mechanisms through which people communicate their desires to the system. The evolution of graphical systems has seen a whole new family of devices provided to assist and enhance this communication. These new mechanisms are most commonly referred to as pointing devices. In this chapter, we will:

- Identify the characteristics and capabilities of various device-based controls:
  - Trackball
  - Joystick
  - Graphic tablet
  - Light pen
  - Touch screen
  - Voice
  - Mouse
  - Keyboard
- Select the proper controls for the user and tasks.

For years the device of choice in display-based systems was the standard keyboard and some human-engineered variations. As graphical systems evolved, emphasis shifted to another device, the mouse and some of its cousins: the trackball and joystick. A few other devices have also been around and have seen extended service through the years: the light pen and the graphic tablet. Some uniquely human devices also exist, touch and voice. A finger has been used in conjunction with touch-sensitive screens. Our vocal chords are being harnessed to speak meaningfully to the computer, not simply to shout words of exasperation. These various alternatives have both strengths and weaknesses. Selecting the proper device-based control to do the required job is critical to system success. A good fit between user and control will lead to fast, accurate performance. A poor fit will result in lower productivity, produce more errors, and increase user fatigue.

We'll begin by reviewing the kinds of tasks being performed using graphical systems. We'll discuss each device and identify its advantages and disadvantages. Then, we'll focus on the most popular control, the mouse, describing it in more detail and presenting a series of design guidelines for its use. The keyboard, because of its versatility and usefulness for text entry tasks, will also be examined in more detail. Finally, pertinent research will be reviewed and guidelines presented to aid in selecting the proper device.

Characteristics of Device-Based Controls

Several specific tasks are performed using graphical systems.

- To point at an object on the screen.
- To select the object or identify it as the focus of attention.
- To drag an object across the screen.
- To draw something free form on the screen.
- To track or follow a moving object.
- To orient or position an object.
- To enter or manipulate data or information.

The various devices vary in how well they can perform these actions. Among the considerations to be reviewed are two very important factors. First, is the mechanism a direct or indirect pointing device? *Direct* devices are operated on the screen itself. Examples include the light pen, the finger, and voice. *Indirect* devices are operated in a location other than the screen, most often on the desktop. Examples include the mouse, trackball, and keyboard. The psychomotor skills involved in learning to use, and using, a direct device are much simpler than those required for an indirect device. Most of these direct device skills were instilled in our formative years.

Second, in terms of *direction, distance,* and *speed,* what is the relationship between movement of the hand-operated device and the corresponding pointer movement on the screen? Does the pointer movement track control movement exactly or does it not? The mouse achieves a coupled relationship in all three aspects of direction, distance, and speed: The pointer on the screen moves in the direction the mouse is pushed, at the speed the mouse is pushed, and the distance the mouse is pushed (there may be some ratios applied). A trackball does not achieve this relationship in all three aspects. The pointer moves the direction the trackball is turned and the speed the ball is turned, but not the distance the ball is moved because the ball does not move forward or backwards; its socket is stationary. Devices possessing coupled relationships in these three aspects require less psychomotor skill learning than those not possessing a coupled relationship in all three aspects.

Trackball

- Description:
  — A spherical object (ball) that rotates freely in all directions in its socket.
  — Direction and speed is tracked and translated into cursor movement.
- Advantages:
  — Direct relationship between hand and pointer movement in terms of direction and speed.
  — Does not obscure vision of screen.
  — Does not require additional desk space (if mounted on keyboard).
- Disadvantages:
  — Movement is indirect, in a plane different from the screen.
  — No direct relationship exists between hand and pointer movement in terms of distance.
  — Requires a degree of eye-hand coordination.
  — Requires hand to be removed from keyboard keys.
  — Requires different hand movements.
  — Requires hand to be removed from keyboard (if not mounted on keyboard).
  — Requires additional desk space (if not mounted on keyboard).
  — May be difficult to control.
  — May be fatiguing to use over extended time.

Description. Commonly used with notebook PCs, the trackball is a ball that rotates freely in all directions in its socket. The ball is rotated with one's fingertips, and its direction and speed are tracked and translated into equivalent screen cursor movement. Trackballs are well suited for navigational control, as in video games or exploration of 3-D environments. In these tasks, smooth movement is more important than fine target acquisition.

Advantages. In terms of direction and speed, a trackball possesses a direct relationship between how it is rolled and how the cursor moves on the screen. The cursor moves in the same direction and speed ratio as the ball is rotated. Many trackballs are mounted on the keyboard itself, permitting the user's hands to remain close to the keys. Trackballs on the keyboard do not require additional desk space, although the keyboard must often be expanded to allow for their inclusion.

Disadvantages. Trackballs share a common problem with several other controls: control movement is in a different plane from the screen, or indirect. The cursor, or pointer, is separated from the control itself—the pointer being on the screen, the control on the keyboard. To effectively use a trackball requires learning the proper psychomotor skills, fine finger movements for accurate pointing, and gross hand movements for moving longer distances. The fine finger movements necessary to use them can be difficult to perform. Over longer periods of use, they can be fatiguing. When paired with keyboard tasks, they require a shift in motor activity from keystrokes to finger/hand movement.

Joystick

- Description:
  - — A stick or bat-shaped device anchored at the bottom.
  - — Variable in size, smaller ones being operated by fingers, larger ones requiring the whole hand.
  - — Variable in cursor direction movement method, force joysticks respond to pressure, movable ones respond to movement.
  - — Variable in degree of movement allowed, from horizontal-vertical only to continuous.
- Advantages:
  - — Direct relationship between hand and pointer movement in terms of direction.
  - — Does not obscure vision of screen.
  - — Does not require additional desk space (if mounted on keyboard).
- Disadvantages:
  - — Movement indirect, in plane different from screen.
  - — Indirect relationship between hand and pointer in terms of speed and distance.
  - — Requires a degree of eye-hand coordination.
  - — Requires hand to be removed from keyboard keys.
  - — Requires different hand movements to use.
  - — Requires hand to be removed from keyboard (if not mounted on keyboard).
  - — Requires additional desk space (if not mounted on keyboard).
  - — May be fatiguing to use over extended time.
  - — May be slow and inaccurate.

Description. A joystick, like its aircraft namesake, is a stick or bat-shaped device usually anchored at the bottom. They come in variable sizes, smaller ones being operated by fingers, larger ones requiring the whole hand. The smaller joysticks require fine motor coordination, the larger ones more gross coordination. Some, called *force* joysticks, are immovable, responding to pressure exerted against them. The direction and amount of pressure is translated into pointer movement direction and speed. Others, called *movable* joysticks, can be moved within a dish-shaped area. The direction and distance of the movements create a similar pointer movement on the screen. Some kinds of joysticks permit continuous movements, others only horizontal and vertical movements. Joysticks may also be mounted on the keyboard. Joysticks are also well suited for navigational control where smooth movement is most important.

Advantages. Joysticks typically possess a direct relationship between hand and cursor movement in terms of direction. They do not obscure vision of the screen and, when mounted on the keyboard, do not require additional desk space.

Disadvantages. Joysticks are also indirect devices, the control and its result being located in different planes. They require developing a skill to use and can be slow and inaccurate. Use over extended time, they may also be fatiguing. When paired with keyboard tasks, they require a shift in motor activity from keystrokes to finger/hand movement.

Graphic Tablet

- Description:
  - — Pressure-, heat-, light-, or light-blockage-sensitive horizontal surfaces that lie on the desktop or keyboard.
  - — May be operated with fingers, light pen, or objects like a stylus or pencil.
  - — Pointer imitates movements on tablet.
- Advantages:
  - — Direct relationship between touch movements and pointer movements in terms of direction, distance, and speed.
  - — More comfortable horizontal operating plane.
  - — Does not obscure vision of screen.
- Disadvantages:
  - — Movement is indirect, in a plane different from screen.
  - — Requires hand to be removed from keyboard.
  - — Requires hand to be removed from keyboard keys.
  - — Requires different hand movements to use.
  - — Requires additional desk space.
  - — Finger may be too large for accuracy with small objects

Description. A graphic tablet, also called a *touch* tablet, is a device with a horizontal surface sensitive to pressure, heat, light, or the blockage of light. It may lie on the desk or may be incorporated on a keyboard, and it is operated with fingers, light pen, or objects like a pencil or stylus. The screen pointer imitates movement on the tablet.

Advantages. With graphic tablets, a direct relationship exists between touch movements and pointer movements in terms of direction, distance, and speed. The screen mimics the tablet. When used with objects like styluses, light pens, or pencils, the operational angle, horizontal, is more comfortable than those vertically oriented.

Disadvantages. Tablets are also indirect controls, creating coordination problems. To use them requires moving one's hand from the keyboard and, if using another device, picking it up. If the finger is the tablet-activation object, accuracy with small objects is difficult. Tablets also require desk space.

Touch Screen

- Description:
  - — A special surface on the screen sensitive to finger or stylus touch.

- Advantages:
  - — Direct relationship between hand and pointer location in terms of direction, distance, and speed.
  - — Movement is direct, in the same plane as screen.
  - — Requires no additional desk space.
  - — Stands up well in high-use environments.
- Disadvantages:
  - — Finger may obscure part of screen.
  - — Finger may be too large for accuracy with small objects.
  - — Requires moving the hand far from the keyboard to use.
  - — Very fatiguing to use for extended period of time.
  - — May soil or damage the screen.
- Design Guidelines:
  - — Screen objects should be at least 3/4″ × 3/4″ in size.
  - — Object separation should be at least 1/8″.
  - — Provide visual feedback in response to activation. Auditory feedback may also be appropriate.
  - — When the consequences are destructive, require confirmation after selection to eliminate inadvertent selection.
  - — Provide an instructional invitation to begin using.

Description. A touch screen is a screen that consists of a special surface sensitive to finger or stylus touch. Objects on the screen are pointed to and touched to select them.

Advantages. Touch screens possess a direct relationship between hand and pointer movement in terms of direction, distance, and speed. This relationship is direct, not indirect, because the control (finger or stylus) is on the same plane as the pointer. Another significant advantage of a touch screen is that it does not require any additional desk space.

Disadvantages. A disadvantage of touch screens is that they are fatiguing to use over an extended period of time. If a finger is the touch mechanism, it may obscure part of the screen and be too large to be accurate with small objects. A stylus is usually more accurate than the finger. Fingers may also soil the screen, and a stylus may damage it. Both finger and stylus require moving a hand from the keyboard, and if a stylus is used, it must also be picked up.

Guidelines. When using touch screens, larger screen objects should always be provided to foster accuracy in use. Objects should be 3/4″ square at a minimum and separated by at least 1/8″. Visual, and perhaps auditory, feedback should be provided in response to activation. When the consequences of selection are destructive, require a confirmation to avoid inadvertent selection. Observational research indicates that touch screen devices placed in public places, for use by the general public, should possess an instructional invitation to begin their use.

Today, other forms of touch screen devices are being used. One type allows placement of a finger on the screen without item selection, selection being accomplished by lifting the finger off the screen. This may allow more accurate item selection. Another method involves placing a cursor on the screen directly above one's finger and moving the cursor as the finger is moved. The cursor permits better target visibility, as well as the detection of smaller targets.

Light Pen

- Description:
  - — A special surface on a screen sensitive to the touch of a special stylus or pen.
- Advantages:
  - — Direct relationship between hand and pointer movement in terms of direction, distance, and speed.
  - — Movement is direct, in the same plane as screen.
  - — Requires minimal additional desk space.
  - — Stands up well in high-use environments.
  - — More accurate than finger touching.
- Disadvantages:
  - — Hand may obscure part of screen.
  - — Requires picking it up to use.
  - — Requires moving the hand far from the keyboard to use.
  - — Very fatiguing to use for extended period of time.

Description. A light pen also utilizes a touch screen, but one that is sensitive in a specific way to one kind of pen or stylus. Advantages and disadvantages are similar to those of the touch screen.

Advantages. Light pens possess a direct relationship between hand and pointer movement in terms of direction, distance, and speed, and are also classified as direct pointing devices because the control (pen or stylus) is on the same plane as the pointer. Another advantage of a light pen is that it does not require any additional desk space, except for a place for the pen to rest. A light pen is usually more accurate than the finger.

Disadvantages. A disadvantage is that they are also fatiguing to use over an extended period of time. Light pens require moving a hand from the keyboard to pick up and use.

Voice

- Description:
  - — Automatic speech recognition by the computer.
- Advantages:
  - — Simple and direct.
  - — Useful for people who cannot use a keyboard.
  - — Useful when the user's hands are occupied.

- Disadvantages:
  - — High error rates due to difficulties in:
    - Recognizing boundaries between spoken words.
    - Blurred word boundaries due to normal speech patterns.
  - — Slower throughput than with typing.
  - — Difficult to use in noisy environments.
  - — Impractical to use in quiet environments.

Description. Automatic speech recognition technology has been under development for more than a quarter of a century. Its progress has been hindered by the disadvantages listed below.

Advantages. Speech is a simple and direct communication medium. It is very useful for people who cannot use a keyboard, or whose hands are otherwise occupied.

Disadvantages. Speech recognition errors are fundamentally different from keying errors. Most keying errors result from a user's inability to always press the correct key. Most speech recognition errors result from the computer speech recognizers' inability to correctly recognize words. People can dictate to a computer at a fairly fast rate, about 105 words per minute (Karat, Halverson, Horn, & Karat, 1999 and Lewis, 1999). After making the required corrections, the input rate becomes about 25 words per minute when transcribing the input. New users had even lower transcribing rates. The most commonly used correction methods are: deleting and repeating the last phrase, deleting and repeating a specific word, deleting and selecting a correct word from a list of alternative words, and retyping the selection.

Several research studies have shown that correcting voice recognition errors using a method other than additional voice recognition speeds up the correction process. Suhm, Myers, and Waibel (1999) found that fast typists made almost three times more corrections per minute than people who made corrections by voice only. Lewis (1999) and Karat et al. (1999) uncovered very similar results.

Speech recognition is also, of course, difficult to utilize in an improper environment. Noise can hinder the process, and it is very impractical, and disturbing, to try and use it in a very quiet location such as a library.

Mouse

- Description:
  - — A rectangular or dome-shaped, movable, desktop control containing from one to three buttons used to manipulate objects and information on the screen.
  - — Movement of screen pointer mimics the mouse movement.
- Advantages:
  - — Direct relationship between hand and pointer movement in terms of direction, distance, and speed.

— Permits a comfortable hand resting position
— Selection mechanisms are included on mouse.
— Does not obscure vision of the screen.

- Disadvantages:
— Movement is indirect, in a plane different from screen.
— Requires hand to be removed from keyboard.
— Requires additional desk space.
— May require long movement distances.
— Requires a degree of eye-hand coordination.

Description. A mouse is a rectangular or dome-shaped, movable, desktop control containing from one to three buttons used to manipulate objects and information on the screen. The movement of the screen pointer mimics the mouse movement. In 1968, Doug Engelbart, a researcher at the Stanford Research Institute, invented what became the mouse. While using a trackball, he was inspired to turn it upside down and let the ball become the bottom of a control that, attached to a cord, was moved across the desk. It was patented as the "x-y position indicator," and finally christened the "mouse" by a colleague of Engelbart's (a colleague whose name is lost in time). In 1997, Engelbart was at long last rewarded for his invention when he received the annual Lemelson-Mit Prize for American Innovation, including a well-deserved and very substantial monetary reward (cnn.com, 1997).

Advantages. There is a direct relationship between hand and pointer movement in terms of direction, distance, and speed. The mouse itself contains some basic controls (buttons) useful for manipulating screen objects. The hand position when using the mouse is generally fairly comfortable, and the mouse does not obscure the screen.

Disadvantages. Disadvantages are that they are also indirect devices, the control and its result being located in different planes. They require developing a skill to use and, when paired with keyboard tasks, they require movement away from the keyboard and a shift in motor activity from keystrokes to finger/hand movement. The mouse also requires extensive additional desk space and long positioning movements. The mouse comes in a variety of configurations, performs some basic functions, and is operated in several ways.

Configurations. A mouse may possess one, two, or three buttons. Most, but not all, windowing systems permit operation using all configurations. Buttons are used to perform three functions to be described. When three mouse buttons are not available, the pointer location or keyboard qualifiers must be used to determine the function to be performed. A multibutton mouse permits a more efficient operation, but a person must remember which button to use to perform each function. A multibutton mouse may usually be configured for left- or right-hand use.

Functions. The functions performed by a mouse are Select, Menu, and Adjust. The Select function is used to manipulate controls, to select alternatives and data, and to select objects that will be affected by actions that follow. *Select* is a mouse's most important function and is the function assigned to a one-button mouse. For a multibutton mouse, it is usually assigned to the leftmost button (assuming a right-handed operation).

The *Menu* function is typically used to request and display a pop-up menu on a screen. A menu appears when the button is depressed within a particular defined area of the screen. This area may be, for example, the entire screen, within a window, or on a window border. This button eliminates the need for a control icon, which must be pointed at and selected. The user, however, must remember that a menu is available. The *Adjust* function extends or reduces the number of items selected. It is the least used of the three functions and is usually assigned last and given the least prominent location on a mouse.

Operations. Several operations can be performed with a mouse. The first, *point*, is the movement and positioning of the mouse pointer over the desired screen object. It prepares for a selection or control operation. To press is to hold the button down without releasing it. It identifies the object to be selected.

To *click* is to press and immediately release a button without moving the mouse. This operation typically selects an item or insertion point, operates a control, or activates an inactive window or control. To *double-click* is to perform two clicks within a predefined time limit without moving the mouse. It is used as a shortcut for common operations such as activating an icon or opening a file.

To *drag* is to press and hold the button down, and then move the pointer in the appropriate direction. It identifies a range of objects or moves or resizes items. To *double-drag* is to perform two clicks and hold the button down, and then move the pointer in the appropriate direction. It identifies a selection by a larger unit, such as a group of words.

Mouse Usage Guidelines

- Provide a "hot zone" around small or thin objects that might require extremely fine mouse positioning.
- Never use double-clicks or double-drags as the only means of carrying out essential operations.
- Do not use mouse plus keystroke combinations.
- Do not require a person to point at a moving target.

If an object is very small and might require fine mouse positioning, provide a large "hot zone" around it. This will increase target size and speed selection. Do not require double-clicks or double-drags as the only way to carry out essential operations. Rapid double-pressing is difficult for some people. Do not use mouse plus keystroke combinations to accomplish actions. This can be awkward. One exception: multiple selections of items in a list. Do not require a person to point at a moving target, except, of course, for a game.

Keyboard

- Description:
  - — Standard typewriter keyboard and cursor movement keys.
- Advantages:
  - — Familiar.
  - — Accurate.
  - — Does not take up additional desk space.
  - — Very useful for:
    - Entering text and alphanumeric data.
    - Inserting in text and alphanumeric data.
    - Keyed shortcuts—accelerators.
    - Keyboard mnemonics—equivalents.
  - — Advantageous for:
    - Performing actions when less than three mouse buttons exist.
    - Use with very large screens.
    - Touch typists.
- Disadvantages:
  - — Slow for non-touch-typists.
  - — Slower than other devices in pointing.
  - — Requires discrete actions to operate.
  - — No direct relationship between finger or hand movement on the keys and cursor movement on screen in terms of speed and distance.

Description. Christopher Latham Sholes invented the standard typewriter keyboard in 1870. Commonly called the QWERTY layout, Sholes' placement of letters was intended to slow down a typist's keying movements so that the potential for key jams was minimized. From a strictly human-engineering perspective, its layout inadequacies included a dominance of the left hand in making keystrokes, frequent successive keystrokes with the same hand, frequent movement between keyboard key rows, and frequently used letter pairs being placed far from each other. In 1936, August Dvorak created a revised and well-human-engineered keyboard that overcame many of these deficiencies. The advantages of the DVORAK layout, as it came to be called, included a right-hand dominance in keying, much less frequent row changes, and more systematic alternation between the right and left hand. With this new layout, finger travel distances were reduced by at least one order of magnitude. Acceptance of this new keyboard was, and continues, to be slow. Most users have seemed unwilling to invest the time and effort to change.

In the 1980s, IBM performed a series of studies comparing the QWERTY keyboard with various sequential key layouts such as ABCDEF or JIHGFE (starting from the upper left or QWERTY location). IBM wanted to determine if a sequential layout was better for users who professed to be non-touch-typists. Their findings were surprising. Non-touch-typist performance results were as good, or better, using the QWERTY layout as using the various systematic layouts. IBM's conclusion: Why change? So they didn't. IBM researchers could only speculate as to why the new systematic layouts fared so poorly. Perhaps, they said, while non-touch-typists profess no knowledge of the QWERTY layout, through experience they have learned the layout, at least well enough to permit effective two-finger typing to be accomplished. Another possibility, they said, was that perhaps some characteristic of the QWERTY layout makes it easy to scan and find needed keys. Speculation number one seems to be the most reasonable explanation, but we may never know for sure.

Advantages. The standard keyboard is familiar, accurate, and does not consume additional desk space. It is useful and efficient for entering or inserting text or alphanumeric data. For tasks requiring heavy text or data entry, shifting the hands between a keyboard and an alternative control, such as a mouse, can be time-consuming and inefficient, especially for a touch typist. The keyboard is flexible enough to accept keyed shortcuts, either keyboard accelerators or mnemonic equivalents. Some systems also permit navigation across a screen through use of keyboard keys such as the space bar, arrows, Tab, and Enter.

Inefficiencies in using other graphical device-based controls can occur, making it advantageous to use a keyboard. A mouse with a limited number of buttons will require use of the keyboard to accomplish some functions, possibly causing frequent shifting between devices. When operations are being performed on very large screens, the user may also find keyboard window management preferable to the long mouse movements frequently required. Therefore, to compensate for these possible inefficiencies, many windowing systems provide alternative keyboard operations for mouse tasks.

Disadvantages. Disadvantages of a keyboard include its requiring discrete finger actions to operate instead of the more fine positioning movements. As a result, no direct relationship exists in terms of speed and distance between finger or hand movement on the keys and cursor movement on the screen. Depending on the layout of the keyboard cursor control keys, direct-relationship direction problems may also exist, because fingers may not move in the same direction as the cursor. Keyboards will also be slower for non-touch-typists and slower than other controls in pointing tasks.

Keyboard Guidelines

- Provide keyboard accelerators.
  - — Assign single keys for frequently performed, small-scale tasks.
  - — Use standard platform accelerators.
  - — Assign Shift-*key* combinations for actions that extend or are complementary to the actions of the key or key combination used without the Shift-*key*.
  - — Assign Ctrl-*key* combinations for:
    - Infrequent actions.
    - Tasks that represent larger-scale versions of the task assigned to the unmodified key.
- Provide keyboard equivalents.
  - — Use standard platform equivalents.

  - — Use the first letter of the item description.
  - — If first letter conflicts exist, use:
    - Another distinctive consonant in the item description.
    - A vowel in the item description.
- Provide window navigation through use of keyboard keys.

Keyboard accelerators. Accelerators provide a way to access menu elements without displaying a menu. They are useful for frequent tasks performed by experienced users. Keys assigned for accelerators should foster efficient performance and be meaningful and conceptually consistent to aid learning. Use standard accelerators as shown in Table 5.7 in Chapter 5 "Menus."

Microsoft suggests that frequently performed, small-scale tasks should be assigned single keys as the keyboard alternative. Actions that extend or are complementary to the actions of a key (or key combination) should be assigned a Shift key in conjunction with the original action. Microsoft, for example, uses a single key, F6, as the key to move clockwise to the next pane of an active window. To move counterclockwise to the next pane, use Shift-F6.

Infrequent actions, or tasks that represent larger-scale versions of the task assigned to the unmodified key, should be assigned Ctrl-*key* combinations. The left arrow key in Microsoft Windows, for example, moves the cursor one character; Ctrl-left arrow moves it one word.

Keyboard equivalents. Keyboard mnemonics enable the selection of a menu choice through the keyboard instead of by pointing. This enables a person's hands to remain on the keyboard during extensive keying tasks. Keyboard mnemonics should be chosen in a meaningful way to aid memorability and foster predictability of those things that may be forgotten. Mnemonics need only be unique within a menu. A simple rule is always to use the first letter of a menu item description. If the first letter of one item conflicts with that of another, choose another distinctive consonant in the item description, preferably, but not always necessarily, the second in the item word (occasionally another consonant may be more meaningful). The last choice would be a vowel in the item description. If standard platform equivalents are available, use them. Standard equivalents were shown in Table 5.6 in Chapter 5.

Window navigation. Also provide ways of navigating through windows by the use of keyboard keys.

Selecting the Proper Device-Based Controls

A number of studies have been performed comparing the various controls for assorted office tasks. Significant findings include the following.

Keyboard versus Mouse

Why do many skilled typists prefer a keyboard to a mouse? Speed is obviously one reason. An experienced typist, through kinesthetic memory, has memorized the location of keyboard keys. The keying process becomes exceptionally fast and well learned. The mouse is slower, and it has a tendency to move about the desk. Its location cannot be memorized. The keyboard keys always remain in the same spot.

Consider the following: When using the mouse, the time to move one's hand from the keyboard, grasp the mouse, and point at a screen object ranges from 1.5 to 2 seconds. A very skilled typist can type 13 to 15 characters in that amount of time; an average typist can type 4 to 6 characters. No wonder the keyboard is often preferred.

Control Research

Which devices work better for which tasks and under what conditions has been addressed by a number of investigators. A survey of the research literature comparing and evaluating different devices yields the following summarization concerning tasks involving pointing and dragging:

- The fastest tools for pointing at stationary targets on screens are the devices that permit direct pointing: the touch screen and light pen. This is most likely due to their high level of eye-hand coordination and because they use an action familiar to people.
- In terms of positioning speed and accuracy for stationary targets, the indirect pointing devices—the mouse, trackball, and graphic tablet, do not differ greatly from one another. The joystick is the slowest, although it is as accurate as the others. Of most importance in selecting one of these devices will be its fit to the user's task and working environment.
- A separate confirmation action that must follow pointer positioning increases pointing accuracy but reduces speed. The mouse offers a very effective design configuration for tasks requiring this confirmation.
- For tracking small, slowly moving targets, the mouse, trackball, and graphic tablet are preferred to the touch screen and light pen because the latter may obscure the user's view of the target.

Another common manipulation task is dragging an object across the screen. Using a mouse, graphic tablet, and trackball for this task, as well as pointing, was studied by MacKenzie, Sellen, and Buxton (1991). They report the following:

- The graphic tablet yielded best performance during pointing.
- The mouse yielded best performance during dragging.
- The trackball was a poor performer for both pointing and dragging, and it had a very high error rate in dragging.

Guidelines for Selecting the Proper Device-Based Control

- Consider the characteristics of the task.
  - — Provide keyboards for tasks involving:
    - Heavy text entry and manipulation.
    - Movement through structured arrays consisting of a few discrete objects.

— Provide an alternative pointing device for graphical or drawing tasks. The following are some suggested best uses:
  - Mouse—pointing, selecting, drawing, and dragging.
  - Joystick—selecting and tracking.
  - Trackball—pointing, selecting and tracking.
  - Touch screen—pointing and selecting.
  - Graphic tablet—pointing, selecting, drawing, and dragging.

— Provide touch screens under the following conditions:
  - The opportunity for training is minimal.
  - Targets are large, discrete, and spread out.
  - Frequency of use is low.
  - Desk space is at a premium.
  - Little or no text input requirement exists.

- Consider user characteristics and preferences.
  — Provide keyboards for touch typists.
- Consider the characteristics of the environment.
- Consider the characteristics of the hardware.
- Consider the characteristics of the device in relation to the application.
- Provide flexibility.
- Minimize eye and hand movements between devices.

Selection of the proper device for an application, then, depends on a host of factors.

Task characteristics. Is the device suited to the task? Standard typewriter keyboards are always necessary for tasks requiring text entry and manipulation; Keyboards (cursor control keys) are usually faster when moving through structured arrays consisting of a few discrete objects.

For graphical and drawing tasks, alternative pointing devices are easier and faster. Use a mouse, joystick, trackball, or graphic tablet for pointing, selecting, drawing, dragging, or tracking. The devices best suited for each kind of task are summarized above.

Provide touch screens when the opportunity for training is minimal; targets are large, discrete, and spread out; frequency of use is low; desk space is at a premium; and little or no text input requirement exists. Touch screens also work well when the usage environment is dirty.

User characteristics and preferences. Will the user be able to easily and comfortably operate the control? Are the fine motor movements required by some devices capable of being performed? Is the user familiar with the standard keyboard? What are the user's preferences? While preferences do not always correspond to performance, it is important that the user be comfortable with the selected device.

Environmental characteristics. Will the device fit easily into the work environment? If desk space is necessary, does it exist and is it large enough?

Hardware characteristics. Is the device itself of a quality that permits easy performance of all the necessary tasks? Joysticks, for example, are quite variable in their movement capabilities.

The device in relation to the application. Is the device satisfactory for the application?

Flexibility. Often task and user needs will vary within an application. Providing more than one kind of device will give the user choices in how to most efficiently accomplish whatever tasks must be performed. A keyboard paired with another kind of pointing device is almost always necessary.

Minimizing eye and hand movements. When multiple devices are used, eye and hand movements between them must be minimized. Structure the task, if possible, to permit the user to stay in one working area. If shifts must be made, they should be as infrequent as possible. It is estimated that, for a good typist, it costs 3 to 8 keystrokes for each jump between the keyboard and a mouse. The general rule is that more than 80 percent of the tasks should be doable using only one device.

Pointer Guidelines

- The pointer:
  — Should be visible at all times.
  — Should contrast well with its background.
  — Should maintain its size across all screen locations and during movement.
  — The hotspot should be easy to locate and see.
  — Location should not warp (change position).
- The user should always position the pointer.
- The shape of a pointer:
  — Should clearly indicate its purpose and meaning.
  — Should be constructed of already defined shapes.
  — Should not be used for any other purpose other than its already defined meaning.
  — Do not create new shapes for already defined standard functions.
- Use only as many shapes as necessary to inform the user about current location and status. Too many shapes can confuse a person.
- Be conservative in making changes as the pointer moves across the screen.
  — Provide a short "time-out" before making noncritical changes on the screen.
- Animation should not:
  — Distract.
  — Restrict one's ability to interact.

Pointer. The focus of the user's attention in most device operations is most often the pointer. Therefore, the pointer image should be used to provide feedback concerning the function being performed, the mode of operation, and the state of the system. For example, the pointer shape image can be changed when it is positioned over a selectable object, signaling to the user that a button action may be performed. When an action is being performed, the pointer can assume the shape of a progress indicator such as a sand timer, providing an indication of processing status.

A pointer should contrast well with its background and be visible at all times. The user should always be in control of its location on the screen. The shape of a pointer should clearly indicate its purpose and meaning. Always use predefined shapes provided by graphical systems. Microsoft Windows, for example, provides about two dozen standard shapes. To aid learning and avoid user confusion, never create new shapes for already defined standard functions or use a shape for any purpose other than its previously defined meaning. Also, use only as many shapes as absolutely necessary to keep the user informed about current position and status. Too many shapes can also confuse a person.

Be conservative in making changes as the pointer moves across the screen. Excessive changes can be distracting to a person. To avoid frequent changes while crossing the screen, establish a short time-out before making noncritical pointer changes. Any pointer animation should not distract the viewer or restrict one's ability to interact with the system.

Multiple Choice Questions

1. Device based controls are often called as
   (a) Input devices
   (b) Output devices
   (c) Both (a) and (b)
   (d) User defined controls

2. Device based controls are used
   (a) To point an object on the screen
   (b) To select the object or identify it as the focus of attention
   (c) Both (a) and (b)
   (d) None of the above

3. Touch screens are
   (a) Input devices
   (b) Output devices
   (c) Both (a) and (b)
   (d) None of the above

4. Trackball possess
   (a) Direct relationship between hand and pointer movement in terms of direction and speed
   (b) Indirect relationship between hand and pointer movement in terms of direction and speed
   (c) Direct relationship between hand and pointer movement in terms of direction
   (d) Indirect relationship between hand and pointer movement in terms of direction
   (e) None of the above

5. Joystick possess
   (a) Direct relationship between hand and pointer movement in terms of direction and speed
   (b) Indirect relationship between hand and pointer movement in terms of direction and speed
   (c) Direct relationship between hand and pointer movement in terms of direction
   (d) Indirect relationship between hand and pointer movement in terms of speed and distance
   (e) None of the above

6. Graphics Tablet possesses
   (a) Direct relationship between touch movements, hand and pointer movement in terms of direction, distance, and speed
   (b) Indirect relationship between touch movements and pointer movement in terms of direction, distance, and speed

(c) Direct relationship between touch movements and pointer movement in terms of direction
(d) Indirect relationship between touch movements and pointer movement in terms of speed and distance
(e) None of the above

7. Touch screen possesses
(a) Direct relationship between hand and pointer movement in terms of direction and speed
(b) Indirect relationship between hand and pointer movement in terms of direction and speed
(c) Direct relationship between hand and pointer movement in terms of direction, distance, and speed
(d) Indirect relationship between hand and pointer movement in terms of speed and distance
(e) None of the above

Review Questions

1. Describe the characteristics of device-based controls.
2. Describe the characteristics of the following devices:
(a) Trackball
(b) Joystick
(c) Graphic tablet
(d) Light pen
(e) Touch screen
(f) Voice
(g) Mouse
(h) Keyboard
3. Describe HCI Guidelines for selecting proper device based controls.
4. Categorize the following devices in term of direct and indirect relationship existing between any of the hand, touch, pointer movement and also in terms of direction, distance and speed.
(a) Trackball
(b) Joystick
(c) Graphic tablet
(d) Light pen
(e) Touch screen
(f) Voice
5. Considering any mini project as a sample, design user interface screens using various interactive devices. Design the interaction screen with and without using interactive devices. Write advantages and disadvantages of interactive devices used.
6. A UI designer wants to design the application for people with difficulty using keyboard. Comment on selecting the proper device based controls for this application.

CHAPTER 8

Screen-Based Controls

Screen-based controls, often simply called *controls* and sometimes called *widgets*, are the elements of a screen that constitute its body. By definition, they are graphic objects that represent the properties or operations of other objects. A control may:

- Permit the entry or selection of a particular value.
- Permit the changing or editing of a particular value.
- Display only a particular piece of text, value, or graphic.
- Cause a command to be performed.
- Possess a contextual pop-up window.

In the last decade, some platforms have expanded the definition of a control to include all specifiable aspects of a screen, including screen text, headings, and group boxes. For the purposes of this discussion, this broader definition of a screen-based control will be assumed. In this chapter we will:

- Identify the characteristics and capabilities of the various screen-based controls, including:
  - Buttons.
  - Text entry/read-only controls.
  - Selection controls.
  - Combination entry/selection controls.
  - Specialized operable controls.
  - Custom controls.

- Presentation controls.
- Web controls.

- Select the proper controls for the user and tasks.

The screen designer is presented with an array of screen-based controls to choose from. Selecting the right one for the user and the task is often difficult. But, as with device-based controls, making the right choice is critical to system success. A proper fit between user and control will lead to fast, accurate performance. A poor fit will result in lower productivity, more errors, and dissatisfaction.

We'll start by describing the types of controls and identifying their advantages, disadvantages, and proper usage. Relevant control design guidelines will also be presented. Not all toolkits or platforms will necessarily possess all the kinds of controls to be described. After describing the controls, we'll look at several research studies addressing the way to choose the best control or controls for particular situations. By the time we look at these studies, their findings will have been incorporated into the control usage and design guidelines already presented. This organization has been chosen because it is more meaningful to first clearly describe each control before discussing it in a research context. We'll finish by providing some general guidance in choosing the proper kind of control to enable tasks to be performed quickly and efficiently by the user.

In describing the controls, we'll break them down into categories that reflect the way they are used. We'll begin with operable controls, those that are manipulable, changeable, or settable. We'll then review presentation controls, those used to inscribe permanent information on a screen or used to give the screen structure. Before starting this review, three extremely important principles regarding controls should be noted:

- A control must:
  - Look the way it works.
  - Work the way it looks.
- A control must be used exactly as its design intended.
- A control must be presented in a standard manner.

The look of a control should make it obvious that it is a control. Its design characteristics should signal "enterability" or "clickability." Microsoft Windows, for example, presents the following simple rules:

- Raised elements can be pressed.
- Recessed elements cannot be pressed.
- Elements on a flat white background can be opened, edited, or moved.

A control must also be presented in a standard and consistent manner, and used exactly as its design intended. The nonstandard design use of controls destroys consistency and aggravates and frustrates users, who have developed expectations based upon their past experiences. Using standard controls allows people to focus on their tasks or the content of the screens with which they are interacting, instead of having to figure out what to do.

Web page design has unleashed and exposed thousands of instances where these basic principles (and others to be described) have been violated. Page designers, all to often it seems, have been placing greater value on personal creativity than on interface usability. Some examples will be presented throughout the following pages.

Operable Controls

Operable controls are those that permit the entry, selection, changing, or editing of a particular value, or cause a command to be performed. Classes include buttons, text entry/read-only, selection, combination entry/selection, and other specialized controls.

Buttons

- Description:
  - — A square or rectangular-shaped control with a label inside that indicates action to be accomplished.
  - — The label may consist of text, graphics, or both.
- Purpose:
  - — To start actions.
  - — To change properties.
  - — To display a pop-up menu.
- Advantages:
  - — Always visible, reminding one of the choices available.
  - — Convenient.
  - — Can be logically organized in the work area.
  - — Can provide meaningful descriptions of the actions that will be performed.
  - — Larger size generally provides faster selection target.
  - — Can possess 3-D appearance:
    - Adds an aesthetically pleasing style to the screen.
    - Provides visual feedback through button movement when activated.
  - — May permit use of keyboard equivalents and accelerators.
  - — Faster than using a two-step menu bar/pull-down sequence.
- Disadvantages:
  - — Consumes screen space.
  - — Size limits the number that may be displayed.
  - — Requires looking away from main working area to activate.
  - — Requires moving the pointer to select.
- Proper usage:
  - — Use for frequently used actions that are specific to a window.
    - To cause something to happen immediately.
    - To display another window.
    - To display a menu of options.
    - To set a mode or property value.

A button comes in three styles. The first resembles the control commonly found on electrical or mechanical devices and is sometimes called a pushbutton. These are most often rectangular, with text that indicates the action to be taken when they are selected or pressed. These buttons are usually placed within a window, and activating them causes the action or command described on them to be performed immediately. This kind of button may take a variety of forms, some of which are illustrated in Figure 8.1. They are often referred to as *command buttons.*

The second style is square or rectangular in shape with an icon or graphic inside. It may have an associated label. This kind of button is illustrated in Figure 8.2. The label may be permanently affixed to the screen within the button, adjacent to it, or only appear when the pointer is moved to the button (called ToolTip, to be discussed). These buttons may appear singly or be placed in groupings commonly called *button bars* or *toolbars.* We'll refer to them as toolbars in this text. They are most frequently used to quickly access commands, many of which are normally accessed through the menu bar, or to initiate other actions or functions. These button groupings are usually placed at the screen's top or side. They are usually relocatable and removable by the user.

The third style is square or rectangular in shape with a symbol inscribed inside, as illustrated in Figure 8.3. The symbol, when learned, identifies the button and the action to be performed when the button is selected. These buttons, specific to a platform and provided by it, are located in the borders of windows and are used to do such things as obtaining a system menu or resizing a window. They have already been described in more detail in Chapter 6 "Windows" and will not be addressed in this chapter. This chapter will focus on *command* and *toolbar* buttons.

Command button advantages. An advantage of a command button is that it is always visible, providing a reminder of its existence. Command buttons are conveniently and logically located in the work area and can be inscribed with meaningful descriptions of what they do. Their ability to assume a fairly large size speeds selection, and their three-dimensional appearance is aesthetically pleasing. Buttons can also provide meaningful visual feedback through the movement of the button when activated. Their activation is much easier and faster than using a two-step menu bar/pull-down sequence.

Figure 8.1 Command buttons.

Figure 8.2 Toolbar buttons without labels.

Figure 8.3 A symbol button.

Command button disadvantages. Among the disadvantages of command buttons is their larger size, which consumes considerable screen space and limits the number that can be displayed.

Toolbar advantages. Advantages of toolbar buttons include their continuous visibility and ease and speed of use. They also, individually, consume a relatively small amount of space.

Toolbar disadvantages. Disadvantages include their location being away from the main work area and their small size, which slows down selection. Another disadvantage is that when a large number of buttons are grouped in a bar, they consume a great deal of screen space, and they can easily create screen clutter. In circumstances where they do not possess a label, the necessity of learning and remembering what they are used for can also cause problems.

Proper usage. Buttons are best for frequently used actions in a window. They can be used to cause actions to occur immediately, such as saving a document, quitting a system, or deleting text. They can be used to display a menu of options, such as colors or fonts. Windows calls a button that leads to a menu a *menu button*. Buttons can also be used to display other secondary windows or dialog boxes, and to expand the dialog or invoke dialog features. Windows calls a button that expands the dialog an *unfolding* button. Buttons may also be used to reflect a mode or property value setting similarly to the use of radio buttons or check boxes. In some kinds of windows, command buttons may be the only command method available to the user.

Web browsers also provide a series of command and toolbar buttons that vary from platform to platform. These buttons are not addressed in this chapter.

Command Buttons

Command button guidelines include the following.

Usage

- For windows with a menu bar:
  — Use to provide fast access to frequently used or critical commands.
- For windows without a menu bar:
  — Use to provide access to all necessary commands.

For fast access to commands contained in a menu bar, especially those frequently used or critical, also provide access by command buttons. Buttons must also be provided for situations where a command is not available through the menu bar. For windows without menu bars, buttons must be provided to provide access to all window commands.

Structure

- Provide a rectangular shape with the label inscribed within it.
- Give the button a raised appearance.
- Maintain consistency in style throughout an application.

The shape of a button can vary. Generally, rectangular-shaped buttons are preferred because they provide the best fit for horizontally arrayed textual captions. Square-cornered rectangles are found in some platforms including Microsoft Windows, while rounded-corner rectangles are found in others. The button style chosen must reflect the three cornerstone principles presented at the beginning of this chapter, including giving it a raised appearance to make it obvious that it is a command but-ton. To do this, drop shadows are used in some platforms, beveled edges in others. "Invisible" buttons must never exist. Web command button styles are noted for their variety in shape and size. The button style chosen is mostly a matter of preference. Web-specific button styles should be consistently designed and maintained through-out the Web site.

Labels

- Use standard button labels when available.
- Provide meaningful descriptions of the actions that will be performed.
- Use single-word labels whenever possible.
  - — Use two-three words for clarity, if necessary.
- Use mixed-case letters with the first letter of each significant label word capitalized.
- Display labels:
  - — In the regular system font.
  - — In the same size font.
- Do not number labels.
- Center the label within the button borders, leaving at least two pixels between the text and the button border.
- Provide consistency in button labeling across all screens.

Labels. Button labels should be clearly spelled out, with meaningful descriptions of the actions they will cause to be performed. Choices should be composed of mixed-case single words. Multiple words are preferred, however, to single words lacking clarity in their intent. If multiple-word labels are used, capitalize the first letter of each word (headline style). Use the same size and style of font in all buttons. The regular system font is preferred. Never change font style or size within buttons; these kinds of changes can be very distracting to the viewer. Center each label within the button borders, leaving at least two pixels between the text and the border.

Common button functions should have standard names and uses. Microsoft windows, for example, provides these standard names and definitions:

OK—Any changed information in the window is accepted and the window is closed.

Cancel—Closes window without implementing unsubmitted changes.

Reset—Resets defaults and cancels any changed information that has not been submitted.

Apply—Any changed information in the window is accepted and again displayed in the window that remains open.

Close—Closes the window.

Help—Opens online Help.

Always follow all platform presentation and usage guidelines for standard button functions.

Size

- Provide as large a button as feasible.
- Maintain consistent button heights and widths.
- Exception: Buttons containing excessively long labels may be wider.

Provide as large a button as possible, consistent with Fitts' Law. Buttons must, at minimum, be wide enough to accommodate the longest label. Leave at least two pixels between labels and button borders. A com-mand button's minimum height should be 25 pixels. Create, however, standard, equal-sized buttons encompassing the majority of system functions. When a button's label will not fit within the standard size, expand the button's size to achieve a proper label fit. Never reduce the font size of some labels to create equal-sized buttons. In this case, but-tons of different widths are preferable. Also, do not create an unnecessarily wide button for aesthetic balance purposes, as illustrated by the Color Palette button in Figure 8.4. The perceptual model we possess in our memory for a button will be lost.

Number

- Restrict the number of buttons on a window to six or fewer.

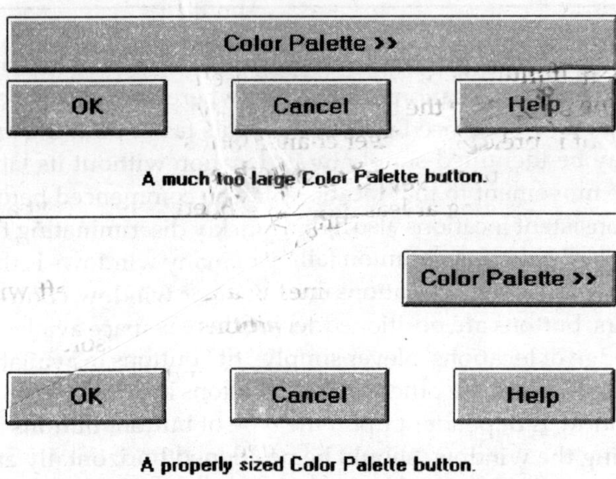

Figure 8.4 Improper and proper button sizes.

The maximum number of buttons on a window must reflect a balance between effectiveness, real estate efficiency, and operational simplicity. Having no more than six buttons per window or dialog box seems to appropriately balance these issues. If an extra button or two is necessary and space is available, they may be included.

Location and Layout

- Maintain consistency in button location between windows.
- Never simply "fit" buttons in available space.
- If buttons are for exiting the dialog:
  — Position them centered and aligned horizontally at the bottom.
- If buttons are used for invoking a dialog feature or expanding the dialog:
  — Position them centered and aligned vertically on the right side.
- If a button has a contingent relationship to another control:
  — Position it adjacent to the related control.
- If a button has a contingent relationship to a group of controls:
  — Position it at the bottom or to right of related controls.
- If, due to space constraints, exiting and expanding/invoking feature buttons must be placed together:
  — If at the bottom, place exiting buttons to the right, separating the groupings by one button's width.
  — If along the right side, place exiting buttons at the bottom, separating the groupings by one button's height.
- For exiting and expanding/invoking feature buttons, do not:
  — Align with the other screen controls.
  — Present displayed within a line border.
- Provide equal and adequate spacing between adjacent buttons.
- Provide adequate spacing between buttons and the screen body controls.

Command buttons should be positioned in consistent positions within a window. This enables a person to memorize button locations and predict where they will appear when a window is presented. For an experienced user this permits faster pointing and activation because a button may be identified simply by its location without its label having to be read, and a mouse movement to that location may be commenced before a window is even displayed. Consistent locations also aid in quickly discriminating the different kinds of buttons described below. A common failing of many windows is that buttons are positioned within windows *after* locations for the other window controls are established. When this occurs, buttons are positioned where there is space available. The result is usually a hodgepodge of locations. Never simply "fit" buttons in available space. Allocate a space for buttons before the other control locations are established.

Button location within a window is dependent upon the type of button. Buttons *exiting* a dialog, and usually closing the window, should be positioned horizontally and centered across the lower part of the window. This positioning places the buttons at the end of the dialog. A study of Web pages (Spool et al., 1997) found that people preferred to scroll to the bottom of a page to press the final buttons. If a button *invokes* a dialog feature or *expands* the dialog, position it centered and aligned vertically along the right side of the window. Maintaining these consistent locations will enable a person to quickly identify what general kind of button it is, and what kind of action will occur if the button is activated. The location of the exiting buttons across the bottom will also allow more efficient use of window real estate when invoking/expanding buttons are not included within a window. Exiting and expanding/invoking feature button locations are illustrated in Figure 8.5. If, due to screen space constraints, exiting and expanding/invoking feature buttons must be positioned together at the screen bottom, place the exiting buttons to the right, separating the groupings by one standard button's width. If they are located together along the right side, place exiting buttons at the bottom, separating the groupings by one button's height.

If a button has a *contingent* relationship to another control, position it adjacent to the related control in the order in which the controls are usually operated, as illustrated in Figure 8.6. If a button possesses a contingent relationship to a group of controls, position it at the bottom or to the right of the grouping, again in logical flow order, as illustrated in Figure 8.7.

For exiting and expanding/invoking feature buttons, do not provide alignment with the other screen controls. Maintain alignment and spacing only within the buttons themselves. Trying to align the buttons to other screen controls will most often create variable spacing between the buttons themselves, which is visually distracting. Also, do not display buttons within a line border; instead present them on the background of the window itself. The unique physical look of the buttons is strong enough for them to create their own visual grouping. Reserve line borders for individual controls or groups of controls that are in greater need of closure. Too many borders can also create visual clutter.

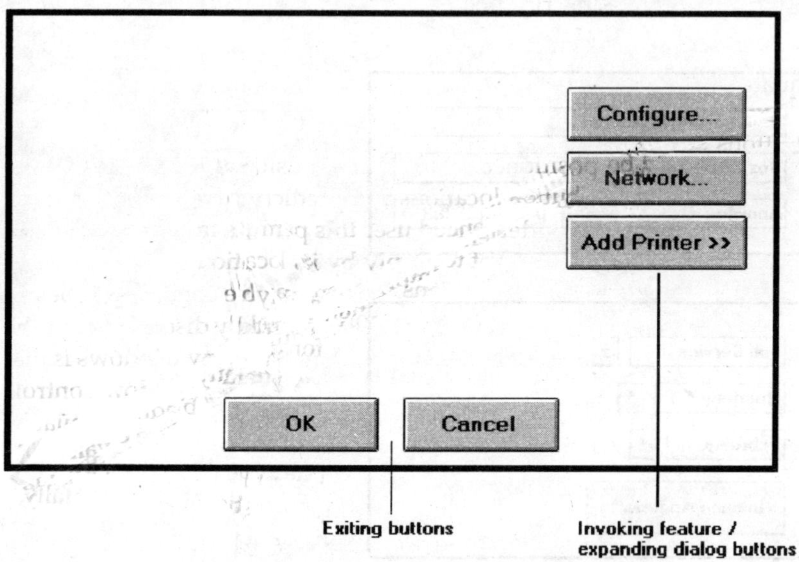

Figure 8.5 Exiting and invoking feature/expanding dialog buttons.

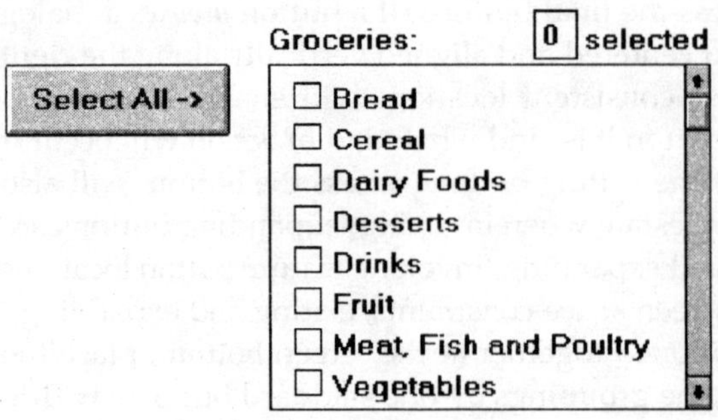

Figure 8.6 Button with contingent relationship to a control.

Provide equal and consistent spacing between adjacent buttons, and groups of buttons. Also, maintain adequate separation between screen buttons and other screen controls.

Organization

- Organize standard buttons in the manner recommended by the platform being used.
- For other buttons, organize them in common and customary grouping schemes.
  - — For buttons ordered left to right, place those for most frequent actions to the left.
  - — For buttons ordered top to bottom, place those for most frequent actions at the top.
- Keep related buttons grouped together.
- Separate potentially destructive buttons from frequently chosen selections.

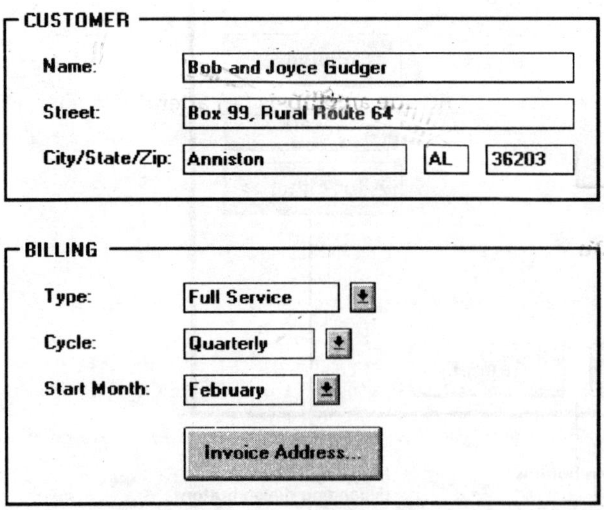

Figure 8.7 Button with contingent relationship to a grouping.

- Buttons found on more than one window should be consistently positioned.
- The order should never change.
- For mutually exclusive actions, use two buttons; do not dynamically change the text.

Follow the standard, consistent ordering schemes recommended by the platform being used. Windows recommends the following:

- An affirmative action to the left (or above).
- The default first.
- OK and Cancel next to each other.
- Help last, if supported.

Other platforms may suggest a different ordering. If differences exist, and people may be using more than one platform, some organizational compromises may be necessary.

Buttons should be ordered logically, such as by frequency of use, sequence of use, or importance. For buttons arrayed left to right, start the ordering from left to right. For buttons arrayed top to bottom, start the ordering from top to bottom.

Keep related buttons grouped together. Separate potentially destructive buttons from frequently chosen selections to avoid inadvertent activation and potentially catastrophic results. Always locate the same buttons that appear on different windows in consistent positions. For mutually exclusive actions, avoid using one button that toggles changing text. This can be confusing. Use two buttons with labels that clearly describe the two actions.

Intent Indicators

- When a button causes an action to be immediately performed, no intent indicator is necessary.

Figure 8.8

- When a button leads to a cascading dialog, include an ellipsis (...) after the label.

Figure 8.9

- When a button leads to a menu, include a triangle pointing in the direction the menu will appear after the label.

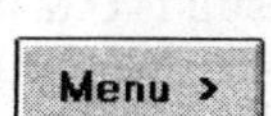

Figure 8.10

- When a button leads to an expanding dialog, include a double arrow (>>) with the label.

Figure 8.11

- When a button has a contingent relationship to another control that must be indicated, include a single arrow (->) pointing at the control.

Figure 8.12

Button intent indicators will follow, where applicable, the same conventions used for menu items. When a button causes a command to be performed immediately, no special intent indicator is necessary on the button. When a button leads to a cascading dialog box, include an *ellipsis* with the label. When a button leads to a menu of choices, include a *triangle* after the label; point the triangle in the direction the menu will appear. If a button expands the dialog, include a *double arrow* with the label. When a button has a contingent relationship to another control, include a *single arrow* pointing at the control. Intent indicators are very useful because they enable the user to predict the consequences of an intended action.

Expansion Buttons

- Gray them out after expansion.
- Provide a contraction button, if necessary.
  - — Locate it beneath, or to right of, the expansion button.
  - — Gray it out when not applicable.

When a button that expands a dialog is activated, and the dialog is expanded, display the button dimmed or grayed out. If the dialog can again be contracted, provide a contraction button beneath the expansion button or to the right of it. Gray this button out when the dialog is contracted; display it at normal intensity when the dialog is expanded.

Defaults

- Intent:
  - — When a window is first displayed, provide a default action, if practical.
- Selection:
  - — A default should be the most likely action:
    - A confirmation.
    - An application of the activity being performed.
    - A positive action such as OK, unless the result is catastrophic.
  - — If a destructive action is performed (such as a deletion), the default should be Cancel.
- Presentation:
  - — Indicate the default action by displaying the button with a bold or double border.
- Procedures:
  - — The default can be changed as the user interacts with the window.
  - — When the user navigates to a button, it can temporarily become the default.

— Use the Enter key to activate a default button.
— If another control requires use of the Enter key, temporarily disable the default while the focus is on the other control.
— Permit double-clicking on a single selection control in a window to also carry out the default command.

When a window with buttons is first displayed, provide a default action whenever practical. The default action should be the most likely action within the window. It may be a confirmation, an application of the activity being performed, or a positive response such as OK. If the default is irreversible or destructive (such as Delete), the default should be Cancel, requiring a person to change the selection in order to perform the destructive action. If none of the buttons is destructive in nature, the default button should be the one most frequently selected.

The default can be changed as the user interacts with a window. When the user navigates to a button, it can temporarily become the default. Return the button to its original state when the focus leaves a button. Permit use of the Enter key to activate a default button. If another control requires use of the Enter key, temporarily disable the default while the focus is on the other control. Permit double-clicking on a single selection control in a window to also carry out the default command.

Unavailable Choices

- Temporarily unavailable choices should be dimmed or grayed out.

A button should visually indicate whether it is available for activation. Dim or gray-out buttons for actions that are not available.

Keyboard Equivalents and Accelerators

- Equivalents:
  — Assign a keyboard equivalent mnemonic to each button to facilitate keyboard selection.
  — The mnemonic should be the first character of the button's label.
    • If duplication exists in first characters, for duplicate items, use another character in the label.
    • Preferably, choose the first succeeding consonant.
  — Designate the mnemonic character by underlining it.
  — Maintain the same mnemonic on all identical buttons on other screens.

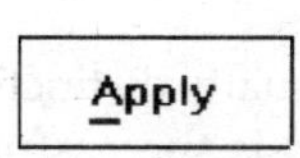

Figure 8.13

- Accelerators:
  — Assign a keyboard accelerator to each button to facilitate keyboard selection.

Enabling the user to select button actions through the typewriter keyboard provides flexibility and efficiency in the dialog. To do this, provide keyboard equivalent, single-character mnemonic codes that, when typed, will cause the action to be performed. The suggested method is to indicate the accelerator by underlining the proper character in the button label.

Keyboard accelerators, a keyboard key or combination of keys, may also be assigned to buttons to facilitate keyboard activation.

Keyboard equivalents and accelerators, including Microsoft Windows standard ones, were more fully described in Chapter 5 "Menus."

Scrolling

- If a window can be scrolled, do not scroll the command buttons.
  - Exception: if the screen cannot scroll independently of the buttons.
- Use buttons to move between multipage forms, not scroll bars.
  - Label buttons Next and Previous.

If scrolling the contents of a window, never scroll the buttons. They should be available at all times. Web page screens, whose content cannot be scrolled independently of buttons, are exceptions to this rule at the moment. Use buttons to move between multipage forms, not scroll bars. Label the buttons Next and Previous.

Button Activation

- Pointing:
  - Highlight the button in some visually distinctive manner when the pointer is resting on it and the button is available for selection.
- Activation:
  - Call attention to the button in another visually distinctive manner when it has been activated or pressed.
  - If a button can be pressed continuously, permit the user to hold the mouse button down and repeat the action.

Highlight the button in some visually distinctive manner when the pointer is resting on it and it is available for selection. This will provide the user with feedback indicating that the selection process may be performed. Some platforms display a brighter button.

Highlight the button in another visually distinctive manner when it has been activated or pressed, to indicate that the action is successful. One platform subdues or grays out the button. Another has raised beveled buttons that appear to sink into the screen when selected. Another alternative is to move the button slightly as if it has been depressed.

If a button can be pressed continuously, permit the mouse button to be held down and the action repeated.

Toolbars

Toolbars are compilations of commands, actions, or functions, usually graphical in structure but sometimes textual, grouped together for speedy access. Microsoft Windows defines a toolbar as a panel that contains a *set* of controls. Toolbars may also be called *button bars, control bars,* or *access bars*. Specialized toolbars may also be referred to as *ribbons, toolboxes,* or *palettes*. Toolbars may also appear in palette windows.

Usage

- To provide easy and fast access to most frequently used commands or options across multiple screens.
- To invoke a subapplication within an application.
- To use in place of certain menu items.

Provide toolbars to allow fast and easy access to a system's most frequently used commands, functions, or options. Also provide toolbars for easily invoking subapplications within an application. Toolbars are considered "fast paths" or expert aids. All toolbar functions must also be obtainable by normal textual menu means, including through use of the menu bar. One exception: if menu text cannot clearly explain an item and a graphical toolbar representation can, the toolbar item may replace the menu item.

Structure

- Images:
  - — Provide buttons of equal size.
  - — Create a meaningful and unique icon.
    - Design them using icon design guidelines.
  - — Center the image within the button.
  - — Give the button a raised appearance.
  - — Ensure that toolbar images are discernible from Web page graphical images.
- Text:
  - — Create a meaningful label, adhering to label guidelines for command buttons.
  - — Create toolbar buttons of equal size, following the size guidelines recently described.
- Consistency:
  - — Use the same icon throughout an application and between applications.

Create meaningful and unique images and icons utilizing the icon design guidelines in Chapter 11 "Graphics, Icons, and Images." Center the image within the button and provide an associated textual label. A label is always necessary to ensure button comprehensibility. One study has found that placing graphics *and* words on buttons, makes them more usable than including graphics only. Create the label following the guidelines for command buttons. The label may be located within the button, positioned beneath it, or presented on demand through a ToolTip control. Labels beneath toolbar button images will provide a larger pointing target. If the label is located within the button and the system will be translated into one or more other languages, allow extra space for the label. A ToolTip control is discussed later in this chapter. Give the button a raised appearance to convey that it is a screen navigation element to be pressed. Ensure that toolbar images are discernible from all Web page graphical images.

For text-only toolbar buttons, create a meaningful label, adhering to the label guidelines for command buttons. Provide consistent icons throughout all applications.

Size

- Button:
  - — 24 (w) by 22 (h) pixels, including border.
  - — 32 (w) by 30 (h) pixels, including border.
  - — Larger buttons can be used on high-resolution displays.
- Label:
  - — 16 (w) by 16 (h) pixels.
  - — 14 (w) by 24 (h) pixels.
- Default:
  - — Provide the smaller size as the default size with a user option to change it.
- Image:
  - — Center the image in the button.

A toolbar button should be large but not too large because of the number that may need to be displayed. Microsoft provides the above guidelines. Other sizing guidelines and much more detailed image guidelines are presented in Chapter 11.

Organization

- Order the buttons based on common and customary grouping schemes.
  - — For buttons ordered left to right, place those for the most frequently used actions to the left.
  - — For buttons ordered top to bottom, place those for the most frequently used actions at the top.
- Keep related buttons grouped together.
- Separate potentially destructive buttons from frequently chosen selections.
- Permit user reconfiguration of button organization.

Toolbar buttons should be ordered logically, such as by frequency of use, sequence of use, or importance. If the buttons reflect a quality on a continuum such as colors or shades, follow standard and expected ordering schemes. For buttons arrayed left to right, start the ordering from left to right. For buttons arrayed top to bottom, start the ordering from top to bottom.

Keep related buttons grouped together. Separate potentially destructive buttons from frequently chosen selections to avoid inadvertent activation and potentially catastrophic results. Permit the user to reconfigure the button organizational structure to better meet his or her unique needs.

Location

- Position main features and functions bar horizontally across top of window just below menu bar.
- Position subtask and subfeatures bars along sides of window.
- Permit the location of the bar to be changed by the user.
- Permit display of the bar to be turned on or off by the user.
  — Also provide access through standard menus.

Locate the main features and functions tool bar horizontally across the top of the window just below the menu bar. Locate subtask and subfeature tool bars along sides of window. Permit the location of the toolbar to be changed by the user. Since a toolbar can create visual noise, permit its display to be turned on or off. Always also provide access to the toolbar actions through standard menus.

Active Items

- Make only currently available toolbar items available.
- Temporarily not available items may be displayed grayed out.

As the user moves around through an application, items at various points that are not applicable do not have to be displayed. Temporarily unavailable items may be grayed out.

Customization

- Permit toolbars to be turned off by the user.
- Allow the customizing of toolbars.
  — Provide a default, however.

Permit the toolbars to be turned off by the user, should their use not be necessary or should more screen space be desired. Also, allow users to customize the toolbar, determining what they would like to add or remove. Many users do not customize them, however, so a default set should always be provided.

Keyboard Equivalents and Accelerators

- Equivalents:
  - — Assign keyboard equivalents to facilitate keyboard selection.
  - — Maintain the same mnemonic on all identical buttons on all screens.
- Accelerators:
  - — Assign a keyboard accelerator to facilitate keyboard selection.

Provide keyboard equivalents and accelerators to facilitate keyboard selection. Maintain the same mnemonic on all identical buttons on all screens. One caution, if a particular mnemonic is being used somewhere else in the window; it may not be available for use on the toolbar.

Button Activation

- Pointing:
  - — Highlight the button in some visually distinctive manner when the pointer is resting on it and the button is available for selection.
- Activation:
  - — Call attention to the button in another visually distinctive manner when it has been activated or pressed.

Highlight the button in some visually distinctive manner when the pointer is resting on it and the button is available for selection. This will provide the user with feedback indicating that the selection process may be performed. Highlight the button in another visually distinctive manner when it has been activated or pressed, to indicate that the action is successful.

Text Entry/Read-Only Controls

A Text Entry/Read-Only control contains text that is exclusively entered or modified through the keyboard. It may also contain entered text being presented for reading or display purposes only.

Text Boxes

- Description:
  - — A control, usually rectangular in shape, in which:
    - • Text may be entered or edited.
    - • Text may be displayed for read-only purposes.
  - — Usually possesses a caption describing the kind of information contained within it.
  - — An outline field border:
    - • Is included for enterable/editable text boxes.
    - • Is not included for read-only text boxes.

  - Two types exist:
    - Single line.
    - Multiple line.
  - When first displayed, the box may be blank or contain an initial value.
- Purpose:
  - To permit the display, entering, or editing of textual information.
  - To display read-only information.
- Advantages:
  - Very flexible.
  - Familiar.
  - Consumes little screen space.
- Disadvantages:
  - Requires use of typewriter keyboard.
  - Requires user to remember what must be keyed.
- Proper usage:
  - Most useful for data that is:
    - Unlimited in scope.
    - Difficult to categorize.
    - Of a variety of different lengths.
  - When using a selection list is not possible.

Two types of *text boxes* exist. One consists of a rectangular box into which information is typed. It may also be referred to as an *edit* control. The second is also rectangular in shape but contains text displayed purely for read-only purposes. The former type has historically been referred to as an *entry field*, the latter as an *inquiry* or *display field*. While display-only text boxes are not operable in the true sense of the word, the information contained within them is capable of being modified by other controls. Hence, they will be reviewed as an operable control since their characteristics, and the characteristics of an entry field, are very similar. Some platforms classify both as text boxes. Text boxes almost always possess a separate caption describing the kind of information to be keyed. An enterable text box is visually presented on the screen, its shape being defined by an outline border, a reversal in screen polarity, a white background, or various combinations of these features. The information in a read-only text field is most effectively displayed on the screen background, not in a box. Therefore, a box does not surround the information contained in read-only text boxes.

Single-Line and Multiple-Line Text Boxes

- Single line:
  - Description:
    - A control consisting of no more than one line of text.
  - Purpose:
    - To make textual entries when the information can be contained within one line of the screen.

— Typical uses:
  - Typing the name of a file to save.
  - Typing the path of a file to copy.
  - Typing variable data on a form.
  - Typing a command.

- Multiple line:
  — Description:
    - A control consisting of a multiline rectangular box for multiple lines of text.
  — Purpose:
    - To type, edit, and read passages of text.
  — Typical uses:
    - Creating or reading an electronic mail message.
    - Displaying and editing text files.

Text boxes exist in two forms: *single line* and *multiple line*. A single-line box is used when the information contained within it can be confined to one screen line. Multiple-line boxes are used when the information exceeds a single line. When first displayed, a text box may be blank or contain an initial value. Text boxes are illustrated in Figure 8.14.

Text boxes are familiar, flexible, and consume little screen space. They do require a typewriter keyboard, which, depending upon one's skill with a keyboard may be an advantage or a disadvantage. A disadvantage to all is that what is keyed into an entry field must often be remembered. They are most useful for data that is difficult to categorize or unlimited in scope, or when use of a selection field is not possible.

Captions

- Structure and size:
  — Provide a descriptive caption to identify the kind of information to be typed, or contained within, the text box.
  — Use a mixed-case font.
  — Display the caption in normal intensity or in a color of moderate brightness.

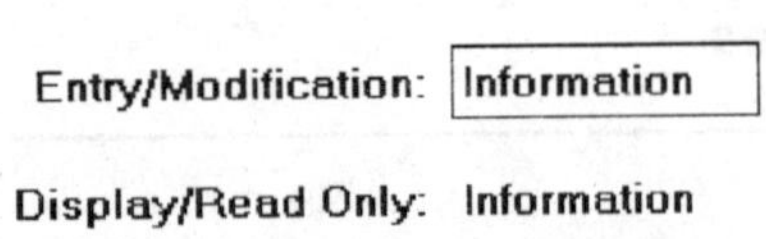

Figure 8.14 Text boxes.

- Formatting:
  - — Single fields:
    - • Position the field caption to the left of the text box.
      - — Place a colon (:) immediately following the caption.
      - — Separate the colon from the text box by one space.

Figure 8.15

- • Alternately, the caption may be placed above the text box.
  - — Place a colon (:) immediately following the caption.
  - — Position above the upper-left corner of the box, flush with the left edge.

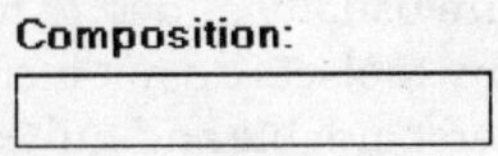

Figure 8.16

- — Multiple occurrence fields:
  - • For entry/modification text boxes:
    - — Position the caption left-justified one line above the column of entry fields.

Figure 8.17

- • For display/read-only boxes:
  - — If the data field is long and fixed-length, or the displayed data is about the same length, center the caption above the displayed text box data.

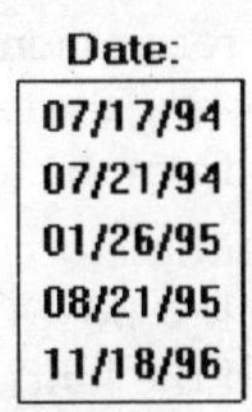

Figure 8.18

- — If the data displayed is alphanumeric, short, or quite variable in length, left-justify the caption above the displayed text box data.

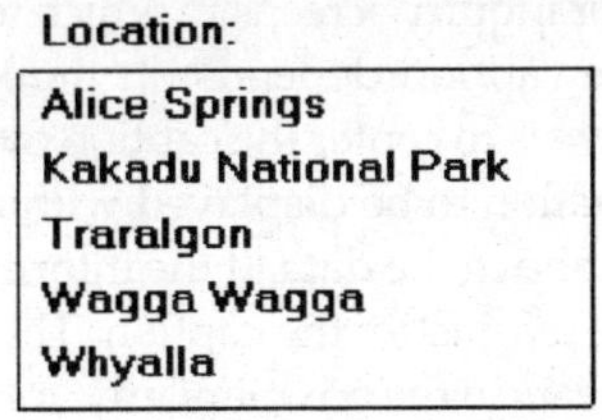

Figure 8.19

— If the data field is numeric and variable in length, right-justify the caption above the displayed text box data.

Balances:

12,642,123.05
53.98
355,125.44
199.13
612.01

Figure 8.20

Structure and size. Captions are usually added to text boxes using *static text* fields, to be described shortly. Many toolsets do not include captions with text box controls. Captions must be understandable and fully spelled out in a language meaningful to the user. In general, abbreviations and contractions should not be used. To achieve the alignment recommendations (to be discussed shortly), however, an occasional abbreviation or contraction may be necessary. If so, choose those that are common in the everyday language of the user or those that are meaningful or easily learned. Use mixed-case text in the headline style, capitalizing only the first letter of each word (except for articles, conjunctions, and prepositions—a, the, and, for, and so on). Acronyms, abbreviations, or proper nouns that are normally capitalized, however, may be capitalized. If the caption is of a sentence-style nature, sentence-style capitalization should be followed. In this case, capitalize only the first letter of the first word of the caption.

In relation to the text box, the caption should be of normal intensity or consist of a moderately bright color. Visual emphasis should always be given to the information in the text box.

Single fields. For single fields, it is recommended that the caption precede the text box. Place a colon (:) directly following the caption to visually separate the caption from the data; separate the colon from the text box by one space.

Multiple occurrence fields. For multiple-occurrence fields, the caption should be positioned above the columnized text boxes. The exact location of the caption will depend on the kind of screen and the kind of data displayed. For entry screens, the caption should be left-justified above the columnized entry fields. This will signal the starting point of the text box and ensure that the caption is positioned directly above the keyed data.

For display/read-only or inquiry screens in which text box information already exists, the positioning of the caption depends on the kind of information displayed within the box. The objective is to center the caption over the information. If the box is fixed-length, or the information to be displayed within it usually fills, or almost fills, the box, center the caption above the data. If the information is alphanumeric and can be quite variable in length, left-justify the caption. This will keep the caption directly above the data when it appears in the box. Similarly, for numeric fields, right-justify the caption to keep it above the data that will be right-justified when it appears.

Fields

- Structure:
  - — Identify entry/modification text boxes with a line border or reverse polarity rectangular box.
    - To visually indicate that it is an enterable field, present the box in a recessed manner.

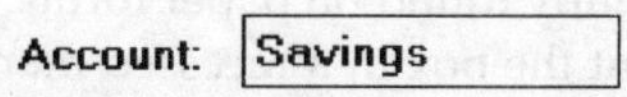

Figure 8.21

- Present display/read-only text boxes on the window background.

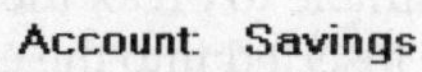

Figure 8.22

- — Break up long text boxes through incorporation of slashes (/), dashes (-), spaces, or other common delimiters.

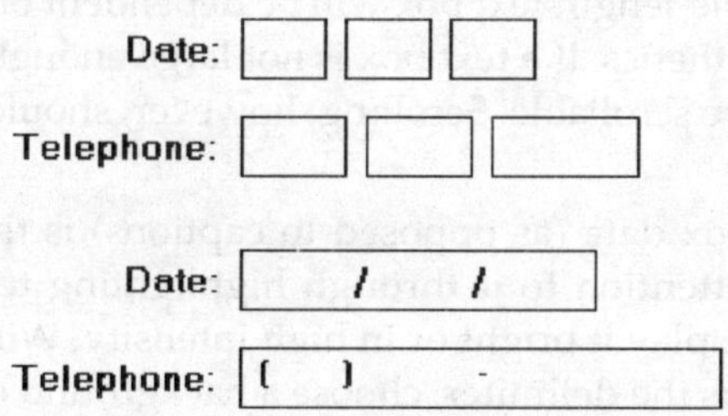

Figure 8.23

- Size:
  - — Size to indicate the approximate length of the field.
  - — Text boxes for fixed-length data must be large enough to contain the entire entry.
  - — Text boxes for variable-length data must be large enough to contain the majority of the entries.
  - — Where entries may be larger than the entry field, scrolling must be provided to permit keying into, or viewing, the entire field.
  - — Employ word wrapping for continuous text in multiple-line text boxes.
- Highlighting:
  - — Call attention to text box data through a highlighting technique.
    - Higher intensity.
    - If color is used, choose one that both complements the screen background and contrasts well with it.
- Unavailable fields:
  - — Gray-out temporarily unavailable text boxes.
- Fonts:
  - — To support multiple fonts, use a *Rich-Text Box*.

Structure. A text box should attract attention, but not detract from the legibility of the data contained within it, be capable of allowing an indication of the structure of the data contained within it, and indicate the appropriate number of characters to be keyed into it. An early study found that, in meeting these objectives, a broken underscore and an outlined box were the best delimiters for screen entry fields. The older text-based screens traditionally have used the underscore as the delimiter; graphical screens, the outlined box. Interestingly, both resemble the coding areas most frequently found on paper forms. To visually indicate that it is an enterable field, present the box in a recessed manner, as is done by Microsoft Windows.

Present display/read-only text boxes on the window background. To make text boxes more readable, it is desirable to break them up into logical pieces. Slashes, dashes, and spaces should be inserted into the entry fields as illustrated.

Size. The size of a field must give an approximate indication of the data length. Text boxes for fixed-length data must be long enough to contain the entry. Variable-length text boxes should be large enough to contain the majority of the entries. The size of a variable-length text box will be dependent on field alignment, space utilization, and aesthetics. If a text box is not large enough to key or view the entire entry, it must be scrollable. Scrolling, however, should be avoided whenever possible.

Highlighting. Text box data (as opposed to captions) is the most important part of a screen. Call attention to it through highlighting techniques. With monochrome screens, display it bright or in high intensity. With color, use the brightest colors. If a box is the delimiter, choose a background color that complements the screen body background and provides good contrast with the color chosen for the data.

Temporarily unavailable. For fields temporarily unavailable for entry, gray-out the box and its associated label. This temporary graying out implies, however, that the user can perform some action that will again make the field enterable.

Rich-Text Boxes. Most text boxes typically support only the standard system font. A Microsoft Windows rich-text box is similar to a text box but provides, in addition, font properties, such as typeface, size, color, bold, and italics. It also supports character and paragraph alignment, tabs, indents, and numbering, as well as printing.

Selection Controls

A selection control presents on the screen all the possible alternatives, conditions, or choices that may exist for an entity, property, or value. The relevant item or items are selected from those displayed. Some selection controls present all the alternatives together, visibly on a screen; others may require an action to retrieve the entire listing and/or scrolling to view all the alternatives. Selection controls include radio buttons, check boxes, list boxes, drop-down/pop-up list boxes, and palettes.

Radio Buttons

- Description:
  - — A two-part control consisting of the following:
    - • Small circles, diamonds, or rectangles.
    - • Choice descriptions.
  - — When a choice is selected:
    - • The option is highlighted.
    - • Any existing choice is automatically unhighlighted and deselected.
- Purpose:
  - — To set one item from a small set of mutually exclusive options (2 to 8).
- Advantages:
  - — Easy-to-access choices.
  - — Easy-to-compare choices.
  - — Preferred by users.
- Disadvantages:
  - — Consume screen space.
  - — Limited number of choices.
- Proper usage:
  - — For setting attributes, properties, or values.
  - — For mutually exclusive choices (that is, only one can be selected).
  - — Where adequate screen space is available.
  - — Most useful for data and choices that are:
    - • Discrete.
    - • Small and fixed in number.
    - • Not easily remembered.
    - • In need of a textual description to meaningfully describe the alternatives.
    - • Most easily understood when the alternatives can be seen together and compared to one another.
    - • Never changed in content.
  - — Do not use:
    - • For commands.
    - • Singly to indicate the presence or absence of a state.

Structure. Controls of this type take several different physical forms. They are most often called *radio buttons* because of their resemblance to similar controls on radios. Microsoft Windows, however, refers to these controls as *option buttons*. One common display method consists of a circle associated with each choice description. When an alternative is selected, the center of the circle is partially or fully filled in to provide a visual indication that it is the active choice. Other styles of radio buttons have also been implemented. Microsoft Windows uses a small depressed circle that contains a small dot when selected. Other presentation methods include small circular buttons that look recessed when not selected and are raised when selected, and small diamond-shaped buttons that look raised when

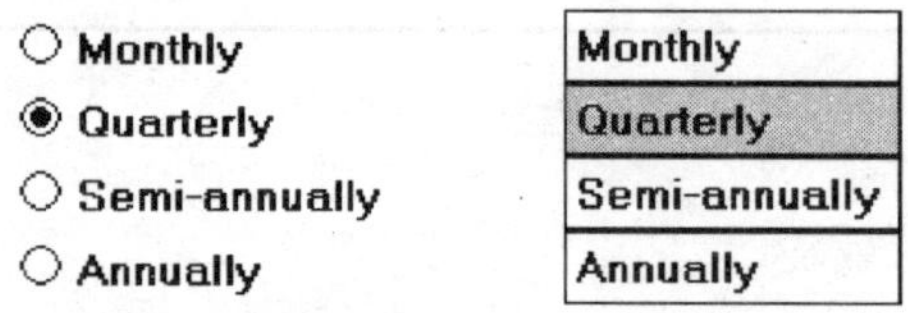

Figure 8.24 Radio buttons.

Figure 8.25 Radio buttons.

not selected and depressed when selected. Another method for presenting exclusive choices is the butted box or button where the alternatives are inscribed in horizontally arrayed adjoining rectangles resembling command buttons. The selected alternative is highlighted in some way. Examples of radio buttons are illustrated in Figures 8.24 and 8.25. Deciding on which style to use seems to be more a matter of preference than performance. No published comparison studies are available for guidance.

Purpose. Radio buttons are used to designate one of a small set of options, no more than about eight. As with a radio, the choices are mutually exclusive, only one frequency or setting is permitted at one time in the presented array.

Advantages/disadvantages. With radio buttons, all alternatives are always visible. Therefore, it is easy to access and compare choices. Two recent studies (Johnsgard, Page, Wilson, and Zeno, 1995; Tullis and Kodimer, 1992) have found radio buttons a preferred and very effective control for presenting mutually exclusive choices. These studies will be described later in this chapter. On the negative side, radio buttons do consume a certain amount of screen real estate, limiting the number of alternatives that can reasonably be displayed.

Proper usage. Radio buttons are useful for setting attributes, properties, or values where adequate screen space is available. The alternatives should be discrete, small in number, and in need of a textual description to identify them meaningfully. Radio buttons are helpful in situations where the alternatives cannot always be easily remembered or where displaying the alternatives together facilitates understanding and selecting the proper choice. The radio button choices displayed should be stable, never changing in content.

Never use radio buttons for implementing commands, such as causing a dialog box to immediately appear based upon a button setting. Commands to the system should result from direct user command actions, such as pressing a command button. This allows control to remain with the user. Unfortunately, use of a radio button to perform an action is a common Web page design problem. Also, do not use one radio button by itself to indicate the presence or absence of a state. A single check box is recommended for this purpose.

Choice Descriptions

- Provide meaningful, fully spelled-out choice descriptions clearly describing the values or effects set by the radio buttons.

- Display in a single line of text.
- Display using mixed-case letters, using the sentence style.
- Position descriptions to the right of the button. Separate them by at least one space from the button.
- When a choice is conditionally unavailable for selection, display the choice description grayed out or dimmed.
- Include a None choice if it adds clarity.

Choice descriptions must be clear, meaningful, fully spelled out, and displayed in a mixed-case text. For multiword descriptions, capitalize the first letter of the description and use the sentence style for the remainder of the description. Small button-type indicators should be located to the left of the choice description; rectangular boxes that resemble a command button will find the description within the box. Small buttons associated with text are advantageous when the choice description must be lengthy. Descriptions in boxes impose restrictions on the number of words that can be inscribed within them. When a choice is unavailable for selection in the present condition, display the choice selection grayed out or dimmed. Where a "None" alternative clarifies the alternatives presented, provide it in the listing.

Size

- Show a minimum of two choices, a maximum of eight.

Generally, selection fields of this style should not present more than eight choices. Displaying more than eight is usually not efficient, wasting screen space. If the number of choices exceeds this maximum, consider using a single selection list box or a drop-down list box. Johnsgard, Page, Wilson and Zeno (1995) have found, however, that even for as many as thirty choices, radio buttons were preferred by users, and performed better, than these other controls.

Defaults

- When the control possesses a state or affect that has been predetermined to have a higher probability of selection than the others, designate it as the default and display its button filled in.
- When the control includes choices whose states cannot be predetermined, display all the buttons without setting a dot, or in the *indeterminate* state.
- When a multiple selection includes choices whose states vary, display the buttons in another unique manner, or in the *mixed value* state.

Provide a default setting for a radio button whenever possible. In some situations, however, a default setting may be difficult to predetermine, or inappropriate to predetermine (sex: male or female?). Microsoft Windows provides for additional settings called the *indeterminate* or *mixed value* states. When a default setting cannot be preestablished because of the nature of the information, leave all the buttons blank or not filled in. If a multiple selection on an object is performed and the values in the selection are mixed or differ, display the applicable radio buttons in another distinctive manner, such as a gray shadow.

Structure

- A columnar orientation is the preferred manner of presentation.
- Left-align the buttons and choice descriptions.

Figure 8.26

- If vertical space on the screen is limited, orient the buttons horizontally.
- Provide adequate separation between choices so that the buttons are associated with the proper description.
  — A distance equal to three spaces is usually sufficient.

Figure 8.27

- Enclose the buttons in a border to visually strengthen the relationship they possess.

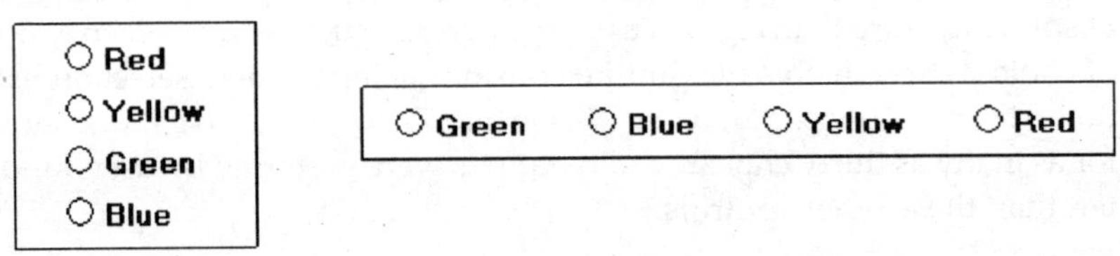

Figure 8.28

The preferred orientation of radio buttons is columnar. This aids visual scanning and choice comparison. Controls with small button indicators usually fit best in this manner because choice descriptions do not have to be restricted in size. Left-align the buttons and choice descriptions. Provide adequate separation—about three spaces—between choices if they must be presented horizontally. Enclose the buttons in a border. Rectangular boxes should be of equal height and/or width and be butted up against one another. This will distinguish them from nonexclusive choice fields (check boxes) that will be separated from one another. Figure 8.29 illustrates the best ways to, and not to, present radio buttons.

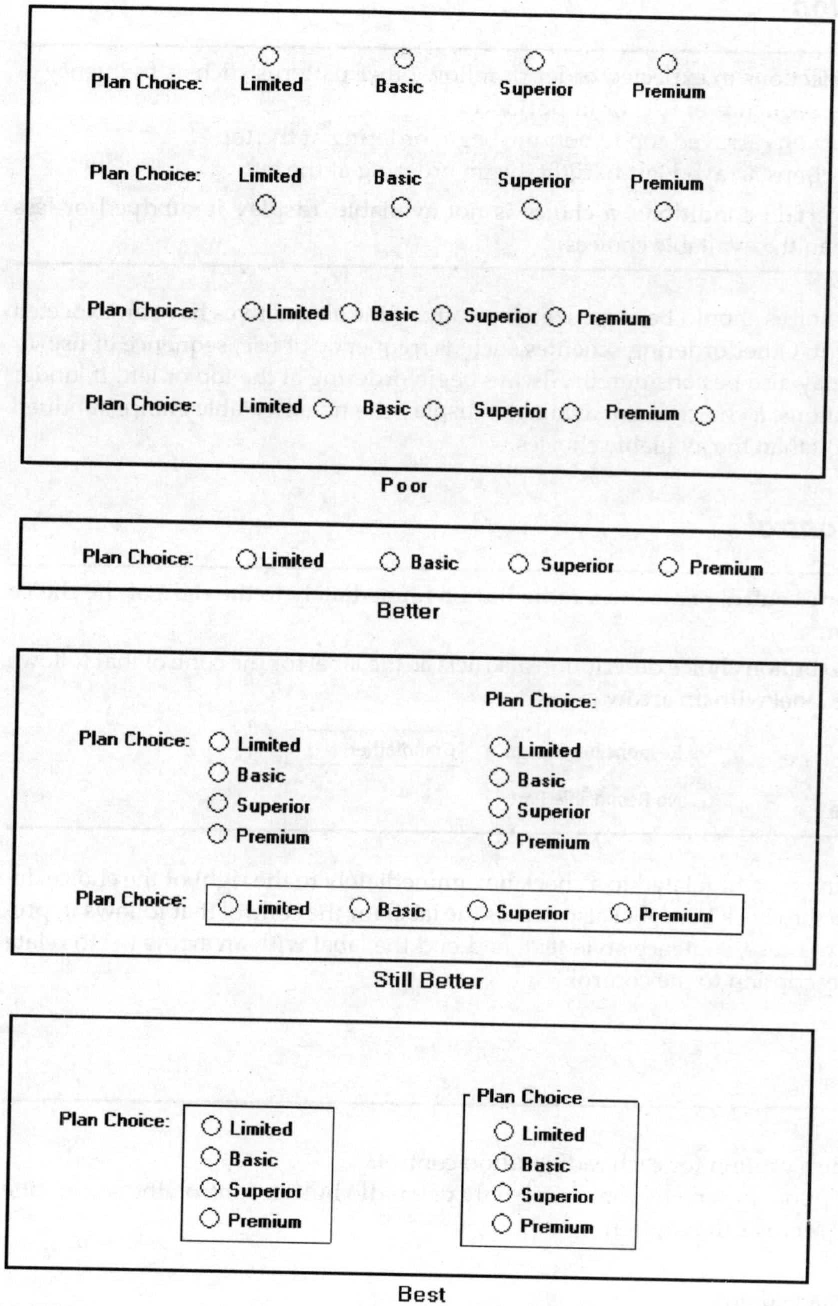

Figure 8.29 Ways to, and not to, present radio buttons.

Organization

- Arrange selections in expected order or follow other patterns such as frequency of occurrence, sequence of use, or importance.
  - — For selections arrayed top to bottom, begin ordering at the top.
  - — For selections arrayed left to right, begin ordering at the left.
- If, under certain conditions, a choice is not available, display it subdued or less brightly than the available choices.

Selection choices should be organized logically. If the alternatives have an expected order, follow it. Other ordering schemes such as frequency of use, sequence of use, or importance may also be considered. Always begin ordering at the top or left. If, under certain conditions, a choice is not available, display the nonselectable choice subdued or less brightly than the available choices.

Related Control

- Position any control related to a radio button immediately to the right of the choice description.
- If the radio button choice description also acts as the label for the control that follows it, end the label with an arrow (>).

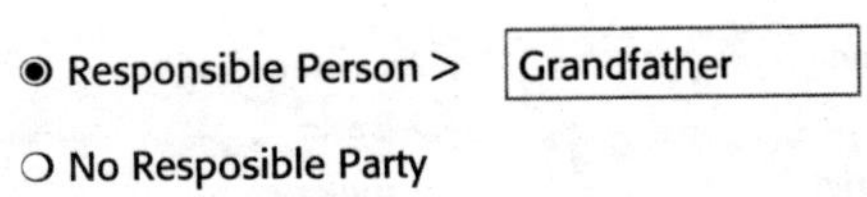

Figure 8.30

Position any control related to a check box immediately to the right of the choice description. If a the check box label also acts as the label for the control that follows it, present it in mixed case, sentence style text, and end the label with an arrow (>) to relate the choice description to the control.

Captions

- Structure:
  - — Provide a caption for each radio button control.
    - Exception: In screens containing only one radio button control, the screen title may serve as the caption.
- Display:
  - — Fully spelled out.
  - — In mixed-case letters, capitalizing the first letter of all significant words.
- Columnar orientation:
  - — With a control border, position the caption:
    - Upper-left-justified within the border.

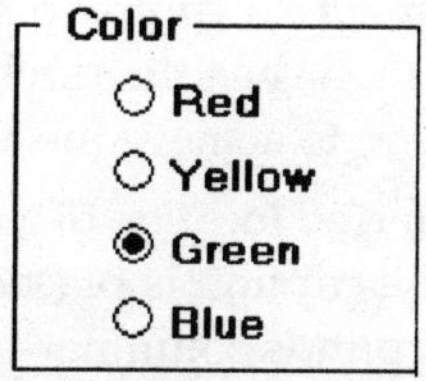

Figure 8.31

- Alternately, the caption may be located to the left of the topmost choice description.

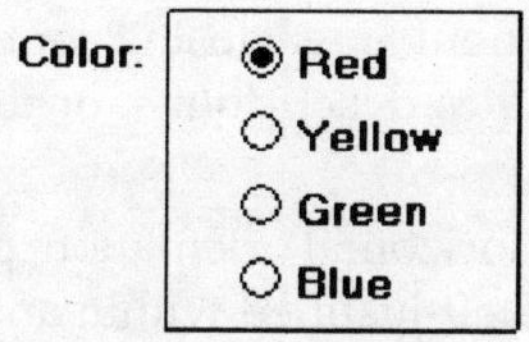

Figure 8.32

— Without an enclosing control border, position the caption:

- Left-justified above the choice descriptions, separated by one space line.

Figure 8.33

- Alternately, the caption may be located to the left of the topmost choice description.

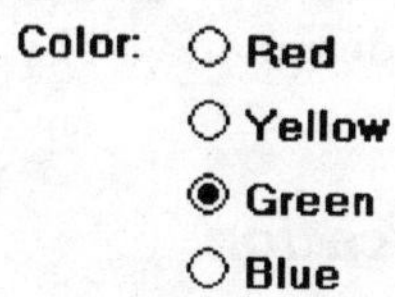

Figure 8.34

- Horizontal orientation:

  — Position the caption to the left of the choice descriptions.

Figure 8.35

- Alternately, with an enclosing control border, left-justified within the border.

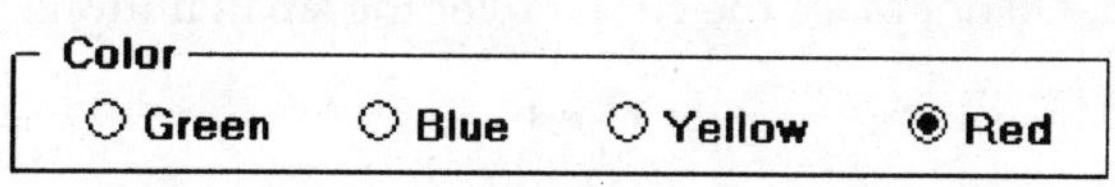

Figure 8.36

— Be consistent in caption style and orientation within a screen.

Structure. Using a *static text* or *group box* control field, display the caption fully spelled out, using mixed-case letters in the headline style. Some occasional common abbreviations may be used, however, to achieve the alignment goals to be specified.

Columnar orientation. The preferred location of a radio button control caption within a screen can vary. Ideally, the caption is placed upper-left-justified within a line border or group box that surrounds columnar-oriented radio buttons, as shown in the example in the above guideline summary. If other controls on a screen possess captions positioned to the left, and the radio button control is aligned with these controls, position the caption to the left of the control. This will help achieve screen efficiency, minimize viewer eye movements, and provide caption and choice distinctiveness. Without an enclosing control border, position the caption left-justified above the choice descriptions, or to the left of the topmost choice description.

Horizontal orientation. In a horizontal orientation, position the caption to the left of the choice descriptions, or left-justified within an enclosing control border. If the screen contains only one radio button control, the screen title may serve as the control caption. Be consistent in caption style and orientation within a screen.

Keyboard Equivalents

- Assign a keyboard mnemonic to each choice description.
- Designate the mnemonic by underlining the applicable letter in the choice description.

Figure 8.37

Assign unique keyboard mnemonics for each alternative in the standard way, choosing the first letter (or another) and designating it by character underlining.

Selection Method and Indication

- Pointing:
  - — The selection target area should be as large as possible.
    - • Include the button and the choice description text.
  - — Highlight the selection choice in some visually distinctive way when the cursor's resting on it and the choice is available for selection.
    - • This cursor should be as long as the longest choice description plus one space at each end. Do not place the cursor over the small button.

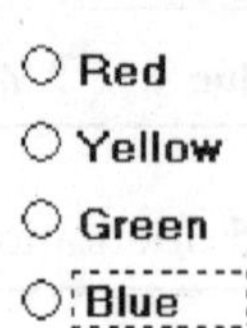

Figure 8.38

- Activation:
  - — When a choice is selected, distinguish it visually from the unselected choices.
    - A radio button should be filled in with a solid dark dot or made to look depressed or higher through use of a shadow.
  - — When a choice is selected, any other selected choice must be deselected.
- Defaults:
  - — If a radio button control is displayed that contains a choice previously selected or a default choice, display the selected choice as set in the control

---

Pointing. The selection target area should be as large as possible in order to make it easy to move to. If a small button is the selection indication method used, the target area should include the button and the choice description text. If the rectangular box selection method is used, the entire box should be the target. Highlight the selection choice in some visually distinctive way when the pointer is resting on it and the choice is available for selection. If a small button is the selection indication method used, a distinctive reverse video, reverse color, or dotted or dashed box selection cursor or bar may be used to surround the selected choice description. This cursor should be as long as the longest description plus one space at each end. The cursor should not cover the small button.

Activation. When a choice is selected, distinguish it visually from the unselected choices. A radio button should be filled in with a solid dark dot or other similar marking (for example, making the button look depressed or higher than the others through the use of a drop shadow). A rectangular box can be highlighted in a manner different from when it is pointed at, or a bolder border can be drawn around it. When a choice is selected, any other selected choice must be deselected or made inactive.

Defaults. If a selection field is displayed with a choice previously selected or a default choice, display the currently active choice in the same manner as when it is selected.

MYTH **Our software is highly usable—it includes all the latest interface widgets.**

Check Boxes

- Description:
  - — A two-part control consisting of a square box and choice description.
  - — Each option acts as a switch and can be either "on" or "off."
    - When an option is selected (on), a mark such as an "X" or "check" appears within the square box, or the box is highlighted in some other manner.
    - Otherwise the square box is unselected or empty (off).
  - — Each box can be:
    - Switched on or off independently.
    - Used alone or grouped in sets.

- Purpose:
  - — To set one or more options as either on or off.
- Advantages
  - — Easy-to-access choices.
  - — Easy-to-compare choices.
  - — Preferred by users.
- Disadvantages:
  - — Consume screen space.
  - — Limited number of choices.
  - — Single check boxes difficult to align with other screen controls.
- Proper usage:
  - — For setting attributes, properties, or values.
  - — For nonexclusive choices (that is, more than one can be selected).
  - — Where adequate screen space is available.
  - — Most useful for data and choices that are:
    - Discrete.
    - Small and fixed in number.
    - Not easily remembered.
    - In need of a textual description to describe meaningfully.
    - Most easily understood when the alternatives can be seen together and compared to one another.
    - Never changed in content.
  - — Can be used to affect other controls.
  - — Use only when both states of a choice are clearly opposite and unambiguous.

Description. *Check box* controls differ from radio buttons in that they permit selection of more than one alternative. Each option acts as a switch and can be either "on" or "off." When an option is selected (on), an X or check appears within the square box, or it is highlighted in some other manner. When not selected, the square box is unselected or empty (off). Each box can be switched on or off independently. Check boxes may be used alone or grouped in sets.

Check boxes, too, may take different physical forms and be called by different names. The most common name is *check boxes*, the name used by Microsoft Windows. Others names include: *toggle buttons*, *switches*, and *two state nonexclusive settings*. Not only their names differ; differences also exist in the way these fields are presented on screens. One very common display method is a check box, which, resembling its namesake, consists of a square placed adjacent to each alternative. When the choice is selected, some systems place an X in the square to provide a visual indication that it is active. Others, including Microsoft Windows, place a check mark in the square, or fill in the selected square or make it look depressed when selected.

Interestingly, in the past decade, Microsoft Windows and others have switched from Xs to checks as the "on" mark in a check box. This has occurred because of possible confusion concerning Xs that have existed in some using communities. In an engineering environment, for example, an X marked in a box means not applicable or not set, while a check mark customarily means active or set. Internationally, also, an X is not universally recognized. (This control is called a check box, isn't it?)

Another style for this type of field is a button or box with the choice description inscribed inside. When selected, the alternative is highlighted in some way. To distinguish these fields visually from similarly constructed fields presenting mutually exclusive choices, the buttons are not adjacent to, or butted up against, one another. Check boxes are illustrated in Figures 8.39 and 8.40. Again, deciding on which style to use seems to be more a matter of preference than performance (other than for the possible confusion of Xs and checks). No published comparison studies are available for guidance.

Purpose. The purpose of a check box, then, is to set one or more options either on or off.

Advantages/disadvantages. With check boxes, all alternatives are always visible. Therefore, it is easy to access and compare choices. Like radio buttons, check boxes were the preferred, and fastest to use, controls in the Johnsgard et al. (1995) study. One disadvantage is the large amount of screen real estate they consume, limiting the number of alternatives that can be efficiently displayed. Another potential disadvantage is that it can be difficult to align a single check box with other arrayed screen controls because they often possess long descriptions for clarity purposes.

Proper usage. Check boxes are useful for setting attributes, properties, or values where adequate screen space is available. The alternatives should be discrete, small in number, and in need of a textual description to identify meaningfully. Check boxes are helpful in situations where the alternatives cannot always be easily remembered and the displaying of the alternatives together aids in understanding and

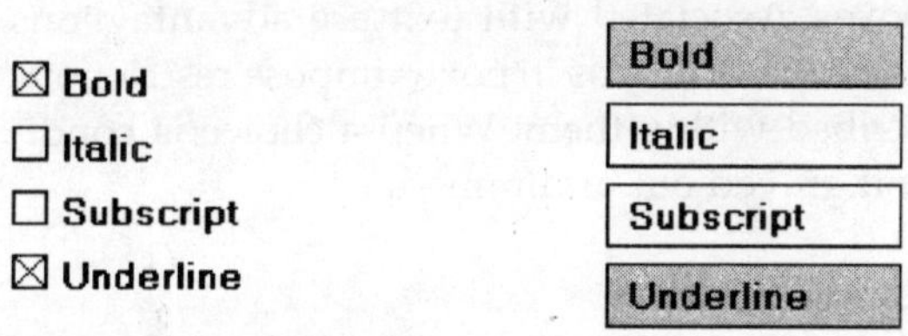

Figure 8.39 Check boxes.

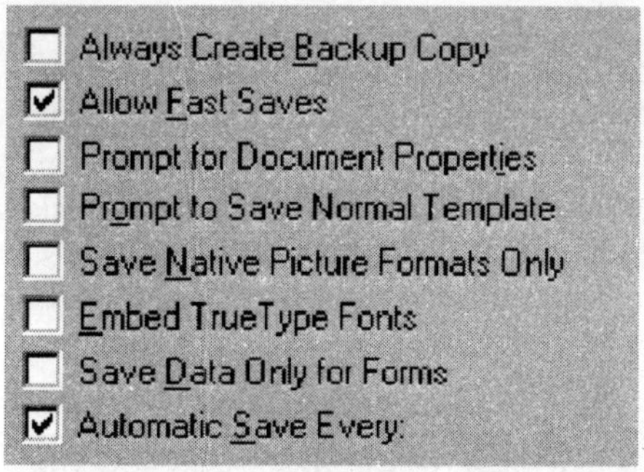

Figure 8.40 Check boxes.

selecting the proper choice. The choices displayed should be stable, never changing in content.

Check boxes can be used to affect other controls. The contents of a list can, for example, be filtered by setting check boxes. Use a check box only when both states of a choice are clearly opposite and unambiguous. If opposite states are not clear, use two radio buttons, clearly stating the opposite states.

Choice Descriptions

- Provide meaningful, fully spelled-out choice descriptions clearly describing the values or effects set by the check boxes.
- Display them in a single line of text.
- Display them using mixed-case letters in sentence style.
- Position descriptions to the right of the check box. Separate by at least one space from the box.
- When a choice is unavailable for selection under a certain condition, display the choice description visually dimmed.

Choice descriptions must be clear, meaningful, fully spelled out, and displayed in a mixed-case text. For multiword descriptions, capitalize the first letter and present the description in the sentence style. Small box-type indicators should be located to the left of the choice description; rectangular boxes that resemble a command button will find the description within the box. Small boxes associated with text are advantageous when the choice description must be lengthy. Descriptions in boxes impose restrictions on the number of words that can be inscribed within them. When a choice is conditionally unavailable for selection, display it grayed out or dimmed.

Size

- Show a minimum of one choice, a maximum of eight.

Generally, selection fields of this style should not offer more than eight choices. Displaying more than eight is usually not efficient because it wastes screen space. If the number of choices exceeds this maximum, consider using a multiple selection list box. Johnsgard et al. (1995) have found, however, that even for as many as 30 choices, check boxes were preferred by users and performed better than other nonexclusive controls.

Defaults

- When the control possesses a state or affect that has been preset, designate it as the default and display its check box marked.

- When a multiple selection includes choices whose states vary, display the buttons in another unique manner, or the *mixed value* state.

Provide a default setting for a check box whenever possible. If a multiple selection is performed and the values in the selection differ, display the applicable check boxes in the *mixed value* state, or in another distinctive manner such as with a gray shadow.

Structure

- Provide groupings of related check boxes.
- A columnar orientation is the preferred manner of presentation for multiple related check boxes.
- Left-align the check boxes and choice descriptions.

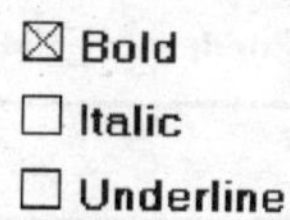

Figure 8.41

- If vertical space on the screen is limited, orient the boxes horizontally.
- Provide adequate separation between boxes so that the buttons are associated with the proper description.
  — A distance equal to three spaces is usually sufficient.

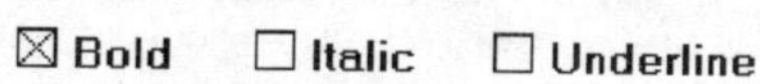

Figure 8.42

- Enclose the boxes in a border to visually strengthen the relationship they possess.

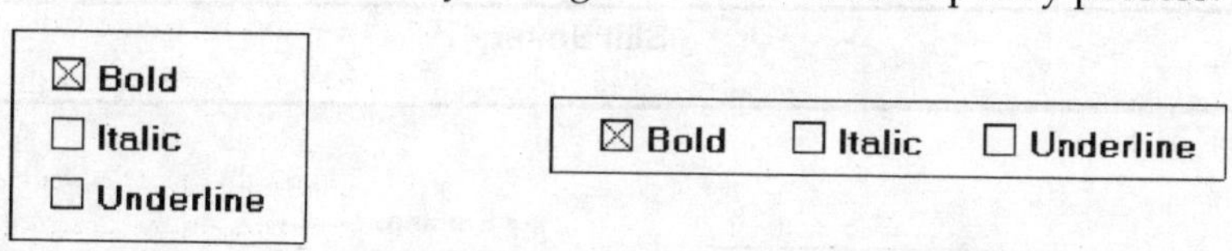

Figure 8.43

Provide groupings of related check boxes. The preferred check box orientation is columnar. This aids scanning and choice comparison. Controls with small box indicators usually fit best in this manner because choice descriptions are not restricted in size. Left-align the check boxes and choice descriptions. Rectangular boxes should be of equal width and separated from one another by small and equidistant spaces. This will distinguish them from mutually exclusive choices that will be butted up against one another. If the boxes must be horizontally oriented, provide adequate separation between them. Enclose the boxes in a border to emphasize their relationship. Figure 8.44 illustrates ways to, and not to, present groupings of check boxes.

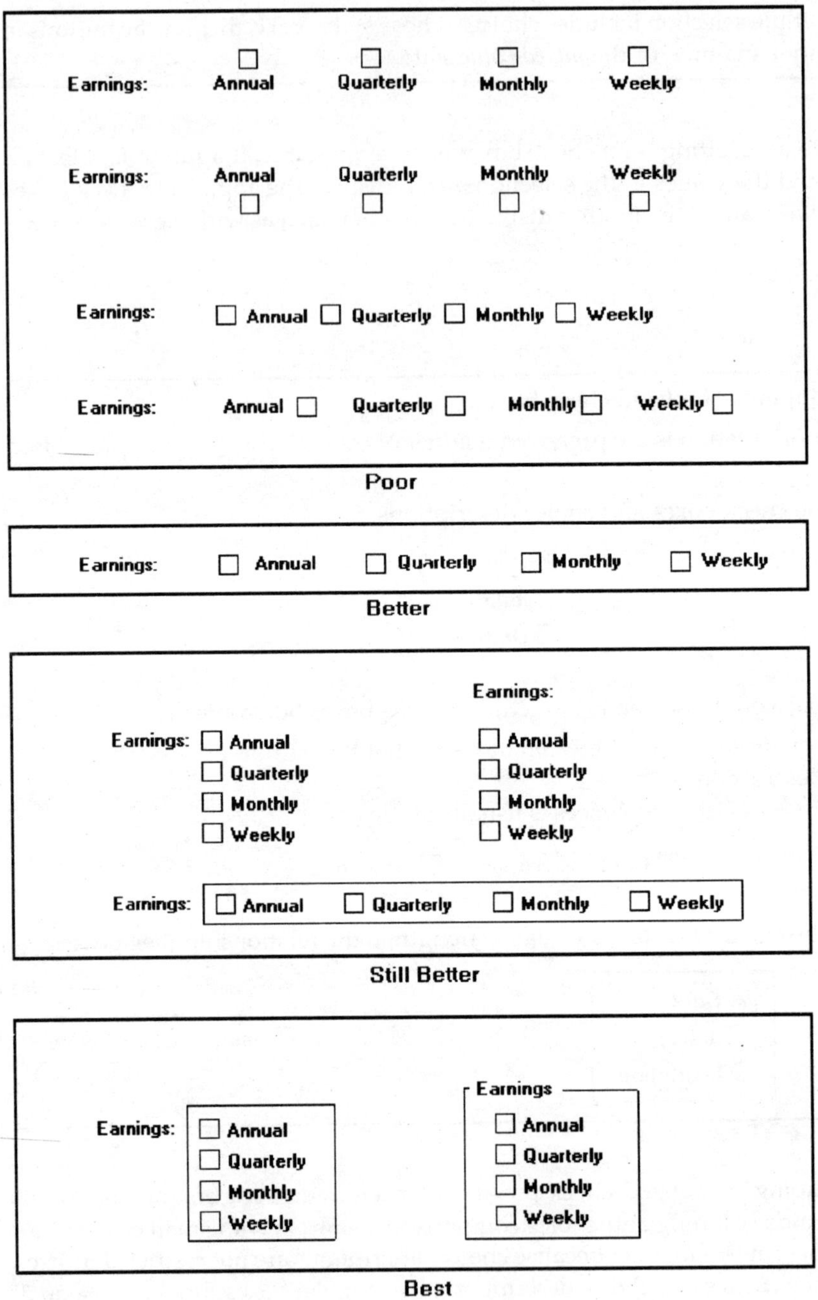

Figure 8.44 Ways to, and not to, present check boxes.

Organization

- Arrange selections in logical order or follow other patterns such as frequency of occurrence, sequence of use, or importance.
  - — For selections arrayed top to bottom, begin ordering at the top.
  - — For selections arrayed left to right, begin ordering at the left.
- If, under certain conditions, a choice is not available, display it subdued or less brightly than the available choices.

Selection choices should be organized logically. If the alternatives have an expected order, follow it. Other ordering schemes such as frequency of use, sequence of use, or importance may also be considered. Always begin the ordering at the top or left. If, under certain conditions, a choice is not available, display the unavailable choice subdued or less brightly than the available choices.

Related Control

- Position any control related to a check box immediately to the right of the choice description.
  - — If a the check box choice description also acts as the label for the control that follows it , end the label with an arrow (>).

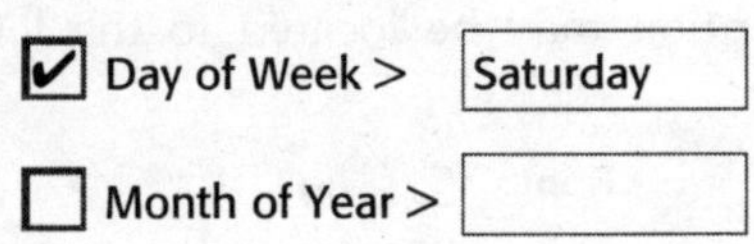

Figure 8.45

Position any control related to a check box immediately to the right of the choice description. If a the check box label also acts as the label for the control that follows it, present it mixed case, sentence style text and end the label with an arrow (>) to relate the choice description to the control.

Captions

- Structure:
  - — Provide a caption for each grouping of related check boxes.
    - Exception: In screens containing only one check box grouping, the screen title may serve as the caption.
  - — Display:
    - Fully spelled out.
    - In mixed-case letters capitalizing the first letter of all significant words.
- Columnar orientation:
  - — With a control border, position the caption:
    - Upper-left-justified within the border.

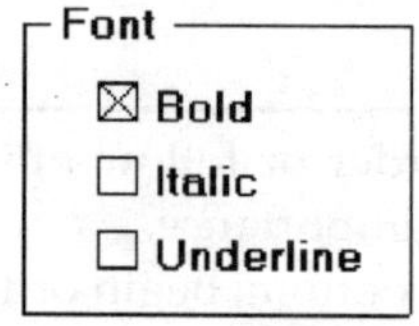

Figure 8.46

- Alternately, the caption may be located to the left of the topmost choice description.

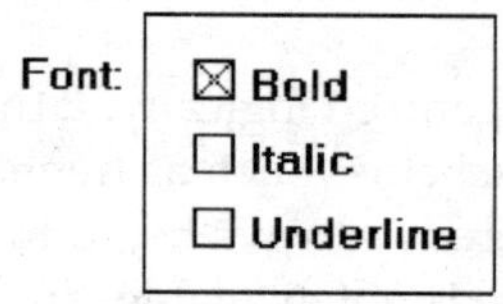

Figure 8.47

— Without an enclosing control border, position the caption:

- Left-justified above the choice descriptions separated by one space line.

Figure 8.48

- Alternately, the caption may be located to the left of the topmost choice description.

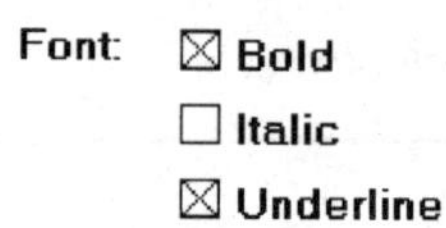

Figure 8.49

■ Horizontal orientation

— Position the caption to the left of the choice descriptions.

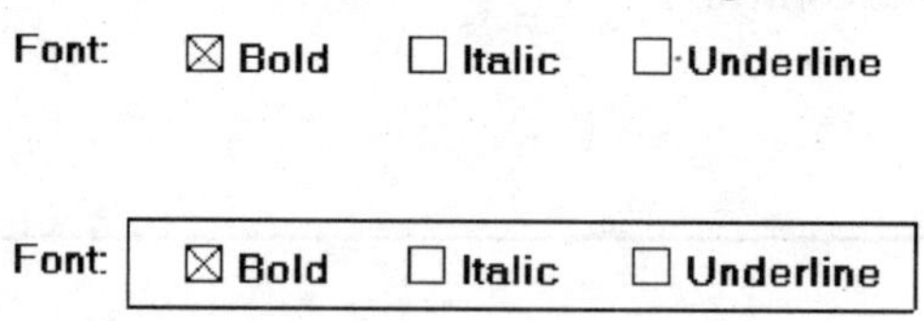

Figure 8.50

- Alternately, with an enclosing control border, it should be left-justified within the border.

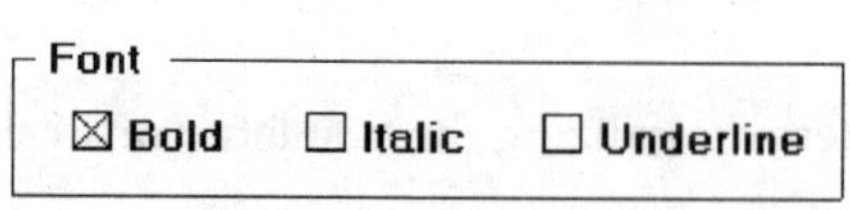

Figure 8.51

— Be consistent in caption style and orientation within a screen.

Structure. Using a *static text* or *group box* control, provide a caption for each grouping of related check boxes. Display the caption fully spelled out using mixed-case letters. Some occasional common abbreviations may be used, however, to achieve the alignment goals to be specified.

Columnar orientation. The preferred location of a check box control caption within a screen can vary. Ideally, the caption is placed upper-left-justified within a line border, or group box, surrounding columnar-oriented check boxes as shown in the first example in the above guideline summary. If other controls on a screen possess captions positioned to the left, and the check box control is aligned with these controls, position the caption to the left of the control. This is the second example illustrated above. This will help achieve screen efficiency, minimize viewer eye movements, and provide caption and choice distinctiveness. Without an enclosing border, position the caption left-justified above the choice descriptions, or to the left of the topmost choice.

Horizontal orientation. If horizontal orientation is necessary, position the caption to the left of the choice descriptions, or left-justified within an enclosing control border. If the screen contains only one related grouping of check boxes, the screen title may serve as the control caption. Be consistent in caption style and orientation within a screen.

Keyboard Equivalents

- Assign a keyboard mnemonic to each check box.
- Designate the mnemonic by underlining the applicable letter in the choice description.

Figure 8.52

Assign unique keyboard mnemonics for each check box in the standard way, choosing the first letter (or another) and designating it by character underlining.

Selection Method and Indication

- Pointing:
  - — The selection target area should be as large as possible.
    - Include the check box and the choice description text.
  - — Highlight the selection choice in some visually distinctive way when the cursor's resting on it and the choice is available for selection.
    - This cursor should be as long as the longest choice description plus one space at each end. Do not place the cursor over the check box.

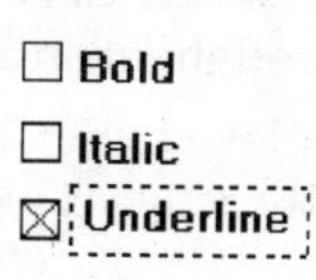

Figure 8.53

- Activation:
  - — When a choice is selected, distinguish it visually from the non-selected choices.
    - A check box should be filled in or made to look depressed or higher through use of a shadow.
- Defaults:
  - — If a check box is displayed that contains a choice previously selected or default choice, display the selected choice as set in the control.
- Select/deselect all:
  - — Do not use *Select All* and *Deselect All* check boxes.
- Mixed-value state:
  - — When a check box represents a value, and a multiple selection encompasses multiple value occurrences set in both the on and off state, display the check box in a *mixed value* state.
    - Fill the check box with another easily differentiable symbol or pattern.

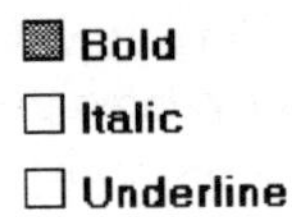

Figure 8.54

  - — Toggle the check box as follows:
    - Selection 1: Set the associated value for all elements. Fill the check box with an "X" or "check."
    - Selection 2: Unset the value for all associated elements. Blank-out the check box.
    - Selection 3: Return all elements to their original state. Fill the check box with the mixed value symbol or pattern.

Pointing. The selection target area should be as large as possible in order to make it easy to move to. If a small check box is the selection indication method used, the target area should include the box and the choice description text. If the rectangular box selection method is used, the entire box should be the target. Highlight the selection choice in some visually distinctive way when the pointer is resting on it and the choice is available for selection. If a check box is the selection indication method used, a distinctive reverse video, reverse color, or dotted or dashed box selection cursor or bar may be used to surround the selected choice description. This cursor should be as long as the longest description plus one space at each end. The cursor should not cover the check box.

Activation. When a choice is selected, distinguish it visually from the unselected choices. A check box may be marked with an X or check or filled in. Other methods include making the button look depressed or raised through appropriate use of drop shadows. A rectangular box can be highlighted in a manner different from when it is pointed at, or a bolder border can be drawn around it. The style chosen must be consistently applied throughout an application or system.

Defaults. If a selection field is displayed with a choice previously selected or a default choice, display the currently active choice in the same manner as when it is selected.

Select/deselect all. Do not use *Select All* and *Deselect All* check boxes. If this option is necessary, consider using a multiple selection list box with command buttons to accomplish these actions.

Mixed-value state. A check box can have three states.

- Checked—the associated property or value is set.
- Cleared—the associated value or property is not set.
- Mixed value—the associated value is set for some, but not all elements of the selection.

An example of the mixed value state would be when a sentence is selected and the selected text is partly bold and partly normal. So, when a check box represents a value, and a selection encompasses multiple value occurrences set in both the on and off state, display the check box in the *mixed value* state. Fill the check box with another easily differentiable symbol or pattern. Toggle the check box through clicking as described in the above guidelines.

Palettes

- Description:
  - — A control consisting of a series of graphical alternatives. The choices themselves are descriptive, being composed of colors, patterns, or images.
  - — In addition to being a standard screen control, a palette may also be presented on a pull-down or pop-up menu or a toolbar.
- Purpose:
  - — To set one of a series of mutually exclusive options presented graphically or pictorially.
- Advantages:
  - — Pictures aid comprehension.
  - — Easy-to-compare choices.
  - — Usually consume less screen space than textual equivalents.
- Disadvantages:
  - — A limited number of choices can be displayed.
  - — Difficult to organize for scanning efficiency.
  - — Requires skill and time to design meaningful and attractive graphical representations.
- Proper usage:
  - — For setting attributes, properties, or values.
  - — For mutually exclusive choices (that is, only one can be selected).
  - — Where adequate screen space is available.
  - — Most useful for data and choices that are:
    - Discrete.
    - Frequently selected.
    - Limited in number.
    - Variable in number.

- Not easily remembered.
- Most easily understood when the alternatives may be seen together and compared to one another.
- Most meaningfully represented pictorially or by example.
- Can be clearly represented pictorially.
- Rarely changed in content.

— Do not use:

- Where the alternatives cannot be meaningfully and clearly represented pictorially.
- Where words are clearer than images.
- Where the choices are going to change.

Description. Like radio buttons, *palettes* can also be used to present two or more mutually exclusive alternatives. The choices presented, however, are visually descriptive within themselves, no choice descriptions being needed to identify them. Examples of palettes might be fill-in colors, patterns, or different shades of a color. A palette may also be referred to as *value set* or *well*. A palette is illustrated in Figure 8.55. In addition to being a standard screen control, a palette may also be presented on a pull-down or pop-up menu, included in a toolbar, or be contained in a Palette window.

Purpose. A palette's purpose is to set one of a series of mutually exclusive options presented in a graphic or pictorial form.

Advantages/disadvantages. Palettes are preferable to radio buttons in that they take up less space and allow the viewer to focus on the visual characteristics of the choice itself, instead of having to read the choice text and cross-reference it to a radio button. Some qualities, such as colors, patterns, and shades, are much more easily comprehended when they are actually seen. While a larger number of choices can be presented than with radio buttons, there is still a limit to how many can be practically displayed. Because of their larger size, palettes are also more difficult to organize for scanning efficiency. Palettes also require skill and time to design meaningful and attractive graphical representations.

Proper usage. Palettes are used for setting attributes, properties, or values of mutually exclusive choices where adequate screen space is available. Consider using a palette when the choices have qualities that can be best described by actual illustration. They are useful for data and choices that are discrete and limited in number. They are most useful when the choices' being seen together and compared to

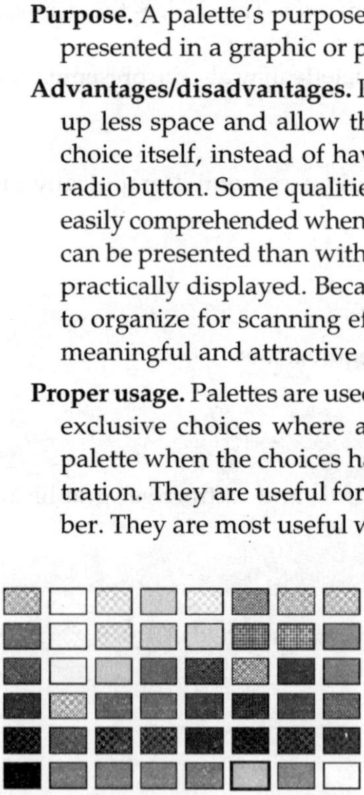

Figure 8.55 Palette.

one another aids identification and selection of the proper alternative. They are also most useful when the alternatives can be meaningfully and clearly represented pictorially or by example. Palettes should rarely change in content.

Palettes should be displayed in the proper manner. If the attributes on a palette must be available at all times, place them on a standard control or fixed palette. If the attributes on the palette are sometimes used frequently and other times used infrequently, place them on a pop-up or tear-off menu. Do not place frequently used palettes on pull-down menus.

Also, from a presentation perspective, do not use a palette if the alternatives cannot be meaningfully and clearly represented pictorially. In addition, do not use one where words are clearer than images, or in situations where the choices are going to change.

Graphical Representations

- Provide meaningful, accurate, and clear illustrations or representations of choices.
- Create images large enough to:
  - — Clearly illustrate the available alternatives.
  - — Permit ease in pointing and selecting.
- Create images of equal size.
- Always test illustrations before implementing them.

Provide meaningful, accurate, and clear illustrations of alternative choices. Create equal size images large enough to illustrate clearly the available alternatives and permit ease in pointing and selecting. Always test illustrations with users before implementing them, to ensure that they will work satisfactorily. While most palettes will not possess textual choice descriptions, under certain circumstances textual descriptions may be needed. For example, a choice might require selection of a style of font. The palette may contain the names of the available styles (such as Roman) with the text displayed as the font style would actually appear.

Size

- Present all available alternatives within the limits imposed by:
  - — The size of the graphical representations.
  - — The screen display's capabilities.

Since palettes will consume less screen space, more choices can be displayed in a given area of a screen than can be displayed when using textual descriptions. Present all available alternatives within the limits imposed by how big the graphical representations must be and the capabilities of the display hardware in creating clear illustrations. Limitations in people's ability to accurately differentiate the kinds of graphical representations being presented must also be considered.

Layout

- Create boxes large enough to:
  — Effectively illustrate the available alternatives.
  — Permit ease in pointing and selecting.
- Create boxes of equal size.
- Position the boxes adjacent to, or butted up against, one another.
- A columnar orientation is the preferred manner.
- If vertical space on the screen is limited, orient the choices horizontally.

Palette boxes must be large enough to illustrate effectively the available alternatives and to maximize ease in selecting. Created boxes should be of equal size and positioned adjacent to, or butted up against one another, since they are mutually exclusive choices. Columns are preferred, but horizontal rows can be used if space constraints exist on the screen.

Organization

- Arrange palettes in expected or normal order.
  — For palettes arrayed top to bottom, begin ordering at the top.
  — For palettes arrayed left to right, begin ordering at the left.
- If an expected or normal order does not exist, arrange choices by frequency of occurrence, sequence of use, importance, or alphabetically (if textual).
- If, under certain conditions, a choice is not available, display it subdued or less brightly than the other choices.

Palettes should be orgánized logically. If the alternatives have an expected order, follow it. Colors, for example, should be ordered from the right or top by their spectral position: red, orange, yellow, green, blue, indigo, and violet. If an expected or normal order does not exist, arrange choices by frequency of occurrence, sequence of use, or importance. Palettes with text may be arranged alphabetically. If, under certain conditions, a choice is not available, display the unavailable choice subdued or less brightly than the available choices.

Captions

- Provide a caption for each palette.
  — On screens containing only one palette, the screen title may serve as the caption.
- Display the caption fully spelled out using mixed-case letters.
- Columnar orientation:
  — The field caption may be positioned left-aligned above the palette.

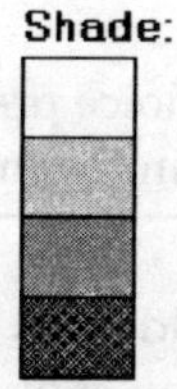

Figure 8.56

— Alternately, the caption may be positioned to the left of the topmost alternative.

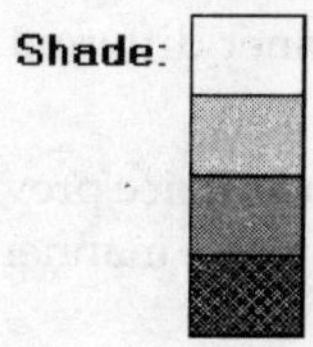

Figure 8.57

- Horizontal orientation:
  — The field caption may be positioned above the palette.

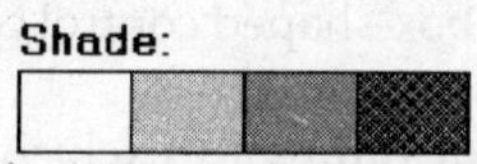

Figure 8.58

— Alternately, the caption may be positioned to the left of the alternatives.

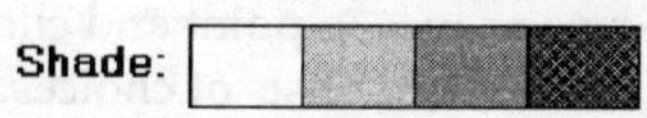

Figure 8.59

Using a *static text* control, provide a caption for each palette. In screens containing only one palette, the screen title may serve as the caption. Display the caption fully spelled out using mixed-case letters, although some abbreviations may be used to achieve the alignment goals to be specified. Captions may be located above or to the left of the palette, as shown above. With a horizontal orientation, the caption may be positioned above the palette or to the left of the alternatives. Positioning on any one screen will be dependent on other caption-control relationships within the screen.

Selection Method and Indication

- Pointing:
  — Highlight the choice in some visually distinctive way when the pointer or cursor is resting on it and the choice is available for selection.
- Activation:
  — When a choice is selected, distinguish it visually from the unselected choices by highlighting it in a manner different from when it is pointed at, or by placing a bold border around it.

- Defaults:
  - — If a palette is displayed with a choice previously selected or a default choice, display the currently active choice in the manner used when it was selected.

Pointing. The selection target should be as large as possible in order to make it easy to move to. Highlight the selection choice in some visually distinctive way when the pointer or cursor is resting on it and the choice is available for selection.

Activation. When a choice is selected, distinguish it visually from the unselected choices by highlighting it in a manner different from when it is pointed at, or by placing a bolder border around it.

Defaults. If a palette is displayed with a choice previously selected or a default choice, display the currently active choice in the manner used when it was selected.

List Boxes

- Description:
  - — A permanently displayed box-shaped control containing a list of attributes or objects from which:
    - A single selection is made (mutually exclusive), or
    - Multiple selections are made (non-mutually-exclusive).
  - — The choice may be text, pictorial representations, or graphics.
  - — Selections are made by using a mouse to point and click.
  - — Capable of being scrolled to view large lists of choices.
  - — No text entry field exists in which to type text.
  - — A list box may be may be associated with a *summary list box* control, which allows the selected choice to be displayed or an item added to the list.
- Purpose:
  - — To display a collection of items containing:
    - Mutually exclusive options.
    - Non-mutually-exclusive options.
- Advantages:
  - — Unlimited number of choices.
  - — Reminds users of available options.
  - — Box always visible.
- Disadvantages:
  - — Consumes screen space.
  - — Often requires an action (scrolling) to see all list choices.
  - — The list content may change, making it hard to find items.
  - — The list may be ordered in an unpredictable way, making it hard to find items.
- Proper usage:
  - — For selecting values or setting attributes.
  - — For choices that are:
    - Mutually exclusive (only one can be selected).
    - Non-mutually-exclusive (one or more may be selected).

— Where screen space is available.
— For data and choices that are:
  - Best represented textually.
  - Not frequently selected.
  - Not well known, easily learned, or remembered.
  - Ordered in an unpredictable fashion.
  - Frequently changed.
  - Large in number.
  - Fixed or variable in list length.
— When screen space or layout considerations make radio buttons or check boxes impractical.

Description. A *list box* is a permanently displayed rectangular box control that contains a list of values or attributes from which single or multiple selections are made. It can also be referred to as a *fixed list box* because it is fixed on the screen. In Java, they are called *lists,* and in HTML, *selection lists/scrolling lists.* The choices are usually text, but they may be pictorial representations or graphics as well. A list box may be scrollable to view large lists, and the user uses a mouse to point and click to make selections. No text entry field exists in which to type text, but a single-selection list box may be associated with a text box where the selected choice is displayed or an item may be added to the list. Examples of single-selection list boxes are illustrated in Figure 8.60.

Purpose. The purpose of a list box is display a collection of items. The choices may be mutually exclusive (single-selection) or not mutually exclusive (multiple-selection).

Advantages/disadvantages. List boxes are always visible, reminding users of the choices available. They permit an unlimited number of options to be displayed. Among their disadvantages are the excessive screen space they consume and the possible necessity for time-consuming scrolling to see all items. Since the list content can change, and items can be ordered in an unpredictable way, it can be hard to find items.

Proper usage. List boxes are used for selecting objects or values or setting attributes, either mutually exclusive or not, where sufficient screen space is available to display 6 to 8 choices. Their best use is for data and choices that are textual; large in number; fixed or variable in list length; not well known, easily learned or

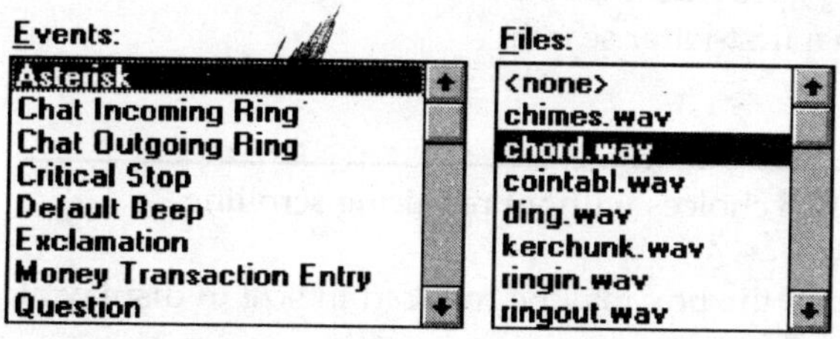

Figure 8.60 List boxes.

remembered; and ordered in an unpredictable fashion. List box items should not have to be selected or changed frequently. List boxes may be used when screen space, list size, and data volatility considerations make use of radio buttons and check boxes impractical. The content of a list box is easier to change than that of radio buttons and check boxes.

List Box General Guidelines

First, general list box guidelines will be presented. Then, specific guidelines for single- and multiple-selection lists will be reviewed.

Selection Descriptions

- Clearly and meaningfully describe the choices available. Spell them out as fully as possible.
  - — Graphical representations must clearly represent the options.
- Present in mixed case, using the sentence style structure.
- Left-align into columns.

Selection descriptions will reflect the selection alternatives available. They should be meaningful, fully spelled out, and follow the sentence style of presentation. Array the descriptions into columns. Meaningful ordering schemes include logical order, frequency of use, sequence of use, and importance. If no such pattern exists, arrange the list alphabetically. Display the list of choices using mixed-case letters.

List Size

- Not actual limit in size.
- Present all available alternatives.
- Require no more than 40 page-downs to search a list.
  - — If more are required, provide a method for using search criteria or scoping the options.

A list being displayed in a fixed list box has no actual size limit. All available alternatives should be capable of being displayed. Searching a very long list, however, can be very time-consuming. A list should not require more than 40 page-downs to completely search it. If more are necessary, provide a method for using search criteria or scoping the options, perhaps through a first-letter search.

Box Size

- Must be long enough to display 6 to 8 choices without requiring scrolling.
  - — Exceptions:
    - If screen space constraints exist, the box may be reduced in size to display at least three items.
    - If it is the major control within a window, the box may be larger.

— If more items are available than are visible in the box, provide vertical scrolling to display all items.

- Must be wide enough to display the longest possible choice.

Figure 8.61

— When box cannot be made wide enough to display the longest entry:
  - Make it wide enough to permit entries to be distinguishable, or,
  - Break the long entries with an ellipsis (...) in the middle, or,
  - Provide horizontal scrolling.

The exact size of a fixed list box will depend on its function and screen space constraints. Generally, boxes should be restricted to displaying no more than eight choices at one time. Slightly larger boxes that eliminate the need for scrolling, however, are preferable to list boxes that require a little scrolling. If screen space constraints exist, the box may be reduced in size to display at least three items. If scrolling is necessary, include a scroll bar on the right side of the box.

The list box should be wide enough to display fully all item wording. When a box cannot be made wide enough to display the longest entry, make it wide enough to permit entries to be distinguishable, or, break the long entries with an ellipsis in the middle. If breaking long entries, preserve the important characteristics needed to distinguish them. When shortening an item's name in this way, include a *ToolTip* that displays the item's full name.

As a last resort, provide horizontal scrolling and a scroll bar at the bottom of the list box. Many people dislike horizontal scrolling, however.

Organization

- Order in a logical and meaningful way to permit easy browsing.
  — Consider using separate controls to enable the user to change the sort order or filter items displayed in the list.
- If a particular choice is not available in the current context, omit it from the list.
  — Exception: If it is important that the existence and unavailability of a particular list item be communicated, display the choice dimmed or grayed out instead of deleting it.

Choices should be organized logically to permit easy browsing. If the alternatives have an expected order, follow it. Other ordering schemes such as frequency of use, sequence of use, or importance may also be considered. When no obvious scheme exists, use alphabetic order. You can provide separate controls to enable the user to change the sort order or filter items displayed in the list.

If a particular choice is not available in the current context, it should be omitted from the list. If it is important that the existence and unavailability of a list item be communicated, however, display the choice dimmed or grayed out instead of deleting it.

Layout and Separation

- Enclose the choices in a box with a solid border.
  — The border should be the same color as the choice descriptions.
- Leave one blank character position between the choice descriptions and the left border.
- Leave one blank character position between the longest choice description in the list and the right border, if possible.

Enclose the box in a solid border in the color of the choice descriptions. To provide adequate legibility, leave one space between the choice descriptions and the left border, and one space between the longest choice description and the right border.

Captions

- Use mixed-case letters.
- The preferred position of the control caption is above the upper-left corner of the list box.

Figure 8.62

- Alternately, the caption may be located to the left of the topmost choice description.

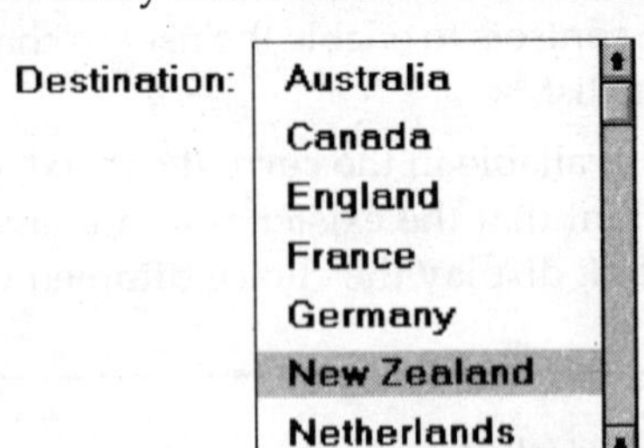

Figure 8.63

- Be consistent in caption style and orientation within a screen, and related screens.

To identify the list box, a field caption in mixed-case letters, with each significant word capitalized is necessary. A list box does not have a caption, so create one using a *static text* control. Place this caption either above the upper-left corner of the box or to the left of the first choice description. The caption style chosen will again be dependent upon caption-control relationships in other controls included within the screen. It should be consistently oriented with the other control captions.

Disabling

- When a list box is disabled, display its caption and show its entries as grayed out or dimmed.

Display a list box's caption and entries as dimmed or grayed when the list box is entirely disabled.

Selection Method and Indication

- Pointing:
  - — Highlight the selection choice in some visually distinctive way when the pointer or cursor is resting on it and the choice is available for selection.
- Selection:
  - — Use a reverse video or reverse color bar to surround the choice description when it is selected.
  - — The cursor should be as wide as the box itself.

Figure 8.64

  - — Mark the selected choice in a distinguishing way.
- Activation:
  - — Require the pressing of a command button when an item, or items, is selected.

Pointing. Highlight the selection choice in some visually distinctive way when the pointer or cursor is resting on it and the choice is available for selection. One method used for this is to place a bold border around the choice.

Selection. Indicate the selected choice through use of a reverse video or reverse color bar, as wide as the box itself. Visually differentiate multiple-choice (nonexclusive) from single-choice (mutually exclusive) fixed list boxes, as described in the following sections.

Activation. Require the pressing of a command button when an item, or items, is selected. Double-clicking is difficult for many people. Always provide for a single click followed by a button press.

Single-Selection List Boxes

- Purpose:
  — To permit selection of only one item from a large listing.
- Design guidelines:
  — Related text box
  - If presented with an associated text box control:
    — Position the list box below and as close as possible to the text box.
    — The list box caption should be worded similarly to the text box caption.

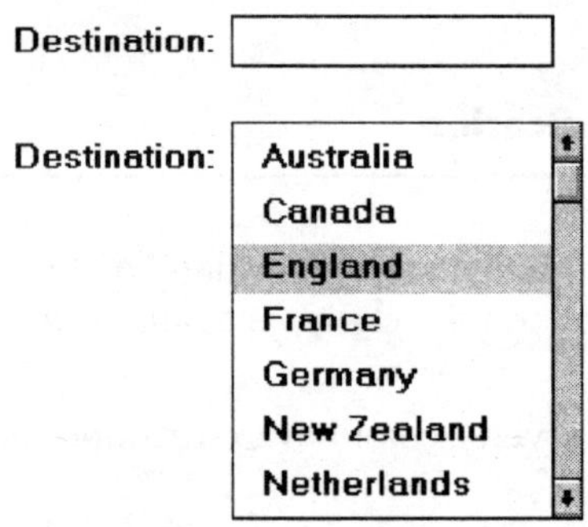

Figure 8.65

— If the related text box and the list box are very close in proximity, the caption may be omitted from the list box.

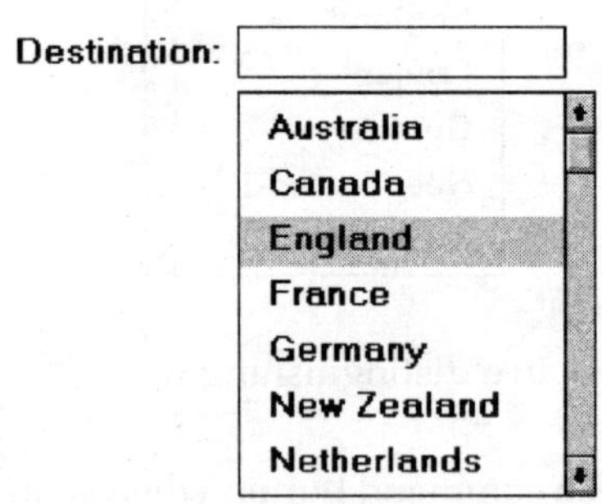

Figure 8.66

— Use the same background color for the text box as is used in the list box.

— Defaults:
  - When the list box is first displayed:
    — Present the currently active choice highlighted or marked with a circle or diamond to the left of the entry.
    — If a choice has not been previously selected, provide a default choice and display it in the same manner that is used in selecting it.

— If the list represents mixed values for a multiple selection, do not highlight an entry.
— Other:
• Follow other relevant list box guidelines.

Purpose. A *single-selection* list box is used for selecting only one item in a list. It provides a mutually exclusive operation similar to a group of radio or option buttons. This kind of list box, however, can handle a large number of items more efficiently.

Related text box. If the list box is associated with a text field, position the list box below and as close as possible to the related text box. If this cannot be accomplished, position the text box to the left. Captions of related text boxes and list boxes must be worded similarly. If, however, the text box and the list box are located in close physical proximity, the caption may be omitted from the list box. Visually relate a list box to a text box by using the same background color for both boxes.

For single-selection fixed list boxes, indicate an active choice by highlighting it or marking it with a circle or diamond to the left of the choice description. If the list represents mixed values for a multiple selection, do not highlight any entry.

Extended and Multiple-Selection List Boxes

- Purpose:
  — To permit selection of more than one item in a long listing.
  • Extended list box: Optimized for individual item or range selection.
  • Multiple-selection list box: Optimized for independent item selection.
- Design guidelines:
  — Selection indication:
  • Mark the selected choice with an X or check mark to the left of the entry.

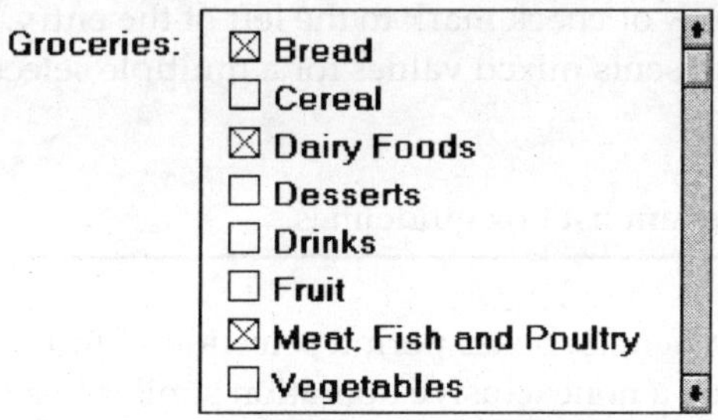

Figure 8.67

• Consider providing a *summary list box*.
  — Position it to the right of the list box.
  — Use the same colors for the summary list box as are used in the list box.

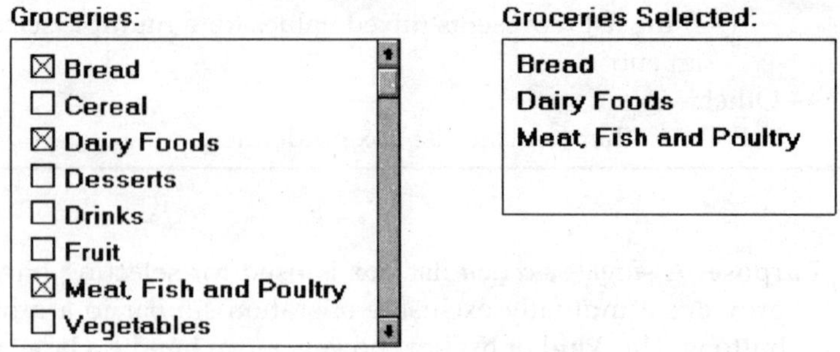

Figure 8.68

— Provide command buttons to *Add* (one item) or *Add All* (items) to the summary list box, and *Remove* (one item) or *Remove All* (items) from the summary list box.

- Consider providing a display-only text control indicating how many choices have been selected.
  — Position it justified upper-right above the list box.

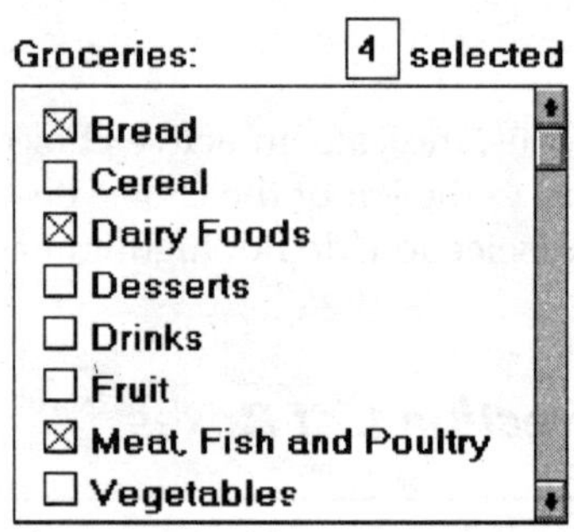

Figure 8.69

— Select All and Deselect All buttons
- Provide command buttons to accomplish fast *Select All* and *Deselect All* actions, when these actions must be frequently or quickly performed.

— Defaults:
- When the list box is first displayed:
  — Display the currently active choices highlighted.
  — Mark with an X or check mark to the left of the entry.
  — If the list represents mixed values for a multiple selection, do not highlight an entry.

— Other:
- Follow other relevant list box guidelines.

Purpose. *Multiple-selection* list boxes permit selection of multiple items from a long listing. They provide a nonexclusive operation similar to a group of check boxes. This kind of list box, however, can handle a large number of items more efficiently. *Extended list* boxes are optimized for individual item or range selection. *Multiple-selection* list boxes are optimized for independent item selection.

Selection indication. For choice selections, mark them with an X or check mark to the left of the entry. Also consider providing a *summary list* box, another list box containing a compilation of the active selections from the multiple-selection list box. This will permit quick scanning and comparison of these active choices and greatly reduce the need for scrolling if the selectable list is lengthy. The summary list box can be made scrollable, if necessary. Position the summary list adjacent to, and to the right of, the multiple-selection list box. Use the same colors for the summary list box and the multiple-selection list box. Include command buttons to *Add* (one item) or *Add All* (items) to the summary list box, and *Remove* (one item) or *Remove All* (items) from the summary list box.

Also consider providing a *display-only text box* control indicating how many choices have been selected in the multiple-selection list box. This text box can be associated with either the multiple-selection or summary list box. It is useful in situations where the multiple selections may be numerous and all the choices cannot be seen without scrolling. It is also useful when the user must know exactly how many choices have been selected. Position this text box justified upper-right above the list box.

Select All and Deselect buttons. Provide command buttons to accomplish fast "select all" and "deselect" actions, when these actions must be frequently or quickly performed.

Defaults. When the list box is first displayed, the active selection will depend on previous activities. If a choice has been previously selected, display the currently active choice in the same manner used when it was selected. If the list represents mixed values for a multiple selection, do not highlight any list entries.

List View Controls

- Description:
  - — A special extended-selection list box that displays a collection of items, consisting of an icon and a label.
  - — The contents can be displayed in four different views:
    - Large Icon: Items appear as a full-sized icon with a label below.
    - Small Icon: Items appear as a small icon with label to the right.
    - List: Items appear as a small icon with label to the right.
      - — Arrayed in a columnar, sorted layout.
    - Report: Items appear as a line in a multicolumn format.
      - — Leftmost column includes icon and its label.
      - — Subsequent columns include application-specific information.
- Purpose and usage:
  - — Where the representation of objects as icons is appropriate.
  - — To represent items with multiple columns of information.

Description. A *list view* control is a special extended-selection list box that displays a collection of items, each consisting of an icon and a label. List view controls can display content in four different views, *large icon*, *small icon*, *list*, and *report*. The control also supports options for aligning, selecting, and sorting icons, and for editing icon labels.

Purpose and usage. Use list views when the representation of objects as icons is appropriate, or to represent items with multiple columns of information.

Drop-down/Pop-up List Boxes

- Description
  - — A single rectangular control that shows one item with a small button to the right side.
    - • The button provides a visual cue that an associated selection box is available but hidden.
  - — When the button is selected, a larger associated box appears, containing a list of choices from which one may be selected.
  - — Selections are made by using the mouse to point and click.
  - — Text may not be typed into the control.
- Purpose:
  - — To select one item from a large list of mutually exclusive options when screen space is limited.
- Advantages:
  - — Unlimited number of choices.
  - — Reminds users of available options.
  - — Conserves screen space.
- Disadvantages:
  - — Requires an extra action to display the list of choices.
  - — When displayed, all choices may not always be visible, requiring scrolling.
  - — The list may be ordered in an unpredictable way, making it hard to find items.
- Proper usage:
  - — For selecting values or setting attributes.
  - — For choices that are mutually exclusive (only one can be selected).
  - — Where screen space is limited.
  - — For data and choices that are:
    - • Best represented textually.
    - • Infrequently selected.
    - • Not well known, easily learned, or remembered.
    - • Ordered in a unpredictable fashion.
    - • Large in number.
    - • Variable or fixed in list length.
  - — Use drop-down/pop-up lists when:
    - • Screen space or layout considerations make radio buttons or single-selection list boxes impractical.
    - • The first, or displayed, item will be selected most of the time.
  - — Do not use a drop-down list if it important that all options be seen together.

Description. A *drop-down/pop-up list box* is a single rectangular field with a small button to the side and an associated hidden list of options. In Java, they are called *choice/pop-up lists*, in HTML, *selection lists/pop-up menus*. The button provides a visual cue to the user that an associated selection box of choices is hidden but available on demand. When requested, a larger associated rectangular box appears containing a scrollable list of choices from which one is selected. Selections are made by using the mouse to point and click. No text field exists in which to type text.

Fields of this nature go by many different names. They are called *drop-down lists* because they appear to drop down from the single-selection field. Microsoft Windows calls them *drop-down list boxes*. Other common names are *pull-down lists, option menus,* and simply *list boxes*. Other list boxes of this type seem to *pop-up* on the screen, either next to or over the selection field. Even a Microsoft Windows "drop-down" will "pop-up" if it is opened near the bottom of the screen. In this discussion, these variously named controls will be given the generic name of *drop-down/pop-up list boxes*. A drop-down list is illustrated in Figures 8.70 and 8.71. Figure 8.72 shows a pop-up list.

Purpose. The purpose of these list boxes is to permit selection from a large set of mutually exclusive choices when screen space is scarce.

Figure 8.70 Drop-down list boxes. There are four unopened boxes, Country, Language, Keyboard Layout, and Measurement.

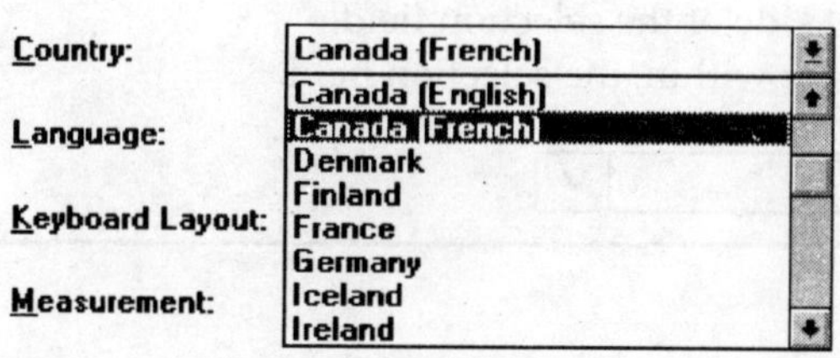

Figure 8.71 Drop-down list box opened for Country.

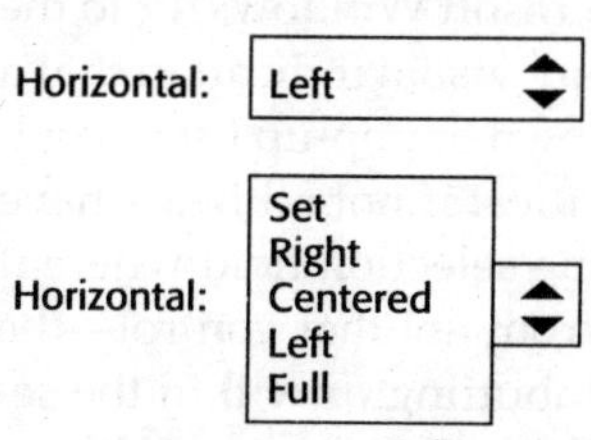

Figure 8.72 Pop-up list box, closed and opened.

Advantages/disadvantages. The most useful feature of drop-down/pop-up list boxes is that they conserve screen space. They may be retrieved on demand, reminding users of the choices available. They permit an unlimited number of options to be displayed.

A significant disadvantage of these lists is that they necessitate an extra step to display the available options. Scrolling may also be necessary to see all items. Since items can be ordered in an unpredictable way, they can be hard to find occasionally. Generally, drop-down/pop-up list boxes require more work on the part of the user than many other screen-based controls because of the activation step and the possible need for scrolling. A study comparing drop-down/pop-up lists to other similar controls will be described later in this chapter.

Proper usage. Drop-down/pop-up list boxes are used much like regular list boxes, except that the choices are not visible at all times. They are used for selecting values or setting attributes when sufficient screen space is not available to display the choices permanently. Their best use is for data and choices that are textual; large in number; fixed or variable in list length; not well known, easily learned or remembered; and ordered in an unpredictable fashion. Items should not have to be selected frequently.

Drop-down/ pop-up lists are most useful when screen space or layout considerations make radio buttons or single-selection list boxes impractical. It is also desirable that most users select the first, or displayed, item in the listing so the box does not have to be opened. Never use a drop-down/pop-up list if it is important that all options be seen together at one time.

Prompt Button

- Provide a visual cue that a box is hidden by including a downward pointing arrow, or other meaningful image, to the right side of the selection field.
  - — Position the button directly against, or within, the selection field.

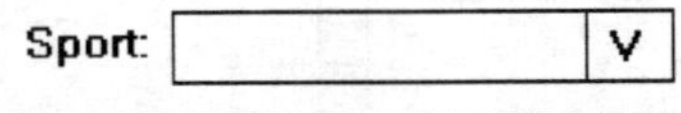

Figure 8.73

Most systems indicate the presence of a drop-down or pop-up list by associating a meaningful icon with the applicable field. This icon can be seen positioned to the left of the selection field, within the selection field as is done by Microsoft Windows, or to the right of the selection field. Other platforms do not provide any visual indication that a hidden list is available. An indication to the user that a drop-down or pop-up list is available should be indicated on the screen. This is especially critical if not all fields have associated hidden lists. The best location is to the right of the selection field where it is out of the way until needed. To visually differentiate it from another control—the drop-down/pop-up combination box—position the button abutting or within the selection field. (A drop-down/pop-up combination box button will be separated by a space.) The indicator should be large enough to provide a good pointing target.

Selection Descriptions

- Clearly and meaningfully describe the choices available. Spell them out as fully as possible.
  — Graphical representations must clearly represent the options.
  — Left-align them in columns.
  — Display the descriptions using mixed-case letters.

Selection descriptions will reflect what choices exist in the control. They should be meaningful, fully spelled out, and organized in columns. Display the list of choices using mixed-case letters. Box descriptions should be displayed in the same color as the selection field text. If a particular choice is not available in the current context, it should be omitted from the list.

List Size

- Not limited in size.
- Present all available alternatives.

A list being displayed in a drop-down/pop-up list box has no size limit. All available alternatives should be capable of being displayed. It would seem practical that for large scrollable lists, the same rules as presented for list boxes should also be applied. Restrict page-downs to no more than 40 and provide a method to scope actions.

Box Size

- Long enough to display 6 to 8 choices without scrolling.
  — If more than eight choices are available, provide vertical scrolling to display all items.
- Wide enough to display the longest possible choice.
- When a box cannot be made wide enough to display the longest entry:
  — Make it wide enough to permit entries to be distinguishable, or,
  — Break long entries with ellipses (...) in the middle, or,
  — Provide horizontal scrolling.

Drop-down/pop-up list boxes should be restricted to eight or fewer choices. If more must be displayed, permit scrolling and include a scroll bar on the right side of the box. The list box should be wide enough to fully display all selection choice wording. When a box cannot be made wide enough to display the longest entry, make it wide enough to permit entries to be distinguishable, or break the long entries, inserting an ellipsis in the middle. If breaking entries, preserve the important characteristics needed to distinguish them. When shortening an item's name in this way, include a *ToolTip* that displays the item's full name. As a last resort, provide horizontal scrolling and a scroll bar at the bottom of the list box. Avoid horizontal scrolling whenever possible, however.

Organization

- Order in a logical and meaningful way to permit easy browsing.
- If a particular choice is not available in the current context, omit it from the list.
  — Exception: If it is important that the existence and unavailability of a particular list item be communicated, display the choice dimmed or grayed out instead of deleting it.

Selection choices should be organized logically. If the alternatives have an expected order, follow it. Other ordering schemes such as frequency of use, sequence of use, or importance, may also be considered. Always begin ordering at the top or left. If, under certain conditions, a choice is not available, display the unavailable choice subdued or less brightly than the available choices.

Layout and Separation

- Enclose the choices in a box composed of a solid line border.
  — The border should be the same color as the choice descriptions.
  — Leave one blank character position between the choices and the left border.
  — Leave one blank character position between the longest choice description in the list and the right border, if possible.

To provide adequate legibility, leave one space between the choice descriptions and the left border, and one space between the longest choice description and the right border. Extending the listing box to the right edge of the prompt button allows the user to move easily from the button to the list. To set off the box from the screen body background, use the same color background for the box as is used in the entry field. Also incorporate a solid line border around the box in the same color as the choice descriptions.

Captions

- Display using mixed-case letters.
- Position the caption to the left of the box.
  — Alternately, it may be positioned left-justified above the box.

To identify the drop-down/pop-up list box, a field caption in mixed-case letters, with each significant word capitalized is necessary. Use a *static text* control to create the caption. The recommended position is to the box's left. Select a positioning consistent with other controls presented on the window.

Defaults

- When the drop-down/pop-up listing is first presented, display the currently set value.
- If a choice has not been previously selected, provide a default choice.

When the drop-down/pop-up listing is first presented, display the currently set value. If a choice has not been previously selected, provide a default choice. The list must be opened to change the choice.

Disabling

- When a drop-down/pop-up list box is disabled, display its caption and entries as disabled or dimmed.

Display a drop-down/pop-up list box's caption and entries as dimmed or grayed out when the list box is entirely disabled.

Selection Method and Indication

- Pointing:
  — Highlight the selection choice in some visually distinctive way when the pointer or cursor is resting on it and the choice is available for selection.
- Activation:
  — Close the drop-down/pop-up list box when an item is selected.

Highlight the selection choice in some visually distinctive way when the pointer or cursor is resting on it and the choice is available for selection. Close the listing when an item is selected.

Combination Entry/Selection Controls

It is possible for a control to possess the characteristics of both a text field and a selection field. In this type of control, information may either be keyed into the field or selected and placed within it. The types of combination entry/selection fields are spin boxes, attached combination boxes, and drop-down/pop-up combination boxes.

Spin Boxes

- Description:
  — A single-line field followed by two small, vertically arranged buttons.
    - The top button has an arrow pointing up.
    - The bottom button has an arrow pointing down.
  — Selection/entry is made by:
    - Using the mouse to point at one of the directional buttons and clicking. Items will change by one unit or step with each click.
    - Keying a value directly into the field itself.

- Purpose:
  - — To make a selection by either scrolling through a small set of meaningful predefined choices or typing text.
- Advantages:
  - — Consumes little screen space.
  - — Flexible, permitting selection or typed entry.
- Disadvantages:
  - — Difficult to compare choices.
  - — Can be awkward to operate.
  - — Useful only for certain kinds of data.
- Proper usage:
  - — For setting attributes, properties, or values.
  - — For mutually exclusive choices (only one can be selected).
  - — When the task requires the option of either key entry or selection from a list.
  - — When the user prefers the option of either key entry or selection from a list.
  - — Where screen space is limited.
  - — Most useful for data and choices that are:
    - Discrete.
    - Infrequently selected.
    - Well known, easily learned or remembered, and meaningful.
    - Ordered in a predictable, customary, or consecutive fashion.
    - Infrequently changed.
    - Small in number.
    - Fixed or variable in list length.

Description. A *spin box,* also called a *spin button,* is a single-line field followed by two small, vertically arranged buttons inscribed with up and down arrows. These buttons may also be referred to as *up-down* buttons. Selection of an item is accomplished using the mouse to point at one of the buttons and clicking. Items in a listing in the display field will change by one unit or step in the direction selected with each click. The list is searched as the ring or circle of alternatives "spins" by. Keying a value directly into the field itself may also complete a spin box. A spin box is illustrated in Figure 8.74.

Advantages/disadvantages. Spin boxes are flexible, permitting either selection or typed entry. They also consume little screen space. On the other hand, spin boxes are useful only for certain kinds of data, that which is predictable or consecutive. Because only one item is displayed at a time, it is difficult to compare choices. Spin

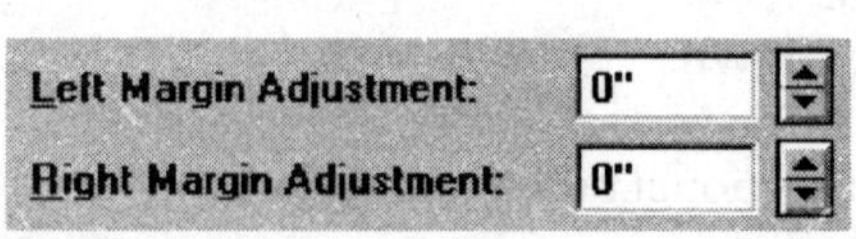

Figure 8.74 Spin boxes.

boxes may also be awkward to operate, often requiring several back and forth iterations to bring the desired value into view.

Proper usage. Spin boxes are used for setting attributes, properties, or values that are mutually exclusive. They are useful when the task requires, or the user prefers, the option of either key entry or selection from a list. Spin boxes are useful for data and choices that are discrete and small in number. The choices themselves should be well known, easily learned or remembered, and meaningful. Choices should be ordered in a predictable, customary, or consecutive fashion so people can anticipate the next not-yet-visible choice. Items in spin boxes should not require frequent selection, and the array of items listed should be stable.

List Size

- Keep the list of items relatively short.
- To reduce the size of potentially long lists, break the listing into subcomponents, if possible.

Since the list must be manipulated to display its contents, it should be as short as feasible. To reduce the size of potentially long lists, break the listing into subcomponents whenever possible. A date, for example, may be broken into its components of month, day, and year.

List Organization

- Order the list in the customary, consecutive, or expected order of the information contained within it.
  — Ensure that the user can always anticipate the next (not-yet-visible) choice.
- When first displayed, present a default choice in the box.

Spin boxes are most effective when the values they contain have a customary or consecutive order that is predictable. Information can be letters or numbers. Examples are days of the week, months of the year, shoe sizes, and so on. The user must always be able to anticipate the next choice before it is displayed. The control should always contain a default value when first displayed.

Other Spin Box Guidelines

- Box size:
  — The spin box should be wide enough to display the longest entry or choice.
- Caption:
  — Display it using mixed-case letters.
  — Position the caption to the left of the box.
    - Alternately, it may be positioned left-justified above the box.

- Entry and selection methods:
  - — Permit completion by:
    - • Typing directly into the box.
    - • Scrolling and selecting with a mouse.
    - • Scrolling and selecting with the up/down arrow keys.
  - — For alphabetical values:
    - • Move down the order using the down arrow.
    - • Move up the order using the up arrow.
  - • For numeric values or magnitudes:
    - • Show a larger value using the up arrow.
    - • Show a smaller value using the down arrow.

Box size. Fully display all alternatives within the spin box. The box should be wide enough to display the longest entry or choice.

Caption. To identify the spin box, use a static text field to provide a field caption in mixed-case letters, with each significant word capitalized. The recommended position is to the box's left. Select a positioning consistent with other controls presented on the window.

Entry and selection. Spin box completion should be possible by typing directly into the field or by scrolling and selecting options with a mouse or keyboard keys. When spinning alphabetical values, move down the order using the down arrow and up the order using the up arrow. For numeric values or magnitudes, display a larger value using the up arrow and a smaller value using the down arrow.

Combo Boxes

- Description:
  - — A single rectangular text box entry field, beneath which is a larger rectangular list box (resembling a drop-down list box) displaying a list of options.
  - — The text box permits a choice to be keyed within it.
  - — The larger box contains a list of mutually exclusive choices from which one may be selected for placement in the entry field.
    - • Selections are made by using a mouse to point and click.
  - — As text is typed into the text box, the list scrolls to the nearest match.
  - — When an item in the list box is selected, it is placed into the text box, replacing the existing content.
  - — Information keyed may not necessarily have to match the list items.
- Purpose:
  - — To allow either typed entry in a text box or selection from a list of options in a permanently displayed list box attached to the text box.
- Advantages:
  - — Unlimited number of entries and choices.
  - — Reminds users of available options.
  - — Flexible, permitting selection or typed entry.

— Entries not necessarily restricted to items selectable from list box.
— List box always visible.

- Disadvantages:
  — Consumes some screen space.
  — All list box choices not always visible, requiring scrolling.
  — Users may have difficulty recalling sufficient information to type entry, making text box unusable.
  — The list may be ordered in an unpredictable way, making it hard to find items.
- Proper usage:
  — For entering or selecting objects or values or setting attributes.
  — For information that is mutually exclusive (only one can be entered or selected).
  — When users may find it practical to, or prefer to, type information rather than selecting it from a list.
  — When users can recall and type information faster than selecting it from a list.
  — When it is useful to provide the users a reminder of the choices available.
  — Where data must be entered that is not contained in the selection list.
  — Where screen space is available.
  — For data and choices that are:
    - Best represented textually.
    - Somewhat familiar or known.
    - Ordered in an unpredictable fashion.
    - Frequently changed.
    - Large in number.
    - Variable or fixed in list length.

Description. A *combo box*, also known as an *attached combination box*, is a single rectangular entry field, beneath which is a larger rectangular box (resembling a drop-down list box) displaying a list of options. In Java combo boxes are called *editable choice pop-up lists*. The entry field permits a choice to be keyed within it, while the larger box contains a list of mutually exclusive choices, from which one may be selected for placement in the entry field. A combo box combines the capabilities of both a text box and a list box. It visually resembles a drop-down list box or drop-down combo box (to be described). The text box and its associated list box have a dependent relationship. As text is typed into the text box, the list scrolls to the nearest match. Also, when an item in the list box is selected, that item is placed within the text box, replacing the existing content. When typing into the field, the information keyed does not have to match the list items. Combo boxes are illustrated in Figure 8.75.

Advantages/disadvantages. Combo boxes are flexible, permitting selection or typed entry. Alternatives are always visible, or retrievable, reminding people of the available options. An unlimited variety of entries and choices are possible. Entries are not necessarily restricted to items selectable from a box.

Combo boxes do consume quite a bit of screen space. Because all box choices may not be visible, some scrolling may be required. It is always possible that people may have difficulty recalling sufficient information to type, making the text

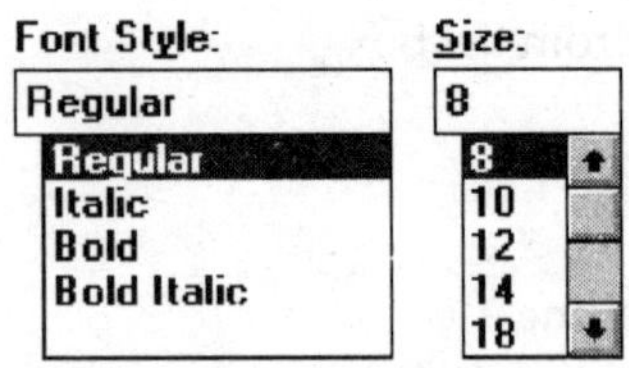

Figure 8.75 Combo boxes.

box unusable. The list may also be ordered in an unpredictable way, making it hard to find items. Additional work is required of the user if selection scrolling must be performed.

Proper usage. Combo boxes are useful for entering or selecting objects or values or setting attributes that are mutually exclusive. They are most valuable when users may find it practical to, or prefer to, type information rather than selecting it from a list, but where reminders of alternatives available must occasionally be provided. They are also useful when the listings are dynamic and changeable, permitting the user to key items not contained on the list in the box. They do require that screen space be available to display them, but they eliminate the extra steps involved in retrieving drop-down lists.

Combo boxes are useful for textual data and choices that are frequently changed and somewhat familiar or known, fostering keyed entry. The lists may be long, variable, and ordered in an unpredictable fashion.

Combo Box Guidelines

For the text box entry field, see "Text Box/Single Line" guidelines. For the list box, see "Drop-down/Pop-up List Box" guidelines.

Drop-down/Pop-up Combo Boxes

- Description:
  - — A single rectangular text box with a small button to the side and an associated hidden list of options.
    - The button provides a visual cue that an associated selection box is available but hidden.
  - — When requested, a larger associated rectangular box appears, containing a scrollable list of choices from which one is selected.
  - — Selections are made by using the mouse to point and click.
  - — Information may also be keyed into the field.
  - — As text is typed into the text box, the list scrolls to the nearest match.
  - — When an item in the list box is selected, it is placed into the text box, replacing the existing content.
  - — The information keyed does not necessarily have to match list items.
  - — Combines the capabilities of both a text box and a drop-down/pop-up list box.

- Purpose:
  - — To allow either typed entry or selection from a list of options in a list box that may be closed and retrieved as needed.
- Advantages:
  - — Unlimited number of entries and choices.
  - — Reminds users of available options.
  - — Flexible, permitting selection or typed entry.
  - — Entries not restricted to items selectable from list box.
  - — Conserves screen space.
- Disadvantages:
  - — Requires an extra step to display the list of choices.
  - — When displayed, all box choices may not always be visible, requiring scrolling.
  - — User may have difficulty in recalling what to type.
  - — The list content may change, making it hard to find items.
  - — The list may be ordered in an unpredictable way, making it hard to find items.
- Proper usage:
  - — For entering or selecting objects or values or setting attributes.
  - — For information that is mutually exclusive (only one can be entered or selected).
  - — When users may find it practical to, or prefer to, type information rather than selecting it from a list.
  - — When users can recall and type information faster than selecting from a list.
  - — When it is useful to provide the users with an occasional reminder of the choices available.
  - — Where data must be entered that is not contained in the selection list.
  - — Where screen space is limited.
  - — For data and choices that are:
    - Best represented textually.
    - Somewhat familiar or known.
    - Ordered in an unpredictable fashion.
    - Frequently changed.
    - Large in number.
    - Variable or fixed in list length.

Description. A *drop-down/pop-up combo box* is a single rectangular field with a small button to the side and an associated hidden list of options. The button provides a visual cue to the user that an associated selection box of choices is available but hidden. When requested, a larger associated rectangular box appears, containing a scrollable list of choices from which one can be selected. One makes selections by using the mouse to point and click. The text box and its associated list box have a dependent relationship. As text is typed into the text box, the list scrolls to the nearest match. Also, when an item in the list box is selected, that item is placed within the text box, replacing the existing content. It closely resembles a drop-down/pop-up list box.

Information, however, may also be keyed into the field. The information keyed does not necessarily have to match items in the list. A drop-down/pop-up

Figure 8.76 Windows 3.1 Drop-down combo box, closed.

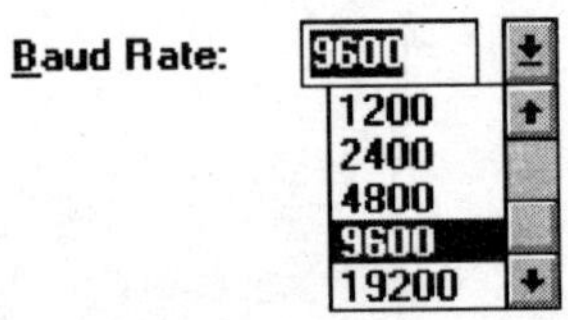

Figure 8.77 Windows 3.1 Drop-down combo box, opened.

combination box, therefore, combines the capabilities of both a text box and a selection field. A drop-down combo box is illustrated in Figures 8.76 and 8.77.

Advantages/disadvantages. Drop-down/pop-up combo boxes are flexible, permitting selection or typed entry. They conserve screen space, but alternatives are always retrievable, reminding people of the available options. An unlimited variety of entries and choices are possible. Entries are not restricted to items selectable from a box.

In terms of disadvantages, they necessitate an extra step to display the available options. Scrolling may also be necessary to see all items. Since the list content can change, and items can be ordered in an unpredictable way, it can be hard to find items. It is always possible also that people may have difficulty recalling sufficient information to type, making the entry field unusable. Generally drop-down/pop-up combination boxes require more work on the part of the user than many other screen-based controls.

Proper usage. Drop-down/pop-up combo boxes are useful for entering or selecting objects or values or setting attributes that are mutually exclusive. They are most valuable when users may find it practical to, or prefer to, type information rather than selecting from a list but where reminders of alternatives available must occasionally be provided. The box may only be retrieved as needed, thereby conserving screen space. They are also useful when the listings are dynamic and changeable, permitting the user to key items not contained on the list in the box.

Drop-down/pop-up combo boxes are useful for textual data and choices that are frequently changed and somewhat familiar or known, fostering keyed entry. The list may be long, variable, and ordered in an unpredictable fashion.

Prompt Button

- Provide a visual cue that a list box is hidden by including a downward-pointing arrow to the right of the text box.
- Separate the button from the text box by a small space.

Figure 8.78

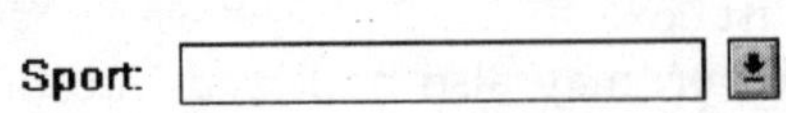

Provide a visual cue that a list box is hidden by including a downward-pointing arrow to the right of the entry field. Unfortunately, Microsoft Windows has provided drop-down list boxes and combo boxes that are visually almost identical. The only way to differentiate the two types is to click and see whether a box can be typed into. This is extremely poor design. Each unique control should be identifiable by the way it looks so trial and error behavior can be avoided. Microsoft, in Windows 3.1, did provide this distinction. The prompt button was slightly separated from the text box, as shown in Figures 8.76 and 8.77. Ideally, then, position the prompt button separated by a space from the associated text box.

Other Guidelines

For the text box entry field, see the "Text Box/Single Line" guidelines. For the box and selection components, see the "Drop-down/Pop-up List Box" guidelines.

Other Operable Controls

Other more specialized operable controls also exist. Among them are sliders, tabs, date-pickers, and scroll bars.

Slider

- Description:
  - — A scale exhibiting degrees of a quality on a continuum.
  - — Includes the following:
    - A shaft or bar.
    - A range of values with appropriate labels.
    - An arm indicating relative setting through its location on the shaft.
    - Optionally, a pair of buttons to permit incremental movement of the slider arm.
    - Optionally, a text box for typing or displaying an exact value.
    - Optionally, a detent position for special values.
  - — May be oriented vertically or horizontally.
  - — Selected by using the mouse to:
    - Drag a slider across the scale until the desired value is reached.
    - Point at the buttons at one end of the scale and clicking to change the value.
    - Keying a value in the associated text box.
- Purpose:
  - — To make a setting when a continuous qualitative adjustment is acceptable, it is useful to see the current value relative to the range of possible values.
- Advantages:
  - — Spatial representation of relative setting.
  - — Visually distinctive.

- Disadvantages:
  - — Not as precise as an alphanumeric indication.
  - — Consumes screen space.
  - — Usually more complex than other controls.
- Proper usage:
  - — To set an attribute.
  - — For mutually exclusive choices.
  - — When an object has a limited range of possible settings.
  - — When the range of values is continuous.
  - — When graduations are relatively fine.
  - — When the choices can increase or decrease in some well-known, predictable, and easily understood way.
  - — When a spatial representation enhances comprehension and interpretation.
  - — When using a slider provides sufficient accuracy.

Description. A *slider* is a scale that exhibits the amount or degree of a quantity or quality on a continuum (see Figure 8.79). It is sometimes called a track bar control. A slider incorporates the range of possible values and includes a shaft or bar representing the range, the values themselves with appropriate labels, and a visual indication of the relative setting through the location of a sliding arm. Optionally, sliders also may include a pair of buttons to permit incremental movement of the slider arm, an entry/display text box for typing and displaying an exact value, and a detent position for special values. A slider may be oriented vertically or horizontally.

Slider values can be set by using the mouse to drag a slider across the scale until the desired value is reached. A visual indication of the relative setting is seen as the setting movement is made. In addition, some sliders may also be set by pointing at slider buttons located at one end of the scale and incrementally moving the arm through button clicks. Finally, keying a value in an associated text box may also set some sliders.

A slider is used to make a setting when a continuous qualitative adjustment is acceptable, and it is advantageous to see the current value relative to all possible values.

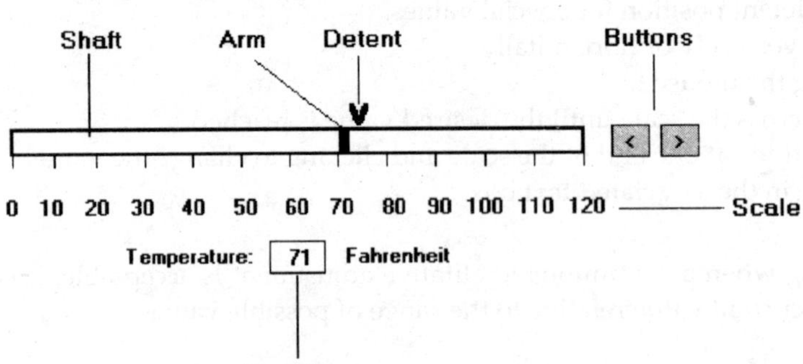

Figure 8.79 Slider.

Advantages/disadvantages. A slider displays a spatial representation of a relative setting, providing an excellent indication of where a value exists within a range of values. They are also visually distinctive and very recognizable. Sliders, however, are not as precise as an alphanumeric indication, unless a display field is provided. They also consume more screen space than other kinds of fields, and they can be more complex to operate.

Proper usage. Sliders are used to set an attribute when a limited range of continuous, relatively fine, possible settings exist. The choices must increase or decrease in some well-known, predictable, and easily understood way. Spatial representation of the attribute should enhance comprehension and interpretation and be sufficiently accurate.

General

- Use standard sliders whenever available.

Use of standard system sliders will speed learning

Caption and Labels

- Caption:
  — Provide meaningful, clear, and consistent captions.
  — Display them using mixed-case letters.
  — Position the caption to the left of the box.
    • Alternately, it may be positioned left-justified above the slider.
- Labels:
  — Provide meaningful and descriptive labels to aid in interpreting the scale.

Caption. The slider caption must clearly reflect the quality being displayed. Use a *static text* or *group box* control to provide a field caption in mixed-case letters with each significant word capitalized. Use a static text field; the recommended position is to the box's left. Alternately, captions may be positioned above the slider, aligned with the left edge. Select a positioning consistent with other controls presented in the window.

Labels. Provide meaningful and descriptive labels to aid in interpreting the scale. A temperature slider will necessitate the inclusion of numeric temperature values. A volume slider may be labeled *low* and *high*. Create the labels using *static* text fields.

Scale

- Show a complete range of choices.
- Mark the low, intermediate, and high ends of the scale.
- Provide scale interval markings, where possible.

- Provide consistent increments.
- Permit the user to change the units of measure.
- If the precise value of a quantity represented is important, display the value set in an adjacent text box.

Provide a complete range of choices on the scale. Mark the low, intermediate, and high ends of the scale. For example, volumes may be indicated by low and high. Provide scale interval markings at consistent increments. Allow the user to change the units of measure, for example, changing a temperature from Fahrenheit to centigrade. If the precise value of a quantity represented is critical, display the set value in an adjacent entry/display text box control. This will also permit typed entry of the desired value.

Slider Arm

- If the user cannot change the value shown in a slider, do not display a slider arm.

Do not display a slider arm if the user cannot change the value shown in a slider. Fill in the shaft in a distinctive way to indicate the relative setting, as illustrated in the guideline for proportions.

Slider Buttons

- Provide slider buttons to permit movement by the smallest increment.
- If the user cannot change the value shown in a slider, do not display slider buttons.

Provide slider buttons to permit movement by the smallest increment. Movement is achieved by pointing and clicking. If the user cannot change the value shown in a slider, do not display slider buttons.

Detents

- Provide detents to set values that have special meaning.
- Permit the user to change the detent value.

For values that have special meaning, provide detents that can be changed by the user.

Proportions

- To indicate the proportion of a value being displayed, fill the slider shaft in some visually distinctive way.
  - — Fill horizontal sliders from left to right.
  - — Fill vertical sliders from bottom to top.

When the proportion of a value is also important, provide proportional indicators by filling in the slider shaft in a distinctive way. Fill it from left to right and bottom to top.

Tabs

- Description:
  - — A window containing tabbed dividers that create pages or sections.
  - — Navigation is permitted between the pages or sections.
- Purpose:
  - — To present information that can be logically organized into pages or sections within the same window.
- Advantages:
  - — Resembles their paper-based cousins.
  - — Visually distinctive.
  - — Effectively organize repetitive, related information.
- Disadvantages:
  - — Visually complex.
- Proper usage:
  - — To present discrete, logically structured, related, information.
  - — To present the setting choices that can be applied to an object.
  - — When a short tab label can meaningfully describe the tab's contents.
  - — When the order of information use varies.

Description. A *tab* control is a window containing tabbed dividers that create pages or sections. Also referred to as a *notebook*, the tabs are analogous to dividers in a file cabinet or notebook. Navigation is permitted between the tabbed pages or sections. Microsoft Windows has a window organization scheme called a *workbook* (See Chapter 5) that is similar to the notebook control. Tabs from Microsoft Windows are illustrated in Figure 8.80.

Advantages/disadvantages. Tabs resemble their paper-based cousins, entities that are familiar to almost everyone. They are very meaningful electronic metaphors. Tabs are visually distinctive, and they permit effective organization of repetitive and related information. One drawback: They may result in a visually more complex screen.

Proper usage. Tabs can be used to present data that can be logically structured into discrete and meaningful pages or sections. They are most useful for presenting the choices that can be applied to an object, for example, a person and the person's descriptive data such as address, employment, family, and so forth. When the information on one tab is heavily dependent on information found on another tab, tabs are a poor choice because the user will have to keep flipping between tabs. Tabs are useful only if a brief tab label can identify their contents. Tabs are also useful when the order in which information is used varies.

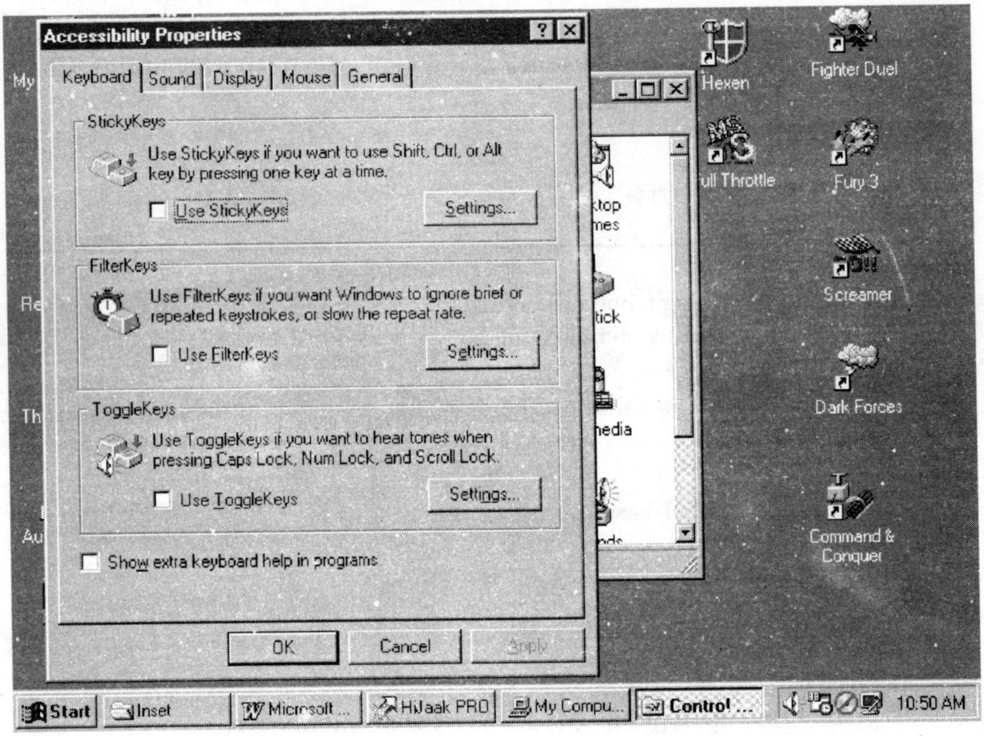

Figure 8.80 Tabs from Microsoft Windows.

Sections and Pages

- Place related information within a page or section.
- Order them meaningfully.
- Arrange pages so they appear to go deeper, left to right and top to bottom.
- Provide pages of equal size.

Place related information within a page or section. Order the pages in a meaningful way, based upon the window's content. Arrange the pages so they appear to go deeper, left to right and top to bottom. Provide pages of equal size.

Location, Size, and Labels

- Place the tabs at the top of the page or section.
- Provide fixed-width tabs for pages or sections of related information.
- Provide textual labels.
  - — Use system fonts.
  - — Keep information brief and the same general length.
    - Nouns are usually better than verbs.

— Use mixed case, capitalizing each significant word.
— Assign a keyboard equivalent for keyboard access.

- Center the labels within the tabs.
- Restrict tabs to only one row.
- Arrange tabs so that they appear to go deeper, left to right and top to bottom.

Place tabs at the top of the page or section. This is the most customary location. Tabs may be capable of being located at all four points of the compass but these positions are not as common. Left and right tabs will provide label readability problems. Fixed-width tabs are preferred but variable-width tabs may be used if screen space constraints exist. For labels, use the standard system fonts in mixed case, capitalizing each significant word. Keep tab text labels brief and of the same general length. Nouns are usually better than verbs. Assign each tab a keyboard equivalent to facilitate keyboard access. Center the labels within the tabs and restrict them to only one row.

Avoid multiple rows of tab or scrolling a single row of tabs. This adds complexity to the interface and makes it harder for the user to read and access a particular tab. As an alternative, consider separating the tabbed pages into sets and using another control to move between sets, or use subordinate dialog boxes. Arrange tabs so that they appear to go deeper, left to right and top to bottom.

Command Buttons

- If they affect only a page or section, locate the buttons on the page or section.
- If they affect the entire tabbed control, locate the buttons outside the tabbed pages.

For command buttons that affect only the tabbed page being displayed, locate the buttons on that page. If they affect the entire tabbed control, position the buttons outside the pages but within the window holding the pages. Tab users often have trouble understanding that command buttons actions within a tab page only affect that page, but that command buttons outside all the pages affect the entire tab window. The users may not always be aware that when the window is closed, actions taken within a window are not "activated" until the *window's* OK button is pressed. Guidance may have to be provided to the users to ensure that all expected user actions are actually performed. Alternatives include providing instructions on the window or providing a confirming message box if the window is closed.

Date-Picker

- Description:
  — A drop-down list box that displays a 1-month calendar in the drop-down list box.
  — The displayed month can be changed through pressing command buttons with left- and right-pointing arrows.

- The left arrow moves backward through the monthly calendars.
- The right arrow moves forward through the monthly calendars.

— A date for the list box can be selected from the drop-down calendar.

- Purpose:
  — To select a date for inscribing in a drop-down list box.
- Advantages:
  — Provides a representation of a physical calendar, a meaningful entity.
  — The calendar listing is ordered in a predictable way.
  — Visually distinctive.
- Disadvantages:
  — Requires an extra step to display the calendar.
  — When displayed, all month choices are not visible, requiring a form of scrolling to access the desired choice.
- Proper usage:
  — To select and display a single date in close monthly proximity to the default month presented on the drop-down list box.

A *date-picker*, illustrated in Figure 8.81, is a drop-down list box that displays a 1-month calendar in the drop-down. The displayed month can be changed by pressing command buttons with left- and right-pointing arrows. A relevant date to be entered in the list box is selected from the calendar drop-down list box. Advantages and disadvantages are similar to drop-down list boxes. Its structure as a calendar is a meaningful representation for most users. Like drop-down list boxes, the date-picker requires exposing the list before the date can be chosen. If the date desired as not within the default month's calendar presented, the calendar must be scrolled to the proper month. If the date is far away in time, excessive scrolling may be required to obtain it. Therefore, it is most useful for dates close in time to the default month presented. A wide range of dates would best be collected through a text box.

Figure 8.81 A date-picker control.

Tree View

- Description:
  - — A special list box control that displays a set of objects as an indented outline, based on the objects' logical hierarchical relationship.
  - — Includes, optionally, buttons that expand and collapse the outline.
    - A button inscribed with a plus (+) expands the outline.
    - A button inscribed with a minus (-) collapses the outline.
  - — Elements that can optionally be displayed are:
    - Icons.
    - Graphics, such as a check box.
    - Lines to illustrate hierarchical relationships.
- Purpose and proper usage:
  - — To display a set of objects as an indented outline to illustrate their logical hierarchical relationship.

A *tree view* control, as illustrated in Figure 8.82, is a special list box control that displays a set of objects as an indented outline, based on their logical hierarchical relationship. The control is used to display the relationship between a set of containers or other hierarchical elements, and, optionally, includes buttons to expand or collapse the

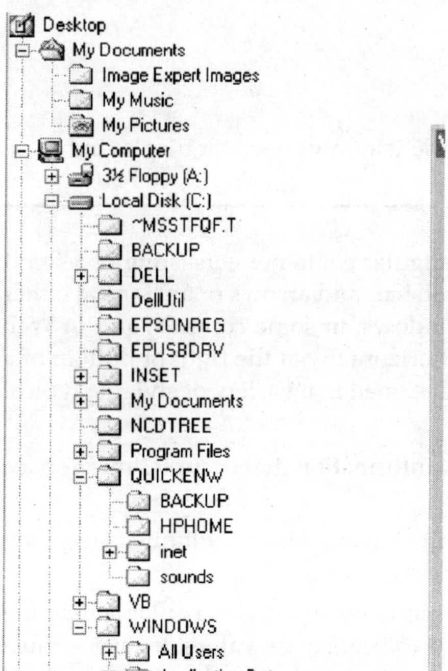

Figure 8.82 A tree view control.

hierarchy. Icons can be included with the text label for each item in the tree. Different icons can be displayed when the tree expands or collapses. A graphic, such as a check box, can be used to reflect state information about the item. The tree view control also supports an optional display of lines to illustrate the hierarchical relationship of the items in the list.

Scroll Bars

- Description:
  - — An elongated rectangular container consisting of:
    - A scroll area.
    - A slider box or elevator inside.
    - Arrows or anchors at either end.
  - — Available, if needed, in primary and secondary windows, some controls, and Web pages.
  - — May be oriented vertically or horizontally at the window or page edge.
- Purpose:
  - — To find and view information that takes more space than the allotted display space.
- Advantages:
  - — Permits viewing data of unlimited size.
- Disadvantages:
  - — Consumes screen space.
  - — Can be cumbersome to operate.
- Proper use:
  - — When more information is available than the window space for displaying it.
  - — Do not use to set values.

Description. A *scroll bar* is an elongated rectangular container consisting of a scroll area, a slider box, or elevator inside the scroll bar, and arrows or anchors at either end. They may be placed, if needed, in windows, in some controls, and in Web pages. They may be oriented vertically or horizontally at the right or bottom of a screen. Historically, scroll bars have been designed in a variety of styles; a typical one is illustrated in Figure 8.83.

Purpose. Scroll bars are used to find and view information that occupies more space than the allotted display space.

Advantages/disadvantages. While they permit viewing data of unlimited size, they do consume screen space and can be cumbersome to operate.

Proper usage. Use a scroll bar, or bars, when more information is available than the window space for displaying it. Do not use scroll bars to set values. If a value must be set or adjusted, use a *slider* or another control such as a *spin box.* Because scroll bars are designed for scrolling through information, using a scroll bar to set values may confuse the user about the purpose or interaction of the control.

Figure 8.83 Scroll bar.

Scroll Bar Design Guidelines

- General:
  - — Provide a scroll bar when invisible information must be seen.
- Scroll area or container:
  - — To indicate that scrolling is available, a scroll area or container should be provided.
    - Construct it of a filled-in bar displayed in a technique that visually contrasts with the window and screen body background.
- Scroll slider box or handle:
  - — To indicate the location and amount of information being viewed, provide a slider box or handle.
    - Constructed of a movable and sizable open area of the scroll area, displayed in a technique that contrasts with the scroll area.
    - By its position, spatially indicate the relative location in the file of the information being viewed.
    - By its size, indicate, proportionately, the percentage of the available information in the file being viewed.
- Scroll directional arrows:
  - — To indicate the direction in which scrolling may be performed, directional arrows should be provided.
    - Construct them as arrows in small boxes, with backgrounds that contrast with the scroll area.
- Selection:
  - — When the slider box/handle has been selected, highlight it in some visually distinctive way.
- Location:
  - — Position a vertical (top-to-bottom) scroll bar to the right of the window.
  - — Position a horizontal (left-to-right) scroll bar at the bottom of the window.
- Size:
  - — A vertical scroll bar should be the height of the scrollable portion of the window body.
  - — A horizontal scroll bar should be at least one-half the width of the scrollable portion of the window body.
- Current state indication:
  - — Whenever the window's size or the position of the information changes, the scroll bar components must also change, reflecting the current state.

— Include scroll bars in all sizable windows.
  - If no information is currently available by scrolling in a particular direction, the relevant directional arrow should be subdued or grayed out.

General. A *scroll bar* provides a method to permit the displaying of information that may not always fit within a window on a screen. A scroll bar should only be included when scrolling may be necessary.

In today's systems, scroll bars come in a variety of styles. Scroll bars consist of three elements: a scroll area or container, a slider box or handle that moves within a track made by the scroll area/container, and directional or scroll arrows.

Scroll area or container. The scroll area or, as it is sometimes called, the scroll container, is an elongated rectangular-shaped bar. Its presence indicates scrolling is available. It usually is constructed of a filled-in area displayed in a technique that visually contrasts with the window and screen body background. The chosen display technique should be of moderate intensity, neither too powerful nor too subtle. A powerful technique will be distracting; a subtle technique may be overlooked.

Slider box or handle. To indicate the location and amount of information being viewed, a slider box or, as it is sometimes called, a scroll handle, is included within the scroll area/container. It is constructed of a movable and sizable portion of the scroll area displayed in a technique that contrasts with the scroll area. It should indicate, by its position, the relative spatial location in the file of the information being viewed. It should indicate by its size, proportionately, the percentage of the available information in the file being viewed. Displaying, within a scrollable screen, the page number of page-organized material being viewed can further enhance the usability of the slider box or handle.

Directional or scroll arrows. To indicate the direction in which scrolling may be performed, directional or scroll arrows are also included. They are constructed of variously shaped arrows in small boxes with backgrounds that contrast with the scroll area/container. They are most often located at each end of the scroll bar, but some systems locate them adjacent to one another within the scroll area/container itself.

Placing directional arrows at opposite ends of the scroll bar is conceptually the clearest. The mouse pointer is moved in the same direction, away from the current position, when either the scroll arrow or scroll handle is manipulated. The distance that the directional arrows are separated by, however, causes increased effort when a window's contents must be adjusted by scrolling in opposite directions.

One platform solved the direction-switching problem by positioning the directional arrows adjacent to one another at one end of the scroll bar. While the forward-backward scrolling is made more efficient, the spatial correspondence between the beginning, middle, and end of the data is lost.

Another platform took another approach, placing the directional arrows at opposite ends of the slider box/handle to maintain the desirable spatial correspondence while at the same time minimizing their separation. Since during a continuous scrolling operation the directional arrows move as the slider box/handle moves, this platform automatically moves the mouse pointer to keep it aligned with the scroll arrow. This eliminates the need for the user to move the pointer during the continuous scrolling operation, but it requires that the user relinquish control of the mouse operation, and may be disorienting.

Using a scroll bar, the scrolling movement can be performed in several ways. The most common actions involve grabbing the slider box/handle and moving it in the desired direction, or selecting the proper directional arrow. Clicking a mouse button while selecting a directional arrow moves the contents of a window one line. Pressing the mouse button scrolls the window's contents continuously until the button is released. One platform provides another more efficient process. A region of the scroll area/container can also be selected, automatically moving the slider box/handle to that point and displaying the proper window contents.

Based upon early scrolling research (Bury, Boyle, Evey, and Neal, 1982), movement of the window data usually follows the window-up or telescope approach, whereby the window moves around over data that appears fixed in location. This causes the data in a window to move in the direction opposite the one indicated by the directional arrow or the direction of movement of the scroll container/handle. Scrolling using window systems, however, seems to be especially mistake-prone, users often assuming the arrows will move the data in the same direction as the directional arrow or scroll container/handle. In other words, it is sensed that the data moves under the window, not the window over the data (Billingsley, 1988). Why this happens is open to conjecture. Billingsley speculates that, because windows seem to move on screens, when data scrolls or moves in a window, people may conclude the data must be moving because the window remains still during the scrolling operation. Or, because of the close physical proximity of the directional arrows in scroll bars to the data, people may feel that the arrows are acting on the data, not the window. The implication is that the scrolling procedure should be rethought and restudied. Some recent applications have devised scrolling methods through actually point at the window data.

Selection. When the slider box/handle has been selected, highlight it in some visually distinctive way. Most systems do provide some visual feedback of this kind.

Location. While, again, no universal agreement exists, the majority of systems locate the vertical (top-to-bottom) scroll bar to the right of the window and the horizontal (left-to-right) scroll bar at the bottom of the window.

Size. A vertical scroll bar should be the height of the scrollable portion of the window body. A horizontal scroll bar should be at least one-half the width of the scrollable portion of the window body.

Current state indication. Whenever the window's size or the position of information changes, the scroll bar components must also change, reflecting the current state of the scrolling process. Providing accurate information about the scrolling location facilitates user navigation and makes it easier to reposition the slider box/container. Include scroll bars in all sizable windows.

If scrolling cannot be performed in a particular direction, the relevant arrow box should be reduced in contrast or grayed out. If all the information in a window is displayed and no information is available for scrolling, both directional arrows should be reduced in contrast or grayed out.

Scroll Bar Usage Guidelines

- Scroll bar style:
  - — Stick with standard, proven design styles.
- Directional preference:
  - — Use vertical (top-to-bottom) scrolling.
  - — Avoid horizontal (left-to-right) scrolling.

Style. The standard, well-known, proven design style used in graphical systems works best. A scroll bar is complex enough that presenting a new style to the user will focus attention away from the screen content as the user struggles to learn how to deal with the new style. This is a form of "senseless" learning and must be avoided.

Directional preferences. Where the choice exists, people prefer and deal better with vertical (top-to-bottom) scrolling rather than horizontal (left-to-right) scrolling. Avoid horizontal scrolling whenever possible.

Media Controls

- For all playable files provide the following controls.
  - — Play.
  - — Pause/Resume.
  - — Stop.
  - — Rewind.
  - — Fast Forward.
  - — Volume.

Some media products provide their own controls. For others, controls may have to be designed. Always provide the above standard media controls.

Custom Controls

- Implement custom controls with caution.
- If used, make the look and behavior of custom controls different from that of standard controls.

Many toolkits and interface builders provide the ability to create custom controls; implement them with caution. The user is currently presented with a multitude of controls whose usage and operation must be learned and remembered. The addition of custom controls adds to this learning and increases system complexity. If custom controls must be developed and implemented, make their look and behavior as different as possible from the standard controls. This will avoid confusion between the various controls.

MAXIM **Fewer is usually better.**

Presentation Controls

Presentation controls are purely informational. They provide details about other screen elements or controls, or assist in giving the screen structure. Common presentation controls are *static text fields, group boxes column headings, ToolTips, balloon tips,* and *progress indicators.*

Static Text Fields

- Description:
  - — Read-only textual information.
- Purpose:
  - — To identify a control by displaying a control caption.
  - — To clarify a screen by providing instructional or prompting information.
  - — To present descriptive information.
- Proper usage:
  - — To display a control caption.
  - — To display instructional or prompting information.
  - — To display descriptive information.

Description. A *static text field*, as illustrated in Figure 8.84, provides read-only textual information. It is a standard Microsoft Windows control.

Purpose/proper usage. Use static text fields to create and present read-only information, including all control captions. Also using static text fields clarify screen usage by providing prompting or instructional information. Other descriptive screen information can also be provided through static text fields. Examples are headings, subheadings, slider scales, progress indicator text, and so on. In Microsoft Windows, static text cannot be selected, so avoid using it for any text the user might want to copy to the clipboard.

Caption:

HEADING

This message is very important!

Figure 8.84 Static text field.

Static Text Field Guidelines

- Captions:
  - — Include a colon (:) as part of the caption.
  - — Include a mnemonic for keyboard access.
  - — When the associated control is disabled, display it dimmed.
  - — Follow all other presented guidelines for caption presentation and layout.
- Instructional or prompting information:
  - — Display it in a unique and consistent font style for easy recognition and differentiation.
  - — Follow all other presented guidelines for prompting and instructional information.
- Descriptive information:
  - — Follow all other guidelines for required screen or control descriptive information.

Captions. Always include a colon as part of the caption. The colon immediately identifies the element as a caption. In Microsoft Windows the colon is also used by screen review utilities. Include a keyboard equivalent (mnemonic) for all captions to provide keyboard access to its associated control. Captions may also provide a means of indicating that their associated controls are disabled. Follow all the rules for caption display presented throughout these guidelines.

Instructional or prompting information. Display in a unique and consistent font style for easy recognition and differentiation. Follow all other presented guidelines for prompting and instructional information. Guidelines for writing instructional or prompting information are found in Chapter 9.

Descriptive information. Other descriptive information includes headings, subheadings, slider scales, progress indicator text, and so forth. Also, follow all the rules for these other kinds of screen information presented throughout these guidelines.

Group Boxes

- Description:
  - — A rectangular frame that surrounds a control or group of controls.
  - — An optional caption may be included in the frame's upper-left corner.
- Purpose:
  - — To visually relate the elements of a control.
  - — To visually relate a group of related controls.
- Proper usage:
  - — To provide a border around radio button or check box controls.
  - — To provide a border around two or more functionally related controls.
- Guidelines:
  - — Label or heading:
    - Typically, use a noun or noun phrase for the label or heading.
    - Provide a brief label or heading, preferably one or two words.

  - Relate label or heading's content to the group box's content.
  - Capitalize the first letter of each significant word.
  - Do not include and ending colon (:).
- — Follow all other guidelines presented for control and section borders.

Description. A *group box is* a standardized rectangular frame that surrounds a control or group of controls. An optional caption may be included in the frame's upper-left corner. Standard Microsoft Windows Group boxes are illustrated in Figure 8.85.

Purpose/proper usage. The purpose of a group box is to visually relate the elements of a single control or a grouping of related controls. Group boxes should be used to provide a border around a radio button control, a grouping of related check boxes, or two or more functionally related controls.

Guidelines. Typically, use a noun or noun phrase for group box labels or headings. Keep the text brief, one or two words. Consider the group box content and relate the control captions inside the group box to the label or heading being created. Use headline-style capitalization, but do not include any ending colon. Refer to all the guidelines presented for control and section borders, in designing group boxes.

Column Headings

- Description:
  - — Read-only textual information that serves as a heading above columns of text or numbers.
  - — Can be divided into two or more parts.
- Purpose:
  - — To identify a column of information contained in a table.
- Proper usage:
  - — To display a heading above a column of information contained in a table.
- Guidelines:
  - — Heading:
    - Provide a brief heading.
    - Can include text and a graphic image.
    - Capitalize the first letter of each significant word.
    - Do not include an ending colon (:).
  - — The width of the column should fit the average size of the column entries.
  - — Does not support keyboard access.

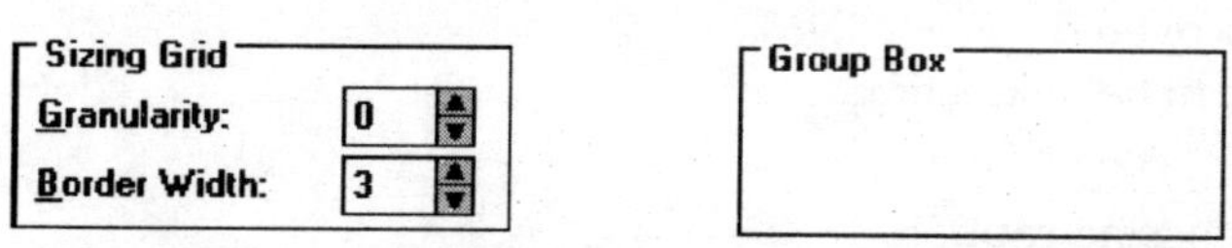

Figure 8.85 Group boxes.

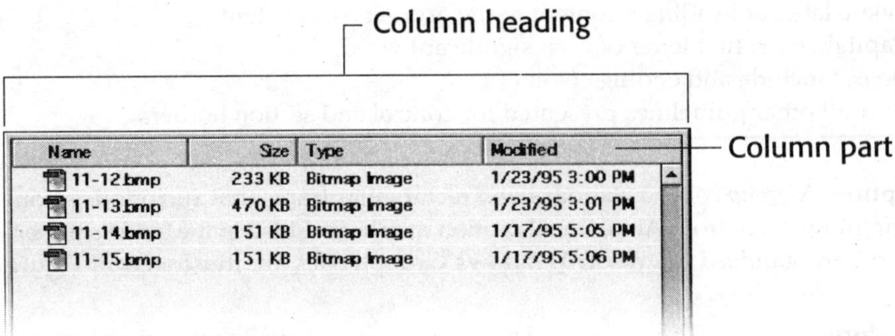

Figure 8.86 Column heading control.

Description. A *column heading control,* also known as a *header control,* is used to display a heading above columns of text or numbers. A column heading is illustrated in Figure 8.86. It can be divided into two or more parts.

Purpose/proper usage. To identify and display a heading above a column of information contained in a table.

Guidelines. Provide a brief heading. Headings can include text as well as a graphic image. Use the headline style of capitalization, without an ending colon. The width of each column should fit the average size of the column entries. Column heading controls do not support keyboard access.

ToolTips

- Description:
  - — A small pop-up window containing descriptive text that appears when a pointer is moved over a control or element either:
    - Not possessing a label.
    - In need of additional descriptive or status information.
- Purpose:
  - — To provide descriptive information about a control or screen element.
- Advantages:
  - — Identifies an otherwise unidentified control.
  - — Reduces possible screen clutter caused by control captions and descriptive information.
  - — Enables control size to be reduced.
- Disadvantages:
  - — Not obvious, must be discovered.
  - — Inadvertent appearance can be distracting.
- Proper usage:
  - — To identify a control that has no caption.
  - — To provide additional descriptive or status information about a screen element.

Description. A *ToolTip*, sometimes called a Screen Tip, is a standard Microsoft Windows control, a small pop-up window that displays descriptive text when the pointer is moved over a control that does not possess a caption, or that possesses only an abbreviated caption. A ToolTip is illustrated in Figure 8.87.

Purpose/proper usage. The purpose of a ToolTip is to simply provide thorough descriptive information about a control when its function must be quickly identified. It is also used to provide additional descriptive or status information about a screen element.

Advantages/disadvantages. A ToolTip provides an easy way to identify an otherwise unidentifiable control, or a control with a cryptic caption. It reduces possible screen clutter caused by control captions, enabling the control size to be reduced. A ToolTip, however, is not obvious and must be discovered. Its appearance when the pointer is positioned incorrectly, or is slowly passing over it, can be distracting to the screen viewer.

ToolTip Guidelines

- Display after a short time-out.
- For toolbars, provide a brief word as a label.
  — Use mixed case in the headline style of presentation with no ending punctuation.
- For other elements, provide a brief phrase presenting descriptive or status information.
  — Use mixed case in the sentence style of presentation.
- Present ToolTips at the lower-right edge of the pointer.
  — Display them fully on the screen.
  — For text boxes, display ToolTips centered under the control.
- Display them in the standard system ToolTip colors.
- Remove the ToolTip when the control is activated or the pointer is moved away.
- Don't substitute ToolTips for good design.

Display the ToolTip on the screen after a short pause, ideally three-quarters of a second. This avoids its appearing briefly as the pointer is just being moved over a control or element that possesses a ToolTip. When used to provide descriptions of toolbar buttons, keep ToolTips brief, usually one or two words that identify the button's action. Use the headline style of capitalization with no ending punctuation. For other elements,

Figure 8.87 ToolTip

descriptive or status information may be provided. In this case, use a short phrase, in sentence-style capitalization, which briefly describes the item or status. Position the ToolTip to the lower-right of the pointer, but fully on the screen. Always adjust the location for a full fit. For text boxes, present the ToolTip centered under the control it relates to. Display it in the system's standard ToolTip colors so it will be immediately recognized as a ToolTip. Remove the ToolTip when the control is clicked or the pointer is moved away.

Don't substitute ToolTips for good design. Presented screen elements should always be designed for maximum comprehension. ToolTips are supplements.

Balloon Tips

- Description:
  - — A small pop-up window that contains information in a word balloon.
  - — Components can include:
    - Title.
    - Body text.
    - Message Icons.
  - — Appear adjacent to the item to which they apply, generally above or to left.
  - — Only one tip, the last posted, is visible at any time.
  - — Tips are removed after a specified time period.
- Purpose:
  - — To provide additional descriptive or status information about a screen element.
- Advantages:
  - — Provides useful reminder and status information.
- Disadvantages:
  - — If overused they lose their attention-getting value.
  - — If overused in situations the user considers not very important, their continual appearance can be aggravating.
- Proper usage:
  - — To display noncritical:
    - Reminder information.
    - Notification information.
  - — Do not use tips to display critical information.

Description. A *balloon tip*, illustrated in Figure 8.88, is a small pop-up window that contains information presented in a word balloon. Its components can include a title, body text, and informational, warning, or critical icons. (These icons are described in Chapter 9.) Custom icons are not supported. Balloon tips appear adjacent to the item to which they apply, generally, above or to the left of the item. However, the system automatically adjusts their position so they remain on-screen. Although a tip can be posted at any time, only one, the last posted, will be visible at any time. Balloon tips used for the taskbar are presented for a specified, within minimum and maximum limits.

Figure 8.88 Balloon tip.

Purpose. To provide additional descriptive or status information about a screen element.

Advantages/disadvantages. Balloon tips can provide useful reminder and status information to the user. Their sudden appearance can at some times be distracting, and perhaps aggravating, however, especially if overused in situations the user considers not very important. If overused the also lose their attention-getting value.

Proper usage. For noncritical reminder or notification information, special conditions, or status information that would otherwise require a message box. They are very useful for informing the user of unexpected system behaviors. Due to their brief nature and frequent out-of-the-way location, never rely on balloon tips to display critical information.

Balloon Tip Guidelines

- General:
  - — Use a notification tip to inform the user about state changes.
  - — Use a reminder tip for state changes that the user might not usually notice.
  - — Point the tip of the balloon to the item it references.
  - — Do not use them to replace ToolTips.
  - — Do not overuse balloon tips.
- Content:
  - — Restrict them to a length of 100 characters, including title and body text.
  - — Title text should:
    - If the tip refers to an icon or other image representing a specific object, include:
      - — The object's name, using its normal capitalization.
      - — The object's status, using sentence-style presentation without ending punctuation.
    - Be presented in bold.
  - — Body text should:
    - Include a description of the situation in one or two brief sentences.
    - Include a brief suggestion for correcting the situation.
    - Be presented using mixed-case in the sentence style.

General. Balloon tips can provide either notifications or reminders. The notification balloon is displayed and then times out. This tip style should be used to notify the user about state changes. The reminder balloon appears at regular intervals. The default interval is 60 minutes. Use the reminder balloon only for state changes that the user might not usually notice. Notification and reminder styles are supported for taskbar components. Other screen elements are only supported by the notification style. Tips are automatically removed when the user clicks it or clicks elsewhere.

Always point the tip of the balloon to the item it references. Balloon tips are not intended to replace standard ToolTips. ToolTips and balloon tips are mutually exclusive; if a ToolTip is currently displayed and a balloon tip is presented, the balloon tip will automatically cause the ToolTip to be removed. ToolTips will not appear until the balloon tip is dismissed. Finally, be careful not to overuse balloon tips. The user may ignore them if they appear too frequently.

Content. The notification balloon tip has a maximum length of 100 characters, including the title and body text. Title text automatically appears as bold text. Body text uses the text style and size of standard ToolTips. For the title text, if the balloon tip refers to an icon or other image representing a specific object, include the object's name using its normal capitalization and its status using sentence-style capitalization without ending punctuation. Otherwise, just display the status text. The body text should include a statement of the problem in one or two brief sentences, followed by a brief suggestion for correcting the problem. Use sentence-style capitalization and appropriate punctuation.

Progress Indicators

- Description:
  - — A rectangular bar that fills as a process is being performed, indicating the percentage of the process that has been completed.
- Purpose:
  - — To provide feedback concerning the completion of a lengthy operation.
- Proper usage:
  - — To provide an indication of the proportion of a process completed.

A *progress indicator* is a rectangular bar that fills as a process is being performed. The filled-in area indicates the percentage of a process that has been completed. A progress indicator, sometimes called a *progress bar*, is illustrated in Figure 8.89.

Progress Indicator Guidelines

- When filling the indicator:
  - — If horizontally arrayed, fill it from left to right.
  - — If vertically arrayed, fill it from bottom to top.
- Fill it with a color or a shade of gray.
- Include descriptive text for the process, as necessary.
- Place text outside of the control.

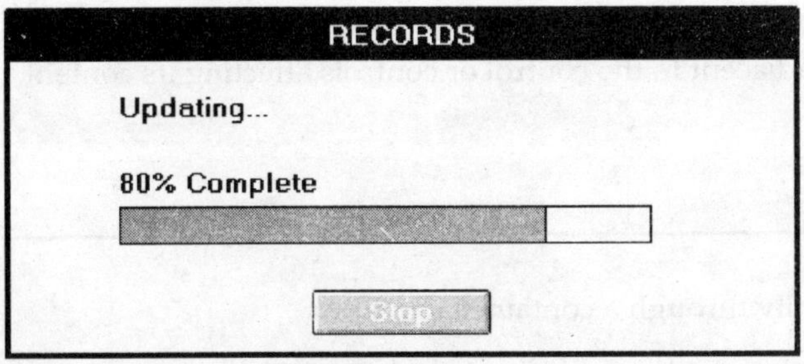

Figure 8.89 Progress indicator.

Fill horizontally arrayed progress indicators from left to right; fill vertically arrayed progress indicators from bottom to top. Fill them with a color or a shade of gray. Create necessary descriptive text using a *static text* control. Position the text outside of the control. Progress indicators are also discussed in Chapter 10.

Sample Box

- Description:
  - — A box illustrating what will show up on the screen based upon the parameter or parameters selected.
  - — May include text, graphics, or both.
- Purpose:
  - — To provide a representation of actual screen content based upon the parameter or parameters selected.
- Guidelines:
  - — Include a brief label.
  - — Use mixed case in the headline style.
  - — Locate it adjacent to the controls upon which it is dependent.

Description. A *sample box* is a box illustrating what will show up on the screen based upon the parameter or parameters currently selected. A common example, shown in Figure 8.90, illustrates a font selected for display on a screen. Sample boxes may include text, graphics, or both.

Purpose. To provide a representation of actual screen content based upon the parameter or parameters selected so that the choice may actually be seen.

Figure 8.90 Sample box.

Guidelines. Include a brief label using mixed case in the headline style. Position the sample box immediately adjacent to the control or controls affecting its content.

Scrolling Tickers

- Description:
  — Text that scrolls horizontally through a container window.
- Advantages:
  — Consume less screen space than full text.
- Disadvantages:
  — Hard to read.
  — Time-consuming to interpret.
  — Distracting.
- Guideline:
  — Do not use.

Description. A *scrolling ticker* is a window that contains text scrolling horizontally.

Advantages/disadvantages. The biggest advantage of a scrolling ticker is its efficient use of screen space. Disadvantages include scrolling text being hard to read and time-consuming to interpret. Human memory being what it is, information scrolled out of sight is difficult to remember, and longer messages may not be understood. Scrolling screen elements are also visually distracting.

Guideline. The most prudent guideline at the moment is: do not use scrolling tickers.

Selecting the Proper Controls

Providing the proper control, or mix of controls, is critical to a system's success. The proper control will enable a person to make needed selections, entries, and changes quickly, efficiently, and with fewer mistakes. Improper selection most often leads to the opposite result.

This section will begin with a survey of several research studies addressing control selection. Studies such as these, while few in number, appear in the research literature. The results of these studies have already been incorporated within the control usage guidelines just discussed. Next, the criteria that must be considered in control selection will be summarized. Finally, some selection guidelines will be presented.

Entry versus Selection—A Comparison

The first studies to be described are a series performed by IBM. These studies (Gould, Boies, Meluson, Rasamny, and Vosburgh, 1988; Greene, Gould, Boies, Meluson, and Rasamny, 1988; Greene, Gould, Boies, Rasamny, and Meluson, 1992) looked at the advantages and disadvantages of using either entry fields or selection fields for data collection. Entry involved keying text; selection was performed by pointing at a choice

SOME THOUGHTS ON POOR SCREEN DESIGN

Following is a collection of control design inadequacies whose most endearing qualities are they *really, really aggravate* the author.

Why do interface designers insist on collecting state codes through drop-down list boxes when all other name and address details are collected through text boxes?

I'm merrily typing away my "mentally programmed" name and address when I encounter the state field and come to a screeching halt. Do I reach for the mouse? Open the drop-down list box with the keyboard? I stumble, grumble, open the drop-down list box, find my home state, Arizona, and select it, thinking all the while how glad I am I live in a state whose name is near the top of the alphabetized list. My condolences go out to friends in places like Illinois and Texas who'll have to scroll to their state name. I return my hands to the keyboard and forge ahead to zip code. Why, I'm now thinking, do they need my zip code? They now have enough information to determine it—but that's another story.

Why am I often penalized by American systems for living in the United States?

Back to the name and address again; now I must indicate country. Can I type USA? Nope, back to a drop-down list box. Opening it, I stare at an alphabetized list of countries within which, I quickly realize, the United States of America lies well submerged. I look at the system's owner (a large hotel chain) and, since 95 percent of their hotels are in the USA, I estimate that the overwhelming majority of guests must be American. Have these people ever thought of another sequence like, perhaps, frequency of use? Or a combination of frequency and alphabetical with the several most frequent possibilities at the top? I guess not, I think, wondering if I should move to Australia to avoid this nonsense. "They're getting even with you for living in Arizona," you may be thinking, and this may be true. My friends in Illinois and Texas are double-whammed, however.

Why do they clear one critical piece of information when they re-present a screen?

With another hotel system, I encounter a "sorry, no room at this inn" for the days I'd like to be there. I select a different hotel and glance at the booking screen. The dates I previously entered are still there as well as well as the room type. I click "send." You didn't tell us whether your trip was for business or pleasure, their error message sternly advises. (Can't I also have pleasure on a business trip, I wonder?) I glance at the top of the screen. The radio buttons designating business or pleasure have magically been cleared, but nothing else on the reservation screen has changed. If I'm looking for another hotel on the same dates as just a moment ago, would I now be doing it for business instead of pleasure (or vice versa), I wonder. Perhaps some hotels are only for business, others only for pleasure—a worthwhile subject for usability research…

Why do they give me a small command button and surround it by acres of white space?

Are they afraid it might be too easy to find? Don't they really want it pressed? Are they testing my perceptual-motors skills? Is an anorexic button beautiful? Have they ever heard of Fitts' Law? Undoubtedly not!

through the keyboard using the cursor control keys (not a mouse). The information compared was of three kinds: dates, text, and data. The first conclusion:

Choosing a Type of Control

- For familiar, meaningful data choose the technique that, in theory, requires the fewest number of keystrokes to complete.
- If the data is unfamiliar or prone to typing errors, choose a selection technique.

The studies found that if the data to be entered was familiar, the technique that required the minimum theoretical number of keystrokes to complete the task was the fastest. Theoretical keystrokes are the minimum number possible, excluding mis-keys, and erroneous cursor or selection movements. However, as the information became less familiar or became subject to spelling or typing errors, the minimum keystroke principle broke down. Selection techniques, and the reminders and structure they provide for unfamiliar items, hard to spell words, and items prone to typing errors becomes advantageous. The point at which the changeover occurs is not known. It would be influenced by the nature of the task and the nature of the user.

These studies point out the advantages of the techniques that permit both typed entry and selection to enter the data (spin box, drop-down/pop-up combination box, and attached combination box).

Aided versus Unaided Entry

- Provide aided entry whenever possible.
  — Absorb any extra and unnecessary keystrokes.
  — Provide an auditory signal that autocompletion has been performed.

The studies also compared unaided typed entry (the entire field had to be keyed) with aided entry (the system automatically and immediately completed the field when enough characters were keyed to make the desired data known). They found that aided entry, also known as autocompletion, was preferred over unaided entry methods, and it was also the fastest. Autocompletion was also preferable to, and faster than, many selection methods. Greene et al. (1992) found that, for keying of difficult to spell words, aided entry was much faster, and significantly reduced errors, when compared to unaided entry.

The result is that, when possible, autocompletion of text entry fields should be provided. Autocompletion will minimize the user's effort by reducing input time and keystrokes. It should also enhance the user's opinion of the system. If aided entry is provided, extra keystrokes must be absorbed by the system. The software will finish spelling a word much faster than a person's fingers are capable of stopping movement. Also, provide some kind of auditory signal that autocompletion has begun. A person may not be looking directly at the control when the completion is performed.

Comparison of GUI Controls

Tullis and Kodimer (1992) compared seven controls used for direct manipulation, selection, and data entry. The task was to reorder four items in a table (Filename, Number, Size, and Date). The controls studied were the following. Complete descriptions of control usage methods are summarized in Table 8.1.

- Direct Manipulation.
  1. Drag and drop on.
  2. Drag and drop between.
- Selection.
  3. Icons.
  4. Radio buttons.
  5. Menus (drop-down list boxes).
- Entry.
  6. One entry area.
  7. Four entry areas.

The direct manipulation methods reflected the perceived strength of graphical systems, namely manipulation of objects on the screen. The selection methods utilized indirect manipulation and illustrated the types of controls available in graphical screen design. The entry methods are a carryover from text-based screens, the only way the task could be accomplished for many years. Study participants were experienced Microsoft Windows users. No instructions were provided on how to carry out the item reorganization tasks. Users had to rely on their experience.

The two fastest methods were radio buttons and the one entry field. The methods most preferred by participants were radio buttons, drop-down list boxes, and one entry field. The direct manipulation methods fared rather poorly, ending midlist in the speed and preference rankings. The surprise, perhaps, was the good showing of an old control: the one entry field, or text box.

Tullis (1993) performed a follow-up to this study by asking a group of programmers to predict the study results (without, of course, being privy to its results). For both reordering speeds and subjective preferences, their predictions were way off the mark. They anticipated that the direct manipulation methods would be the fastest and most preferred. This, of course, was not at all the case. They predicted that radio buttons would be midway in the speed and preference ordering and that one entry field would be near the bottom. Again, they were quite mistaken. The correlation between their predictions and actual reordering speed was a dismal .07. They did slightly better on predicting preferences, the correlation being .31.

Based on these studies, Tullis concludes that control selection decisions made according to convention and intuition may not necessarily yield the best results. We might modify that conclusion to say, with a great deal of justification, that such decisions made using *common sense* may not even yield *good* results. Just because a control or process is new does not necessarily make it better. Just because the control has been around a long time does not necessarily make it poorer. Controls should be selected on the basis

Table 8.1 Controls Evaluated by Tullis and Kodimer (1992)

DIRECT MANIPULATION

1. Drag and Drop On
   - The items are arrayed horizontally. An item is dragged to a new location above another item and released. The item in that position moves to the old location of the arriving item.
2. Drag and Drop Between
   - The items are arrayed horizontally. An item is dragged to a new location between two other items and released. The items are readjusted into new positions, including, when necessary, automatic wrap-around for items located at the end of the line.

SELECTION

3. Icons
   - The items are arrayed horizontally. Icons are positioned between each pair of items. Selecting an icon switches the positions of each adjacent item.
4. Radio Buttons
   - The items are presented in a matrix, item name along the left side, item position numbers across the top. Radio buttons in the matrix are selected to represent each item's position.
5. Menus (Drop-down List Boxes)
   - Items are positioned horizontally. A drop-down listing is activated, and the item for that location selected.

ENTRY

6. One Entry Area
   - A single text entry field is provided. A one-character mnemonic (F,N,S,D) is provided for each choice. The mnemonics are keyed in the order in which the items are to be arrayed.
7. Four Entry Areas
   - Four text entry fields, labeled with the item names are arranged vertically. A number (1-4) is keyed into each field, indicating the manner in which the items are to be ordered.

of the objectives they are to achieve, and they should be subjected to the same rigorous testing as all other parts of the system.

Another control comparison study was conducted by Johnsgard et al. (1995). They evaluated a variety of controls including check boxes, drop-down list boxes, drop-down combination boxes, text boxes, list boxes, radio buttons, sliders, and spin boxes. Speeds, errors, and preferences were obtained for the various controls under various conditions.

Mutually Exclusive Choice Controls

For a small set of options (5), a medium set (12), and a large set (30), radio buttons were significantly faster than the other mutually exclusive controls. They were also the most accurate and most preferred by the study participants. This result is consistent with the results of the Tullis and Kodimer (1992) study. Among other findings: as control set sizes increased, control activation speeds significantly increased (took longer), and sets organized in a meaningful way were searched significantly faster than those in random orders.

The medium and large set sizes (12 and 30) are larger than generally recommended for radio buttons (8 or less). The results indicate that radio buttons may effectively be used for these larger quantities, if sufficient screen space exists for their presentation. Controls requiring scrolling to see all the choices, or require an action to display a listing of choices (drop-downs), seem to significantly impede selection speeds.

Nonexclusive Choice Controls

For a small set of options (5) with two selected choices, a medium set (12) with three selected choices, and a large set (30) with eight selected choices, check boxes were significantly faster than the other nonexclusive controls. Check boxes were also the most preferred by the study participants. Among other findings: like radio buttons, as control set sizes increased, control activation speeds increased (took longer), and sets organized in a meaningful way were searched significantly faster than those in random order.

The medium and large set sizes (12 and 30) are also larger than generally recommended for check boxes (8 or less). The results also seem to indicate that check boxes may effectively be used for these larger quantities, if sufficient screen space exists for their presentation. Again scrolling and retrieving lists slow one down.

Combination Selection and Entry Controls

Two controls were compared: a drop-down combination box and an array of radio buttons, including an "other" choice with an associated text entry field for keying the "other" value. The fastest, most accurate, and preferred: radio buttons with the text entry field.

Controls for Selecting a Value within a Range

Setting range values included indicating a time, a percentage, or the transmission frequency of a radio station. Controls evaluated were the spin button, text entry field, and the slider. The spin button was the most accurate, and the text entry field fastest and most preferred. The slider finished last in all three measurement categories.

The study's general conclusions are:

- Making all options always visible will enhance performance.
- Requiring additional actions to make further options visible slows performance.
- For longer lists, scrolling tends to degrade performance more than the action associated with retrieving a hidden list.

As set size increases, performance times increase more for controls that require scrolling than for those that do not. For a large set size (30 options) scrolling slowed performance more than the action to retrieve a list.

Control Selection Criteria

Selection of the proper control, then, depends on several factors. The first is the structure and characteristics of the property or data itself. Other considerations include the nature of the task, the nature of the user, and the limitations of the display screen itself.

Property or data considerations reflect the characteristics of the data itself. Some kinds of controls are very restrictive in that they permit only specific kinds of information with specific qualities to be presented within them. Other kinds of controls may not be as restrictive concerning a data's qualities, but they are not well suited to the kind of data being used. Data considerations include the following:

- Is the property or data *mutually exclusive* or *nonexclusive*? Does entry/selection require single or multiple items?
- Is the property or data *discrete* or *continuous*? Discrete data can be meaningfully specified and categorized, while continuous data cannot.
- Is the property or data *limited* or *unlimited* in scope? If limited, how many items will the data normally not exceed?
- Is the property or data *fixed* or *variable* in list length? Are there always a fixed number of items, or will it vary?
- Is the property or data ordered in a *predictable* or *unpredictable* fashion? If predictable, will the user be able to anticipate the next, unseen, item?
- Can the property or data be *represented pictorially*? Will a picture or graphic be as meaningful as a textual description?

Task considerations reflect the nature of the job. Considerations include the following:

- *How often* is an item *entered* or *selected*?
- *How often* is an item *changed*?
- How *precisely* must the item be entered or selected?

User considerations reflect the characteristics of the user. Important considerations:

- How much *training* in control operation will be provided?
- How *meaningful* or *known* is the property or data to the user?
- How *easily remembered or learned* by the user is the property or data?
- How *frequently used* will the system be?
- Is the user an *experienced typist*?

Display considerations reflect the characteristics of the screen and hardware.

- How much *screen space* is available to display the various controls?

Choosing a Control Form

In light of the above research and considerations, and the known characteristics of the various controls, some guidance in control selection can be presented.

When to Permit Text Entry

- Permit text entry if any of the following questions can be answered *Yes*:
  - — Is the data unlimited in size and scope?
  - — Is the data familiar?
  - — Is the data *not* conducive to typing errors?
  - — Will typing be faster than choice selection?
  - — Is the user an experienced typist?

Permit text entry when any of the above conditions exist. The use of combination controls is almost always the best alternative, permitting the user to *choose* when to type and when to point and select.

What Kind of Control to Choose

Next are two tables providing some control recommendations based upon a control's known advantages, disadvantages, and proper usage characteristics. Table 8.2 is a simple decision chart for small listings, based upon Johnsgard et al. (1995). Table 8.3 is more thorough and is based upon the known characteristics of the controls described in this chapter.

The recommendations presented by Johnsgard et al., in these tables are based upon their research study. The names of some controls have been modified to reflect the control classification scheme found in this text. It would seem worth considering for controls containing a small number of choices. All controls in their study, except *setting a value within a range*, were limited to 30 options. For more than 30 choices, the use of radio buttons or check boxes still seems inappropriate at this time. More research is needed in this area.

Table 8.2 Best Controls for Certain Tasks and Screen Conditions

TASK	BEST CONTROL	IF SCREEN SPACE CONSTRAINTS EXIST
Mutually Exclusive	Radio Buttons	Drop-down/Pop-up List Box
Not Mutually Exclusive	Check Boxes	Multiple-Selection List Box
Select or Type a Value Text Entry Field	Radio Buttons with "Other"	Drop-down Combo Box
Setting a Value within a Range	Spin Button	Text Box

From Johnsgard et al., 1995

Table 8.3 Suggested Uses for Graphical Controls

1. IF:	*USE:*
• *Mutually exclusive* alternatives. • Discrete data. • Best represented verbally. • Very limited in number (2 to 8).	
AND: • Typed entry is never necessary. • Content can never change. • Adequate screen space is available.	Radio Buttons
OR: • Typed entry is never necessary. • Content can never change. • Adequate screen space is not available.	Drop-down/Pop-up List Box
OR: • Typed entry may be necessary. • Content can change. • Adequate screen space is available.	Combo box
OR: • Typed entry may be necessary. • Content can change. • Adequate screen space is not available.	Drop-down/Pop-up Combo Box
2. IF:	*USE:*
• *Mutually exclusive* alternatives. • Discrete data. • Best represented verbally. • Potentially large in number (9 or more).	
AND: • Typed entry is never necessary. • Content can never change. • Adequate screen space is available.	Single-Selection List Box
OR: • Typed entry is never necessary. • Content can never change. • Adequate screen space is not available.	Drop-down/Pop-up List Box
OR: • Typed entry may be necessary. • Content can change. • Adequate screen space is available.	Combo Box
OR: • Typed entry may be necessary. • Content can change. • Adequate screen space is not available.	Drop-down/Pop-up Combo Box

Table 8.3 Continued

IF:	USE:
3. IF:	**USE:**
• *Mutually exclusive* alternatives. • Discrete data. • Best represented graphically. • Content rarely changes. • Small or large number of items.	Palette
4. IF:	**USE:**
• *Mutually exclusive* alternatives. • Not frequently selected. • Content does not change. • Well-known, easily remembered data. • Predictable, consecutive data. • Typed entry sometimes desirable. *AND:* • Adequate screen space is not available.	Spin Box
OR: • Adequate screen space is available.	Combo Box
5. IF:	**USE:**
• *Mutually exclusive* alternatives. • Continuous data with a limited range of settings. • Value increases/decreases in a well-known, predictable way. • Spatial representation enhances comprehension.	Slider
6. IF:	**USE:**
• *Nonexclusive* alternatives. • Discrete data. • Best represented verbally. • Typed entry is never necessary. • Content can never change. • Adequate screen space is available. *AND:* • Very limited in number (2 to 8).	Check Boxes
OR: • Potentially large in number (9 or more).	Multiple-Selection List Box

Table 8.4 Choosing a Command Form

IF THE COMMANDS:	USE:
Are standard commands provided by a tool set.	Commands provided by the tool set
Total seven or more, and can be arranged hierarchically into groups.	Menu bar and pull-downs
Total six or fewer, are selected frequently, and affect an entire window.	Buttons in a window
Total seven or more, are selected frequently, and affect an entire window.	Buttons in a toolbar
Are used with other controls, or are complicated commands and need to be simplified.	Buttons in a dialog box
Are sometimes used frequently and are sometimes used infrequently.	Buttons in a dialog box
Are frequently accessed and have only two conditions.	Toggled menu item

Choosing between Buttons and Menus for Commands

Determining the proper way to present a command also depends on several factors. The following considerations are involved in choosing the correct command form:

- Whether or not the command part of a *standard tool set.*
- The total *number* of commands in the application.
- The *complexity* of the commands.
- The *frequency* with which commands are used.
- Whether or not the command is used in association *with another control.*

Guidelines for choosing the proper command form are presented in Table 8.4.

Examples

Improper and proper usage of several controls are illustrated and discussed.

Example 1

This is an instance of improper and proper presentation of command buttons.

Screen 1.1

Here the design and display of buttons is poor. Problems include: (1) The buttons are split between the left and right side of the screen, causing a wide separation. Positioning buttons to the left, from a screen usage and flow standpoint, is illogical. (2) Differences in sizes exist between buttons. OK, a very frequently used button is the smallest, slowing down selection speed if a pointer is used. (3) Different size labels also exist (OK and Search). (4) There appears to be redundancy in button use and purpose. How does OK differ from Save? What does Edit do? (5) From an organization standpoint, standard and application buttons appear to be intermixed. (6) The Back and Next actions are widely separated, making fast reversal of actions more difficult.

Screen 1.2

This shows a much better button design and presentation. Enhancements include: (1) The buttons are located at the bottom of the screen, in a position following the screen usage flow. (2) Button size is standardized, presenting generally larger targets. (3) Button label size is standardized. (4) The seemingly redundant buttons are eliminated. (5) Function-specific buttons are grouped separately from standard buttons, and button groupings are created through a larger spacing between Print and OK. (6) Back, now called Previous, and Next are positioned together for fast paging reversal.

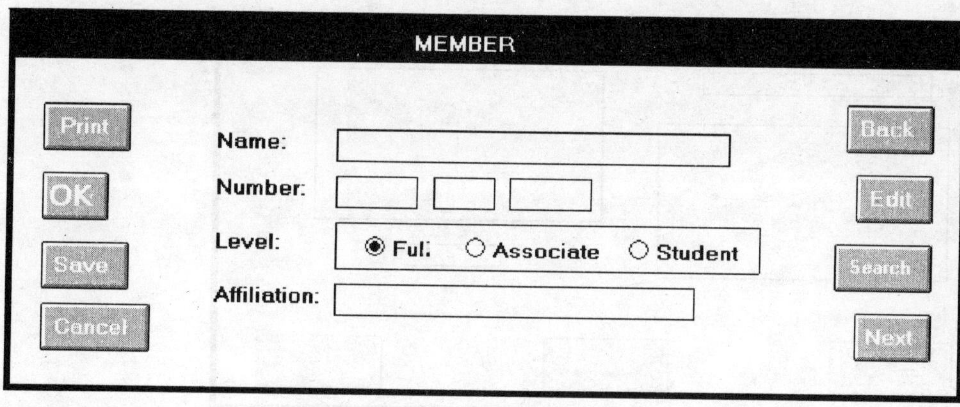

Screen 1.1

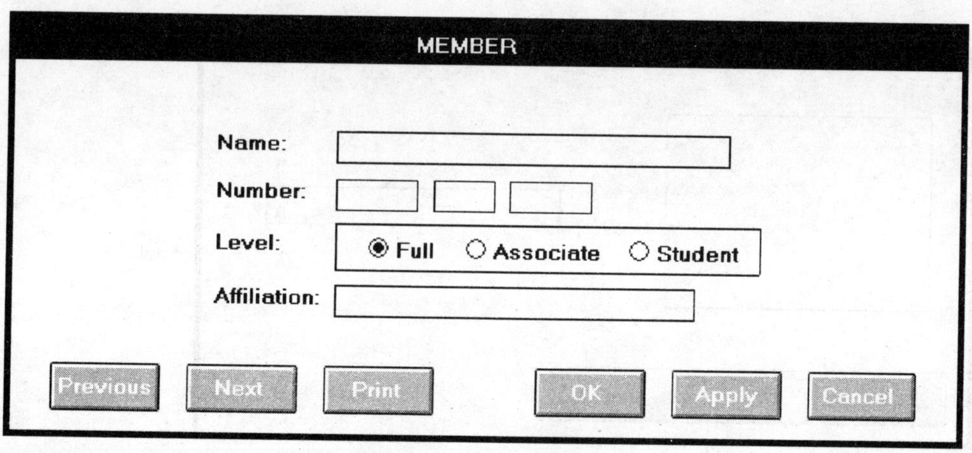

Screen 1.2

Example 2

Here we are dealing with inconsistent location of command buttons.

Screens 2.1 to 2.4

These are the button locations found on four windows within a graphical system. Positions include spread out across the window's bottom (Screen 2.1), left-justified at the bottom (Screen 2.2), centered along the right side (Screen 2.3), and top-justified along the right side (Screen 2.4). Memorization and prediction of button location will be very difficult, slowing down the experienced user.

Screen 2.5

Proper positioning would have found *all* the command buttons consistently positioned, as at the bottom center as illustrated in Screen 2.5.

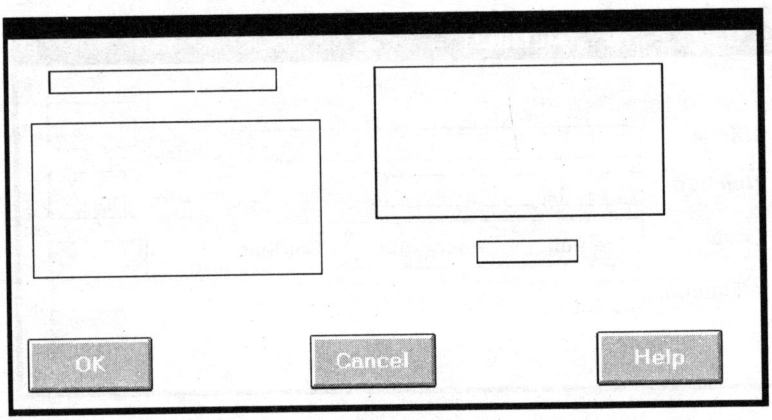

Screen 2.1

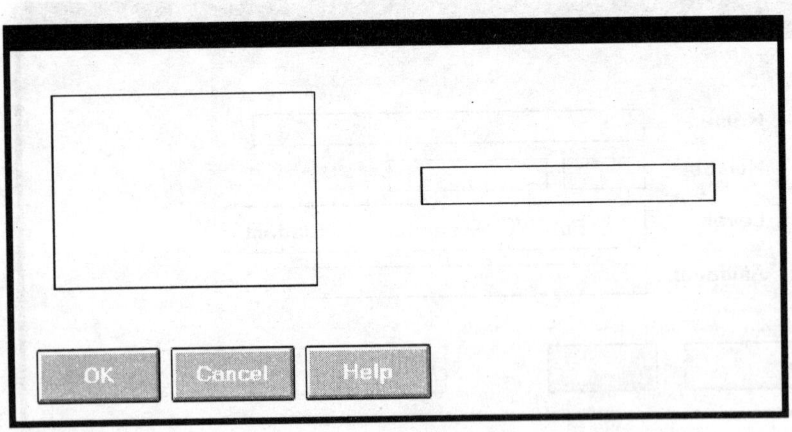

Screen 2.2

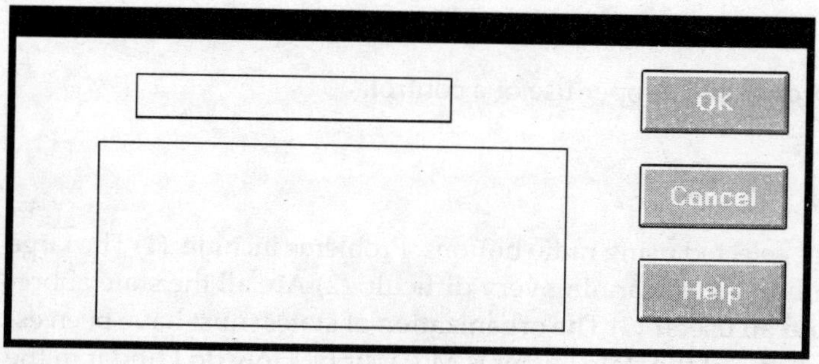

Screen 2.3

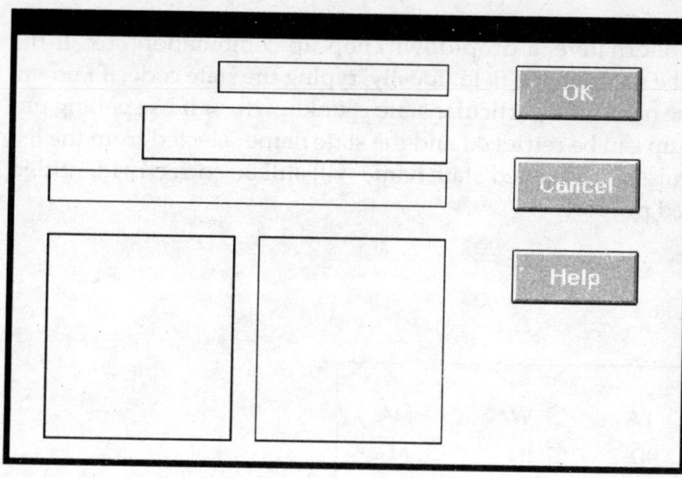

Screen 2.4

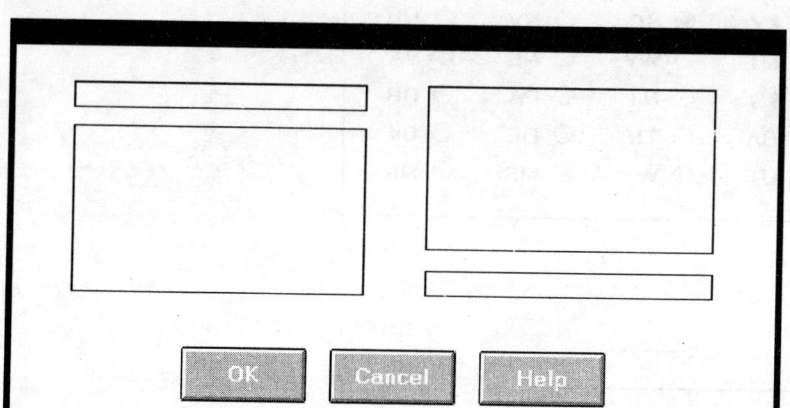

Screen 2.5

Example 3

This is an example of improper and proper use of a control.

Control 3.1

The names of states must be selected using radio buttons. Problems include: (1) The large number of choices presented makes scanning very difficult. (2) Are all the state abbreviations familiar to you, and all users? (3) The organization of states must have been established by a lottery. The name of the state I want is Mississippi. How do I find it in the array?

Control 3.2

This shows a much better alternative, a drop-down/pop-up combination box. If the state name is known, it can be typed in the field. Ideally, typing the state code, if known, will also be acceptable. If the name of a particular state is unknown, or if its spelling unclear, the drop-down/pop-up can be retrieved and the state name selected from the list presented. Ideally, also, a misspelled keyed state name will still be correctly identified by the system and displayed properly.

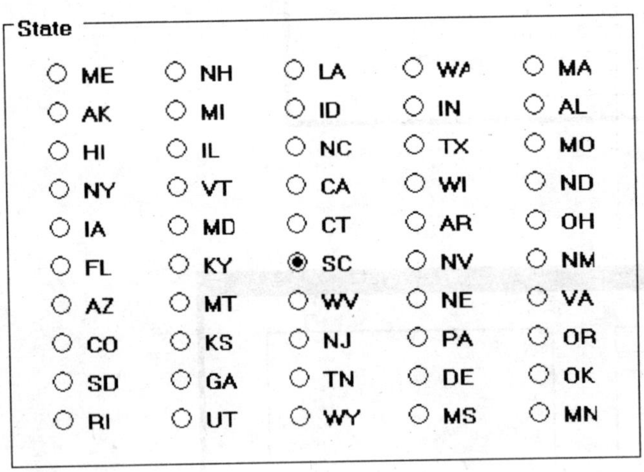

Control 3.1

Control 3.2

Example 4

Here is another instance of improper and proper use of a control.

Screen 4.1

A listing of names is being collected. A courtesy title is selected through list box; last name, first name, and middle initial are typed. The problem: The task is heavily keyboard intensive. To select a title requires shifting to an alternative device control, such as a mouse, or tabbing through the list box listing to find the proper title. This slows down the keying process and may be awkward. The list box also consumes a great deal of space on the screen.

Screen 4.2

A solution: Collect the courtesy title using a pop-up/drop-down combination box. Familiar titles may be quickly typed, along with the remainder of the name data. Rare or unusual titles may be identified by selecting, displaying, and searching the listing of all alternatives. The title may then be entered in the field by selecting from the list or keying it into the field.

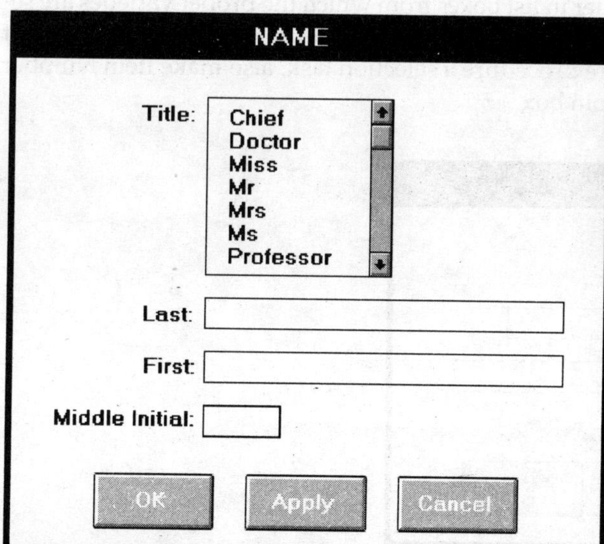

Screen 4.1

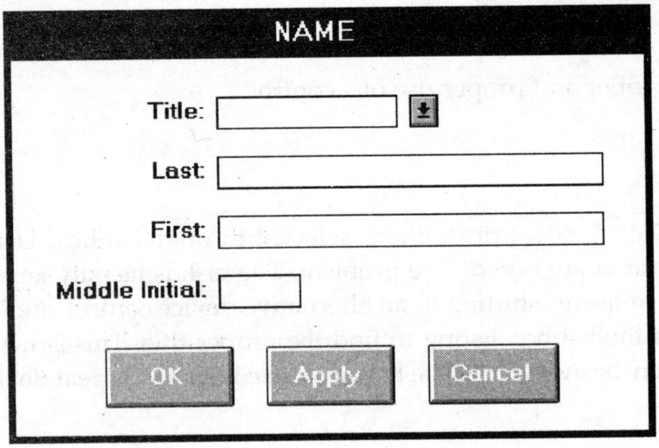

Screen 4.2

Example 5

Again, improper and proper use of controls.

Screen 5.1

A collection of seashells is being cataloged by class and order. Text boxes are provided for the task. The catalog process includes typing words such as "Cephalopoda" and "Eulamellibranchia." The process is slow and conducive to spelling errors.

Screen 5.2

A solution: Present Class and Order in list boxes from which the proper varieties are selected. This will speed up the cataloguing process and eliminate the possibility of spelling errors. To make the entire procedure a selection task, also make Item Number a selectable and incrementable spin box.

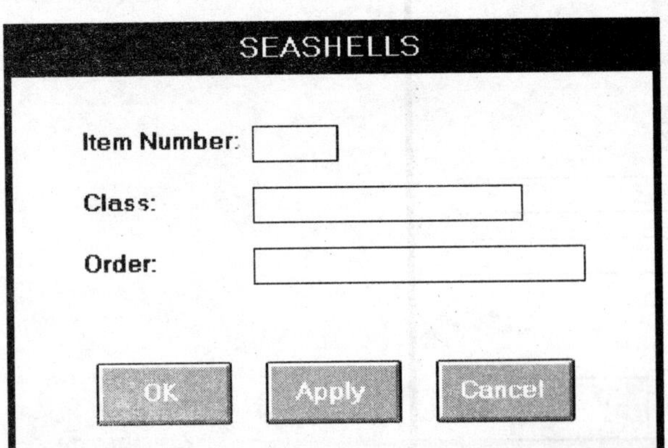

Screen 5.1

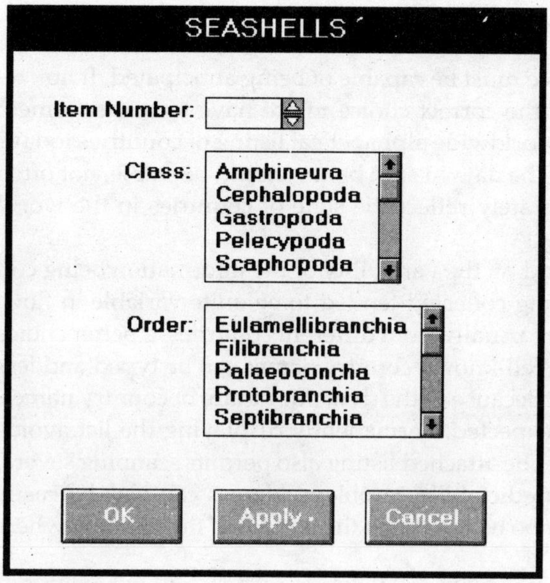

Screen 5.2

Example 6

Again, improper and proper use of a control.

Screen 6.1

An international corporation is setting up a worldwide account database. Names from dozens of different countries are added each day. Country is collected though a spin box. Is this proper usage for a spin box?

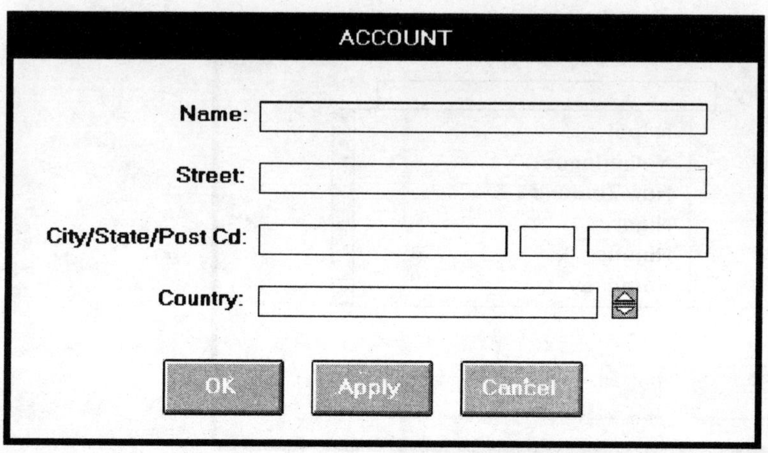

Screen 6.1

Screens 6.2 and 6.3

With a spin box, the next unseen choice must be capable of being anticipated. If not, tedious clicking and searching to find the correct choice might have to be performed. (What country follows Greece in the worldwide alphabetical listing of countries today? Guatemala—at least at this writing.) The data in spin boxes should be stable, not often changing. This quality does not accurately reflect the state of countries in the world today.

The best choice would really depend on the variability of the information being collected. If the account information being collected tended to be quite variable in flow, that is, successive account entries were usually from different countries, a better choice would be a combo box (Screen 6.2). Well-known country names can be typed and less well-known ones found in the listing. Because of the dynamic nature of country names, frequent reference to the list can be expected. Permanently displaying the list avoids the step of retrieving it when needed. The attached listing also permits scanning several names at one time, alleviating the predictability problem. Names can also be easily added or changed as needed. The combo box is also at the bottom of the window where it tends to be out of the way.

If successive account entries tended to be from the same country, that is, the information is batched, a pop-up/drop-down combination would be more appropriate (Screen 6.3). The box can remain closed through successive same country entries and only need be opened occasionally when actually needed.

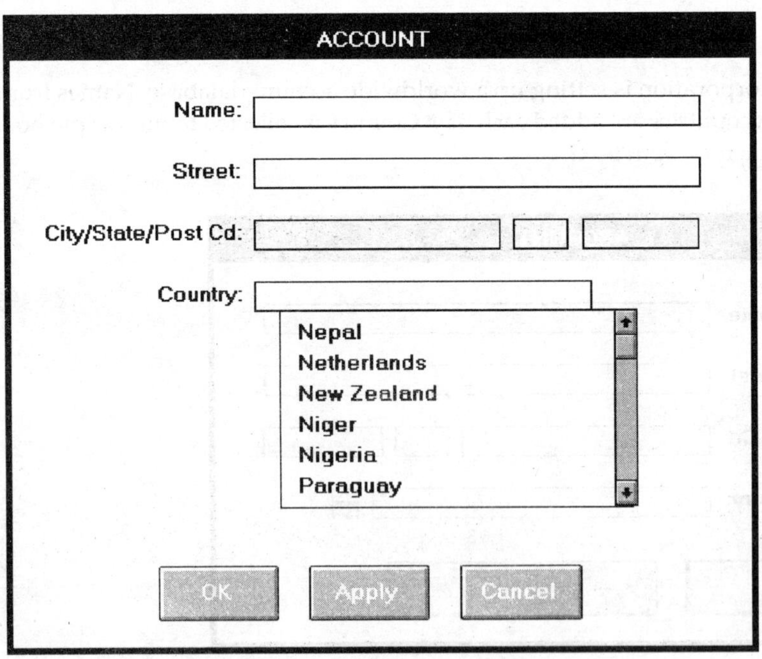

Screen 6.2

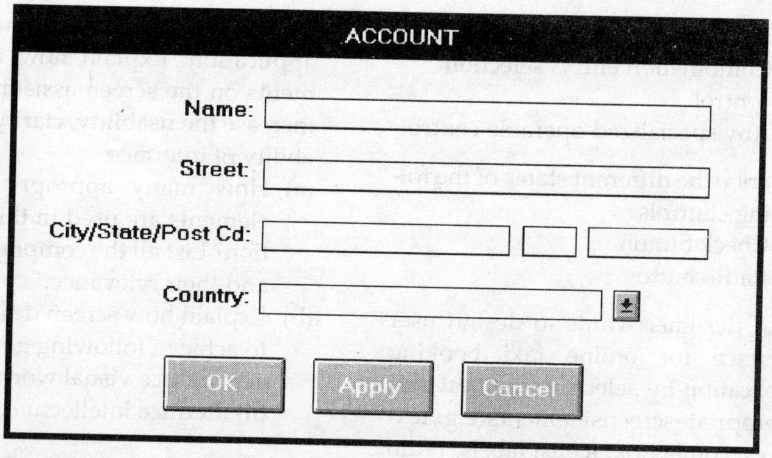

Screen 6.3

Multiple Choice Questions

1. ToolTip control is an example of
   (a) Selection control
   (b) Combination Entry/Selection control
   (c) Presentation control
   (d) Both (a) and (b)
   (e) None of the above
2. Radio Button control is an example of
   (a) Selection control
   (b) Combination Entry/Selection control
   (c) Presentation control
   (d) Both (a) and (b)
   (e) None of the above
3. Spin box control is an example of
   (a) Selection control
   (b) Combination Entry/Selection control
   (c) Presentation control
   (d) Both (a) and (b)
   (e) None of the above
4. Slider control is an example of
   (a) Selection control
   (b) Specialized operable control
   (c) Presentation control
   (d) Both (a) and (b)
   (e) None of the above
5. Balloon Tips control is an example of
   (a) Selection control
   (b) Specialized operable control
   (c) Presentation control
   (d) Both (a) and (b)
   (e) None of the above

Review Questions

1. Describe the criteria for selecting screen based control for GUI applications.
2. Discuss the following screen based controls and explain their types:
   (a) Selection control
   (b) Presentation controls
3. Describe the characteristics and capabilities of the following screen based controls:

(a) Buttons
(b) Combination entry/selection control
(c) Any specialized operable control

4. Describe the different states of the following controls:
   (a) Check button
   (b) Radio button

5. A UI designer wants to design user interface for online taxi booking application by selecting the best and appropriate screens elements (e.g., text boxes, combobox, icons, labels, radio button, check boxes etc.) suitable for application. Explain how these elements on the screen assisting user to increase the usability, clarity, predictability of interface.
   (a) How many appropriate screen elements are used in this application? List all the components used and their relevance.
   (b) Explain how screen design is able to achieve following goals:
      (i) Reduce visual work
      (ii) Reduce intellectual work

Unit

Four

Communication

CHAPTER

9

Text Messages

The wording of the interface and its screens is the basic form of communication with the user. Clear and meaningfully crafted words, messages, and text lead to greatly enhanced system usability and minimize user confusion that leads to errors and possibly even system rejection. In this chapter, general guidelines for choosing the proper words and writing clear messages and text will be presented. These general guidelines will be followed by a discussion of some Web-specific guidelines.

Words, Sentences, Messages, and Text

All communications should simply, clearly, and politely provide the information one must have to effectively use a system. The design of these communications must take into account the user's experience and knowledge of the system topic, and how much information the user actually needs to efficiently interact with the system. Like all aspects of interface design, knowing the user is the first step in choosing the proper words and creating acceptable messages and text.

Words

- Do not use:
  - — Jargon, words, or terms:
    - Unique to the computer profession.
    - With different meanings outside of the computer profession.
    - Made up to describe special functions or conditions.

— Abbreviations or acronyms.
  - Unless the abbreviation or acronym is as familiar as a full word or phrase.

— Word contractions, suffixes, and prefixes.

- Use:
  — Short, familiar words.
  — Standard alphabetic characters.
  — Complete words.
  — Positive terms.
  — Simple action words; avoid noun strings.
  — The "more" dimension when comparing.
  — Consistent words.
- Do not:
  — Stack words.
  — Hyphenate words.
  — Include punctuation for abbreviations, mnemonics, and acronyms.

Jargon. Jargon may take several forms. It may be words or terms that are unique to the computer profession such as *filespec, abend,* or *spool*; words with different meaning outside of information systems such as *boot* or *abort*; or made-up words used to describe special functions or actions such as *ungroup* or *dearchive*. Avoid jargon because it will have to be learned, and it may be interpreted incorrectly.

Abbreviations or acronyms. Avoid using abbreviations and acronyms unless they are as familiar as the fully spelled-out word or phrase. (An example of a familiar acronym is IBM for International Business Machines.) The reason again, it must be understood and learned. Familiar abbreviations and acronyms, if legal to use, may be used following these guidelines:

- **Always use the fully spelled-out form the first time it is encountered in the interface.** Present the abbreviation or acronym in parentheses following the fully spelled-out form.
- **Use the abbreviation or acronym in any subsequent locations in the dialog reached directly, and only directly, from the place where it is defined.** If these subsequent locations can be reached from places in the dialog other than the location where the abbreviation or acronym was defined (as in Web page design), then do not use the abbreviation or acronym alone.

Contractions or short forms. While contractions (*won't* instead of *will not*) save space and lend an informal tone to the interface, be cautious in their use. Never form a contraction from a subject and it's verb, *he'll* instead of *he will*. Words can also be more difficult to understand if they contain prefixes and suffixes, like "un-," or "-ness." A study found that word comprehension often involves a person decomposing more complex terms to establish their basic root meaning and then modifying the meaning to account for the various prefixes and suffixes. Structural complexity hinders comprehension.

Short, familiar words. Shorter words tend to be used more often in everyday conversation, so they are more familiar and easier to understand. The most important factor, however, is familiarity, not length. A longer but familiar word is better than a short, unfamiliar word.

Standard alphabetic characters. Standard alphabetic characters are most familiar to screen viewers. Never use restricted alphabetic sets. Symbols should be used only if they are familiar to all who are using the screen. Common symbols that may be considered as substitutes for alphabetic characters are # for number, % for percent, and $ for dollar. Again, all potential screen users must be familiar with a symbol if it is used as a substitute for alphabet characters.

Complete words. Instead of contractions or short forms, use complete words. Complete words are understood better and faster.

Positive terms. It is generally easier to understand positive, affirmative information than the same information expressed in a negative way. Therefore, avoid the prefixes "ir-," "in-," "dis-," and "un-." Implicitly negative terms, such as "decrease," should be replaced with positive terms, such as "increase."

Simple action words. Replace noun strings with simple action words. Instead of saying, for example, "Project Status Listing" say "*List* Project Status."

"More" dimension. When using comparative terms, the "more" dimension is easier to deal with. The opposite of the "more" is usually considered the "negative." So, use "longer" rather than "shorter," "bigger" rather than "smaller."

Consistency. Words chosen for use in an interface should be used consistently throughout the interface. Never use different words to describe identical functions.

Stacking words. Multiple-word phrases are more readable if the entire phrase is on one line, not stacked vertically.

Hyphenating words. Again, for better readability, never break a word between two lines. Hyphenation was created for ease in production, not ease in comprehension.

Punctuation. Abbreviations, mnemonics, and acronyms should not include punctuation. This permits better readability and avoids confusion between the punctuation and other screen elements.

Some words to forget. Words should be meaningful to, understandable by, and acceptable to, all users. As mentioned above, words perceived as "computerese" may confuse or place an unnecessary intellectual demands on the user. Other words may have a particularly harsh meaning or invoke unpleasant associations (abort, execute, kill), or have vague meanings (abend, boot). These problem words, summarized in Table 9.1, should be avoided in communications whenever possible. Suggested alternative words are presented.

Sentences and Messages

- Sentences and messages must be:
  - — Brief and simple.
  - — Directly and immediately usable.
  - — An affirmative statement.
  - — In an active voice.

— In the temporal sequence of events.
— Structured so that the main topic is near the beginning.
— Of parallel construction.

- Sentences and messages must be of the proper tone:
  — Nonauthoritarian.
  — Nonthreatening.
  — Nonanthropomorphic.
  — Nonpatronizing.
  — Nonpunishing.
  — Cautious in the use of humor.

A sentence, and a message, must minimize ambiguity and confusion, allowing easy, correct, and fast interpretation. It must also have the proper tone, reflecting the needs of the users. Threatening, rude, or impolite messages most often evoke negative responses. The following guidelines will lead to easy, correct, and fast message interpretation and acceptance. A study restructuring error messages along such guidelines has found higher success rates in problem resolution, lower error rates, and improved user satisfaction.

Brief and simple. A message that has to be explained does not communicate. It fails as a message. Brief, simple sentences are more readily understood than longer sen-

Table 9.1 Some Words to Forget

AVOID	USE
Abend	End, Cancel, Stop
Abort	End, Cancel, Stop
Access	Get, Ready, Display
Available	Ready
Boot	Start, Run
Error	–
Execute	Complete
Hit	Press, Depress
Implement	Do, Use, Put Into
Invalid	Not Correct, Not Good, Not Valid
Key	Type, Enter
Kill	End, Cancel
Output	Report, List, Display
Return Key	Enter, Transmit
Terminate	End, Exit

tences containing multiple clauses. Research indicates that sentences over 20 words in length cause a loss in reading comprehension with each additional sentence word. Another research study created messages at three levels of reading ability (fifth, tenth, and fifteenth grade) and tested them on people of varying verbal abilities. The fifth-grade version was found to be best for all levels. People of high verbal ability did not perceive the fifth-grade version as insulting, as some had feared. So, break long sentences into two or more simple sentences if this can be done without changing the meaning. Always write at the eighth grade level, or less.

Directly and immediately usable. Searching through reference material to translate a message is unacceptable, as are requirements for transposing, computing, interpolating, or mentally translating messages into other units.

Affirmative statement. Affirmative statements are easier to understand than negative statements. For example, *"Complete entry before returning to menu."* is easier to grasp than *"Do not return to menu before completing entry."* Tell a person what to do rather than what to avoid. There is an exception, of course. The user may be told how to avoid a situation with disastrous consequences.

Active voice. The active voice is usually easier to understand than passive voice. For example, *"Send the message by depressing TRANSMIT"* is more understandable than *"The message is sent by depressing TRANSMIT."*

Temporal sequence. If a sentence describes a temporal sequence of events, the order of words should correspond to this sequence. A prompt should say, *"Complete address and page forward"* rather than *"Page forward after completing address."*

Main topic at beginning. Information that must be remembered should be placed at the beginning of a message or sentence. A person can remember something longer if it appears at the start. Items in the middle of a sentence or message are hardest to remember.

Parallel construction. Use the same grammatical structure for elements of sentences or messages that provide the same kind of information. For example, say, *"Use this control to select one choice"* and *"Use this menu to select one option."* Not, *"To select one choice use this control,"* and *"This menu is used to select one option."*

Nonauthoritarian. Imply that the system is awaiting the user's direction, not that the system is directing the user. For example, phrase a message as *"Ready for the next command,"* not *"Enter the next command."*

Nonthreatening. Negative tones or actions, or threats, are not very friendly. Since errors are often the result of a failure to understand, mistakes, or trial-and-error behavior, the user may feel confused, inadequate, or anxious. Blaming the user for problems can heighten anxiety, making error correction more difficult and increasing the chance of more errors. Therefore, harsh words like "illegal," "bad," or "fatal" should be avoided.

Also, avoid using the word "error" in messages when it implies a user error. "Error" tends to focus the attention on the person involved rather than on the problem. For example, instead of saying *"Error—Numbers are illegal,"* say, *"Months must be entered by name."* Since the computer does not have an ego to be bruised, an excellent design approach would be to have it assume the blame for all miscommunications.

Nonanthropomorphic. Having the computer "talk" like a person should be avoided for several reasons. An attribution of knowledge or intelligence will, first, imply a much higher level of computer "knowledge" than actually exists, creating shattered user expectations. Second, this attribute eliminates the distinction that actually exists between people and computers. People "control" computers; they "respect the desires" of other human beings. Third, many people express anxiety about using computers by saying things like "they make you feel dumb." The feeling of interacting with another person who is evaluating your proficiency can heighten this anxiety. There is also some research evidence that a nonanthropomorphic approach is best, being seen as more honest, preferred, and easier to use.

The best advice at this moment is do not give a human personality to a machine. Imply that the system is awaiting the user's direction, not vice versa. Say, for example, "*What do you need?*" not "*How can I help you?*"

Nonpatronizing. Patronizing messages can be embarrassing. "*Very good, you did it right*" may thrill a fourth-grader, but would be somewhat less than thrilling to an adult. Being told "*You forgot again*" once may be acceptable, but being told three or four times in one minute is another story. In a commonly available video golf game, after a player makes a high score on a golf hole, the program returns with the suggestion to the player to "*Try another sport.*" A golf professional that played this game took great offense to this advice and walked away. Would Tiger Woods appreciate this kind of suggestion? A person may disagree with patronizing conclusions, so why risk the offense?

Punishment and humor. Until an optimal computer personality is developed, messages should remain factual and informative, and should not attempt humor or punishment. Humor is a transitory and changeable thing. What is funny today may not be funny tomorrow, and what is funny to some may not be to others. Punishment is never a desirable way to force a change in behavior, especially among adults.

Messages

Messages are communications provided on the screen to the screen viewer. Several different types of messages exist, and they may be displayed in different forms and locations. A message should possess the proper tone and style and be consistent within itself and with other messages.

Screen messages fall into two broad categories: system and instructional. *System* messages are generated by the system to keep the user informed of the system's state and activities. They are customarily presented within message boxes. They reflect the system state, as it exists at that moment in time. *Instructional* messages, sometimes referred to as *prompting* messages, are messages that tell the user how to work with, or complete, the screen displayed. They may be provided in messages boxes and also within the screen itself.

System messages. System messages are of several types, each reflecting a different purpose. The various platforms have developed standard message boxes, with standard components, for these different types. Message box elements include a standard icon to assist in fast recognition of message kind, the message itself, and standard command buttons. The types of message boxes in Microsoft Windows are illustrated in Figures 9.1, 9.2, and 9.3.

Common message types are:

Status messages. A status message is used for providing information concerning the progress of a lengthy operation. It usually contains a progress indicator and a short message describing the kind of operation being performed. It typically only possesses a *Cancel* button, to stop the operation being performed. *Pause* and *Resume* buttons may also be included, if desired.

Informational messages. Informational messages, also called *notification* messages, provide information about the state of the system when it is not immediately obvious to the user. They may confirm that non-obvious processing is taking place or is completed. They may also be used to provide intermediate feedback when normal feedback is delayed. This kind of message is usually identified by an "I" icon to the left of the message. In Microsoft Windows "I" is in a balloon. No user actions are normally necessary with these kinds of messages, although confirmation that the message has been seen can be requested. A Microsoft Windows informational message box is illustrated in Figure 9.1.

Warning messages. Warning messages call attention to a situation that may be undesirable. They are usually identified by an "!" icon to the left of the message. The user must determine whether the situation is in fact a problem and may be asked to advise the system whether or not to proceed. A deletion request by a user is an action that commonly generates a warning message. When a user requests a deletion, a message asking for confirmation of the deletion is usually presented. A warning message can also be used for field edit error messages. A Microsoft Windows warning message box is illustrated in Figure 9.2.

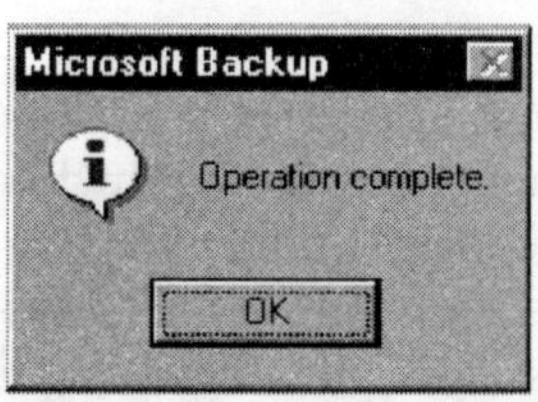

Figure 9.1 Informational message box from Microsoft Windows with icon, text, and button.

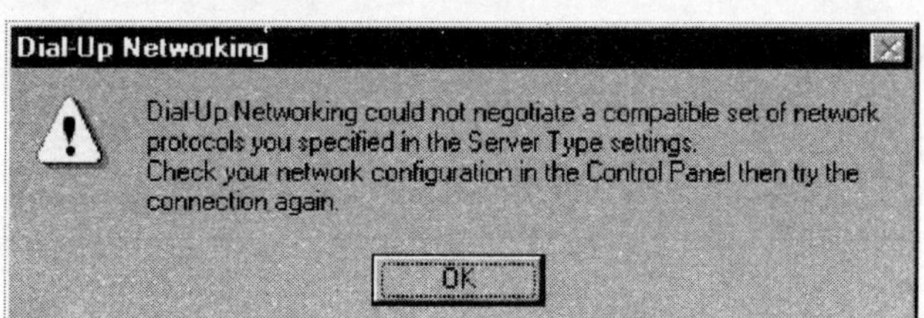

Figure 9.2 Warning message box from Microsoft Windows with icon, text, and button.

Figure 9.3 Critical message box from Microsoft Windows with icon, text, and button.

Critical messages. Critical messages, sometimes called *action* messages, call attention to conditions that require a user action before the system can proceed. A message describing an erroneous situation is usually presented as a critical message. Some inconsistency currently exists in the icons used to designate this kind of message. Some products use a "Do Not" symbol while others use a "Stop" sign. An X in a circle is used by Microsoft Windows. Additionally, one platform provides the option of using a "?" icon if the user's attention to the problem may not be immediately needed (for example, Printer is out of paper). Critical messages require a user action to continue. A Microsoft Windows critical message box is illustrated in Figure 9.3.

Question messages. Question messages are another kind of message type sometimes seen. A question message asks a question and offers a choice of options for selection. It is designated by a "?" icon preceding the message text. This type may be used when there is a question to be asked and the message does not appear to be suited to the above types. Before using a question message, remember that one platform uses the "?" icon for certain kinds of critical messages. Also, Microsoft Windows no longer recommends the "?" icon because of possible confusion with help dialogs.

Messages that are too generic or poorly written frustrate users, increase support costs, and ultimately reflect poorly on the quality of the product. Therefore, it is worthwhile to design effective message boxes. It is even better to avoid creating situations that require displaying such a message. For example, if the user does not have sufficient disk space to perform an operation, check for available disk space before the user attempts the operation and disable the command if necessary. A balloon tip or status bar message can be used to notify the user about why the command is unavailable.

MYTH If the users need an explanation they'll always read the documentation.

Writing Message Box Text

- Title bar:
  — Clearly identify the source of the message.
    - The name of the object to which it refers.
    - The name of the application to which it refers.

— Do not include an indication of message type.
— Use mixed case in the headline style.

- Message box:
  — Provide a clear and concise description of the condition causing the message box to be displayed.
    - Use complete sentences with ending punctuation.
    - State the problem, its probable cause (if known), and what the user can do about it.
    - Avoid contractions.
    - Avoid technical jargon and system-oriented information.
    - Provide only as much background information as necessary for the message to be understood.
    - Show only one message box about the cause of condition in a single message.
    - Make the solution an option offered in the message.
    - Avoid multistep solutions.
    - Use consistent words and phrasing for similar situations.
    - Use the word "please" conservatively.

  — Do not exceed two or three lines.
  — Include the relevant icon identifying the type of message to the left of the text.
  — Center the message text in window.

Microsoft recommends these message box guidelines.

Title Bar Text

Clearly identify the source of the message in the message box title bar. This may be the name of the object to which it refers, or the name of the application to which it refers. A clear title is particularly important in the Windows multitasking environment because message boxes that appear might not always be the result of current user interaction. In addition, because objects supported by different applications can be embedded in the same document, different application code may be running when the user activates the object for editing. Therefore, the title of a message box plays a vital role in communicating the source of a message.

Do not include in the title an indication of message type. (*Warning* or *caution*, for example.) The icon contained within the message box conveys the nature of the message. Never include the word "error" in the title, for reasons previously mentioned. Use mixed case in the headline style to present the message box title.

Message Box Text

Provide a clear and concise description of the condition causing the message box to be displayed, in terminology the user understands. Use complete sentences with ending punctuation. State the problem, its probable cause (if known), and what the user can do about it, no matter how obvious the solution. To aid user comprehension, avoid contractions, technical jargon, and system-oriented information.

Provide only as much background information as necessary for the message to be understood. To supplement the amount of information in the message box text, include a *Help* button to access more complete descriptive information.

Make messages as specific as possible. Show only one message box regarding a condition in a single message; avoid combining two or more conditions in a single message. For example, if something cannot be done for several reasons, provide a specific message describing each reason.

Make the solution an option offered in the message. For example, if an object such as a string of text will not fit within a certain boundary, and another boundary is available within which it will fit, provide the option to switch to the larger boundary. Do not simply say "The text will not fit."

Avoid multistep solutions. People have difficulty remembering more than two or three simple steps after a message box closes. If multiple steps are necessary, provide general instructions or add a Help button that displays a relevant Help topic. Always present the steps in the order they should be completed. Use consistent words and phrasing for similar situations.

Use the word *please* conservatively. Overuse will diminish its effectiveness. Consider using it in the following situations:

- When the user is asked to wait while the program completes an action.
- When the user is asked to retype information that is required before the user can continue.
- When the user is inconvenienced in some other way.

Do not exceed two or three lines of text. Include the relevant icon identifying the type of message to the left of the text, and center the message text in window.

Message Box Controls

- Command buttons:
  - — If a message requires no choices to be made but only acknowledgment:
    - Include an *OK* button.
  - — If a message requires a choice be made, provide a command button for each option:
    - Include *OK* and *Cancel* buttons only when the user has the option of continuing or stopping the action.
    - Include *Yes* and *No* buttons when the user must decide how to continue.
    - If these choices are too ambiguous, label the command buttons with the names of specific actions.
  - — If a message allows initiation of an action to correct the situation described:
    - Include a properly labeled button initiating the corrective action.
  - — If a message describes an interrupted process whose state cannot be restored:
    - Provide a *Stop* button.
  - — If a message offers an opportunity to cancel a process as well as to perform or not perform an action:
    - Provide a *Cancel* button.
  - — If more details about a message topic must be presented:
    - Provide a *Help* button.
  - — Designate the most frequent or least destructive option as the default.

— Display a message box only when the window of an application is active.
— Display only one message box for a specific condition.

- Close box:
  — Enable the title bar *Close* box only if the message includes a Cancel button.

Command buttons. A user response to a message box is usually accomplished though a command button. The kind, or kinds, of command buttons included depend upon the reason the message box was presented. If a message requires no user choices to be made but only an acknowledgment of the message, include an *OK* button. If the message requires the user to make a choice, include a command button for each option. Include *OK* and *Cancel* buttons only when the user has the option of continuing or stopping the action. Use *Yes* and *No* buttons when the user must decide how to continue. If these choices are too ambiguous, label the command buttons with the names of specific actions to be performed, *Save* and *Delete* for example.

If a message allows initiation of a user action to correct the situation described, include a properly labeled button initiating the corrective action. If, for example, the message indicates that the user must switch to another application window to take corrective action, include a button that opens that application window. Be sure to clearly label the button and the results the user can expect from pressing it. If a message describes an interrupted process whose state cannot be restored, provide a *Stop* button. (Cancel implies restoring the state of the process or task that initiated the message.) If a message offers an opportunity to cancel a process as well as to perform or not perform an action, provide a *Cancel* button. Clearly label the button and the results the user can expect from selecting it. If more details about a message topic must be presented, provide a *Help* button. This enables the message text to be succinctly presented.

Designate the most frequent or least destructive command option as the default. Because a message box disrupts the user's current task, it is best to display a message box only when the window of the application to which the message refers is active. If the application's window is not active, use the application's button entry on the taskbar to alert the user. After the user activates the application, the message box can be displayed. Display only one message box for a specific condition. Displaying a sequential set of message boxes tends to confuse users.

Command buttons allow the message box interaction to be simple and efficient. If other types of controls are considered, always be aware of the potential increase in interface complexity.

Close box. Enable the title bar *Close* box only if the message includes a Cancel button. To leave it available in other situations can confuse users.

Message Location

- Use the message line for messages that must not interfere with screen information.
- Pop-up windows may be used for all kinds of messages, if available.
- Pop-up windows should always be used for critical messages.

Messages may also be displayed either in the message line as well as within pop-up windows, with pop-up windows being recommended location. All critical messages should be displayed in a pop-up window. A research study compared locating messages in pop-up windows with messages presented in permanently displayed fixed locations, such as at the screen's bottom or top. The study found pop-up windows were detected more often, and faster, than those permanently affixed in standard locations on the screen.

Other Message Considerations

- Abbreviated, more concise versions of messages should be available.
- Something that must be remembered should be at the beginning of the text.
- Do not include code numbers with messages.

Abbreviated versions. People are impatient with uninformative or redundant computer messages. A problem, however, is that the degree of computer-to-person message redundancy depends on the person's experience with the system. And it may vary with different parts of a system. So the availability of abbreviated and detailed messages allows the tailoring of the system to the needs of each user. During system training and early implementation stages, detailed versions can be used. Individuals can switch to abbreviated versions as their familiarity with the system increases. People using abbreviated messages should, however, be able to request detailed messages at any time.

Important at beginning of text. One can remember something longer if it appears at the beginning of a message. Items in the middle of a message are hardest to remember.

Code numbers. Messages that begin with a strange code number do not meet the user's needs. A code number, if needed at all, is only necessary after reading the message and should, therefore, be placed in parentheses at the end of the message.

Instructional Messages

- Provide instructional information at the depth of detail needed by the user.
- Locate it at strategic positions on the screen.
- Display it in a manner that visually differentiates it from other screen elements.
- In writing, follow all relevant writing guidelines for words, sentences, and messages.

The second categories of messages, *instructional* or prompting messages, are guidance messages that tell the user how to work with, or complete, the screen displayed. They may be permanently affixed to a screen, or they may appear as the result of a help request.

Depth of detail. Instructional messages are of most benefit to the novice or casual system user. Instructions for these kinds of users must be more detailed than for experienced users. Experienced users usually require only cryptic reminders. To balance the needs of a wide range of users with varying experience levels, accessing instructions through a *Help* function is the best solution.

Location. Locate instructions at strategic points on screens. They should be placed at spots just preceding the controls or elements to which they apply. Never, however, place an instruction on one screen that applies to elements on a following screen. They will not be remembered.

Visual differentiation. Display instructions in a manner that visually differentiates them from all other screen elements. This will allow them to be easily ignored by users who do not need them.

Writing. In writing instructions, follow all relevant writing guidelines recently described for words, sentences, and messages. Also refer to Table 9.2 for the proper terms to use when interacting with a screen control.

In conclusion, the following "error message" was recently encountered using the Web site of a popular cable TV channel:

> ERROR!
> PLEASE HIT YOUR BACK BUTTON AND ENTER A SEARCH.

In this brief 10-word message, the message writer managed to use three nonrecommended words (error, hit, and enter). Wouldn't the following have been much more agreeable?

> THE SEARCH FIELD DID NOT CONTAIN AN ENTRY.
> PLEASE CLICK THE BACK BUTTON AND TYPE A SEARCH VALUE.

The original message writer gets one point for including *Please*, however.

Table 9.2 Instructional Interaction Terms

TO INTERACT WITH THIS CONTROL:	USE THIS TERM:
For a command button, to activate.	Click
For a text box, to type or paste information.	Type
For a list box, to select an item, or items.	Select
To either type or select an option.	Enter
For a check box: To add a component. To clear a component.	 Select Clear
For a radio button.	Select
For a slider interaction.	Move
For a tab interaction.	Click

Text

Text, by a very general definition, is any textual element that appears on a screen, including field captions, headings, words, sentences, messages, and instructions. Text, in the following discussion, refers to *body* text, a large compilation of words whose smallest element is a paragraph and whose maximum length is unlimited, its size being governed by the reason for its existence.

Presenting Text

- Fonts:
  - — Use plain and simple fonts.
  - — Choose a minimum point size of 12 to 14.
  - — Use proportional fonts.
- Width:
  - — Include no more than 40 to 60 characters on each line.
    - A double column of 30 to 35 characters separated by five spaces is also acceptable.
  - — Do not right-justify.
  - — Do not hyphenate words.
- Content:
  - — Use headings to introduce a new topic.
  - — Separate paragraphs by at least one blank line.
  - — Start a fresh topic on a new page.
  - — Use lists to present facts.
  - — Emphasize important things by:
    - Positioning.
    - Boxes.
    - Bold typefaces.
    - Indented margins.
- Miscellaneous:
  - — Use paging (not scrolling).
  - — Provide a screen design philosophy consistent with other parts of the system.

Fonts. Fonts chosen for text should be plain and simple and of adequate size for easy reading, either 12 or 14 points. Proportional spacing (width governed by actual letter size, when an *l* is narrower than an *m*) is preferred to nonproportional spacing.

Width. A typical screen is a little too wide for comfortable reading of text. It is difficult for the eye to keep its place as it moves from the end of one line to the beginning of the next line. Studies find that a line of text should contain no more than 40 to 60 characters, or be confined to 1.5 lowercase alphabets or 39 characters. For greater screen efficiency, consider using two columns of text, each about 30 or 35 characters wide. Confine double-columns to one screen of information, however. Never require scrolling up and down multiple times to read all the text.

Studies also find that non-right-justified (or ragged-right edge) text lines are just as legible as justified text lines. Large spaces left in right-justified text interrupt eye movement and impede reading. The reading speed of right-justified text was actually found to be 8 to 10 percent slower than non-right-justified text in one study. Non-right-justified text has another advantage in that word hyphenation is not required. Experts also say that non-right-justified text creates more visual interest, and is best for very narrow columns of text. Full left- and right-justification, may be considered for long works that require continuous reading and concentration, such as long text, newspapers, and novels.

Content. Headings to introduce new topics provide breaks or pause points for the reader. They provide obvious closure points. Starting new topics on new pages reinforces the needed breaks. Separating paragraphs by a blank line will result in more cohesive groupings and alleviate the impression of a dense screen.

Use lists to present facts. Lists are convenient, simple, and uncluttered and can effectively break up long strings of text. Designate items in a list with a "bullet" or other simple symbol. Emphasize important points by placing them in unusual places, drawing boxes around them, using bold typefaces, or providing indented left and right margins. In addition to their emphasizing capabilities, they also make the screen more visually interesting.

Miscellaneous. Paging through screens, rather than scrolling, has been found to yield better performance and to be preferred by many system users. A severe disadvantage of scrolling for novices is loss of orienta-tion. While experts can handle scrolling, the best choice if all users are considered is paging.

If scrolling is going to be used, the preferred approach is *telescoping*, in which the window moves around the data. This method is more natural and causes fewer errors than the *microscope* approach, in which the data appears to move under a fixed viewing window.

MAXIM **Clear communication is not shouting VERY, VERY LOUD.**

Writing Text

- Sentences and paragraphs:
  - — Use short sentences composed of familiar, personal words.
    - Cut the excess words.
    - Try to keep the number of words in a sentence to 20 or less.
  - — Cut the number of sentences.
  - — Use separate sentences for separate ideas.
  - — Keep the paragraphs short.
  - — Restrict a paragraph to only one idea.
- Style:
  - — Use the active writing style.
  - — Use the personal writing style, if appropriate.

— Write as you talk.
— Use subjective opinion.
— Use specific examples.
— Read it out loud.

Sentences and paragraphs. Simple words and short sentences are the cornerstones of good writing. As mentioned above, research indicates that sentences over 20 words in length cause a loss in reading comprehension with each additional sentence word. Long sentences often result from trying to express more than one idea in the sentence, or from using unnecessary words. Table 9.3, derived from Microsoft (2001), lists some common "wordy" phrases to avoid and their replacement words. It also describes some redundant word pairings to avoid. These redundancies are also known as *baby puppies,* a concept that was graciously explained to me by the editor of my first book many years ago. Use separate sentences for separate ideas. Place multiple items in a list format, and delete all unnecessary words. Short paragraphs are less threatening to the user and more frequently read. They also provide visual breaking points in a screen or page.

Style. The style chosen should reflect the needs and characteristics of the user. The style will affect the readability and comprehensibility of the text. The active writing style is easier to read and understand. It almost always uses fewer words and leaves no unanswered questions (contrast the passive "The customer name should be typed" with the active "Type the customer name"). The personal style, the use of "you" and "I" ("Now you must press the Enter key"), keeps the writing active, makes writing directly relevant to the reader, and is more interesting. Materials read by a wide variety of people for informational purposes only, however, should not use the personal style.

Write in the way you would say something to the reader. Also, use subjective opinion ("This screen is not used very often") to reinforce the users' understanding of what they are reading. It does not tell anything specific, but reinforces facts already read or about to be read. Do not overuse subjective opinion, however, and make sure it is correct. Overuse makes facts harder to find, and an incorrect opinion casts suspicion on all the facts being presented.

The best way to explain a general rule is to show how it applies through examples. Examples should be short, relevant, and easy for the reader to relate to. They should also be made visually different from the main text, either through indentation, boxing, or some other technique. Finally, read what you have written out loud to yourself. If it sounds wordy, stilted, or difficult, it will sound this way to the reader, too. Rewrite it.

Window Title

- All windows must have a title located in a centered position at the top.
  — Exception: Windows containing messages.
- Clearly and concisely describe the purpose of the window.
- Spell it out fully using an uppercase or mixed-case font.

- If title truncation is necessary, truncate it from right to left.
- If presented above a menu bar, display it with a background that contrasts with the bar.

The window title should be positioned at the top center and fully spelled out using either uppercase letters or mixed case in the headline style. Using an uppercase font will give it the needed moderate emphasis, aiding in setting it off from the screen body (IBM's SAA CUA and Microsoft's Windows guidelines display the title, like all screen components, in mixed-case letters). Windows containing messages, however, need not have a title. The title should clearly and concisely describe the screen's purpose. If the window appears as a result of a previous selection, the title should clearly reflect the wording of the selection made to retrieve it. For small windows, where title truncation is necessary, truncate from right to left.

If the title appears above the menu bar, the title's background should contrast with that of the bar. A recommendation is to use the same background color and caption color as the screen body. A title can always be identified by its topmost location on the screen, so using a color different from other screen components may add to visual confusion.

Conventions

- Establish conventions for referring to:
  - — Individual keyboard keys.
  - — Keys to be pressed at the same time.
  - — Field captions.
  - — Names supplied by users or defined by the system.
  - — Commands and actions.

Table 9.3 Wordy Phrases and Word Redundancies

INSTEAD OF THIS PHRASE:	SAY THIS:	WORD REDUNDANCIES
By means of	By	Surrounding Environment
For the purposes of	For	Absolutely Complete
In many cases	Often	Exactly identical
In the event that	If	Repeat again
Is able to	Can	Final conclusion
The way in which	The way, how	Knowledge and awareness
In order to	To	Each and every
Prior to	Before	Complete overview
Is required to	Must	Advance planning
		Full and complete

Derived from Microsoft (2001)

In messages and text it is often necessary to refer to keyboard keys, field captions, filenames, commands, or actions. These components should be described in the same manner whenever referenced. Keyboard keys should always be referenced as they are inscribed on the keyboard. (They usually appear in a mixed-case text format.) A useful convention for referring to keys that should be pressed at the same time is a plus (+) sign between the key descriptions (Alt+F10). Names may be enclosed in quotes ("Pending").

Sequence Control Guidance

- Consider providing a guidance message telling how to continue at points in the dialog when:
  — A decision must be made.
  — A response needs to be made to continue.
- Consider indicating what control options exist at points in the dialog where several alternatives may be available.
- Permit these prompts to be turned on or off by the user.

Consider providing prompts telling the user how to continue when a decision and response must be made to continue. For example, it might be indicated that:

INFORMATION IS CURRENT THROUGH AUGUST 26, 2001.
PRESS ENTER TO CONTINUE.

Where several control options exist, consider providing a prompt such as:

PRESS S TO SAVE, D TO DELETE, OR P TO PRINT.
TYPE C TO CREATE A NEW FILE, OR E TO EDIT A NEW FILE: _

For experienced users, these kinds of prompts can become visual noise. Allow users to turn them on or off as needed.

Text for Web Pages

Text for Web pages will generally follow the aforementioned guidelines for words, sentences, messages, instructions, and text. The unique characteristics of the Web, however, require a separate set of supplemental guidelines for several Web topics, including, word usage, error message presentation, and text, heading, and title writing. Additionally, the writing of links must be addressed. This section focuses on these topics.

Words

- Minimize the use of words that call attention to the Web.

Generally, avoid using words that are specific to the Web. A few Web-specific terms are "This Web site," "Click here," and "Follow this link." A good test of this guideline is to print out a page, read it, and see if it makes as much sense on paper as it does on the screen.

Error Messages

- Provide helpful error messages for:
  - — Incomplete or incorrectly keyed, entered, or selected data.
  - — Requests for documents that do not exist or cannot be found.
- Redisplay a message on the page to which it relates.
- Present them in a visually distinctive and noticeable manner.

Provide helpful error messages for data that has been incompletely or incorrectly entered. Also provide messages for requested documents that do not exist or cannot be found. In a graphical interface, an error message is displayed in a message box overlaying the error-causing screen. The underlying screen is visible and can be viewed in conjunction with the error-correction instructions. The message box remains displayed until the user acknowledges its presence. In Web page design, displaying the error message on a separate page is accomplished at the expense of the error-causing page disappearing from view. Human memory being what it is, a possible solution now exists to a problem whose details are now vague. Problem resolution typically involves paging back and forth between the error message and the related Web page, an inefficient operation.

The alternate solution is to present the error message on the page where the error exists. This is the recommended choice. Context is maintained, and both elements can be viewed in fairly close proximity to each other. The error message must be displayed in a visually distinctive manner as close to the problem as possible. Visual distinctiveness can be achieved through displaying the message in a larger, bolder, and distinctive font. The user's attention will probably be directed to the part of the page on which actions can be performed, so the message should be made as obvious as possible. A message in the same font style as the page will be less likely to be noticed.

Keep in mind, however, that it is better to prevent errors than handle them. This topic will be addressed next in Chapter 10 "Feedback and Guidance."

Instructions

- Do not use phrasing that indicates a certain page order or flow.
- Explain where "Up" leads too.
- Phrase them in a browser-independent manner.
- Minimize "Click here" instructions.
  - — Say "Select this link."

Do not use phrasing that indicates a certain page order or flow. How the visitor arrived at the site is unknown. Do not use "Return to" instructions; it cannot be assumed that the term is meaningful in the new context. Describe where an "Up" button leads, where the user will go, and what will be found there. Make sure instructions are detailed enough to be understood without being specific to one browser version or brand. Don't use the phrase "click here." Some users will not use a mouse and may feel alienated. A more proper instruction for all users is "Select this link."

Text

Web page text must be legible and properly written for the medium.

Presentation

- Provide text that contrasts highly with the background.

Text legibility can be a severe problem if insufficient contrast exists between the text and its background. Patterned backgrounds can severely impact legibility, as do many colors. A common characteristic of the best Web sites is they contain text highly contrasting with its background. Overall, the best combination is black text on a white background.

Writing

- Style:
  - Use a style reflecting the needs of the site users.
  - Write objectively.
  - Use the inverted pyramid organization.
  - Be concise, using only about half the number of words of conventional text.
  - Each paragraph should:
    - Be short.
    - Contain only one main idea.
- Links:
  - Minimize within-text links.
  - Place them at the beginning or end of paragraphs or sections of text.
- Scanning:
  - Make text scannable by using:
    - Bulleted listings.
    - Tables.
    - Headings.
    - Bold type.
- Testing:
  - Test for legibility and readability.

Style. Web users can be characterized as being multicultural with multi-interests, multi-needs, and multi-just about everything else. Writing styles will vary, depending on the needs of the target audience. Establishing the proper style depends on who the viewers are, what they know, where they normally get similar information, and the nature of the material. A business application will be written differently than an entertainment site. A product sales site differently than that of a business application or entertainment site. Writing style depends less on medium differences than on answers to the above questions. Writing style, then, should reflect the tone of similar copy published for the target audience in other media. Generally speaking, writing that strays too far from what is conventional for the target audience draws attention to itself at the expense of content. If Web writing does have one quality that sets it apart from print writing, however, it is its informality. Users seem to prefer a more informal writing style.

Users also prefer writing, says research, that is *objective* rather than filled with overly hyped or boastful promotional claims or sprinkled with "marketese-isms." Subjective adjectives, such as outstanding, experienced, reliable, and dynamic, have been shown to inspire mistrust on the part of the user, and also to increase the user's cognitive load as the "irrelevant stuff" must first be comprehended and then discarded. So, always be objective in writing style.

The *inverted pyramid* organization starts with a conclusion or summary of key points and follows with the supporting details or background information. This organization scheme, also commonly found in newspaper articles, lets the user quickly identify an article's content and assess whether continued reading is warranted.

Be *concise,* succinct, and to the point, using only about half the number of words of conventional text. Pack the maximum meaning into minimum text, so users will get the message in the shortest possible time. Keep the writing tight and nonverbose. Use short sentences and the shortest form of a word or an idea. Minimize "fluff," useless, and inessential information, or words that do not add meaning to what is being said. Avoid words with three syllables. Research shows that concise and short writing reduces the user's cognitive load, resulting in faster and more efficient information processing.

Each *paragraph* should contain only one main thought. Make the paragraph's intentions plain in the first sentence. For additional ideas or points use additional paragraphs. Users tend to skip over more than one point or ideas in a paragraph as they scan. Keep paragraphs short, no longer than five sentences encompassing no more than 75 words. Provide clear paragraph breaks.

Links. Too many links embedded within text can disrupt reading continuity and content understanding. Minimize within-text links and, where possible and appropriate, place them at the beginning or end of paragraphs or sections of text.

Scanning. Make texts more scannable by using bulleted listings, tables, headings, and bold type. Key information will be found faster.

Testing. Test for readability. Print out text to carefully proofread it; errors will be more easily caught. Also, write and edit with international readers in mind.

Links

- Create wording that makes links:
  - — Descriptive.
  - — Differentiable.
  - — Predictive.
- Create concisely worded links.
- Integrate embedded links smoothly into the text.
  - — Make only a few words the active link.
  - — Do not spread links over two lines.
- Standalone links should not exceed one sentence in length.

Descriptive, differentiable, and predictive. The success of a link is determined by how well the user can predict where the link leads. Link differentiability and descriptiveness aids prediction. Understanding of a link's purpose reduces disorientation, because irrelevant links are less likely to be followed. Link text should clearly communicate the link's nature and purpose, and contain enough information to let users decide whether or not to follow it. The links of the best-rated Web sites are textual and descriptive, letting the user know what to expect

Concise. Create links that are brief and to the point, avoiding wordiness. Generally, a link has to strike a proper balance between enough words to make it descriptive and differentiable, and few enough words to make it most easily readable and legible. Underlining does slow reading of text.

Embedded links. Write text containing embedded links as if there were no links in it. The links must integrate smoothly and continuously into the text. Choose the most relevant words or phrase as the active link. Embedded links must not be continued over two lines. They may be mistaken for two links.

Standalone links. Standalone links should not exceed one sentence in length.

Examples of proper link writing are shown in Figure 9.4. Placing links in headings always make them easier to find.

POOR >	Paragraphs with embedded links are sometimes useful for a variety of reasons.
BETTER >	Paragraphs with embedded links are sometimes useful for a variety of reasons.
BEST >	Embedded Links Paragraphs with embedded links are sometimes useful for a variety of reasons.

Figure 9.4 Writing links.

Link Titles

- Provide link titles that describe:
  - — The name of site the link will lead to (if different from current site).
  - — The name of subsection the link will lead to (if staying within current site).
  - — The kind of information to be found at the destination.
  - — How the linked information relates to the anchor link and the current page content.
  - — How large the linked information is.
  - — Warnings about possible problems to be encountered at the other end.
- Restrict them to no more than 60 characters.

Some Web browsers have added the ability to pop up a short explanation of a link before the user selects the link. This explanation, called a *link title*, gives a more thorough preview of where the link goes, greatly enhancing predictiveness. Types of information that may be included in a link title are summarized above. Link titles should be reserved for supplementary information to help clarify the link's purpose. They do not eliminate need for a link and its surrounding text to be understandable. Generally, a link title should not exceed 60 characters in length.

Page Title

- Provide a page title:
  - — That possesses meaningful keywords.
  - — Whose first word is its most important descriptor.
  - — That makes sense when viewed completely out of context.
  - — That is different from other page titles.
  - — Is written in mixed case using the headline style.
- Do not highlight keywords.

Page titles must be carefully designed to provide useful information. They should contain as many keywords as possible. While a title may contain 60 characters, ensure that the first 40 characters adequately describe the page topic. Titles are often truncated in navigation menus and by search facilities. The title's first word should be its most important descriptor. This word is most easily noticed in the scanning of long lists. Never begin a title with a generic term such as "Welcome" or "Page," or with an article such as "The." Give different titles to different pages. If page titles addressing the same topic must begin with same word, end the title with words that explain the differences between them.

A title must also make sense when viewed completely out of context, with no supporting content or arrayed in a listing with other titles. Write titles in mixed case using the headline style. Do not use highlighting for keywords. A single keyword might be emphasized through putting it in upper case, but be conservative in this regard. Never use upper case for the first word in a title; its position is sufficient emphasis.

Headings and Headlines

- Create meaningful headings and headlines that quickly communicate the content of what follows.
  - — Make the first word an important information-carrying one.
  - — Skip leading articles (the and a).
- Create meaningful subheadings to break up large blocks of text.

Headings and headlines are often scanned to find screen content of interest. Their wording must provide a strong clue as to the content they relate to. Headings should be descriptive and straightforward. Headlines must often be made sense of out of context. Clever, cute or funny headlines or headings, or teasers to entice, should be avoided. A study has found that users prefer straightforward headlines to funny or cute ones. The first word in a heading or headline is the most important information-carrying one. Make it as distinctive as possible, especially if the heading or headline will be contained in an alphabetized listing. Skip leading articles (the and a) to also achieve distinctiveness. Distinctive first words will be easier to find in scanning. Use subheads to break up large blocks of text for visual appeal and ease of scanning.

Multiple Choice Questions

1. User should follow the following guidelines for Writing Clear Text and Messages:
   (a) Do not use jargon
   (b) Do not use abbreviations, mnemonics
   (c) Do not use simple letters
   (d) Do not use icons
   (e) All of the above

2. A status message is used for providing
   (a) Information about the state of the system when it is not immediately obvious to the user
   (b) Information about the progress of a lengthy operation
   (c) Information that brings attention to an undesirable situation
   (d) Both (a) and (b)
   (e) None of the above

3. An Informational message is used for providing
   (a) Information about the state of the system when it is not immediately obvious to the user
   (b) Information about the progress of a lengthy operation
   (c) Information that brings attention to an undesirable situation
   (d) Both (a) and (b)
   (e) None of the above

4. A warning message is used for providing
   (a) Information about the state of the system when it is not immediately obvious to the user
   (b) Information about the progress of a lengthy operation
   (c) Information that brings attention to an undesirable situation
   (d) Both (b) and (c)
   (e) None of the above

5. A critical message is used for providing

(a) Information about the state of the system when it is not immediately obvious to the user
(b) Information that brings attention to conditions that require a user action before the system can proceed
(c) Information that brings attention to an undesirable situation
(d) Both (a) and (c)
(e) None of the above

6. A question message is used for providing
(a) Information about the choices of options selection
(b) Information that brings attention to conditions that require a user action before the system can proceed
(c) Information that brings attention to an undesirable situation
(d) Both (a) and (c)
(e) None of the above

7. All windows must have a **title** located in a ________ position at the top.
(a) Left aligned
(b) Centered
(c) Right aligned
(d) All of the above

Review Questions

1. Explain what is wrong with the following interface dialogs of a file manager system and also state which of the rules of the interface design it violates:
   (a) An error message says

   You cannot use CTRLD to delete a file.

   (b) After the user request to delete the document, the following message appears:

   Are you sure you want to delete the selected document? Press 'OK'.

2. Describe the different forms of message box Controls used for simple, clear and polite communication which enhances systems usability.

3. How can the jargons and abbreviations or acronym affect communication with user interface. Give one example with proper use of words.

4. Describe the general guideline for easy, correct and fast message interpretation and acceptance.

5. Describe the different types of messages used in user interface.

6. Distinguish between informational messages and warning messages.

7. Distinguish between critical messages and question messages.

8. State the guidelines for writing Message Box text.

9. State the guidelines for using Message Box controls like command buttons.

10. Describe instructional messages with suitable examples.

11. What are the guidelines to be used by UI designer while presenting text on user screen?

12. What are the guidelines to be used by UI designer while writing text on user screen?

13. What are the guidelines to be used by UI designer while using text for web pages?

14. Describe the different types of worded links used in web pages.

CHAPTER

10

Feedback and Guidance

All user actions must be reacted to in some way. Feedback, as has been noted, shapes human performance. Without it, we cannot learn. To aid user learning and avoid frustration, it is also important to provide thorough and timely guidance and assistance. In this chapter, the following feedback topics are addressed:

- Acceptable response times.
- Dealing with time delays.
- Blinking for attention.
- The use of sound.

This will be followed by a review of guidance and assistance, including:

- Preventing errors and problem management.
- The types of guidance and assistance to provide.
  - Instructions or prompting.
  - A Help facility.
  - Contextual Help.
  - Task-oriented Help.
  - Reference Help.
  - Wizards.
  - Hints or tips.

Providing the Proper Feedback

To be effective, feedback to the user for an action must occur within certain time limits. Excessive delays can be annoying, interrupt concentration, cause the user concern, and impair productivity as one's memory limitations begin to be tested.

Response Time

- System responsiveness should match the speed and flow of human thought processes.
  - If continuity of thinking is required and information must be remembered throughout several responses, response time should be less than one or two seconds.
  - If human task closures exist, high levels of concentration are not necessary, and moderate short-term memory requirements are imposed; response times of 2 to 4 seconds are acceptable.
  - If major task closures exist, minimal short-term memory requirements are imposed; responses within 4 to 15 seconds are acceptable.
  - When the user is free to do other things and return when convenient, response time can be greater than 15 seconds.
- Constant delays are preferable to variable delays.

What the ideal system response time is has been the subject of numerous studies. Unfortunately, there still does not exist definitive time or times that are acceptable under all conditions. What is clear is that dissatisfaction with response time is very dependent on user expectations. It is also clear that expectations can vary, depending on the task as well as the situation. The ideal condition is one in which a person perceives no delays. Generally, a response time is too long for a person when one *notices* that something is taking too long. The following paragraphs summarize some study conclusions and some tentative findings.

The optimum response time is dependent upon the task. There is an optimum work pace that depends on the task being performed. Longer or shorter response times than the optimum lead to more errors. In general, response times should be geared to the user's short-term memory load and to the way he or she has grouped the activities being performed. Intense short-term memory loads necessitate short response times. While completing chunks of work at task closures, users can withstand longer response delays.

The human *now*, or psychological present, is under 2 to 3 seconds. This is why continuity of thinking requires a response time within this limit. Research indicates that for many creative tasks, response times under one second, in the range of four-tenths to nine-tenths of a second, can yield dramatic increases in productivity, even greater in proportion to the decrease in response time. The probable reason is the elimination of restrictions caused by short-term memory limitations. For data entry tasks, research has found no advantages for having response times less than 1 second.

If human task closures exist, high levels of concentration are not necessary, and moderate short-term memory requirements are imposed; response times of two to four seconds are acceptable. If major task closures exist, minimal short-term memory requirements are imposed, and responses within 4 to 15 seconds are acceptable. As the response-time interval increases beyond 10 to 15 seconds, however, continuity of thought becomes increasingly difficult to maintain. It has been suggested that this happens because the sequence of actions stored in short-term memory becomes badly disrupted and must be reloaded.

The response time guidelines above, then, relate to the general tasks being performed. Their applicability to every situation can never be guaranteed.

Satisfaction with response time is a function of expectations. Expectations are based, in part, on past experiences. These experiences may be derived from working with a computer, from the world in general, or from the perceived complexity of the task the computer is performing. These expectations vary enormously across individuals and tasks.

Dissatisfaction with response time is a function of one's uncertainty about delay. The degree of frustration with delay may depend on such psychological factors as a person's uncertainty concerning how long the delay will be, the extent to which the actual delay contradicts those expectations, and what the person thinks is causing the delay. Such uncertainty concerning how long a wait there will be for a computer's response may in some cases be a greater source of annoyance and frustration than the delay itself.

People will change work habits to conform to response time. As response time increases, so does think time. People also work more carefully with longer response times because the time penalty for each error made increases. In some cases, more errors have been found with very short response times. This may not necessarily be bad if the errors are the result of trial-and-error learning that is enhanced by very fast response times.

Constant delays are preferable to variable delays. It is the variability of delays, not their length, that most frequently distresses people. From a consistency standpoint, a good rule of thumb is that response-time deviations should never exceed half the mean response time. For example, if the mean response time is 4 seconds, a 2-second deviation is permissible. Variations should range from 3 to 5 seconds. Variation should never exceed 20 percent, however, because lower response time variability has been found to yield better performance, but small variations may be tolerated.

More experienced people prefer shorter response times. People work faster as they gain experience, a fact that leads Shneiderman (1987) to conclude that it may be useful to let people set their own pace of interaction. He also suggests that in the absence of cost or technical feasibility constraints, people will eventually force response time to well under 1 second. In general, the longer people interact with a system, the less delay they will tolerate.

Very fast or slow response times can lead to symptoms of stress. There is a point at which a person can be overwhelmed by information presented more quickly than it can be comprehended. There is also some evidence indicating that when a system responds too quickly, there is subconscious pressure on users to respond quickly also, possibly threatening their overall comfort, increasing their blood pressure, or causing them to exhibit other signs of anxious behavior. Symptoms of job burnout have been reported after substantial reductions in response time.

Slow and variable response times have also been shown to lead to a significant build-up of mood disturbances and somatic discomfort over time, culminating in symptoms of work stress, including frustration, impatience, and irritation.

Web response time. Bouch, Kuchinsky, and Bhatti (2000) performed three related studies. Web pages were presented at preestablished delays ranging from 2 to 73 seconds. Delay was defined as the time between a page's request and its complete displaying on the screen. Test participants rated the response times with the following results:

- *High (Good):* Up to 5 seconds.
- *Average:* From 6 to 10 seconds.
- *Low (Poor):* Over 10 seconds.

In the second study, test participants were presented a button labeled "Increase Quality" and asked to press it when response time became unacceptable. The average button-pressing time was 8.6 seconds. In the third study, the Web pages were loaded incrementally, the banner first, the text second, and the graphics last. The test participants were much more tolerant of delays under these conditions. Response times up to 39 seconds were rated as "good," and response times over 56 seconds were rated as "poor."

Selvidge, Chaparro, and Bender (2000) studied the effect of downloading delays on user performance. For delays of 1, 30, and 60 seconds they examined task success, task efficiency, and participant frustration. They found that participants were less frustrated with the 1-second delay, but task success and efficiency were not affected by any of the response times. Ramsay, Barbesi, and Preece (1998) evaluated people's reactions to a Web page's quality in relation to downloading times ranging between 2 and 120 seconds. Pages with longer delays, over 41 seconds, were rated as less interesting and more difficult to scan.

In general, these studies seem to indicate that the same factors affecting optimum computer response times in general also operate in the world of the Web, although longer downloading times may be more readily accepted due to the graphical nature of the Web's content. Slower response times, from a practical standpoint, however, would appear to reduce the amount of work that can be performed, and probably lead to increased user frustration.

Dealing with Time Delays

- Button click acknowledgement:
  — Acknowledge all button clicks by visual or aural feedback within one-tenth of a second.

- Waits up to 10 seconds:
  - — If an operation takes 10 seconds or less to complete, present a "busy" signal until the operation is complete.
    - • Display, for example, an animated hourglass pointer.
- Waits of 10 seconds to 1 minute:
  - — If an operation takes longer than 10 seconds to complete, display:
    - • A rolling barber's pole or other large animated object.
    - • Additionally, a progress indicator, percent complete message, or elapsed time message.
- Waits over 1 minute:
  - — Present an estimate of the length of the wait.
  - — Display a progress indicator, percent complete message, or elapsed time message.
  - — When a long operation is completed, present an acknowledgment that it is completed.
    - • A significantly changed screen appearance.
    - • An auditory tone.
  - — If an operation is very time-consuming:
    - • Consider breaking the operation into subtasks and providing progress indicators for each subtask.
    - • Allow users to start a new activity while waiting.
- Long, invisible operations:
  - — When an operation not visible to the user is completed, present an acknowledgment that it is completed.
    - • A message.
    - • An auditory tone.
- Progress indicator:
  - — A long rectangular bar that is initially empty but filled as the operation proceeds.
    - • Dynamically fill the bar.
    - • Fill it with a color or shade of gray.
    - • Fill it from left to right or bottom to top.
- Percent complete message:
  - — A message that indicates the percent of the operation that is complete.
  - — Useful if a progress indicator takes too long to update.
- Elapsed time message:
  - — A message that shows the amount of elapsed time that the operation is consuming.
  - — Useful if:
    - • The length of the operation is not known in advance.
    - • A particular part of the operation will take an unusually long time to complete.
- Web page downloads:
  - — For pages requiring download times greater that 5 seconds, give the user something to do while waiting.
    - • Quickly present, at the top of the downloading page, some text or links.

Elapsing time is in the eye of the beholder. What is important is *perceived* passing time, not actual time as measured by a clock. Dealing with time delays involves providing feedback that the system is truly working, and that the system's processing will be completed at some foreseeable and predictable time. Dealing with time delays also involves diverting people's attention away from a delay by engaging them in some meaningful interim activities.

Button clicks. Acknowledge all button clicks by visual or aural feedback within one-tenth of a second. This assures the user that a requested action has been received by the system.

Waits up to 10 seconds. If an operation takes 10 seconds or less to complete, present a "busy" signal until the operation is finished. An hourglass pointer is the customary signal. A "Please wait..." message can be presented to indicate that more complex processing is occurring or has been delayed. When the process is finished, provide an indication that the user may precede.

Waits of 10 seconds to 1 minute. If an operation takes longer than 10 seconds to complete, display a rolling barber's pole or other large animated object. Additionally, present a progress indicator, percent complete message, or elapsed time message. When the process is finished, provide an indication that the user may precede.

Waits over 1 minute. For waits exceeding one minute, present an estimate of the length of the wait. If the length is unknown, an educated guess is better than a "Don't Know" or no estimate at all. A time estimate allows the user to decide what to do next—wait, go to lunch, or start some other task. For these waits, display a progress indicator, percent complete message, or elapsed time message. If an operation is very time-consuming, consider breaking the operation into subtasks and providing progress indicators for each subtask. Also allow users to start a new activity while waiting so a delay will not be unproductive. Also, consider offering engaging text messages to keep users informed and entertained while they are waiting for process completion. Provide a clear indication of when the process is finished, significantly changing the screen's appearance so the change may be recognized from some distance away. Also include an auditory tone to attract the user's attention back to the screen.

Long, invisible operations. When a long operation not visible to the user is completed, present an acknowledgment message that it is completed. For example, upon completion of a search with no positive results, "Search complete, Jones not found" might be displayed. Also provide an auditory signal, since the user's attention may be directed to another part of the screen, or entirely away from the screen.

Progress indicator. A *progress indicator* is a long rectangular bar that is initially empty but filled as the operation proceeds. Dynamically fill the bar with a color or shade of gray. Fill all bars from left to right or bottom to top. A progress indicator is illustrated in Figure 10.1.

Percent complete message. A *percent complete* message provides an indication of the percent of an operation that is complete. It is useful if a progress indicator takes too long to update. An indication of the percentage of processing that has been ac-

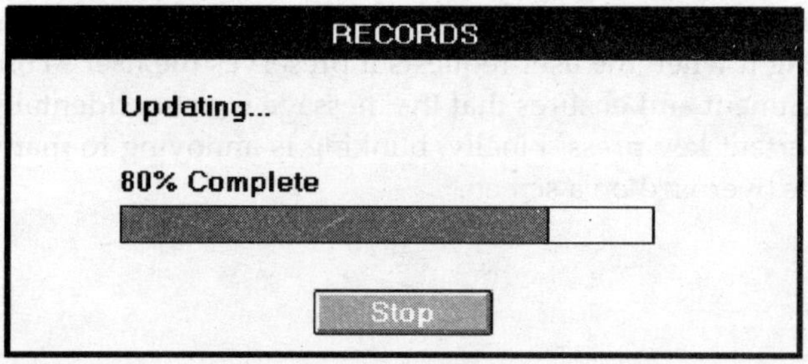

Figure 10.1 Processing progress indicator.

complished can also be given through a message such as "22 of 27 transactions have been processed."

Elapsed time message. An *elapsed time* message shows the amount of elapsed time the operation has consumed. It is useful if the length of the operation is not known in advance, or if a particular part of the operation will take an unusually long time to complete.

Web page downloads. For pages requiring download times greater that 5 seconds, give the user something to do while waiting. Quickly provide at the downloading page top some text to hold one's interest, or some links to act upon. These diversions will reduce impatience while images load.

Blinking for Attention

- Attract attention by flashing an indicator when an application is inactive but must display a message to the user.
  - — If a window, flash the title bar.
  - — If minimized, flash its icon.
- To provide an additional message indication, also provide an auditory signal (one or two beeps).
  - — Very useful if:
    - The window or icon is hidden.
    - The user's attention is frequently directed away from the screen.
- Display the message:
  - — When the application is activated.
  - — When requested by the user.

Attention. Flashing an element on the screen will usually capture a person's attention. If a window is displayed on the screen, flash its title bar. If the window is minimized, flash its icon.

Auditory signal. To provide an additional indication that a message is waiting, also provide an auditory signal (one or two beeps). This will be useful if the window or icon is hidden or the user's attention is frequently directed away from the screen.

Message display. Display the message when an application is activated or when the user requests it. Displaying it when the user requests it preserves the user's control over the work environment and ensures that the message is not accidentally closed through an inadvertent key press. Finally, blinking is annoying to many people, so it should not be overused on a screen.

Use of Sound

- Always use in conjunction with a visual indication.
- Use no more than six different tones.
  — Ensure that people can discriminate among them.
- Do not use:
  — Jingles or tunes.
  — Loud signals.
- Use tones consistently.
  — Provide unique but similar tones for similar situations.
- Provide signal frequencies between 500 and 1,000 Hz.
- Allow the user to adjust the volume or turn the sound off altogether.
- Test the sounds with users over extended trial periods.
- Use sounds sparingly because they:
  — Are annoying to many people, including other users and nonusers in the vicinity.
  — Can easily be overused, increasing the possibility that they will be ignored.
  — Are not reliable because:
    - Some people are hard of hearing.
    - If they are not heard, they leave no permanent record of having occurred.
    - The user can turn them off.

Sounds, sometimes called *earcons,* are useful for alerting the user:

- To minor and obvious mistakes.
- When something unexpected happens.
- Where visual attention is directed away from the screen and immediate attention is required.
- When a long process is finished.

Tones used must be discriminable, nonannoying, and consistently used. Therefore, they must be thoroughly tested for discrimination and effectiveness. Brewster, Wright, and Edwards (1993) have found that high levels of recognition can be achieved by careful use of earcon pitch, rhythm, and timbre. They recommend:

- Timbre: Use synthesized musical instrument timbres, where possible with multiple harmonics.
- Pitch: Do not use on its own unless there are very big differences between the pitches used.

- Register: Acceptable to use alone to differentiate earcons; otherwise large differences of three or more octaves should be used.
- Rhythm: Make rhythms as different as possible. Including a different number of notes in each rhythm is very effective.
- Intensity: 10dB to 20dB above threshold. Since sound level will be under control of the user, it should be kept in a close range.
- Combinations: Leave a delay of 0.01 second between successively played earcons.

Since sounds can be annoying to some people, they should be capable of being turned down or off by the user. Playing jingles or tunes, or loud sounds, focuses attention on the sound itself, which is distracting. Loud sounds can also be irritating, especially to those with sensitive hearing.

Never consider sounds reliable; because they can be turned off, they leave no permanent record of their existence, and not all users will be able to hear all tones because of hearing defects. Sounds should always be used in conjunction with a visual indication of some kind.

Guidance and Assistance

We'll begin by first looking at ways to prevent errors from occurring in the first place. Then, we will look at how to gracefully handle them when they do occur. Finally, we'll look at guidance and assistance and its components, including the various forms of Help typically available in a system.

Preventing Errors

In spite of our lofty design goals, people will make errors using even the most well-designed system. When errors occur they must be properly managed. The magnitude of errors in computer systems is astounding. Studies have found error rates in commands, tasks, or transactions as high as 46 percent. In addition to stranding the user and wasting time, errors interrupt planning and cause deep frustration.

Errors can be classified as slips or mistakes. A *slip* is automatic behavior gone awry. One's hands navigate the keyboard improperly and the wrong key is accidentally pressed. The wrong menu bar item is chosen because of inattentiveness. An inference error is made due to carelessness. A person often detects a slip because it is usually noticeable. The wrong letter appears within a word or the expected action is not performed. Slips are usually, but not always, corrected fairly easily. Slips can be reduced through proper application of human factors in design (for example, by providing adequate separation between elements to be selected).

A *mistake* results from forming a wrong model or goal and then acting on it. A mistake may not be easily detected because the action may be proper for the perceived goal—it is the goal that is wrong. Anticipating a mistake in design is also more difficult. Mistakes can be reduced, however, by eliminating ambiguity from design. Doing usability testing and watching for nonsensical (to the designer) requests and actions can also detect mistake-conducive situations.

Some experts have argued that there is no such thing as an "error" in using a system; they are simply iterations toward a goal. There is much truth to that statement. It is also said "to err is human." The corollary to that statement, at least in computer systems, might be, ". . . to forgive is good design." Whatever we call them, errors will occur. People should be able to correct them as soon as they are detected, as simply and easily as they were made.

MAXIM **Everyone makes mistakes, so every mistake should be fixable.**

Problem Management

- Prevention:
  - — Disable inapplicable choices.
  - — Use selection instead of entry controls.
  - — Use aided entry.
  - — Accept common misspellings, whenever possible.
  - — Before an action is performed:
    - Permit it to be reviewed.
    - Permit it to be changed or undone.
  - — Provide a common action mechanism.
  - — Force confirmation of destructive actions.
    - Let expert users disable this.
  - — Provide an automatic and continuous Save function.
- Detection:
  - — For conversational dialogs, validate entries as close to point of entry as possible.
    - At character level.
    - At control level.
    - When the transaction is completed or the window closed.
  - — For high speed, head-down data entry.
    - When the transaction is completed or the window closed.
  - — Leave window open.
  - — Maintain the item in error on the screen.
  - — Visually highlight the item in error.
  - — Display an error message in a window.
    - Do not obscure item in error.
  - — Handle errors as gracefully as possible.
    - The greater the error, the more dramatic should be the warning.
  - — Use auditory signals conservatively.
- Correction:
  - — Preserve as much of the user's work as possible.
  - — At window-level validation, use a modeless dialog box to display an error list.
    - Highlight first error in the list.
    - Place cursor at first control with error.
    - Permit fixing one error and continuing to next error.
  - — Always give a person something to do when an error occurs.

    - Something to enter/save/reverse.
    - A Help button.
    - Someone to call.
- Provide a constructive correction message saying:
    - What problem was detected.
    - Which items are in error.
    - What corrective action is necessary.
- Initiate a clarification dialog if necessary.

Preventing, detecting, and correcting errors involves doing the following.

Prevention. It is always better to prevent errors than handle them. Errors can be reduced in a number of ways. First, disable all choices that are not applicable at any one moment. Make improper alternatives impossible to select or activate. Next, after considering the task and user, if practical, design screens using selection instead of entry controls. Selection error rates tend to be lower than entry error rates. Use aided entry if at all possible. The computer has been found to be a better speller than most people. When entry is performed, human misspellings of commands and requests should be accepted by the system. Person-to-person communication does not require perfection. Person-to-computer communication should impose no more rigor than that imposed between people. Use of the Shift key should also be discouraged, since it is such a large cause of keying errors. Actions about to be performed should also be reviewable and changeable. Keying or selection slips will occasionally occur.

A common send mechanism should be provided to transmit an action to the system. The existence of two or more keys to accomplish the same purpose, especially if their use is mandated by different conditions, can be confusing and more prone to error. Finally, if an action causes an irreversible change and the change is critical, the user should be requested to confirm the change. A separate key should be used for this purpose, not the Send key. Let expert users disable the confirmation request, if the action is recoverable. Finally, provide an automatic continuous *Save* function so that users never lose their work due to a system (or user) malfunction.

Detection. Errors should be detected quickly, but without disrupting a person's thought patterns and actions if this can be avoided. Generally, the longer the wait before editing is performed, the longer the time to accomplish the editing. So, validate according to how important accuracy is to the user, and the characteristics of the task being performed. It is also preferable to wait for a closure point in the dialog. For conversational dialogs, accuracy is usually more important than speed, actions are slower paced, and more closure points usually exist. In these situations, validate as close to the point of input as possible: at the character level or at the control level, and when the transaction is completed or the window closed. High-speed, head-down data entry is generally fast paced. Constant interruptions for errors can be a great speed detriment. In this situation, validate when the transaction is completed or the window closed. This is usually the only task closure point.

All errors should be maintained on the screen and identified to the user through a highlighting display technique (for example, high intensity or contrasting color). Display an error message in a dialog box and position it on the screen so it does not obscure the item in error. Handle all errors as gracefully as possible, avoiding discouraging, embarrassing, or alarming words. Words with such intent can compound the frustration a person already feels in having made an error. For minor problems, provide less intrusive warnings. The greater the error, the more dramatic may be the warning.

Be cautious in using auditory signals to notify of an error. Many people, especially those with status or position, do not want their inefficiencies advertised, especially to peers and subordinates.

Correction. Preserve as much of the user's work as possible. It can be irritating to have to reenter an entire screen when only one field is in error. At the window level of validation, use a modeless dialog box to display a list of errors. Highlight the first error in the list and place the cursor at the first control with error. Permit fixing one error, and then continuing on to the next error. If multiple errors occur, and it is impossible to display messages about all of them at one time, provide an indication that there are additional messages. Say, for example, "+ 2 other problems." Also, provide a distinct visual difference if the same error message is displayed more than once, because the first attempt to correct the problem failed. A person may not notice a repeated message that looks identical to the previous one. Always give a person something to do when an error occurs: something to enter, save, or reverse, or someone to call. Also provide a Help button. The Help button *must* be helpful, though.

Explicit and constructive error messages should be provided. These messages should describe what error occurred, and how it should be corrected. Corrective actions will be clearer if phrased with words like "must be" or "must have." A study addressing restructuring messages following guidelines such as these, and others previously described, found improved success rates in fixing errors, lower overall error rates, and improved user satisfaction.

Any error ambiguities should be resolved by having the system query the user. Errors should be corrected with minimal typing. Another important error control measure is to have the system identify and store errors. This will allow tracking of common errors so that appropriate prevention programs can be implemented.

Providing Guidance and Assistance

New users must go through a learning process that involves developing a conceptual or mental model to explain the system's behavior and the task being performed. Guidance in the form of the system's hard-copy, online documentation, computer-based training, instructional or prompting messages, and system messages serves as a cognitive development tool to aid this process. So does assistance provided by another form of online documentation, the Help function. Broadly speaking, online documentation is *every* communication provided online to help people to do their work effectively.

While it is desirable that the human-computer interface be so "self-evident" and "intelligent" that people never experience difficulties, this goal will not be achieved in the foreseeable future. So a great deal of emphasis should be placed on creating good guidance and assistance, and managing the trouble that does occur. Indeed one survey found that documentation was the second most important factor influencing the decision to purchase something. (Quality was first.)

Useful guidance and assistance answers the following questions:

- What is this?
- What does it do?
- How do I make it do it?
- What is its role in the overall scheme of things?

Technical information, unlike works of fiction, is seldom read for pleasure. People turn to it only when a question has to be answered. Failure to provide the guidance and assistance needed in learning, answering questions, and problem solving makes it very difficult for the user to recover from trouble on his or her own and to avoid future trouble by learning from his or her mistakes. The result is most often more errors and great frustration.

Problems with Documentation

Wright (1991) feels that poor documentation is usually not the result of stupid and careless writing. Most writers, professional or not, she says, try to communicate their ideas as well as they can. Poor products, however, suggest that being a native speaker of the language is not a sufficient qualification to ensure communicative success. Rather, four other factors contribute to bad design.

Organizational factors. First are organizational factors including management decisions concerning who does the writing: product developers or specialist technical authors. Product developers, by their nature, are more interested in the technical aspects and seldom have time to focus on writing. Another organizational factor is the frequency and nature of the contact between writers and developers. Successful writing requires that frequent contact be maintained between writers and developers. If not, modifications may go undocumented, and functionality may occur that is difficult to explain.

Time scale. Second is the time scale allocated for the writing process. Successful writing also involves detailed early planning, drafting, testing, and considerable revising. Without adequate time being made available for the writing process, the planning, testing, and revising processes are limited, thereby increasing the potential for a mismatch between the final product and its documentation.

Theoretical rationale. Third, there is not yet a clear theoretical rationale about what content should be included in documentation and how this information should be presented. Until this is developed, one cannot be sure that the documentation being developed is the most effective that it can be.

Resources. Finally, Wright concludes, there are the resources. Adequate resources are needed to include people with different skills in the documentation development process. Required are people good at visual layout, writing, and test and evaluation. Rarely does the same person possess more than one of these skills. Without the proper expertise, documentation will also suffer.

Another problem with documentation is created by the need for translation in our shrinking world. The following is found in a current user guide: "The color deviation from the original is thus resulted." (KYE Systems, 1995) The product manufacturer is guilty of Wright's sins number two and four above.

How Users Interact with Documentation

There are three broad stages through which a reader interacts with documentation: finding information that is relevant, understanding what the documentation says, and applying that understanding to the current task in order to solve the problem that prompted turning to the documentation in the first place.

Finding information is enhanced through use of contents pages and index lists. It is also enhanced if browsing is made easy through clearly visible page headings and subheadings. Pictures and symbols can also be used to draw the reader's attention to particular kinds of information. Understanding information is achieved through a variety of factors. Included are following good writing principles. Understanding can also be maximized through testing and revision of materials as necessary.

Instructions or Prompting

Instructional or prompting information is placed *within the body* of a screen. It may take the form of messages or other advice, such as the values to be keyed into a field. Prompting is provided to assist a person in providing what is necessary to complete a screen.

Inexperienced users find prompting a valuable aid in learning a system. Experienced users, however, often find prompting undesirable. It slows them down, then adds "noise" to the screen, and may reduce the amount of working information that can be displayed at one time.

Since instructions or prompting can easily create screen noise, be cautious in placing it on a screen. Use it only if all screen usage will be casual or infrequent. If people with a wide range of experience will be using a screen, it should be selectable, capable of being turned on or off as needed. As an alternative, two separate sets of screens could be made available, one with prompts and the other without. Guidelines for writing instructions and prompts were covered in Chapter 9 "Text Messages."

Help Facility

The most common form of online documentation is the Help system. The overall objective of a Help facility is to assist people in remembering what to do. Its benefits include improving the usability of a system, providing insurance against design flaws that may develop, and accommodating user differences that may exist (novice versus expert). Typical methods of invoking Help include: through a typed command, by pressing a Help key or button, or by selecting a Help option from a multiple-item menu. Help may also automatically appear on the screen.

Some studies have found a Help system can aid performance, others have concluded that a Help function can impair performance if it is not task-oriented, and if it makes the interface more complex. One potential danger of the Help facility, as one study found, is that a person's recall of command operations is related to frequency of Help facility access; fewer Help requests were associated with better command recall. The researchers speculate that the availability of Help may become a crutch and lead to less effective retention. People may implement a passive cognitive strategy. A Help facility, then, may influence performance in systematic and subtle ways.

The specific design characteristics that enhance an online Help are still being identified. Three broad areas of Help that must be addressed in creating Help are: its content, its presentation, and its access mechanisms. Of these, presentation and access are best understood.

Elkerton and Palmiter (1991) propose that the content (and structure) of an effective online Help can be specified using the GOMS (goals, operators, methods, selection rules) model (Card, Moran, and Newell, 1983). Using GOMS, information is provided to the user on *goals* for meaningful tasks, on *operators* for actions required to be performed, on *methods* for accomplishing the goals, and where multiple interface methods exist, and on *selection rules* for choosing a specific method. Gugerty, Halgren, Gosbee, and Rudisill (1991) found that this structure was useful in remembering medical procedures. Elkerton (1988) presents a set of suggested principles for online assistance (which he calls *online aiding*). These principles are reproduced in Table 10.1.

Next, we'll look at some general Help guidelines. Then, we'll address some specific considerations for contextual Help, task-oriented Help, reference Help, and wizards.

Help Facility Guidelines

- Kind:
  - — Collect data to determine what types of Help are needed.
- Training:
  - — Inform users of availability and purpose of Help.
- Availability:
  - — Provide availability throughout the dialog.
  - — If no Help is available for a specific situation, inform the user of this and provide directions to where relevant Help may exist.
- Structure:
  - — Make them as specific as possible.
  - — Provide a hierarchical framework.
    - Brief operational definitions and input rules.
    - Summary explanations in text.
    - Typical task-oriented examples.
- Interaction:
  - — Provide easy accessibility.

Table 10.1 Suggested Design Principles for Providing Online Advice Based on the GOMS Model

USE *GOALS* IN ONLINE AIDING TO DO THE FOLLOWING:
1. Describe what can be done in task-oriented terms (interface actions and objects) for improved initial skill learning.
2. Provide an adjustable level of detail on interface procedures for accommodating the information needs of a wide range of users.
3. Provide procedurally incomplete advice so that users can actively learn for improved long-term performance with and understanding of the interface.
4. Provide feedback to users that may help in reminding them of appropriate procedures to use, particularly when recovering from errors.
5. Develop modular assistance and instructional dialogs that can be used to describe similar and dissimilar procedural elements of the interface.
USE *OPERATORS* IN ONLINE AIDING TO DO THE FOLLOWING:
1. Describe simple actions, such as pressing specific keys or finding specific objects on the display, that are common to many interface procedures, to assist the user in current task performance.
2. Provide detailed information on interface procedures that inexperienced users can actively learn and that more skilled users can combine with other procedural knowledge to improve long-term performance and understanding of the interface.
3. Monitor users' actions to provide context-sensitive Help or to diagnose user problems actively.
USE *METHODS* IN ONLINE AIDING TO DO THE FOLLOWING:
1. Present step-by-step interface procedures to assist the user with specific problems.
2. Improve user understanding and acceptance of online advice.
3. Decrease the cognitive load of users who are learning a new interface task by providing an explicit procedure for users to follow.
4. Provide procedural demonstrations of interface procedures so that users can quickly learn simple operations.
5. Map sequences of users' actions to a reduced set of interface goals to help provide context-sensitive advice to users.
USE *SELECTION RULES* IN ONLINE AIDING TO DO THE FOLLOWING:
1. Help users choose between multiple interface methods.
2. Provide users with an understanding of representative tasks to increase their knowledge of when to apply specific interface skills.

From Elkerton (1988)

— Leave the Help displayed until:
    • The user exits.
    • The action eliminating the need for Help is performed.
— Provide instructions for exiting.
— Return to original position in dialog when Help is completed.

■ Location:
— Minimize the obscuring of screen content.
— If in a window, position priorities are: right, left, above, and below.

■ Content:
— Minimize the Help's length.
— Develop modular dialogs that can be used to describe similar and dissimilar procedural elements of the interface.
— Provide step-by-step interface procedures to assist the user with specific problems.
— Provide procedural demonstrations of interface procedures to aid quick learning of simple operations.
— Provide information to help users select between multiple interface methods.
— Provide users with an understanding of representative tasks to increase their knowledge of when to apply specific skills.

■ Style:
— Provide easy browsing and a distinctive format.
    • Contents screens and indexes.
    • Screen headings and subheadings.
    • Location indicators.
    • Descriptive words in the margin.
    • Visual differentiation of screen components.
    • Emphasized critical information.
— Use concise, familiar, action-oriented wording.
— Refer to other materials, when necessary.
— Never use Help to compensate for poor interface design.

■ Consistency:
— Provide a design philosophy consistent with other parts of the system.

■ Title:
— Place the word "Help" in all Help screen titles.

Kind. The two most common reasons people use Help are: (1) Confusion exists about something located on the screen, and (2) information about a specific function is needed. All system usability problems should be systematically identified through testing and evaluation. Monitoring users' actions can also be a useful tool in identifying user problems. Online Help can then be developed to address these problems.

Training. Inform users of the availability and purpose of various types of Help. Never assume that this will be obvious.

Availability. Make Help available at all points in the dialog. It is especially critical that Help be available consistently in all similar situations. For example, if one particular system menu has Help, ensure that all menus provide Help. If no Help is available for a specific situation, inform the user of this and provide directions to where relevant Help may exist, including hard-copy materials.

Structure. The Help response should be as specific as possible, tailored to the task and the user's current position. When accessed, the Help facility should be aware of the kind of difficulties a person is having and respond with relevant information. Only the information necessary to solve the immediate problem or to answer the immediate question should be presented. If the Help facility is unsure of the request, it should work with the user through prompts and questions to resolve the problem.

A Help facility should be multilevel, proceeding from very general to successively more detailed and specific explanations to accommodate a wide range of users. The first level should provide brief definitions and rules, simple reminders, and memory joggers sufficient for skilled users. The second level should incorporate more detailed explanations in a textual format. The final, and deepest, level should provide guidance in the form of task-oriented examples.

Interaction. A Help facility should be retrievable simply, quickly, and consistently by a key action, selection, or command. Leave the Help displayed until the user explicitly exits the Help, or performs the action eliminating the need for Help. Instructions for exiting the Help process should always be provided. These may take the form of displayed pushbuttons, function keys, or something similar.

Help should not disrupt processing. Easy return to the point of the problem should be permitted. Ideally, the problem or work should be retained on the screen when Help is accessed, but this will not always be possible unless the system provides a windowing capability.

Location. When Help is displayed, minimize the obscuring of relevant screen content. If Help is displayed within a window, position priorities are right, left, above, and below.

Content. Minimize the Help's length, whenever possible. Carroll, Smith-Kerker, Ford, and Mazur (1986) recommend the development of Help text in the form of "minimal manuals." These manuals are explicit and focus on real tasks and activities, and they have been found to be significantly better than traditional Help texts (Black, Carroll, and McGuigan, 1987; Carroll, et al., 1986).

Elkerton (1988) suggests that few Help users want detailed, fact-oriented knowledge such as a hierarchical list showing the syntax of a command. Instead, they want to know the methods to complete a task. Without knowledge of how to do things, users are left to browse through a wealth of information with little understanding of what may be useful. Hence, he recommends, among other things, providing the following:

- Step-by-step interface procedures to assist the user with specific problems.
- Procedural demonstrations of interface procedures to aid quick learning of simple operations.
- Information to help users choose between multiple interface methods.
- Users with an understanding of representative tasks to increase their knowledge of when to apply specific skills.

When procedural steps are presented, consecutive numbering will make them easy to follow.

Style. Provide easy browsing and a distinctive format. Often the exact location of information needed to answer a question cannot be definitely established. Providing information in a format that can be easily skimmed aids the search process and also helps the user become familiar with the information being presented. The following techniques enhance the skimming process:

- Contents screens and indexes.
- Screen headings and subheadings.
- Location indicators.
- Descriptive words in the margin.
- Visual differentiation of screen components.
- Emphasized critical information.

An index has been found to be one of the first place users turn when they have a problem. Help wording should also be concise, familiar, and action oriented. Reference to outside material may be included in the Help text, especially if the Help information cannot be provided in a concise way. Never use Help to compensate for poor interface design.

Consistency. The Help design philosophy should be consistent with the philosophy used in other parts of the system. This includes presentation techniques, style, procedures, and all other aspects.

Title. For easy identification, place the word "Help" in all Help screen titles.

Contextual Help

Contextual Help provides information within the context of a task being performed, or about a specific object being operated upon. Common kinds of contextual Help include Help command buttons, status bar messages, and ToolTips. Microsoft Windows has also introduced what is called the What's This? Command.

Help Command Button

- Description:
  — A command button.
- Purpose:
  — To provide an overview of, summary assistance for, or explanatory information about the purpose or contents of a window being displayed.
- Design guidelines:
  — Present the Help in a secondary window or dialog box.

Description and purpose. The proper usage of a command button labeled Help, illustrated in Figure 10.2, is to provide supplemental Help for a secondary window,

Figure 10.2 Help command button.

dialog box, or message box. It should provide an overview of, summary assistance for, or explanatory information about, the purpose or contents of a window.

Design guideline. Present this form of Help in a secondary window or dialog box. Microsoft Windows considers this Help an optional secondary form of contextual assistance, and not a substitute for the *What's This?* command to be described shortly. The guidance and assistance provided by a Help command button differs from the "What's This?" In that more general assistance is provided rather than information specific to the control that has the current input focus.

Status Bar Message

- Description:
  - — An abbreviated, context-sensitive message related to the screen item with the focus.
  - — Appears in window's status bar when the primary mouse button is pressed over an item (or keyboard focus is achieved).
- Purpose:
  - — To provide explanatory information about the object with the focus.
  - — Use to:
    - Describe the use of a control, menu item, button, or toolbar.
    - Provide the context of activity within a window.
    - Present a progress indicator or other forms of feedback when the view of a window must not be obscured.
  - — Do not use for information or access to functions essential to basic system operations unless another form of Help is provided elsewhere in the Help system.
  - — If extended Help is available and must be presented, place "Press F1 for Help" in bar.
- Writing guidelines:
  - — Be constructive, not simply descriptive.
  - — Be brief, but not cryptic.
  - — Begin with a verb in the present tense.
  - — If a command has multiple functions, summarize them.
  - — If a command is disabled, explain why.

Description. An abbreviated, context-sensitive message related to the screen item with focus. The message appears in the screen's status bar, as shown in Figure 10.3 when the primary mouse button is pressed over an item (or keyboard focus achieved).

Purpose. A status bar message's purpose is to provide explanatory information about the screen object with focus. Because the user may not always notice a mes-

Figure 10.3 Status bar message.

sage displayed in the bar, or the bar may be turned off and not displayed, it must be considered a form of secondary or supplemental assistance.

Use a status bar message to provide context for the activity being performed in window, or to describe the use of toolbars, menu items, or buttons being displayed. When the primary mouse button is clicked over one of these items (or keyboard focus achieved) display a short message describing the use of the associated command.

The bar may also be used for presentation of a progress indicator, or other forms of feedback, when the view of a window must not be obscured. Never use the bar for information or access to functions essential to basic system operations, unless another form of Help for this operation is provided elsewhere in the interface. If extended Help must be provided, and displaying it in the bar is not possible, place "Press F1 for Help" in the bar.

Writing. Do not simply describe something but explain it in a constructive manner Be as brief as possible so the text can be read easily, but do not make the text so short that it is cryptic Begin all messages with a verb in the present tense. If a command with multiple functions has focus, summarize its multiple uses. If a command is disabled, explain why.

ToolTip

- Description:
  - — A small pop-up window that appears adjacent to control.
  - — Presented when the pointer remains over a control a short period of time.
- Purpose:
  - — Use to display the name of a control when the control has no text label.
- Design guidelines:
  - — Make application-specific ToolTips consistent with system-supplied ToolTips.
  - — Use system color setting for ToolTips above to distinguish them.

Description. A ToolTip is a small pop-up window with a label that appears adjacent to a control without a label (such as a toolbar) when the pointer is positioned over the control. It is displayed after the pointer remains over the control for a short period of time. This avoids the distracting effect of a ToolTip appearing when a pointer is simply being moved past a control.

Purpose. To display the name of a control when the control has no text label.

Design guidelines. Make application-specific ToolTips consistent in size and structure with system-supplied ToolTips, including using the system's color setting to distinguish them. ToolTips were also described in Chapter 8 "Screen-Based Controls."

What's This? Command

- Description:
  - — A command located on the Help drop-down menu on a primary window.
  - — A button on the title bar of a secondary window.
  - — A command on a pop-up menu for a specific object.
  - — A button on a toolbar.
- Purpose:
  - — Use to provide contextual information about any screen object.
- Design guidelines:
  - — Phrase to answer the question "What is this?"
  - — Indicate the action associated with the item.
  - — Begin the description with a verb.
  - — Include "why," if helpful.
  - — Include "how to," if task requires multiple steps.
  - — For command buttons, use an imperative form: "Click this to...."

Description and purpose. A *What's This* command may take the form of a command in a menu or a button, as summarized above. It's purpose is to provide contextual information about any screen object, including controls, dialog boxes, and property sheets.

Design guidelines. Phrase the label or caption to answer the question "What is this?" Indicate the action associated with the item and begin description with a verb. If helpful, include an answer to "Why?" as well. Include a "how to" if the task requires multiple steps. For command buttons, use an imperative form, "Click this to. . . ."

The guidance and assistance provided by "What's This? differs from that of a command button. With command button Help, more general assistance is provided rather than information specific to the control that has the current input focus.

Task-Oriented Help

- Description:
  - — A primary window typically accessed through the Help Topics browser.
  - — Includes a set of command buttons at the top; at minimum:
    - A button to display the Help Topics browser dialog box.
    - A Back button to return to the previous topic.
    - Buttons that provide access to other functions such as Copy or Print.

- Purpose:
  - — To describe the procedural steps for carrying out a task.
  - — Focuses on *how* to do something.
- Design guidelines:
  - — Provide one procedure to complete a task, the simplest and most common.
  - — Provide an explanation of the task's goals and organizational structure at the start.
  - — Divide procedural instructions into small steps.
  - — Present each step in the order to be executed.
  - — Label each step.
  - — Explicitly state information necessary to complete each step.
  - — Provide visuals that accurately depict the procedural steps.
  - — Accompany visuals with some form of written or spoken instructions.
  - — Begin any spoken instructions simultaneously with or slightly after a visual is presented.
  - — Segment any animation to focus attention on specific parts.
  - — Segment instructions.
  - — Delay the opportunity to perform the procedure until all the procedure's steps have been illustrated.
- Presentation guidelines:
  - — The window should consume a minimum amount of screen space, but be large enough to present the information without scrolling.
  - — Normally, do not exceed four steps per window.
  - — Use a different window color to distinguish task-oriented Help windows from other windows.
- Writing guidelines:
  - — Write simply and clearly, following all previously presented guidelines.
  - — Focus on *how* information, rather than *what* or *why*.
  - — Do not include introductory, conceptual, or reference material.
  - — Limit steps to four or fewer to avoid scrolling or multiple windows.
  - — If a control is referred to by its label, bold the label to set it off.
  - — Include the topic title as part of the body.

Description. *Task-oriented Help,* sometimes called *procedural Help* is presented on a primary window accessed through the Help Topics browser dialog box in Microsoft Windows. It includes a set of command buttons at the top, minimally, a button to display the Help Topics browser dialog box, a Back button to return to the previous topic. And buttons that provide access to other functions such as Copy or Print.

Purpose. Task-oriented Help details the procedural steps for carrying out a task. People prefer task-oriented Help to product-oriented Help, and research evidence shows a productivity gain using it. It is not surprising that task-oriented Help has such a preference and benefits, because people think in terms of tasks, not functions. This form of Help focuses on *how* to do something, rather than the *what* or *why*. Its purpose is not to document everything there is to know about a subject.

Design guidelines. The following guidelines are mostly derived from Harrison (1995). First, present only one procedure to complete a task, the simplest and most common. (If information about alternate methods is included, place it in a Notes or Related Topic section.)

At the beginning, provide an explanation of the task's goals and organizational structure. Divide procedural instructions into small steps and present them in the order they are to be executed. Clearly label each step. Explicitly state what information is necessary in order to complete each step, presenting the most important information first.

Provide visuals that accurately depict the procedural steps. People prefer to follow visual examples rather than instructions, and visuals minimize orientation errors. Accompany the visuals with some form of written or, if possible, spoken instructions. Instructions provide cues as to most important aspects of the procedure. Begin any spoken instructions simultaneously with or slightly after a visual is presented. If animation is included, segment it to focus attention on specific parts. Segment the instructions to reinforce the concept of chunks or steps. Finally, delay the opportunity to perform the procedure until all the procedure's steps have been illustrated.

Presentation guidelines. A task-oriented Help window should consume a minimum amount of screen space, but be large enough to cover all the necessary information without requiring cumbersome scrolling. Normally, this means do not exceed four steps per window. To distinguish task-oriented Help windows from other windows, use a different window color to present them.

Writing guidelines. Write simply and clearly, following all previously presented text guidelines. Focus on *how* information, rather than *what* or *why*. Do not include introductory, conceptual, or reference material. If a control is referred to by its label, bold the label to set it off. Include the topic title as part of the body.

Reference Help

- Description:
  - — An online reference book.
  - — Typically accessed through a:
    - Command in a Help drop-down menu.
    - Toolbar button.
- Purpose:
  - — To present reference Help information, either:
    - Reference oriented.
    - User guide oriented.
- Design guidelines:
  - — Provide a consistent presentation style, following all previously presented guidelines.
  - — Include a combination of contextual Help, and task-oriented Help, as necessary.
  - — Include text, graphics, animation, video, and audio effects, as necessary.
  - — Make displayed toolbar buttons contextual to the topic being viewed.

— Provide jumps, a button or interactive area that triggers an event when it is selected, such as:
  - Moving from one topic to another.
  - Displaying a pop-up window.
  - Carrying out a command.

— Visually distinguish a jump by:
  - Displaying it as a button.
  - Using a distinguishing color or font to identify it.
  - Changing the pointer image when it is over it.

- Presentation guidelines:
  — Provide a nonscrolling region for long topics to keep the topic title and other key information visible.
- Writing guidelines:
  — Write simply and clearly, following all previously presented guidelines.
  — Provide meaningful topic titles.

Description and purpose. *Reference Help* is another form of online documentation. Its purpose is to present Help information that may be reference-oriented, documenting the features of a product, or it may serve as a user's guide to a product. It is typically accessed through a command in a Help drop-down menu, or a toolbar button. Reference-oriented Help is usually organized by functions and features and includes more text than other types of Help. User-guide-oriented Help is usually organized by tasks and may include more illustrations than other types of Help.

Design guidelines. Provide a consistent presentation style, following all previously presented guidelines. Include a combination of contextual Help, and task-oriented Help, as necessary. Include text, graphics, animation, video, and audio effects, as necessary and as available. Make toolbar buttons contextual to the topic being viewed in the Help window.

Provide *jumps*, a button or interactive area that triggers an event when it is selected. The action may be to move from one topic to another, to display a pop-up window, or to carry out a command. Jumps, when in button form are called *shortcut buttons* in Microsoft Windows. They automatically perform a task, thereby providing efficiency by reducing the amount of information necessary to present for reading by the viewer. Do not use a jump, however, if the goal is to enable the user to perform the task. Consider a balance for common tasks. Provide information that explains how to perform a task and also provide a shortcut button to accomplish the task, making stepping through the task easier. Visually distinguish a jump by displaying it as a unique style button or using a distinguishing color or font to identify it. The system default for a textual jump in Microsoft Windows is green underlined text. Also, change the pointer image when the pointer is positioned over the jump.

Presentation guidelines. If scrolling is necessary, provide a nonscrolling region for long topics to keep the topic title and other key information visible.

Writing guidelines. Write simply and clearly, following all previously presented guidelines. Also, provide meaningful topic titles.

Wizards

- Description:
  - — A series of presentation pages displayed in a secondary window.
  - — Include:
    - Controls to collect input.
    - Navigation command buttons.
  - — Typically accessed through:
    - Toolbar buttons.
    - Icons.
- Purpose:
  - — To perform a complex series of steps.
  - — To perform a task that requires making several critical decisions.
  - — To enter critical data and for use when the cost of errors is high.
  - — To perform an infrequently accomplished task.
  - — The necessary knowledge or experience to perform a task is lacking.
  - — Not suited to teaching how to do something.
- Design guidelines:
  - — Provide a greater number of simple screens with fewer choices, rather than a smaller number of more complex screens with too many options or too much text.
  - — Provide screens of the exact same size.
  - — Include on the first page:
    - A graphic on the left side to establish a reference point or theme.
    - A welcoming paragraph on the right side to explain what the wizard does.
  - — Include on subsequent pages:
    - A graphic for consistency.
    - Instructional text.
    - Controls for user input.
  - — Maintain consistent the locations for all elements.
  - — Make it visually clear that the graphic is not interactive.
    - Vary from normal size or render it as an abstract representation.
  - — Include default values or settings for all controls when possible.
  - — For frequently used wizards, place a check box with the text "Do not show this Welcome page again" at the bottom of the Welcome page.
  - — Include a Finish button at the point where the task can be completed.
  - — Do not require the user to leave a wizard to complete a task.
  - — Make sure the design alternatives offered yield positive results.
  - — Make certain it is obvious how to proceed when the wizard has completed its process.
- Presentation guidelines:
  - — Display the wizard window so it is immediately recognized as the primary point of input.
  - — Present a single window at one time.
  - — Do not advance pages automatically.

- Writing guidelines:
  - — Clearly identify the wizard's purpose in title bar.
  - — At the top right of the wizard window, title the Welcome page "Welcome to the *Wizard Name* Wizard."
    - • Use mixed case in headline style and no ending punctuation.
  - — Write simply, concisely, and clearly, following all previously presented guidelines.
  - — Use a conversational rather than instructional style.
  - — Use words like "you" and "your."
  - — Start most questions with phrases like "Which option do you want . . ." or "Would you like . . ."

Description. A *Wizard* is a structured set of screens that guides the user through a decision-making or data entry process. Wizards are displayed in a secondary window. The screens include controls to collect input, and navigation command buttons located at the page bottom (Back, Next, Finish, and Cancel). A wizard is typically accessed through toolbar buttons or icons.

Purpose. A wizard's purpose is to assist a user by automating a task and walking the user through the process. It may not appear as an explicit part of the Help interface. Wizards are useful for complex or infrequently occurring tasks that people may have difficulty learning or doing. Wizards are designed to hide many of the steps and much of the complexity in doing something. They are not suited to teaching how to do something, and should be considered a supplement to the actual performance of the task. An experienced user who knows a process will usually find a wizard inefficient or lacking access to all necessary functionality. A wizard can be accessed through toolbar buttons or icons. Microsoft (2001) suggests the following guidelines.

Design guidelines. Provide a greater number of simple pages with fewer choices, rather than a smaller number of more complex pages with too many options or too much text. Fewer pages will make it easier to understand the wizard and the process. Create screens of the exact same size. Include on the first page a graphic on the left side to establish a reference point or theme and a welcoming paragraph on the right side to explain what the wizard does. The graphic's purpose is to establish a reference point, or theme, or present a preview of the wizard's result. Include on subsequent pages a graphic for consistency, instructional text, and the necessary controls for user input. (If screen space is critical, graphics on subsequent pages may be omitted.)

Make it visually clear that the graphic is not interactive by varying it from normal size or rendering it as an abstract representation. Do not require the user to leave a wizard to complete a task. The user, often a novice, may lose context if asked to leave. Everything must be done from within the wizard. Make sure the design alternatives offered to the user yield positive results.

For frequently used wizards, place a check box with the text "Do not show this Welcome page again" at the bottom of the Welcome page. Include a Finish button at the point where the task can be completed. Make certain it is obvious how to proceed when the wizard has completed its process by including proper closing text on the last page.

Presentation guidelines. Display the wizard window so it is immediately recognized as the primary point of input. Present a single window at one time, overlaying underlying windows so they are not visible. Do not advance pages automatically. The viewer may be unable to read all the information, and control of the dialog is removed from the user and placed in the hands of the computer.

Writing guidelines. Clearly identify the wizard's purpose in the title bar. At the top right of the wizard window, title the Welcome page "Welcome to the *Wizard Name* Wizard." Use mixed case in the headline style of presentation, and no ending punctuation. Write simply, concisely, and clearly, following all previously presented guidelines. Use a conversational rather than instructional style, and words like "you" and "your." Start most questions with phrases like "Which option do you want?" or "Would you like . . .?" People react better to phrasing that implies they are in control, rather than phrasing telling them what to do.

Hints or Tips

- Description:
  - — A command button labeled Hints or Tips.
- Purpose:
  - — To provide a few important contextual, but specific, items of information related to a displayed screen.
- Design guidelines:
  - — Provide guidance on only two or three important points.
  - — Locate the button near where its guidance applies.
  - — Write concisely and to the point.

Description. A *Hint* or *Tip* is a command button placed on a screen and labeled as such.

Purpose. To provide a few important contextual, but specific, items of information related to a displayed screen. It is a supplement to the standard Help facility, but more easily accessible and relevant to the current situation. The objective is to quickly get the user back on track when disorientation or confusion occurs.

Design guidelines. Provide guidance on only two or three important points. Locate the button near the location where its guidance applies and write concisely and to the point.

For more information on Hints and Tips, see User Interface Engineering (2001).

Multiple Choice Questions

1. Which of the following control is to be used if any operation takes longer than 10 seconds to complete?
   (a) An auditory tone
   (b) Progress indicator
   (c) A message box
   (d) Elapsed time message
   (e) None of the above
2. Which of the following control is to be used if any operation waits upto 10 seconds or less to complete?
   (a) Hourglass pointer
   (b) Progress indicator
   (c) Busy signal
   (d) Elapsed time message
   (e) None of the above
3. Which of the following control is to be used if any operation takes over 1 minute to complete?
   (a) An auditory tone
   (b) Progress indicator
   (c) A message box
   (d) Elapsed time message
   (e) None of the above
4. Which of the following control is to be used it for long invisible operation?
   (a) An auditory tone
   (b) Progress indicator
   (c) A message box
   (d) Elapsed time message
   (e) None of the above
5. Elapsed time message is referred as
   (a) A message that shows the amount of elapsed time that the operation is consuming.
   (b) A message that indicates the percent of the operation that is complete.
   (c) A long rectangular bar that is initially empty but filled as the operation proceeds.
   (d) Both (a) and (b)
   (e) None of the above
6. For active window, attention can be attracted by
   (a) Flashing the icon.
   (b) Flashing the title bar
   (c) Flashing the status bar
   (d) Both (a) and (b)
   (e) None of the above
7. One's hands navigate the keyboard improperly and the wrong key is accidentally pressed. This type of error is referred to as
   (a) Mistake
   (b) Slip
   (c) Both (a) and (b)
   (d) None of the above
8. An error may not be easily detected because the action may be proper for the perceived goal—it is the goal that is wrong, is referred to as
   (a) Mistake
   (b) Slip
   (c) Both (a) and (b)
   (d) None of the above
9. Status bar message are used
   (a) To provide explanatory information about the object with the focus.
   (b) To display the name of a control when the control has no text label.
   (c) To provide contextual information about any screen object.
   (d) Both (a) and (b)
   (e) None of the above
10. ToolTip are used
   (a) To provide explanatory information about the object with the focus.
   (b) To display the name of a control when the control has no text label.

(c) To provide contextual information about any screen object.
(d) Both (a) and (b)
(e) None of the above

11. What's This? command is used
(a) To provide explanatory information about the object with the focus.
(b) To display the name of a control when the control has no text label.
(c) To provide contextual information about any screen object.
(d) Both (a) and (b)
(e) None of the above

12. Reference Help are used
(a) To provide explanatory information about the object with the focus.
(b) To present reference Help information
(c) To provide contextual information about any screen object.
(d) Both (a) and (b)
(e) None of the above

13. Wizards are used
(a) To perform a complex series of steps.
(b) To present reference Help information.
(c) To perform a task that requires making several critical decisions.
(d) Both (a) and (c)
(e) None of the above

Review Questions

1. Describe the different ways and means to provide an effective feedback while designing HCI application with suitable examples.
2. Describe the various interface controls used for proving feedback of the task.
3. "Dissatisfaction with response time is very dependent on user expectations". Justify.
4. How can UI designer deal with time delays to avoid frustration and bringing people's attention on interim ongoing tasks?
5. What are audio and visual representations of feedback in GUI?
6. Comment on the following terms:
   (a) Errors as a "slip"
   (b) Errors as a "mistake"
7. Describe the assistance provided by UI designer for User while interacting with documentation.
8. Describe how the help facility can be designed in UI application like Word Processor or spreadsheet.
9. What are types of help facility designed in UI Application for documentation?
10. How are ToolTip and Balloon Tip used for notification in UI application?
11. What are Wizards? State the guidelines for designing Wizards.

CHAPTER

11

Graphics, Icons and Images

The graphics era in interface and screen design began with the Xerox Star computer in the 1970s and fully blossomed with the advent of Apple's Lisa and Macintosh in the mid-1980s. GUI systems rapidly began to supplement the earlier text-based systems that had been in existence for three decades. When Microsoft finally entered the picture with their Windows system, GUI systems quickly became the dominant user interface. The significant graphical feature of a GUI system is the use of *icons* (the symbolic representation of objects, such as applications, office tools, and storage locations) and the symbolic representation of actions that could be applied to objects. The faces of many 1990s and beyond GUI screens scarcely resembled their older text-based siblings of the mid- to late-twentieth century.

The graphical evolution in interface design was further expanded in the 1990s with the maturing of the World Wide Web. The Web permitted easy inclusion of other media on a screen, including images, photographs, video, diagrams, drawings, and spoken audio. Since these media, including icons, could be combined in various ways, the term *multimedia* was coined to describe these combinations. A Web interface, then, has its foundation in GUI systems, but it has added its own unique elements to screen design.

Screen graphics, if used properly, can be a powerful communication and attention-getting technique. They can hold the user's attention, add interest to a screen, and quickly convey information. Improperly used graphics, however, can confuse the user, lead to navigation inefficiencies, and be distracting. Screen graphics must always serve a useful purpose.

This chapter will provide design guidelines for the various graphical techniques avail-able in GUI and Web screen design. It will begin with a discussion of icons, the kinds available, their characteristics, and their usability influences. It will then address how icons are chosen and the icon design process. Finally, design guidelines for the various other graphical media will be presented.

Icons

Icons are most often used to represent objects and actions with which users can interact with or that they can manipulate. These types of icons may stand alone on a desktop or in a window, or be grouped together in a toolbar. A secondary use of an icon is to reinforce important information, a warning icon in a dialog message box, for example.

Kinds of Icons

The use of icons to reflect objects, ideas, and actions is not new to mankind. We've been there before. Early humans (100,000 years or so ago) used pictographs and then ideographs to communicate. Some of these early communications can still be found today on rock walls and in caves around the world. Until recent times, this was also the only way to communicate in some cultures (Native Americans and Australian aborigines, for example).

Word writing is traced back to Chinese writing from about 6000 BC and Egyptian hieroglyphics from about 3000 BC. This was followed by cuneiform (Babylonia and Assyria) from about 1900 BC, and the contemporary Chinese vocabulary (numbering about 50,000) around 1500 BC. In 1000 BC the Phoenicians developed a 22-sign alphabet that the Greeks adopted about 800–600 BC. The Greeks passed this alphabet on to the Romans about 400 BC, who then developed a 23-character alphabet. This alphabet has been modified and embellished but has remained essentially the same for the last 2000 years.

Pictorial representations, then, have played a prominent role in mankind's history. Word writing, however, unleashed much more flexibility and richness in communication. This has caused some skeptics to wonder why, after taking 2500 years to get rid of iconic shapes, we have now revived them on screens.

Whatever the past, today, objects or actions *are* depicted on screens by icons. The term icon by itself, however, is not very specific and can actually represent very different things. An attempt has been made by some to define the actual types of icons that do exist. Marcus (1984) suggests icons fall into these categories:

Icon. Something that looks like what it means.

Index. A sign that was caused by the thing to which it refers.

Symbol. A sign that may be completely arbitrary in appearance.

He states that what are commonly referred to as icons may really be indexes or symbols. A true icon is something that looks like what it means. It is representational and easy to understand. A picture of a telephone or a clock on a screen is a true icon. An index is a sign caused by the thing to which it refers. An open door with a broken window indicates the possible presence of a burglar. The meaning of an index may or may not be clear, depending upon one's past experiences. A symbol is a sign that may be completely arbitrary in appearance and whose meaning must be learned. The menu and sizing icons on screens are examples of symbols. From this perspective, strictly speaking, so-called icons on screens are probably a mixture of true icons, signs, and indexes.

Rogers (1989) provided an expanded definition for icon kinds.

- Resemblance—An image that looks like what it means.
- Symbolic—An abstract image representing something.
- Exemplar—An image illustrating an example or characteristic of something.
- Arbitrary—An image completely arbitrary in appearance whose meaning must be learned.
- Analogy—An image physically or semantically associated with something.

She suggests that an icon is *used* in a number of different ways: for *objects* such as a document, *object attributes* such as a color or fill pattern, *actions* such as to paste, *system states* such as ready or busy, and *message types* like critical or warning.

The different ways icons are used may then be represented by different design schemes. A *resemblance* icon is an image that looks like what it means—a book, for example, to represent a dictionary. This is equivalent to Marcus's icon. A *symbolic* icon is an abstract image that represents something. A cracked glass, for example, can represent something fragile. Marcus's symbol would be similar. An *exemplar* icon represents an example or characteristic of something. A sign at a freeway exit picturing a knife and fork has come to indicate a restaurant. An *arbitrary* icon is not directly related in any way and must be learned. Marcus's symbol would be an equivalent. Finally, an *analogy* icon is an image physically or semantically associated with something—a wheelbarrow full of bricks for the move command, for example. Marcus's symbol would also be similar.

In a study looking at various kinds of icons, Rogers found that those depicting both an action and an object were quite effective. For example, a drawing of a page and an arrow pointing up means "go to the top of the page." She also found that arbitrary icons were only meaningful in very small sets, and that icons based on analogies were relatively ineffective.

Characteristics of Icons

An icon possesses the technical qualities of syntactics, semantics, and pragmatics (Marcus, 1984). *Syntactics* refers to an icon's physical structure. Is it square, round, red, green, big, small? Are the similarities and differences obvious? Similar shapes and colors can be used to classify a group of related icons, communicating a common relationship. *Semantics* is the icon's meaning. To what does it refer—a file, a wastebasket, or some other object? Is this clear? *Pragmatics* is how the icons are physically produced and depicted. Is the screen resolution sufficient to illustrate the icon clearly? Syntactics, semantics, and pragmatics determine an icon's effectiveness and usability.

Influences on Icon Usability

Simply providing an icon on a screen does the user no particular favor, unless it is carefully designed to present a natural and meaningful association between the icon itself and what it stands for. Unfortunately, a sampling of many current systems finds icons that do not achieve this objective. Icons are included because "this is the thing to do" in a graphical system today. Little concern is given to effectiveness. The result is too often a cluttered and confusing screen that is visually overwhelming. So, proper icon design is important from an acceptance, learning, and productivity perspective. The following factors influence an icon's usability:

- Provide icons that are:
  - — Familiar.
  - — Clear and Legible.
  - — Simple.
  - — Consistent.
  - — Direct.
  - — Efficient.
  - — Discriminable.
- Also consider the:
  - — Context in which the icon is used.
  - — Expectancies of users.
  - — Complexity of task.

Familiarity. How familiar is the object being depicted? Familiarity will reduce learning time. How familiar are the commonly seen icons in Figure 11.1? Lack of familiarity requires learning the icons' meanings. Very unfamiliar icons require a great deal of learning.

Experience often makes words and numbers more familiar to a person than symbols. Confusion matrices have been developed through extensive research for alphanumeric data (0 versus O, 1 versus I). Graphic symbols may be more visually similar to each other.

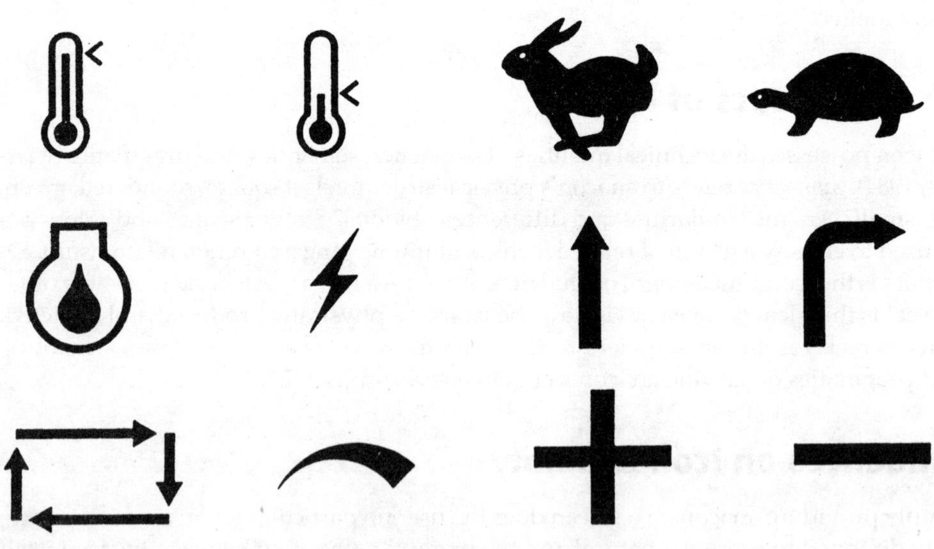

Figure 11.1 Some common icons. What do they stand for? Answers are on the next page.

From Micro Switch (1984)

The icons depicted in Figure 11.1 have the following meanings:

Hot	**Cold**	**Fast**	**Slow**
Engine Oil	**Ammeter/Generator**	**Straight**	**Turn**
Automatic	**Variable Regulation (Increase/Decrease)**	**Plus/Positive**	**Minus/Negative**

Clarity. Is the icon legible? Does the shape, structure, and formation technique on the screen permit a clear and unambiguous depiction of what it is? Screen resolution should be sufficiently fine to establish clear differences of form at the normal working distance. The resolution and pixel shapes for screens differ from one another. Icons must appear correctly and consistently no matter what kind of screen is used. If color is used, it should contrast well with the background. Poor clarity will lead to identification errors and slower performance.

Simplicity. Is the icon simple? Is the shape clean and devoid of unnecessary embellishments? Too many parts will only confuse the screen viewer.

Consistency. Are families of icons consistent in structure and shape? Are the same icons displayed on different screens consistent in shape and structure? Are the same icons displayed in different sizes also consistent in structure and shape?

Directness. How "sign-like" is the icon; how well does it convey its intended meaning? For concrete objects and actions, direct links are more easily established. Adjectives, adverbs, conjunctions, and prepositions can cause problems, however. Also, how does one easily convey concepts such as bigger, smaller, wider, or narrower?

Efficiency. In some situations, a graphics screen may be less efficient, consuming more screen display space than a word or requiring more physical actions by the user than text. A telephone directory of 50 names and numbers listed on an alphanumeric screen may consume the same screen space required for, and manipulation of, 15 file cards. Raising an arm or moving a mouse may be slower than simply typing. In other situations, icons can be more effective than words in communicating concepts in a smaller area of space. Icons' strength lies in situations where this occurs.

Discriminability. The symbols chosen must be visually distinguishable from other symbols. A person's powers of differentiation for shapes and other forms of codes have been experimentally determined over the years. The maximum number of codes that can be effectively differentiated by a human being, including geometric shapes, is summarized in Table 11.1. A person's ability to discriminate alphabetic or alphanumeric information is much more potent.

Context. The context of a symbol may change its meaning. Does the rabbit symbol illustrated in Figure 11.1, if seen on a road sign in a national park, mean, "go faster"? From this contextual perspective, icons are similar to words.

Expectancies. The symbol may be comprehended, but a false conclusion may be reached about the desired action because of an incorrect expectancy. A study of international road signs found that eight percent of all drivers never saw the "do not do" slash through a symbol on a road sign. Their expectancy was that they could do it, not "not do it."

Table 11.1 Maximum Number of Codes for Effective Human Differentiation

ENCODING METHOD	RECOMMENDED MAXIMUM	COMMENTS
Alphanumerics	Unlimited	Highly versatile. Meaning usually self-evident. Location time may be longer than for graphic coding.
Geometric Shapes	10–20	High mnemonic value. Very effective if shape relates to object or operation being represented.
Size	3–5	Fair. Considerable space required. Location time longer than for colors and shapes.
Line Length	3–4	Will clutter the display if many are used.
Line Width	2–3	Good.
Line Style	5–9	Good.
Line Angle	8–11	Good in special cases (such as wind direction).
Solid and Broken Lines	3–4	Good.
Number of Dots or Marks	5	Minimize number for quick assimilation.
Brightness	2–3	Creates problems on screens with poor contrast.
Flashing/Blinking	2–3	Confusing for general encoding but the best way to attract attention. Interacts poorly with other codes. Annoying if overused. Limit to small fields.
Underlining	No data	Useful but can reduce text legibility.
Reverse Video	No data	Effective for making data stand out. Flicker easily perceived in large areas, however.
Orientation (location on display surface)	4–8	—
Color	6–8	Attractive and efficient. Short location time. Excessive use confusing. Poor for the color blind.
Combinations of Codes	Unlimited	Can reinforce coding but complex combinations can be confusing.

Data derived from Martin, 1973; Barmack and Sinaiko, 1966; Mallory et al., 1980; Damodaran et al., 1980; and Maguire, 1985.

Complexity of task. The more abstract or complex the symbol, the more difficult it is to extract or interpret its intended meaning. It has been found that more concrete graphic messages are easier to comprehend than the more abstract. Icons, therefore, cannot completely replace words in more complex situations.

Choosing Icons

Icon design is an important process. Meaningful and recognizable icons will speed learning and recall and yield a much more effective system. Poor design will lead to errors, delays, and confusion. While the art of icon design is still evolving, it is agreed that the usability of a system is aided by adhering to the following icon design guidelines.

A Successful Icon

- Looks different from all other icons.
- Is obvious what it does or represents.
- Is recognizable when no larger than 16 pixels square.
- Looks as good in black and white as in color.

Fowler and Stanwick (1995) provide these general guidelines. An icon must look different from all other product icons, making it discriminable and differentiable. What it does or represents must also be obvious so it is interpretable. It must be recognizable when no larger than 16 pixels square. Finally, it must look as good in black and white as in color. Color is always an enhancing quality of an icon.

Size

- Supply in all standard sizes.
  - — 16 × 16 pixels.
    - 16- and 256-color versions.
  - — 32 × 32 pixels
    - 16- and 256-color versions.
    - Effective: 24 × 24 or 26 × 26 in 32 × 32 icon.
  - — 48 × 48 pixels
    - 16- and 256-color versions.
- Use colors from the system palette.
- Use an odd number of pixels along each side.
  - — Provides center pixel around which to focus design.
- Minimum sizes for easy selection:
  - — With stylus or pen: 15 pixels square.
  - — With mouse: 20 pixels square.
  - — With finger: 40 pixels square.
- Provide as large a hot zone as possible.

Size. Typically, icons come in three standard sizes, 16, 32 and 48 pixels square. For clarity, 16 x 16 should be an icon's minimum size. An effective combination for an image is a 24 × 24 or 26 × 26 in a 32-pixel square icon.

Colors. Microsoft suggests that while 256 colors may be used in the smaller sizes than 48 × 48 pixels, to do so increases icon storage requirements, and they may not be displayable on all computer configurations. If 256 colors are used for icons, they suggest that the standard 16-color format should *always* be provided. Also, use colors from the system palette to ensure that the icons look correct in all color configurations.

Odd number of pixels. Horton (1994) recommends using an odd number of pixels along each side of the matrix. This provides a center pixel around which to focus, thus simplifying the design process.

Icon selection. For easy selection the following are minimum icon sizes: with a stylus or pen, 15 pixels square; with a mouse, 20 pixels square; with one's finger, 40 pixels square.

Hot zone. An icon's hot zone, the area within it that allows it to be selected, should be as large as possible, preferably the entire size of the icon. This allows easier selection.

Choosing Images

- Use existing icons when available.
- Use images for nouns, not verbs.
- Use traditional images.
- Consider user cultural and social norms.

Existing icons. Many standard icons have already been developed for graphical systems. Use these standard icons where they are available. This will promote consistency across systems, yielding all the performance benefits that consistency provides. Where standard icons are not available, determine if any applicable icons have already been developed by industries and trade or standards organizations. The International Standards Organization (ISO), for example, has developed standard shapes for a variety of purposes. Always consult all relevant reference books before inventing new symbols or modifying existing ones.

Nouns. An object, or noun, is much easier to represent pictorially than an action or verb. Choose nouns for icons whenever possible.

Traditional images. Old-fashioned, traditional images often work better than newer ones. They have been around longer, and more people recognize them.

Cultural and social norms. Consider users' cultural and social norms. Improper design of icons can create problems internationally. Social norms vary, so great variations exist in what is recognizable and acceptable throughout the world. What one culture recognizes may have no meaning in another. What is acceptable in one country may not be in another.

Creating Images

- Create familiar and concrete shapes.
- Create visually and conceptually distinct shapes.
  - — Incorporate unique features of an object.
  - — Do not display within a border.
- Clearly reflect objects represented.
- Simply reflect objects represented, avoiding excessive detail.
- Create as a set, communicating relationships to one another through common shapes.
- Provide consistency in icon type.
- Create shapes of the proper emotional tone.

Concrete and familiar shapes. Ideally, an icon's meaning should be self-evident. This is enhanced when concrete shapes are provided, those that look like what they are. An icon should also be intuitive or obvious, based upon a person's preexisting knowledge. Familiar shapes are those images that are well learned. Figure 11.2 illustrates concrete and familiar icons for a file folder, book, and telephone as well as images for the same objects that are more abstract and unfamiliar. A study found that concrete, familiar icons were preferred to abstract, unfamiliar ones.

Keep in mind, however that familiarity is in the eye of the viewer. The concrete images pictured may be familiar to us, readers of this book, but not to a tribal chief living in a remote area of the world where these objects do not exist. Similarly, items familiar to those working on the factory floor may not be at all familiar in the office or in the home, and vice versa. Mayhew (1992) also cautions that some

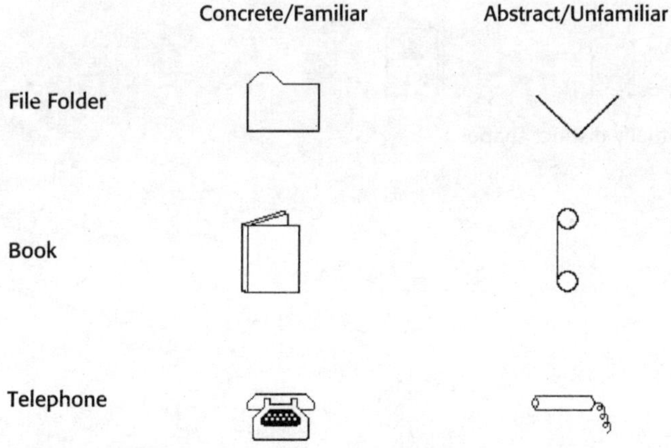

Figure 11.2 Concrete and familiar shapes.

abstract images should not be discounted because they have become familiar, in spite of their being abstract. On a road sign, for example, an angled red bar inscribed over an object means do not do what is pictured beneath (at least to most people, as described earlier). While abstract, it is a very familiar shape today. If an abstract image must be used, it should be capable of being learned quickly and easily recalled. Familiarity can only be determined through knowing one's user.

Visually and conceptually distinct shapes. It must be easy to tell icons apart so the chances of confusing them are minimized. Differentiation is aided when icons are visually different from one another. It is also aided when icons are conceptually different—that is, when they portray specific features of an object that are relatively unique within the entire set of objects to be displayed. Figure 11.3, based upon Mayhew (1992), illustrates how distinctiveness may be achieved for two similar items, a dictionary and a telephone book. Visual distinctiveness is achieved by incorporating unique features of each: for the dictionary, it is its content of letters and words, for the telephone book, numbers and the telephone bell.

Visual distinctiveness is degraded when borders are placed around icons, as illustrated in Figure 11.4. Borders tend to obscure the shape of the object being displayed.

Clearly reflect objects. The characteristics of the display itself should permit drawings of adequate quality. Poorly formed or fuzzy shapes will inhibit recognition.

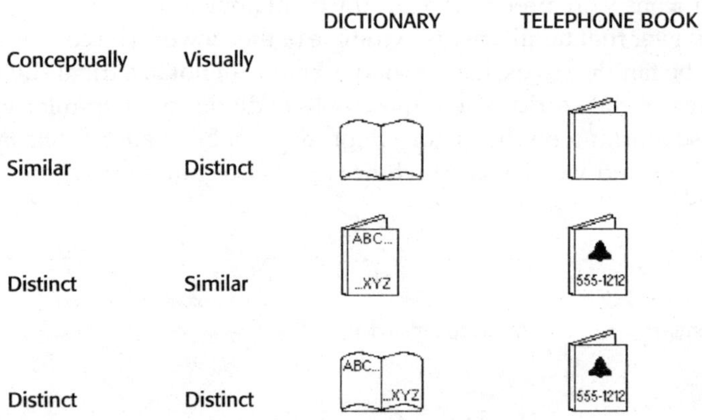

Figure 11.3 Visually and conceptually distinct shapes.

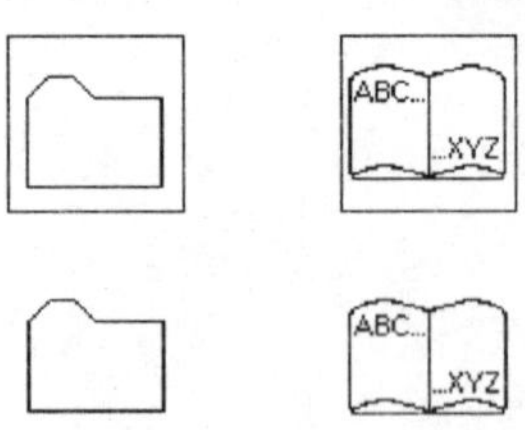

Figure 11.4 Borders degrading icon distinctiveness.

Simply reflect objects. Construct icons with as few graphical components as necessary, using no more than two or three, if possible. Also, use simple, clean lines, avoiding ornamentation. Byrne (1993) found that simple icons, icons containing fewer graphical elements, were located faster in a visual search task than complex icons, icons with more components. He concluded that complex icons seemed to clutter a screen with information that people were unable to employ to their advantage. Too much detail inhibits rather than facilitates perception, as illustrated in Figure 11.5. For real-world objects, use only enough detail to permit recognition and recall.

Design as a set. Do not design icons in isolation, but as a family considering their relationships to each other and the user's tasks. Provide a common style. When icons are part of an overall related set, create shapes that visually communicate these relationships. Objects within a class, for example, may possess the same overall shape but vary in their other design details, as illustrated in Figure 11.6. Color may also be used to achieve this design goal. In creating sets, always avoid repeating unrelated elements.

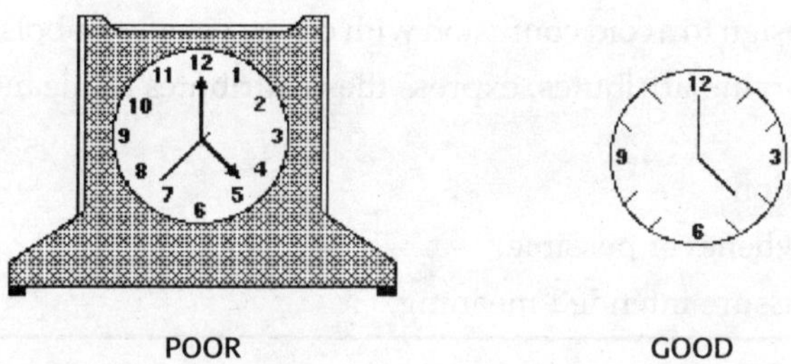

Figure 11.5 Avoid excessive detail in icon design.

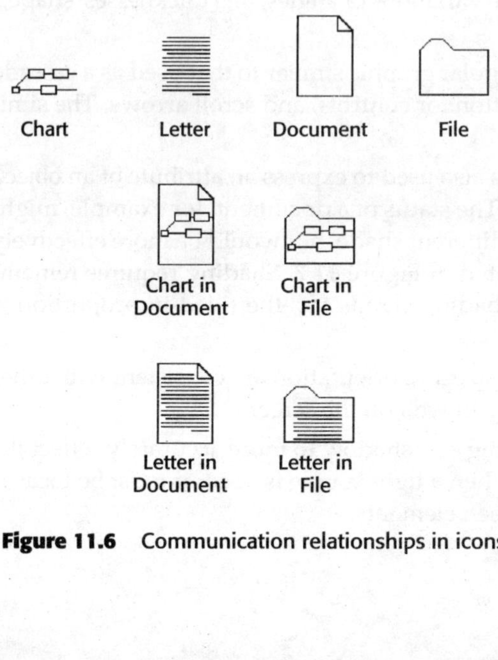

Figure 11.6 Communication relationships in icons.

Consistency in icon type. As previously noted, there are many different kinds of design schemes for icons (resemblance, symbolic, arbitrary, and so on). All these schemes might be used to create a meaningful family of icons for an application. Learning the meaning of icons and searching for the right icon, however, will be aided if the same design scheme is used for all icons within a family. In presenting a series of icons for actions such as paint, cut, and so on, one could, for example, (1) depict a before-after representation of the action, (2) depict the action itself being performed, or (3) picture the tool to perform the action. While a series of meaningful icons could be developed using each scheme, the best approach would be to use only one of these schemes to develop the entire family of icons.

Proper emotional tone. The icon should appropriately reflect the environment in which it is used. A sewage disposal system would be an inappropriate metaphor for an electronic mail system wastebasket.

Drawing Images

- Provide consistency in shape over varying sizes.
- Do not use triangular arrows in design to avoid confusion with other system symbols.
- When icons are used to reflect varying attributes, express these attributes as meaningfully as possible.
- Provide proper scale and orientation.
- Use perspective and dimension whenever possible.
- Accompany icon with a label to assure intended meaning.

Consistency. When drawing images, create consistency in shapes for identical icons of differing sizing. Preserve the general shape and any distinctive detail. Consistency is achieved through limiting the variations of angles, line thicknesses, shapes, and amount of empty space.

Triangular arrows. Avoid using a triangular graphic similar to that used as a cascade symbol for menus, a drop-down button for controls, and scroll arrows. The similarity may cause confusion.

Meaningful attributes. When an icon is also used to express an attribute of an object, do this as meaningfully as possible. The status of a document, for example, might be represented by displaying it in a different shade, but would be more effectively illustrated by filling it in, as illustrated in Figure 11.7. Shading requires remembering what each specific type of shading stands for; the filled-in proportion is more intuitively obvious.

Scale and orientation. Ensure that the size and orientation are consistent with other related objects. Also ensure that they fit well on the screen.

Perspective and dimension. Use lighting and shadow to more accurately reflect the real-world experiences of people. When a light source is used, it must be located upper left, as is done with other screen elements.

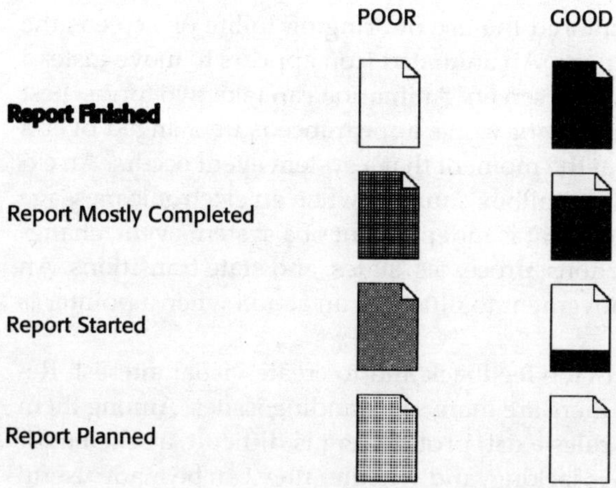

Figure 11.7 Expressing attributes in icon design.

Caption or label. Since icons may not be used often, the ability to comprehend, learn, and recall an icon's meaning can be greatly improved by attaching textual captions or labels to them. Labels beneath the icon also provide a larger target, speeding selection. Labels should always be related to icons in a consistent positional way. "Mystery icons," icons with no caption or label to explain them, lead to a user guessing game and many errors. While ToolTips can be used to present labels, they are time-consuming to present, taking about two-thirds of a second to appear and be comprehended. Scanning an entire row of 15 icons with ToolTips, therefore, will consume about 10 extra seconds.

MAXIM **If people must remember hieroglyphics, they won't stick around long.**

Icon Animation and Audition

- Animation:
  - — Use:
    - To provide feedback.
    - For visual interest.
  - — Make it interruptible or independent of user's primary interaction.
  - — Do not use it for decoration.
  - — Permit it to be turned off by the user.
  - — For fluid animation, present images at 16 or more frames per second.
- Audition:
  - — Consider auditory icons.

Animation. Recent research has explored the use of bringing to life on screens the icons representing objects and actions. An animated icon appears to move instead of maintaining a static position on the screen. Animation can take two forms, best described as static and dynamic. A *static* icon's appearance is unchanged over a period of time and changes only at the moment that a system event occurs. An example would be the open door of a mailbox shutting when an electronic message is received. A *dynamic* icon's movement is independent of a system event, changing appearance to represent functions, processes, states, and state transitions. An example is an icon that begins movement to illustrate an action when a pointer is moved close to it.

Animation can be used to provide feedback and to create visual interest. Researchers caution, however, that there are many outstanding issues. Among them are that few animation creation rules exist, prototyping is difficult, a scheme for how they fit into a larger system is lacking, and whether they can be made useful for more complex and abstract concepts is not known. Morimoto, Kurokawa, and Nishimura, (1993) found that dynamic animation of the type in the example above did not increase the comprehensibility of icons. Its only advantage was its entertainment value.

Some general guidelines, however, seem appropriate. First, do not prevent the user from interacting with the system while the animation is performed. Unless the animation is part of a process, it should be independent of what the user is doing. It should also be interruptible. Be conservative in its use; do not use animation simply for decoration. It can be very distracting or annoying. Finally, provide the user with the option of turning it on or off, as desired

Microsoft recommends that to achieve fluidity in movement, images should be presented at a speed of at least 16 frames per second. The reader interested in more information on animation is referred to Baecker and Small (1990).

Audition. Objects make sounds as they are touched, dragged, bumped against one another, opened, activated, and thrown away. Auditory icons are computer sounds replicating everyday sound-producing events. When a printer near one's desk begins printing, the sound of the printing mechanism is heard. This provides auditory feedback that a print operation one has just asked for has successfully started. An auditory icon would be the same sound, generated by the computer. Another example would be to convey information about an object's dimensions. If a file is large, it can sound large. If an object is dragged over a new surface, the new surface is heard. If an ongoing process starts running more quickly, it sounds quicker.

Sounds can convey information about many events in computer systems, permitting people to listen to computers as we do in the everyday world. It may be well suited to providing information:

- About previous and possible interactions.
- Indicating ongoing processes and modes.
- Useful for navigation.
- To support collaboration.

Auditory icons are distinct from *earcons*, abstract synthetic tones used in structured combinations to create sound messages. Auditory icons may also be susceptible to the distracting influences that sounds can cause to listeners, especially others. The use of sound was more fully discussed in Chapter 10 "Feedback and Guidance." The reader in need of more information on auditory icons is referred to Garver (1993).

The Design Process

- Define the icon's purpose and use.
- Collect, evaluate, and sketch ideas.
- Draw in black and white.
- Draw using an icon-editing utility or drawing package.
- Test for user:
  - — Expectations.
  - — Recognition.
  - — Learning.
- Test for legibility.
- Register new icons in the system's registry.

Define purpose. To begin the design process, first define the icon's purpose and use. Have the design team brainstorm about possible ideas, considering real-world metaphors. Simple metaphors, analogies, or models with a minimal set of concepts are the best places to start in developing icons.

Collect, evaluate, and sketch ideas. Start by designing on paper, not on the computer (Fowler and Stanwick, 1995). Ask everyone to sketch his or her ideas. Do not worry about too much detail; exact pixel requirements are not necessary at this time.

Draw in black and white. Many icons will be displayed in monochrome. Color is an enhancing property; consider it as such.

Test for expectation, recognition, and learning. Choosing the objects and actions, and the icons to represent them, is not a precise process, and will not be easy. So, as in any screen design activity, adequate testing and possible refinement of developed images must be built into the design process. Icon recognition and learning should both be measured as part of the normal testing process.

Test for legibility. Verify the legibility and clarity of the icons in general. Also, verify the legibility of the icons on the screen backgrounds chosen. White or gray backgrounds may create difficulties. An icon mapped in color, then displayed on a monochrome screen, may not present itself satisfactorily. Be prepared to redraw it in black and white, if necessary.

Register new icons in the system's registry. Create and maintain a registry of all system icons. Provide a detailed and distinctive description of all new icons.

Screen Presentation

- Follow all relevant general guidelines for screen design.
- Limit the number of symbols to 12, if possible, and at most 20.
- Arrange icons:
  - — In a meaningful way, reflecting the organization of the real world.
  - — To facilitate visual scanning.
  - — Consistently.
- Place object and action icons in different groups.
- Present an interactive icon as a raised screen element.
- Ensure that a selected icon is differentiable from unselected icons.
- Permit arrangement of icons by the user.
- Permit the user to choose between iconic and text display of objects and actions.

In designing, or establishing, screen layout rules; adhere to the following presentation rules.

General guidelines. Follow all relevant general guidelines for screen design. Icons are but one part of a larger picture.

Number of icons. A person's ability to identify shapes is limited (see Figure 11.1). A literature review, suggest using no more than eight to twelve or so functions that require icons at one time. At most, present no more than 20. If labels are attached to icons, however, the meaning of the icon is greatly clarified. Too many icons on a screen, though, will greatly increase screen clutter and create confusion. In general, fewer are better.

Arranging icons. Organize icons in a way that reflects the *real-world* organization of the user. Place object icons and action icons within different groupings. *Visual scanning* studies, in a non-iconic world, universally find that a top-to-bottom scan of columnar-oriented information is fastest. Generalization of these findings to an icon screen may not necessarily be warranted if icons have attached labels. Columnar orientation icons (with labels below the icons) will separate the labels from one another by the icons themselves. The labels will be farther apart and fewer icons will fit in a column than in a horizontal or row orientation. A row orientation would seem to be more efficient in many cases, as adjacent icons will be in closer physical proximity. Until research evidence is established to the contrary, organizing icons either in a column or a row seems appropriate. In either case, a *consistent* straight eye movement must be maintained through the icons.

Object and action icons. Conceptually similar items should always be arrayed together. Locating them will be easier.

Interactive icons. To provide a visual indication that an icon is interactive or "clickable," present it in a three-dimensional state raised from the screen background.

Selected icon. Ensure a selected icon is visually differentiable from unselected icons. One common method to achieve this is to present the selected icon in a three-dimensional "pressed" state.

User arrangement. Allow the user to arrange the icons in a manner that is meaningful for the task. A default arrangement should be provided, however.

Iconic or text display. In some situations, and for some users, pure text labels may be more meaningful than icons. The option to display text only should always be provided.

Multimedia

The graphical flexibility of the Web permits inclusion of other media on a screen, including images, photographs, video, diagrams, drawings, and spoken audio. The availability of these additional interface elements has, however, been a double-edged sword. On the one hand, the various media can be powerful communication and attention-getting techniques. Multimedia can hold the user's attention, add interest to a screen, entertain, and quickly convey information that is more difficult to present textually. It can also make the Web much more accessible to people with disabilities. On the other hand, effective use of multimedia in design has been hindered by a lack of knowledge concerning how the various media may best be used, and a scarcity of applied design guidelines. (GUI guidelines relevant to Web page design have been available for years, but their existence was either unknown or ignored.) Effective multimedia use has also been hindered by the "let's use it because we have it" attitude exhibited by many designers. (To be fair, early GUI design has suffered from the same problem.) The resulting usability problems, user confusion and frustration, poor screen legibility, and slow downloads, and so on have created situations where the user was too often denied an efficient and meaningful Web experience.

As a result, recent studies (Spool et al., 1997, for example) have found that the most difficult to use Web sites were those that were graphically intense, and the top Web sites were characterized by little, if any, multimedia. Studies have also found that for users, text is currently a much more important Web site component than graphics. (At least at this stage in Web evolution.) Today, consequently, good interface design employs multimedia in a conservative and appropriate manner. The objective is good interaction design, not "sparkle." In the future, experts say, multimedia elements will be much better integrated with browsers, alleviating many of today's usability problems.

Graphics

- Use graphics to:
  - — Supplement the textual content, not as a substitute for it.
  - — Convey information that can't be effectively accomplished using text.

— Enhance navigation through:
  - Presenting a site overview
  - Identifying site pages.
  - Identifying content areas.
- Limit the use of graphics that take a long time to load.
- Coordinate the graphics with all other page elements.

Graphics contained in Web pages serve several distinct purposes, which can be classified as follows:

Navigational. To identify links that may be followed.

Representational. To illustrate items mentioned in the text.

Organizational. To depict relationships among items mentioned in text.

Explanative. To show how things or processes work.

Decorative. To provide visual appeal and emphasis.

Graphics must always be used for a specific purpose. This purpose must be determined before designing or choosing the graphic itself. Graphics should only be used when they add to a Web site's message. Graphics that do not relate to a Web site's purpose, and do not strengthen the Web site's message should never be used.

Supplement textual content. Use graphics to supplement text, not as a substitute for it. Graphics are not easily accessible to search facilities and screen reviewers, and are slower to download than text. As studies have shown, people prefer textual page content to graphical content. So, never use graphics when text will do the job. If a graphic will help people understand the text they are reading, then certainly use it.

Convey information not possible using text. Use graphics to convey information that can't be effectively conveyed using text. In some cases the old adage "a picture is worth a thousand words" is indeed true. Photographs, for example, can be used to communicate the exact appearance of objects. Video is useful for showing objects or things that move. Diagrams can be used to present an object's structure. Drawings are useful when selected parts of an object need to be emphasized or represented. If a graphic does a better job of communicating an idea or concept than text, then use it. (Remember, however, text descriptions or transcripts of the graphic will always be necessary for accessibility reasons.)

Enhance navigation. Graphics can be used to enhance navigation. A graphical *overview* of a site's organizational scheme will enable the user to conceptualize and learn the site's structure faster than can be done through textual overviews. *Site pages* can be related through a consistent graphical theme carried from page to page. This will reinforce the browsing user's sense of place. Graphics can also be used to identify and represent major site *content areas*. The experienced user will locate and identify the content areas faster using meaningful graphical identifiers rather than text.

Limit long-loading graphics. Limit the use of graphics that take a long time to load In general, all graphics must be smaller on the Web than on the printed page. Large graphics take longer to download testing the user's patience. If a large graphic is needed, present a small version and link it to a page containing the large version. Richly colored graphics and pages containing numerous graphics are also slower to load.

Coordinate graphics. Graphics are only one component of a Web page. The graphics must fit in with the style of typography used, the colors used, and the page layout itself. Use of plain and simple fonts are best coordinated with simple graphics. Realistic graphics work best with elements like three-dimensional effects and more complex typography.

Images

- General:
  - — Use standard images.
  - — Use images consistently.
  - — Produce legible images.
  - — Provide descriptive text or labels with all images.
  - — Distinguish navigational images from decorative images.
  - — Minimize:
    - The number of presented images.
    - The size of presented images.
      - — Restrict single images to 5K.
      - — Restrict page images to 20K.
      - — Provide thumbnail size images.
    - Image animation.
  - — Avoid extraneous or gratuitous images.
- Color:
  - — Minimize the number of colors in an image.
- Format:
  - — Produce images in the most appropriate format.
    - GIF.
    - JPEG.
- Internationalization:
  - -— Provide for image internationalization.
- Screen design:
  - — Reuse images on multiple pages.

Standard images. Whenever possible, use standard images that have already been developed and tested. This will promote consistency across systems, yielding all the performance benefits that consistency provides. These standard images may be found in guideline books, company or organizational documentation, or in industry, trade, or standards organizations' documentation. The International Standards Organization (ISO), for example, has developed standard image shapes for a variety of purposes. Always consult all relevant reference books before inventing new images or modifying existing ones.

Consistency. Use an image consistently throughout an application or Web site. Multiple images with the same meaning will be difficult to learn.

Legibility. Create legible images, images that are easy to identify from a variety of viewing distances and angles. Legibility is affected by a number of factors, including contrast with the background, image complexity, and image size. Images with a minimum amount of detail are usually easier to comprehend and faster to load. If an image with more detail is needed, provide a link to a page containing the detailed version. An image that is perfectly legible when it is drawn or rendered large may, when shrunk for placing on a page, become incomprehensible.

Descriptive text or labels. Many images are not immediately clear, even if well designed. The ability to comprehend, learn, and recall an image's meaning, especially if it is used for navigation, can be greatly improved by providing images with descriptive text or labels. Also, many people browse the Web with their graphics turned off. Without alternate, text an image's purpose and function will not be known. Alternate text for an image also provides the following benefits:

- It provides vision-impaired users with access to content through a screen-review utility.
- It helps sighted users determine whether they want to wait for the image to fully load.
- It enables users to read a description of a linked image and activate the link before image fully loads.

Navigational and decorative images. Clearly indicate which graphical images on the screen are used for navigation by providing a visual indication that an image is interactive or "clickable." Possibilities include giving the image a raised or three-dimensional appearance (like a navigational icon) or underlining any descriptive text contained within it (like a textual link). Navigational images that cannot be distinguished from decorative images force users to "mouse over" each image to determine which are interactive. (Once they are over their initial state of confusion.) This is time-consuming, and important navigation links may be missed.

Minimize number of images. The more images presented on a Web page, the slower the download time. Use text whenever possible

Minimize size of images. Oversized images also take a long time to load. Slow-loading graphics rarely add value to text, and people often don't bother to stick around for them. The design goal is to produce images that load quickly. Make the graphic as small as possible while still retaining sufficient image quality. In general, restrict *single images* to 5K, *page images* to no more than 20K. A 200K file can take several minutes to load. Never put borders around an image with a drawing program because this also adds to the file size.

Thumbnail size. A thumbnail is a small version of an image, usually fairly low in quality. This small image will load quickly because of its small file size. Link this thumbnail image to a large high-quality version of the image. Users can then decide whether or not they want to retrieve and view the full-size version. Always let the user know the size of the full-size image. Thumbnails are especially useful when several images, or a collection of images, must be displayed on a Web page.

Minimize animation. Animated images take a long time to load and are distracting to many people. Only use animation when it serves a useful purpose.

Extraneous or gratuitous images. Similarly, do not present extraneous or gratuitous images. Images take longer to load than text, and Web users prefer text. Images must always serve a useful purpose.

Minimize the number of colors. To reduce the size of image files, reduce the size of the color palette and the number of colors in the image. Color-rich images tend to be large. If the image color palette is too small, however, the image will be degraded. The objective is to retain sufficient image quality while making the file as small as possible. To create images of sufficient color quality while at the same time reducing file size, begin with a high-quality image and create versions using successively smaller color palettes. Stop when the image degradation becomes apparent. (Guidelines for the use of color in screen design are addressed in Chapter 12 "Colors.")

Appropriate format. Produce images in the most appropriate format, GIF or JPEG. CompuServe developed the GIF format (Graphics Interchange Format) in 1987. The JPEG (Joint Photographic Experts Group) was developed for the transfer of photographic images over the Internet.

GIF. Most Web color images and backgrounds are GIF files. They are usually smaller and load faster than JPEGs. They are particularly useful for images that contain flat areas of color. Since GIFs are limited to 256 colors, they are ideal for graphics that use only a few colors. GIFs exist in either a *dithered* or *nondithered* format. Dithering is the color-mixing process a computer goes through when it encounters a color not in its palette. In this process palette colors are mixed to approximate the appearance of the desired color. The resulting color may be grainy or unacceptable. The dithering will be most apparent in gradations, shadows, and feathered edges. A nondithered GIF attempts to match the closest colors from the palette to the image. This is referred to as *banding*. This banding may also create an unacceptable image.

One way to control the dithering process is to create images that only use nondithering colors. The 216 colors that are shared by PCs and Macintoshes are called the Web palette or browser-safe colors. These colors display properly across all platforms without dithering.

GIFs may also be *interlaced*. Interlacing is the gradual display of an image in a series of passes on the screen. The first pass displays a low-resolution out-of focus image and each succeeding pass creates a clearer view until finally a complete image is displayed. With interlacing, users see a complete, although not clear, image much more quickly. An impression that the image is loading much faster is achieved, and users can quickly determine if they are interested in the image. With a *noninterlaced* GIF, the graphic unfolds more slowly one row at a time. Use interlaced GIFs to give users a preview of graphics while they unfold.

Most Web servers call up to four GIFs at a time for display. Limiting GIF images on a page to four will allow pages to load much faster.

JPEG. JPEG formats are superior for images such as photographs that contain numerous changes in color tonality. They look best on monitors capable of displaying 16 million colors. A JEPG's range of colors cannot be produced in monitors displaying 256 or fewer colors. Images that contain flat areas of color may also find that JEPGs introduce unwanted artifacts. JPEGs usually take longer to download than GIFs.

JPEGs may be displayed as progressive or standard. *Progressive* images gradually fade into view like interlaced GIFs, each pass an increasingly higher quality scan. *Standard* images are drawn from top to bottom like noninterlaced GIFs. Use progressive JPEGs to give users a preview of the graphics while they are unloaded.

Internationalization. When designing for international or multilingual users, using images may eliminate the need for translating words.

Reuse images. Repeat the same images on multiple pages. Repeated images will be stored in a *cache*, the browser's temporary storage area. Loading an image from cache significantly reduces an image's downloading time.

Image Maps

- Use:
  - — To provide navigation links to other content.
- Advantages:
  - — Can be arrayed in a meaningful and obvious structure.
  - — Faster to load than separate images.
- Disadvantages:
  - — Consume a significant amount of screen space.
  - — "Hot spots" not always obvious.
  - — One's location within image map is not always obvious.
- Guidelines:
  - — Use with caution.
  - — Provide effective visual cues and emphasis to make it easy to identify link boundaries.
  - — Ensure image maps are accessible to the vision impaired.

Use. An *image map* is a complete image containing individual segments with navigation links to other content. It primary use is to present a meaningfully structured image within which the links are contained.

Advantages/disadvantages. An *advantage* of an image map is its meaningful and obvious structure. It can reflect the user's mental model of an object, minimizing organizational learning requirements. An image map may be a map of a country, for example, with areas reflecting regions that can be selected as links to more detailed content. An image map can also be an image reflecting a site's organization. Image maps, because of their graphical nature, can aid conceptualization of a Web site and how it is organized. Another image map advantage is that they are faster to load than individual images, at least for users accessing the Web through a modem.

There are several *disadvantages* of image maps. First, they are quite wasteful of screen space. Providing large enough "hot spots" or "clickable" areas for each element often necessitates creating very large maps. Within the maps, clickable regions are also not always obvious because they cannot be seen. Whether to click on the map, or where to click, is not always known. This can be confusing for the new user. Unclear or poorly designed image maps can cost users a great deal of time when they make erroneous navigation selections. Selected image map links are also not obvious to the user. A link just selected may be again selected, directing the user right back to the page displayed with no indication that anything has changed. User confusion can again exist. Another disadvantage is that search facilities may not be able to index an image map.

MYTH **Cool = Usable**

Guidelines. Because of these disadvantages, be cautious in the use of image maps. Some experts recommend not using them at all. If used, provide effective visual cues and emphasis to make it easy to identify individual selectable segments and where link boundaries exist. Consider supplementing the image map graphic with text to inform users what they will see when they select a particular area. Finally, ensure that image maps are accessible to vision-impaired users.

Photographs/Pictures

- Use:
  - When every aspect of the image is relevant.
- Guidelines:
  - Use JPEG format.
  - On the initial page:
    - Display a small version.
      - A thumbnail size image.
      - Zoom-in on most relevant detail.
    - Link to larger photos showing as much detail as needed.

Use. When every aspect of an image or object is relevant, present a picture or photograph of it. A photo or picture will capture all visible aspects.

Guidelines. The *JPEG* format was developed for presenting photographs that contain numerous changes in color tonality. Pictures or photos look best on monitors capable of displaying 16 million colors.

A large photo will have an excessively long downloading time. To minimize this time, on the initial page display a small version of the photo and provide a link to a larger, high-quality, complete photo on another page. The small version may be a *thumbnail* image, a complete miniature photograph, usually fairly low in quality. Because of the complexity of a photographic image, a thumbnail may not always be legible. When legibility is a problem, instead of resizing the image to a miniature photo, provide a *zoom-in* on the most relevant photo detail, cropping and resizing as necessary to provide a meaningful and legible image.

For linked full-size photographs provide as much detail as the users need and always inform the users of the image's size. Also, if necessary, provide a zoom or rotation capability for the photograph on the linked page.

Video

- Uses:
  - — To show things that move or change over time.
  - — To show the proper way to perform a task.
  - — To provide a personal message.
  - — To grab attention.
- Disadvantages:
  - — Expensive to produce.
  - — Slow to download.
  - — Small and difficult to discern detail.
- Guidelines:
  - — Never automatically download a video into a page.
  - — Create short segments.
  - — Provide controls, including those for playing, pausing, and stopping.
  - — Consider using:
    - Existing video.
    - Audio only.
    - A slide show with audio.

Uses. Video is especially suited to showing things that move or change over time. Examples include product demonstrations, how to repair a piece of equipment, or how to perform a dance step. Videos can also be used to present personal messages, although the speaker's "presence" may not always have the desired emotional effect. Because of their animation, videos can also be used to grab attention.

Disadvantages. Videos are expensive to produce and slow to download and play. They are also small and limited in the detail they can present. Always inform the user of a video's size so a choice of whether or not to download it can be made. Depending on a video's purpose, its animation may also be distracting to the user.

Guidelines. Do not *automatically download* a video into a loading Web page. Create *short segments*. There are many distractions people may encounter while using a video (the telephone or interruptions by people, and so on), so long segments should be avoided. A 60 to 90 second video is considered long so keep a video's length well within these limits. For all playable files provide the following *controls*: Play, Pause/Resume, Stop, Rewind, Fast Forward, and Volume.

Because of a video's disadvantages consider using existing videos, audio alone, or a slide show with audio. Reusing an *existing video* will save production time and money. A new voice-over may be all that is necessary. *Audio alone* may be as powerful a tool as a video, since the human voice is an important aspect of all videos. Determine whether audio alone will accomplish the video's objectives. An *audio slide show* may also be a good substitute for a video. The impression of movement is still achieved as the slides change, but they are quicker and easier to create and download.

Diagrams

- Uses:
  - — To show the structure of objects.
  - — To show the relationship of objects.
  - — To show the flow of a process or task.
  - — To reveal a temporal or spatial order.
- Guidelines:
  - — Provide simple diagrams.
  - — Provide cutaway diagrams or exploded views to illustrate key points.

Uses. Diagrams are useful for illustrating the structure of an object, its key parts and how they are related to each other. Diagrams are also useful for illustrating the relationships of objects, the structure of an organization, or the structure of a Web site. Other uses are to illustrate the flow of a process or task, a software program, or an airline passenger check-in sequence, for example. Diagrams can also be used to reveal temporal or spatial order, including activities such as the sequence in which an object's parts should be assembled.

Guidelines. Provide simple diagrams showing only as much detail as necessary to clearly illustrate the diagram's objective. Simpler diagrams will also load faster on a Web page. To illustrate key points, provide cutaway diagrams or exploded diagram views.

Drawings

- Use:
  - — When selective parts need to be emphasized or represented.
- Guidelines:
  - — Provide simple drawings showing minimal detail.
  - — Provide a link to a complete drawing.

Use. Use a drawing when only certain parts of an image are of relevance, and these parts must be emphasized or clearly represented. If the working of a specific object is to be described, a diagram illustrating its relevant parts should be used.

Guidelines. Provide simple drawings showing minimal detail. They are easier to view and understand and they also load more quickly. Photographs are likely to be less effective since they contain information that is not relevant, they lack clarity, and they take longer to load on a Web page. If the user is also in need of a detailed drawing, provide a link to a page containing a complete drawing.

Animation

- Uses:
  - — To explain ideas involving a change in:
    - Time.
    - Position.
  - — To illustrate the location or state of a process.
  - — To show continuity in transitions.
  - — To enrich graphical representations.
  - — To aid visualization of three-dimensional structures.
  - — To attract attention.
- Disadvantages:
  - — Very distracting.
  - — Slow loading.
- Guidelines:
  - — Use only when an integral part of the content.
  - — Create short segments.
  - — Provide a freeze frame and stop mode.
  - — Avoid distracting animation.

Uses. Only use animation when it serves a useful purpose. Animations can be used to enhance textual explanations of objects changing over *time.* A map illustrating population growth can be animated to illustrate population densities and patterns over a sequence of years or centuries. Proper sequential body *positions* needed to skillfully perform a sport can also be illustrated as they are textually described. The current *location* within, or the state of, a process can be highlighted through animating flow arrows or process steps.

Continuity in transitions can also be illustrated. The changing of states of an element with two or more states will be easier to understand if the transitions are animated instead of being instantaneous. In Windows, actually seeing an icon moving as it is dragged from a desktop to the Recycle Bin or the My Documents file strengthens one's understanding of the task and the results. *Graphical representations* can also be enriched. Some kinds of information are easier to visualize with movement rather than with still pictures. *Visualization* of three-dimensional structures can also be aided. While a two-dimensional screen can never provide a full understanding of a three-dimensional element, animating the element by slowly turning it aids in understanding its structure. Animation can also be used to *attract attention*. The user's attention can be directed to an important screen element or alerted to an important condition.

MAXIM ***Content* is always more important than graphics.**

Disadvantages. Any discussion of screen image animation includes a strong caution concerning animation's side effects. Screen animation is difficult to ignore, often overpowering a person's peripheral vision. Peripheral vision competes with foveal vision for a person's attention. That sensed in the periphery is passed on to our information-processing system along with what is actively being viewed foveally. It is, in a sense, visual noise. Mori and Hayashi (1993) experimentally evaluated the effect of windows in both a foveal and peripheral relationship and found that performance on a foveal window deteriorates when there are peripheral windows, and the performance degradation is even *greater* if the information in the peripheral is dynamic or moving. Reeves and Nass (1996) measured brain waves with an EEG and found that attention increased every time motion appeared on a screen. Permanently moving animation on a screen makes it very hard for people to concentrate on reading text, if the brain wants to attend to the motion. Animation can also be very annoying.

Another current negative side effect of Web page animation is its close association with advertising. Animation, including scrolling text, is frequently being used by advertisers to try and gather the users' attention. Studies suggest that people have started equating animation with advertising, so animation as a screen element is being routinely ignored. Important animation may, therefore, be missed. Animated images also take longer to load.

Guidelines. Use animation sparingly. Only use it when it is an *integral part* of the textual content, or reinforces the content. Create *short segments*. There are many distractions people may encounter while watching animation, so long segments should be avoided. Animation, when used, should be capable of being *stopped* by the user so an image may be studied in detail. It should also be capable of being ended entirely so it is eliminated as a visual distraction. In conclusion, always avoid animation or special effects that detract from the screen's message.

Audition

- Uses:
  - — As a supplement to text and graphics.
  - — To establish atmosphere.
  - — To create a sense of place.
  - — To teach.
  - — To sample.
- Advantages:
  - — Does not obscure information on the screen.
  - — Shorter downloading time than video.

- Disadvantages:
  - — Is annoying to many people, including users and nonusers in the vicinity.
  - — Can easily be overused, increasing the possibility that it will be ignored.
  - — Is not reliable because:
    - Some people are hard of hearing.
    - If it is not heard, it may leave no permanent record of having occurred.
    - The user can turn it off.
    - Audio capability may not exist for the user.
- Guidelines:
  - — When words are spoken:
    - The content should be simple.
    - The speed of narration should be about 160 words per minute.
  - — When used to introduce new ideas or concepts the narration should be slowed.
  - — Off-screen narration should be used rather than on-screen narration.
    - Unless the narrator is a recognized authority on the topic.
  - — Create short segments.
  - — Provide segments of high quality.
  - — Provide audio controls.
  - — Play background audio softly.

This discussion of audition focuses on sound as a communication medium for presenting meaningful information, words, music, and so on A discussion of sounds used to alert the user is found in Chapter 10.

Uses. Use audio as a *supplement* to text and graphics and only to reinforce visual content. Audio should never be used alone because of the disadvantages listed above. Audio can also be used to establish *atmosphere.* A particular type of music reflecting a Web site's content can be played to establish ambience and also to create orientation signposts fostering a *sense of place*. Audio can also be used to *teach* word pronunciation or to provide *samples* of music.

Advantages. An advantage of audio is its ability to offering commentary or help for a visual display. Audio does not obscure information on the screen, and it downloads faster than most other types of graphics.

Disadvantages. Audio's disadvantages are similar to those of sounds described in Chapter 10. Audio can be annoying to many people, including users and nonusers in the vicinity. It can easily be overused, increasing the possibility that it will be ignored. Audio is also not reliable because some people are hard of hearing, it may leave no permanent record of having occurred, it may not be available to the user, or it may be turned off. Loud audio can also be irritating, especially to those with sen-sitive hearing.

Guidelines. Williams (1998) in a multimedia literature review extracted most of the following guidelines. When words are spoken, the content should be simple, and the speed of narration should be about 160 words per minute. When the narration is used to introduce new ideas or new concepts the narration should be slowed. Off-screen (invisible) narration should be used rather than on-screen narration.

On-screen narration is acceptable, however if the narrator is a recognized authority on the topic being presented.

Other audition guidelines include these: Create *short segments*. There are many distractions people may encounter while listening to audio, so long segments should be avoided. Always provide audio segments of *high quality*. Research has found (Reeves and Nass, 1996) that while people will accept poor video, they are very affected by poor audio. Let users control the playing of audio. Provide the following *controls*: Play, Pause/Resume, Stop, Rewind, Fast Forward, and Volume. Any *background* audio should be subdued so it does not interfere with main information being presented on the screen.

Combining Mediums

- Combinations:
  - — Use sensory combinations that work best together:
    - Auditory text with visual graphics.
    - Screen text with visual graphics.
- Integration:
  - — Closely integrate screen text with graphics.
- Relevance:
  - — Both the visual and auditory information should be totally relevant to the task being performed.
- Presentation:
  - — Visual and auditory textual narrative should be presented simultaneously, or the visuals should precede the narrative by no more than 7 seconds.
  - — To control attention, reveal information systematically.
    - Limit elements revealed to one item at a time and use sequential revelations for related elements.
  - — Animation must show action initiation as well as the action's result.
  - — Avoid animation that distracts from other more important information.
- Downloading times:
  - — Consider downloading times when choosing a media.
- Testing:
  - — Thoroughly test all graphics for:
    - Legibility.
    - Comprehensibility.
    - Acceptance.

Interface technology encourages inclusion of the various graphical media (images, photos, video, diagrams, drawings, and audio) along with text on a screen. The design issue is which mediums work best with other mediums, and which mediums should not be employed together. Before reviewing research on this topic, which does find performance advantages for certain combinations of multimedia, theories for why this may happen will be summarized.

The first theory is called the *dual code* theory. It proposes that people store information in two ways in memory: verbally and pictorially. This theory postulates that, because of this dual-storage capability, information communicated to a person in both a verbal and pictorial manner has a greater likelihood of being remembered than information arriving in only one format. Also postulated is that too much information arriving in one format can overtax that particular memory. Combining verbal audio with displayed text is one such overtaxing combination.

The second theory also proposes two independent working memories, but is slightly different in concept. The first type of memory is a visual-spatial sketchpad in which information accumulated visually is stored. This visual information may be graphical or textual in nature. The second type of working memory is a phonological loop for dealing with and storing auditory information. This theory postulates that performance may be improved for certain more complex tasks because working memory is expanded through the application of two senses. The general conclusion is that combining visual and verbal auditory information can lead to enhanced comprehension, when compared to relying on one sense alone.

The two theories diverge on the storage of audio. The former suggests that verbal audio and displayed text is stored together; the latter suggests that they are stored separately.

Combinations and integration. Williams (1998) in a literature review found that combining visual and verbal auditory information in multimedia design can lead to enhanced comprehension, when compared to use of these medias alone. Several recent studies have also explored the effects of various media, or combinations of media, on user performance. One such study is that of Lee and Bowers (1997). These researchers evaluated various mediums to see which yielded the best learning. The results, summarized in Table 11.2, compared a control group to groups learning material by the various methods described.

Another series of three studies were those of Tindall-Ford, Chandler, and Sweller (1997). They compared combinations of the following multimedia conditions for learning and performance:

Table 11.2 Learning Improvements for Various Media

MEDIUM	PERCENT MORE LEARNING
Hearing spoken text and viewing graphics	91%
Viewing graphics alone	63%
Viewing text and viewing graphics	56%
Hearing spoken text, viewing text, and viewing graphics	46%
Hearing spoken text and viewing text	32%
Viewing text alone	12%
Hearing spoken text alone	7%

From Lee and Bowers (1997).

- A visual diagram or table and separated visual text.
- A visual diagram and integrated visual text.
- A visual diagram or table and spoken instructions.

They found that the visual-audio combinations yielded reliably better performance for complex tasks, but no differences were found for easy tasks. They also found that visual text integrated into a diagram yielded better performance than separated visual text. They attributed the better results for the audiovisual combination and the integrated text and diagram alternative to reduced demands on working memory.

What can we conclude from these studies?

- **The proper multimedia combinations can improve learning and performance.** Hearing spoken text combined with a visual graphic is an especially useful combination, especially for complex tasks. All studies found this pairing useful.
- **Visual graphics do enhance learning and performance.** In the Bowers and Lee study, the various graphical combinations yielded the higher learning rates.
- **Single-dimensional textual media are not as successful when used alone.** In the Bowers and Lee study, viewing text or hearing spoken text alone yielded the lowest learning rates.
- **Hearing spoken text and viewing text at the same time may not be great, but it may not be terrible, either.** This combination yielded "middle-of-the-road" results in the Bowers and Lee study. The dual code theory would suggest, however, that its use be minimized. Exercise caution in this area.
- **Visual text should always be integrated with related visual graphics.** Tindall-Ford et al. found much better user performance when visual text was closely integrated with, or adjacent to, related visual graphics. It will be much easier for user to coordinate and integrate the visual materials. Presenting spatially separated text and related graphics places greater demands on working memory.

Relevance. Both the visual and auditory information should be totally relevant to the task being performed. All spoken text should reinforce presented graphics.

Presentation. Faraday and Sutcliffe (1997) also conducted a series of studies addressing multimedia design. Like the above-mentioned studies, they found displayed graphics (images and animation) improved user performance, specifically the recall of information. Based upon these studies, they developed the following guidelines. Provide sufficient *time* for reading screen graphic captions. Present simultaneously all visual and auditory *narrative information* to the user, or have the visual information precede the auditory narrative by no more than 7 seconds. To control the users' attention, *reveal* or expose information systematically on the screen, either from left to right or from top to bottom. Limit the information revealed to one item at a time, and sequentially reveal related elements. Finally, any *animation* must show an action being initiated as well as the action's result, and avoid any animation that distracts from other more important screen information.

Downloading times. Consider times in choosing a graphical medium. In general, downloading times range from the fastest, audio, to the slowest, video.

Testing. Thoroughly test all graphics for *legibility*. Make sure visual graphics are easy to see from a variety of viewing distances. Also test them for *comprehensibility*. Are visual graphics and related audio clear and understandable? Are the graphics *acceptable* to the using audience? This is especially critical if the users are multicultural. Always test graphics with all representative user groups.

Multiple Choice Questions

1. An image that looks like what it means falls into the following kind of icon:
   (a) Resemblance (b) Symbolic
   (c) Exemplar (d) Arbitrary
   (e) Analogy

2. An abstract image representing something falls into the following kind of icon:
   (a) Resemblance (b) Symbolic
   (c) Exemplar (d) Arbitrary
   (e) Analogy

3. An image illustrating an example or characteristic of something falls into the following kind of icon:
   (a) Resemblance (b) Symbolic
   (c) Exemplar (d) Arbitrary
   (e) Analogy

4. An image completely arbitrary in appearance whose meaning must be learned falls into the following kind of icon:
   (a) Resemblance (b) Symbolic
   (c) Exemplar (d) Arbitrary
   (e) Analogy

5. An image physically or semantically associated with something falls into the following kind of icon:
   (a) Resemblance (b) Symbolic
   (c) Exemplar (d) Arbitrary
   (e) Analogy

6. The purpose of Navigational graphics is
   (a) To illustrate items mentioned in the text
   (b) To identify links that may be followed
   (c) To depict relationships among items mentioned in text
   (d) To show how things or processes work
   (e) To provide visual appeal and emphasis

7. The purpose of Representational graphics is
   (a) To illustrate items mentioned in the text
   (b) To identify links that may be followed
   (c) To depict relationships among items mentioned in text
   (d) To show how things or processes work
   (e) To provide visual appeal and emphasis

8. The purpose of Organizational graphics is
   (a) To illustrate items mentioned in the text
   (b) To identify links that may be followed
   (c) To show how things or processes work
   (d) To depict relationships among items mentioned in text
   (e) To provide visual appeal and emphasis

9. The purpose of Decorative graphics is
   (a) To illustrate items mentioned in the text
   (b) To identify links that may be followed
   (c) To show how things or processes work
   (d) To depict relationships among items mentioned in text
   (e) To provide visual appeal and emphasis

10. The purpose of Explanative graphics is
    (a) To illustrate items mentioned in the text
    (b) To identify links that may be followed
    (c) To show how things or processes work
    (d) To depict relationships among items mentioned in text
    (e) To provide visual appeal and emphasis

Review Questions

1. What is an Icon? Describe the various categories of Icons used in UI application.
2. List the characteristics of Icon.
3. State the design process for designing an Icon.
4. Explain the icon design guidelines with examples.
5. State the design rules for presenting Icons on screen layout.
6. Consider the User Interface for Zoo information kiosk.
   (a) Draw the screen layout for Zoo information kiosk.
   (b) State how Icons can be designed using animation and audition feature.
   (c) State the advantage and disadvantage of the choosing icons.
7. Describe the use of graphics in UI and Web Interface design.
8. State the general guidelines for choosing images for Screen UI design.
9. State the advantage and disadvantage of using videos and animation component for UI design.

CHAPTER 12

Colors

Color adds dimension, or realism, to screen usability. Color draws attention because it attracts a person's eye. If used properly, it can emphasize the logical organization of information, facilitate the discrimination of screen components, accentuate differences among elements, and make displays more interesting. If used improperly, color can be distracting and possibly visually fatiguing, impairing the system's usability. In this chapter we will:

- Come to understand color's characteristics.
  - What color is.
  - The uses of color.
  - Possible problems and cautions when working with color.
  - The results of color research.
  - Color and human vision.
- Come to understand how to use color.
- Choose the proper colors for textual graphic screens.
- Choose the proper colors for statistical graphics screens.
- Choose the proper color for Web screen text and images.

Effective use of color in screen design has taken great steps forward in the last four decades. Earlier text-based displays could only present a few colors, and many of the colors were not very legible. Color was often overused in combinations that reminded one more of a Christmas tree than of an effective source of communication. The evolution to graphical screens expanded the use of color, but did not immediately eliminate some of the color problems. Today, because technology has improved, as well as our understanding of what constitutes good design, colors in screens are being used much more effectively. Pastels have replaced bright reds and dark blues, and the number of colors presented at one time on a screen has been reduced, dramatically in some cases. This is not to say, however, that all the problems have been solved. A tour around the office will usually uncover some questionable, or awful, uses of color. Two of two most common problems are screen backgrounds being more attention-grabbing than the screen data (which is the most important element of a screen), and overuse of color as a graphic language or code (the color itself meaning something to the screen viewer). This latter kind of use forces the user to interpret a color's meaning *before* the message it is communicating can be reacted to.

In recent years, the development of the Web and the availability of monitors with significantly expanded color capability have initiated a replay of the early color-use problems that surfaced in both text-based and graphical systems. Infatuated with the almost unlimited supply of available colors, developers have eagerly raced to include a multitude of colors on Web pages, with too little thought given to the consequences for users. The "Christmas tree effect" has lived on as users struggled with illegible text and numerous visual distractions. Today, the use of color in Web pages has improved somewhat. Too many site designers still, however, associate good design with "splashy" color.

The discussion to follow begins by defining color. Next is a review of how color may be used in screen design and some critical cautions on its use. Then, the human visual system and its implications for color are discussed. Continuing, a series of general screen guidelines are presented for choosing and using colors. This is followed by a compilation of guidelines for specific kinds of screens: textual and graphical, statistical graphics, and Web screens and their associated graphical elements.

Color—What Is It?

Wavelengths of light themselves are not colored. What is perceived as actual color results from the stimulation of the proper receptor in the eye by a received light wave. The name that a color is given is a learned phenomenon, based on previous experiences and associations of specific visual sensations with color names. Therefore, a color can only be described in terms of a person's report of his or her perceptions. The visual spectrum of wavelengths to which the eye is sensitive ranges from about 400 to 700 millimicrons. Objects in the visual environment often emit or reflect light waves in a limited area of this visual spectrum, absorbing light waves in other areas of the spectrum. The dominant wavelength being "seen" is the one that we come to associate with a specific color name. The visible color spectrum and the names commonly associated with the various light wavelengths are shown in Table 12.1.

To describe a color, it is useful to refer to the three properties it possesses: hue, chroma or saturation, and value or intensity, as illustrated in Figure 12.1. *Hue* is the spectral wavelength composition of a color. It is to this we attach a meaning such as green or red. *Chroma* or *saturation* is the purity of a color in a scale from gray to the most vivid version of the color. The more saturated a hue is, the more visible it is at a distance. The less

Table 12.1 The Visible Spectrum

APPROXIMATE COLOR WAVELENGTHS IN MILLIMICRONS	
Red	700
Orange	600
Yellow	570
Yellow-green	535
Green	500
Blue-green	493
Blue	470
Violet	400

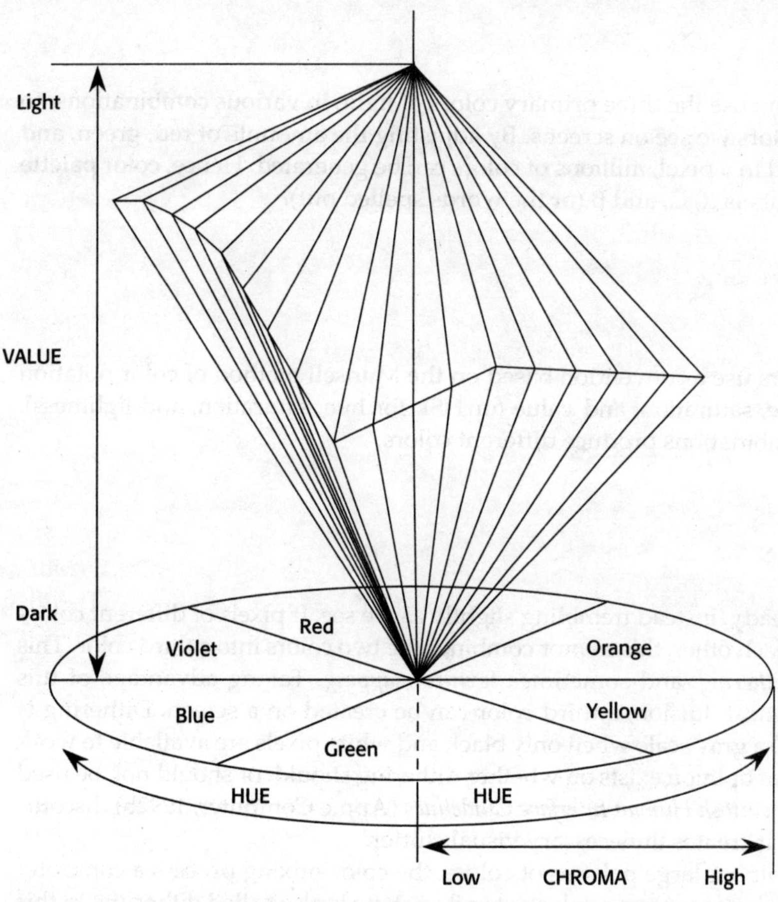

Figure 12.1 The relationship of hue, chroma, and value.

saturated, the less visible it is. *Value* or *intensity* is the relative lightness or darkness of a color in a range from black to white. Two-word descriptors, such as light red or dark blue, are usually used to describe lightness differences. Some hues are inherently lighter or darker than others, for example, yellow is very light and violet is very dark.

The primary colors of illuminated light are red, green, and blue, whose wavelengths additively combine in pairs to produce magenta, cyan, and yellow, and all the other visible colors in the spectrum. The three primary colors additively combine to produce white. The long-wavelength colors (red) are commonly referred to as warm, and short-wavelength colors (blue) as cool.

Color, then, is a combination of hue, chroma, and value. In any one instance what we call "blue" may actually be one of several hundred thousand "blues." This problem has confounded color research over the years. A "blue" may be unacceptable in one situation because it is highly saturated and dark, but perfectly acceptable in another, being less saturated and light. The exact measures of a color are rarely reported in the literature.

RGB

Many color monitors use the three primary colors of light, in various combinations, to create the many colors we see on screens. By adjusting the amounts of red, green, and blue light presented in a pixel, millions of colors can be generated. Hence, color palette editors exist with labels R, G, and B (or the words spelled out).

HSV

Some palette editors use a convention based on the Munsell method of color notation called HSV, for hue, saturation, and value (or HSL for hue, saturation, and lightness). Again, various combinations produce different colors.

Dithering

The eye is never steady, instead trembling slightly as we see. If pixels of different colors are placed next to each other, this tremor combines the two colors into a third color. This is referred to as *dithering*, and sometimes *texture mapping*. Taking advantage of this phenomena, an optical illusion, a third color can be created on a screen. Dithering is often used to create a gray scale when only black and white pixels are available to work with. A difference of opinion exists on whether dithering should, or should not, be used on a screen. *The Macintosh Human Interface Guidelines* (Apple Computer, 1992b) discourage its use, stating it creates unnecessary visual clutter.

In systems containing large palettes of colors, the color-mixing process a computer goes through when it encounters a color not in its palette is also called dithering. In this process palette colors are mixed to approximate the appearance of the desired color.

Color Uses

- Use color to assist in formatting a screen:
  - — Relating or tying elements into groupings.
  - — Breaking apart separate groupings of information.
  - — Associating information that is widely separated on the screen.
  - — Highlighting or calling attention to important information by setting it off from the other information.
- Use color as a visual code to identify:
  - — Screen components.
  - — The logical structure of ideas, processes, or sequences.
  - — Sources of information.
  - — Status of information.
- Use color to:
  - — Realistically portray natural objects.
  - — Increase screen appeal.

Color may be used as a formatting aid in structuring a screen, or it may be used as a visual code to categorize and identify information or data. It may also be used to portray objects naturally and make a screen more appealing to look at.

Color as a Formatting Aid

As a formatting aid, color can provide better structure and meaning to a screen. It is especially useful when large amounts of information must be included on a screen and spacing to differentiate components is problematic. For example, displaying groupings of information in different colors can enhance differentiation of the groupings. Spatially separated but related fields can also be tied together through a color scheme.

Color can also replace highlighting as a means of calling attention to information. Color is much more flexible than other techniques because of the number of colors that are available. Color, as an attention-getting mechanism must, however, be chosen in light of the psychological and physiological considerations to be described shortly.

Color as a Visual Code

A color code indicates what category the information being displayed falls into. It has meaning to the screen's user. A properly selected color-coding scheme permits a person to identify a relevant information category quickly, without having to read its contents first. This permits focusing on this category, while the remaining information is excluded from attention.

One common color-coding scheme used to differentiate screen components is to display screen captions and data in different colors. Another is to identify information from different sources—information added to a process from different locations, or text added to a message from different departments, may be colored differently. Using color-coding to convey status might involve displaying, in a different color, information that passed or failed system edits. Color can also be used as a prompt, guiding a person through a complex transaction.

To be effective, color as a visual code must be relevant and known. Relevance is achieved when the color enables a person to attend to only the information that is needed, and easily exclude that which is not needed. A relevant code, however, will be useless unless its meaning is also understood by the person who must use it. If a color's meaning is not known, one must first interpret its meaning. This can place burdens on a person's memory. It can also impede performance, requiring one to consult a manual or a legend in order to understand it.

Other Color Uses

Color can also be used to more realistically portray objects in the world around us that must be displayed on a screen. It is also thought that the addition of color increases a screen's appeal and makes working with a display more pleasant.

Possible Problems with Color

The simple addition of color to a screen will not guarantee improved performance. What may have been a poorly designed product will simply become a colorful poorly designed product. When used improperly, color may even impair performance by distracting the viewer and interfering with the handling of information. Possible problems may be caused by the perceptual system itself or the physiological characteristics of the human eye.

High Attention-Getting Capacity

Color has an extremely high attention-getting capacity. This quality causes the screen viewer to associate, or tie together, screen elements of the same color, whether or not such an association should be made. A person might search for relationships and differences that do not exist, or that are not valid. The result is often bewilderment, confusion, and slower reading. The effect achieved is often described as the Christmas tree mentioned earlier.

Interference with Use of Other Screens

Indiscriminate or poor use of color on some screens will diminish the effectiveness of color on other screens. The rationale for color will be difficult to understand and its attention-getting capacity severely restricted.

Varying Sensitivity of the Eye to Different Colors

All colors are not equal in the eye of the viewer. The eye is more sensitive to those in the middle of the visual spectrum (yellow and green), which appear brighter than those at the extremes (blue and red). Thus, text composed of colors at the extremes is thought to be more difficult to read. Research evidence on this topic is mixed. Several studies have found that acuity, contrast sensitivity, target recognition, legibility, and performance were not influenced by color. On the other hand, other studies have found advantages for central spectral colors in reaction times, resolution, and error rates.

Also, it is thought that some combinations of screen colors can strain the eye's accommodation mechanism. The wavelengths of light that produce blue are normally focused in front of the eye's retina, the red wavelengths behind it. Simultaneous or sequential viewing of red and blue causes the eye to continually refocus to bring the image directly onto the retina, thereby increasing the potential for eye fatigue. Again, the research evidence is mixed. Some studies have found this a problem while others have not.

What does one conclude after looking at the research addressing the above problems? The reasonable assumption is that they have neither been proved nor disproved. We have not properly defined all the terminal-based tasks being performed, and the exact qualities of the colors being studied. Also, the studies have used only a few of the many devices in existence. And, a firm definition of "visual fatigue" remains elusive. Finally, none of the studies have addressed extended terminal viewing. The prudent course is to be cautious and avoid using colors and combinations that color theory suggests can create problems.

The perceived appearance of a color is also affected by a variety of other factors, including the size of the area of color, the ambient illumination level, and other colors in the viewing area. Also, larger changes in wavelength are needed in some areas of the visual spectrum for a color change to be noticed by the eye. Small changes in extreme reds and purples are more difficult to detect than small changes in yellow and blue-green. Failure to consider the eye and how it handles color, then, can also lead to mistakes in color identification, misinterpretations, slower reading, and, perhaps, visual fatigue.

Color-Viewing Deficiencies

Another disadvantage of color is that about 8 percent of males and 0.4 percent of females have some form of color-perception deficiency—color blindness, as it is commonly called. In actuality, very few people are truly color-blind; most of those with problems simply have difficulties discriminating certain colors. A red viewing deficiency is called *protanopia*, a green deficiency is called *deuteranopia*, and a blue deficiency is called *tritanopia*. These common color deficiencies, their results, and the percentage of people who experience these problems, are summarized in Table 12.2. Total color blindness affects no more than 0.005 percent of both sexes. For an individual with color-perception deficiency, all the normal colors may not be discernible, but often differences in lightness or intensity can be seen. The important point: a person experiencing any form of color deficiency must not be prohibited from effectively using a screen.

Table 12.2 Results of Color-Defective Vision

ACTUAL COLOR	COLOR SEEN WITH: RED-VIEWING DEFICIENCY (2.04%)	GREEN-VIEWING DEFICIENCY (6.39%)	BLUE-VIEWING DEFICIENCY (0.003%)
Red	Brown	—	—
Yellow	Greenish-Yellow	Orange	Deeper Yellow
Purple	Dark Blue	Red	Deep Red
Green	—	Light Brown	—
Brown	—	Reddish-Brown	—
Blue	—	—	Green

From Barnett (1993); Fowler and Stanwick (1995).

Cross-Disciplinary and Cross-Cultural Differences

Colors can have different meanings in different situations to different people. A color used in an unexpected way can cause confusion. An error signaled in green would contradict the expected association of red with stop or danger. The same color may also have a different connotation, depending upon its viewer. The color blue has the following quite different meanings:

- For financial managers—Corporate qualities or reliability.
- For health care professionals—Death.
- For nuclear reactor monitors—Coolness or water.
- For American movie audiences—Tenderness or pornography.

Differences in color connotations also exist between cultures. Red, for example, in the United States is associated with danger, in Egypt with death, and in India with life. Incorrect use in a different culture may cause severe problems.

Color appeal is also subjective. People have different tastes in color, what is pleasing to one person may be distasteful or unusable by someone else.

The proper use of color, then, requires an analysis of the expectations and experiences of the screen viewer. The use of color in design must always keep these possible problems clearly in focus. The designer must work to minimize their disruptive and destructive effects.

MAXIM **Poor use of color is worse than not using it at all.**

Color—What the Research Shows

The effectiveness of color in improving the usability of a display has been studied for many years. The research results have been mixed. To illustrate, on a positive note, color has been shown to improve performance (Kopala, 1981; Nagy and Sanchez, 1992; Sidorsky, 1982), to improve visual search time (Christ, 1975; Carter, 1982), to be useful for organizing information (Engel, 1980), to aid memory (Marcus, 1986b), and to demarcate a portion of a screen (as opposed to lines or type font, Wopking, Pastoor, and Beldie 1985). Color has also created positive user reactions (Tullis, 1981), was preferred to monochromatic screens for being less monotonous and reducing eyestrain and fatigue (Christ, 1975), and is more enjoyable (Marcus, 1986b).

On the other hand, it has also been shown that color does not improve performance (Tullis, 1981), does not have much of an effect on reading text (Legge and Rubin, 1986), may impair performance (Christ and Teichner, 1973; Christ, 1975), and is less important than display spacing (Haubner and Benz, 1983). It has also been demonstrated that poor character-background color combinations lead to poorer performance (McTyre and Frommer, 1985). Finally, no evidence has been produced that color, as compared to black and white, can significantly improve aesthetics or legibility or reduce eyestrain (Pastoor, 1990).

Research has found, moreover, that as the number of colors on a display increases, the time to respond to a single color increases, and the probability of color confusion increases (Luria, Neri, and Jacobsen 1986). Many studies have found that the maximum number of colors that a person can handle is in the range of 4 to 10, with emphasis on the lower numbers (for example, Brooks, 1965; Halsey and Chapanis, 1951; Luria, Neri, and Jacobsen, 1986).

The conclusion to be derived from these studies is that for simple displays, color may have no dramatic impact. Indeed, a monochromatic display may serve the purpose just as well. As display complexity increases, however, so does the value of color. A second conclusion is that people like using color and think it has a positive influence on their productivity, even though it may not.

To be effective, color must be properly used. Poor use of color will actually impair performance, not help it. When using color, keep in mind its value will be dependent upon the task being performed, the colors selected, the number of colors used, and the viewing environment.

Color and Human Vision

To understand how color should be used on a screen, it is helpful to know something of the physiology of the human eye.

The Lens

Muscles control the lens of the eye. These muscles focus received wavelengths of light on the retina. The lens itself is not color corrected. The wavelengths of light that create different colors are focused at different distances behind the lens, the longer wavelengths (red) being focused farther back than the shorter wavelengths (blue). The result is that colors of a different wavelength from the color actually being focused by the lens will appear out of focus. To create a sharp image of the out-of-focus colors requires a refocusing of the eye. Excessive refocusing (such as between red and blue) can lead to eye fatigue.

The effect of this focusing for most people is that blues appear more distant and reds appear closer. This can give a three-dimensional appearance to what is being viewed. A critical problem is that the wavelength of light that creates blues can never be brought into focus on the retina but is always focused in front of it. A sharp blue image is impossible to obtain. Very pure or saturated colors require more refocusing than less pure or unsaturated colors. Therefore, a color with a large white component will require less refocusing.

The lens does not transmit all light wavelengths equally. It absorbs more wavelengths in the blue region of the spectrum than those in the other regions. Additionally, as the lens ages, it tends to yellow, filtering out the shorter blue wavelengths. Thus, as people get older, their sensitivity to blue decreases. The lens also refocuses for light waves of different brightness. Sharp contrasts in brightness in things being viewed can lead to visual fatigue as the eye continually makes muscular adjustments. Driving an automobile through a forest of trees on a bright sunny day illustrates this effect. The eye continually adjusts as the auto sequentially moves through areas of bright sunlight and patches of shadows.

The Retina

The retina is the light-sensitive surface of the eye. It comprises two kinds of receptors, rods and cones, which translate the incoming light into nervous impulses. Rods are sensitive to lower light levels and function primarily at night. Cones are stimulated by higher light levels and react to color. The sensitivity of cones to colors varies, different cones possessing maximum sensitivity to different wavelengths of light. About two-thirds (64 percent) of the cones are maximally sensitive to longer light wavelengths, showing a peak response at about 575 millimicrons. These cones have traditionally been referred to as "red" sensitive cones. In actuality, however, the peak sensitivity is in the yellow portion of the visual spectrum (see Table 12.1). About one-third (32 percent) of the cones achieve maximum sensitivity at about 535 millimicrons and are commonly referred to as "green" sensitive cones. The remainder (2 percent) primarily react to short light wavelengths, achieving maximum sensitivity at about 445 millimicrons. These are known as "blue" sensitive cones. Any light wave impinging on the retina evokes a response, to a greater or lesser degree, from most or all of these cones. A perceived "color" results from the proportion of stimulation of the various cone kinds.

Rods and cones vary in distribution across the retina. The center is tightly packed with cones and has no rods. Toward the periphery of the retina, rods increase and cones decrease. Thus, color sensitivity does not exist at the retina's outer edges, although yellows and blues can be detected further into the periphery than reds and greens. The very center of the retina is devoid of blue cones, creating a "blue-blindness" for small objects being looked at.

The receptors in the eye also adjust, or adapt, their level of sensitivity to the overall light level and the color being viewed. Adaptation to increases in brightness improves color sensitivity. Color adaptation "softens" colors.

The brightness sensitivity of the eye to different colors also varies. It is governed by output from the red and green cones. The greater the output, the higher the brightness, which results in the eye being most sensitive to colors in the middle of the visual spectrum and less sensitive to colors at the extremes. A blue or red must be of a much greater intensity than a green or yellow even to be perceived.

The ability of the eye to detect a form is accomplished by focusing the viewed image on the body of receptors to establish edges. Distinct edges yield distinct images. Edges formed by color differences alone cannot be accurately brought into focus and thus create fuzzy and indistinct images. A clear, sharp image requires a difference in brightness between adjacent objects, as well as differences in color.

The components of the eye—the lens and retina—govern the choices, and combinations, of colors to be displayed on a screen. The proper colors will enhance performance; improper colors will have the opposite effect, as well as increase the probability of visual fatigue.

MYTH **If we can't do it right, do it big. If we can't do it big, do it in color.**

Choosing Colors

When choosing colors for display, one must consider these factors: the human visual system, the possible problems that the colors' use may cause, the viewing environment in which the display is used, the task of the user, how the colors will be used, and the hardware on which the colors will be displayed. The primary objective in using color is communication, to aid the transfer of information from the screen to the user.

Choosing Colors for Categories of Information

- Choosing colors for categories of information requires a clear understanding of how the information will be used.
- Some examples:
  - — If different parts of the screen are attended to separately, color-code the different parts to focus selective attention on each in turn.
  - — If decisions are made based on the status of certain types of information on the screen, color-code the types of status that the information may possess.
  - — If screen searching is performed to locate information of a particular kind or quality, color-code these kinds or qualities for contrast.
  - — If the sequence of information use is constrained or ordered, use color to identify the sequence.
  - — If the information displayed on a screen is packed or crowded, use color to provide visual groupings.
- Use color as a redundant screen code.

Categories. Color chosen to organize information or data on a screen must aid the transfer of information from the display to the user. This requires a clear understanding of how the information is selected and used. The examples above describe some common ways of classifying information for color-coding purposes.

Redundancy. Never rely on color as the only way of identifying a screen element or process. Users with a color-viewing deficiency may not be able identify a specific color when it is important. It is also important to remember that information on one screen may be used in more than one way. What is useful in one context may not be in another and may only cause interference. Therefore, when developing a color strategy, always consider how spatial formatting, highlighting, and messages may also be useful and employ these structural and coding methods as well.

Colors in Context

Colors are subject to contextual effects. The size of a colored image, the color of images adjacent to it, and the ambient illumination all exert an influence on what is actually perceived. At the normal viewing distance for a screen, maximal color sensitivity is not reached until the size of a colored area exceeds about a 3-inch square. Smaller images become desaturated (having a greater white component) and change slightly in color. Also, small differences in actual color may not be discernible. Blues and yellows are particularly susceptible to difficulties in detecting slight changes. Finally, small adjacent colored images may appear to the eye to merge or mix. Red and green, for example, might appear as yellow.

Adjacent images can influence the perceived color. A color on a dark background will look lighter and brighter than the same color on a light background, for example. A color can be *induced* into a neutral foreground area (gray) by the presence of a colored background. A red background can change a gray into a green. Induced colors are the complement of the inducing color. Looking at a saturated color for a period of time can also induce complementary afterimages. Colors also change as light levels change. Higher levels of ambient light tend to desaturate colors. Saturated colors will also appear larger than desaturated colors.

Usage

- Design for monochrome first.
- Use colors conservatively.
  — Do not use color where other identification techniques, such as location, are available.

Monochrome. Design for monochrome first, or in shades of black, white and gray. A screen should be as capable of being effectively used as if it were located in a monochrome environment. Spatial formatting, consistent locations, and display techniques such as highlighting and multiple font styles, should all be utilized to give information a structure independent of the color. Doing this will permit the screen to be effectively used:

- By people with a color-viewing deficiency.
- On monochrome displays.
- In conditions where ambient lighting distorts the perceived color.
- If the color ever fails.

Conservative Use. Use color sparingly since it has such a high attention-getting quality. Only enough colors to achieve the design objective should be used. More colors increase response times, increase the chance of errors due to color confusion, and increase the chance of the Christmas tree effect. If two colors serve the need, use two colors. If three colors are needed, by all means use three. A way to minimize the need for too many colors is not to use color in situations where other identification methods are available. A menu bar, for example, will always be located at the top of the screen. Its position and structure will identify it as a menu bar. To color-code it would be redundant.

Discrimination and Harmony

- For best absolute discrimination, select no more than four or five colors widely spaced on the color spectrum.
  — Good colors: red, yellow, green, blue, and brown.
- For best comparative discrimination, select no more than six or seven colors widely spaced on the color spectrum.
  — Other acceptable colors: orange, yellow-green, cyan, violet, and magenta.
- Choose harmonious colors.
  — One color plus two colors on either side of its complement.
  — Three colors at equidistant points around the color circle.
- For extended viewing or older viewers, use brighter colors.

Absolute discrimination. The population of measurable colors is about 7.5 million. From this vast number, the eye cannot effectively distinguish many more than a handful. If color memorization and absolute discrimination is necessary (a color must be correctly identified while no other color is in the field of vision), select no more than 4 to 5 colors widely spaced along the color spectrum. Selecting widely spaced colors will maximize the probability of their being correctly identified. Good choices are red, yellow, green, blue, and brown.

Two good color opponent pairs are red/green and yellow/blue. All of these colors except blue are easy to resolve visually. Again, be cautious in using blue for data, text, or small symbols on screens because it may not always be legible. If the meaning for each of more than five colors is absolutely necessary, a legend should be provided illustrating the colors and describing their associated meanings.

Comparative discrimination. If comparative discrimination will be performed (a color must be correctly identified while other colors are in the field of vision), select no more than six or seven colors widely spaced along the visual spectrum. In addition to those above, other colors could be chosen from orange, yellow-green, cyan, violet, and magenta. Again, be cautious of using blue for data, text, or small symbols. If the intent is to portray natural objects realistically, the use of more colors is acceptable.

Harmony. Choose harmonious colors. Harmonious colors are those that work well together or meet without sharp contrast. Harmony is most easily achieved with a monochromatic palette. For each background color, different lightness or values are established through mixing it with black and white. Marcus (1986a) suggests a minimum of three values should be obtained.

Harmonious combinations in a multicolor environment are more difficult to obtain. Marcus recommends avoiding complementary colors—those at opposite sides of the circle of hues in the Munsell color system, a standard commercial color system. He suggests using split complements, one color plus two colors on either side of its complement, or choosing three colors at equidistant points around the color circle.

Extended viewing. For older viewers or extended viewing, use bright colors. As eye capacity diminishes with age, data, text, and symbols in the less bright colors may be harder to read. Distinguishing colors may also become more difficult. For any viewer, long viewing periods result in the eye adapting to the brightness level. Brighter colors will be needed if either of these conditions exists.

Emphasis

- To draw attention or to emphasize elements, use bright or highlighted colors. To deemphasize elements, use less bright colors.
  - — The perceived brightness of colors from most to least is white, yellow, green, blue, red.
- To emphasize separation, use contrasting colors.
  - — Red and green, blue and yellow.
- To convey similarity, use similar colors.
  - — Orange and yellow, blue and violet.

Drawing attention. To draw attention or emphasize, use bright colors. The eye is drawn to brighter or highlighted colors, so use them for the more important screen components. The data or text is the most important component on most screens, so it is a good candidate for highlighting or the brightest color. Danger signals should also be brighter or highlighted. The perceived brightness of colors, from most to least, is white, yellow, green, blue, and red.

Keep in mind, however, that under levels of high ambient illumination, colors frequently appear washed out or unsaturated. If some means of light attenuation is not possible, or if the colors chosen are not bright enough to counter the illumination, color should be used with caution.

Emphasizing separation. Use contrasting colors to emphasize separation. The greater the contrast, the better the visibility of adjacent elements. To emphasize the separation of screen components, use contrasting colors. Possible pairs would be red/green and blue/yellow.

Similarity. Use similar colors to convey similarity. Displaying elements in a similar color can bring related screen components together. Blue and green, for example, are more closely related than red and green.

Common Meanings

- To indicate that actions are necessary, use warm colors.
  — Red, orange, yellow.
- To provide status or background information, use cool colors.
  — Green, blue, violet, purple.
- Conform to human expectations.
  — In the job.
  — In the world at large.

Actions. The warm colors, red, yellow, and orange, imply active situations or that actions are necessary. Warm colors advance, forcing attention.

Status or background. The cool colors, green, blue, violet, and purple, imply background or status information. Cool colors recede or draw away.

Expectations. Conform to human expectations. Use color meanings that already exist in a person's job or the world at large. They are ingrained in behavior and difficult to unlearn. Some common color associations are the following:

- Red—Stop, fire, hot, danger.
- Yellow—Caution, slow, test.
- Green—Go, OK, clear, vegetation, safety.
- Blue—Cold, water, calm, sky, neutrality.
- Gray—Neutrality.
- White—Neutrality.
- Warm colors—Action, response required, spatial closeness.
- Cool colors—Status, background information, spatial remoteness.

Some typical implications of color with dramatic portrayal are:

- High illumination—Hot, active, comic situations.
- Low illumination—Emotional, tense, tragic, melodramatic, romantic situations.
- High saturation—Emotional, tense, hot, melodramatic, comic situations.
- Warm colors—Active, leisure, recreation, comic situations.
- Cool colors—Efficiency, work, tragic and romantic situations.

Proper use of color also requires consideration of the experiences and expectations of the screen viewers.

Location

- In the center of the visual field, use red and green.
- For peripheral viewing, use blue, yellow, black, and white.
- Use adjacent colors that differ by hue and value or lightness.

Central vision. The eye is most sensitive to red and green in the center of the visual field. The edges of the retina are not sensitive to these colors. If used in the viewing periphery, some other attention-getting method such as blinking must also be used.

Peripheral vision. For peripheral viewing, use blue, yellow, black, or white. The retina is most sensitive to these colors at its periphery.

Adjacent colors. Colors that appear adjacent to one another should differ in hue and lightness for a sharp edge and maximum differentiation. Also, adjacent colors that differ only in their blue component should not be used so that differentiation is possible. The eye is poorly suited for dealing with blue.

Ordering

- Order colors by their spectral position.
  - — Red, orange, yellow, green, blue, indigo, violet.

If an ordering of colors is needed, such as from high to low, by levels of depth, and so on, arrange colors by their spectral position. There is evidence that people see the spectral order as a natural one. The spectral order is red, orange, yellow, green, blue, indigo, and violet, most easily remembered as "ROY G. BIV."

Foregrounds and Backgrounds

- Foregrounds:
  - — Use colors that highly contrast with the background color.
  - — For text or data, use:
    - Black.
    - Desaturated or spectrum center colors such as white, yellow, or green.
    - Warmer more active colors.
  - — Use colors that possess the same saturation and lightness.
  - — To emphasize an element, highlight it in a light value of the foreground color, pure white, or yellow.
  - — To deemphasize an element, lowlight it in a dark value of the foreground color.

- Backgrounds:
  - — Use a background color to organize a group of elements into a unified whole.
  - — Use colors that do not compete with the foreground.
  - — Use:
    - Light-colored backgrounds of low intensity: Off-white or light gray.
    - Desaturated colors.
    - Cool, dark colors such as blue or black.
    - Colors on the spectral extremes.

Foregrounds

Foreground colors should be as different as possible from background colors. A widely different foreground will maximize text legibility. With today's high-resolution monitors, the most recommended text color is black presented on a light-colored background of low intensity, either off-white or light gray. Bright white backgrounds should be avoided because of the harsh contrast between the dark text and the background.

Desaturated spectrum center colors, such white, yellow, or green, on dark backgrounds also work well. These colors do not excessively stimulate the eye and appear brighter to the eye. Saturated colors excessively stimulate the eye. Color theory also suggests using warmer, more active colors for foregrounds. Warmer colors advance, forcing attention. Exercise caution in using more fully saturated red and orange, however. They may be difficult to distinguish from one another.

Use foreground colors that possess the same saturation and lightness. Highlight elements in a light value of the foreground color. If off-white is the foreground color, highlight elements in pure white. Yellow can also be used to highlight elements. To deemphasize an element, lowlight it in a darker value of the foreground color. When lowlighting, a strong enough contrast with both the background and the non-lowlighted element must be maintained so that legibility and visual differentiation is possible.

The simultaneous use of highlighting and lowlighting should be avoided. Used together they may confuse the viewer. Also, as with other display techniques, be conservative in using highlighting and lowlighting, so that simplicity and clarity are maintained.

Backgrounds

A background color should organize a group of elements into a unified whole, isolating them from the remainder of the screen. Use colors that do not compete with the foreground. A background must be subtle and subservient to the data, text, or symbols on top of it.

As mentioned above, with today's high-resolution monitors, the most recommended background color is a low-intensity off-white or gray with black text. Pastoor (1990), in a study to be described shortly, also found that desaturated backgrounds in almost any color work well. Foreground colors must be chosen with consideration of the background color, however.

For dark backgrounds, use the cool, dark colors. Cool, dark colors visually recede, providing good contrast to the advancing lighter, foreground colors. Blue is especially good because of the eye's lack of sensitivity to it in the retina's central area and increased sensitivity to it in the periphery. Lalomia and Happ (1987), also in a study to be described shortly, found the best background colors to be black and blue. In a similar study, Pastoor (1990) found that cool colors, blue and bluish cyan, were preferred for dark background screens.

Also consider colors at the extreme end of the color spectrum. Marcus (1986a) recommends, in order of priority, the following background colors: blue, black, gray, brown, red, green, and purple.

Three-Dimensional Look

- Use at least five colors or color values to create a 3-D look on a screen.
  - — Background: The control itself and the window on which it appears.
  - — Foreground: Captions and lines for buttons, icons, and other objects.
    - Usually black or white.
  - — Selected mode: The color used when the item is selected.
  - — Top shadow: The bezel on the top and left of the control.
  - — Bottom shadow: The bezel on the bottom and right of the control.

At least five colors or color values are needed to create a three-dimensional look on a screen (Fowler and Stanwick, 1995): the backgrounds of the control and the surface on which it is placed, the foreground (captions, lines, and so on), the selected mode, and the top and bottom shadows of the controls. These shadows assume an upper-left light source. Motif has created an algorithm to automatically calculate the top and bottom shadows, and the select color based upon the background (Kobara, 1991). Briefly, it recommends the following:

- **Background.** Midrange colors, 155–175 on the RGB scale.
- **Foreground.** Black or white, depending on the lightness or darkness of the background.
- **Selected mode.** About 15 percent darker than the background color, halfway between the background and bottom shadow. (Calculate this by multiplying the background color's RGB value by 0.85.)
- **Top shadow.** About 40 to 50 percent brighter than the background color. (Calculate this by multiplying the background color's RGB by 1.50.)
- **Bottom shadow.** About 45 to 60 percent darker than the background color. (Calculate this by multiplying the background's RGB values by 0.50.)

One reminder: A raised look should only be used on operable controls.

Color Palette, Defaults, and Customization

- Permit users to customize their colors.
- Provide a default set of colors for all screen components.
- Provide a palette of six or seven foreground colors.
  — Provide 2 to 5 values or lightness shades for each foreground color.
- Provide a palette of six or seven background colors.
- Never refer to a screen element by its color.

Customization. Because color preference is subjective, permit users to customize their displayed colors. While little research has been performed on color customization, Familant and Detweiler (1995) have measured the frequency of color changes by users. Compared were displayed color combinations that were judged to be "good" or "poor." They found that users with the poorer color combinations changed their screen colors more often than those with good combinations. Color satisfaction for those with "poor" color combinations must be fleeting. When color customization is permitted, whenever possible allow users to see the results of their color choices before they are applied. Include a sample screen in a preview function within the customization process.

Default set. While some users experiment with different color combinations, many others take what is provided them and never attempt to change it. Actually, many people do not know how to apply color to create a clear and appealing screen. Others may have the talent and skills but not the time to choose a proper combination. For these users, a preselected set of default colors should be developed for all screen elements.

Both the Macintosh and Microsoft Windows provide standard, well thought out color schemes. While thousands of colors may be available for display on a screen, most platforms recommend the use of restricted palettes. This is actually a good thing, reducing the probability of very poor color combinations and Christmas trees. Most Macintosh colors are subdued to avoid a "circus" effect on the screen (Apple, 1992b). Microsoft offers a number of predefined schemes such as "Arizona."

Do not provide the color spectrum; limit the number of choices available. A maximum of six or seven foreground and background colors will provide the necessary variety. It is also worthwhile to note that 2 to 5 values or lightnesses for each foreground color be developed.

With these palettes, however, some sort of guidance concerning maximum number of colors to use and what are good and poor combinations should be provided. Macintosh, for example, suggests that, if you create your own color schemes, colors compatible with the ones on the Color Control Panel be used. Guidelines will make the color selection process more efficient and reduce the likelihood of visually straining conditions developing.

Color reference. Finally, never refer to a screen element by its designed color. What was originally on the screen in yellow may not now be so on some users' screens.

Gray Scale

- For fine discriminations use a black-gray-white scale.
  - — Recommended values are white, light gray, medium gray, dark gray, black.

The perception of fine detail is poor with color. The eye resolves fine detail much better on a black-white scale. Marcus (1986b) recommends five tonal values for black and white, higher-resolution screens: black, dark gray, medium gray, light gray, and white. He suggests the following general uses:

White:	Screen background. Text located in any black area.
Light Gray:	Pushbutton background area.
Medium Gray:	Icon background area. Menu drop shadow. Window drop shadow. Inside area of system icons. Filename bar.
Dark gray:	Window border.
Black:	Text. Window title bar. Icon border. Icon elements. Ruled lines.

Motif presents the following scheme for designing windows in a gray scale (Kobara, 1991).

Background:	A 30 percent light gray (RGB 79, 79, 79).
Foreground:	White (RGB 0, 0, 0).
Selected mode:	A 70 percent dark gray (RGB 181, 181, 181).
Top Shadow:	White.
Bottom Shadow:	Black (RGB 255, 255, 255).

Gray scale values must differ by at least 20 to 30 percent (White, 1990).

Text in Color

- When switching text from black to color:
  - — Double the width of lines.
  - — Use bold or larger type:
  - — If originally 8 to 12 points, increase by 1 to 2 points.
  - — If originally 14 to 24 points, increase by 2 to 4 points.
- Check legibility by squinting at text.
  - — Too-light type will recede or even disappear.

Text in color is not as visible as it is in black. Fowler and Stanwick (1995) report that the size of text has to be increased to maintain legibility when the text is switched from black to color. Lines should be doubled in width and type made larger or bolder. If the existing type ranges from 8 to 12 points, increase it one or two points. If the existing type ranges from 14 to 24 points, increase it by 2 to 4 points. They suggest that by squinting at it, you can check the legibility of type. A type that is too light will recede, or even disappear, from view.

Monochromatic Screens

- At the standard viewing distance, white, orange, or green are acceptable colors.
- At a far viewing distance, white is the best choice.
- Over all viewing distances, from near to far, white is the best choice.

Monochromatic, or one-color, screens are still found in graphical systems, most frequently on notebook PCs. In a study by Hewlett-Packard (Wichansky, 1986) white, orange, and green monochrome desktop display device screens were evaluated for performance and readability at various viewing distances. At the standard screen viewing distance (18 to 24 inches), no performance differences were found between white, orange, and green phosphor in either polarity (light characters on a dark background, or dark characters on a light background). Subjective ratings of ease of reading were highest for green and orange light background screens as compared to dark background screens, while no differences in ease of reading were found for either polarity with white phosphor at this distance. At a far viewing distance (4 to 5 feet), orange and green light background screens could be seen more clearly than dark background screens, while white screens were equally legible in either polarity. More errors were found with green than the other two colors.

A green screen yielded red or pink afterimages for 35 percent of the screen viewers; orange, blue afterimages for 20 percent; white yielded afterimages for 5 percent. A 35 percent pink afterimage rate for green screen viewing was also found by Galitz (1968).

Some conclusions:

- At standard viewing distances, no significant performance differences exist for white, orange, or green. All are acceptable. Subjective preferences may vary, however, so providing the viewer a choice of any of these colors is desirable.
- At far viewing distances, white is the more legible color and therefore the best choice.
- Over all viewing distances, white is the best choice.
- White has the lowest probability for creating visual afterimages.

Consistency

- Be consistent in color use.

Consistency in color usage should exist within a screen, a set of screens, and a system. A person can sense the relatedness of color in space and over time, thereby linking elements not seen immediately together. An identical background color in windows on different screens, for example, will be seen as related. Changing specific color meanings must be avoided. It will lead to difficulties in interpretation, confusion, and errors. In general, broadly defined meanings (such as red indicating a problem) permit more scope for variations without inconsistency.

Cultural, Disciplinary, and Accessibility Considerations

- Consider the impact of specific colors on:
  — Users of various cultures.
  — Users of various disciplines.
  — Users with color-viewing deficiencies.
  — Users relying on accessibility utilities.

As previously described, colors may possess different meanings and interpretations in different cultures and disciplines. Where applicable, color choices for screen elements should reflect these differences and not be offensive. Also consider users with a color-viewing deficiency. If color is used as a code, it must be recognizable by all users. It is best to use color as a supplement to other coding methods such as location, size, or element orientation. See Table 12.2 for a summary of problem-creating colors for people with defective color vision. Colors chosen should also consider the impact of users relying on accessibility utilities. Some utilities, such as the Magnifier accessory included with Windows, alter the colors displayed on a screen.

Choosing Colors for Textual Graphic Screens

For displaying data, text, and symbols on a textual graphical screen (as opposed to statistical graphics screens to be described shortly) colors selected should have adequate visibility, meaning, contrast, and harmony.

- Use effective foreground/background combinations.
- Use effective foreground combinations.
- Choose the background color first.
- Display no more than four colors at one time.
- Use colors in toolbars sparingly.
- Test the chosen colors.

Effective Foreground/Background Combinations

Lalomia and Happ (1987) established effective foreground/background color combinations for the IBM 5153 Color Display. From a color set of 16 different foregrounds and 8 different backgrounds, 120 color combinations were evaluated for (1) response time to identify characters, and (2) subjective preferences of users. The results from each measure were ranked and combined to derive an overall measure of color combination effectiveness. The best and poorest color combinations are summarized in Table 12.3. In this table "Best" means the specified combination was in the top 20 percent for overall effectiveness; "Poor" means it was in the bottom 20 percent. Those combinations composing the "middle" 60 percent are not marked.

The results yield some interesting conclusions:

- The majority of good combinations possess a bright or high-intensity color as the foreground color.
- The majority of poor combinations are those with low contrast.
- The best overall color is black.

Table 12.3 Effective Foreground/Background Combinations

	BACKGROUND							
FOREGROUND	**BLACK**	**BLUE**	**GREEN**	**CYAN**	**RED**	**MAGENTA**	**BROWN**	**WHITE**
BLACK	x			Good		Good		Good
BLUE		x			Poor			Good
H.I. BLUE			Poor	Poor			Poor	Poor
CYAN	Good		Poor	x			Poor	
H.I. CYAN	Good	Good		Good	Good	Good		
GREEN	Good	Good	x	Poor	Good		Poor	Poor
H.I. GREEN		Good						
YELLOW	Good	Good		Good		Good		
RED			Poor		x	Poor	Poor	
H.!. RED			Poor					
MAGENTA			Poor		Poor	x	Poor	
H.I. MAGENTA	Good		Good			Poor		
BROWN			Poor			Poor	x	
GRAY		Poor			Poor		Poor	
WHITE		Good		Poor				x
H.I. WHITE	Good		Good	Good				

(H.I. = High Intensity)

From Lalomia and Happ (1987).

- The poorest overall color is brown.
- Maximum flexibility and variety in choosing a foreground color exists with black or blue backgrounds. (These backgrounds account for almost one-half of the good combinations.)
- Brown and green are the poorest background choices.

Bailey and Bailey (1989), in their screen creation utility Protoscreens, have a table summarizing research-derived good foreground/background combinations. This table, which uses the results of the Lalomia and Happ study plus some others, is shown in modified form in Table 12.4.

The studies referenced above did not control character-background luminance-contrast ratios. Because of the characteristics of the eye, some colors appear brighter to it than others. A conclusion of the Lalomia and Happ study was that good combinations usually possessed a bright or high-intensity foreground color.

Table 12.4 Preferred Foreground/Background Combinations from Protoscreens

BACKGROUNDS	ACCEPTABLE FOREGROUNDS	
Black	Dark Cyan Dark Yellow Dark White	Light Green Light Cyan Light Magenta Light Yellow Light White
Blue	Dark Green Dark Yellow Dark White	Light Green Light Cyan Light Yellow Light White
Green	Black Dark Blue	Light Yellow Light White
Cyan	Black Dark Blue	Light Yellow Light White
Red		Light Green Light Cyan Light Yellow Light White
Magenta	Black	Light Cyan Light Yellow Light White
Yellow	Black Dark Blue Dark Red	
White	Black Dark Blue	

Pastoor (1990) equalized luminance-contrast ratios at preoptimized levels for about 800 foreground/background color combinations. For light foregrounds and dark backgrounds, the ratio was 10:1; for light backgrounds and dark foregrounds, 1:6.5. He then had the combinations rated with the following results:

- For dark on light polarity:
  - Any foreground color is acceptable if the background color is chosen properly.
  - Increased saturation of the foreground only marginally affected ratings, implying that any dark, saturated, foreground color is satisfactory.
  - Saturated backgrounds yield unsatisfactory ratings.
  - Less saturated backgrounds generally receive high ratings with any foreground color.
- For light on dark polarity:
  - Combinations involving saturated colors tend to be unsatisfactory.
  - As foreground color saturation increases, the number of background colors yielding high ratings diminishes.
  - Generally, desaturated foreground/background color combinations yielded the best ratings.
  - Short wavelength, cool colors were preferred for backgrounds (blue, bluish cyan, cyan).

In general, Pastoor concluded that: (1) there was no evidence suggesting a differential effect of color on subjective ratings or performance (except that for light on dark polarity, blue, bluish cyan, or cyan were preferred as backgrounds), and (2) overall, desaturated color combinations yielded the best results.

Choose the Background First

When choosing colors to display, it is best to select the background color first. Then, choose acceptable foreground colors.

Maximum of Four Colors

While not experimentally verified, experience indicates that displaying more than four colors at one time on a textual screen gives rise to a feeling of "too much." Marcus (1986a) suggests an even more conservative approach, a maximum of three foreground colors and, even better, only two. An application of good use of color can often be viewed in one's living room. Note the use of color by the television networks when textual or tabular information is presented (for example, sport scores, news highlights, and so on). The use of only two, or sometimes three, colors is most commonly seen.

So, while more than four colors may be displayed over a period of time or on a series of screens, do not display more than four colors at one time on a single screen. For most cases, restrict the number of colors to two or three.

Use Colors in Toolbars Sparingly

Toolbar icons are usually small in size. Presenting them in color is rarely useful, most often disrupting legibility. Use color in toolbar icons simply and conservatively, and only if the color aids icon identification, makes it easier to distinguish icons, or adds meaning. A file folder in yellow or a "stop" icon in red are examples of good uses of color.

Test the Colors

Because color is such a complex phenomenon, because definitions of a color can vary, and because the hardware on which a color is used can affect its look, always test all chosen colors as part of the system testing process.

Choosing Colors for Statistical Graphics Screens

The visual, spatial, or physical representation of information—as opposed to numeric, alphanumeric, textual, or symbol representation—is known as *statistical* or data graphics. Common kinds of statistical graphics include bar graphs, line graphs, scatterplots, and pie charts. Color can also be used to render a statistical graphic screen more legible and meaningful.

Emphasis

- Emphasize the graphic's data.

The main emphasis of color in a statistical graphics screen should be in the data area. Brighter colors and highlighting should attract the eye to the presented data so that trends and conclusions can be quickly perceived. Supporting text, numbers, and legends should receive slightly less emphasis. Aids in data interpretation such as grids should receive the least emphasis.

Number of Colors

- Use no more than six colors at one time.
- Use one color of five values or lightness.

Experience indicates that displaying more than six colors at one time on statistical graphics screens is "too much." Even five or six colors, however, may be distracting or confusing if they are not properly chosen or are not harmonious. Marcus (1986a) suggests a more pleasing arrangement can often be achieved for graphics with five or less segments by using one color and displaying each segment in a different value or lightness.

Backgrounds

- Surround images:
  - — In a neutral color.
  - — In a color complementary to the main image.

A neutral background will help set off a full color. A background in the complementary color of the main image will minimize visual afterimages.

Size

- Provide images of an adequate size for the task.
- If the image changes in size, use colors that exhibit a minimum shift in hue or lightness.
  - — White, yellow, and red on dark backgrounds.

As color areas decrease in size, they appear to change in lightness and saturation. Similar colors may look different, and different colors may look similar. Interactions with the background color also increase. Thin gray images (lines or borders, for example) appear as a desaturated color complement of their background.

Provide *adequately sized* images. Where color identification is important, an image should be large enough to eliminate these distortions. For images *changing in size*, use colors that exhibit minimal hue or lightness shifts. Marcus (1986b) recommends that white, yellow, and red be used for light text, thin lines, and small shapes on dark backgrounds (blue, green, red, light gray).

Status

- To indicate a status, use the following colors:
  - — *Proper, normal, or OK:* Green, white, or blue.
  - — *Caution:* Yellow or gold.
  - — *Emergency or abnormal:* Red.

To indicate a status, use green, white, or blue to indicate OK; yellow or gold for caution; and red for emergency or abnormal. The use of red, yellow, and green are well-learned color conventions.

Measurements and Area-Fill Patterns

- Display measurements in the following colors:
  - — Grids: Gray
  - — Data points: Yellow

— Variance or error bars: Blue
— Out of specified range data: Red
— Captions and labels: Lavender, lime green, or cyan

- Display area-fill patterns in the following colors:
  — Widely spaced dots: Red
  — Closely spaced dots: Green
  — Wide dashed lines: Magenta
  — Narrow dashed lines: Cyan
  — Wide crosshatch: Blue
  — Narrow crosshatch: Yellow

For *measurements,* Smith (1986) recommends the above. They balance emphasis considerations (gray for grids, yellow for data points, lavender, lime green, or cyan for labels) and human expectations (red for out-of-specified range). Marcus (1986a) recommends that all text and the horizontal and vertical axis lines of a statistical graphic should be off-white. This will aid in focusing users' main attention on the colored data. To ensure that fill-in area patterns are identifiable, discriminable, and free from unintended brightness effects, Smith (1988) recommends the above.

Physical Impressions

- Size:
  — To convey an impression of:
    - Larger: Use bright or saturated colors.
    - Smaller: Use dark or desaturated colors.
    - Similar: Use colors of equal lightness.
- Weight:
  — To convey an impression of:
    - Heavy: Use dark, saturated colors.
    - Light: Use light, desaturated colors.
- Distance:
  — To convey an impression of:
    - Close: Use saturated, bright, long-wavelength (red) colors.
    - Far: Use saturated, dark, short-wavelength (blue) colors.
- Height:
  — To convey an impression of height, use desaturated, light colors.
- Depth:
  — To convey an impression of depth, use saturated, dark colors.
- Concentration level:
  — To convey an impression of concentration level, use:
    - High: Saturated colors.
    - Low: Desaturated colors.

- Magnitude of change:
  - — To convey an impression of magnitude of change, use:
    - Lowest: Short-wavelength (blue) colors.
    - Highest: Long-wavelength (red) colors.
- Actions:
  - — To convey an impression of action, use:
    - Required: Long-wavelength (red) colors.
    - Not required: Short-wavelength (blue) colors.
- Order:
  - — To convey an impression of order with color, use:
    - Low end of a continuum: Short-wavelength (blue) colors.
    - High end of a continuum: Long-wavelength (red) colors.
  - — When displaying an array of ordered colors, position:
    - Short-wavelength colors at the left side or at the bottom.
    - Long-wavelength colors at the right side or at the top.
  - — To convey an impression of order with value or lightness, use the lightness order of a color (darkest to lightest or vice versa).
- Neutrality:
  - — To convey an impression of neutrality, use black, gray, and white.

Colors yield different physical impressions. Bright, saturated colors convey a feeling of large and close. Dark, saturated colors mean heavy, far, and impression of depth. Desaturated, light colors indicate a light weight and height. Desaturated dark colors mean smaller. Long-wavelength (red) colors are associated with high rate of change, action required, and the high end of a continuum. Short-wavelength (blue) colors are associated with low rate of change, no actions required, and the low end of a continuum. Neutrality is best indicated by black, gray, or white.

Choosing Colors for Web Pages

- Purpose:
  - — Color must always have a meaningful purpose.
- Palette:
  - — Use the browser 216-color palette.
- Presentation:
  - — Minimize the number of presented colors.
  - — Always consider color in context.
  - — Use similar or the same color schemes throughout.
    - For foregrounds: Use black or strong colors for text and headings.
  - — For backgrounds: Use weaker contrasting colors such as off-white or light gray.
  - — Use a uniform color in large areas.

— The smaller the element, the more contrast is required between it and its background.
— Larger images should use:
  • Flat, Web-safe colors.
  • Fewer colors than small images.
— Select colors that can be easily reproduced in black and white.

- Links:
  — Use default colors for links.
    • Make unselected/unvisited links blue.
    • Make selected/visited links purple.
  — Do not display non-link text in link colors.
- Testing:
  — Test all colors.

Purpose. Color should always be used for a meaningful purpose. Acceptable uses include highlighting or calling attention to information, grouping related information, designating selected links, giving a site an identity, or communicating realism for images. Color without a purpose is gratuitous and visually distracting.

Palette. Use colors that succeed on a variety of platforms or browsers. There are 216 colors (out of the standard 256 colors) that will always look the same on any monitor at any resolution. This is called the *browser-safe* palette, and it is illustrated on several Web sites. A search on "color palette" or a similar term will lead to these Web sites.

Presentation. Colors should be carefully chosen to aid users in understanding content, to keep a page well balanced, and to keep it graphically simple. Always *minimize* the number of presented colors. Too much color makes it difficult for people to notice something that might be really important, and makes it difficult to comprehend how color is being used to aid in understanding the screen's content. Christmas trees should be reserved for December 25; the "Las Vegas effect" (as the gratuitous use of color is also sometimes called) should be confined to a region in southern Nevada. Minimizing the use of color will also have page download benefits. Fewer colors means faster downloads.

Always consider color in *context,* never in isolation. One background color interacts with other background colors. Foreground text colors and graphics interact with background colors. When choosing colors, consider these interactions and use colors that work well together. Use *similar* or the same color schemes throughout a Web site. This will give the site an identity and help the user maintain a sense of place.

Foreground colors should be as different as possible from *background* colors. A contrasting foreground will maximize text legibility. A background color should organize a group of elements into a unified whole, isolating them from the remainder of the screen. Use background colors that do not compete with the foreground. A background must be subtle and subservient to the data, text, or symbols on top of it. With today's high-resolution monitors, the most recommended foreground text color is black presented on a light-colored background of low intensity, either off-white or light gray. Most other pastel colors, especially spectrum center colors, have also been found to be acceptable as backgrounds

(Pastoor, 1990). Use dark backgrounds only when establishing contrast between an area of the screen and the main screen body. High intensity colors as backgrounds (such as red, magenta and bright green) must be avoided as they can be visually fatiguing when viewed for a period of time. Short wavelength, cool colors (blue and black) have been found to be preferred for dark backgrounds (Lalomia and Happ, 1987). Cool, dark colors visually recede, providing good contrast to the advancing lighter, foreground colors. Blue is especially good because of the eye's lack of sensitivity to it in the retina's central area and increased sensitivity to it in the periphery.

When choosing foreground and background colors, ensure that contrasting combinations are selected. See Tables 12-3 and 12-4 for color selection guidance. Also, always test all selected foreground and background colors. What may look good in theory may not always look as good in reality.

Use a *uniform* color in large screen areas. Large areas of the same color download faster. They compress well and are an efficient use of the GIF format. The *smaller* the element, the more contrast is required between it and its background. To reduce image file sizes for *larger* images, use flat Web-safe colors. Also use fewer colors with smaller images. Finally, select colors that can be easily *reproduced* in black and white on a screen or printer. This ensures that those who use a monochrome display or print in black and white will have a faithful reproduction of the intended screen.

MAXIM ***Content* is always more important than color.**

Links. Unselected/unvisited links must be distinguishable from selected/visited links. Stick with the default colors of *blue* for links already followed and *purple* for links not yet ventured down. While the choice of blue as a text color was poor because of its degraded reading ability, it is well learned, its use is recommended because it is now very familiar. Using nonstandard link colors can lead to severe problems. It is difficult to remember what color means what, increasing link selection errors. It can also lead to confusion with normal underlined text in a document. Never display general screen text in the link colors of blue and purple. This will create confusion between linked and non-linked text. It is acceptable, however, to use these colors in text that is large and decorative in nature and acting as a graphic and not plain text.

Testing. The possibility always exists that identical colors may appear differently on different monitors and platforms. Color choices should be tested on a variety of displays.

Uses of Color to Avoid

- Relying exclusively on color.
- Too many colors at one time.
- Highly saturated, spectrally extreme colors together:
  — Red and blue, yellow and purple.
- Low-brightness colors for extended viewing or older viewers.

- Colors of equal brightness.
- Colors lacking contrast:
  — For example, yellow and white; black and brown; reds, blues, and browns against a light background.
- Fully saturated colors for text or other frequently read screen components.
- Pure blue for text, thin lines, and small shapes.
- Colors in small areas.
- Color for fine details.
- Non-opponent colors.
- Red and green in the periphery of large-scale displays.
- Adjacent colors that only differ in the amount of blue they possess.
- Single-color distinctions for color-deficient users.
- Using colors in unexpected ways.
- Using color to improve legibility of densely packed text.

The proper use of color in screen design also suggests some things to avoid.

Relying exclusively on color. Consider the needs of color-blind viewers and the effects of ambient lighting on color perception. Do not underestimate the value and role of other techniques such as spatial formatting and component locations in good screen design.

Too many colors at one time. Using too many colors at one time can eliminate the benefits of color. Response times are increased, erroneous associations made, the handling of information is interfered with, and confusion is created. The objective is a screen that communicates; a colorful screen is not the objective. Use just enough colors to create effective communication. Again, consider the value of other techniques such as spatial formatting and consistent component locations in good design.

Highly saturated, spectrally extreme colors together. Spectrally extreme combinations can create eye focus problems, vibrations, illusions of shadows, and afterimages. In addition to red/blue and yellow/purple, other combinations that might cause problems are yellow/blue, green/blue, and red/green.

Low-brightness colors for extended viewing or older viewers. The eye adapts to color during extended viewing. The eye's capability also diminishes with age as the amount of light passing through the lens decreases. All colors will look less bright, and colors that are dim to begin with may not be legible. Brighter colors are needed to prevent reading problems.

Colors of equal brightness. Colors of equal brightness cannot be easily distinguished. A brightness difference must exist between adjacent colors.

Colors lacking contrast. Colors lacking contrast also cannot be easily distinguished. Similar foreground and background colors often do not have sufficient contrast with each other.

Fully saturated colors for frequently read screen components. Fully saturated colors excessively stimulate the eye, possibly causing visual confusion and fatigue.

Pure blue for text, thin lines, and small shapes. Because of its physical make-up, the eye has difficulty creating a clear and legible image of small blue shapes. They will look fuzzy.

Colors in small areas. Distortions in color, lightness, and saturation may occur for small areas of color.

Colors for fine details. Black, gray, and white will provide much better resolution. Reserve other colors for large areas or attracting attention.

Non-opponent colors. Non-opponent colors, red/yellow or green/blue, produce poorer images. Opponent colors, red/green or yellow/blue are good combinations for simple displays.

Red and green in the periphery of large-scale displays. The edges of the retina are not particularly sensitive to red and green. Avoid these colors in the periphery, especially for small symbols and shapes. Yellow and blue are much better peripheral colors.

Adjacent colors only differing in the amount of blue they possess. Because of the eye's difficulty in dealing with blue, differences in color based upon varying amounts of blue in the color's mixture will not be noticed.

Single color distinctions for color-deficient users. For those people with colorviewing deficiencies, distinguishing certain colors may be difficult or impossible. Always provide a redundant coding scheme.

Using colors in unexpected ways. Colors have become associated with certain meanings. Red, for example, is always associated with stop or danger. To display a c ritical or error message in green would violate an ingrained association and cause confusion. Always use colors in the way people expect them to be used.

Using color to improve legibility of densely packed text. Space lines between paragraphs of text or after about every five lines of data will work much better.

Too many colors at one time (again). Never overuse color (again, this is important). Too many colors at one time may make a screen confusing or unpleasant to look at. Use only enough color to fulfill the system's objectives.

Multiple Choice Questions

1. Hue is defined as
   (a) the purity of a color in a scale from gray to the most vivid version of the color
   (b) the spectral wave-length composition of a color
   (c) the relative lightness or darkness of a color in a range from black to white
   (d) Both (a) and (b)
   (e) None of the above
2. Chroma is defined as
   (a) the purity of a color in a scale from gray to the most vivid version of the color
   (b) the spectral wave-length composition of a color
   (c) the relative lightness or darkness of a color in a range from black to white

(d) Both (b) and (c)
(e) None of the above

3. Intensity is defined as
   (a) the purity of a color in a scale from gray to the most vivid version of the color
   (b) the spectral wave-length composition of a color
   (c) the relative lightness or darkness of a color in a range from black to white
   (d) Both (a) and (c)
   (e) None of the above

4. The following color has maximum wavelength:
   (a) Violet (b) Yellow
   (c) Green (d) Red
   (e) Blue

5. The following color has shortest wavelength:
   (a) Violet (b) Yellow
   (c) Green (d) Red
   (e) Blue

6. If different parts of the screen are attended to separately, then:
   (a) color-code the types of status that the information may possess
   (b) color-code the different parts to focus selective attention on each in turn
   (c) use color to provide visual groupings
   (d) Both (a) and (c)
   (e) All of the above

7. If decisions are made based on the status of certain types of information on the screen, then:
   (a) color-code the types of status that the information may possess
   (b) color-code the different parts to focus selective attention on each in turn
   (c) use color to provide visual groupings
   (d) Both (a) and (b)
   (e) All of the above

8. If screen searching is performed to locate information of a particular kind or quality, then
   (a) color-code the types of status that the information may possess
   (b) color-code the different parts to focus selective attention on each in turn
   (c) use color to provide visual groupings
   (d) color-code these kinds or qualities for contrast
   (e) All of the above

9. The following warm colors are used to indicate necessary actions:
   (a) Green (b) Red
   (c) Orange (d) Purple
   (e) All of the above

10. The following cool colors are used to indicate necessary actions:
    (a) Green (b) Violet
    (c) Orange (d) Purple
    (e) All of the above

Review Questions

1. Explain how color can be used as formatting aid and visual code.
2. What type of problems should arise while using colors for UI screen component?
3. Explain the guidelines for color selection for textual graphics screen.
4. Explain the guidelines for color selection for statistical graphics screen.
5. Explain the guidelines for color selection for Web pages.

CHAPTER 13

Experiments

An Application to Teach Math

Title: Maths for children
Aim: To design an interface that can teach math to children of 4 to 5 years age.
Theory:

i. Analysis of children behaviour, for example, their preferences, interests, etc.
ii. What kinds of interfaces will they like and why?
iii. Existing apps—analyze and rate them
iv. What will be your choice of screen elements?
v. How will your app be better than the existing ones?

Implementation: Code and snapshots.
Conclusion: Rate your application on HCI principles.

Digital Diary for Young Teens

Title: Teenagers.
Aim: To design a digital diary for teenagers.
Theory: A digital diary for young teens can help them overcome various social pressures they deal with during their teens. This diary should act like a self-help tool and deal with incidents like bullying, peer pressure, etc.

i. Analysis of teenagers, for example, their problems, interests, needs, etc.
ii. What kinds of interfaces will they like and why?
iii. Existing apps—analyze and rate them
iv. What will be your choice of screen elements?
v. How will your app be better than the existing ones?

Implementation: Snapshots of UI.
Conclusion: Rate your application based on HCI principles.

Online Payment Portal for Older Generation

Title: The older generation
Aim: To design an online bill pay portal for the older generation.
Theory: Older generation finds it hard to learn the online payment concept and when they do, they become very skeptical to use it, as they learn of the threats too. But it will be easier for them to pay their utility bills, insurance, etc. online. Design a system that can help them pay their bills on time and educate them on safe online payments. (Old people may have visual problems, slow motor skills, color identification issues, etc.)

i. Analysis of old people, for example, their nature, interests, needs, etc.
ii. What kinds of interfaces will they like and why?
iii. Existing apps—analyze and rate them
iv. What will be your choice of screen elements?
v. How will your app be better than the existing ones?

Implementation: Snapshots of UI.
Conclusion: Rate your UI based on HCI principles.

ATVM for Train Ticketing in Rural Area

Title: ATVM machine for metro trains
Aim: To design an interface of ATVM machine for metro trains
Theory:

i. Behavioral analysis: who will be most common commuters, how much time they may have to buy a ticket, their level of computer skills, languages known, etc.
ii. What kind of interfaces will they like and why?
iii. Existing apps—analyze and rate them.
iv. What will be your choice of screen elements?
v. How will your app be better than the existing ones?

Implementation: Code and snapshots.
Conclusion: Rate your application on HCI principles.

Redesign Interfaces of Home Appliances

Title: Microwave ovens
Aim: To design an interface for microwave ovens.
Theory:

i. Who are your end users? Analyze their behavior, for example, level of expertise, etc.
ii. What kind of interfaces will they like and why?
iii. Existing interfaces—analyze and rate them.
iv. What will be your choice of screen elements?
v. How will your interface be better than the existing ones?

Implementation: Code and snapshots.
Conclusion: Rate your application on HCI principles.

Heuristic Evaluation Using Design Principles

Title: Understand the principles of good screen design by heuristic evaluation.
Aim: To understand the HCI principles by comparing websites.
Theory: Identify five websites catering to one specific goal (e.g., goal: shopping – eBay, Amazon, Flipkart, Zovi, Myntra) and perform a competitive analysis on them to understand how each one caters to the goal. Prepare a report.
Implementation: Snapshots to compare these sites.
Conclusion: Declare which site is the best.

Website Redesign for Better Navigation

Title: Menus and navigation
Aim: To understand the use and importance of menus and navigation in web pages.
Theory: Redesign a news website. Usually they are cluttered and take the users a few minutes to find the info he wanted. Your design may be less cluttered, provide relevant info (e.g., area specific), order news items based on his interests (learnt from previous searches).

i. Analysis of the types of people who read newspaper online, and why do they read an e-paper.
ii. What kinds of interfaces will they like and why?
iii. Analyze existing website based on HCI principles.
iv. How will your design be better than the existing ones?

Implementation: Snapshots of your UI.
Conclusion: Compare your UI with existing website based on HCI principles.

Service Design—Connect Humans

Title: Service design
Aim: To design an experience for passengers to deal with the long wait hours in an airport.
Theory: How often do you find yourself waiting for a flight that has been delayed, or you have missed your flight and the next one is after four hours, or waiting for a connecting flight.

i. Analysis of people waiting at an airport—their anxiety, boredom, etc.
ii. How can your app help them?
iii. Existing ways used to keep them relaxed.
iv. How can your app be better than that?
v. Choice of your screen elements and purpose.

Implementation: Code and snapshots.
Conclusion: Rate your application on HCI principles.

Statistical Graphics—Expense Tracker

Title: Statistical graphics
Aim: To realize the use and importance of statistical graphics in GUI.
Theory: Matt is a young engineer who has just started working on his first job. His parents want him to handle his finances himself. He is looking for a tool/app/software that can help him budget his finances, create goals, track his expenses, categorize his credit card spending, etc. He would also need help and motivation to start saving. Suggest various investment options

i. Analysis of your client—his routine, interests, requirements, etc.
ii. Existing apps—analyze and rate them.
iii. Introduce new and better icons (*.ico or *.png files). Design an interface to show how these icons can be used.

Implementation: Snapshots of your UI.
Conclusion: Rate your application based on HCI principles.

Graphics—Way Finding

Title: Way finding
Aim: To introduce a new method for text input.
Theory: Design an map for someone who is trying to find his ways to commute in a new city/town/village.

i. Who will need your app?
ii. Why will they need your app and how is your app going to help them?
iii. Existing apps—analyze and rate them.
iv. What will be your choice of screen elements?
v. How will your app be better than the existing ones?

Implementation: Code and snapshots.
Conclusion: Rate your application on HCI principles.

Icon Designing

Title: Icon designing
Aim: To understand how to design appropriate icons.
Theory: Form groups dealing each dealing with a separate line of business (e.g., medical, greeting cards, law, androids, etc.).

i. Analysis of your client—their business, customers, etc.
ii. Existing icons—analyze and rate them based on the characteristics and guidelines of icon designing.
iii. What will be your choice of screen elements?
iv. How will your app be better than the existing ones?

Implementation: Snapshots of your app.
Conclusion: Rate your icons based on usability.

Colors and Animation

Title: Use of colors
Aim: To realize the use and importance of colors in GUI designing.
Theory: Design a website for a celebrity, who is famous in some kind of art (e.g., painting, music, dance, fights, etc.). This website must be a true portrayal of his character.

i. Analysis of your client—preferences, likes, dislikes, lifestyle, reputation, etc.
ii. What kinds of interfaces will they like and why?
iii. Existing websites for similar celebrities.
iv. What will be your choice of colors?
v. How will your UI be better than the existing ones?

Implementation: Snapshots of your UI.
Conclusion: Rate your application based on HCI principles.

Concept Generation—Input Methods

Title: Concept generation exercise
Aim: To introduce a new method for text input.
Theory: Study the various technologies for typing—standard keyboard (QWERTY), T9 (predictive), touchscreen (swipe), gestures. Brainstorm on the various ways you can improve the existing technologies. You can choose any of the different input types.

i. Analysis of people who type, their need, skill, device used, etc.
ii. Existing methods used for typing.
iii. What are the problems of existing methods?
iv. What you can introduce to ease out these problems?

Implementation: Code and snapshots.
Conclusion: Rate your application on HCI principles.

Chart for evaluating HMI applications

Sl. No	Principles	Poor	Average	Good	Very good	Excellent
1	*Aesthetically pleasing*					
2	*Compatibility*					
3	*Comprehensibility*					
4	*Consistency*					
5	*Control*					
6	*Efficiency*					
7	*Flexibility*					
8	*Forgiveness*					
9	*Recovery*					
10	*Responsiveness*					

Note:

1. All the applications must be designed by following the HMI guidelines.
2. Apply HMI principles to evaluate the user interface.
3. Any tool or technology can be used for implementation.

CHAPTER

14

Case Studies for Practice

Voice Enabled Android Application for Vehicular Complaint System

Summary: It presents the architecture of a Voice Enabled Global Positioning System (GPS) based approach for reporting vehicular complaints on an Android platform. The complaint is registered via the Short Message Service (SMS) over the Global System for Mobile Communications (GSM). GPS tracking enhances the accuracy and competence of the complaint system by mapping the location where the complaint was issued. This will aid the authorities to identify the spot and have the problems resolved responsively. The system serves as a facilitative platform for road commuters to send complaints to the relevant authorities, in addition to the existing channels, so that these issues could be addressed in a timely manner.

This application provides for a voice to text conversion utility which increases the convenience of use by reducing the user's dependency on typing, hence enabling him to register his complaint even when driving. Using the real time GPS tracking feature, the exact location of the problem is captured. All this collected information is then sent to the concerned authorities via an SMS over the GSM network. This information is saved into a database and the location parameters are used to plot the point of complaint on Google Maps. Thus, the method provides a way for the user to register the complaint and for the authorities to resolve the issue. The scope of this work can be increased by making it applicable for other uses such as reporting accidents, road problem tracking (for example potholes) and live traffic updates, etc. The complaint data can be further analyzed to determine accident zones, bottlenecks and problematic locations so as to take immediate actions.

Applying Human Computer Interaction to Individual Security Using Mobile Application

Summary: Ability to ensure individual security is of prime importance in case of attacks or emergencies. In order to cater to this requirement, we have proposed a mobile application based solution following the principles of HCI in order to enhance simplicity, usability and ease of access. Mobile Application development has witnessed revolutionary changes in the past decade. The suggested solution activates the security application in one's mobile device by voice, since in case of emergencies or attacks it is highly possible that one may not be in physical contact with the device. Upon activation the application sends a message along with current location to the pre-selected contacts list. Other features like button-sequence activation, recording the sounds for a specified time and loud siren sound to attract help when the application is activated are proposed to enhance safety. The proposed solution is constructed based on the comparative analysis of existing security applications and survey results. Though developing the suggested application is challenging, but it can be achieved by the advent in mobile application development technologies. Also to enhance the effectiveness, multi-lingual support and sound-clipping algorithms can be added to reduce the battery usage. This solution can be of great assistance in times of emergencies and attacks as it reduces the communication time and truly makes your mobile device, your safety device.

Machine Learning Applied to Human Learning

Summary: With the ever-increasing data around us, remembering information is becoming an increasingly difficult task. It is becoming essential to find ways to remember information. In order to memorize information, humans use various methods: mnemonics, visualization and relating the information to already known information. Despite these efforts, memorizing information is a difficult task for humans. On the other hand, a computer can easily memorize information. Using this ability of computers, our research tried to make memorizing word meanings easier for humans. We focused on building de-contextualized vocabulary (words and their meaning), which is used in vocabulary-based tests.

As a human needs to be reminded of the information at intervals (that need not be equally spaced) in order to register the information in the memory, our aim was to find the assessment intervals and the number of times the word and its meaning needs to be reiterated, using the data from the previous assessments, so that the word and its meaning gets registered in the student's memory.

In this research, there are two factors under consideration: the time factor and the assessment factor. Time factor was used to keep track of the time interval that has passed and to determine the next interval at which the student needs to be assessed.

Assessment factor was to take into account all the assessments done so far. We maintained a record for each student consisting of whether the student failed or passed in giving the right meaning of the word. Thus, for each student, we had an Assessment tuple with 1 corresponding to correct answer and 0 corresponding to wrong answer and another tuple containing the timestamp for the assessment. With the help of these tuples, we calculated the probability of the student passing in the next assessment, and if it was above the threshold value (the minimum probability required to become confident that the student would answer correctly the next time), then we did not assess the student on the same word again.

This data was gathered by assessing a set of students in the third year of Computer Engineering. They were assessed on an English word and its meaning, at predefined time intervals. We used Logistic Regression in order to classify our dataset. Our proposed algorithm was intuitive in nature, and we compared its outcome with logistic regression's outcome. The factors of both the algorithms depended majorly upon the correct answers given by the student till date, thus making them personalized. It was found that the coefficient for history is positive i.e. as the ratio of the number of correct answers to the number of answers given increases the probability of the student recollecting the word and its meaning increases. Also, as the time from first viewing of the word and its meaning increases the probability of recollecting the word and its meaning decreases. This analysis coupled with logical regression helped us in developing an algorithm to determine how many times and at what time interval should a student be assessed so as to make it certain that the student has learnt a particular word and its meaning.

Educative Games for Autistic Children

Introduction

Autism is a *developmental disorder* found in children when they are around eighteen months. These children usually suffer from communication problems, recognition problems, and social impairments and display a very repetitive behavior. This paper proposes an educative game that shall create situations where the autistic child has to think out of the box to move ahead. This game looks to not only cure them of their repetitive behavior, and improve on their communication and recognition skills, but also measure their level of autism, and indicate progress.

Research Observations

- Autistic children have varying levels of IQ.
- Levels of repetitive behavior vary from every child.
- Communication is a problem, as they are not able to channel their thoughts.
- Recognition is a problem, as they are not able to recollect things, people or events from the past.
- Some children take a long time to trust others, hence do not take guidance or mingle well.

- All children respond very well to music.
- Some children with autism and motor disabilities will not be able to use a computer.

Interfaces for the Autistic

- Large and colorful target buttons.
- Audio guidance and acknowledgement.
- Verbal and audio instructions for each task.
- Full screen visual.
- Touch screen interface.
- Minimal screen items.
- Use minimal words. More of photographs than cartoon images for icons.

Proposed System

1. **GUI:** An interface friendly for autistic children with 3D animated characters and environment. It shall provide audio guidance, acknowledgement and encouragement at every step. The game will gradually increase in complexity. Initially it will only introduce a daily routine activity to the child, and then he will be given challenges. The game will be customizable. The child can choose the name of the character, gender and siblings. Language customization will be the future scope of the project.
2. **SPEECH RECOGNITION:** The child needs to interact with the game verbally. He will be prompted to greet his friends, make a telephone call, or enter into a casual conversation with another on-screen character. This speech recognition module can translate the child's voice into words.

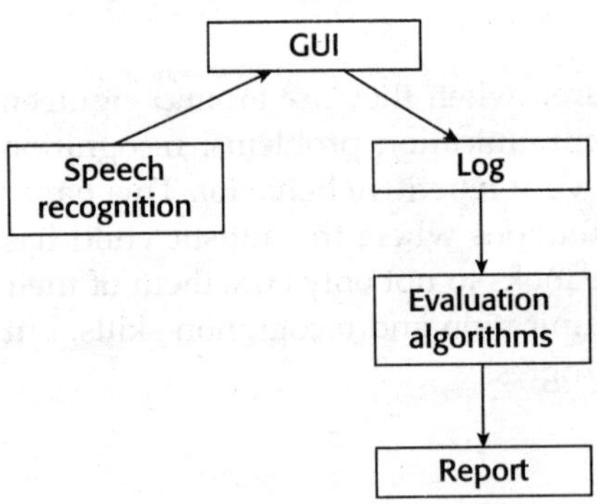

Block diagram of the proposed game.

3. **LOG MAINTENANCE:** Regular logs of the child's actions will be maintained. This includes the choices he makes, the time he takes to respond, the time he takes to complete a task, etc.
4. **EVALUATION ALGORITHMS:** By analyzing the logs, we must be able to declare the level of autism in the child. We can compare various inputs, like the

level of game at which the child is, with the number of hours he has spent on the game till now, and so on.

Assuming the following are inputs:

- Game Level
- Number of hours played.
- Amount of time taken to finish a task.
- Number of attempts to finish a task.
- Number of toys or pets he owns.

These inputs can be represented using fuzzy variables and can be described using 4–5 linguistic descriptors each. Similarly the output, which is the level of autism, can also be addressed using fuzzy variables like VERY LOW, LOW, AVERAGE, HIGH and SEVERE.

Conclusion

A research on autistic children has yielded observations about their behavior that are useful in designing interfaces for them. The proposed game shall be built using these guidelines.

ISSAC Intelligent System for Streamlined Accelerometric Control

Introduction

It is highly likely that in the near future wearable devices like smartwatches will be commonplace. Strong sales of devices like Apple Watch and Android Wear are indicators of this trend. ISSAC was a project designed to leverage this new trend as a new way to interact with computers. The goal was to let users interact with computers using their hand movement data from their wrist worn smartwatches instead of using computationally expensive image processing. ISSAC consists of a wearable hardware device featuring an accelerometer, gyroscope and gravitational sensors (smartwatch), along with an application on the device that communicates with the computer being controlled. Depending on the data received, the gesture is recognized and the intended action is executed.

Design

The wearable device can be paired with multiple PCs by means of QR code or NFC. When pairing, the wearable records the direction the PC is facing using compass data. Later when the user makes gestures, the wearable can intelligently send data to only the PC which is in front of the user. The actual data itself is sent wirelessly using WiFi or Bluetooth.

Once data arrives on the PC, the companion application performs some decompression and transformation and routes the data through a transient databank. Other extension modules can then be built that make use of the data flowing through the databank. These modules can do things like detect clicks, mouse movements, etc. using a finite state machine or similar approaches. There is also a globally accessible Status Module that can be used by other modules to smartly save power by knowing when the user inactive.

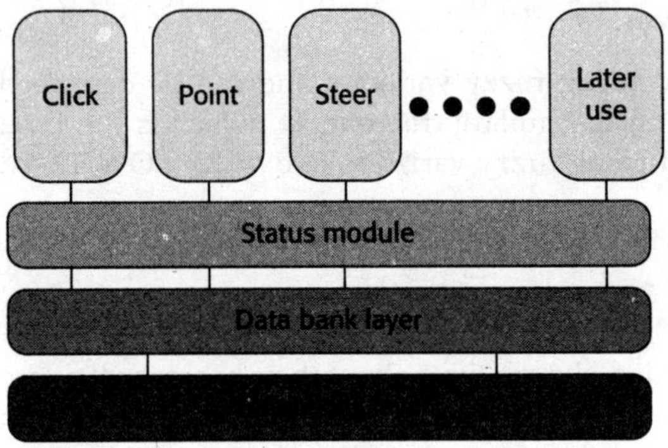

Results/Applications

We explored two potential applications of the system.

1. **Virtual Mouse:** We could provide users the ability to move the mouse on the screen and click or right click on things by simply making gestures in the air in front of the computer. Previously such an application would have to use the data from the webcam and perform image processing on it.

Virtual mouse.

2. **Game Controller (Steering Wheel, Boxing, etc.):** We enabled the user to move his hands like a virtual steering wheel to play racing games. We also built a boxing game that let the user win by virtually punching opponents while wearing the ISSAC wearable device.

Steering Wheel Application.

Design Case Study (Goal Directed Design)

Typewriting is the essential skill for almost all the computer users. There are very few users who know the systematic type writing. When typewriters were innovated there were lots many evolutions of key boards. Type writers now available have QWERTY keyboards and QWERTY was invented considering the maximum used alphabets and symbols in normal English language.

Following is the typical QWERTY Keyboard Layout:

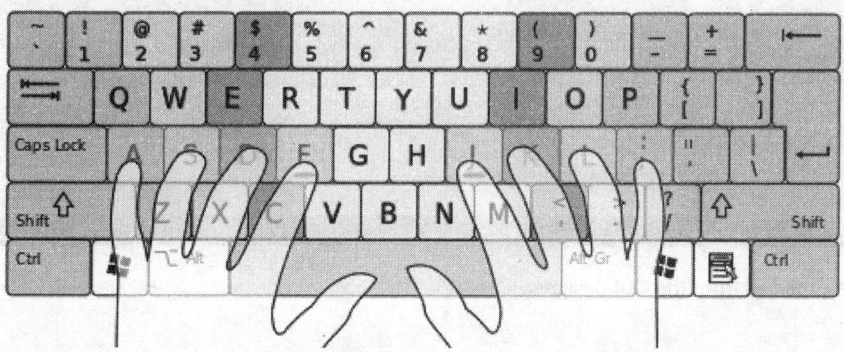

QWERTY Keyboard Layout (Current key pads).

We have already discussed in the goal directed design that typewriting skills are obtained by typing practice sets.

The major expectation is to propose a graphical user interface design to train the beginner to achieve typewriting skills. There are various lesson sets available; using the same or similar lesson sets it is necessary to provide the user a state of an art environment for self learning.

User will practice the lesson by actually typing on the screen using his own key board. The system will provide necessary dashboard to make necessary changes in his lesson provided for typing practice.

The business logic in this system is that the system will count the number of words typewritten by the learner and will help learner to change its experience level from beginner to expert. There should be a GUI that adopts all interaction design guidelines and a visually pleasant composition.

Following is the proposed typewriting trainer prototype. Identify the complete system design requirements that need to be considered while designing the system. Also identify functional and non functional requirements. Provide special features for experts in the type writing. As shown in the figure there should be on screen typing practice text box and easy navigation to switch from one lesson to other lesson. This is just a reference taken from http://www.learntyping.org a state of an art online typing tutor. The students or practitioners creativity will definitely win accolades.

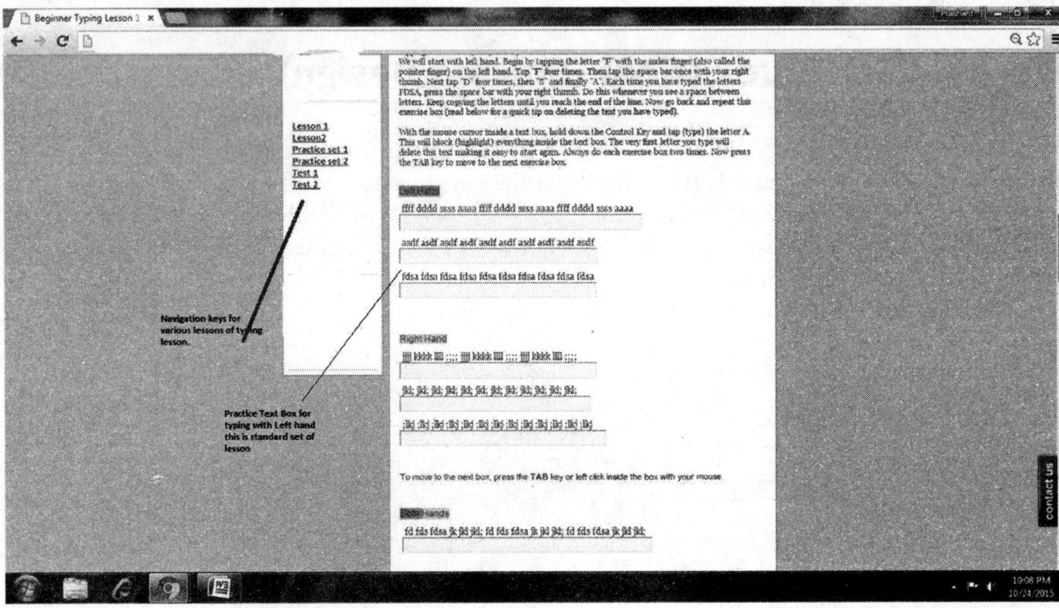

Design prototype that is expected from the GUI designer.

References

Andre, A.D. and Wickeans, C.D. (1995). "When users want what's NOT best for them." *Ergonomics in Design*. October.

Apple Computer, Inc. (1992a). *Guide to Macintosh Software Localization*. Reading, MA: Addison-Wesley.

Apple Computer, Inc. (1992b). *Macintosh Human Interface Guidelines*. Reading, MA: Addison-Wesley.

Baca, B. and Cassidy, A. (1999). "Intranet development and design that works," *Proceedings of the Human Factors and Ergonomics Society—1999*, 777–790.

Baddeley, A. (1992). "Working memory." *Science*, 255, 556–559.

Baecker, R., and Small, I. (1990). "Animation at the interface." In *The Art of Human-Computer Interface Design*, B. Laurel (ed.). Reading, MA: Addison-Wesley.

Bailey and Bailey Software Corporation. (1989). *Protoscreens*. Ogden, UT: Bailey and Bailey Software Corporation.

Bailey, Bob. (1999a) *UI Design Update Newsletter*. http://www.humanfactors.com/library/feb992.htm. February.

Bailey, Bob. (1999b) *UI Design Update Newsletter*. http://www.humanfactors.com/library/may992.htm, May.

Bailey, Bob. (1999c) *UI Design Update Newsletter*. http://www.humanfactors.com/library/dec992.htm, December.

Bailey, Bob. (2000) *UI Design Update Newsletter*. http://www.humanfactors.com/library/aug002.htm, August.

Bailey, Bob. (2001) *UI Design Update Newsletter*. http://www.humanfactors.com/library/jan012.htm, January.

Bailey, R.W., Allan, R.W., and Raiello, P. (1992). "Usability testing vs. heuristic evaluation: A head-to-head comparison." *Proceedings of the Human Factors Society 36th Annual Meeting*, Santa Monica, CA: Human Factors Society.

Barmack, J.E. and Sinaiko, H.W. (1966). *Human Factors Problems in Computer-Generated Graphic Displays*. Institute for Defense Analysis (AD-636170).

Barnett, R. (1993). *Forms Analysis and Design*. Belconnen ACT, Australia: Robert Barnett and Associates Pty. Ltd.

Beasley, R. and Waugh, M. (1997). "Predominant Initial and Review Pattern Navigation in a Fully Constrained Hypermedia Hierarchy: An Empirical Study" (11 Aug. 1997) Retrieved via Netscape. http://aace.virginia.edu/aacr/pubs/jemh/v6n2.html#Predominant.

Beer, T., Anodenko, T., and Sears, A. (1997). "A Pair of Techniques for Effective Interface Evaluation: Cognitive Walkthroughs and Think-Aloud Evaluations," *Proceedings of the Human Factors and Ergonomics Society 41st Annual Meeting*, 380–384.

Bennett, J.L. (1979). "The commercial impact of usability in interactive systems." *Man-Computer Communication, Infotech State-of-the-Art*, Vol. 2. B. Schackel, ed. Maidenhead: Infotech International.

Bennett, J.L. (1984). "Managing to meet usability requirements." In *Visual Display Terminals: Usability Issues and Health Concerns*. J.L. Bennett, D. Case, J. Sandelin, and M. Smith, eds. Englewood Cliffs, NJ: Prentice Hall.

Berry, Dick. (2000) "The user experience #2 It's a matter of style—GUI versus the Web," User Experience Design, IBM Ease of Use Team, http://www-106.ibm.om/developerworks/library/w-berry2.html, October.

Bias, Randolph G. and Mayhew, Deborah J. (Eds.). (1994). *Cost-Justifying Usability*. Boston Academic Press.

Billingsley, P. (1988). "Taking panes: Issues in the design of windowing systems." In *Handbook of Human-Computer Interactions*, M. Helander, ed. Amsterdam: Elsevier Science Publishers.

Billingsley, P. (1996). "Standards: Simplifying conformance." *SIGCHI Bulletin*. 28: 36–38.

Bishu, Ram R. and Zhan, P. (1992). "Increasing or decreasing? The menu direction effect on user performance." *Proceedings of the Human Factors Society 36th Annual Meeting*, Santa Monica, CA: Human Factors Society.

Black, J.B., Carroll, J.M., and McGuigan, S.M. (1987). "What kind of minimal instruction manual is most effective?" *Proceedings of CHI+GI*. 1987. New York.

Blinn, B. and Biers, D.W. (1999). "Searching hard-copy (paper) vs. electronic (CRT) documents: Role of experience, amount of text displayed, and the book metaphor." *Proceedings of the Human Factors and Ergonomics Society*, 447-451.

Bonsiepe, G. (1968). "A method of quantifying order in typographic design." *Journal of Typographic Research*, 2, 203–220.

Bouch, A., Kuchinsky, A., and Bhatti, N. (2000). "Quality is in the eye of the beholder: Meeting users' requirements for Internet quality of service," *CHI 2000*, 297–304.

Bouma, H. (1970). "Interaction effects in parafoveal letter recognition." *Nature*. 226: 177–178.

Boyarski, D., Neuwirth, C., Forlizzi, J., and Regli, S.H. (1998). "A study of fonts designed for screen display." *CHI 98 Conference Proceedings*, 87–94.

Brewster, S.A., Wright, P.C., and Edwards, A.D.N. (1993). "An evaluation of earcons for use in auditory human-computer interfaces." *INTERCHI 93*. Amsterdam.

Brooks, R. (1965). "Search time and color coding." *Psychonomic Science*. 2: 281–282.

Brown, C.M. (1988). *Human-Computer Interface Design Guidelines*. Norwood, NJ: Ablex Publishing Co.

Bury, K.F., Boyle, M. , Evey, R.J., and Neal, A.S. (1982). "Windowing versus scrolling on a visual display terminal." *Human Factors* 24: 385–394.

Byrne, M.D. (1993). "Using icons to find documents: simplicity is critical." *INTERCHI 93*. Amsterdam, April 24–29.

Byrne, M.D., John, B.E., Wehrle, N.S., and Crow, D.C. (1999). "The tangled web we wove: A taskonomy of WWW use." *CHI 99 Conference Proceedings*, 544–551.

Card, S.K., Moran, T.P., and Newell, A. (1983). *The Psychology of Human-Computer Interaction*. Hillsdale, NJ: Lawrence Erlbaum.

Carroll, J.M., and Carrithers, C. (1984). "Blocking learner error states in a training-wheels system." *Human Factors* 26: (4)377–389.

Carroll, J.M., Smith-Kerker, P.L., Ford, J.R., and Mazur, S.A. (1986). *The Minimal Manual* (Research Report RC 11637). Yorktown Heights, NY: IBM T.J. Watson Research Center.

Carter, R.L. (1982). "Visual search with color." *Journal of Experimental Psychology: Human Perception and Performance*. 8: 127–136.

CAST.org. "Welcome to Bobby Worldwide (2001)," http://www.cast.org/bobby/.

Catani, M.B. and Biers, D.W. (1998). "Usability evaluation and prototype fidelity: Users and usability professionals," *Proceedings of the Human Factors and Ergonomics Society 42nd Annual Meeting*, 1331–1335.

Charness, N. and Dijkstra, K. (1999). "Age, luminance, and print legibility in homes, offices, and public places." *Human Factors*, 41 (2)173–193.

Christ, R.E., and Teichner, W.H. (1973). "Color research for visual displays." *JANAIR* (Report No. 730703), New Mexico: New Mexico State University.

Christ, R.E. (1975). "Review and analysis of color coding research for visual displays." *Human Factors* 17: (6)542–570.

CNN. (April 9, 1997). "Inventor of Computer 'Mouse' Finally Cashes a Big Check." www.cnn.com/TECH/9704/09/mouse.inventor/.

Cohen, S. (1994). "Most comfortable listening level as a function of age," *Ergonomics*, 37 (7)1269–1274.

Coll, R.A., Coll, J.H., and Thakur, G. (1994). "Graphs and tables: A four-factor experiment." *Communications of the ACM*. l77–85.

Cope, M.E. and Uliano, K.C. (1995). "Cost-justifying usability engineering: A real world example." *Proceedings of the Human Factors Society 39th Annual Meeting*, Santa Monica, CA: Human Factors Society.

Czaja, S.J. (1997) "Computer technology and older adults," In *Handbook of Human-Computer Interaction (2nd Edition)*, M.E. Helander, T.K. Landauer and P. Prabhu (eds.) New York: Elsevier, 797–812.

Damodaran, L., Simpson, A., and P. Wilson. (1980). "Designing systems for people." *NCC*. Manchester and Loughborough University of Technology.

Danchak, M.M. (1976). "CRT displays for power plants." *Instrumentation Technology*. 23: (10)29–36.

del Galdo, E. (1990). "Internationalization and translation: Some guidelines for the design of human-computer interfaces." *Designing User Interfaces for International Use*, J. Nielsen, (ed.). Amsterdam: Elsevier Science Publishers.

Digital Equipment Corp. (1988). *XUI Style Guide* (Order No. AA-MG20A-TE). Maynard, MA.

Dillon, A. (1992). " Reading from paper versus screen: A critical review of the empirical litereature," *Ergonomics*, 35 (10)1297–1326.

DiPierro, C., Nachman, G., and Raderman, (2000) "Screen Size and Web Browsing."*UI Design Update Newsletter*, February.

Dumas, Joseph S. and Redish, Janice C. (1993) *A Practical Guide to Usability Testing*. Norwood, NJ: Ablex Publishing.

Dvorak, A., Merrick N.F., Dealey, W.L., and Ford, G.C. (1936) "Typewriting Behavior: Psychology Applied to Teaching and Learning Typewriting." New York: American Book Co.

Eberts, R. (1997). "Cognitive modeling." In *Handbook of Human Factors and Ergonomics*, Second Edition, G. Salvendy (ed.). New York: John Wiley and Sons.

Elkerton, J. (1988). "Online aiding for human-computer interfaces." In *Handbook of Human-Computer Interaction*. M. Helander, ed. Amsterdam: Elsevier Science Publishers.

Elkerton, J. and Palmiter, S.L. (1991). "Designing help using a GOMS model: An information retrieval evaluation." *Human Factors* 33: (2)185–204.

Ellis, R.D. and Kurniawan, S.H. (2000). "Increasing the usability of online information for older users: A case study in participatory design," *International Journal of Human-Computer Interaction*, 12 (2)263–276.

Engel, F.L. (1980). "Information selection from visual displays." In *Ergonomic Aspects of Visual Display Terminals*, E. Grandjean and E. Vigliani (eds.). London: Taylor and Francis Ltd.

Faraday, P. and Sutcliffe, A. (1997). "Designing Effective Multimedia Presentations," *Proceedings of CHI'97*, 272–278.

Fath, J.L. and Henneman, R. L. (1999). "On the development of user interface design guidelines for electronic commerce." *Proceedings of the Human Factors and Ergonomics Society—1999*, 192–198.

Familant, M.E., and M.C. Detweiler. (1995). "Do human factors color recommendations have any practical value?" *Proceedings of the Human Factors and Ergonomics Society 39th Annual Meeting*, Santa Monica, CA: Human Factors Society.

Festa, P. (1998). *Web design not what you pay for*. http://www.news.com/News/Item/0,4,21150,00.html.

Fitts, P.M. (1954). "The information capacity of the human motor system in controlling the amplitude of movement." *Journal of Experimental Psychology*, *47*, 381–391.

Fowler, S.L., and Stanwick, V.R. (1995). *The GUI Style Guide*, Cambridge, MA: Academic Press.

Fuccella, Jeanette, Pizzolato, Jack, and Franks, Jack. (1999). "Finding out what users want from your Web site: Techniques for gathering requirements and tasks." June.

Galitz, W.O. (1968). "CRT viewing and visual aftereffects." *UNIVAC Internal Report*. Roseville, MN.

Galitz, W.O. (1980). *Human Factors in Office Automation*. Atlanta, GA: Life Office Management Association.

Galitz, W.O. (1981). *Handbook of Screen Format Design*. Wellesley, MA: QED Publishing Group.

Galitz, W.O. (1992). *User-Interface Screen Design*. Wellesley, MA: QED Publishing Group.

Galitz, W.O. and DiMatteo, A. (1974). "EIS forms and screens design manual." *International Report*. Philadelphia, PA: INA Corporation.

Garver, W.W. (1993). "Synthesizing auditory icons." *INTERCHI 93*. April 24–29, Amsterdam.

Gerhardt-Powals, J. (1996). "Cognitive engineering principles for enhancing human-computer performance," *International Journal of Human-Computer Interaction*, 8 (2), 189–211.

Gould, J.D. (1988). "How to design usable systems." *Handbook of Human-Computer Interaction*, M. Helander (ed.). Amsterdam: Elsevier Science Publishers.

Gould, J.D., Boies, S.J., Meluson, M., Rasamny, M., and Vosburgh, A.M. (1988). "Empirical evaluation of entry and selection methods for specifying dates." *Proceedings of the Human Factors Society 32nd Annual Meeting*, Santa Monica, CA: Human Factors Society.

Greene, S.L., Gould, J.D., Boies, S.JU., Meluson, A., and Rasamny, M. (1988). "Entry-based versus selection-based interaction methods." *Proceedings of the Human Factors Society 32nd Annual Meeting*, Santa Monica, CA: Human Factors Society.

Greene, S.L., Gould, J.D., Boies, M.R., Rasamny, M., and Meluson, A. (1992). "Entry and selection based methods of human-computer interaction." *Human Factors* 34: (1)97–113.

Grose, E., Parush, A., Nadir, R., and Shtub, A. (1998). "Evaluating the layout of graphical user interface screens: validation of a numerical computerized model." *International Journal of Human-Computer Interaction*, 10 (4)343–360.

Grok Dot Com, www.grokdot.com.com

Guastello, S.J., Traut, M., and Korienek, G. (1989). "Verbal versus pictorial representation of objects in a human-computer interface." *International Journal of Man-Machine Studies*. 31: 99–120.

Gugerty, L., Halgren, S., Gosbee, J., and Rudisill, M. (1991). "Using GOMS models and hypertext to create representations of medical procedures for online display." *Proceedings of the Human Factors Society 35th Annual Meeting*, Santa Monica, CA: Human Factors Society.

Gujar, A.U., Harrison, B.L., and Fishkin, K.P. (1998). "A comparative evaluation of display technologies for reading." *Proceedings of the Human Factors and Ergonomics Society 42nd Annual Meeting*, 527–531.

Halsey, R.M. and Chapanis, A. (1951). "On the number absolutely identifiable spectral hues." *Journal of Optical Society of America*. 41: 1057–1058.

Harrison, S.M. (1995). "A comparison of still, animated, or nonillustrated on-line help with written or spoken instructions in a graphical user interface." *Proceedings of CHI 95*. May 7–11, Denver, CO.

Hatfield, D. (1981). *Conference on Easier and More Productive Use of Computer Systems*. Ann Arbor, MI. (In Shneiderman, 1986).

Haubner, P., and Benz, C. (1983). "Information display on monochrome and colour screens." *Abstracts: International Scientific Conference on Ergonomic and Health Aspects in Modern Offices*. November 7–9, Turin, Italy.

Haubner, P. and Neumann, F. (1986). "Structuring alphanumerically coded information on visual display units." *Proceedings: International Scientific Conference: Work with Display Units*. May 12–15, Stockholm, Sweden.

Hicks, R. and Essinger, J. (1991). *Making Computers More Human: Designing for Human-Computer Interaction*. Oxford: Elsevier Advanced Technology.

Hollands, J.G. and Spence, I. (1992). "Judgments of Change and Proportion in Graphical Perception." *Human Factors*, 34: (3)313–334.

Hornof, A.J., and Kieras, D.E. (1997). "Cognitive Modeling Reveals Menu Search Is Both Random and Systematic," *Proceedings of CHI '97*, 107–114.

Hornof, A.J. and Kieras, D.E. (1999). "Cognitive modeling demonstrates how people use and anticipate location knowledge of menu items." *CHI 99 Conference Proceedings*, 410–417.

Horton, W. (1994). *The Icon Book*. New York: John Wiley and Sons.

Howe, Walt. (2001). "A Brief History of the Internet." http://www.walthowe.com/navnet/history.html.

Howlett, V. (1995). *Visual Interface Design for Windows*. John Wiley and Sons.

Hulteen, Eric, (1988) in Walker, 1989.

Hutchins, E.L., Hollan, J.D., and Norman, D.A. (1986). "Direct manipulation interfaces." In *User Centered System Design: New Perspectives on Human-Computer Interaction*. Hillsdale, NJ: Lawrence Erlbaum Associates.

International Business Machines Corporation (IBM). (1987). *Systems Application Architecture Common User Access, Panel Design and User Interaction* (SC26-4351-0). Boca Raton, FL: IBM.

International Business Machines Corporation (IBM). (1989a). *System Application Architecture Common User Access, Advanced Interface Design Guide* (SC26-4582). Cary, NC: IBM.

International Business Machines Corporation (IBM). (1989b). *Systems Application Architecture Common User Access, Basic Interface Design Guide* (SC26-4583). Cary, NC: IBM.

International Business Machines Corporation (IBM). (1991). *Systems Application Architecture Common User Access Advanced Interface Design Reference* (SC34-4289).

International Business Machines Corporation (IBM). (1992). *Object-Oriented Interface Design: IBM Common User Access Guidelines*. Carmel, IN: Que Corporation.

International Business Machines (IBM). (2001). "Cost Justifying Ease of Use." http://www-3.ibm.com/ibm/easy/eou_ext.nsf/Publish/23.

Intons-Peterson, M.J., Rocchi, P., West. T., McLellan, K., and Hackney, A. (1998). "Aging, optimal testing times, and negative priming." *Journal of Experimental Psychology: Learning, Memory, and Cognition*, 24 (2)362–376.

Intons-Peterson, M.J., Rocchi, P., West. T., McLellan, K., and Hackney, A. (1999). "Age, testing at preferred or nonpreferred times (testing optimality), and false memory." *Journal of Experimental Psychology: Learning, Memory, and Cognition*, 25 (1) 23-40.

Johnsgard, T.J., Page, S.R., Wilson, R.D., and Zeno, R.J. (1995). "A comparison of graphical user interface widgets for various tasks." *Proceedings of the Human Factors and Ergonomics Society 39th Annual Meeting*, Santa Monica, CA: Human Factors Society.

Karat, C. (1997). "Cost-justifying usability engineering in the software life cycle." In *Handbook of Human-Computer Interaction*, M. Helander, T. Landauer, and P. Prabhu (eds.). Elsevier Science, Amsterdam.

Karat, C.M., Halverson, C., Horn, D., and Karat, J. (1999). "Patterns of Entry and Correction in Large Vocabulary Continuous Speech Recognition Systems," *CHI 99 Conference Proceedings*, 568–575.

Karat, C.M., Halverson, C., Horn, D., and Karat, J. (1999). "Patterns of entry and correction in large vocabulary continuous speech recognition systems, *CHI99 Conference Proceedings*, 568–175.

Keil, M., and Carmel, E. (1995). "Customer-developer links." *Communications of the ACM*. 38: (5)33–34.

Kobara, S. (1991). *Visual Design with OSF/Motif*. Reading, MA: Hewlett-Packard/Addison-Wesley.

Koenemann, J. and Belkin, N. (1996). "A case for interaction: a study of interactive information retrieval behavior and effectiveness." *Proceedings CHI 96: Human Factors in Computing Systems*, ACM Press, New York, NY, 205–212.

Kohl, J.R., Barclay, R.O., Pinelli, T.E., Keene, M.L., and Kennedy, J.M. (1993). "The impact of language and culture on technical communication in Japan." *Technical Communication*.

Kopala, C.J. (1981). "The use of color coded symbols in a highly dense situation display." *Proceedings of the Human Factors Society 23rd Annual Meeting*, Santa Monica, CA: Human Factors Society.

KYE Systems Corp. (1995). *Genius EasyScan/Color PRO User's Guide*.

Lai, Y. and Waugh, M.L. (1995). "Effects of three different hypertextual menu designs on various information searching activities." *Journal of Multimedia and Hypermedia*, 4: (1)25–52.

Lalomia, M.J. and Happ, A.J. (1987). "The effective use of color for text on the IBM 5153 color display. *Proceedings of the Human Factors Society 31st Annual Meeting*, Santa Monica, CA: Human Factors Society.

Larson, K., and Czerwinski, M. (1998). "Web page design: Implications for memory, structure and scent for information retrieval." *CHI 98 Conference Proceedings*, 25–32.

Lee, A.Y. and Bowers, A.N. (1997). "The Effect of Multimedia Components on Learning," *Proceedings of the Human Factors and Ergonomics Society 41st Annual Meeting*, 340–344.

Legge, G.E. and Rubin, G.S. (1986). "Psychophysics of reading IV. Wavelengths effects in normal and low vision." *Journal of the Optical Society of America*. 3: 40–51.

Levi, Michael D. and Conrad, Frederick G. (1996). "Usability Testing of World Wide Web Sites," http://stats.bls.gov/ore/htm_papers/st960150.htm.

Levine, R. (1995) "*Guide to Web Style.*" Sun Microsystems, Inc. http://www.sun.com/styleguide.

Lewis, J.R. (1999). "Effect of Error Correction Strategy on Speech Dictation Throughput." *Proceedings of the Human Factors and Ergonomics Society*, 457–461.

Lind, N.E., Johnson, M., and Sandblad, B. (1992). "The art of the obvious." *CHI 95*. May 3–7, Monterey, CA.

Luria, S.M., Neri, D.F., and Jacobsen, A.R. (1986). "The effects of set size on color matching using CRT displays." *Proceedings of the Human Factors Society 30th Annual Meeting*, Santa Monica, CA: Human Factors Society.

MacKenzie, J.S., Sellen, A., and Buxton, W. (1991). "A comparison of input devices in elemental pointing and dragging tasks." *CHI 91*.

Maguire, M.C. (1985). "A review of human factors guidelines and techniques for the design of graphical human-computer interfaces." *Comput and Graphics* 9: (3)25.

Mallory, K., et al. (1980). "Human engineering guide to control room evaluation. Essex Corporation." *Technical Report NUREG/CR-1580*. Alexandria, VA.

Mandel, T. (1994). *The GUI-OOUI War: Windows vs. OS/2, the Designer's Guide to Human-Computer Interfaces*. New York: Van Nostrand Reinhold.

Marcus, A. (1984). "Icon design requires clarity, consistency." *Computer Graphics Today*.

Marcus, A. (1986a). "Proper color, type use improve instruction." *Computer Graphics Today*.

Marcus, A. (1986b). "Ten commandments of color." *Computer Graphics Today*.

Marcus, A. (1992). *Graphic Design for Electronic Documents and User Interfaces*. New York: ACM Press.

Martin, J. (1973). *Design of Man-Computer Dialogues*. Englewood Cliffs, NJ: Prentice Hall.

Mayhew, D.J. (1992). *Principles and Guidelines in Software User Interface Design*. Englewood Cliffs, NJ: Prentice Hall.

McTyre, J.H. and Frommer, W.D. (1985). "Effects of character/background color combinations on CRT character legibility." *Proceedings of the Human Factors Society 29th Annual Meeting*, Santa Monica, CA: Human Factors Society.

Mead, S.E., Spaulding, R.A., Sit, B.M., and Walker, N. (1997). "Effects of age and training on World Wide Web navigation strategies." *Proceedings of the Human Factor and Ergonomics Society 41st Annual Meeting*, 152–156.

Microsoft Corporation. (1992). *The Windows Interface: An Application Design Guide*. Redmond, WA: Microsoft Press.

Microsoft Corporation. (1995). *The Windows Interface Guidelines for Software Design*. Redmond, WA: Microsoft Press.

Microsoft 2001, msdn.Microsoft.com.library, 2001.

Microswitch (A Honeywell Division). (1984). *Applying Manual Controls and Displays: A Practical Guide to Panel Design*. Freeport, IL: Microswitch.

Miller, G.A. (1956). "The magical number seven, plus or minus two: Some limits on our capability for processing information." *Psychological Science*. 63: 87–97.

Molich, R. and Nielsen, J. (1990). "Improving a human-computer dialogue," *Communications of the ACM*, 33 (3)338–348.

Mori, H. and Hayashi, Y. (1993). "Visual interference with user's tasks on multi-window system." *Proceedings of the Fifth International Conference on Human-Computer Interaction*. 80–85.

Morimoto, K., Kurokawa, T., and Nishimura, T. (1993). "Dynamic representation of icons in human-computer interaction." *Proceedings of the Fifth International Conference on Human-Computer Interaction*.

Morrison, J.B., Pirolli, P., and Card, S.K. (2001). "A Taxonomic Analysis of What World Wide Web Activities Significantly Impact People's Decisions and Actions." Interactive poster, presented at the Association for Computing Machinery's *Conference on Human Factors in Computing Systems*, Seattle, March 31–April 5, 2001.

Nagy, A.L. and Sanchez, R.R. (1992). "Chromaticity and luminance as coding dimensions in visual search." *Human Factors* 34: 601–614.

National Language Technical Center. (1991). *National Language Design Guide: Designing Enabled Products*. Vol. 1. Canada: National Language Technical Center.

Nelson, T. (1980). "Interactive systems and the design of virtuality." *Creative Computing*. l6 (11)56 ff., and 6 (12)94 ff.

Nielsen, J. (1990). "Usability testing of international interfaces." In *Designing User Interfaces for International Use*, J. Nielson (ed.). New York: Elsevier.

Nielsen, J. (1992). "Finding usability problems through heuristic evaluation." *Proceedings: CHI 95*. May 3–7, Monterey, CA.

Nielsen, J. (1994). "Enhancing the explanatory power of usability heuristics," *CHI'94 Conference Proceedings.*

Nielsen, Jakob (1993). "Usability Engineering." Boston, MA: Academic Press .

Nielsen, Jakob (1996). "Top Ten Mistakes in Web Design." *Jakob Nielsen's Alertbox for May 1996*. www.useit.com/alertbox/9605.html.

Nielsen, Jakob (1997a). "The Difference Between Web Design and GUI Design." *Jakob Nielsen's Alertbox for May 1, 1997*. www.useit.com/alertbox/9705a.html.

Nielsen, Jakob (1997b). "The Difference Between Intranet and Internet Design." *Jakob Nielsen's Alertbox for September 15, 1997*. www.useit.com/alertbox/9709b.html.

Nielsen, Jakob (1999a). "Intranet Portals: The Corporate Information Infrastructure," *Jakob Nielsen's Alertbox*. www.useit.com/alertbox/990404.html, April 4.

Nielsen, Jakob (1999b). "'Top Ten Mistakes' Revisited Three Years Later." *Jakob Nielsen's Alertbo*. www.useit.com/alertbox/990502.html, May 2.

Nielsen, Jakob (2000). "Is Navigation Useful?" *Jakob Nielsen's Alertbox*. www.useit.com/alertbox/20000109.html, January 9.

Nielsen, Jacob, and Mack, Robert L. (Eds.) (1994). *Usability Inspection Methods*. New York: John Wiley and Sons.

NIST, 2001, www.nist.gov/webmetrics.

Omanson, R. C., Cline, J.A., Kilpatrick. C.E., and Dunkerton, M.C. (1998). "Dimensions affecting Web site identity." *Proceedings of the Human Factors and Ergonomics Society 42nd Annual Meeting*, 429–433.

Omoigui, N., He, L., Gupta, A., Grudin, J. and Sanocki, E. (1999). "Time-compression: Systems, concerns, usage, and benefits, *CHI 99 Conference Proceedings*, 136–143.

Open Software Foundation. (1993). *OSF/Motif Style Guide*. Englewood Cliffs, NJ: Prentice Hall.

Ozok, A.A. and Salvendy, G. (2000). "Measuring consistency of Web page design and its effects on performance and satisfaction, *Ergonomics*, Vol. 43, No. 4, 443–460.

PBS Life on the Internet, http://www.pbs.org/internet/timeline/timeline-txt.html.

Pastoor, S. (1990). "Legibility and subjective preference for color combinations in text." *Human Factors* 32: (2)157–171.

Piolat, A., Roussey, J.Y., and Thunin, O. (1998). "Effects of screen presentation on text reading and revising." *International Journal of Human Computer Studies*, 47, 585–589.

Popowicz, A. (1995). "Collecting user information on a limited budget." *SIGCHI Bulletin*. 27: (4)23–28.

Pressman, R.S. (1992). "Software Engineering: A Practitioner's Approach." New York: McGraw Hill.

Ramsay, J., Barbesi, A., and Preece, J. (1998). "A psychological investigation of long retrieval times on the World Wide Web," *Interacting with Computers*, 10, 77–86.

Reeves, B., and Nass, C. (1996). "The media equation: How people treat computers, television, and new media like real people and places." New York: Cambridge University Press.

Rogers, Y. (1989). "Icons at the interface: Their usefulness." *Interacting with Computers: The Interdisciplinary Journal of Human-Computer Interaction*. 1: (1)105–117.

Rooden, M.J., Green, W.S., and Kanis, H. (1999). "Difficulties in usage of a coffeemaker predicted on the basis of design models," *Proceedings of the Human Factors and Ergonomics Society*, 476–480.

Russo, P., and S. Boor. (1993). "How fluent is your interface? Designing for international users." *INTER 93*. April 24–29, Amsterdam.

Rutkowski, C. (1982). "An introduction to the human applications standard computer interface, part 1: Theory and principles," *BYTE 7*. 11: 291–310.

Schrier, J.R. (1992). "Reducing stress associated with participating in a usability test." *Proceedings of the Human Factors Society 36th Annual Meeting*, Santa Monica, CA: Human Factors Society.

Selvidge, P.R., Chaparro, B., and Bender, G.T. (2000). "The world wide wait: Effects of delays on user performance," *Proceedings of the IEA 2000/HGES 2000 Congress*, 1-416 to 1-419.

Shackel, B. (1981). "The concept of usability." *Proceedings of IBM Software and Information Usability Symposium*. September 15–18, Poughkeepsie, NY.

Shackel, B. (1991). "Usability—context, framework, definition, design and evaluation." In *Human Factors for Informatics Usability*, B. Schackel and S.J. Richardson (eds.). Cambridge, U.K.: Cambridge University Press.

Shannon, C.E. and Weaver, W. (1949). *The Mathematical Theory of Communication*. Urbana, IL: The University of Illinois Press.

Sharit, J. and Czaja, S.J. (1994). "Ageing, computer-based task performance, and stress: Issues and challenges," *Ergonomics*, 37 (4)559–577.

Shneiderman, B. (1982). "The future of interactive systems and the emergence of direct manipulation." *Behaviour and Information Technology, I*. 237–256.

Shneiderman, B. (1987). *Designing the User Interface: Strategies for Effective Human-Computer Interaction*. Readir.g, MA: Addison-Wesley.

Shurtleff, M. (1993). "Say cheese! Guidelines for the use of photorealism in graphical user interfaces." *CSTG Bulletin*. 15–17.

Sidorsky, R.C. (1982). "Color coding in tactical displays: Help or hindrance." *Army Research Institute Research Report*.

Simkin, D. and Hastie, R. (1987). "An information-processing analysis of graph perception." *Journal of the American Statistical Association*. 82: 454–465.

Simmons, T. and Manahan, M. (1999). "The Effects of Monitor Size on User Performance and Preference," *Proceedings of the Human Factors and Ergonomics Society*.

Smith, D.C., Harslem, E.F., Irby, C.H., Kimball, R.B., and Verplank, W.L. (1982). "Designing the star user interface." *Byte*.

Smith, S.L., and J.N. Mosier. (1986). *Guidelines for Designing User-Interface Software* (Mitre ESD-TR-86-278 MTR 10090). Hanscom AFB, MA.

Smith, W. (1986). "Computer color: Psychophysics, task application, and aesthetics." *Proceedings: International Scientific Conference: Work with Display Units*. May 12–15, Stockholm, Sweden.

Smith, W. (1988). "Standardizing colors for computer screens." *Proceedings of the Human Factors Society 32nd Annual Meeting*, Santa Monica, CA: Human Factors Society.

Spool, J.M., Scanlon, T., Schroeder, W., Snyder, C., and DeAngelo, T. (1997). "Web Site Usability: A Designer's Guide." North Andover, MA: User Interface Engineering.

Stanton, N.A. and Stevenage, S.V. (1998). "Learning to predict human error: Issues of acceptability, reliability and validity," *Ergonomics*, 41 (11)1737–1747.

Streveler, D.J. and Wasserman, A.I. (1984). "Quantitative measures of the spatial properties of screen designs." *INTERACT '95. Human-Computer Interaction*. England.

Stromoski, R. (1993). "Fighting the futz factor." *Information Week*. February 15: 55.

Suhm, B., Myers, B., and Waibel, A. (1999). "Model-Based and Evaluation of Multimodal Interactive Error Correction." *CHI 99 Conference Proceedings*, 584–591.

Sukaviriya, P. and Moran, L. (1990). "User interfaces for Asia." In *Designing User Interfaces for International Use*, J. Nielsen (ed.). New York: Elsevier.

Sun Microsystems, Inc. (1990). *Open Look Graphical User Interface Application Style Guidelines*. Reading, MA: Addison-Wesley.

Sun Microsystems, Inc. (1998), www.sun.com/sunonnet/.

Taylor, D. (1992). *Global Software*. New York: Springer Verlag.

Thacker, P. (1987). "Tabular displays: A human factors study." *CSTG Bulletin*. 14: (1)13.

Thecounter.com. (2001) www.thecounter.com/stats/.

Thovtrup, H., and Nielsen, J. (1991). "Assessing the usability of a user interface standard." *Proceedings: CHI 91*. 335–342.

Tindall-Ford, S., Chandler, P., and Sweller, J. (1997). "When two sensory modes are better than one," *Journal of Experimental Psychology;* Applied, 3 (4)257–287.

Tinker, M.A. (1955). "Prolonged reading tasks in visual research." *Journal of Applied Psychology*, 39: 444–446.

Tripathi, P.D. (1992). "English: 'The Chosen Tongue,'" *English Today*. 8 (4)3–11.

Tufte, E.R. (1983). *The Visual Display of Quantitative Information*. Cheshire, CT: Graphics Press.

Tullis, T. (1981). "An evaluation of alphanumeric, graphic, and color information displays." *Human Factors* 23: 541–550.

Tullis, T. (1983). "Predicting the usability of alphanumeric displays." Ph.D. diss., Rice University.

Tullis, T. (1993). "Is user interface design just common sense?" *Proceedings of the Fifth International Conference on Human-Computer Interaction*. 9–14.

Tullis, T. and Kodimer, M.L. (1992). "A comparison of direct-manipulation, selection, and data-entry techniques for reordering fields in a table." *Proceedings of the Human Factors Society 36th Annual Meeting*, Santa Monica, CA: Human Factors Society.

Uceta, F.A., Dixon, M.A., and Resnick. M.L. (1998). "Adding Interactivity to Paper Prototypes," *Proceedings of the Human Factors and Ergonomics Society 42nd Annual Meeting*, 506–511.

Usability.gov/guidelines.

useit.com, "Severity Ratings for Usability Problems," http://www.useit.com/papers/heuristic/severityrating.html.

User Interface Engineering. (2001) http://world.std.com/~uieweb/tips.htm.

Verplank, B. (1988). "Designing graphical user interfaces." *Proceedings: CHI 88*. May 15.

Vitz, P.C. (1966). "Preference for different amounts of visual complexity." *Behavioral Science*, 2: 105–114.

Walker, M.A. (1989). "Natural language in a desktop environment." In *Designing and Using Human-Computer Interfaces and Knowledge Based Systems*, G. Salvendy and M.J. Smith (eds.). Amsterdam: Elsevier Science Publishers.

Weinschenk, S. (1995). "Storyboarding the information process." *Session Proceedings, BFMA The 26th International Symposium on Forms and Information Systems*. May 7–11, St. Louis, MO.

Weinschenk, S. (2001). "Page Design for Web Documents." http://www.wein schenk.com/guidelinesdemo/presweb.html.

White, J.V. (1990). *Color for the Electronic Age*. New York: Watson-Guptill Publications.

Whiteside, J., Jones, S., Levy, P.S., and Wixon, D. (1985). "User performance with command, menu, and iconic interfaces." *Proceedings CHI 85*.

Wichansky, A.M. (1986). "Legibility and user acceptance of monochrome display phospher colors." *Proceedings: International Scientific Conference: Work with Display Units*. May 12–15, Stockholm, Sweden.

Williams, J.R. (1998). "Guidelines for the Use of Multimedia in Instruction." *Proceedings of the Human Factors and Ergonomics Society 42nd Annual Meeting*, 1447–1451.

Winograd, T. (1995). "From programming environments to environments for designing." *Communications of the ACM*. 38: (10)65–74.

Wopking, M., Pastoor, S., and Beldie, I.O. (1985). "Design of user guidance in videotex systems." *Proceedings of the 11th International Symposium on Human Factors in Telecommunications*. Boston: Information Gatekeepers.

World Wide Web Consortium. (2001). www.w3.org.

Wright, P. (1991). "Designing and evaluating documentation for I.T. users." In *Human Factors for Informatics Usability*, B. Shackel and S.J. Richardson (eds.). Cambridge U.K.: Cambridge University Press.

Wright, P., Lickorish, A., and Milroy, R. (1994). "Remember while mousing: The cognitive cost of mouse clicks." *SIGCHI Bulletin*, 26: (1)41–45.

Zahn, C.T. (1971). "Graph-theoretical methods for detecting and describing gestalt clusters." *IEEE Transactions on Computers, X-20*. 68–86.

Zaphiris, P. and Mtei, L. (1998). "Depth versus breadth in the arrangement of Web links." www.otal.umd.edu/Shore/bs04/.

Zhan, P., Bishu, R.R., and Riley, M.W. (1993). "Screen layout and semantic structure in iconic menu design." *Proceedings of the Fifth International Conference on Human-Computer Interaction*.

Ziefle, M. (1998). "Effects of display resolution on visual performance." *Human Factors*, 40 (4)555–568.

References for Case Studies for Practice

1. Voice Enabled Android Application for Vehicular Complaint System

Mhapsekar Aditi; Kulkarni, Priyanka; Nagarsekar, Uma; Kalbande, Dhananjay R. "Voice Enabled Android Application for Vehicular Complaint System" in IEEE sponsored International Conf. on Information and Communication Technologies (WICT), Trivendrum Oct 30, 2012, DOI: 10.1109/WICT.2012.6409133, Publication Year: 2012, Page(s): 520–524.

2. **Applying Human Computer Interaction to Individual Security using Mobile Application**

Save, Shraddha; Gala, Mansi; Patil, Surabhi; Kalbande, Dhananjay R. "Applying Human Computer Interaction to Individual Security using Mobile Application", IEEE Conference (ICCICT-2015 Approved by IEEE), Jan 15–17, 2015, Mumbai. DOI: 10.1109/ICCICT.2015.7045691, Publication Year: 2015, Page(s): 1–6.

3. **Machine Learning Applied To Human Learning**

Chandnani, Kanchan; Chavan, Deepti; Desai, Pratiti; Kalbande, Dhananjay R., "Machine Learning Applied To Human Learning", IEEE International Conference IEEE INDICON 2013,13–15 Jan 2013, IIT Bombay, Mumbai, India.

4. **Educative Games for Autistic Children**

Iyer, Sridhari; Kalbande, Dhananjay R., "Educative Games for Autistic Children" IEEE Conference (CSCITA –Approved by IEEE), April 4–5 2014, Mumbai.

5. **ISSAC Intelligent System for Streamlined Accelerometric Control**

Sumit, G.; Karande, O.; Pandya, A.; Kalbande, Dhananjay R. "Gesture Detection System Using Smart Watch Based Motion Sensors", IEEE Conference (CSCITA – Approved by IEEE), April 4–5 2014, Mumbai.

Additional Reading Material

1. Norman, Don (2013), The Design of Everyday Things, Perseus Books Group.
2. Cooper, Alan; Reimann, Robert; Cronin, David (2007), *About Face 3: Essentials of Interaction Design*, John Wiley and Sons.
3. Human Centric Design, http://jnd.org/dn.mss/human-centered_design_considered_harmful.html

Index

W